A COMPANION
TO HORACE

BLACKWELL COMPANIONS TO THE ANCIENT WORLD

This series provides sophisticated and authoritative overviews of periods of ancient history, genres of classical literature, and the most important themes in ancient culture. Each volume comprises between twenty-five and forty concise essays written by individual scholars within their area of specialization. The essays are written in a clear, provocative, and lively manner, designed for an international audience of scholars, students, and general readers.

ANCIENT HISTORY

Published

A Companion to the Roman Army
Edited by Paul Erdkamp

A Companion to the Roman Republic
Edited by Nathan Rosenstein and Robert Morstein-Marx

A Companion to the Roman Empire
Edited by David S. Potter

A Companion to the Classical Greek World
Edited by Konrad H. Kinzl

A Companion to the Ancient Near East
Edited by Daniel C. Snell

A Companion to the Hellenistic World
Edited by Andrew Erskine

A Companion to Late Antiquity
Edited by Philip Rousseau

A Companion to Ancient History
Edited by Andrew Erskine

A Companion to Archaic Greece
Edited by Kurt A. Raaflaub and Hans van Wees

A Companion to Julius Caesar
Edited by Miriam Griffin

In preparation

A Companion to Byzantium
Edited by Elizabeth James

A Companion to Ancient Macedonia
Edited by Ian Worthington and Joseph Roisman

A Companion to the Punic Wars
Edited by Dexter Hoyos

A Companion to Ancient Egypt
Edited by Alan Lloyd

A Companion to Sparta
Edited by Anton Powell

LITERATURE AND CULTURE

Published

A Companion to Classical Receptions
Edited by Lorna Hardwick and Christopher Stray

A Companion to Greek and Roman Historiography
Edited by John Marincola

A Companion to Catullus
Edited by Marilyn B. Skinner

A Companion to Roman Religion
Edited by Jörg Rüpke

A Companion to Greek Religion
Edited by Daniel Ogden

A Companion to the Classical Tradition
Edited by Craig W. Kallendorf

A Companion to Roman Rhetoric
Edited by William Dominik and Jon Hall

A Companion to Greek Rhetoric
Edited by Ian Worthington

A Companion to Ancient Epic
Edited by John Miles Foley

A Companion to Greek Tragedy
Edited by Justina Gregory

A Companion to Latin Literature
Edited by Stephen Harrison

A Companion to Greek and Roman Political Thought
Edited by Ryan K. Balot

A Companion to Ovid
Edited by Peter E. Knox

A Companion to the Ancient Greek Language
Edited by Egbert Bakker

A Companion to Hellenistic Literature
Edited by Martine Cuypers and James J. Clauss

A Companion to Vergil's Aeneid and its Tradition
Edited by Joseph Farrell and Michael C. J. Putnam

A Companion to Horace
Edited by Gregson Davis

In preparation

A Companion to Food in the Ancient World
Edited by John Wilkins

A Companion to the Latin Language
Edited by James Clackson

A Companion to Classical Mythology
Edited by Ken Dowden and Niall Livingstone

A Companion to Sophocles
Edited by Kirk Ormand

A Companion to Aeschylus
Edited by Peter Burian

A Companion to Greek Art
Edited by Tyler Jo Smith and Dimitris Plantzos

A Companion to Families in the Greek and Roman World
Edited by Beryl Rawson

A Companion to Tacitus
Edited by Victoria Pagán

A Companion to the Archaeology of the Ancient Near East
Edited by Daniel Potts

A COMPANION
TO HORACE

Edited by

Gregson Davis

A John Wiley & Sons, Ltd., Publication

Blackwell Publishing was acquired by John Wiley & Sons in February 2007. Blackwell's publishing program has been merged with Wiley's global Scientific, Technical, and Medical business to form Wiley-Blackwell.

Registered Office
John Wiley & Sons Ltd, The Atrium, Southern Gate, Chichester, West Sussex, PO19 8SQ, United Kingdom

Editorial Offices
350 Main Street, Malden, MA 02148-5020, USA
9600 Garsington Road, Oxford, OX4 2DQ, UK
The Atrium, Southern Gate, Chichester, West Sussex, PO19 8SQ, UK

For details of our global editorial offices, for customer services, and for information about how to apply for permission to reuse the copyright material in this book please see our website at www.wiley.com/wiley-blackwell.

Library of Congress Cataloging-in-Publication Data

A companion to Horace / edited by Gregson Davis.
    p.   cm. – (Blackwell companions to the ancient world)
  Includes bibliographical references and index.
  ISBN 978-1-4051-5540-3 (hardcover : alk. paper)   1. Horace   2. Horace–Criticism and interpretation.   3. Poets, Latin–Biography.   4. Epistolary poetry, Latin–History and criticism.   5. Laudatory poetry, Latin–History and criticism.   6. Verse satire, Latin–History and criticism.   7. Rome–In literature.   I. Davis, Gregson.
  PA6411.C592 2010
  871′.01–dc22

                                        2009050261

A catalogue record for this book is available from the British Library.

Set in 10.5 on 13 pt Galliard by Toppan Best-set Premedia Limited
Printed and bound in Singapore by Fabulous Printers Pte Ltd

I   2010

Contents

Figures

Notes on Contributors

William Anderson is Professor of Latin Emeritus of the University of California, Berkeley. His extensive publications on Latin poetry include: *The Art of the Aeneid* (1969); *Essays on Roman Satire* (1982); *Ovid's Metamorphoses 6–10* (1972) and *Ovid's Metamorphoses 1–5* (1997); *Ovidius: Metamophoses* (Leipzig, 1977); *Barbarian Play: Plautus' Roman Comedy* (1993). He has edited a collection of interpretations entitled *Why Horace?* (1999). His latest study is *A Terence Reader* (2009).

Ronnie Ancona is the author of *Time and the Erotic in Horace's Odes* (1994), *Horace: Selected Odes and Satire 1.9* (1999, 2nd edn. 2005), and *Writing Passion: A Catullus Reader* (2004), co-editor of *Gendered Dynamics in Latin Love Poetry* (2005), editor of *A Concise Guide to Teaching Latin Literature* (2007), and co-author of *Horace: A LEGAMUS Transitional Reader* (2008). She co-edits a series on women in antiquity forthcoming from Oxford University Press and edits the BC Latin Readers series from Bolchazy-Carducci Publishers. She is currently Professor of Classics at Hunter College and the Graduate Center (CUNY).

David Armstrong is Professor Emeritus of Classics at the University of Texas, Austin. He is the author of *Horace* in the Yale University Press *Hermes* series (1989). Besides writing on Horace and other topics he has worked for fifteen years on the Epicurean papyri from Herculaneum. He has published several essays on Epicureanism, as known from these texts, and its reflections in Roman literature, for example, *Vergil, Philodemus and the Augustans* (2004).

Phebe Lowell Bowditch is Associate Professor of Classics at the University of Oregon. She is the author of *Horace and the Gift Economy of Patronage* (2001) and articles on Horace, Propertius, Ovid, and translation. Her current research focuses on love elegy and Roman imperialism.

Susanna Braund moved to the University of British Columbia in 2007 to take up a Canada Research Chair in Latin Poetry and its Reception after teaching previously at Stanford, Yale, and the Universities of London, Bristol, and Exeter.

She has published extensively on Roman satire and Latin epic poetry and has translated Lucan (for the Oxford World's Classics series) and Persius and Juvenal (for the Loeb Classical Library) (2004).

Jenny Strauss Clay is William R. Kenan Jr Professor of Classics at the University of Virginia. Her publications include *The Wrath of Athena: Gods and Men in Homer's Odyssey* (1983); *The Politics of Olympus: Form and Meaning in the Major Homeric Hymns* (2006), *Hesiod's Cosmos* (2003*)*, as well as numerous articles on Greek and Roman poetry.

Andrea Cucchiarelli is Associate Professor at the University of Rome "La Sapienza." He has published articles on Lucretius, Virgil, Horace, and Petronius, and he is the author of two books: *La satira e il poeta. Orazio tra Epodi e Sermones* (2001), and *La veglia di Venere-Pervigilium Veneris* (2003).

Gregson Davis is Andrew W. Mellon Distinguished Professor in the Humanities at Duke University in the Department of Classical Studies and in the Program in Literature. He has taught both Classics and Comparative Literature at Stanford University (1966–89) and at Cornell University (1989–93). He has published articles on the poetry of Horace, Catullus, Vergil, and Ausonius, as well as on the contemporary Caribbean poets Derek Walcott and Aimé Césaire. He is the author of two monographs on Augustan poets: *The Death of Procris: "Amor" and the Hunt in Ovid's Metamorphoses* (1983) and *Polyhymnia: The Rhetoric of Horatian Lyric Discourse* (1984). He is currently at work on a book on Vergil's *Eclogues*.

Lowell Edmunds is Professor of Classics Emeritus at Rutgers University. His *From a Sabine Jar: Reading Horace, Odes 1.9* appeared in 1991. His most recent book is *Oedipus* (2006), in the Routledge series Gods and Heroes in the Ancient World. He is working on a book on minor Roman poetry.

Kirk Freudenburg is Professor of Latin in the Department of Classics at Yale University. His published works focus on the cultural life of Roman letters, and they include several books on Roman Satire: *The Walking Muse: Horace on the Theory of Satire* (1993), *Satires of Rome: Threatening Poses from Lucilius to Juvenal* (2001), and *The Cambridge Companion to Roman Satire* (2005). He also edited the *Oxford Readings in Horace, Satires and Epistles* (2009). His current projects include a commentary on Horace *Sermones* Book 2 (for the Cambridge Greens and Yellows), articles on Lucilius and Varro, and a book on the self in Roman personal poetry.

Bernard Frischer is Director of the Virtual World Heritage Laboratory and a professor of Art History and Classics at the University of Virginia. He received his B.A. in Classics from Wesleyan University (1971) and his Ph.D. in Classics from Heidelberg University (1975). The author or co-author of six print and three electronic books on Classics, the Classical Tradition, and virtual archaeology, he has been Professor of Classics at the University of California at Los Angeles (1976–2004), as well as Professor-in-Charge of the Intercollegiate Center for Classical Studies in Rome (2001–2), guest professor at the University of Bologna (1993), and a fellow (1974–6) and trustee (2007–2010) of the American Academy in Rome. From 1996 to 2003 he directed the Horace's Villa Project.

Leon Golden is Professor Emeritus of Classical Languages and Humanities at Florida State University. He is the author of *In Praise of Prometheus* (1966), *Aristotle on Tragic and Comic Mimesis* (1992), *Understanding the Iliad* (2005), *Achilles and Yossarian* (2009), and a number of articles on Classical literary theory and criticism.

W. R. Johnson is John Matthews Manly Distinguished Service Professor of Classics and Comparative Literature, Emeritus at the University of Chicago. He is the author of several books on Latin poetry, including *Horace and the Dialectic of Freedom: Readings in Epistles 1* (1993) and, most recently, *A Latin Lover in Ancient Rome: Readings in Propertius and his Genre* (2009). He is providing the Introduction to Stanley Lombardo's translation of Ovid's *Metamorphoses.*

Michèle Lowrie is Professor of Classics and the College at the University of Chicago. She has published *Horace's Narrative Odes* (Oxford 1997) and *Writing, Performance, and Authority in Augustan Rome* (Oxford 2009), as well as edited *The Aesthetics of Empire and the Reception of Vergil* (co-editor Sarah Spence, special volume of *Literary Imagination* 8.3 [2006]) and *Oxford Readings in Classical Studies: Horace's Odes and Epodes* (2009). She has written articles on Latin literature in the Republican and Augustan periods and its reception in nineteenth- and twentieth-century literature and political thought. Current research projects focus on the *exemplum*, foundation, security, and state violence.

David Mankin is Associate Professor of Classics at Cornell University. He received his PhD from the University of Virginia in 1985. He is the author of *Horace, Epodes* (Cambridge 1995), of articles and reviews on Latin poetry, and of the forthcoming *Cicero, de Oratore 3* for the series: Cambridge Greek and Latin Classics.

Michael C. J. Putnam is W. Duncan MacMillan Professor of Classics and Professor of Comparative Literature Emeritus at Brown University. He is the author or editor of many volumes devoted primarily to Latin poetry of the late Republic and early empire, and to its tradition, including: *Artifices of eternity: Horace's Fourth Book of Odes* (1986) and *Horace's Carmen Saeculare: Ritual Magic and the Poet's Art* (2000). He is a member of the American Philosophical Society and a fellow of the American Academy of Arts and Sciences. A former president of the American Philological Association, he is also a Trustee of the American Academy in Rome.

William H. Race is the George L. Paddison Professor of Classics at the University of North Carolina at Chapel Hill. He has published articles on both Greek and Roman poetry. His major books include *Pindar* (1997) and *Apollonius Rhodius* (2008) in the Loeb Classical Library.

Catherine Schlegel, Associate Professor of Classics at the University of Notre Dame, is the author of *Satire and the Threat of Speech: Horace's Satires Book I* (2005) and (with the poet Henry Weinfield) a translation of Hesiod's *Theogony and Works and Days*, for which she also wrote the commentary (2006). She is currently working on a book on literary and philosophical considerations of emotion in Greek and Roman literature.

Hans Peter Syndikus is former Studiendirecktor at the Gymnasium Weilheim, Bavaria. His major publications on Latin poetry include: *Lucans Gedicht vom Bürgerkrieg* (1958), *Die Lyrik des Horaz: Eine Interpretation der Oden* (1972–3; 3rd edn. 2001), and *Catull: Eine Interpretation* (1984–90; 3rd edn. 2001). An interpretation of the elegies of Propertius is forthcoming in 2010.

Abbreviations Used

AJPh	American Journal of Philology
ANRW	Aufstieg und Niedergang der römischen Welt
ClAnt	Classical Antiquity
CompLit	Comparative Literature
CPCP	California Publications in Classical Philology
CPh	Classical Philology
CQ	Classical Quarterly
CSCA	California Studies in Classical Antiquity
CW	The Classical World
EL	Études de Lettres: Bulletin de la Faculté des Lettres de l'Université de Lausanne et de la Société des Études de Lettres
EMC	Échos du Monde Classique (Classical Views)
GRBS	Greek, Roman and Byzantine Studies
HSPh	Harvard Studies in Classical Philology
ICS	Illinois Classical Studies
IJCT	International Journal of the Classical Tradition
JDAI	Jahrbuch des Deutschen Archäologischen Instituts
JHI	Journal of the History of Ideas
JRS	Journal of Roman Studies
MCr	Museum Criticum
MD	Materiali e Discussioni per l'Analisi dei Testi Classici
MH	Museum Helveticum
MPhL	Museum Philologum Londiniense
PCPhS	Proceedings of the Cambridge Philological Society
QUCC	Quaderni Urbinati di Cultura Classica
RFIC	Rivista di Filologia e di Istruzione Classica

RhM	Rheinisches Museum für Philologie
SIFC	Studi Italiani di Filologia Classica
TAPhA	Transactions and Proceedings of the American Philological Society
YClS	Yale Classical Studies
ZPE	Zeitschrift für Papyrologie und Epigraphik

Author's Note

Horace's works are normally referred to in this volume without abbreviation as follows:

Epodes   *Epistles*
Odes   *Ars Poetica*
Satires   *Carmen Saeculare*

Italics are employed for these works where specific titles (rather than general references to the genre) are invoked, e.g.:

Epistles 1.1; *Odes* 1.1.   [specific titles of works]
The Epistles; The Odes   [general references to genre]

Ars Poetica and *Carmen Saeculare* are italicized throughout.

Acknowledgments

The editor and publisher gratefully acknowledge the permission granted to reproduce the copyright material in this book:

Excerpts from Miller, A. 1996. *Greek Lyric: An Anthology in Translation* (Hackett Publishing Company, Indianapolis and Cambridge).

Citations in Chapter 19 from O. B. Hardison and Leon Golden, eds., *Horace for Students of Literature: The "Ars Poetica" and its Tradition* (University Press of Florida, 1995) are reprinted by permission of the University Press of Florida.

Excerpted English translations in Chapter 12 from *Horace: Satires, Epistles, The Art of Poetry* (Loeb Classical Library, Volume 194, translated by H. R. Fairclough, Cambridge, Mass.: Harvard University Press, 1926), are reprinted by permission of the publishers and the Trustees of the Loeb Classical Library.

Every effort has been made to trace copyright holders and to obtain their permission for the use of copyright material. The publisher apologizes for any errors or omissions in the above list and would be grateful if notified of any corrections that should be incorporated in future reprints or editions of this book.

Introduction

Few poets of the Greco-Roman canon have exerted as profound and enduring an influence on European letters as Horace, and among the foremost poets of Augustan Rome, only Vergil, Horace's close friend and fellow-poet, has surpassed him in his role as composer of "classic" works of Latin literature. His unabashed boast in the concluding poem of his Third Book of Odes, "I have completed a work more enduring than bronze," famously predicts this posthumous renown, and has taken its ordained place in the galaxy of purple passages and quotable lines that Horace's poetry has generated. The lyric corpus (Odes), in particular, has inspired copious translators and imitators in all the major European languages. In the case of the English tradition, at least two substantial anthologies of translations of the Odes have been assembled, with examples that include some of the greatest practitioners of English lyric, such as John Milton, and A. E. Housman.[1] Horace's impact on literary criticism through his *Art of Poetry* (*Epistle to the Pisos*) has also been enormously influential at various periods of literary history. In the Renaissance, in particular, it enjoyed an almost august status, along with Aristotle's *Poetics*, as a source of authoritative prescriptions on how to achieve excellence as a poet.

The literary scholar who seeks to offer cogent interpretations of Horace's poetic output faces the formidable challenge of having to reconstruct conventions that belong to an alien cultural tradition. By the term "cultural" I here mean to subsume an entire network of social, political, historical, and religious values. A deep knowledge of cultural values, in turn, entails familiarity with an array of rhetorical conventions, as well as with the interplay of ideas that are more or less latent in the poetic texts. Though the essays in this volume employ different hermeneutical perspectives in their approach to Horatian poetics, they all share the aim of exploring the hazardous terrain that lies at the intersection of genre, rhetoric, and philosophy within the intellectual horizon of the Augustan period.

As a versatile poet who left his mark on a variety of genres (lyric, satiric, epistolary, didactic), Horace inhabits and "performs" multiple personae that are germane to the rhetorical conventions of particular types of poetry in the

Greco-Roman tradition. Rather than seeing himself as rigidly bound by those conventions, however, he manipulates the knowledgeable readers' expectations in such as way as to negotiate a unique space for his verbal art. At the same time, we recognize (or so imagine) that there is an overarching, if often elusive, persona that is retrievable through the shifting stances of the other diverse, generically shaped, personae that he adopts in his works. In my view, this residual persona (call him "Horace") is most clearly identifiable at the level of ideas and philosophical outlook. The voice of this Horace reminds us in several passages in the *Epistles* and *Satires* that he had a life-long passion for philosophy, and his poetry reflects an abiding concern with articulating a set of values that embody his eclectic version of practical wisdom (*sapientia*).

Since genre is the main organizing principle that governs the selection of topics in this collection, it is worth posing the question whether it is possible to reconstruct the Roman poets' own fundamental conception of literary typologies. In the case of Horace and his contemporaries we are fortunate to be able to extrapolate their underlying assumptions about the nature of genre from the many passages in their poetry that broach the topic of generic choice. All the major Augustan poets without exception (Horace, Vergil, Tibullus, Propertius, Ovid) engage in "programmatic" rhetorical prologues in which they characterize their works in relation to inherited generic conventions. A synchronic examination of these passages of inter-generic negotiation (commonly referred to under the label of *recusatio* ("refusal") in the literature, but more properly understood as "disavowals") allows us to pinpoint the key constituents of their generic discriminations. A genre, as conceived by the Latin poets of the late Republic, may be succinctly defined as a set of conventions and expectations regarding the correlation of subject matter (content) and stylistic level (form). Stylistic levels, in turn, are usually associated with normative choices of meter. It is important to stress, however, that the system of correlations was elastic: in their practice poets asserted their originality by consciously manipulating the reader's expectations while openly challenging the traditional correlations.

The image chosen for the jacket cover of this volume may be taken as a cultural reflection of the flexibility that characterized the Augustan poets' robust dramatizations of their chosen level of style in regard to individual poems. The provenance of the image is a spectacular wall-painting in the *triclinium* (dining-room) of a villa excavated in the environs of the buried city of Pompei,[2] and it depicts the Muse Calliope bearing a *stylus* (writing instrument), in one hand, and a writing tablet in the other. In one of his most ambitious odes, composed in a notably elevated style (*Odes* 3.4), Horace calls upon Calliope in an elaborate proem to inspire his song, and he boldly goes on to describe her as having manifestly heeded his call in the evolving poem. Since the majority of the Odes occupy a less exalted stylistic domain than this poem (and are far briefer in compass), the invocation of Calliope in this instance is a salient clue to the reader to ramp up his/her expectations regarding the tone of the ensuing narrative of the poet's literary career.

Horace refers to his own published collections according to certain generic labels: for example, *Iambi* (Epodes); *Carmina* (Odes); *Sermones* (Satires). In each category of poem he playfully stretches the limits of convention in highly nuanced ways that repay detailed investigation. The essays in this volume address this entire array of genres, as well as special thematic subgroups within it. Without attempting to summarize each scholarly contribution, it may be useful to present an overview of the main topics in the four parts into which the *Companion* is divided.

The essays in Part I explore issues of biographical and social context that are relevant to an understanding of the tastes of the poet and his contemporaries. Horace's literary œuvre was circulated in his life-time among close friends and acquaintances, some of whom were writers of distinction, such as the poet Vergil. The inner circle also included his wealthy patron, Maecenas, and the *princeps* himself, Augustus, whose rule marked the transition from Republic to Empire, and is generally agreed to have ushered in a Golden Age of literary production. Though Horace's poems contain many overt references to incidents and circumstances of his life, as well as to matters of momentous historical, social, and political import, it is a truism worth recalling that such references should not be read as unmediated transcriptions of reality. The constructed *bios* (life-story) serves rhetorical no less than quasi-documentary purposes. Whether the poet is narrating his participation at the battle of Philippi (when he was rescued by Mercury after abandoning his shield), or his privileged witnessing of a Dionysiac epiphany, or the episode of his having been miraculously protected by the Muses as a sleeping infant, the sophisticated reader must bear in mind that he is humorously blurring the distinction between the fictitious and the real in the interest of persuasive discourse. The four essays in this section bring revisionist perspectives to bear on analogous issues: the social status of the author as a member of the equestrian rank (Armstrong); the deconstruction of the notion of the "circle of Maecenas" (Anderson); the decoding of the complex social relations between artistic client and imperial patron (Bowditch); and, on the material side, the re-examination of the archaeological evidence to determine the true dimensions of Horace's Sabine estate (Frischer).

The Odes and Epodes are discussed in Part II primarily, though not exclusively, from the standpoint of Horace's debt to his Greek models. The "iambic" persona that inhabits the Epodes is derivative in part from the invective poetry of Archilochus, and is subjected to subtle transfigurations and extensions in the hands of the Roman poet (Mankin); the "lyric ethos" of the *Carmina* is analyzed in relation to the non-invective poetry of the same Archaic Greek master (Davis); the scope of the poet's debt to Lesbian *melos* (foregrounded in his inaugural *carmen*) is circumscribed by Clay, while his appropriation of Pindaric encomiastic techniques is the topic of the contribution by Race. Encomiastic strategies as they relate to the occasion of lyric performance are examined by Putnam with respect to the commissioned choral hymn, the *Carmen Saeculare*. Lowrie considers the poet's redefinition of lyric imperatives in connection with the separately published collection of *Carmina* (Book Four). Thematic, as opposed to strictly generic, considerations determine the choice of topics in two of the essays on the lyric corpus: the coherence and political referentiality of the subgroup of Odes in Book III conventionally designated the "Roman Odes" (Syndikus), and the representation of female figures in the Odes (Ancona).

In Part III, which features approaches to Horatian poetics focused on the Satires and Epistles, the vexed question of malleable and evolving personae or "selves" is a common preoccupation, to varying degrees, of the four contributors. Interpretative frames represented in this segment comprise: the Horatian reformulation of the satiric persona against the foil of a major Latin predecessor, Lucilius (Schlegel); the nature and degree of ambivalent "self-revelation" that may be discerned across the generic boundaries of satire and lyric (Freudenburg); the self-reflective conversation that takes place between the personae of the Epistles and the Satires (Cucchiarelli); and the author's epistolary dialogues with himself on such philosophical concerns as how to come to terms with advancing old age and physical decline (Johnson).

Reception studies—the major theme of Part IV—have attracted increasing attention from Classical scholars since the final decades of the twentieth century. As these have proliferated, so has the inter-cultural range and theoretical sophistication of the investigations with respect to both time and place. At the analytical level, there is now more general acknowledgment among philologists that the phenomenon of "reception" is not confined to readers from later eras, but rather is coeval with the poet's contemporary readers and early commentators. Theoretical as well as empirical insights into the historical reception of Horatian verse are provided in this final section with reference to the major genres: *Odes* (Edmunds); *Sermones* and *Epistulae* (Braund); *Ars Poetica* (Golden).

A guiding principle determining the ensemble of essays in this volume has been to go beyond the synoptic norms of the typical handbook to embrace provocative and revisionist perspectives on well-worn issues of interpretation of Horace's works. Appended to each contribution is a Guide to Further Reading that furnishes suggestions for those readers who may be stimulated to venture into the vast domain of the secondary literature on Horace's poetry.

NOTES

1   See, e.g., Carne-Ross and Haynes 1996.
2   The well-preserved fresco, which has been dated to the first century CE, was found on the left wall of a *triclinium* excavated in the town of Moregine, south of Pompei's Porta Stabia: see Mattusch 2009: 246–7.

PART I

Biographical and Social Contexts

CHAPTER ONE

The Biographical and Social Foundations of Horace's Poetic Voice[1]

David Armstrong

Descende caelo et dic age tibia
Regina longum Calliope melos,
    seu uoce nunc mauis acuta
        seu fidibus citharaue Phoebi.

Auditis? An me ludit amabilis   5
insania? Audire et uideor pios
    errare per lucos, amoenae
        quos et aquae subeunt et aurae.

Me fabulosae Volture in Apulo
nutricis extra limen Apuliae   10
    ludo fatigatumque somno
        fronde noua puerum palumbes

texere, mirum quod foret omnibus
quicumque celsae nidum Aceruntiae
    saltusque Bantinos et aruum
        pingue tenent humilis Forenti,   15

ut tuto ab atris corpore uiperis
dormirem et ursis, ut premerer sacra
    lauroque conlataque myrto,
        non sine dis animosus infans.   20

Vester, Camenae, uester in arduos
tollor Sabinos, seu mihi frigidum
    Praeneste seu Tibur supinum
        seu liquidae placuere Baiae;

uestris amicum fontibus et choris   25
non me Philippis uersa acies retro,
        deuota non extinxit arbor
            nec Sicula Palinurus unda.

Vtcumque mecum uos eritis, libens
insanientem nauita Bosphorum
        temptabo et urentis harenas   30
            litoris Assyrii uiator,

uisam Britannos hospitibus feros
et laetum equino sanguine Concanum,
        uisam pharetratos Gelonos   35
            et Scythicum inuiolatus amnem.

Come down from heaven, sing to the flute,
queen Calliope, lasting music,
let your piercing voice sound over it,
or choose Apollo's harp, or lyre.

Do you all hear it? sweet madness playing
with me? I hear and seem to wander
through sacred groves, with pleasant waters
drifting through them, and pleasant breezes.

There is a fable that fabulous doves
in Apulia, on the Vultures' Mountain,
outside my nurse's Apulian threshold,[2]
strewed me, a child, with fresh-grown leaves

(tired out with play, tired out with sleep),
and hid me—a miracle known to all
that live in Acherontia, the Eagle's Nest,
and the groves of Bantium halfway up
and the rich farms of flat Forentum—

that I might sleep there, already covered
in sacred laurel heaped with myrtle,
safe from black vipers and forest bears,
by the gods' favor, precocious infant!

Still yours in the Sabine hills, Italian Muses:
yours halfway up in cool Praeneste,
yours further down in the canyons of Tibur,
or if I like in breezy Baiae.

Neither the rout at Philippi's field
nor the accursed tree could kill me,
charmed by your sacred springs and dances,
nor storms from Sicily, come to the cape
of Palinurus: with you I'd tempt

the raging Bosphorus as a sailor,
and be a traveller through the sands
that burn on the Assyrian shore,

to Britons, savages to guests,
to Spaniards drunk on the blood of horses,
Ukrainian archers and their quivers,
or the Don's frozen mouth, safe always. (Horace, *Odes* 3.4.1–36) [3]

This is poetry, or at least the original Latin is, as exalted and complex in its lengthy periodic phrasing as even Horace ever attempts. Its obvious theme is poetry and opening spaces by it, yet nothing about it is obvious or simple. Doves carry ambrosia to Zeus (*Odyssey* 12.62), and bees fed Pindar as a child, and similar miracles are told of Stesichorus and Aeschylus. In the second part of the poem, 37–80, Horace will tell Augustus the story of the war between Zeus and the Olympians and the Giants, as a parable of the new emperor's own hard work to establish the *Pax Romana* across the Roman and the known world. He ventures up the scale of difficulty in poetic imitation to the greatest height yet heard of in lyric, to Pindaric models, particularly to the *First Pythian*. There a similar comparison is made between Zeus' wars and triumphs over the Titans and Giants and the king of Syracuse, Hiero, triumphant in a chariot victory at Delphi, triumphant over Carthage and Etruria, but old, sick, and with many enemies at home. The doves, which feed Zeus the stuff of immortality and keep Zeus strong to keep the world at peace, along with the legendary infancy of great poets, are the points of comparison for Horace's childhood. The poet is the helper of the king, and the same gods inspire him as inspire Augustus. This is foreshadowed even at the beginning. The laurel and myrtle that the doves pile over Horace to hide him from beasts are both the typical crowns of poets and Roman military crowns, for laurel crowns were the triumphs for great military victories and myrtle crowns were for the ovation for lesser or peaceful victories, laurel the crown of Apollo and myrtle the crown of Venus.

But this is an essay on Horace's biography, and its relation to his poetry.[4] And the spaces opened to Horace by the Muses are all literal, historically attested, autobiographical spaces that were opened to him in life in one way or another—especially Philippi, where he fought at age 23 as a legionary officer *against* Octavian, the future Augustus, and Antonius, Octavian's rival. For that, the two triumvirs confiscated his properties in his native town of Venusia in Apulia, now Venosa, located in the middle of a vast plain of farmland that it still serves as a farm-town. But by the time Horace published *Odes* 1–3 in 23 BCE, Augustus' court and inner circle included many who, like Horace, had once served with Brutus and Cassius against him, and others who had served with Antony and Cleopatra, and some who had done both. Horace throughout his poetry addresses as patrons and friends many veterans of Brutus' wars with Caesar and Antonius, and of Antonius' wars with Caesar, now safe and forgiven, like himself, under Augustus' regime and a testimony to Augustus' clemency and willingness to forget the past.

Venosa lies several miles from a broad, long-extinct volcano, Monte Volture, and from Venosa the little villages Horace describes, Acerenza high up, Banzi halfway down, Forenza in the plain, are still visible.[5] What we can verify about Horace's life and times is essential to understanding his poetry, even the details of his upbringing, property, and status. All the first readers of Horace's publications knew that even in the lyrics he would not have fictionalized his claims to status as an ex-military officer, a Roman knight, a scribe of the treasury, a *iudex selectus*. All of them knew what the land, on the other side of the Italian boot from the Bay of Naples, where he came from, was like. Italy is a small country, and not all the north of it was even "Italian" in Horace's lifetime, and all Italian citizens were also by then citizens of Rome, and all prosperous Italian citizens had and did business there.

His birthplace was a historic Roman town, a quiet farm-town, and in Horace's day a favorite retirement place for ex-soldiers. Probably a dozen tourists who know something about ancient history go to see the Sabine Farm outside Rome near Vicovaro, for every tourist that goes all the way to Venosa, far out in the southeastern countryside around the ankle of the Italian boot, looking for yet further light on Horace. Venosa is still small even now (12,000 people), still a farm-town, with a few handsome buildings and churches, and some attractive Roman ruins near it. It also features a statue of Horace in the town square, put up as late as 1898, with the unadventurous inscription Q HORATIO FLACCO/VENUSIA/MDCCCXCVIII, suggesting that the local schoolmasters hesitated even to choose a quotation from the works of the most famous citizen ever to have lived there. Horace was a *pugliese*, an Apulian, and harks back to his homeland all his life: in lines 9–10 of *Odes* 3.4 (whatever the text of line 10) he emphasizes that twice. An earlier text shows him uncertain whether his territory is far enough west from the coast toward Greece to be also Lucanian: *Lucanus an Apulus anceps*, he calls himself ("I might be either", *Satires* 2.1.34). Before we were quite at Monte Vulture, driving from Naples on our way there in 1986, I remember being charmed to see a two-armed fingerpost roadsign painted "LUCANIA" on one arm and "APULIA" on the other, as if to embody this question. Monte Vulture is several miles long and looms, at its height of blue-gray stone, 3,000 feet above the fertile plain first created around its volcano, extinct half a million years. It is still cooler in summer there at the top, of course, than the plain below, which is why the infant Horace was sent there by his businessman father. Its top is crowned with resorts, which we drove through, and also to Acerenza, 2,500 feet up at one side, and Banzi, 12 miles southeast of Venosa, and 1,900 feet up. Horace's Forenza was in the plain, which is 1,300 feet above sea level, but it comes with a view of all three places. Deforestation has made it hard to picture Horace's "bears" roaming the mountain any more (they did then), but his native towns are all still instructive to see.

Our poem claims that everyone up and down the mountain and in the plain knew of the miracle of Horace's childhood. Little had happened in history to Venosa. It was made a Roman colony with the limited form of citizenship called *ius Latii*, Latin rights, in 291 BCE. It served as a refuge for defeated troops fleeing from the defeat at Cannae in 216. In the Social War, 91–88 BCE, it was the only city with Latin rights to join a pan-Italian revolt against the Romans. Though its inhabitants won their full citizenship in the end, the city was taken during the war and many were enslaved. Horace's father was a freed slave, and perhaps he was one of these, and had to earn his freedom all over again. Horace *never* speaks of himself as anything but Italian, a pose that would have gotten him derision had it been false. Most scholars assume that, though a slave, Horace's father was born Italian also.

"Freedmen" like Horace's father—*libertini*—could be found in every economic class in the Roman Empire, from the poorest to the wealthiest. When Horace was born, on whatever day may have been indicated by what we call "December 8, 65 BCE," according to the calendar before Julius Caesar revised it, possibly in early autumn.[6] His father, who was perhaps born between 100 and 90 BCE, was already free and already prosperous enough to send his son in summer as a matter of course up the mountain and away from the heat, to the house of a nurse, whether free or slave. And his father was well enough known and respected, in an area the size of a large American county, that "everyone" who lived round the mountains and plains knew, before Horace was more than an adolescent, that he had a brilliant and promising son. Thus Horace did not begin his life without space to roam in—that of a whole rural county where he was known and respected—even before his father took him to Rome and bought a house there, from which to supervise his education.

Horace's father, like many freedmen who succeeded in business, was eager to advance his son further in life, and open more space to him, than he could himself ever climb or travel. The ambitions of freedmen of Roman citizens and towns, some of whom had already acquired substantial property before being freed, legally theirs (called their *peculium* and including even personal slaves), were one of the great engines of Roman business. Such talented slaves, like all freedmen of Roman citizens or Roman cities with the franchise, had Roman citizenship on being freed, and could hope for yet more social progress for their children and descendants. And though Horace's father came from a country district, he had easy access to the rest of south Italy, and to the area from Rome, down to Naples, round to Rhegium, Tarentum, and Brundisium, which was the heart of the whole Mediterranean business and trade of the Empire, and to all the resort towns and villa towns on the Bay of Naples, like Baiae and Salerno. Horace's poetry continually evokes these landscapes as well as those of his native district.

We have at least a brief digest of Suetonius' *Life* of Horace. Both it and the poems (no fragment of written prose or of anything supposed to have been said by Horace in conversation survives, but all but a few of the poems are spoken in Horace's own *persona*) give us a number of facts about Horace, particularly about his class, property, and standing. It was not socially acceptable or, as far as property and standing and offices held go legal, for him to misrepresent these in writing. Whatever you could get away with in the provinces, in Rome itself pretenders to rank were mercilessly ridiculed, even prosecuted in court.[7] Horace was born a free Roman citizen, and to parents who were most probably *both* freed slaves, though we know nothing about his mother. His father was a freedman, and freedmen tended to marry freedwomen. He was also an auction broker, *coactor auctionum*, a lucrative profession at the heart of Roman business, which depended on the conversion of goods and real estate into coin. Dull as Venosa was, its inhabitants had been Roman citizens since the Social War of 81–78 BCE. By Roman law, whatever Roman inhabitant freed the elder Horatius (if it was not the town of Venosa itself, whose *servus publicus* he could equally well have been) gave him and his children Roman citizenship. It was full citizenship with all privileges, but with the limitations the law imposed on freedmen. You should behave as the faithful client of whoever freed you for the rest of your life or his. However much wealth you accumulated, you could never wear the gold ring that identified the two highest classes of citizens, to which all Horace's great patrons and friends belonged, the senators and the knights. You could acquire many times the legally required property for the status, yet could never be a Roman knight, *eques Romanus*, which gave you immense privileges in civil law even above ordinary Roman citizens throughout the rest of the Empire. Much less could you be a senator, a lifetime privilege which required election to at least one major magistracy in Rome in addition. The rich freedman Trimalchio in Petronius' *Satyricon* only dares to wear a gold ring "covered with iron ornaments like stars" (32). And that although he is rich enough to buy and sell many a Roman knight, and both he and his guests make the point explicitly that he could do so if he chose.

Horace's father was debarred from these ranks, but he had a son—evidently an only or only surviving son, for Horace mentions no brothers and sisters, and he and his father are apparently thought of as a pair confiding in each other alone when he describes their relationship in *Satires* 1.4 and 1.6. How far freedmen's sons could rise in rank was a gray area of the law. Five years before Horace's birth, in 70 BCE, came the last census ever successfully conducted by the ex-consuls who were chosen as censors by the laws of the Republic.[8] After that, for forty years, the census was often started but always abandoned. The power the censors had to strike Roman citizens from the list and cancel their privileges exercised all over the empire, such as their tax exemptions, the superior status in provincial governors' law courts, or their right of freeing slaves and paying a 5 percent tax on their value to convert them into Roman citizen clients of their own, was too frightening. So also the censors' power of dismissing even senators from their lifelong status as senators, and *equites* from their "public horse," was too explosive and controversial for two senior senators, however respected, to exercise it successfully on their own sole responsibility. When Augustus finally revised the lists of the senate, knights and people in 28 BCE, having awarded himself and Agrippa censorial powers, he was accompanied to the Senate to announce his new list of senators by soldiers concealing arms under their togas. It encapsulates some important aspects of Horace's career that the *equites*, one of whom he now was, and the *plebs* were generally as willing to accept the new census as they were to accept nearly everything else the new regime did. But Horace was an enthusiastic convert to the new regime, and his status remained unquestioned.

The law required that to be *eques* or *senator* you should have property valued at 400,000 sesterces, which were only units of account and not really coins in Horace's youth, or 100,000 denarii, the real currency of daily life in Italy. Augustus thought proper in revising the Senate to raise the qualification to 1,000,000 sesterces for senators. But that really only brought to full definition a view which Horace endorses, that senators ought to have and spend more to support their rank than the *equites*. In *Satires* 1.6, published at age 30, he already claims that he could be a senator if he liked, but it would cost too much and gain him too little. When he pictures in *Satires* 2.3.168–86 a self-made Italian businessman, "Oppidius," *dives antiquo censu*, "rich by standards of earlier times," telling his two sons he will curse them and disinherit them in his will if they waste his money buying their way into the Senate, just for the "vain titles" of aedile or praetor, he is picturing a situation similar to his own and his father's, though I think no commentary says this explicitly. Whatever one chooses to make of this claim, it seems plausible at face value. Thus in 35 BCE, while Octavian and Antony were still disputing the leadership of the Roman world and would for another four years, the 35-year-old Horace can write of himself as one who could be not just a Roman knight but a marginal senator, one of the 600 in the House of Lords of the Roman Empire. However, he knows he could have a status among the aristocracy equivalent only to that of a Labor life peer, not that of a hereditary earl or duke. His father is spoken of already in this book as no longer living, but it is doubtful that his wildest dreams for Horace's future status went even that far.

The beautiful denarii of the Republic, with which Italy was fairly well monetized in Horace's day—at least by the standards of the ancient world—are still not expensive to buy at coin sales, at least in common types ($25 in average condition on Ebay as of February 2009). In terms of US dollars in 2009, their purchasing power seems to have been that of the common currency that stuffs our wallets, $20 bills, or perhaps not quite: I thought of denarii as $5 bills when I first wrote about this subject in 1986, but probably the $20 bill will not even be enough before long. A person with a secure net worth of two million dollars in our society in 2009 has about the sort of status and influence the equestrian class claimed in the Roman world. On this equestrian minimum census of 100,000 denarii you could expect a yield of 5 percent, or 20,000 sesterces a year, in a society where bare subsistence could be had for 200–400 sesterces. So Juvenal's disappointed male gigolo Naevolus, who mentions this income (9.140) as his minimum that he had hoped for, was hoping to be *pauper … et eques* (Martial, 4. 40.4), on the minimum census. Martial thinks you can even get 6 percent out of the minimum equestrian fortune (cf. Courtney on Juvenal 9.140) and have 24,000 a year. I know that ancient and modern incomes are difficult to compare, but $120,000 a year in New York City and that notionally equivalent income in Rome c.100 BCE—100 CE seem at the beginning of 2009 a fair comparison none the less.

Money had depreciated a little from Horace's day to Martial's and Juvenal's, but the minimal equestrian census even then still made you a person of respect, even in Rome, let alone the countryside. You could also have lots more than that, and be *eques splendidus* and *clarus* to distinguish you from the herd. Indeed, you could be like Horace's immensely rich patron Maecenas or (at a more reasonable level) Cicero's friend Atticus, who had two million sesterces of *census,* which made him moderately rich, and twelve million after an inheritance, which made him very rich. And still, like both these men, you could refuse to enter the Senate, and simply keep the rank of *eques Romanus.* Horace's colleague in poetry, Vergil, another rich knight, died worth twenty million sesterces, richer even than Atticus. At all levels, the equestrian class was proud of its business abilities and its endless interactions with greater people as patrons and clients. Yet even for the most merciless Roman businessmen and moneylenders a pretence of leisure and landowning and a wish to retire from the City to the country for quiet was part and parcel of equestrian rank. Thus Horace's poetry, especially after Maecenas had given him the Sabine Farm (by 30 BCE, when he was 35), is full of what his rank required of him, unenthusiastic references to the boredom of business work in Rome as *scriba* and *iudex,* and idealizations of country quiet, study, and peace at the farm (*Satires* 2.6–7). For that matter in *Satires* 1.6.111–31, as part of his self-portrait as a potential senator, he makes perfectly clear that even in Rome he already had abundant leisure, daylong if he liked.

How did Horace reach this enviable position, even before Maecenas became his patron? Wealth and *census* were denominated in theoretical denarii, not real ones. Very much revenue was in kind, and property in land, houses, and slaves had also to be realized into silver coins when they were sold (Augustus and his successors introduced gold and bronze on a large scale). All this coin was carefully realized, collected, and guarded by commission brokers and dealers. "Auctioneers" were at the cash foundation of Roman business life. That was the business Horace's father was in, probably for both private persons, and for the local, and later on the central, Roman government. Horace calls him (and so does the *Life*) a *coactor,* goods gatherer, for the auctions. But probably he could double as a *praeco* or goods-barking auctioneer, or as *argentarius*, collector of money from bidders. These were not always separate roles. There were 1 percent commissions from the state and from private persons for each of these to earn from this trade, and these commissions built the houses—for example—of such Pompeiian freedmen as L. Caecilius Jucundus, some of whose auction account books survive, and the Vettii brothers. Probably the tough survivor's face of Jucundus' portrait statue is the sort of thing to think of in picturing Horace's father. But it is worth noting that art historians are beginning to discard the theory that these big, handsome town houses with their elegant and discreetly erotic decorations are mere McMansions in imitation of the greater artistic culture of the aristocratic villas outside the towns.[9] Horace's poetry, particularly his earliest publications, the two books of Satires, published at age 30 and age 35 in 35 and 30 BCE, is full of clues and explicit statements about his upbringing and about the exact rank it bought for him. And while poetry and imagination to some extent color these statements, they can be shown to have a factual basis.

The first of these factual claims made in the Satires is that Horace's father moved him to Rome, and bought a house there on the Esquiline, to a city where already for a hundred years visiting client kings had famously found themselves too poor to rent anything that suited their station, without planning elaborately in advance. He could, says Horace, have sent his son to school at Venusia with the sons of centurions—these made nearly half an *eques'* minimum income in the army, and were important people in small towns—but moved him to Rome, and gave him an education that put him squarely among the two upper ranks.

> macro pauper agello
> noluit in Flavi ludum me mittere, magni
> quo pueri magnis e centurionibus orti
> laevo suspensi loculos tabulamque lacerto
> ibant octonos referentes idibus aeris,   75
> sed puerum est ausus Romam portare docendum
> artis quas doceat quivis eques atque senator
> semet prognatos. vestem servosque sequentis,
> in magno ut populo, siqui vidisset, avita
> ex re praeberi sumptus mihi crederet illos.
> ipse mihi custos incorruptissimus omnis
> circum doctores aderat.

> Low born, and not rich in land,
> he would not have me sent to Flavius' day-school,
> where hulking centurions' hulking louts of sons,
> with pack and tablets hung on their left arms,
> went clutching their eight brass pennies on the Ides:
> but dared to take his son to Rome and teach him
> whatever studies the greatest knight or senator
> would teach his sons. My clothes and my train of slaves,

> as is necessary in crowded cities, whoever saw
> would believe an ancestral fortune supported my spending.
> He himself, the most incorruptible of protectors,
> went with me to all my teachers'... (*Satires* 1.6.71–82)

Horace's father must have been born about 100–90 BCE. He was declaring a certain amount of leisure from business by now (c.50 BCE, in the middle of the civil wars caused by the First Triumvirate), just by taking off work and accompanying his son back and forth from his Roman house to school. But the rewards for auction-broking in Rome itself were the greatest in the Empire, and no doubt his south Italian connections made him a success. One of the fashionable teachers we know he hired for Horace was from south Italy, not far from Venosa, Orbilius of Beneventum, now Benevento, who taught Horace the early Latin poets (Horace mentions Livius Andronicus) and was famous for inflicting beatings on his students. Orbilius was remembered affectionately by them, as were many brutal Victorian schoolmasters by their aristocratic students (like John Keate, DD, 1773–1832, headmaster of Eton, who was adored by his students throughout their later life though he once flogged eighty of them in one day). Such parallels with the *plagosus Orbilius* are often mentioned in Horace commentaries of the nineteenth century, but they do not often enough draw the obvious conclusion that Horace was being educated among schoolmates of the two higher ranks in the Republic, in order to push himself as high in rank as he could be made to go. Where Horace is testing the reader's credulity is in saying immediately about his father:

> nec timuit, sibi ne vitio quis verteret, olim
> si praeco parvas, aut ut fuit ipse, coactor
> mercedes sequerem: neque ego essem questus: at hoc nunc
> laus illi debetur et a me gratia maior.

> He was never afraid it would be a reproach to him
> if as auctioneer or, as he was, auction broker,
> I piled up small gains: nor would I complain: as things are,
> I owe him praise and gratitude all the more.

These lines suggest that Horace's father, by pushing him ahead in society, enabled him to attain the rank of Roman *eques*, with several times the necessary fortune. Horace goes on to assert that at Rome, in his house there, he can spend all the day free from business if he wants (*Satires* 1.6.110–31). The morning has no business duties, the afternoon can be spent wandering around lonely as a cloud, checking out the goings-on in the Forum and attending services at one temple or another, and then having dinner by himself at home, a dinner "served by only three slaves." (116) Commentators have sometimes talked as if these were the only slaves he had at his Roman house. But Horace characterizes in the same book Tigellius, a monster of excess in both directions, as being someone he has seen sometimes rich enough to keep 200 slaves (therefore a rich senator's household) and sometimes so poor he is down to his last ten (*Satires* 1.3.11–12). Horace's point is that he only needs three of his slaves to serve him dinner *when he dines by himself*. This assertion does not appear to be a mark of ostentation. Along with the house they served him in—for owning one's own house in Rome was as unusual as in modern New York City—it places him clearly in a certain class and rank. The house alone will have had two or three dozen slaves at least, not to mention his other properties.[10]

This is in the first of his books, published at age 30, and we know something about how he got to this point. His father sent him to Athens, to be educated with "senators' and knights' sons" like those he had gone to school with. And like the fashionable Roman boys' schools, it cost him a lot. Philosophy, studied at Athens, was the culmination of aristocratic educations. Cicero gave his son the income of an entire apartment house he owned to live on during his philosophical studies at Athens, and if Horace had not been able to hold up his head in this sort of society, one of the central events of his life would never have happened. He began philosophical studies that he claims lasted the rest of his life, and he clearly values this knowledge both in itself (he kept a lifelong but skeptical preference for the Epicureans, as Cicero kept a skeptical preference for the Stoics) and as a class marker and bond with aristocratic Roman amateurs of philosophy. When he was 22, not long after the assassination of Julius Caesar, Brutus and Cassius the Liberators arrived in Athens and enlisted all the young aristocrats there who would come into their army against Octavian, Antony, and Lepidus, the new Triumvirs. We may assume on the evidence of the *Life* that Brutus personally conferred, probably at the request of Horace's friends, the rank of *tribunus militum* on Horace. As one of the board of six officers who formed the officer corps of a legion, the rank conferred the equestrian gold ring for life, as monuments show,[11] in its most unquestionable form, earned by military office in youth; the grant of the *equus publicus*, a cavalry horse paid for by the state; and the right for life to sit not just in the front fourteen rows at spectacles and theatre performances that were reserved for the *equites*, but in the first two of these rows. In other words, officer service, for the upper classes, was repaid with lifetime, upper-class privileges.

In the end, after the loss at Philippi, Horace expressed no great affection for Brutus at any time in his life. In *Satires* 1.7 he pictures Brutus as a distant, contemptuous presence, listening to two noisy litigants, both wealthy Romans, in a business case. Brutus does this in his role as provincial governor, on which his right to lead his army was founded. The litigant Persius calls Brutus "the sun of Asia, and his suite of companions lifegiving stars," *Satires* 1.7.23–4, for the court of a governor and the governor himself were sometimes addressed even by Romans in language appropriate to regal flattery. But his opponent Rex is the Dog Star, and since Brutus cuts kings' throats, the satire concludes, why not Rex's throat also? [12]

Whatever he thought of Brutus as a person, Horace is clearly proud that he won this distinction in the last armies of the Republic, rather than from the triumvirs or the emperor. Though he says the appointment was controversial, with soldiers in camp chanting the words *libertino patre natus*, "born of a freedman for a father," (*Satires* 1.6.45–8) and the defeat cost him much property, by confiscation (*Epistles* 2.2.49–53), he had enough left to buy the *scriptus quaestorius* when he returned.

He could have lived the rest of his life in ease in this position, a splendid "job" in both senses of the word, both several ranks higher in the state service than the state's auctioneers and auction brokers, and far more of a sinecure. The board of scribes to the annually elected quaestors who ran the treasury had the equestrian census, or near it, though the freedmen among them could not wear the ring. Indeed, the office itself cannot have cost less than the equestrian census, because it gave the holder a 4 percent commission on the revenues he registered, and this must have been far more than the 24,000 sesterces the minimum equestrian property could yield at best. This generous commission was not considered an instance of corruption,[13] and it implies a lot of practical work which Horace does not describe. It was so profitable that one did not exercise it every year, and thus attended board meetings and committees only in off years.

Horace will probably have bought the position of scribe at about age 25, in 40 BCE. We know this was the minimum age to be an equestrian *iudex selectus*, or justice/judge of the peace, as Horace became at some point in the thirties BCE. He may even have attained the rank this early, as an ex-tribune of the soldiers.

Then his friend the poet Vergil, and the tragic poet Varius, sponsored his introduction as a promising writer to Maecenas, with Agrippa, one of Octavian's two most trusted associates. Maecenas' circle of friends, and now Horace's, included not only Vergil and Varius but Plotius Tucca, later Vergil's editor after his death, and the literary critic Quintilius Varus. All four of these wealthy young men of equestrian rank, together, are now known to have been addressees of a treatise written in the forties BCE by the Epicurean poet and philosopher Philodemus (c.110–c.35 BCE), whose verses and even prose treatises are referred to by Horace, among his many other models, throughout his poetic career. All four names occur frequently together in Horace's early poetry, but Maecenas', as his principal patron, the most often.

There was a third equestrian rank, or the equivalent, that Horace held, probably in 35 BCE when he wrote *Satires* 1, and certainly in 30 BCE when he wrote *Satires* 2: *iudex selectus*. In *Satires* 1.4, he pictured his father holding the Roman *iudices selecti* up for admiration to him, as a boy, and clearly hoping his behavior would merit comparison with theirs and possible admission to their rank (*Satires* 1.4.120–3).[14]

For the whole last hundred years of the Republic, the right to be a *iudex* and decide on one's own authority smaller cases between parties and smaller criminal offences, as well as sit on larger juries and permanent legal commissions for larger cases, had been battled over by senators, *equites* of high rank, and *equites* and marginal census-holders of lower rank. Horace was one of these *iudices*. It was a time-consuming occupation for gentlemen of leisure, similar to the duties of a landed gentleman or rich Londoner who is "justice of the peace" in a Victorian novel. These also were required, not to be legal experts, but to have legal experts (juris consulti) accessible for consultation, and, like Roman *iudices*, were unpaid, and expected to be vital elements in the maintenance of order and upper-class rule. Aulus Gellius was a *iudex selectus* under Hadrian, and describes with some pride his duties and the required consultations with aristocratic jurisconsults it entailed to make decisions correctly,[15] even as Horace flaunts his acquaintance with the two Epicurean-leaning jurisconsults, Trebatius Testa (*Satires* 2.1) and Manlius Torquatus[16] (*Epistles* 1.5). Recognized moral character in business matters was required for this office, as his father had told him (he claims) in his boyhood, not just in business matters, but even in sexual relations. Romans disapproved of adultery and of interference with freemen's children, and also valued chastity in childhood at least until the assumption of the *toga candida* at 14 or 15. This Horace's father required of him (*Satires* 1.4.103–26). He seems to have attained the ranks of *eques equo publico* (far from the poorest among these), *scriba quaestorius*, and *iudex selectus*. That is as much and more than his father, now dead, had hoped, though he would supposedly have settled for less.

More surprisingly, in his first book publication, Horace asserts in detail in *Satires* 1.6 that he has the money and influence to get himself even the rank of senator. He could easily be elected as *quaestor*, the first of the elected ranks that made you a senator for life. He could even borrow money as did a certain foolish "Tillius,"[17] a mirror of what would happen to Horace if he went too far with this imaginary career-track (*Satires* 1.6.24–5, 105–9). He could (one supposes, by giving the expensive games or doing the expensive public works demanded of senators of the next rank, the aediles) raise himself to be one of the praetors. The board of these officials doubled as army generals during their term and provincial governors after it, but they were also the supreme judges that preside over the *album iudicum* Horace belonged to as *iudex selectus*, though his fantasies do not include the ultimate honor of the consulship. This too is a claim that would have made him ridiculous if not supported by facts.[18] But like his patron Maecenas, who (cf. *Satires* 1.8) was already building a palace on the Esquiline that astounded all Rome by its magnificence and yet did not think the Senate worth entering, he would rather keep his leisure than overcome doubts about his birth on the part of the public by offering himself at the election, or risk more doubts from any possible set of censors that came along. His right to be *eques Romanus* was presumably already secure. Moreover, he would be merely wasting time and money. "Tillius" was compelled, first as quaestor and then praetor, to appear in public with *servos sequentes*, a train of five slaves, in Tillius' case carrying his chamber-pot and wine-jar (107). But this is far too few for a person of praetorian rank, even on Tillius' journey to suburban Tibur, presumably already known as Horace's own summer resort.

> nunc mihi curto
> ire licet mulo vel si libet usque Tarentum
> mantica cui lumbos onere ulceret atque eques armos:
> obiciet nemo sordes mihi quas tibi, Tilli.

> As things are, if I like,
> *I* can go on a bob-tailed mule as far as Tarentum,
> a pack irritating its loins, and a Roman *Eques*
> on its shoulders, and no one calling me cheap, like you...
> (*Satires* 1.6.103–5)

He had already said, in *Satires* 1.4, in describing his first visit to Maecenas,

> ut veni coram, singultim pauca locutus,
> infans namque pudor prohibebat plura profari,
>   non ego me claro natum patre, non ego circum
>   me Satureiano vectari rura caballo,
>   sed quod eram narro.

> When I came before you, talking in gulps and briefly,
> for speechless modesty kept me from babbling out more,
> I did not say my father was noble, nor round my fields
> there was a nag from Tarentum carrying—me,
> but I told you what I was. (*Satires* 1.4.56–60)

Maecenas had perhaps asked, why are you wearing the equestrian gold ring? Horace replied that he had the rank but was not high-born, a freedman's son, but without immense landed property, though he had property in south Italy (whatever he lost at Venusia). Nor was there a "nag from Tarentum," a *caballus*, the popular word for horse, carrying this particular *eques*. His joke is that he is an *eques* on a *caballus*, or even, if he felt like it, a *mulus*.[19]

Presumably Horace even had business interests at Tarentum, a commercial port on the sea at the middle of the sole of the Italian boot, since he parades journeys there in his Odes and even asks a friend, Septimius, to invest with him there in real estate, *Odes* 2.6.9–24.[20] In *Odes* 1.28, 29, the speaker is sailing to Tarentum for profit, 27–9. The corpse of the dead man lying on the shore who asks the speaker for burial addresses the speaker, whom I take to be Horace, as being a citizen of Venusia (26), and also remarks that the ancient philosopher Archytas had been buried, as he wishes to be, on the "Matinian shore," near Tarentum (3). Horace famously contrasts himself to Pindar, the Theban Eagle, as the "Matinian Bee," *Odes* 4.2.27–8.

However that may be, his Epicurean circle and their connections raised his prosperity still higher. Between 35 and 30 BCE, Maecenas gave Horace a farm with several tenant farms in the Sabine hills above Rome to the northeast. Horace already had a house in Rome that had probably been his father's. We do not know when in the twenties Augustus gave Horace, or he bought, property in Tibur, now Tivoli, but he had a house there too by the time he published the Odes in 23 BCE. Nor do we know whether Horace had yet another house north of Rome and above it at Praeneste, now Palestrina, or merely liked to stay there for extended periods. He later—in *Epistles* Book I, published three years later in 20 BCE—claims to have read all the way through both Homeric epics during a stay at Palestrina, in order to versify what proves to be Philodemus' allegory of Homer's teachings about good and bad "kings," and apply it to Roman people of rank, *Epistles* 1.2.2.[21] As for Baiae, also mentioned in *Odes* 3.4 among the spaces opened to Horace by his success and his patrons, he probably visited resorts on the other side of south Italy from his birthplace whenever he liked, particularly in winter, but did *not* own property there. For he was perfectly willing, according to *Epistles* I, to change Baiae for Velia (Elea) and Salerno for the winter on the advice of his doctor, Antonius Musa, who was also Augustus' doctor (*Epistles* 1.15.1–3). Horace apparently contemplates both renting lodging in these places, as he will have done yearly in Baiae before, and buying himself better wine and concubines than his Sabine farm could provide (15.18–21). He asks a senatorial friend, Numonius Vala, whose ancient and illustrious family were the hereditary patrons of the Greek city of Paestum nearby, about how to travel there. But he explicitly classes himself below those few, like Vala, who were rich enough to *own* seaside villas at the great resorts on the Bay of Naples:

> Nam tuta et parvula laudo
> cum res deficient, satis inter vilia fortis:
> verum ubi quid melius contigit et unctius, idem
> vos sapere et solos aio bene vivere, quorum
> conspicitur nitidis fundata pecunia villis.

> for I praise what is safe and small,
> when my balance is low, brave enough to live on the cheap side;
> but when things are better and richer for me, I hold
> that only you are the wise men and know how to live
> whose solid funds are on show in your glorious villas. (15.42–6)

Horace separates himself deliberately, as an equestrian of rank, from the villa-owning classes but moves in their circle.

We can return at last to the claims Horace makes for himself at age 42, in 23 BCE, in the passage from *Odes* 3.4 with which we began. As a favored poet of Augustus' new regime, at the time of publication of the three first books of odes in 23 BCE (indeed, on some datings, already in 28 BCE, if *Odes* 3.4 was written separately, or reflects his situation five years earlier as well as at the time of publication), all Italy is open to him. He owns country houses both in the Sabine hills, at what is now Licenza, 4,500 feet above sea level, and farther down at Tibur, now Tivoli, 770 feet above sea level. He can summer at Praeneste, 1,500 feet above sea level, and winter at Baiae down on the Gulf of Naples, if he likes, theoretically a health resort with hot baths and sulphur treatments, but also famous throughout both the life and the literature of the Republic and the Empire as (literally) a byword for expense, luxury, and decadence. These are the parallels for high Acerenza, medium-high Banzi, and flat Forenza and Venosa where he came from. Life had not been without challenge. Horace once risked his life to fight the Triumvirs—that is, Caesar, later Augustus himself, his addressee, along with Mark Antony—in the army of Brutus and Cassius. Later times were more peaceful, but he was nearly killed by a falling tree on his Sabine estate, and on one of his numerous visits to his native south Italy, he was nearly drowned in a shipwreck off Cape Palinurus south of Salerno. All these places are real.

But in imagination, Horace claims in *Odes* 3.4, he would gladly face the further challenge of traveling as a tourist round the whole Roman Empire. Not just to provinces already visited by Roman armies and open to Roman conquest, like Spain or Britain, but places not yet conquered. Even to places unthinkable for ordinary Romans when he was born, like the land of the Geloni, whose name means the "frost people," in Ukraine, or the burning Assyrian sands, or the mouth of the Tanais, now the Don, but even so not entirely beyond Augustus' and Agrippa's ambitious projects for foreign relations and conquest. He will see them as a boat traveler, *navita*, and a land traveler, *viator*, and just for the pleasure of seeing them, *visam*, "I shall go sightseeing": *visere* is to travel for the pleasure of travelling. We do not actually know that Horace ever left Italy for the rest of his life, even for easy places like Greece, after he returned from Philippi to find his lands confiscated at Venosa and took up the scribeship and his literary pursuits for a living. But there is much more here than the literal meaning. Juno has just said in the previous Ode, 3.3, that when she abandons her temporary hostility to Rome, the one portrayed in the *Aeneid*, she will open it up to the Romans both to conquer, and to tour as avid sightseers, the whole known world:

> quicumque mundo terminus obstitit,
>   hunc tanget armis, visere gestiens,
>   qua parte debacchentur ignes,
>   qua nebulae pluviique rores.
>
> whatever limit is set the world
>   he shall reach in conquest, longing for new sights,
>   wherever the fires, wherever the clouds
>   rage highest and the storms of rain. (*Odes* 3.3.53–6)

The ancient commentary handed down as "Porphyrio" is quite right to explain that *Odes* 3.4 begins with *descende caelo*, "come down from heaven," as a reference to Horace's concluding deprecation of his pretence to know Juno's exact words at the end of 3.3 (69–72). It is quite impossible to understand Horace's reason for these grandiose travel plans without looking at the previous poem also, for Horace would only look silly if he had issued *Odes* 3.4 on a sheet by itself. *Odes* 3.3.53–6 is essential to explain what he means in *Odes* 3.4.30–6. Like the Roman soldier of 3.3 he can travel in book form until the world ends, travel both in time and in space. Julius Caesar had conquered Gaul and had wanted to conquer Parthia as well, and had named for himself a month in the Julian calendar. Augustus had already named August for himself and put it right after July, and Augustus' and Agrippa's cartographers were already making up the maps of world organization, conquest, and frontier diplomacy that resulted in such monuments as the great Map of Agrippa, set up in Rome in the *Porticus Vipsania* not long after Horace's death. Their propaganda during Horace's lifetime was centered on pacification and expansion now that the long era of civil war was over and Rome united under the Principate. But Horace has a third meaning which is not literal, and which only works in the context of the Roman Odes as a set and of the three books of Odes as a whole. In the real world other Romans than himself may conquer and travel, in his lifetime and after his death, *but they will take his poetry with them.* Already in his lifetime he values the Roman peace for his personal safety, as he makes clear in *Odes* 3.14.14–16, and believes as long as Augustus rules the whole earth, the civil wars will not return,

> ego nec tumultum
> nec mori per vim metuam, tenente
> Caesare terras,

> nor shall I fear
> insurrection or death in riots if Caesar
> keeps hold of the world.[22]

But if Horace ever left Italy and Sicily again after his return from Philippi, even to go as far as Greece, he does not mention it and neither does any ancient source. He means the reader to take in what looks like the literal meaning, that Horace will personally travel and sail under the Muses' protection anywhere currently under Roman rule in 23 BCE as the book is published, or even in diplomatic contact with Rome, and then discard it.

For Horace's figurative meaning, the real one, is set forth fully at the end of Book 2 of the *Odes*, 2.20, where he forbids mourning at his funeral: he is already in his lifetime turning into a swan that will fly over the whole map of empire. He will live forever all over it in the memory of provincials now not civilized enough to read, like the Spaniards, currently drinking horse's blood, who will later read Horace once they know how:

> Iam Daedaleo notior Icaro
> visam gementis litora Bospori
> Syrtisque Gaetulas canorus
> ales Hyperboreosque campos.

Me Colchus et qui dissimulat metum
Marsae cohortis Dacus et ultimi
    noscent Geloni, me peritus
      discet Hiber Rhodanique potor.

More famous than Icarus the craftsman's son
I shall explore the shores of Bosphorus
and the sands of Africa, a singing
bird, and the Hyperborean fields;

Medea's countrymen, Dacians pretending
no fear of South Italian soldiers,
the farthest, frozen men, and learned
Spaniards, and those by the Rhone shall learn me
by heart[23]... (*Odes* 2.20.13–20)

Horace assumes you have already read this concluding Ode of Book 2, if you are
to understand *Odes* 3.4.1–36 and his "travel plans" there.

Thus the grand Pindaric passage with which we began turns out to be solidly
factual and autobiographical as well. It is even a fact that Horace is still read,
even memorized, in more countries today than Agrippa's map contained, including all the ones he mentions. But the claim to have won status in Rome and
space of his own all throughout Italy, and all over the Empire for his poetry,
from a start in the rustic farmlands of the south, is historically accurate. Yet the
passage shows satisfyingly, thus taken, that though perhaps a poem here and there
is to be taken as written and read to friends earlier than the publication of the
whole, the Roman Odes, 3.1–6, are meant to be read together rather than separately, and even with the last odes of Book 2 as a background.[24] Horace places
himself through this series of poems in the whole context of time and space, of
vast and expanding empire, of the sense of all the centuries of Roman history
coming to a climactic point, of a memory of this climactic point that will last for
ages, that the optimistic art of the early Augustan period loved to portray.

All four of the satirists, Lucilius, Horace, Persius, and Juvenal, and also the
epigrammatist Martial, their congener, make it clear that they were Roman
equites, and proud of their rank (as were many other Roman writers; and the
three senatorial literary men one thinks of first, Cicero, Lucan, and Seneca, were
all born to equestrian families). All five, though rich by everyone's standards but
those of the few thousand greatest men in the Empire, claim that they are men
of moderation occupying an ideal mean in their life style, an *aurea mediocritas*
between the truly great and the poor, but none at such length and in such detail
as Horace. Why Horace says more about his rank than the others is clear enough.
He was a freedman's son, and it was important to him, and presumably to Maecenas' circle, including the future Augustus, to create a self-portrait explaining
his title to be among them. But all the equestrian poets who mention their rank,
and many like Lucretius and Vergil who do not explicitly do so, are assuming

not just the *otium equestre*, the equestrian leisure from senatorial politics, but the *libertas equestris*, the freedom of speech and comment, which their property and rights and interest in the welfare of the Roman state give them. This is a freedom the poor do not have, nor anyone who is compelled to please a patron, whose side he has to take or renounce his friendship, including even the rich freedmen, whose political interests were legally required to be their patron's; or even the marginal knights who are booed by the people or actually removed by the ushers for entering the fourteen rows. The *equites* incurred neither the expense nor the responsibilities of senatorial politics, nor did they receive the great rewards that came with commanding armies and governing provinces. But even where they were themselves dependent on patrons, they had the title of *amici primae admissionis*, friends of the first admission, let in by the slaves ahead of the crowd, and the opportunity of friendship on terms of something like equality, even with grandees and their families.

And by the terms of Roman friendship, they were occasionally *obliged* to speak their mind if they were not to be written off as mere flatterers. Horace details the difficulties felt by equestrian clients of the great in balancing between the required flattery and the required freedom of speech vividly in *Epistles* 1.17.41–57 and especially *Epistles* 1.18.1–20. And by the terms of Roman society, since they were both *clientes*, clients, or rather *amici* ("friends" as a formal term denoting clients on terms of greater equality) of the rich, and *patroni* of poorer men,[25] they occupied a station in Roman politics that required them to protect inferiors and speak independently now and then for themselves and their clients to superiors.[26]

This sounds like a precarious freedom of speech, and open only to a few, a class of several thousand Romans in Italy ranking just below the senators. But Lucilius (a richer and better-born knight than Horace, for Horace says he was *infra Lucili censum*, "not so rich as Lucilius," *Satires* 2.1.75) seems to have had little trouble exercising it when the Roman Republic was really a Republic, if not in any way a democracy. Persius avoids politics, since he lives under Nero, as a young and orphaned *eques* with country estates where he can study philosophy and poetry instead. Juvenal's and Martial's experience of equestrian rank conforms with what both senatorial and equestrian rank became in the full light of Empire: primarily ranks in the imperial civil service, entitling you to jobs in Rome and jobs in the provinces. Horace was born to something that was still like Lucilius' way of thinking about the two top ranks and Lucilius' way of asserting position and *auctoritas* among them. His books show him stage by stage accepting that, for senators and *equites* alike, the world in his time was in the first stages of becoming like Persius' and Juvenal's and Martial's: the senators as those capable of high imperial commands, and the equestrians *puro nomine* as those who were capable of lesser profitable offices given by the emperor.

Indeed, he lived to be offered late in life by Augustus, presumably between 20 and 10 BCE, what became a fairly high equestrian court office similar to that held by Suetonius under Hadrian, the post of *ab epistulis privatis*, secretary of the imperial private correspondence. This would have placed him in the center of imperial politics and made him more a patron of his own aristocratic patrons than a client. He declined it—a piece of independence Suetonius noted in the original of our present *Life*, along with his refusal to write poetry to Augustus in the character of a personal friend, which was also explicitly requested of Horace by Augustus and declined. Hadrian would not have taken either of these refusals easily. Horace's father would not have known what to make either of the offer of so magnificent a position or of his son's refusal of it.

It is an indication, however, that we know some things about Horace's life but only a few. This position, which would have made him *the* example and poster-child for the transition from ordinary equestrian rank in society to a leading rank among imperial bureaucrats, would not have been offered him had he not been as good at managing business, *negotium*, as at enjoying his leisure, *otium*. We know nothing about his prose or his conversation. Augustus' letters to Horace and to Maecenas were there for Suetonius to cite, preserved in the palace files, but what we have of the *Life* does not cite their replies. But if Horace had not been a complete master of Latin prose styles, formal and informal (we can know from his poetic transformations of epistolary style in *Epistles* 1 that he was a student of such models as Cicero's correspondence), a shrewd and politic manager of people, and a hard worker when he worked, Augustus would not have made him this offer. Yet about his prose, conversation, and work style this conjecture must suffice. This side of his life is as closed to us as the cases he decided and voted on as *iudex selectus*, or his activities as a scribe of the treasury. Horace constantly represents himself, for his own amusement, as too idle to write a new poem, even as he in fact writes one (*Satires* 2.3.1–6, the opening of a satire three times longer than all the others, *Epistles* 1.1.1–12, *Epistles* 2.1.1–4, 2.2.1–25). What little we know about him can be supplemented from both the history of events and from social and legal history, but it is all that he wants us to know: he also had a work life and social life barely hinted at in his poems.

Horace's poems reflect this change in what was expected of people of his rank at every stage of their publication. He is most like Lucilius, the prosperous Republican knight and onlooker (but much more reserved) during the period of the Second Triumvirate, *Satires* 1, 35 BCE,[27] when the Republic still lived in lively elections to the lower, and even the higher, levels of the Senate. Octavian is described there as *Caesar qui cogere posset*, "Caesar who can get what he wants," in just one offhand phrase (*Satires* 1.3.4), but his power is not a theme. Just as the Triumvirate ended and Octavian became master of the world, but before his return to Rome (cf. *Satires* 2 and the Epodes, which date to 30 BCE), Horace's role has changed a little. Now he is at the margins of the court of the victorious Triumvir, but still at the center of his assertion of this fact is Maecenas, not Octavian. In *Satires* 2 he only hints once (1.10–20) that he might be expected to sing Octavian's conquest of the world, and he deprecates this expectation with a mock *recusatio*. But in the Epodes, though Horace rejoices that Caesar won the battle of Actium in 31 BCE shortly before their publication (1 and 9) the two epodes where he exercises the *libertas fandi*, the *parrhêsia*, of a Roman knight do not mention Caesar's name, though their subject is that the Roman state is in evil case from civil wars and needs reforming, or even a mass migration to the Isles of the Blessed in order to cleanse it (7 and 16).

In the Odes two different stages of the Augustan monarchy are portrayed, and these correlate with their dates of publication, Books 1–3, 23 BCE, and Book 4, 13 BCE. *Epistles* 1, 20 BCE, is also important in reflecting the growing confidence and stability of Augustus' government, and so is the *Carmen Saeculare* written in 17 BCE for the great celebration of the Secular Games, one of the two greatest triumphal shows of the new regime, the other being the dedication of the Ara Pacis Augustae in 13 BCE, the same year as Book 4 of the Odes was published. In 23 BCE the regime was approaching a crisis: Maecenas' circle was feeling threatened by what would shortly be the triumph of his rival for second place in the regime, Agrippa, after the death the next year of Augustus' first choice for his successor, his nephew Marcellus. Augustus and his conquests in time and space and the new peace he has brought the Roman world are a constant theme: yet the books end with odes to Maecenas and an address by Horace to himself on the immortality he has won himself (3.29.30), and not with one of the odes in praise of Augustus, like 3.28.

His later poems reflect a world in which the imperial regime solidifies. Maecenas becomes more retired in relation to Agrippa and his and Livia's family, the new heirs of the regime. Horace accepts, not a high position in the regime at the top of the equestrian service, though this was offered him, but at any rate the position of laureate to Augustus and his family. In *Epistles* 1, the familiar contrast of Rome and the Sabine farm is expanded spatially as Horace follows the progress of Tiberius, the son of Livia, across the Roman world to receive the peaceful submission of the Parthians and the return of the Roman eagles lost by Crassus in 54 (20 BCE). Friends and patrons of Horace's own serve in Tiberius' suite (*Epistles* 1.3.1.8, 1.9, 1.11, 12.25–9). The *Carmen Saeculare* sung to Apollo and Diana by a chorus of patrician boys and girls at Horace's own direction before the emperor and all Rome in 15 BCE was so much the climax of Horace's poetic career that he wrote another and far more magnificent ode about the thrill of directing its performance (4.6). Maecenas is demoted to a bare mention in *Odes* 4.11.18–20. Now that the princes of the imperial family, Tiberius and Drusus, are more like imperial royalty than republican generals, their easy conquest of Switzerland and south Germany up to Augsburg in 15 BCE, along with the Empire's other immense conquests of new space, and the vast imperial peace, are celebrated, also without irony, throughout. Only the central Odes, 4.7 and 4.8, of the fifteen remind us that death too rules over all space and time, and takes away Aeneas (4.7.15), the recently dead Vergil's hero, Augustus' prototype, as easily as Lucretius' example, which Horace borrows, Ancus Martius (Lucr. *De*

Rerum Natura 3.1025). Gods and heroes, Romulus, Dionysus, Hercules, are alike the creation of the poets' imagination (4.8.22–34, and 4.9.25–8). *Odes* 4.7–8 cast a tone of Epicurean disillusion and distance over the religious and political imagery of the book as a whole. If Horace praised the Empire with unreserved energy and without irony, he still did not give himself entirely to the task. His late poems all treat Augustus as a great ruler. But the Emperor's request (in his own words as given in the *Life*) for poems in which *mecum potissimum loquaris*, "you should address yourself rather to me," only produced according to Suetonius the late *Epistle to Augustus*, in which Horace addresses him indeed for a few lines at the beginning, and for fifty lines at the end, but as a busy public figure and a patron of poets, not in any way as an intimate friend. The other two long late epistles, 2.2 to Florus and 2.3, the *Ars Poetica*, addressed to the family of the Epicurean Philodemus' patrons, the Calpurnii Pisones, mention Augustus not at all.

If we know anything from factual history, however, it is that none of this affected Horace's and Maecenas' *amicitia*, or probably either of their friendships with Augustus. For when Maecenas died in 8 BCE, he left Augustus the instruction, *Horati Flacci ut mei memor esto*, "remember Horatius Flaccus as if he were myself," which implies (to say the least) that he had little to complain of in Augustus. And when Horace died suddenly a month or two later, just before his 57th birthday, thus fulfilling in reality a promise he made in verse to accompany Maecenas both in life and in death (*Odes* 2.17.9–12), he left all his property by word of mouth to Augustus. He is the only distinguished Roman we know by name to have left a declaratory will, legal as these were. Romans of property built their monuments while they were living, and disposed of their property as diligently to family and long lists of friends as modern people would dispose of Christmas cards and thank-you notes. His tomb, clearly by both their wish, was placed (apparently after his death) next to Maecenas' on the Esquiline hill, and Suetonius' life implied it was still shown to tourists, as were Horace's house in Tibur and the Sabine Farm, a hundred years later.

In this brief essay I have tried to delineate the social foundations of Horace's *auctoritas* as a poet speaking of Roman life in his days. This authority, which is well portrayed in modern criticism,[28] is exercised in striking and interesting ways. Horace portrays himself always as a "have" and nearly never as a "have-not," as MacMullen puts it, and interested mainly in the society of other "haves" and his precise position in that society. He is a little interested in social injustice committed by rich against poor, but not much. In Roman society freed slaves and their families were instantly identified with the free and not slaves. Horace identifies himself as free. Some of his comments about vulgar freedmen, slaves, and the pretensions of such people as centurions and city officials in small cities outside Rome are hard to take. Michael Wigodsky has suggested to me[29] that the bankrupt Damasippus, the Stoic speaker to an unsympathetic Epicurean Horace in *Satires* 2.3, and the slave Davus, who has learned Stoicism from a philosopher's doorkeeper and lectures Horace on it in *Satires* 2.7, represent an uncomfortable and honest acknowledgment on Horace's part that those who were really up against it in life needed a harder and more uncompromising philosophy than that of Epicurus to deal with their problems. Against that, one might set Horace's sometimes astonishing (to a modern person) insensitivity, unbuffered by irony, in talking about slaves. Apparently he was wholeheartedly with Augustus in promoting family values—as the Romans understood them. But he sees nothing wrong with the remark of the elder Cato that prostitutes keep one away from free men's wives, and a young man had better use them than commit adultery (*Satires* 1.2.31–5). Even more startlingly he says in the same poem that "when your private parts swell up, and a maid or a home-born boy is right there" (he means, a slave not remarkable for beauty or bought specially for it) "and you can attack him or her right there, why burst with frustrated lust? Not I, for I like ready and easy sex." He also says "Do not let some maidservant or boy stir your lust inside the marble doors of your powerful friend, for the pretty boy's or dear girl's owner may make them his cheap gift to you," thus cheating you of something more valuable, "or torment you with his jealousy," *Epistles* 1.18.72–5. This is a remarkable detail of Roman "good manners," and again said apparently with no irony, at least of the kind we would expect.

On the other hand this adumbration of sexual mores which might be compared to the brutality of the television series *Rome* about sexual and class matters, or the anything-goes attitude of another television series, *Sex and the City*, is not all to the bad for his poetry. Many of those who find his preference for Epicurean friendship, *amicitia*, with his lovers, mostly female but some male, over such passionate *amor* as one finds in Catullus or Propertius is cold and off-putting are not valuing for itself his upper-middle-class realism. Nor the attractive portrait he offers of Roman bachelor life among a whole gallery of free, wealthy, and equal sexual opportunists, centered perpetually in the Odes round the Campus Martius, the beautiful exercise ground of Rome. There the military exercise grounds and the jump-off points for healthy swims in the Tiber are also meeting-grounds for all kinds of lovers, and a vantage-point for the connoisseurs of beautiful bodies. Among these connoisseurs (*Odes* 1.3) are even the dignified consul Sestius. He was once a comrade-in-arms in Brutus' army, now is just appointed consul for the year 23 BCE in which *Odes* 1–3 are published. He is reminded of the inevitability of death and the shortness of the precious time available to admire the youth and beauty before him.

If Horace had been a poet of passionate love for one woman, we would have been deprived of his picture of a splendid society of male and female "haves" with their own houses and slaves, free, emancipated and available, but increasingly frustrated as their poet and his lovers grow older and older, and finally, like Lucretius' good-mannered guest at the table of life, are compelled to leave gracefully before they are thrown out by the young. Jasper Griffin's picture of this kind of society (1998) is a model for further research. And America at the beginning of 2009, troubled and in recession at last after two decades of dubious, showy conquest and prosperity, is a fine place to follow Horace's adventurous rise to the top of the great City's society, and share his privileged view of the possibilities of an empire larger in space and more durable in time than anything ever seen before it, in the opening decades of a brilliant new reign whose darker final years he did not live to see.

GUIDE TO FURTHER READING

What we know of Horace's social status or philosophical attitudes, or about his patrons as they appear in other historical sources, or any other such topics from the world of *Realien*, is precious because it illuminates the poetry and gives it more complexity and mystery, not less. We know more about the generalities of his rank and the attitudes it entailed in him than the specifics of his life. Rome wrote him: Horace provides only enough details to explain his own tone and voice as the specific kind of Roman he was, and the ancient *Vita* only a little more.

There are two easily available surveys of Horace's work and life in English: Perret (1964) and the Twayne's World Authors volume by Kenneth Reckford (1969), valuable for deep historical scholarship lightly worn. I began by thinking these two critics more nimble and subtle by far than Fraenkel (1957), with its famous index entry *s.v.* Horace ("never lies"), and by admiring Steele Commager's *The Odes of Horace* (1962), which first introduced the ambiguities and subtleties of New Criticism into a large-scale reading of Horace. I do not think any of these books are too dated for the general reader trying to form an overall picture of Horace and the real world round him. Indeed, the picture would be very much like that in Philip Hills, *Horace* (2005) forty years later. For treatments of biographical issues that avoid the literalness of interpretation that limits Fraenkel's kind of criticism, I admire and recommend the accumulation of historical information in Lyne's *Horace: Behind the Public Poetry* (1995), without being much alienated by its pose of cynicism. Besides what I have cited in the body of the text, there are also the essays of Gordon Williams on Horace' background (1995), and Roland Mayer on Horace's ascent in Roman society (1995), whose spirit I hope I have echoed.

NOTES

1   I am very much obliged to the editor for asking me to contribute this essay, and for his patience and help, his questions and corrections, both stylistic and scholarly. My friend Michael Wigodsky has also removed some of my errors and contributed valuable advice. All remaining faults are my own entirely.

2   The reading in line 10 is uncertain, but some sort of sound play on the letters APVL- is certain.

[*Editor's note*: The received text of line 10 is almost certainly corrupt. The variant ms. reading, *limina Pulliae*, adopted by several modern editions (including the two Teubner editions of Borzsák and Shackleton Bailey) is grotesquely incongruous with the hymnal tone and stylistic elevation of the proem. Of the plethora of emendations so far proposed, see the attractive conjecture of Courtney 1986: 319–21. A rhetorically grounded analysis of the whole proem is available in Davis 1991: 98–103]

3 My own translation, as are the others in the essay.

4 I gratefully acknowledge the editor's and Blackwell's offer of a chance to expand and revise some views I have published earlier here and there, particularly in Armstrong 1986 and 1989.

5 Throughout this essay I have been immensely helped by the massive scholarly and historical information available in the *Enciclopedia Oraziana*, 1998, particularly its reviews of people and places mentioned in Horace, and such excellent commentaries on the purely historical aspects of the *Odes* as Nisbet and Hubbard on 1–2 (1970, 1978) and Nisbet and Rudd on 3 (2004) as well as treatments of these topics in Taylor 1925, 1968; Nicolet 1966: 44–56; 1974: 914–15; Zanker 1975, and Lyne 1995. I am also indebted to the commentaries of Michael Brown, *Satires* 1 (1993), Frances Muecke, *Satires* 2 (1993), and Roland Mayer, *Epistles* 1 (1994).

6 Cf. the account of the imperial aspects of this calendar transformation in Feeney 2007: chs. 1–5. The conquest of the Julian calendar proclaimed in 45 BCE when Horace was 20, over the confused and irregular calendars that preceded it in Rome and the Mediterranean world, the Romanizing of time, is no less an influence on Horace's poetry than the Romanizing of the imperial map, a major theme of *Odes* 3.4 (for mapmaking as an influence on Augustan culture, embodying visions of conquest and peace, see Nicolet 1991). For an amusing review of the evidence (and a conjecture of 64 for the birth) Bradshaw 2002.

7 Cf. in particular Reinhold 2002, 25–53; Lendon 1997: 173–236 on the system Horace would have been defying by making these claims in published writings. Even in the thirties BCE, Sarmentus, a freedman in Maecenas' circle and a *scriba quaestorius* exactly like Horace, who pictures him as a buffoon (*Satires* 1.5.51–70), was booed by the people out of the equestrian seats at the theatre when he tried to sit there (scholiast on Juvenal 5.3) and taken to court over his claim of status. So important was the distinction even between freedmen themselves and their freeborn sons—especially in eligibility for offices requiring the gold ring—that Horace would have been vulnerable to ridicule, had he misrepresented his status even in this detail.

8 Wiseman 1969.

9 Petersen 2006 gives a new view of the society and houses of rich freedmen like Horace's father in Pompeii and Herculaneum: they were people of far superior culture to Trimalchio's.

10 So also it is often said that the Sabine Farm, which according to Horace had five substantial tenant farms attached to it (*Epistles* 1.14.3), was worked with a mere eight slaves, because he threatens his sarcastic slave Davus with sending him there as the ninth fieldhand: *accedes opera agro nona Sabino*: *Satires* 2.7.118. *Opera* is the word for fieldhand, so there were more house-slaves also, and bailiffs there. But Ps. Acro's note is both more likely historically and much funnier, in a brutal way: *quasi octo servos in ergastula miserit agri Sabini*, "as though Horace had sent off eight slaves

to the chain-gang at the Sabine Farm (already)." I believe, and so does Bernard Frischer (private conversation) that what one sees at "Horace's Villa" at Licenza is more suitable for one of the tenant farms. (If it had anything to do with Horace at all, which is doubtful.) It may plausibly be assumed the real villa was somewhere nearby. See Frischer 2006a, 2006b, and 2006c; and his essay (Chapter 4) in this volume.

11 Zanker 1975: 304–5 w. fig. 44; Armstrong 1986: 256–7, a relief of a contemporary freedman and freedwoman's son, Appuleius, wearing an oversize gold ring, as ex-*tribunus militum* (so the inscription says), and standing between his admiring parents.

12 Cf. Henderson (1994).

13 In spite of the disapproval of MacMullen (1990: 124–6), a good description of the *apparitores'* "rake-offs" in the late Republic and the early Empire. No doubt Horace's aristocratic friends from Brutus' army helped him find this position, whatever he paid for it.

14 This scene has long been known to be borrowed from a comedy of Terence, and only an idealization of what his father said in real life, cf. Leach 1971. But that does not affect the point about *iudices selecti* as objects of admiration, which is not in Terence. Cf. Horace's more explicit claim to possess the equestrian ring and to be a *iudex selectus* at *Satires* 2.7.53–4.

15 There are good descriptions of the sort of work equestrian judges did in casework in Holford-Strevens 1988: 22–5, and 294–301, emphasizing both the amateur standing of these "judges" in the law (shared by the praetors who assigned them cases) and the necessity for learned consultants, like Trebatius and Torquatus. They served on juries in great civil and criminal cases also, but did not think of themselves primarily as "jurymen."

16 The addressee also of the Epicurean ode on death, quoting Lucretius, *C*. 4.8: on the interrelation between the two poems, see Putnam 2006.

17 On Tillius cf. most recently Toher 2005.

18 Historians seem to see nothing extravagant in taking this claim at its face value, e.g. Talbert 1984: 24 n. 60, on the concluding lines 5.130–1, Oliensis 1998: 30–6.

19 See Armstrong 1986: 259–61, where I interpret *Satires* 1.6.58–61 and 100–11, apparently for the first time in the exegetical literature, as being Horace's oblique references to himself as *eques* but with a *mulus* or *caballus* to suit his low birth. Other passages in Horace's works appear to corroborate the hypothesis that *eques* may be plausibly taken to refer to rank with implicit application to the speaker. For example, the famous line *Odes* 3.1.40 (*post equitem sedet atra cura*, "depression sits behind even the *eques* (horseman, person of rank like myself)". See also *Epistles* 1.15.11–14, where Horace the lonely *eques* and his *equus* are in the same situation as Horace the lonely *eques* on his *mulus* at *Satires* 1.6.100–11.

20 So I construe the praise of Tarentum's farms and farm-products and the promise Horace will always be there as a companion for Septimius (if he accepts), 9–24. Cf. Shackleton Bailey 1982: 57; Lyne 1995: 10–11.

21 I have detailed some of Horace's many intertextualities with Philodemus, *On the Good King according to Homer*, in Armstrong 2004: 267–98; see also the introduction, 1–22.

22 *tumultus,* of wars like the Social War in which Venusia took part; see Nisbet-Rudd 2004.

23 I take it that *noscent* and *discet* reinforce each other.

24 Nisbet and Rudd 2004 are conservative enough to analyze the Roman Odes as being as many as six separate entities, but I prefer very much the approach of critics like Santirocco 1986, Putnam 1986, or Zetzel 1980, which hardly entails a concept of forced organic unity in poetry books as a whole, only the amount of unity necessary to make them a coherent performance as a whole and encourage the reading of them all together. See the essay by H.P. Syndikus in this volume, Chapter 10.

25 Horace had clients of his own, whom he portrays in his poems, like the guests he sends away unfed to have dinner with Maecenas, *Satires* 2.7.32–4.

26 The concept of the "tactless" and of "sapping" one's praise of "grandees" with implied criticism, which runs through Lyne's useful book (1995) would be better described as exercise of friendly (cf. Plutarch, *How to tell a flatterer from a friend*) and philosophical (Philodemus, *On Frank Criticism*, 1998) *parrhêsia* or freedom of speech as Roman friendship and the pursuit of philosophy required: cf. Armstrong (997: 394–400).

27 See *Satires* 1, written circa 35 BCE. Cf. the classic essay of Du Quesnay 1984a.

28 Perhaps nowhere better than in Oliensis 1998.

29 Private conversation.

CHAPTER TWO

Horace's Friendship: Adaptation of a Circular Argument

William Anderson

Among students of Latin literature and culture, it has proved tempting to collect the writers of particular eras, group them around one scintillating representative, and christen the group a "circle." The "circle" receives the name of its apparently leading figure, not so much a writer himself but an inspiration to other writers. And thus it became conventional from the nineteenth century to talk of the Scipionic Circle of the mid-second century, of the Circle of Maecenas in the second half of the first century BCE and of the Circle of Augustus that succeeded it in the late decades of the century. In the meantime, students have become restless with the notion of these "circles," because Latin writers of those early times hardly thought of themselves as circles focused around a man of distinction and centered by a system of mutual benefits.

The Scipionic Circle—analogy for later Horace?

What has happened to the Scipionic Circle may represent the difficulties produced by the metaphorical term "circle" and prepare the way for my discussion in this essay of the Circle of Maecenas and my suggestion that we should change our thinking about the people in that group and view it, if as a "circle," then as Horace's Circle. Today, scholars, following A. E. Astin, entertain serious doubts about the so-called Scipionic Circle.[1] The Scipio of the Scipionic Circle was Aemilianus, second son of Aemilius Paullus, the distinguished victor over Macedonian Perseus at the battle of Pydna, born in 185 BCE, who died, possibly murdered for political reasons, in 129. His father, having four sons and a second wife, let him be adopted by the family of Scipios. From the few surviving texts about him, I find it tempting to see him as more important politically and military than culturally. Though only 18, he followed his father on the Macedonian campaign. A precocious military genius, he won the Third Carthaginian War before he was 40, brought discipline to Roman troops in Spain and so won the campaign at Numantia in 133. And he was embroiled in partisan political struggles at the time of his unexpected death (murder?).

Those who cling to the cultural significance of the Scipionic Circle turn to the youth of Scipio, just after the battle of Pydna. Scipio himself, a young man of 19, was immersed in Greek culture as a result of his father's victory. The Greek library of Perseus was transferred to Rome; 1,000 Greek hostages were taken from distinguished families and sent to Rome, among them Polybius, an admirer of Rome and frequent companion of Scipio. The poet Terence, adapter of Greek Menander, wrote his last comedy, *The Brothers*, for Scipio and his older brother, who staged funeral games in honor of their father after his death in 160. Terence's birth is not securely dated, and I myself believe that he was fifteen years older than Scipio, like Polybius. Also uncertain is the birth date of Lucilius, who was a close friend of Scipio and the inventor of the formally striking verse that became Roman satire. He was a few or many years younger than Scipio. Scipio was one of the wealthiest men in Rome, having inherited three sizable fortunes by the time he was 25. With such financial ease, he could have supported the philhellenic interest in various concrete ways, including public buildings, but there is little indication that he did so. It has been tempting to regard Scipio as the banner-bearer of philhellenism in second-century Rome, but the uncertainty of dates and the paucity of literary output among Scipio's Roman friends have persuaded students today to be cautious about their picture of the Scipionic Circle. Cicero, in his essay "On Friendship," with more enthusiasm than fact, imagined the situation after Scipio's death, when his closest friend, Laelius, warmly reminisced about Scipio's role as a model of friendship. There was, he regretfully declared, a special quantity of excellences that belonged to Scipio and operated "in our, if I may call it so, herd or flock" (*in nostro, ut ita dicam, grege*).[2] The metaphor of a "herd" is not the same as the misleading one of "circle" applied later to Scipio, but it has become a much-used justification for the terminology and imagery of the Scipionic Circle.

The Circle of Maecenas and Horace as poet-friend

Maecenas (and Agrippa, too, future general and city-planner) enter history as near-contemporaries of C. Octavius (heir of Julius Caesar, destined to be honored as Augustus). Octavius was 18 when Caesar was assassinated in 44 BCE, and since he was born in the month of September, his birth was in 63. The birth-dates of Maecenas and Agrippa (and of Salvidienus Rufus, the third of the trio of companions whom Caesar had chosen to accompany his heir-to-be) cannot be much before 63. Horace was born in December, 65. Caesar was on the verge of an Eastern campaign against the Parthians when he was brought down by the conspirators, and in preparation for this expedition, he had planned to bring along for the experience Octavius and these three friends of his, sending them ahead to Apollonia in Illyria, where the army was to assemble later in the Spring. (Scipio, too, received his baptism of fire at the age of 18 when he served his father Aemilius Paullus in Macedon.) Instead of watching the greatest military genius of the era wage his campaign in Parthia, Octavius suddenly found himself battling for his inheritance and life back in Rome and using his three friends as trusted, though inexperienced, legates in the negotiations and conflicts that followed rapidly on the Ides of March. Rufus made the first false step and secretly started to deal with Mark Antony as early as 40, for which he was executed. Surer friends, Maecenas and Agrippa remained trusted and reliable until their natural deaths thirty-five years later. Agrippa was the man to whom Augustus turned in military crises and in the reorganization and improvement of Rome; Maecenas rich and proud of his Etruscan heritage, was an invaluable political advisor, negotiator, and substitute ruler in Rome during the critical absences of Augustus. Agrippa advanced his career by three ever more promising marriages, the third in 21 to Augustus' only child, Julia, by whom he had three sons marked for succession; Maecenas kept his wife Terentia and showed no great political ambition.

The *Sermones*: circle or circulation?

We do not see or hear much of Maecenas during the months and four years after the Ides of March. Nor is Octavianus a major player at first. It was almost impossible to claim respect as an inexperienced 18-year-old from the confident and powerful men who had surrounded Julius Caesar. Much had to happen between 44 and 40, when some of the clouds cleared, and we encounter Maecenas and Horace and other minor and major "friends" in one of their typically ambiguous situations of friendship and cut-throat politics. By that time, Hirtius and Pansa had fallen in victory against Antonius; the murderers of Caesar had been defeated at Philippi; in Italy, Antony's brother Lucius, a consul, had staged a revolt against Octavianus and been besieged and forced to surrender; the Second Triumvirate had been patched together in favor of Mark Antony, with subordinate roles for Lepidus and an even more subordinate one for Octavianus, for the time being. The latter had the problem of dealing with the powerful fleet of Sextus Pompeius and his control of Sicily and the grain route to Rome.

   By 40 BCE, Horace, through his friend Vergil, had been introduced to Octavian's favorite negotiator, Maecenas, and the two poets had been invited on a desultory trip from Rome to Brundisium, where Maecenas would try to patch things up with Antony and his negotiators. To relieve the boredom of the trip, arrangements were made that three poet friends, Vergil, Varius, and Plotius, should join the statesmen at Sinuessae. It seems likely that they had been invited by Maecenas or one of the other political travelers, and that they in turn had invited their younger poet-friend Horace, with the concurrence of Maecenas. This is not the operation of Maecenas' literary circle, and it is implied that, if anything is important, it is not Roman poetry but the crucial state of Roman politics. As Horace with studied naivete narrates the episode here in *Satires* 1.5, he started out with one companion, a Greek rhetorician, setting forth on the Via Appia in a southerly direction. He does not seem to know where he is going or why and does not alert us to the more distinguished companions, literary and political, who will be joining the group. At Anxur, the political retinue, Maecenas acting for Octavianus, Fonteius Capito representing Antonius, meet up with the so-far small group. They may have had some preliminary discussions before linking up with Horace, but Horace does not act as if he knows much about that, and he does not report any verbal exchanges with the key political operators, not even a word spoken by or to Maecenas. Vergil and his two friends join them a couple of days later, and this is the moment for a warm display of friendship that very much includes Horace. But no poetry nor politics. Instead of a recitation of poetry, the group is entertained by a barrage of insults voiced against each other by two lowly parasites. And when they all—minus Varius, who left them at Canusium for some personal business[3]—get to Brundisium, that's it: no more travel and no more wasted paper. Probably Maecenas was amused by this minimal poetic version of the trip, but he had more serious things on his mind: how to stop war between his master Octavian and Antony.[4]

At a more relaxed time somewhat before this expedition, Horace had his first contact with Maecenas, thanks to the introduction and recommendations of first Vergil, then Varius. That would imply that Horace was recommended for his literary talents years before he published his first book of *Sermones*, but he calls himself companion and friend. Indirectly, he admits that he had commanded a small detachment of troops as military tribune at the battle of Philippi back in 42, not so long ago that he could deny that he had taken arms against Octavian and lost. But that was status that smacked of ambition as well as republican enthusiasm, whereas gaining friendship with Maecenas now, by choice of Maecenas and by the inclination of Horace himself, is a development "free of the corruption of ambition" (*prava ambitione procul*).[5] To be the affable companion (*convictor*) of Maecenas rather than the proud equestrian and tribune of a legion at the fateful engagement at Philippi suggests that Horace has taken measure of himself and the times and chosen to live amiably on the edges of the literary creators. It also suggests that that is what Maecenas wants of such friends: no pushing forward for political or financial promotion. A defeated Horace had little to offer except his apolitical conversation and the novel poetry that he was writing to revive the successes of Lucilius. Along with Vergil, Varius, and Plotius, he might have helped form an interesting poetic quartet of considerable talent,

but we never see Maecenas treating these poets as anything but *convictores,* nor
does Horace report being seriously noticed at this time by the busy advisor of
Octavian. The trip to Brundisium is the only narrative that brings these poets
together before Actium, and Horace does not present the older trio or his junior
self as special literary talents in a circle carefully governed by a relaxed
Maecenas.

That long diplomatic trip seasoned with literary talent and wit seems to have
been a unique experience for Horace, who otherwise locates himself quietly in
urban Rome, observing and meditating on the various people he encounters in
the frantically busy, changing city. It is filled with people who are openly ambitious and eager to claw their way into the locus of political power and self-pro-
motion that Maecenas represents for their envious eyes and purposes. Horace
deals with such people there in Rome of the mid-thirties in *Satires* 1.9, where
he represents himself struggling to escape a very talkative and pushy man who is
looking for contact with Maecenas and the political opportunities of his association. The contrast between the escapist Horace and the ambitious type who ruins
Horace's perambulation through the heart of Rome, on the Via Sacra, implicitly
defines Maecenas' friends in an ideal way, as activated by non-political motives.
Poor Horace is trying to think about some poetic ideas before the pushy man
drives everything but escape out of his mind. The man misinterprets Horace and
Maecenas' friends as political opportunists, precisely what Horace shows he is
not. As he brings Book 1 of the *Satires* to a close in the tenth poem, Horace
tells us that he is focused on literary matters, trying to bring Lucilius up to date
in style and polish. He lists his supporters at the end, and they include the same
literary trio who joined him on the road to Brundisium, making up with Maecenas a distinguished hexameter,[6] and an impressive set of others. Once again,
Horace also emphasizes the absence of political ambition in the literary goals of
these supporters.[7] Maecenas is named, with no suggestion that he is other than
a notable friend of poetry, far less the manipulator of pro-Octavianic literature.

In the years that closely followed Horace's publication of Book 1 of the *Satires,*
the most important event was Maecenas' gift of the Sabine property. This was a
kind of farm, for the handful of servants whom Horace used to operate it, but
it was not subsistence-farming for the owner, and he used the property more as
a place to withdraw to ever more frequently, a modest villa where he could write
and avoid the crowded Rome to which he had been confined.[8] The gift has been
inspected closely by archaeologists and suspicious readers of Maecenas' and
Horace's political relationship. Is it the definitive sign of Maecenas' influence
over the poet, of the poet's acceptance of the political subordination of literature
to the purposes of Augustus and his advisers? Or does the fact that other poet-
friends of Maecenas languish, despite creative triumphs, un-gifted in such an
outstanding way, point to a special signficance? Horace treated his Sabine asylum
as the answer both to his moral search for wisdom and to his search for an Eden
in nature, where he could wax lyrical over its special properties. Maecenas is never

reported by Horace to have visited him at the villa nor even to have turned one of their innocent conversations to the subject. Whatever the gift signified for Maecenas, we are not invited to conjecture; but poem after poem by Horace construes its rich meaning for the poet.

During the five years from 35 to 30, Horace adjusted himself happily to the Sabine Villa and to the public reputation that he gained, especially in relation to Maecenas. He mentions Maecenas in four of the eight Satires of Book 2: he is said by a sardonic slave, Davus,[9] to be wildly eager at the last moment to dine with Maecenas and he misses out on an invitation to Nasidienus' dinner along with Maecenas.[10] And unreliable Damasippus mocks Horace for trying to act big like Maecenas in *Satires* 2.3.312 ff. All three passages enable the poet to engage the criticism he stirs by this special connection with Maecenas (including, of course, the amazing gift of the Sabine estate). Far more serious and extensive is the defense Horace offers for his new property in *Satires* 2.6. rarely naming his friend the donor, but continuously alluding to him and the twisted notions that his critics voice of their friendship. The poem opens with words of thankfulness by Horace, grateful that he has received this ideal spot in the country and fully committed to live in it and enjoy it. The place is a "citadel" (16) where he can take refuge from the busyness of Rome and from the envious people who misread his friendship with Maecenas as politically motivated. Yet it cannot totally protect him from interruptions of his quiet rustic pleasure. Thus, although he seems to have imagined himself in the Sabine country at the start, he soon corrects the image to one in which he is rushed back to the lawcourts in Rome to give surety for someone. That is the beginning of a day largely wasted in the political ordeals of city life. He tries to get to the Esquiline to wish Maecenas good morning, but his path is constantly blocked by people who want to exploit his closeness to the great man. Although he gives trivial examples of his non-political association with Maecenas, nobody believes he would waste his opportunities for self-profit, and they keep underestimating Horace's kind of friendship.

As the day wears frustratingly later, Horace finds himself longing for the country and the innocuous kinds of pleasure with his neighbors that he fondly imagines: the simple-minded but honest ethical questions that interest the country people (not the competitive issues that provoke passionate conversation in Rome). At the end, he quotes the folk-wisdom of Cervius, who adapts a fable from Aesop about the country mouse and the city. The country mouse is the ultimate hero of the tale, as he learns from his credulity about the city's easy pleasures to be thankful for the protection which his little hole gives him from violent intrusions.[11] He is a parody of Horace, just a little anxious rodent who knows where he can be safe. The Satire then ends with a victory of understanding for the mouse, but a trapped feeling for Horace there in Rome. However, in reality he started from thanksgiving in the Sabine Villa, and every other locale where he places himself is imagined. So the somewhat vulnerable "citadel" of the farm proves to be the final positive scene where the poet is and belongs.

Actium and Epodes: a circuitous route towards lyric

While Horace worked on these satiric themes in Book 2, fitting the Sabine Farm into a new, more complex picture of useful contentment, a mocking answer to those who interpreted that gifted farm as the symbol of political and poetic success through Maecenas, Horace was also exploring in a series of Epodes lyric poetry in the iambic mode of Archilochus. These poems were the seed from which the later Odes sprang, as their metrical experimentation indicates as well as their substantial move from serious ethical themes and, of course, from preoccupation with the Sabine Farm and the political allure of Maecenas. Horace addressed four of the seventeen Epodes to Maecenas, from which no idea of a literary circle is posited or can be deduced. Two Epodes are strategically placed as the first and middle poems, both in special ways dealing with the battle of Actium of 31. In Epode 1, Horace imagines the eve of Actium, when Maecenas was planning to join Octavian in the fight, and therefore the thought occurs to him that he should join Maecenas there, too. There are reasons, including the evidence of Velleius Paterculus, to indicate that Maecenas, no general or fighting man, was absent from the battle, probably remaining in Rome where his executive skills were needed. And if Maecenas stayed home, so did Horace. We do hear him thanking Maecenas for the farm and honoring his generosity (*benignitas*, 31) in words that recall *Satires* 2.6. Actium becomes a possible scene of friendship with Maecenas, not a heroic display of patriotism or gesture of political opportunism.

Epode 9 uses Actium, too, as its occasion, but now the sea-battle has been fought and lost by Antonius and Cleopatra. The poet gives a few vague details of the military situation, but his main concern is the bibulous celebration of victory, not at or near Actium or with the fleet, but back in Rome in Maecenas' lofty palace on the Esquiline (*sub alta domo*, 3–4), where some excellent Caecuban has been reserved for the occasion. That may be additional evidence that neither Maecenas nor Horace participated in battle.

The other two poems where the poet addresses Maecenas remove themselves entirely from Roman politics and that relationship with Maecenas. Or we might rather say that they dwell on light aspects of their friendship. In Epode 3, Horace spends the first eighteen lines fulminating in an exaggerated, playful manner over some very strong garlic in his food. Only then does he reveal in the final four lines that his "poisoner" is trickster Maecenas, his host—no evidence for a literary circle in this! Epode 14 *is* on literary matters: it affects to explain why Horace has been so dilatory about completing this promised book of iambics. The god forbids him from finishing. What god? The god of love, who has diverted our poet from iambs to Anacreontic meters and thoroughly distracted him from proper poetry. We might guess that Horace refers to Maecenas' poetic expectations of him as a member of the Circle. But this would be to misconstrue the rhetoric of generic disavowal (*recusatio*). Moreover, no other poets are mentioned, and this poet evades the circular metaphor by reminding Maecenas at the end that he, too, is a victim of Amor.

The Odes: Circle poet Horace, not Maecenas

Once Actium had ended the political menace of opponents of Octavian, the years after 30 BCE could be devoted to reconstruction and new construction. Agrippa used his consulship in 27 to do major work in the Campus Martius, baths, aqueducts, and even the original version of the Pantheon. Maecenas presumably was a major counselor in the move from *princeps* to Augustus in that same year. Vergil was composing the *Georgics* and Horace his three books of Odes. All the men who had worked faithfully with Octavian since 44 were now in their thirties, mature and practiced men of state, markedly different from the ambitious and ungovernable Antonius. In what ways, if at all, do the Odes reflect this new positive energy of the Augustan Era in its first years? Was this the time when Maecenas could devote himself to his Circle? Or does this period, with its increased freedom and confidence, rather confirm the absence of Maecenas' literary Circle?

It is obvious that Horace gives Maecenas a special position in the Odes, addressing eight of the eighty to his friend. With the first word of *Odes* 1.1, he dedicates the collection to Maecenas in vocative address. Two lines at start and end focus on the special friendship Horace receives from Maecenas and his hope to be ranked by him among the masters of Greek lyric. The interior thirty-two lines which the words to Maecenas frame constitute a very long priamel that reaches its goal in Horace's declaration that his ambition is not to achieve the mundane things that most people desire, but to be a poet blessed by the Muses. The other poem from Book 1.1.20, invites Maecenas for a modest drink (of Sabine wine or poetry), which Horace bottled at the Sabine Villa on the joyous day when Maecenas returned to public cheers after recovering from a serious illness. This little poem of three Sapphic stanzas shows how versatile Horace could be in his use of lyric and his friendly treatment of Maecenas.

Maecenas enters Book 2 at the approximate center, with 2.12, putting a decisive ending to the alternation of Alcaics and Sapphics. Horace imagines a situation in which he deftly refuses to turn Roman history into lyric or to try his hand at Greek myths, and he leaves to Maecenas the task of composing a prose history in honor of Augustus' wars. Instead, he prefers to write of the singing and dancing of charming Licymnia, whoever she may be, and he gets Maecenas to agree that she is indeed an attractive topic. It might seem that Maecenas is exerting his power as patron over the poet of his Circle, but this is all we ever hear about Licymnia or these abortive topics that Horace rejects, and I read this as a typical poem of free choices. Horace goes on in 2.17 from the hypothetical situation that Maecenas, feeling gloomy and sorry for himself, works on the poet's sympathies by predicting that he would die before Horace. But the poet answers this self-pity and urges in extreme terms that no fierce monster could possibly separate them in their last moments; and besides each has positive proof that the gods favor them both. Look at Maecenas' cure from sickness and the almost mythical escape Horace had from the falling tree. The final poem of the book, 2.20, follows up with a cheerful scene of Horace's imaginary death or rather metamorphosis into a swan-bard who will range the world, known and admired as a supreme poet. All three odes of this book focus on the freedom and fame of the lyric poet, but the idea of a Circle centered on Maecenas is disruptive and irrelevant to what Horace accomplishes with his imagination, and he tends to place Maecenas in a subordinate position to his poetic endeavor.

In *Odes* 3.8, Maecenas is supposedly amazed to find Horace celebrating on the day of women's Matronalia, but it turns out that the poet commemorates his escape from the falling tree a year earlier. In his festive mood, then, the poet tries to get Maecenas to celebrate, too, to forget the pressing political problems that he deals with in Rome during Augustus' necessary absence.

The foreign crises are not very serious these days, so enjoy the present happiness of the Roman world and leave behind gravity. It is better to be a clown like Horace than to grimly worry about the distant West and East. A second contrast between the two friends is developed in 3.16, as the poet compares the anxiety over acquiring monumental amounts of gold and his own preference for merely avoiding abject poverty. He is not poor, but his words serve to emphasize by contrast the immense riches of Maecenas' equestrian friends and their senseless anxiety over their possessions. And in his simple satisfaction with what a god has given him, Horace alludes to his Sabine Farm. The next to last Ode, 3.29, links with 1.1 and its words about Maecenas and offers a virtual frame for the entire collection. It is summer, and Horace invites Maecenas to leave his worries in Rome and join him for a friendly drink of wine (and some dinner?) at the Sabine Villa, where they can celebrate what is really important in their comfortable, unendangered existence. All three poems of Book Three concentrate serenely on the pleasure which is available to people like these two, now that Actium has ended civil war.

The poet has come a long way in both independence and self-confidence as he has composed his many Odes during the peaceful thirties. He talks to Maecenas as to an equal, and he does not confine himself to the daily trivialities, but he comments on the political concerns of his friend with a directness that defies the old prejudice of the pushy crowds in Rome. They either no longer matter to him with their spiteful words, or he can show that he is involved with Maecenas on a different basis, but still not opportunistic. He frankly considers, for example, in 2.17, friendship as a pairing of equals, and he wittily plays with the supposed identity of their horoscopes and the similarity of their escapes from danger. Instead of listening to the central figure of a literary circle making significant suggestions and demands on his poetic efforts, he uses the Odes and his status as genuine friend, to assume the role of advisor to Maecenas (and other prominent Romans). If there were ever a Circle focused on Maecenas, where timid Horace was gently admitted, that structure has disappeared. Horace makes himself the central figure of the collection of over eighty Odes and draws his various addressees around him, not to effect political or economic or social advantages for himself, but to generate the image of a mutually friendly group, advised and charmed by the poet.

Consider how he planned his addressees in the Parade Odes, 1.1 through 1.11. Each poem is a polished display of a new Greek meter and of a personal confidence towards the powerful leaders of Rome and towards the amatory involvements of young and old. Maecenas, Augustus Caesar, Vergil, Sestius, Pyrrha, Agrippa, Plancus, in 1.1–7, are followed by various lovers, male and female, and Mercury in 1.8–11. The poet is not embarrassed by the riches of his material: he has practical, non-political advice for the politicians; he does not assert his genius as a poet, nor does he refrain from playing with Vergil as would-be composer of the *Aeneid*, and he treats lightly and evasively Agrippa's ambition to be commemorated by an epic poem. When he adopts an amatory situation, he especially likes triangular affairs where he (or the speaker) is a third member of the lovers and a good-natured self-ironic commentator on others' doubtful success and his own rueful failures. In spite of (or because of) his cheerful irony towards himself and his addressees, Horace's special lyric voice generates the unifying and authoritative *persona* for the Odes.

Epistles 1: Horace as the center of friendship

The three books of Odes appeared for the public in 23, though private readings had probably made many of the eighty poems known before publication. For reasons that we cannot fully determine, Horace decided to abandon lyric for a while and experiment with the possibilities of the poetic epistle over the next three years. The result, as in the case of the Odes, was something close to formal perfection: twenty letters to a variety of addressees with varying reasons for being written to by the poet, who adopted a new *persona* after the one he created for his lyrics. As he sends out these letters, he stamps them with his more serious interests, not topics which Maecenas wanted and urged on him so as to enhance the propaganda of Augustus' new order. He leaves the political questions to Maecenas and Agrippa and their like: he is interested in the moral questions that arise in middle age, for one who is 45 at the time of publication in 20 BCE. From his self-questioning status, he speaks to the problems and enthusiasms of his often-younger addressees and thus creates an imaginary give and take in these epistles, as he gently recommends to his readers a change of direction.

It might seem that Maecenas attempted and failed to deter the poet's choice of letters. The initial epistle addresses Maecenas in two laudatory lines (as at the start of the Odes) and then indicates that Horace's friend has been pushing for more odes, not these personal letters. He compares himself to a long-surviving and exhausted gladiator who has finally been discharged (awarded the wooden sword), but now Maecenas is trying to put him back in training and shut him up in the discipline.[12] The gladiatorial show may be for Maecenas a "sport" or "game," but for the retired poet it is likely to result in shameful defeat and anxious appeal for his life to the disgusted crowd. In more direct terms, the poet claims that he is no longer young enough or motivated in the same way as he was when previously composing lyric odes.[13] In strong reaction against his recent work, Horace declares in highly ambiguous words that he abandons "verse and all the other playful things" (10). However, whereas he seems to suggest that he has called a halt to all poetry and the ironic subjects and manner of the Odes, there he is composing a perfect hexameter and embellishing his sober thoughts with clever metaphor and the comic comparison of his tubby person with the hardened physique of an experienced gladiator. The next line, on the contrary, functions to demonstrate that the "poet" has vanished and allowed himself to write a careless and lumpish hexameter while urgently claiming how very serious he is about non-trivial ethical material. He allows his key ideas to be smashed down by elisions and creates a wordiness of twelve terms, four of which make up the ugly final two feet. Which is the Horace we want: the ambiguous absolute non-poet who writes easy hexameters while disowning poetry, or the awkward moralist who can barely scribble a tolerable poetic line?

It would have been easy for Horace to stress the epistolary elements of this first poem, contrasting, for instance, the location from which he is writing (Sabine Farm?) with the expectable presence of Maecenas in Rome. That is the contrast Horace stresses in *Odes* 3.29. He could also have talked of what he is doing, what he can see and hear from where he is, and then emphasized the political concerns of Maecenas that stand in the way of his leading a happy ethical life. But Horace does not choose to talk of the customary matters of epistles to close friends, no concrete details but rather entertaining metaphors and anecdotes that distract us from a particular rural or urban setting. Maecenas seems to enter the scene near the end of the poem, when Horace uses him (or an indefinite second person singular) to exemplify the misplaced emphasis on appearance and attire, which supposedly Maecenas takes too particularly. He laughs at the poet's haircut and at his clothes, as almost childish blunders; whereas, when it comes to moral thinking and action, he lets inconsistencies and wrong ideas pass without laughing or getting angry. Line 105 strengthens the likelihood that Maecenas is being addressed, though so playfully that he occupies a position different from Horace. Yet he is "the friend that he depends on and refers to." The heart of the Epistle focuses on the urgency Horace voices of his drive to live engrossed in moral improvement. He is like a child in such matters, like a naive new student, not even sure of his teacher, Stoic or Aristippus, distracted by the competing advice of popular morality—money before all else, gained in the easiest and often dishonest way—and the childish nonsense of boys' punning songs about being king (*rex*) if one acts rightly (*recte*, 60). In effect, however, he establishes an important range of interest for the entire book of Epistles that he will be presenting to his audience: a moderate engagement with moral subjects from the perspective of a beginner, not technical nor scholastic, not Greek but everyday Roman. Here in the opening poem, he moves from the playful lyric world of the Odes into what he pretends is a more prosaic but serious environment, using Maecenas as a typical addressee of this and other letters. A different kind of playfulness persists, one that is appropriate to the tentative dedication to *sapientia* in these epistles. Horace establishes his dramatic status in *Epistles* 1.2: he is older than his addressee, Lollius Maximus (*puer*, 68), enjoying the cool hills of Praeneste while Lollius is sweating in Rome; working with the text of Homer more responsibly and thus able to draw on the epic episodes which Lollius has been tossing off as mere subjects of flashy declamation. He finds more ethical learning in Homer than in formal philosophers, and he goes on to show the allegorical significance of certain episodes in the epic. Ulysses serves him as the model of *virtus* and *sapientia* (17), values which he proclaimed in the First Epistle. He moves from his elucidation of Homer to general moral protreptic, and there he marks a slight difference between himself and Lollius: he is already en route toward moral practice, and he urges his young friend to start out after him.

It is characteristic of Horace to devote a good number of Epistles to young men, whom he urges to take their unserious ways into seriousness, locating the moral themes that underlie the literature or life style which they have made the center of their rather trivial lives. Lollius did not read Homer but declaimed his text unthinkingly. In Epistle Three, Horace, the admired poet, writes from Rome or nearby to what he indulgently calls the *studiosa cohors* of Tiberius, several young writers and poets who have accompanied the prince to Asia Minor while he deals with imperial politics, especially Parthia, and they dabble in their poetry. Horace says nothing about himself, but he has lots to say to the members of this "studious cohort" to get them to match their studies with moral and artistic development. One unnamed has taken on an epic in honor of Augustus; Titius is boldly imitating Pindar (unlike Horace); Celsus risks failure by being too imitative of Greek masterpieces; and Florus is making the unwise choice of writing lyric, not an easy task after the successes of Horace. Florus also should be reminded of the path of *caelestis sapientia* (27) and of the need to rectify his unfriendly relationship with Munatius there in the literary group.

In *Epistles* 1.4, Horace writes from his farm to nearby Tibullus at Pedum, during the period when the latter is publishing elegiacs to Delia and Nemesis.

Without paying much attention to Tibullus' topics or success, Horace zeroes in on the apparent melancholy of his friend, who is about a decade younger and therefore worthy of encouragement. He has almost every advantage of intelligence and comfortable possessions, but he seems unable to put all that into perspective, to enjoy the present and play down the inevitable threat of death (which came early for Tibullus). After reminding his neighbor of his advantages, Horace ends with two humorous lines about himself, in the hope that he can bring a smile to Tibullus' face. Instead of inviting the poet over for dinner or some good wine, he offers him the comic sight of himself, sleek and fat, a perfect image of a contented Epicurean pig. But to get that cheerful sight, Tibullus would have to leave his pessimism for a while and share Horace's world. No advice on his poetry is needed.

Horace invites in *Epistles* 1.5 the affluent lawyer Torquatus to a modest dinner in Rome and argues that he knows how to utilize his good fortune and to enjoy the occasion for drinking. With unknown Numicius in 1.6, he produces a moral essay on what things are truly worthy of admiration. Then, he returns to Maecenas in Seven, in what is probably the most serious and complex of all Epistles in the book. These three poems illustrate how Horace varies his addressee, his occasion, his personal exposure, but maintains his friendly, advisory mood throughout. He is the center, who has collected these friends of different ages and concerns, and he remains the same friendly moralist. How can he presume to be didactic and ethical with Maecenas, who had done so much for him? Most readers of *Epistles* 1.7 feel that Horace is tiptoeing along a very dangerous path. But he is the friend that he projects into this collection of poems, not even as critical or didactic as with his younger friends.

The letter presupposes physical separation between poet and Maecenas, a situation that is exacerbated, if Maecenas were irritable, by the frank choice of Horace to increase the length of the separation from a mere five days in August to the better part of a year, until next spring.

We never have a quotation from Maecenas, by which we can infer his agreement or disagreement with Horace's announcements. The separation seems to have started when the poet went out to his Sabine Farm (*rure*, 1) for a few days of rural quiet in August. Having promised to be away only five days, however, he has remained absent the entire month, without apparently excusing himself until now. That shows independence and a touch of defiance: he is not Maecenas' parasite, nor does he accuse Maecenas of any such arrogance. But the great man has got the situation between the friends a little twisted. Horace goes on to emphasize this error by insisting that he may well be absent the entire fall and winter, returning to Rome with the spring.

By a series of inexact analogies, Horace tries to sort out the honorable way in which Maecenas has enriched him with the Sabine Farm and the proper way in which he has accepted the bounty. Horace knows what is good for him better than Maecenas does, and Maecenas has chosen a perfect gift, not the cast-off things of his wealth. Their friendship does not depend on gifts granted and received; gifts do not establish a lien on Horace's new possessions or on his relationship with the donor. The major false analogy develops a story about the politician Philippus and the second-hand dealer Vulteius Mena, in which Philippus is vaguely reminiscent of Maecenas, and Vulteius plays a role somewhat like Horace's. Philippus overcomes Vulteius' caution about getting mixed up with politicians and leaving his life of laziness in Rome, and he essentially traps him into dependence and an amateurish interest in running a farm. He does not give Vulteius an agricultural villa, but arranges his indebtedness and his choice of a piece of rural property where he will be engaged in subsistence farming.

All this is remotely similar to Maecenas' gift of the Sabine Farm, but Horace is no would-be farmer, not working in the fields for his livelihood, and not in debt to Maecenas, who is not toying with Horace's love of the comforts of retiring from Rome. Vulteius ends up as a wretched misfit and bankrupt in a demanding farm, laughed at unsympathetically by Philippus, whereas Horace reluctantly leaves his over-extended rest at his villa-farm, delighted with its ownership, but ready to give it up if strings are tied to its possession.

This ingenious epistle works out Horace's independence in friendship, as it traces the ways in which he balances his connection with Maecenas' Rome and the countryside, with Maecenas' commitment to Rome and its political obligations and, on the other hand, his own drive toward apolitical freedom, which he associates with the country and poetic creativity. The independence toward Maecenas seems at times almost truculent or at least rather careless of Maecenas' feelings as close friend. But in terms of the *persona* that Horace has been developing in the Epistles so far, it is not an accident that Horace here faces Maecenas not as an equal so much as a concerned friend who needs his independence and insists on it.

In *Epistles* 1.8, Horace writes to Albinovanus Celsus, one of the literary men accompanying Tiberius, using the Muse as his spokesperson, aptly for one who sets a high store by his own poetry. But Horace concentrates on his spiritual dissatisfaction, which includes an indecisive love of Rome and the farm (12), and he only assumes the authority of friendship in the final line, with advice for Celsus that also applies to Horace's own unhappiness. The Ninth Epistle goes to Tiberius himself: a recommendation for another young member of his staff, a political piece of writing that makes the poet feel awkward. And the Tenth is at last a full discussion of the city–country tension in Horace's life, written to Aristius Fuscus in Rome. Fuscus was a friend of Horace, roughly of the same age, and he had played a teasing role in *Satires* 1.9, when Horace had his troubles with the ambitious busybody in the Forum. Now, Fuscus lives in Rome, but Horace has escaped its crowds and ambitions to enjoy the rural pleasures, which make him a kind of "king" (8, 33) in the quiet Sabine world. By contrast, living in Rome turns one into a slave to material things. In the fable of Aesop, which Horace tells, he suggests that city-dwellers resemble the horse who vied with a stag for possession of the pastures. When defeated by the stag, the horse looked to a stronger ally and became his mount and servant in return for driving the stag away. It was a bad exchange: the horse gained a master whom he could not get rid of, and similarly Aristius and other city-slaves cannot free themselves from dependence on urban things.

Epistles 1.11 and 1.12 address two younger friends who have escaped Rome, to be sure, but have not found spiritual peace or love of nature in their retreats: Bullatius touring the famous sites of Classical Greece and Iccius managing an estate for Agrippa in Sicily. From his Sabine refuge, Horace talks to these two men who, unlike him, fail to find satisfaction living away from the moral dangers of Rome. The poet in his rural contentment can equally advise Aristius in Rome and his two unhappy friends abroad: what they need is balance (*animus aequus*). Moral balance can be found anywhere by the right attitude, even in desolate Italian Ulubrae, he reminds the tired tourist Bullatius. Iccius is a different problem. Unlike Bullatius, who has the wealth to indulge in expensive tourist travel, Iccius is not rich and forced to work for funds, even though he has a good job serving Agrippa. But he spends too much time regretting his limited means, in feeling cramped in his pursuit of philosophy, and, alas, in being absent from Rome, the center of the contemporary world, and from the political and military activities that radiate from there. So Horace reports on what Iccius is missing. Agrippa is in Spain and Tiberius in Armenia (along with other young friends of the poet, who need advice), and a cornucopia of prosperity pours out its golden fruits on agriculture in Italy. Can Iccius reconcile himself to his Sicilian absence?

The position of Horace among his many friends is quite different in Epistle Thirteen, where he no longer presides over young and old, advising them for their own good to seek independence from material things and equanimity towards the changes arising in life. Horace is the anxious one, fussing over the collection of Odes and trying to make sure that his presentation of the three books makes a strong and positive impression on Augustus. It is not the Odes themselves that worry him: it is rather the trivial correctness that he wishes to achieve by the manner of presentation, and thereby he makes himself into a joke for his friends and Augustus, who already recognize the poetic masterpiece he has composed. In the circle of Horace's friends it is somewhat of relief that he proves vulnerable in ways that he softly criticizes in others. He is presumably writing in his Sabine Villa while the three books of Odes make their way to Augustus in Rome.

In *Epistles* 1.14, Horace would dearly like to be in his rural home, but he has been trapped by duties in Rome, providing consolation to his friend Lamia on the death of his brother. He writes with ill-concealed envy of the bailiff of his Sabine Farm, who, far from appreciating his good fortune to live and work there, wants only to escape to the city, its bars and prostitutes, away from hard physical farm labor. Thus, in this fictitious letter to a man who would not be able to read it and would not be moved by its ideas, Horace compares their distinct lots in life. The bailiff simply dislikes the country as a place, whereas Horace mocks what the man sees in Rome because he continues to pursue cheap material and sexual pleasures there.

Horace has already shown that friendship keeps him briefly in the city, and he rhapsodizes over the rural setting, not for its material advantages, but for the chance it gives him of studying and correcting himself. In both city and country, his moral practices are the object of attention, not the material advantages or disadvantages of the environment. Horace even performs physical tasks in the country, to the amusement of his neighbors and to the disgust of the bailiff. Once again, the poet advises with the generalization that in truth it is not the place that should be blamed but the moral attitude, which lacks the necessary equanimity (12–13). And he concludes by advising that any person should grate-fully practice the art which he knows. That seems apt for Horace, who is doing that; but the bailiff does not have an "art" he recognizes, so he cannot adapt to the ideal life he resents there in Sabine country.

In *Epistles* 1.15, Horace again makes fun of himself and his choice of ideally comfortable refuges. It may be that he is writing from the Sabine Farm at the end of the summer season to his friend Vala at Velia on the coast, to prepare himself a good spot for winter. (That could relate to his warning to Maecenas in *Epistles* 1.7 that, instead of returning directly from the Farm, he might well go south to warm shores for the winter.) What happens in this letter is that Horace represents himself doing exactly what he nobly advised against, taking major interest in the place and its physical conveniences and ignoring the moral appeal and support of simple nature as well as the pleasure of being with friends. Not that he is unaware of the inconsistencies of his style of living and ethical positions. He can endure a restricted diet and call himself "strong" or what we admire as "robust" when forced to live cheaply. But when he does get the opportunity to eat rich food, he laughingly admits, he has to confess that wealthy men like Vala really are wise (*sapere*, 45) and know how to live well on expensive foods.

Thus, the moral term for the announced goal of Horace's abandonment of lyric becomes perverted into an aesthetic "smartness," and wisdom becomes too human. It is easy to be "wise" when wealthy, but the danger that faces those of limited and varying means is that they are close to being parasites, anxious about their meals and stooping to earn them ignominiously and unwisely from their so-called affluent friends.

The basic opposition between the truly wise man and one who poses dishon-estly as such among the people of Rome allows Horace to exempt himself from criticism in his virtuous refuge at the Sabine Villa. Instead, in *Epistles* 1.16 he addresses his negative judgment to a second person singular who is masked behind the politically experienced and honored Quinctius. The average politician finds the goal of good and wise man too restrictive to his ambitions. He may gain the cheers of the populace and fool the voters with his reputation, but the operation of PR is not fool-proof. All too soon, the public vote dismisses the fake man of honor. While he pretends to pray loudly to Apollo, a favorite deity of Augustus, in order to justify his pretense to be the proverbial good man, he barely moves his lips as he begs the help of Laverna in his theft of public funds. Horace relaxes happily in the country, while Quinctius faces the fact that politics, even for a man who tries to be honest, involves too many people and temptations to allow him to choose and achieve honor or the wisdom of goodness. This is neither a playful or cheerful letter and is devoid of self-irony, once Horace removes himself and his farm from consideration and focuses on the tarnished life of politics in Rome. Quinctius seems to be a contemporary of Horace or even a little older.

The next two letters function as a pair, addressing two younger men who have ambitions to achieve the success, such as it seems to be, of a Quinctius by sordid (if necessary) and humiliating means. The years of the civil wars have passed, and political opportunities lie in humble service to the older generation. It is a galling experience, but it is even more painful to realize that the kind of service demanded of one abases and turns one into the proverbial parasite. Horace places us entirely in the environment of his unknown addressee in *Epistles* 1.17, not using his own experiences in his advice. We may imagine that he enjoys himself un-ambitiously on the farm, in stark contrast to the worries of Scaeva, who tries to figure out how to use or exploit the more powerful (*maioribus uti*, 2) in and outside Rome. Young Lollius whom we met in *Epistles* 1.2 comes back with new problems in 1.18: he claims to be an independent man—or at least Horace addresses him as *liberrime*, 1—but his outspoken frankness annoys the politicians he is trying to impress. Unless he modifies his truculence, he will lose friendly support from the great. Instead of fixing on one of these extremes, frankness or subservience, he needs to be more flexible in his search for "useful" friendship. Horace, a generation older and blessed with his relationship to Maecenas, can comfortably write him from the farm, the symbol of his own ideal independence in friendship (104ff.).

The last two letters deal with Horace's poetry. *Epistles* 1.19 addresses Maecenas, who agitated to have the Odes continued in the first letter. So he serves as a sympathetic ear while the poet denounces his critics and their sneers at his lack of originality in lyric. Its acerbic tone contrasts markedly with that of *Epistles* 1.20, a witty, self-ironic poem on the book of Epistles which Horace herewith publishes. Now, his addressee is an imaginary spirit in the book which defies the advice of its poet and confidently, but unwisely, trusts its inexperienced young judgment. The book is a handsome slave who intends to sell itself to admirers, a dangerous project in the city of Rome. But unable to get his advice heard, the poet sends him off with some last biographical data for the world, modest claims of Horace's achievement in his forty-four years of living and writing. His final audience is a version of himself and then the literary public, charmed by this self-criticism.

Conclusion: Horace encircled

I have stopped here, leaving un-praised Book 2 of the Epistles and Book 4 of the Odes, but I did so consciously: Book 1 of the Epistles is a decisive refutation of the theory of Horace's incorporation in the so-called Circle of Maecenas, and the poet moves on from that point in his last works. In the Epistles, his voice and personality, in all their variety dominate. Horace collects friends, advises them in amiable manner, and engages us, his larger audience, in the decision to be poet and moralist. He is polite and friendly to Maecenas in three letters, but Maecenas does not control them, and indeed Horace presents himself from the start as choosing the genre in spite of Maecenas' wishes. That voice of contrariety is strong in terms also of Horace's independent moral choices in relation to the Sabine Farm in *Epistles* 1.7, where the ideal spot in Italy fails to distract the determination of the poet from leading a good and wise life, with equanimity, no matter what material pressures are exerted on him. As he says to the tyrant Pentheus, the worst that can happen to me is that I should die (16.79). That's better than being a slavish parasite.

GUIDE TO FURTHER READING

The inclination to seek and find literary circles dominated by a great political figure was strong as late as 1950, as can be seen by articles in the *Oxford Classical Dictionary* on Scipio Aemilianus and the Scipionic Circle. Twenty years later, the biography of A. E. Astin, *Scipio Aemilianus*, and his contribution to a newer edition of the *OCD* raised insuperable doubts about this Circle and opened up questions about any such circles in Roman culture. Scholars then modified the investigation to study the practices of literary patronage and the response of poets and writers to the favors of the Roman nobility and imperial rulers. A system was discovered that likened patronage to the anthropology of gift-giving and -receiving. This seemed to make sense of the literary explosion that involved the civil wars of the first century and the development of imperial powers: there was a loose exchange of gifts, in the form of material patronage for the poets and poetry dedicated explicitly or implicitly by the poets to their patrons. It was an amiable exchange. See Saller (1982), and White (1993), which stirred doubts about literary patronage. Hence, I have here suggested that Horace, not Maecenas, determines the course of his poetry.

NOTES

1 Astin 1947 and his entry *s.v.* in *Oxford Classical Dictionary*, 1949.
2 Cicero, *De Amicitia* 69.

3 *Satires* 1.5.93.
4 My discussion of Maecenas' Circle and Horace owes much to the ingenious arguments of Peter White 1993.
5 *Satires* 1.6.51–2.
6 *Plotius et Varius, Maecenas Vergiliusque* (81).
7 *ambitione relegata* (83)
8 For the complicated archaeological data on the villa, see Frischer, Crawford, and De Simone 2006. See also the essay by Bernard Frischer in this volume, Chapter 4.
9 *Satires* 2.7.33
10 *Satires* 2.8.21–2.
11 *tutus ab insidiis* 2.6.117.
12 *Epistles* 1.1.2–3: *quaeris ... iterum antiquo me includere ludo.*
13 1.1.4: *non eadem est aetas, non mens.*

CHAPTER THREE

Horace and Imperial Patronage

Phebe Lowell Bowditch

Addressing an epistle to his friend Florus some time after the publication of the *Odes* 1–3, Horace—or rather, his epistolary persona—excuses his tardy letter writing and failure to send lyric poems that he had promised by drawing a series of analogies.[1] In one, he describes a soldier who, losing all his money to a thief, responds with great—and possibly displaced—fury at the enemy: he fights fiercely, storms a tower, and is rewarded with enormous wealth; when the opportunity arises to fight again, however, the soldier demurs and recommends that his officer find another man whose savings have been taken. Following this analogy are some of the most seemingly candid lines in the Horatian corpus (*Epistles* 2.2.46–52). As a young man pursuing a liberal arts education in Athens, the speaker tells us about being caught up in the tumult of the civil wars, when Julius Caesar's heir, Octavian, and the liberators, Brutus and Cassius, clashed arms in the showdown at Philippi, a battle that plucked the would-be poet from his ivory-tower ease. A tribune in Brutus' army—an honor that was unconventionally accorded to the son of a freedman (*Satires* 1.6.45–50)—the student turned military officer fought on the losing side and returned to Italy where, he claims, "bold penury compelled [him], lacking paternal land and estate, to write poetry" (*inopemque paterni/ et laris et fundi, paupertas impulit audax/ ut versus facerem: Epistles* 2.2.50–2). Taken at face value, these lines would retrospectively comment on the poet's early sense of the material advantages to be gained from his poetic talent. However, as Horatian scholars of the last two decades have increasingly emphasized, Horace constructs various faces for himself (e.g. Oliensis 1998; McNeill 2001), fashioning his self-image in response to his different audiences. How, then, should we read these lines? As unmediated autobiography? Or, does the preceding anecdote of the soldier stimulated by loss, and later comfortable with his assets, in fact rhetorically shape the terms of Horace's self-fashioning, both in the interest of a persuasive excuse to Florus and to make a cagey nod to readers of posterity? The speaker does not say outright that his paternal property was in fact stolen, but the analogy of the soldier's loss coyly invites—even dares—us to make this inference, particularly given the backdrop of wide-scale land expropriations during the civil wars. Writing verse, goes the implication, allowed the poet to regain confiscated wealth. And yet, Horatian verse clearly transcends such easy commodification—and this is the irony of the statement—as we cannot reduce the poems to pure objects of economic exchange.

For all that poets during the Augustan period continuously draw on their patronal relationships as rich subject matter for their poems, they tend rather to eschew any overt representation of poetry as an activity intentionally practiced for material gain. Despite the speaker's ironic admission of his own youthful aspirations, he elsewhere claims that poets act to their disadvantage, when they write with the expectation that they will be immediately noticed and granted support (*Epistles* 2.1.226–8). Horace more than his compatriots Vergil and Propertius returns repeatedly to his experience as a beneficiary of literary patronage, but his self-representations generally display him either as a decorously grateful recipient, as in the Satires and Epodes, or as delicately negotiating his independence, as in *Epistles* 1. To describe the role of imperial patronage in Horace's career—the subject of this essay—requires both judicious, at times skeptical, treatment of the autobiographical statements he makes about himself in his poems—this is often all we have as evidence—and a willingness to "read between the lines," that is, to interpret the more oblique, allegorical, and indirect images through which he constructs his self and his development as a poet. Some statements can be corroborated or fleshed out by other sources—Suetonius' biography of the poet, including snippets of Augustus' letters, for example—but so compelling is the author's own self-portrait that it is easy to forget how often we are simply taking Horace's word for it. In contrast to the biographical criticism that dominated classical scholarship for so long, Horatian studies now recognize the futility of seeking the "real" Horace and acknowledge that his poems seductively dangle an array of constructed selves before his readers, personae not only shaped by audience and the conventions of genre (Anderson 1982: 66; Freudenburg 1993), but also fashioned by the social and cultural practices and codes dominant in Rome at the time. History may not be—is not, in fact—wholly recoverable, but neither can it be erased, and the Horatian speaker's own issues of liberty, slavery, compliance, and self-assertion, with regard to his patrons, inevitably take on a more far-reaching political dimension in the context of the changes following the civil wars.

Literary patronage in ancient Rome

Before examining the poetic passages that best trace the contours and implications of the patronal experience Horace constructs for his readers, we should consider both the terminology and the structure of patronage as a relationship that fostered literary production. Although scholars have conventionally referred to the social relations between a poet and his benefactor as "literary patronage," the English phrase does not accurately translate the terms that ancient Romans employed. Historically, "patronage" translates *patrocinium*, which applied to two kinds of relationships: either the sponsorship and protection of a community or city by an individual or the state, or the relationship between citizens of the higher orders who held or aspired to office and those of the *plebs*—including freedmen— to whom, in exchange for their attendance and political support, the elite pro- vided material and legal protection (Brunt 1988: 382–442; Wallace-Hadrill 1989: 63–87; Drummond 1989: 89–115; Deniaux 1993: 1–13). Members of the elite tended to avoid the terms *patronus* ("patron") and *cliens* ("client") to refer to relations between a benefactor and his aristocratic protégé, preferring the more egalitarian and emotive connotations of *amicitia*, or "friendship." As Cicero famously asserts, aristocratic Romans thought it "like death to be called clients or to benefit from patronage" (*patrocinio vero se usos aut clientes appellari mortis instar putant: De Officiis* 2.69); and even when clear differences in status separated two men, terms such as *magnus amicus* or *potens amicus* ("great friend," "powerful friend") would both acknowledge and soften such distinctions (e.g. Horace, *Epistles* 1.18.44). Recently, scholars have challenged the dominant view of such language as a decorous if misleading convention: this preference for the terms of friendship among the elite, it is argued, indicates precisely that—the strength of an emotional attachment (Konstan 1997), or the sympathy of inter- ests and values (White 1993: 13–14), between two individuals in a relationship that may all the same serve a utilitarian purpose.

Richard Saller's classic definition of patronage sees three criteria that must be present in order to justify the critic's use of the term: reciprocity or an exchange of goods and services, asymmetry in the social standing of the two parties and types of goods exchanged, and duration of the relationship (1982: 1). From one perspective, the Augustan writers who benefited from Maecenas' generosity— Vergil, Horace, and Propertius—shared the same social status as their benefactor: all were *equites*, or knights, Horace having become one by virtue of the tribune- ship in Brutus' army (Mayer 1995: 280; Taylor 1968); however, Maecenas' greater wealth, Etruscan regal ancestry (*Satires* 1.6.1–3; *Odes* 1.1, *Odes* 3.29.1), and closer proximity to Augustus, the center of power, raised the Emperor's "right-hand man" above the writers he enriched. Horace, moreover, came from humble origins—his father was a freedman (*Satires* 1.6.45–6; *Epistles* 1.20.20).[2] As for goods exchanged in the relationship, however, the differences were dis- tinctly qualitative: a patron could offer the material benefits of gifts of land or money as well as venues, audience, endorsement, and subject matter for a poet's verse; the poet, in turn, provided companionship, and, most important, verse.[3] In poems, everything from the dedicatory convention of a poetry book, to panegyric content, to, ultimately, the boon of immortality qualified as a "good"—symbolic if not material. Reflecting on patronage in general, Andrew Wallace-Hadrill has asked, "Is it a pattern of relationships that exists objectively in certain societies whether or not the participants themselves acknowledge or approve it, or is it a way in which the actors perceive and formulate the relationships in which they are engaged? That is to say, are we talking about a structure or an ideology?" (1989: 65). His answer that both structure and ideology are components of patronage suggests that the language of friendship, parity, and affection among the elite may also have fostered the semblance of disinterested giving—an "ideology of voluntarism"—in a situation where, in fact, both parties actively profit but resist appearing to manipulate the system and its reciprocity ethic (Bowditch 2001: 22).

Indeed, passages in Seneca's *De Beneficiis* ("On Benefactions") and Cicero's *De Officiis* ("On Duties")—philosophic treatises and handbooks for the proper behavior of the elite—reveal tensions and contradictions between the voluntarism underlying the "art of giving" in ancient Rome and the expectation of reciprocity by which it in fact functioned. Using a monetary metaphor, Seneca asserts that "In benefits the book-keeping is simple—so much is paid out; if anything comes back, it is gain, if nothing comes back, there is no loss. I made the gift for the sake of giving ... The good man never thinks of [benefits] unless he is reminded of them by having them returned ...To regard a benefit as an amount advanced is putting it out at shameful interest." And yet, in contrast to this decorum of disinterested benefaction is the advice for the recipient "to surpass in deed and spirit those who have placed us under obligation, for he who has a debt of gratitude to pay never catches up with the favor unless he outstrips it" (*De Beneficiis* 1.2.3; 1.4.3, trans. Basore 1935). Cicero, in turn, openly addresses the discrepancy between the ideology of giving and the actual exploitation to which the system inclined: "In granting favors ... the most important function of duty ... is to enrich above all the person who is most in need of riches. But people generally do exactly the opposite; for they defer above all to him from whom they expect the most, even though he does not need them" (*De Officiis* 1.49, trans. Atkins).

In many ways, the Roman system of benefaction, and its subset of literary patronage, display features of what anthropologists analyze as a "gift economy" (Veyne 1990; Dixon 1993; Bowditch 2001: 31–63). These characteristics include expenditure for the purpose of establishing prestige and status, the social cohesion that arises from gift-giving, an obligation to make a return gift, a perpetual disequilibrium of indebtedness—who is more indebted to whom?—and, perhaps most tellingly, a delay between an initial gift and its reciprocation, a temporal lag that, as Bourdieu points out (1977: 171), serves to mystify the economic aspect underlying an ideology of voluntarism in this form of exchange. The desire to amass "symbolic capital"—both public status and the debt or obligation imposed by a gift—drives such giving and reveals the implicit economic calculation beneath its decorum.

All these features of a gift economy arguably appear in Horace's experience of patronage, to the degree that we can reconstruct it, and shape his self-representations. The early period of Horace's career has a mythic rags-to-riches appeal; for after the defeat of Brutus and Cassius at Philippi in 42 BCE, the future poet returned to Rome, obtained pardon for having fought with the Republican army, and secured a post as clerk in a quaestor's office (*Epistles* 2.2.49–52; *Satires* 2.6.36; Suet. *Vita Hor.*). Although the income may have given him financial independence, Horace's status, literary opportunities, and landed wealth significantly increased as he became established in Maecenas' network of friends, associates, and beneficiaries. As Octavian's closest political advisor during the thirties as well as the twenties, while the *puer vindex*, or "avenging boy," recreated himself as the merciful Augustus, Maecenas recognized the value of literature engaged with the political and moral issues of the day. Horace's first three collections of verse are all dedicated to his patron and, judging by internal evidence of the poems themselves, can be dated to 35 BCE (*Satires* 1) and 30 BCE (*Satires* 2 and the Epodes), the politically tumultuous period leading up to and just following the decisive battle of Actium in 31 BCE. At a point just prior to, if not simultaneous with, Octavian's victory over Marc Antony, Maecenas endowed Horace with the celebrated Sabine Farm, the first of potentially five gifts of property from either himself or Augustus (*Satires* 2.6; Suet. *Vita Hor.*; Lyne 1995: 9–11), and certainly the most visible poetic symbol of their relationship and the poet's newly acquired elite status. After this gift came a decisive shift in genre, as the poet spent the following seven to eight years—a transitional period for the regime as well—writing his lyric masterpiece, the *Odes* 1–3, which "came out" to the public at a significant date, in 23 BCE, when Augustus orchestrated the second sweeping reorganization of governmental powers that ceded authority to himself while appearing to restore the Republic (on the reorganization of government, see Eder 1990, 2005; Gruen 2005). This sequence of dates, coupled with the historical timing of the Odes' publication, suggests the economic calculus underlying the voluntarism of a gift economy.

When we come to the content of the verse itself, the Horatian speaker, in key poems across the Satires, Odes, and Epistles, invokes and thematically explores the tensions and contradictions between a semblance of disinterested giving and an expectation of reciprocity, between a rhetoric of expenditure and the symbolic capital such spending accrues. Although few, if any, scholars would characterize Horace as the paid hack of his patrons, either in the early triumviral period, or later, as Augustus became more securely established, scholarship has often been divided about the degree of compulsion the poet experienced and the "sincerity" of his political voice. Historians and literary critics display a spectrum of opinions, ranging from patronal gifts as "no-strings attached," leaving the Augustan poet free to compose what or even when he wanted (e.g. White 1993: 17) to a view of patronage as implicitly coercive despite poetic strategies to suggest the contrary (e.g. Williams 1990). To appreciate the complexity of Horace's own experience and his sophisticated treatment of it requires both a sense of the chronology and backdrop of his poetic production and a nuanced reading of his poems.

The early years: portraits of patronage

The two books of Satires and the Epodes display the impact of Horace's patrons in various ways—in subtle or overt support of Octavian, in the themes of friendship and political ambition, in deftly constructed images of the poet's relations with Maecenas and his network. Horace composed the first book of Satires during the early thirties, a time when the alliances of the "second triumvirate," Octavian, Antony, and Lepidus, continuously shifted, broke up, and reformed. The "Sicilian War" with Sextus Pompey, commanding the seas and islands west of Italy, contributed to this landscape of civil unrest. Book 1 of the Satires never directly addresses this political backdrop (*Satires* 1.7 looks further back to a scene remembered from Philippi, in 42), but the subjects of many satires—the ethical issues of *amicitia* (*Satires* 1.3), Lucilian "frank speech" or *libertas* (*Satires* 1.4 and 10), luxury and indulgence as corrosive vices (*Satires* 1.2), and so forth—all have bearing on the factional politics of the period and the wars of rhetoric that attended them (DuQuesnay 1984: 19–58). In contrast to such indirect engagement with public issues, the speaker willingly details the beginnings of his own personal relationship with Maecenas, providing a portrait that gives information, defends his character and motives, and decorously pays tribute to his benefactor:

> I return to myself as a freedman's son, whom everyone slanders as a freedman's son, now because I share your table, Maecenas; but formerly because I commanded a Roman legion at the rank of tribune. These are different issues; although someone might justifiably begrudge me the military office, he should not question my friendship with you, who are particularly careful to choose worthy men, lacking crooked ambition. I could not say that I was lucky in this, that I acquired your friendship by chance ... at one time noblest Virgil, after him Varius described my character. When I met you in person, after speaking a few isolated words, tongue-tied shame kept me from saying more ... you replied, as is your custom, a few words; I left; and after nine months you called me back and bid that I be included in your group of friends (*iubesque/ esse in amicorum numero*). I consider this important—that I pleased you, someone who distinguishes an upright from a base character not by a father's social standing but by a man's life and pure heart. (*Satires* 1.6, 45–64)

In the highly stratified society of status-conscious Rome, the speaker's swift ascent and inclusion among Maecenas' close associates provoked social envy from those outside the halls of power. The image fashioned here aims as much to deflect the ill will of this potential readership as it does to cultivate an "autobiography" for posterity or to distinguish Horace's group of friends. What is perhaps most striking, however, is the way this early account focuses not on Horace's literary aspirations but rather on his freedman origins—and humble versus aristocratic birth—in relation to political office. Here, the speaker takes pains to distance himself from charges of "crooked ambition," and he does this skillfully by allowing Maecenas to vouch for his upright character, thus complimenting his benefactor's discernment in the process. Nor did idle luck put him in the path of the great—his literary friends, Vergil and Varius, spoke on his behalf and introduced him. Horace's poetic talents are implicit here, evident in the identities of those he mentions, but the emphasis remains on the speaker's inner worth as a person. All the same, the picture of Horace reduced to stuttering in his initial "interview" and the grand man's "summons" after nine months for Horace to be included in his "number of friends and associates" (*in numero amicorum*—possibly an official list; Horsfall 1981: 5) underscore both the social disparity between the two (Williams 1990: 264) and the mere convention of the term *amicus*, or "friend," at this point in the relationship.

The previous satire, 1.5, provides another glimpse of Horace's relations with Maecenas, here focusing on trusted companionship as one of the features of *amicitia*. Commonly called "the Journey to Brundisium," this satire describes a trip that historically required urgent diplomatic action. The so-called "Treaty of Brundisium" between the triumvirs had taken place in 40 BCE, but this poem, modeled on a satire of Lucilius, refers to a second journey in 38 BCE, ultimately to Athens, where delicate negotiations conducted through Maecenas and others aimed to secure Antony's aid for Octavian's battle with Sextus Pompey. Despite the momentousness of the occasion, Horace focuses on all the quotidian aspects of travel—insomnia due to mosquitoes, a stove fire, entertainment at an inn—and assiduously avoids any but the briefest mention of the greater context. By drawing attention to his lack of involvement in the politics of the trip, the poet in fact underscores his disciplined discretion (Griffin 1984: 197–8), an indispensable asset in a "*junior amicus*," as Horace later writes to his friend Lollius, in *Epistles* 1.18.37–8.

All these self-portraits not only take Horace's relationship with Maecenas as thematic material but they also constitute a "good" in their own right, poetry that both compliments and reassures. Poems in this sense have no precise quantifiable value, but by reinforcing Maecenas' status in the present and conferring immortality on him for posterity, Horatian verse reciprocates and transforms into "symbolic capital"—here the prestige value of verse—the material wealth that the speaker gratefully and explicitly acknowledges in the first epode: "Enough and more has your generosity enriched me" (*satis superque me benignitas tua/ ditavit. Epodes* 1.31–2). A dedication poem for the collection that came out in 30 BCE, *Epode* 1 also displays the theme of companionship—the poet's tender solicitude for and desire to join Maecenas, who is envisioned as accompanying Octavian to encounter Antony and Cleopatra.

This epode does not mention specific gifts, but a variation of the phrase "enough and more" appears in *Satires* 2.6, a poem often interpreted as a "thank-you" note for the Sabine estate. The opening lines implicitly contrast patronal gift-giving with market exchange dependent on coin:

> This was in my prayers: a measure of land not so large, with a garden and near the house a spring of pure water and, in addition, a little patch of woods. The gods have given me more and better (*auctius atque … melius*). It is good. I ask for nothing more, son of Maia, except that you make these gifts lasting [or truly mine] … if foolishly I pray for none of these things: "Oh, if that nearby corner could be added, which now skews my farm's shape! Oh, if lucky chance would reveal to me a pot of money, as it did for him, who, once the treasure was found, plowed as an owner the same field which he had as a hired laborer, made wealthy by his friend Hercules!" If what is here now pleases me, grateful for it, with this prayer I ask: fatten the master's flock and all else but his talent, and, as you are accustomed, always be my greatest guardian.

In language similar to that used by the shepherd Tityrus in Vergil's first eclogue, the Horatian speaker expresses his gratitude to "gods" who have blessed him with a gift of property—a *modus*, or measure, of land. Just as the historical figure of Octavian hovers behind *praesentis divos*, or "incarnate gods," as responsible for recovering Tityrus' land, so Horace's gods point to Maecenas, with the vocative form for Mercury as son of Maia—*Maia nate*—echoing the patron's name (Oliensis 1998: 48). These metaphors of divinity serve at once to compliment benefactors through a discourse of Hellenistic king-worship (DuQuesnay 1981: 102 on Tityrus'speech; cf. Sen. *De Beneficiis* 3.15.4) and to decorously avoid outright articulation of the historical figures involved. But the satire soon enough demotes the speaker's reverential use of deifying language to a form of street slang, an ironic acknowledgement of the political realities of land redistribution, made by a passerby who observes the poet's relationships: "Tell me, my good man, for you must know, since you fortunately have contact with the gods … is Caesar going to give his soldiers promised rewards in Sicily or from Italian land?" (*Satires* 2.6.51–6). Referring to the settlement of veteran soldiers after Actium, this question puts the "gifts from the gods" at the opening of the satire in a different light. Vergil, Horace, and Propertius as well, appear all to have lost their ancestral or paternal lands in the confiscations of a decade earlier, those undertaken for soldiers discharged after the battle of Philippi. With this historical subtext, the "gods" take on a potentially more capricious identity, one that, for example, resembles the depiction of Jove who both gives and takes away, at the end of *Epistles* 1.18 to Lollius. And not only does Horace receive land that may well have been earlier confiscated from another, but the question from the "man on the street" unwittingly implies that such gifts to poets comprise part of a cultural strategy that parallels the land grants by which a general secured loyalty from his soldiers, after they left the military (Bowditch 2001: 4–5).

This historical context of the land expropriations occurring early in Octavian's career subtly resonates in the imagery through which the poet explores patronal relationships, whether his own or others. We see a certain anxiety of ownership expressed in the foolish wish of the opening of *Satires* 2.6, a "forbidden wish" the rejection of which becomes the condition for the speaker's prayer to Mercury to forever enjoy his property. The speaker must not wish for money like the man who, having discovered such, bought and kept tilling the property that he had previously worked for hire. Now why is this wish foolish? Presumably, on an overt level, because Horace now has and recognizes the leisure conferred by the gift, in contrast to the farmer as owner, who continues to work with his physical labor the same piece of land as before. And yet the status of ownership was far preferable to being a *mercennarius*, or "hired laborer." Although we must be wary about making reductive one-to-one correspondences in the various exempla that Horace uses to flesh out the points he makes, the contrast between property ownership and hired labor here invites us—however fleetingly—to place the speaker, newly in possession of his Sabine estate as a gift, somewhere on the spectrum between these two poles. The speaker's convoluted rhetoric here may well betray a forbidden desire for the freedom that monetary purchase brings, a wish to be free of the reciprocations that gratitude for gifts requires (Bowditch 2001:144–50). On yet another level, then, it is the recent context of the civil wars and the wide-scale confiscations of land that make such a wish foolish, for uninterrupted enjoyment of his property may be all that is possible. That the speaker's gratitude for such pleasure is indeed implicated in poetic production subtly appears in the allusion at the end of the satire's opening: the prayer for a fat flock but lean talent echoes the famous lines of Callimachus' *Aetia*, where Apollo instructs the poet to "feed the sacrificial victim to be as fat as possible but to keep the Muse slender" (*Aet.* 1.23). In keeping with such Alexandrian affiliations, Horatian political poetry—whether *Epodes* 1 and 9 on the lead-up to and aftermath of Actium, or the civic-minded verse of the Odes—eschewed epic in favor of lyric.

The Odes 1–3

How Horace's Odes participate in the socioeconomics of patronage has always been a complex and somewhat contentious issue. Scholarly opinion for much of the twentieth century persistently addressed the ways in which the political poetry, and the Roman Odes (3.1–6) in particular, endorsed "Augustan" ideology. Whether we adduce the seemingly militaristic patriotism of *Odes* 3.2, the anticipated divine status of Augustus in 3.3, the Gigantomachy as allegory for the civil wars in 3.4, or the condemnation of religious impiety in 3.6, this sequence of odes conveys attitudes that many have identified with "pro-Augustan" sentiment. Significantly, although the Roman Odes probably became a sequence after their initial composition, they all date to the years 29–26 BCE, thus roughly coinciding with the major redistribution of political powers in 27 BCE, in which Octavian took the name of Augustus and acquired considerable proconsular authority. For critics convinced of the poet's own investment in the regime and admiration for Augustus the question of patronal pressure was moot (Fraenkel 1957; Doblhofer 1966). Others have doubted the poet's own conviction in the political poems (e.g. La Penna 1963; Lyne 1995). Over the last two decades criticism has departed from the stark terms of "pro-" vs. "anti-" Augustan readings (see Brink 1982: 523–6; Kennedy 1992 on this division) and views the poems as actively creating ideology (e.g. Santirocco 1995), rather than "reflecting" it; for some, fissures in the poetic fabric of the text undermine the viability of panegyric as a coherent mode (Lowrie 1997); or ambiguity characterizes the encomium (Putnam 1990). But for all their different emphases, many Horatian critics themselves invest in an "ideology of voluntarism" that parallels the ancient literature on benefaction. Whether by viewing the poet as entirely in control of his rhetorical game or, in contrast, by maintaining a strict separation between the biographical poet and his text, critics tend to protect Horace's *libertas* or agency, an inclination that goes full circle back to the prominence of this concept in his poetry.

The rhetoric of the Odes draws on various social practices for a range of poetic figures and conventions connected to patronage, but sacrificial motifs and images of priestly euergetism contribute specifically to the image of the poet as voluntarily engaged in the contemporary political and moral issues associated with Augustus' rise to power. The rhetoric of sacrificial expenditure and religious expiation displays the speaker writing poems that become symbolic sacrifices or "gifts" made not for Augustus but for the collective benefit of the Roman people. Following the dedication poem of the collection and thus signaling its manifest importance, the theme of expiation appears initially in *Odes* 1.2, where the gods, angered over the civil wars, have caused the Tiber to flood, a "natural disaster" interpreted as a prodigy that must be expiated. The speaker invests Augustus here, a secular avatar of Mercury, with the divine authority for the job. As though building up to the grand sequence of the Roman Odes, the next treatment of expiation as a theme occurs in the dedication poem of Book 2, addressed to Asinius Pollio. A staunch defender of Republican *libertas* who remained neutral after Actium, Pollio has turned to writing a history on the origins of the civil wars, "a work full of dangerous hazard," involving "doomed friendships, capricious fortune, and arms smeared with blood yet to be expiated (*arma/ nondum expiatis uncta cruoribus*)" (*Odes* 2.1.4–6). Pollio's tragic Muse has left the stage and now inspires the genre of historical narrative, producing a form of catharsis in the speaker. The poem becomes a kind of choral lament for the dead and, in the last stanza, the speaker draws his own Muse up short, rebuking her for taking up "the office of the Cean dirge" (*Odes* 2.1.38), an allusion to Simonides of Ceos.

The word for "office" here, *munera*, has several connotations that poetically implicate the social practice of patronage in other systems of expenditure. First, as a word that also means "gifts" or "offerings to the dead," in the context of the Ode to Pollio it suggests funereal sacrifices that perform the expiation called for at the beginning (Bowditch 2001: 81–2). Second, as a word that here combines both the sense of public office and the poems themselves as sacrificial gifts, "*munera*" looks forward to Horace's most solemn and civic-minded persona as "priest of the Muses" (*sacerdos Musarum*), adopted for the Roman Odes, 3.1–6. In contrast to the metaphor of the poet as visionary seer or *vates*, a posture assumed by other Augustan poets (Newman 1967) as well as Horace in *Odes* 1.1, the office of *sacerdotes* refers specifically to priests in their official capacity to oversee public ritual and to advise on religious matters (Beard and Crawford 1985: 30–1). By calling himself a *sacerdos*, the speaker simultaneously tropes his poems as sacrifices, a metaphor reinforced by the ritual silence he seeks at the beginning of 3.1. The third Roman Ode also invokes this context of religious expiation: echoing the "wanton" (*procax*, 2.1.37) Muse of the Pollio Ode, engaged in funereal song, the speaker's Muse of 3.3 "stubbornly reports" (*pervicax referre*, 70) Juno's speech on the mythic origins of the civil wars—the curse of Laomedon who cheated the gods of payment—as an initial disturbance of the *pax deorum*, the harmony between the mortal and divine levels that must be restored. *Odes* 3.6, in turn, reinforces this idea that Rome's successive generations of turmoil in fact issue from religious impiety, an ideological construction that reframes the political and socioeconomic sources of war as an inherited debt to the gods (Gordon 1990: 194–5; Bowditch 2001: 108). But the speaker as priest offers his poems both as sacrificial expiation that will pay off this debt and as counsel for those willing to listen: ritual silence allows the admonitory voices of Juno, in 3.3, and Regulus, in 3.5, to be heard.

By recasting the history of the civil wars in religious terms the Roman Odes also serve to recreate Augustus and to legitimize a monarchic and divinely endorsed vision of his power. Modeled on the divinity of Romulus as a gift from Juno in 3.3.30–6, Augustus' own godhead and the conditions of empire seem similarly implicated in the process of sacrificial expenditure that restores the *pax deorum*. This vision appears implicitly in the second stanza of 3.1 where, following the speaker's call for ritual silence as though for sacrifice, the orderly cosmos features Jupiter powerful over kings who, in turn, hold sway over their people. "Famous for his triumph in battle with the Giants" (3.1.6–7), Jupiter here looks ahead to his role in 3.4, where his victory allegorically signifies Octavian's defeat of Antony. Just preceding Horace's treatment of the Gigantomachy, the ode draws attention to all these ideologically potent images of Augustus as poetic constructions: "In your Pierian cave, you [Muses] refresh and recreate (*recreatis*) noble Caesar seeking an end to his toil ... beneficent, you give gentle counsel and rejoice in it, once given" (3.4.37–42). Here, we have an emphasis on the gifts of poetry to Augustus, with the Muse as a kind of patron.[4] Indeed, in the first half of 3.4, the speaker engages in a mythic tribute to the power of the Muses whose protection has also ensured his own safety at key moments of his autobiographical narrative. The language employed here is decidedly patronal: "yours, Muses, yours, I am borne up into the steep Sabine country ... a friend of your waters and choruses, the abandoned shield and flight at Philippi did not destroy me" (*vester, Camenae, vester in arduos/ tollor Sabinos...vestris amicum fontibus et choris/ non me Philippis versa acies retro ... extinxit,* 3.4.21–6) By poetically treating the Muses as patronal figures who lavish their gifts and sanctuary on both the speaker and Augustus alike, the poet in fact diverts attention from the regime as the actual source of his benefactions.

To what degree can these and related poems be considered propaganda acquired through patronal gifts? As critics point out, for all that the Roman Odes address key political issues, they also display the same split between private and public themes that characterizes the Odes as a collection overall. The references to the speaker's personal experiences, however rhetorically crafted, and to the Sabine countryside in 3.4 as well as at the end of 3.1, emphasize a private persona that contrasts with and arguably undermines the civic role of public priest. And yet these images suggest more than a crack in the poet's public façade (Lyne 1995: 162), for they connect the private poet as beneficiary with the civic-minded *sacerdos.* "Why should I exchange my Sabine vale for burdensome riches?" queries the speaker at 3.1.47–8. In spite of the typically Horatian gesture embracing modest means, the verb here—*permutem*—points to a certain "exchange" value of the Sabine estate, the most celebrated gift from Maecenas and the Augustan regime—the *munera* of *Satires* 2.6 that the satirist prays will be truly his and everlasting, provided he display his gratitude. By assuming the office of *sacerdos,* the lyric speaker reciprocates these gifts, but by offering his poems as symbolic sacrifices (*munera*) for the Roman people, he makes a form of voluntary expenditure that veils any immediate quid pro quo exchange between poet and patron (Bowditch 2001: 113). All the same, the gift of land circulates as symbolic capital—as poetry of expiation that ideally creates social cohesion and loyalty to the regime.

Maecenas, too, plays a prominent role in Horace's first collection of lyric, appearing as the addressee in no fewer than eight odes (1.1, 1.20, 2.12, 2.17, 2.20, 3.8, 3.16, 3.29), many of which emphasize the social and convivial aspect of patronage and aristocratic friendship. Six of these poems dedicate, close, or "rededicate" one of the books of Odes (1.1, 1.20, 2.12, 2.20, 3.16, 3.29), while three may be classed as "invitation" poems (1.20, 3.8, 3.29). One poem, 2.12, constitutes a *recusatio,* or "refusal poem," a conventional form adopted also by the elegists, in which the speaker typically declares that he would write historical or mythological epic but that his talents are incompatible with, or inadequate to, such elevated genres. Such poems typically address public themes and, in an abbreviated form, assimilate elements of the "disavowed genre" into the very gesture of refusal (Davis 1991: 11, 28–30). This posture rhetorically enables poets to cultivate personae who write at some distance from their patrons (Williams 1982: 16; Santirocco 1995: 231), engaging in political topics or panegyric only voluntarily. Thus the speaker of 2.12 declines to write either about the Carthaginian wars or about mythological topics, claiming that they are ill suited to the lyric genre and that Maecenas, instead, will relate the wars of Caesar in prose. In pointed contrast to Horace's seeming demurral here is the following poem addressed to his benefactor, 2.17, in which the poet, anguishing that Maecenas might die before himself, declares him the "great glory and foundation of my affairs" and "half my soul." These three different appellations, *mearum/grande decus columenque rerum*, and *meae…partem animae* (2.17.3–5), recall the dedication of *Odes* 1.1 ("Maecenas, descended from ancient kings, my sweet glory [*dulce decus meum*] and defense [*praesidium*]," 1–2) and reflect the varied inflections allowed by the term *amicitia*—the more public or formal relation of patronage, conferring status on and lending support to a beneficiary, and the intimacy, even identity, of friendship (cf. Cic. *Amic.* 15 on friendship as the "highest agreement in wishes, pursuits and opinions").

The language of ornament in the poems to Maecenas (*dulce decus meum*, 1.1, 2; *grande decus*, 2.17, 4) reflects not just the status enjoyed by Horace in his association with his patron, but also the power of individual poems and books as prestige gifts on a level beyond the text. Dedication and inclusion as an addressee suggest the role of poetry as symbolic capital that distinguishes the status and shores up the interaffiliation of the elite. All the historical addressees of Horace's poems reap the benefit: for example, Augustus, Virgil, Sestius, Agrippa, Plancus, Varus, Fuscus, Iccius, and Tibullus, all partake of this "sweet glory" conferred by the poet, enjoying a ring or network of social distinction in which aristocratic relations mutually enforce and illumine each other. In the invitation poems, poetry becomes objectified as a gift in other ways (Pavlock 1982), notably through the metaphor of wine: *Odes* 1.20 famously refers to the "humble Sabine wine" that Maecenas will drink, wine sealed by the poet himself in a Greek jar, suggesting Horace's Latin lyric in Greek meters. Similarly, the invitation to Maecenas to visit the Sabine estate in 3.29 includes the offer to him of a "smooth wine from a jar not previously opened" (*non ante verso lene merum cado*, 2). The past participle here—*verso*—allows the sense of "poetic forms never before turned," a telling anticipation of the verse epistles to which Horace turns in his next collection (Bowditch 2001: 179).

Epistles I

Horace's first book of Epistles presents one of the richest sources of material concerning patronage in all of Latin literature. Published in 20–19 BCE, four years after the publication of *Odes* 1–3, this collection of verse-letters analyzes and redefines Horace's own relations with Maecenas even as it displays the poet himself in the role of patron or "powerful friend," *magnus amicus*, dispensing the gift of advice or providing coveted introductions to others. The varied addressees exhibit an almost encyclopedic spectrum of Roman social status, ranging from the humble slave of 1.14, the bailiff on Horace's estate, to Tiberius in 1.9, the Emperor Augustus' stepson, to whom the poet writes a letter of recommendation on behalf of Septimius, his friend. *Epistles* 1.13, a letter giving jocose instructions to a messenger delivering a copy of *Odes* 1–3 to Augustus, clearly has the Emperor's readership in mind, while in other poems the speaker writes as an equal, one friend to another, as in his sensitive and humorous attempt to cajole the poet Tibullus (1.4) from his melancholy. As the speaker claims in the first epistle, he has taken up the study of philosophy, and these novel verse-letters do engage an eclectic blend of Hellenistic ethical thought. Friendship and social relationships in particular, however, shape the aesthetic form of this unique genre, and they inevitably figure as themes as well. Closely wrapped up with the ethics of human relations is the value of liberty in all its inflections—whether the freedom to speak directly or to live as one chooses, the freedom allowed by *otium* ("leisure") or the freedom of refusal.

The three epistles to Maecenas, 1.1, 1.7, and 1.19, show the speaker delicately negotiating his relationship with his patron, withdrawing from expectations and asserting his independence. In some ways, the opening of 1.1 conforms to the convention of the refusal poem in that the poet declines a request from Maecenas, but excuses himself on the grounds of age, temperament, and weariness, rather than for lack of talent. Moreover, the striking metaphor through which the speaker communicates his condition implies that Maecenas seeks more lyric, not the usual epic on historical or mythological subjects to which a *recusatio* makes a polite nod in its demurral. After an elegant dedication that reflexively underscores its power to celebrate Maecenas, the speaker compares himself to a gladiator: "By my first Muse glorified (*dicte*), to be glorified (*dicende*) by my last, you, Maecenas, seek to confine (*includere*) me again in the old school (*ludo*), though I have been sufficiently proven and gazed upon and already awarded the foil of discharge" (1–3). The word for gladiatorial school here, *ludus*, echoes in *includere*, "to confine, shut in," even as it connotes light, erotic poetry, as Catullus' use of the related verb form attests (Cat. 50.1–2). But Horace's blend of political and erotic symposiastic lyric in the Odes implies that *ludus* refers to public civic poems as well. How are we to interpret this image of Horace, given that "writing poetry is not like being condemned to hack one's way out of the theater of death" (Johnson 1993: 12)? Ironic humor is certainly at play here (Williams 1968: 4; Kilpatrick 1986: 2), but the rhetoric of expenditure in the implied gladiatorial shows (*munera; ludi*) from which the speaker, in terms of the metaphor, seeks to retire, tellingly resonates with the earlier images of patronal gifts and religious sacrifice that we see in the Satires and the Odes. " 'Giving gladiators'," as Paul Veyne points out, "became the best way to make oneself popular," and turned in the late Republic and early Empire into *euergesia*, "pure and simple," a form of electoral corruption (1990: 222). Horatian lyric as gladiatorial display suggests the Augustan regime's political interest in sponsoring poetry as a means of engendering symbolic capital or loyalty to the regime (Bowditch 2001: 2, 174).

However, the speaker claims to have been rewarded with his foil, and thus no longer in service. When he then asserts that he is "bound over to swear by the words of no master" (*nullius addictus iurare in verba magistri*, 14), economic implications again undercut the ironic humor of the gladiatorial image. Being *addictus* or "bound over" has three references here: in its immediate context, it responds to the preceding question attributed to the addressee—"lest you ask with what leader or dwelling I reside" (13)—and points to the lack of any one philosophical orientation on the speaker's part; but the term also refers to a gladiator's allegiance to his owner and, finally, to a situation of debt in which the debtor is the property of the creditor. This last definition of *addictus* may be the least overt in Horace's usage here, but the term's echo of *dicte* in the first line, referring to the glory conferred on Maecenas by Horace's poetry, suggests the economic subtext that the speaker is no longer "bound," because he has paid off his debt (Bowditch 2001: 173). (The gerundive, *dicende*, looks ahead to *Epistles* 1.19 which, by the time the collection is published, fulfills the anticipated obligation as the "last" poem—or Muse—excepting the *sphragis* or "seal" of authorship, addressed to Maecenas.) This subtext of "no longer bound to a patron" echoes in *Epistles* 1.18, addressed to Lollius Maximus, where the speaker elaborates on the distinction between an *amicus* who values his *libertas* ("freedom") and a *scurra*, or parasite, an extreme version of the *cliens* in a relationship of patronage (Damon 1997: 105–45). The *scurra* trembles at the nod of his wealthy patron, repeating his speech and dropped words (*verba cadentia*) like a schoolboy rehearsing his lessons for a cruel master (*dictata magistro/reddere*, 1.18.11–14). The verbal echoes here—*verba … dictata … magistro*—of the earlier line referring to a gladiator's oath or a debtor's servitude suggestively resonate in the context of the speaker's representations of his own experience of patronage, even despite the irony of his exaggerated rhetoric.

Indeed, although all these analogies depict an extreme or "far-end" of the spectrum of a patron–client relationship, as rhetorical images with diction echoing beyond their immediate epistolary context they project a consistent picture of what the speaker rejects, either for himself or others. At the end of the first epistle, after a digressive and leisurely inquiry into the benefits of philosophy, the speaker returns to his relationship with Maecenas and complains that his friend and benefactor reacts more to his outward appearance than to his mental well-being:

> If I run into you when my hair is cut unevenly [*inaequali tonsore*], you laugh; if it happens that the shirt under my brand-new tunic is worn-out [*subucula pexae/trita subest tunicae*], or if my toga, ill-fitting, sits askew [*toga dissidet impar*], you laugh: what about when my thought is at war with itself…? You think that I rage my usual fits and you neither laugh at me nor think that I'm in need of a doctor or guardian

appointed by the praetor, though you are the caretaker of my affairs and get angry
over a crookedly cut nail on the friend [*amicus*] who depends on you, who looks
to you for all. (94–105)

For all that the speaker uses the term *amicus*, "friend," here, and delicately
reproaches Maecenas with the permissive intimacy of genuine friendship, he
characterizes his benefactor as focused on externals, a concern with visibility more
typical of patronage where clients serve to reflect the status of their patrons
(Wallace-Hadrill 1989: 83). The stratified hierarchy of such relations appears
tellingly embedded in the diction referring to an "uneven haircut" (*inaequali
tonsore*) and an "ill-fitting toga" (*toga … impar*). The public aspect of this repudiated vision of their relationship arguably surfaces one final time in *Epistles* 1.19,
where the gladiatorial imagery recalls the opening of the first epistle. In this
penultimate poem of the collection, the speaker reflects on poetry as a vocation
and defends the originality of the Odes as unprecedented in the Latin lyric tradition. The reading public, he claims, only disparages his poems because he declines
to canvass for votes with "the expense of dinners and gift[s] of worn-out clothing" (*impensis cenarum et tritae munere vestis*, 1.19.38). The figural language of
patronage here evolves into a hypothetical encounter engendered by the speaker's
dislike for public recitation: should he decline to participate in such author-
events, he is accused by another of saving his verse for the ears of Jove—the circle
of Augustus—and to this attack he replies by seeking a "time-out" from the
gladiatorial contest (*diludia posco*, 1.19.47). In this rhetorical sequence, where
the worn-out clothing recalls the speaker's characterization of his own appearance
in *Epistles* 1.1, the public visibility of and expenditure on the client's role explicitly
overlaps with the gladiatorial image for recitation and suggests once again the
past sponsorship of the regime. However, within the figural terms of these metaphors, the speaker no longer occupies the role of client (or gladiator) even as he
rejects the identity of patron canvassing the public for approval of his poems,
preferring the egalitarian if elitist circle around Augustus.

If *Epistles* 1.19 shows the speaker as having already repudiated the stratified
relations of patronage, the seventh epistle arguably effects this poetic reformulation or negotiation of Horace's relationship with Maecenas. Traditionally understood as a declaration of the poet's independence, either as a letter actually sent
or as a poetic treatment of the theme, *Epistles* 1.7 has discomfited critics for both
the apparent directness of its "autobiographical" statements and its more enig-
matic *ainoi*, or illustrative tales, fables, and exempla, demanding interpretation.
The poem takes as its occasion Maecenas' longing for the poet's company:
"Having promised you that I would be away in the country for five days, I—a
liar—am missed for the entire sixth month" (1–2). The play with numbers here—
five days, sixth month, seventh epistle—indicates that this poem does not qualify
as unmediated autobiography: the speaker's absence from his patron and withdrawal from the city suggests as much a sabbatical from lyric—he has been away

for six epistles and is on his seventh—as an actual departure for the country. And yet, whether literary pretext or not, Maecenas' request for physical companionship elicits not only a refusal in the short term—the speaker will return next spring—but also a series of vignettes that ultimately condition how one interprets the apparent statement that, if pressed by his patron's demands, the speaker would return all his gifts.

This startling and problematic claim follows the fable of a fox that, having crept into a corn bin and eaten his fill, now fattened tries in vain to return through the slender crack by which he entered. A weasel, witnessing this, says, "if you wish to escape from there, you will seek again the narrow hole as thin as when you entered" (32–3). The speaker then asserts, "If I am summoned by this picture, I restore everything" (*hac ego si compellor imagine, cuncta resigno*, 34). A few lines later, after reminding Maecenas how often he has praised the poet's modesty, and heard the traditional patronal epithets *rexque paterque* ("king and father"), in both his presence and absence, the speaker issues a similar challenge, "see if I am able happily to put back what has been given" (*inspice si possum donata reponere laetus*, 39). Despite the seeming lack of ambiguity about these two versions of the same claim, many critics have resisted investing them with any real intentionality: If the epistle is a fictional exploration of patronage, then the poet should not be confused with his fictive, if autobiographical persona.[5] Alternately, the diction of the statements has allowed for readings that modify the boldness of their surface meanings: *si compellor* in the sense "if I am accused" has led to the interpretation of *cuncta resigno* as "I refute the entire charge" (Kilpatrick 1986: 190), a reading that rejects the premise of the fable as applied to the poet's life—that acceptance of his patron's gifts compromises his freedom.

Indeed, the Homeric exemplum that follows the second assertion, issued as a challenge—"see if I am able..."—also permits varied interpretations. When Telemachus visits Sparta for news of his father, the young man refuses Menelaus' initial guest-gift: "Ithaca is not a suitable place for horses, since it offers neither flat open space nor much grass: son of Atreus, I will leave your gifts as more suited to you" (41–3). The Horatian speaker then goes on to say, "Small things befit a small man: royal Rome does not please me now, but rather idle Tibur or peaceful Tarentum" (44–5). If we closely examine (*inspice*) the speaker's claim in light of this Homeric anecdote and the following lines, it becomes more problematic: for Telemachus does not give back gifts already given and received—*donata*—but rather pre-emptively turns down Menelaus' current offer—*dona relinquam*. Similarly, we may infer that the speaker declines Maecenas' present offer, somehow obliging his return to Rome, but not that he would cheerfully return past gifts—*donata*.

One of the difficulties of this epistle is distinguishing between the ironic and non-ironic levels of discourse (Berres 1992: 219). The Horatian speaker in fact signals, at the very beginning of the poem, the slipperiness of his autobiographical persona: although jocose in tone, the speaker's self-reproach as a "liar" or *mendax* anticipates the subtle complexity, if not outright disingenuousness, that colors many of his statements and illustrative examples. In typical Horatian fashion, however, the poet employs such irony to get at deeper truths, in this case to probe the economics of the reciprocity ethic—and its potential for exploitation—that lies beneath the ideology of voluntarism to which patronage aspires. Thus, when the speaker refuses to return to the city not only in the deadly heat of the summer, but also during the winter, he tells Maecenas that at that time, "your poet [*vates*] will go down to the sea and go light on himself and, huddled up [*contractusque*], will read" (11–12). The past participle here—*contractus*—is generally translated to mean "drawn together," as a person's response to the cold or to straightened circumstances, but it can also refer to being bound by a legal contract, a subtext that casts patronage in terms of compulsory rather than voluntary exchange.

That Horace taunts Maecenas with this extreme and distorting view of patronage—even in the early Republic, actual contracts were never involved (Drummond 1989: 99)—appears also in the lines preceding the fable of the fox in the corn bin:

> But if you wish me never to leave, you will return [*reddes*] my strong body, my black hair on a once narrow forehead, you will return my knack for sweet speech and elegant laughter [*reddes dulce loqui, reddes ridere decorum*] and for mourning, in drink, bold Cinara's flight. (1.7.25–8)

Although the speaker presents a humorous *adunaton* ("impossibility") as the condition for never leaving Maecenas' side—the demand that he return the poet's lost youth—the trope nonetheless raises the issue of time's irrevocability even as it presents a subtle picture of Horace's poetic labor as a kind of commodity equated with his bodily self (Bowditch 2001: 195): decorous laughter signals the *Satires* even as sweet speech and elegant laughter in a sympotic context imply the lyric *Odes*—we hear the echo of "sweetly laughing Lalage" (*dulce ridentem Lalagen*, 1.22.23)—and the erotic odes metonymically imply the political lyric as well. But the adjectives "sweet" and "decorous" (*dulce...decorum*) conjure up civic lyric on their own, alluding to the memorable line of military sacrifice in the second Roman Ode, "it is sweet and fitting to die for one's country" (*dulce et decorum est pro patria mori*, *Odes* 3.2.13). Finally, the lines recall the speaker's epithet for Maecenas as *dulce decus meum* (*Odes* 1.1.2), "my sweet ornament," in the dedication of the *Odes*, an allusion that *ridere decorum* extends to the dedication of the *Satires* as well. By making the impossible demand for the return of a past self, as labor that has been reified in his poetry, the speaker demystifies the voluntarism of his own poetic sacrifices—his *munera*—and, reversing the "symbolic alchemy which transmutes the price of labor into an unsolicited gift" (Bourdieu 1977: 173), construes the reciprocity ethic as approaching contractual exchange. The use of the verb *reddere* reinforces this vision of patronage as one of economic exchanges, for it looks ahead to *Epistles* 1.13, where the speaker instructs Vinnius Asina to deliver—*reddes*—*Odes* 1–3 to Augustus (*Epistles* 1.13.2), and it also calls to mind Seneca's distinction between *reddere*, "to pay back" in a monetary context, and *referre gratiam*, "to show gratitude," in the context of ideal benefaction (Sen. *Epistulae* 81.9–10).

And yet the very impossibility of the speaker's humorous demand looks ahead to the final *ainos* of the epistle, a long anecdote that contains seductive, if misleading, points of resemblance to Horace's biography. Philippus, a lawyer, comes upon a freedman, Vulteius Mena, and initiates a relationship that leads to a combined monetary gift and loan to purchase a farm in Sabine country. After a run of bad luck—disease, theft of his animals, and failing crops—Mena begs Philippus, calling him *patrone*, to "return me to my former life" (*vitae me redde priori*, 1.7.95). The speaker then draws the conclusion, "The one who recognizes, at last, how far what he abandoned surpasses what he sought, let him return in time and seek again what was left behind." Despite the evident differences here between Mena's and Horace's situations—Philippus makes a loan in addition to a gift and cynically exploits Mena for his amusement—the vignette invites the reader to speculate that, if pressed, Horace would return the Sabine Farm. Horace's own estate, however, is never mentioned in this poem, although it figures prominently in *Epistles* 1.14 and 1.16, and structurally constitutes the rural "elsewhere" from which the speaker engages in the new genre of epistolary verse. In this seventh epistle, the absence of direct mention of the estate allows it to figure in contradictory ways—as the place associated with the poet's leisure and gestures of independence, and as the most celebrated of the gifts that the poet seems to offer to give back. And yet, in this last *ainos*, patronage verges on *nexum*, a form of debt-bondage in the early Republic (Watson 1975: 111), and Philippus alone has the power "to make a return" (*reddere*), in this case by forgiving Mena his loan. By contrast, the example of Telemachus, the only *ainos* considered by some as not contrary to the poet's situation (e.g. Kilpatrick 1986: 122), construes *amicitia* in the light of Homeric *xenia* or guest-host relations, where a voluntary exchange of gifts cultivates relationship and distinguishes the elite status of giver and recipient. The speaker invites Maecenas—his addressee and specific audience—to reject the "contractual" vision of patronage and to view his relations with the poet in Homeric terms of gift-exchange and aristocratic friendship.[6]

Carmen Saeculare, *Odes* 4, Epistle to Augustus

Ironically, after the publication of the first book of Epistles and its moving exploration of the poet's relationship with his friend and patron, Maecenas fades from sight, his name appearing only once in the fourth book of Odes, in the third person, in an occasional poem celebrating his birthday (4.11). Scholars have advanced different theories for the apparent decline of Maecenas' influence in the later works of Horace, ranging from an indiscretion that angered the Emperor to a premeditated withdrawal that allowed Augustus to step in.[7] Whatever the reasons, after 18 BCE the Emperor became more directly involved in literary patronage, a change also visible in the poetry of Propertius and the marked transition from the primarily elegiac themes of his first three books to the more patriotic verse, ironic or otherwise, of his fourth book. But in Horace's case, our evidence for the Emperor's patronage comes from Suetonius, including a letter he quotes from Augustus, chiding the poet for ignoring him as an epistolary or satiric addressee:

> As to his writings, Augustus rated them so high, and was so convinced that they would be immortal, that he not only appointed [*iniunxerit*] him to write the Secular Hymn, but also bade him celebrate the victory of his stepsons Tiberius and Drusus over the Vindelici, and so compelled [*coegerit*] him to add a fourth to his three books of lyrics after a long silence. Furthermore, after reading several of his "talks," the Emperor thus expressed his pique that no mention was made of him: "you must know that I am not pleased with you, that in your numerous writings of this kind you do not talk with me, rather than with others. Are you afraid that your reputation with posterity will suffer because it appears that you were my friend?" In this way he forced [*expressit*] from Horace the selection which begins with these words [...] (Suet. *Vita Hor.*, trans. Rolfe 1924 [1914], Loeb edition)

The passage then continues with the beginning of the Epistle to Augustus, 2.1. Scholars have seized on the verbs employed here by Suetonius—*iniunxerit*, *coegerit*, *expressit*—and either interpret them as distinct expressions of power (e.g. Williams 1990: 269–70), while recognizing actual compulsion as absurd, or perceive them as conventional diction used by poets and friends when discussing ideas for poetry (White 1993: 114–15). Eduard Fraenkel (1957: 383) attributed their force to the post-Domitian period in which Suetonius wrote. Regardless, both the *Carmen Saeculare* and *Odes* 4 display a more fulsome panegyric of Augustus and all he had achieved (and some of what he had not) than the cautionary note struck by the political poems—by the voices of Juno, Regulus, or the sacerdotal speaker himself—in *Odes* 1–3. In part this reflects their later dates of composition, 17 BCE (*Carmen Saeculare*) and 13 BCE (*Odes* 4), and the sustained peace and prosperity that the Emperor had by then brought to the Roman world. Addressed to Diana and Apollo, the *Carmen Saeculare* resonates with images of abundance (17–20, 29–32, 59–60). In *Odes* 4.5 the Emperor himself shines his light like the Apollinian sun, bringing the brightness of spring with his presence (*instar veris enim vultus ubi tuus/ adfulsit populo*, 6–7). The stability of empire, conjured in images of geographic expanse and foreign peoples subdued, also marks this later poetry—4.15, 21–4 speaks of drinkers of the Danube, Getae, Seres, and Parthian all obeying the Julian edict; and in the Epistle to Augustus, the "wars completed throughout the world under [his] auspices" would be the speaker's subject, if only he had the talent to match his desire (254–57).

Invoking the motif of the *recusatio*, a "generic disavowal" (Davis 1991: 11, 28–30) or stylized "refusal" to celebrate deeds in the high style even as tribute is made, *Epistles* 2.1 argues for the importance of contemporary poetry and contrasts Augustus' practice of imperial patronage with that of Alexander the Great. After elaborating a story about the poor encomium that Alexander received from the poet Choerilus, who received coin for his efforts, the speaker praises Augustus' discernment, assuring him that "Vergil and Varius, poets cherished by you, dishonor neither your judgment about them nor your gifts [*munera*] that, to the great glory of the giver, they have borne away" (245–7). Although Augustus may well have made benefactions of money, the epistle draws a clear distinction between the *philippi* that Alexander pays Choerilus—coins exchanged for poetry in a market situation—and the *munera* or gifts that encourage the verse of Vergil and Varius. Choerilus' poems are "badly formed" and "ill-conceived" (*incultis... male natis*, 233), a result, the anecdote implies, of commodifying poetry. By contrast, the lines describing Augustus' relations with his poets display patronage ideally functioning as a gift economy: gifts to Vergil and Varius issue from the Emperor's cultivation of these poets; such *munera*, in turn, create symbolic capital—both the glory of the giver's reputation and the sense of debt, and loyalty, that eventuates in verse bringing no dishonor to the Emperor's judgment.

Gifts made with discernment elicit gratitude and good poetry—such is the message here—but the speaker's own talents fall short of those required to celebrate the Emperor, or so he claims. A paradoxical form that enacts elements of the disavowed genre, Horace's *recusatio* here in fact lauds Augustus even as the poem gratifies his request for a conversational poem, suggesting Macrobius' dictum that "power compels, not only if it invites but even if it beseeches" (Macrob. *Sat.* 2.7; see Griffin 1984). Whether in response to such power or to the more subtle persuasions of gifts, Horace wrote poems that cannot be dissociated from the socioeconomics of patronage. And yet both poetry and biography testify to the deep and abiding friendship that developed alongside the patronal relationships: even as the poet called Maecenas "half my soul" (*Odes* 2.17.5) so the latter, anticipating his death, instructed Augustus to "look after Horace as you would myself" (Suet. *Hor. Vita*).

GUIDE TO FURTHER READING

This essay has examined the rhetoric of Horace's poems as shaped by the socioeconomics of ancient patronage as a form of "gift economy." Twentieth-century anthropological literature on gift-exchange and reciprocity draws substantially from the fieldwork of

Malinowski (1961 [1922]) and the seminal analysis of Mauss (1990 [1950]) and develops in the work of Sahlins (1965, 1972). On the concepts of "symbolic and cultural capital" in relation to anthropological theory on the gift, see the dense studies of Bourdieu (1977, 1984). Gregory (1982) provides a clear introduction to the distinction between gifts and commodities. The essays in Appadurai (1986) combine economic, anthropological and sociological approaches to the "social life of things."

Scholarship on ancient Greece has engaged anthropological theory to a greater degree than have studies of the Roman world. The literary criticism of Kurke (1991, 1999) and Seaford (1994) and the collected essays in Gill, Postlethwaite and Seaford (1998) all display paradigms of gift-exchange and reciprocity as central to the study of Greek texts. As for the Roman side, the analysis of imperial euergetism in Veyne (1990) and the study of patronage in Dixon (1993) reflect the impact of Mauss and those he influenced. For other important discussions of patronage, see Saller (1982), the chapters in Brunt (1988) on both *clientela* ("clientship") and *amicitia* ("friendship"), the essays in Wallace-Hadrill (1989), Deniaux (1993), and Damon (1997) on the figure of the parasite. Verboven (2002) examines the economics of *amicitia*. For a thorough analysis of the concept of *gratia*—"gratitude, debt, influence," and so forth—see Moussy (1966).

For an overview of literary patronage in both Greece and Rome, see Gold (1987) and for ancient Rome in particular, see the collected essays in Gold (1982). On the role of Augustus as patron, see Griffin (1984), Williams (1990), and White (1991). For literary patronage in the Augustan era as embedded in the social relations of elite friendship, see White (1993). Recent interpretations of Horace and his patrons include Oliensis (1998), Bowditch (2001), and McNeill (2001).

NOTES

1   See Brink 1982: 552 on dating.
2   Williams 1995 challenges the evidence.
3   Gold 1987: 1–3; White 1993: 14–27; Nauta 2002: 26–7, 78–87.
4   See Zetzel 1982: 96 on the motif of the "displaced patron."
5   Williams 1968: 21–2; McGann 1969: 95–9; for more nuanced readings that acknowl-edge the bite of Horace's words, see Johnson 1993: 44–5, following Courbaud 1914: 298–301, and Oliensis 1998: 159–60.
6   On levels of audience in 1.7, see Bowditch 2001: 181–210.
7   Syme 1939: 342; Brink 1982: 528–9; Williams 1990: 258–75; White 1991: 130–8.

CHAPTER FOUR

The Roman Site Identified as Horace's Villa at Licenza, Italy

Bernard Frischer

Since the eighteenth century, a site (fig. 1) with archaeological remains near Licenza, Italy (fig. 2) has been identified as Horace's Sabine Villa.

The aim of this chapter is to address the issue of the ancient ownership of "Horace's Villa"[1] and to give an overview of what is known about it, especially after the new excavations and studies undertaken from 1996 to 2003 under my direction and with the institutional sponsorship of the American Academy in Rome and the Soprintendenza Archeologica per il Lazio (Frischer, Crawford, and De Simone 2006). To anticipate our team's main findings, application of the technique of stratigraphic excavation, and reconsideration of the material found by our predecessors (especially the architectural terracottas, mosaics, and the fresco fragments) suggested that what the earlier excavators considered Augustan should really be assigned to a period six or more decades later. As for Horatian ownership of the site, a study of inscriptions on pipes, tiles, and bricks brought forth the names of a number of people who owned the villa in the first century BCE through the second century CE. Unfortunately, Horace's name did not appear on our list. But, as we will see, this does not necessarily mean that Horace was not one of the owners of the property in antiquity.

The site and its location

"Horace's Villa" (fig. 3) is situated c. 30 miles northeast of Rome in the Licenza valley on a parcel of land whose name since at least the eighteenth century has been "Vigne di San Pietro." Settlement of the Licenza valley appears generally to have developed along the ancient road corresponding to the modern Via Licinese, which runs between S. Cosimato, on the Via Valeria, and Trebula

Figure 4.1   View of "Horace's Villa," Licenza, Italy. Source: Bernard Frischer.

Mutuesca (Monteleone Sabino) on the Via Salaria (Mari 1993: 18). The Licinese starts near the twenty-eighth mile of the Via Valeria, which dates to the late fourth century BCE (Mari 1993 18). The Via Valeria runs through the Anio river valley and beyond to the Adriatic. It was an important transportation corridor since it penetrated the barrier of the Apennines and linked the Tivoli region to the area which in antiquity was inhabited by the Sabines, Aequi, Marsi, and Samnites.

In the second or first century BCE, villas begin to appear in the area. In the zone between the Via Valeria near Mandela and Vicovaro and the hill town of Licenza, Mari identified traces of twelve villa sites (Mari 1993 *passim*). The Augustan age marks an increase in prosperity in the area. By the first century CE, several luxury villas had been built, or rebuilt, on the site of earlier country houses. These include five examples located between Roccagiovine and Mandela-Vicovaro. The mid- to late first-century CE phase at "Horace's Villa" is the northernmost example of this class.

"Horace's Villa" occupies an area of about 110×70 meters, with its long axis oriented roughly north–south (fig. 3). The residence (fig. 3, A) was a two-storey

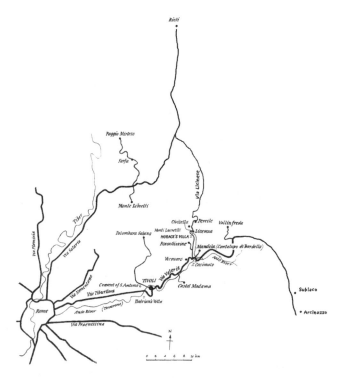

Figure 4.2   Map showing Licenza and the location of the villa in the Vigne di San Pietro. Source: Bernard Frischer and Alan Bartram. Bartram's version is taken from in B. Frischer and I. G. Brown, eds., *Allan Ramsay and the Search for Horace's Villa* (Aldershot: Ashgate, 2001), p. xviii.

structure containing c. 600 square meters of built space. It stood on a higher level at the northern end of the site. Adjacent to the south was a garden area with a central pool (fig. 3, B). Surrounding the garden was a quadriporticus (fig. 3, C), which is joined to the residence on its northern side by a veranda (fig. 3, nr. 13). The quadriporticus gives onto the garden and must have had windows and doors to provide the corridors with light, air, and access from the garden. The connection between the different levels was provided by three ramps, two lateral ones for the long porticated wings and a central one for the uncovered area. Running along the north side of the residence and quadriporticus was a large bath complex (fig. 3, D). These structures, which are situated on the saddle between two hills, only partly conform to the natural gradient, which falls away to the south. The residence is situated on a partially artificial terrace that levels out the grade. Except for the veranda (fig. 3, nr. 13), transitional element between the residence and quadriporticus, the quadriporticus was constructed following the natural slope.

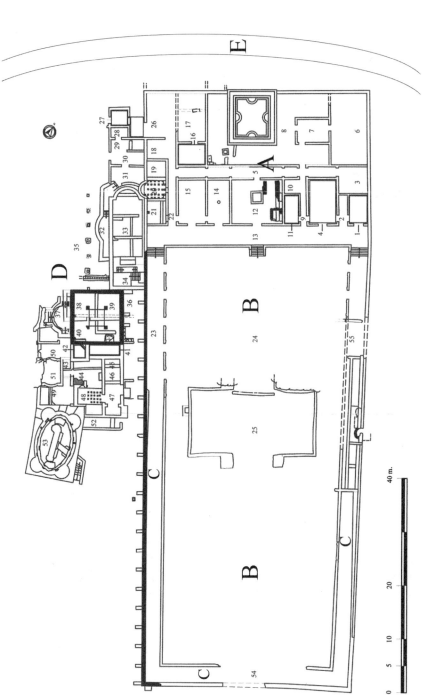

Figure 4.3 Plan of Horace's Villa. A = Residence; B = Garden; C = Quadriporticus; D = Bath Complex; E = gravel road to north of site. Features dating from the late first century BCE are highlighted. Source: Bernard Frischer and Monica De Simone. De Simone's version is taken from: B. Frischer, J. Crawford, and M. De Simone, *The "Horace's Villa" Project, 1997–2003*, vol. 2 (Oxford: Archaeopress, 2006), 727 (fig. 21).

The identification of the site as Horace's Villa

That Horace had a villa in the Sabine country northeast of Rome is a certainty: in a dozen of his poems, Horace writes about what he calls his *villula*, his little country escape (Frischer 2007: 389–91). It was here that the famous wolf of the *integer vitae* ode ran off in fright while hearing Horace chant his song in praise of Lalage; here that the infamous tree almost killed Horace when it unexpectedly fell near him; and here where after dinner he and his friends discussed philosophy and told the story of the town mouse and his friend, the country mouse.[2] It is no wonder that these memorable poems inspired his admirers since the Renaissance to wander through the Sabinum in search of the site of Horace's Villa.

It is well known that we have the names of the owners of practically none of the thousands of Roman villas scattered around western Europe and England. There are some famous exceptions, of course, such as the Villa of Livia at Prima Porta, the villas of Tiberius at Sperlonga and on Capri, Nero's estate at Subiaco, Domitian's retreat at Castel Gandolfo, Hadrian's Villa at Tivoli or Trajan's at Arcinazzo. But the fact remains that the average Roman site (particularly if not owned by a member of the imperial family) is hard, if not impossible, to attribute on the basis of solid evidence to a known historical figure (Pappalardo 2000: 10; Millar 1977: 24; Morley 1996: 101). Why should Horace's Sabinum be any different?

The reason is the poetry of Horace. Not surprisingly, he never gives a very precise location of his Sabine property but does imply that it was near a number of geographical features. Some of these cannot be identified today, such as the valley of *Ustica* (*Odes* 1.17, 11) and the *Mons Lucretilis* (*Odes* 1.17, 1). Other toponyms mentioned by Horace can be placed on the map with certainty or at least some probability. Thus the *Digentia* river (*Epistles* 1.18, 104) is probably the Licenza river. *Varia* is the modern town of Vicovaro (*Epistles* 1.14, 3). *Mandela* (*Epistles* 1.18, 105) is the modern town of the same name. The *fanum Vacunae* (*Epistles* 1.10, 49) is perhaps Roccagiovine. Horace also provides evidence that his villa was near and to the north of Roccagiovane: in *Epistles* 1.10, 49, he says that he is writing "behind the ruined shrine of Vacuna," and "behind" has been reasonably taken to imply that the place where he was writing the poem was on the side of the shrine away from Rome, that is to the north. Now, the territory in which these sites are located has been well surveyed over the past three centuries (Mari 1993: 17–76). North of Roccagiovine, there is just one villa site that has ever been found, our site in the Vigne di San Pietro. It was on the basis of such circumstantial evidence that antiquarians in the 1750s identified this site as Horace's Sabine Villa (for details see Frischer 2006b: 20–9). With very little dissent in the intervening 250 years, the identification has stuck but never been confirmed by indisputable evidence.

Excavations of the site

Shortly after the site was identified as Horace's in the 1750s by antiquarians associated with the Accademia degli Arcadi in Rome (Frischer 2006b: 23), the first excavations in the Vigne di S. Pietro were undertaken by the Baron de Saint'Odile, the Tuscan ambassador to Rome (Frischer 1998). We do not know where and how much he excavated, only that in c. 1760 he exposed some structures as well as an underground passageway and some lead water pipes. In the mid-1770s, the Scottish painter Allan Ramsay exposed the mosaics in rooms 1 and 4 (Frischer 2001). The area was reburied, but not forgotten: visitors in the nineteenth century reported seeing these and several other mosaics now vanished.

At the end of the nineteenth century the city council of Licenza pressed for new excavations and in the early years of the twentieth century, an effective publicity campaign conducted by the Classicist Vincenzo Ussani persuaded the Ministry of Education to undertake the task of investigating the site (Frischer 2006b: 27). In 1911, as a result of these efforts, Angelo Pasqui, the Director of the Office of Excavations for the Ancient Lazio, was given the task of undertaking the excavation of the villa. Pasqui's activity extended until October of 1914 (Frischer 2006b: 29–32). It was in this period that most of the remains visible on the site today were brought to light. The ruins were conserved, and, indeed, in no small measure rebuilt (De Simone 2006), and the site itself was opened to the public. Pasqui died before he was able to present his final publication (for his preliminary report, see Pasqui 1916). The excavations were then resumed in 1930–1 by Thomas Price, a Fellow of the American Academy in Rome, and by Giuseppe Lugli, who in 1926 had published a long account of Pasqui's project (Lugli 1926). The intervention of Price and Lugli was a fairly minor project, lasting just a couple of months and mainly concentrating on the still unexcavated eastern arm of the quadriporticus (Price 1932).

New fieldwork

None of these interventions utilized the stratigraphic method, an approach associated with the British archaeologists Mortimer Wheeler (1954), Philip Barker (1977), and Edward Harris (1989; and cf. Roskams 2001: 17–18) and widely adopted by Italian archaeologists as a result of their collaboration on the UNESCO-sponsored international excavations at Carthage in the 1970s (Carandini 1996; Barbanera 1998: 179). Stratigraphic excavation defines the goal of an archaeological investigation as reconstructing what happened on a site in as full and objective a manner as possible (Roskams 2001: 7–39). The physical evidence of each event is left in the stratigraphic unit. An excavation following the stratigraphic method thus proceeds by identifying a unit, documenting it in plan and section, and setting the unit into its proper spatio-temporal relationship to the other units uncovered. At "Horace's Villa" work prior to 1996 was done using the very different method known as "wall chasing," whose aim is to find and expose the walls remaining above and below the surface. When walls are chased, little or no attention is paid to the relationship between the wall and the soil through which the wall runs or on which it stands. Thus, at the Vigne di San Pietro, materials were removed, restorations were made to the walls in some cases on the basis of hypothesis alone, and the structures considered post-Roman were even demolished without being completely documented.

In 1997 the Horace's Villa Project was begun with the objective of collecting all the data that had emerged thus far and to integrate them with new data in order to increase our understanding of this important but, by then, rather neglected site. A new campaign of stratigraphic excavations was opened, whose main focus on four areas: the residence, the bath complex, the quadriporticus, and the garden.

Residence

Since the eighteenth century, a series of well-preserved mosaics has been found in the residence. Since the eighteenth century these have been dated to the Augustan age and their presence has thus helped to identify the villa as a property that Horace might have owned. We commissioned mosaic-expert Klaus Werner to reexamine this matter (Werner 2006).

In the cubiculum we called room n. 1 (see fig. 3), the mosaic is divided into two zones. The first is decorated using an orthogonal pattern with eight-pointed stars in white on a black ground. The second zone features intertwined white circles on a black ground. Less complex but still of high quality is the mosaic of room 4. Its design is based on a meander pattern of black tesserae on a white ground. In room 11 is seen a diagonal grid in black on a white ground.

For all their differences in design and motifs, the technique and style of the pavements of rooms 1, 4, and 11 are quite similar. Lugli, and all scholars before him, dated them to the Augustan age. But Werner was able to take advantage of another eighty years of discovery and study of Roman mosaics to make a convincing case that the examples in rooms 1, 4, and 11 are datable to a period no earlier than the second half of the first century CE. Thus Werner concludes that at Licenza "we do not have to do with precious 'Horatian'-era mosaics but with pavements in every way typical of the second half of the first century CE. ..." (Werner 2006: 259).

In addition to reexamining material previously found in the residence, we also conducted one excavation and three small soundings (De Simone and Cerri 2006; for the areas, see the areas highlighted on the plan in fig. 3). The excavation took place in the eastern half of area 12 and it was due to the discovery of a document in the archives. The document (illustrated in Frischer, Crawford, and De Simone 2006: 653, figs. 1a and 1b) consists of a sketch plan and its related sections and it was drawn during Pasqui's excavations. It shows features never before published and no longer visible on the surface. Cleaning and stratigraphic excavation were undertaken in order to verify the document and to clarify the nature, date, and function of the features it shows. We uncovered what was shown in the sketch: foundation walls otherwise not visible and part of a square basin.

Humble as these finds were, they are important because they represent a phase earlier than the terraced residence. They may be related to the productive zone of the earlier humble farm. As for the date, Pasqui's earlier work here cleaned out all the ancient stratigraphy that might have provided good dating material. So all we could say was that the basin predates the terraced residence and its pavements. As we have seen from the discussion of the mosaic floors, the residence must date to the second half of the first century CE. So the basin is earlier: but exactly how much earlier, we cannot at present say.

The bath complex

The bath complex (rooms 27–53) was the second area of new fieldwork. It runs along the northwest side of the site. Here, two parts and two construction phases can be distinguished. The older part consists of rooms 32–34, which are built of brick and *opus reticulatum*. In the later phase, the second part of the bath complex was built. The rooms here were also furnished with heating systems and plumbing. The second phase consists of rooms 35 to 53. It differs from the first by the extensive use of brick and also by a more complex architectural design. Some of the rooms, particularly nr. 53, are of notable architectural interest. The investigations from 1997 to 1999 concentrated on the northern area of the baths. Various occupation phases were identified over a long period of time stretching from the late Republic to the early Middle Ages.

Excavations in the area of rooms 38, 39, and 40 brought to light structures and stratigraphy datable to last decades of the first century BCE. The principal feature was a tetrastyle atrium with an impluvium. These features probably belong to the earliest phase of the villa and were possibly contemporaneous with the basin we saw a moment ago in area 12. This would mean that in the Augustan age, and possibly earlier, the arrangement of space was quite different from what it came to be in the later half of the first century CE. At first, the residence was at the western end of the site, not on the north, as it later came to be. If this really was ever Horace's villa, this very different and—from what little we have to go on—much more humble farm was what he would have known.[3]

The whole area underwent a radical transformation as a result of the construction of the bath complex. The atrium and impluvium were replaced at a higher level by the frigidarium of the new baths, which was paved in mosaic (rooms 38, 39, 40). To the west was constructed the apsidal basin (37), which also had a mosaic pavement and whose walls were reveted with marble. To the north of the frigidarium seven piers were erected in a north–south alignment (35). They probably were part of a portico facing one of the gardens of the villa.

In a secondary deposit, in area 35 of the bath complex, numerous fragments of architectonic terracottas were found during the excavation. They can be traced back to a single model plaque that functioned as a crowning sima. Reproduced in several variants, it was characterized by a motif in which palmettes alternated with small columns According to Maria José Strazzulla, a leading expert on this material, our type has comparanda dating to the second half of the first century CE (Strazzulla 2006). Interestingly enough, Strazzulla also notes that before the 1980s, the type was misdated to the Augustan age.

Most of the fresco fragments found at Horace's Villa in the excavations of 1911–14 have no provenance and were dated to the Augustan and Flavian periods. We found numerous fragments with similar designs. Both the older and new finds were studied by Stephan Mols who found that they have their best parallels in Fourth Style paintings of the early Flavian period (i.e., before CE 79; see Mols 2006). This includes the older fragments dated to the Augustan period by Giuseppe Lugli and, more recently, by Rosanna Cappelli (1994). The two paintings (or perhaps parts of one painting) that Cappelli attributes to the Augustan period have *aediculae* with *acroteria*, one with griffins and the other with seated grotesque, partly female, partly monstrous or floral figures (Cappelli 1994: 120–4, 152, and figs. 2 and 3). Cappelli rightly states that griffins appear in Roman paintings of the Second Style. As *acroteria* they are not very common in Second and Third Style paintings, but they do frequently occur during the Fourth Style. The Licenza griffins differ from the late Second Style griffins in that they are very slender and have long legs, and these features are more typical of Fourth Style examples. It is therefore to this period of Roman wall painting to which Mols assigns the Licenza examples.

Quadriporticus and garden

The quadriporticus (13, 23, 55, 54 on the plan in fig. 3; c. 42 m. × 85 m.) harmonizes and dominates the design of the villa. Its northern side (13), which functions as the front porch of the residence, is raised to a higher level than its other three arms. From here two staircases give access to the two long sides on the east (55) and west (23), and a central staircase leads to the open area of the garden (24). The two long sides follow the natural slope from north to south. In the eastern arm of the quadriporticus a fountain or a decorative structure (55) was added, perhaps serving in part as a retaining wall for the hill rising to the east.

The most recent investigations have added to our understanding of the quadriporticus (De Simone, Nerucci, and Passalacqua 2006). Several building phases
have been identified: in the oldest phase (I B.C.) the garden was surrounded by
a simple wall in *opus incertum*. Later (I-II A.D.), the passageways with doors and
windows facing the green space were built on a higher level. This rise should
probably be related to a general remodeling of the villa that is also noticeable in
other parts of the complex. The walls of the passageways must have been decorated with painted plaster, as is attested by some fragments still surviving *in situ*.

Several exploratory studies of the garden (24) inside the quadriporticus were
undertaken by a team led by garden archaeologist Kathryn Gleason (Gleason,
Schryver, and Passalacqua 2006). Perhaps the best results came from a 4 m × 5 m
trial trench at the north end of the garden below the central staircase of the
veranda. Here the excavations of 1997–2000 identified two distinct archaeological levels, of which the older can be dated to the first century BCE. A new and
more complex organization of the green zone appears to have been undertaken
during the Flavian period in the last three decades of the first century CE. Among
the various traces found that are useful for reconstructing the ancient appearance
of the garden, the most interesting is the find *in situ* of a flower pot. Another
flower pot had been found in the excavations of Pasqui and is now on display in
the local museum (Macaulay 2006). The Romans planted their flowers and plants
in such pots, placing them in the ground in geometric patterns along walkways
and water channels.

Phasing of the walls

An important wall study was conducted by Monica De Simone (De Simone
2006). She wanted to establish what is actually ancient (as opposed to modern
restoration) and to divide the genuine ancient remains into building phases.
Besides the direct analysis of all extant masonry, the study of correspondence
among earlier excavators and of archival photographs also furnished a great deal
of surprising information. It turns out that the early twentieth-century restorations aimed not only at reconstructing some walls, but also at the demolition of
others, particularly those thought to be of the medieval period. Some walls and
doorways were invented out of whole cloth. In interpreting the site, care must
be taken not to base an argument on a feature visible on the site before first
having consulted De Simone's report to ensure that it is truly ancient.

The owners

In his recent study of Roman villas, Pappalardo (2000:10) observes: "over 3,000
Roman villas are known in the West, but hardly any owners' names." As our

project historian, Vasily Rudich pointed out, "Horace's Villa at Licenza proves a remarkable exception" (Rudich 2006: 315). Whether or not Horace ever owned the property, Rudich established a series of ancient owners who are noteworthy in their own right.

Of course, the Romans did not put their names on the front door or façade of their villa, so how can we identify the owners of a villa? It was not uncommon for owners to inscribe their names, or those of other members of their family, on three sorts of objects: water pipes, bricks and roof tiles, and honorary monuments such as statues. At "Horace's Villa," we have no inscribed monuments, but we do have names on bricks, tiles, and pipes.

Generally, the names appearing in the stamps on bricks and roof-tiles belong not to the owners of the properties where they are found but to the persons responsible for manufacturing them. An expert in this field, Giorgio Filippi, studied our material and identified seven names of people who owned the Licenza villa (Filippi 2006). The names on our water pipes were studied by Christer Bruun (2006), who is well known for his work on this class of objects.

The earliest brick stamps attest the name of Manius Naevius. Filippi dates these to the second half of the first century BCE. In 2007, one year after our final report was published, a new Naevius brickstamp was found *in situ* in bath structure 33,[4] a part of the complex that our building expert, De Simone, had dated on other grounds to the middle to late first century BCE. This dating is now strengthened by the newly found instance of the stamp. If Horace did own our villa, Naevius must have been the proprietor some time just prior to his tenure. As far as we can tell, the villa in this period was quite a modest place, as the poems of Horace would lead us to have expected.

The next owner we can identify and date is a woman who lived several decades later in period of Claudius and Nero: Claudia Epicharis. Rudich presents cogent reasons for believing that she is the freedwoman whom Tacitus (*Ann.* 15.51, 57; cf. Dip–Xiph. 62.27, 3) describes as one of the key participants in the abortive Pisonian conspiracy against Nero in CE 65 (*PIR*[2] E72; RE VI.1.34 (Stein). Rudich further suggests that the Licentine Claudia Epicharis was the same as the Claudia Epicharis who erected a preserved funerary inscription (*CIL* VI.8411, now in the Capitoline Museums) for her husband, Ti. Claudius Abascantus. As the inscription states, he was an official in Nero's treasury, possibly the treasurer himself. The quadriporticus, residence, and parts of the bath complex with their Fourth Style wall paintings and beautiful frescoes can all be dated to the late Julio-Claudian or early Flavian period. These impressive additions are consistent with owners like Abascantus and Epicharis who were members of the freedmen elite that served the emperor.

Epicharis was truly a remarkable woman. Tacitus recounts how alone of the arrested conspirators arrested in the plot to kill Nero, Epicharis behaved honorably by refusing to denounce others, even though she was pitilessly tortured. He writes:

Nero ... assuming that female flesh and blood must be unequal to the pain ... ordered her to be racked. But neither the lash nor fire, nor yet the anger of the torturers, who redoubled their efforts rather than be braved by a woman, broke down her denial of the allegations. Thus the first day of torment had been defied. On the next, as she was being dragged back in a chair to a repetition of her agony— her dislocated limbs were unable to support her—she fastened the breast-band (which she had stripped from her bosom) in a sort of noose to the canopy of the chair, thrust her neck into it, and, throwing the weight of her body into the effort, squeezed out such feeble breath as remained to her. An emancipated slave and a woman, by shielding, under this dire coercion, men unconnected with her and all but unknown, she had set an example which shone the brighter at a time when persons freeborn and male, roman knights and senators, untouched by the torture, were betraying each his nearest and dearest. ... (Tac. *Ann.* 15. 57 [trans. Jackson 1969])

Our next owner is no less interesting. He probably came into the property a decade or two after Epicharis' death. In the eighteenth century, De Chaupy published an inscription found on one of the lead pipes on the site. It bore the name Claudius Burrus. Burrus is attested on the historical record as the son of Emperor Domitian's powerful freedman chamberlain (*cubicularius*) Ti. Claudius Parthenius.[5] Martial celebrated Burrus' fifth birthday in an epigram of the year CE 88 (4.45; cf. 5.6.6). It is plausible to assume that, in the aftermath of the failed Pisonian plot and Epicharis' suicide, the villa was confiscated and became an imperial property. If so, Parthenius could have purchased it from the imperial holdings or been given it as a gift. Strangely enough, Ti. Claudius Parthenius in turn conspired against the emperor of his day. This time the plot succeeded, and Parthenius arranged the murder of Domitian on September 18, CE 96 (Suetonius *Domit.* 16f.). At first, people were pleased with Parthenius since they were glad to be rid of the tyrant Domitian. But then the Praetorian Guard persuaded Domitian's successor, Nerva, that it was a dangerous precedent not to punish the murderer of an emperor. If we can believe the anonymous author of the so-called *Epitome De Caesaribus* (12.8), Parthenius was executed in a most gruesome way: he was castrated and then strangled on his testicles. So it seems that, whether or not we should call the Roman site in the Vigne di San Pietro "Horace's Villa," it could certainly be called the Villa of the Imperial Assassins, as Rudich proposes.

 This brings us to Hostilius Firminus, the last ancient we can identify as an owner of the property. As Rudich (2006: 324) notes, the combination of this *gentilicium* and *cognomen* is rare, and almost certainly refers to the senator P. Hostilius Firminus.[6] As legate in Africa, he was involved in a scandalous case of corruption and was tried and convicted under Trajan (Pliny *Epistles* 2.1.23f; 2.12.1–5). The appearance of his name on the water pipe found in the bath complex suggests that he might have expanded this part of the villa. This would be consistent with Pliny's report that his lifestyle was extravagant.[7]

Conclusion

There may have been specific social and geographical reasons behind the embellishment of the site in late Julio-Claudian and Flavian periods (cf. Frischer 2006a). As we have seen, two high-ranking imperial freedmen were associated with known owners in this period: Ti. Claudius Abascantus, an official in Nero's treasury, and Ti. Claudius Parthenius, Domitian's chamberlain. This fact suggests that the imperial court took an interest in the site. Why might this have been the case?

The Vigne di San Pietro site enjoyed an ample, year-round water supply, something rare in central Italy (Morley 1996: 104). Its remoteness from major population centers offered security. For someone coming here from Rome, an even more important advantage was its location c. 28.5 miles from the center of the city, along public roads: the Via Tiburtina, from Rome to Tivoli (16.5 miles); the Via Valeria to Vicovaro (7.6 miles); and up the Via Licinese to the villa (4.4 miles).[8] This made our site a convenient one-day trip from the center of Rome, since, as Casson (1994: 184–5) observed, the Romans did not like to travel more than 25 to 35 miles in a day before stopping for the night.[9]

Before the late Julio-Claudian period, the situation of the property would not have been important to the imperial court since no emperors are known to have had villas beyond Licenza (as one travels from Rome) before Nero built his impressive estate at Subiaco (Leppert 1974: 23; Mielsch 1997: 141–60). But Nero's retreat was c. 44 miles from Rome. This meant that some place had to be found that could suitably accommodate for at least one night the emperor and his entourage of hundreds of officials, escorts, bodyguards, family members, and so on.[10] "Horace's Villa" was the right distance from both Rome (28.5 miles) and Subiaco (20 miles) to make it a suitable rest stop. The way that it was enlarged suggests that it was intended to be used in two modes: by a small group of people who slept in bedrooms 1, 4, 11, 14, and 15; and by a much larger group that could be accommodated in the quadriporticus and perhaps in the garden. In this regard, Pasqui's (1916: 12) odd idea that the bath complex was a public building coincidentally located next to a private villa makes a certain amount of sense: he thought that the baths were too big in comparison with the residence. But the baths would be an appropriate size for the occasional troupe of attendants accompanying an emperor from Rome to a villa like that at Subiaco. In the ancient sources, we hear that, starting with Augustus, emperors visited the villas of their freedmen.[11] Perhaps the villa in the Vigne di San Pietro was a case in point: Nero might have sold or given it to Abascantus with the understanding that he could use it as a stopping point on his way to Subiaco.

Under Vespasian, "Horace's Villa" could have served the same purpose for imperial visits to Subiaco, which continued to be used after Nero's death (Mari 1995: 50), and also for the new emperor's trips to his villa near Reate, where he spent his summers (Suet., *Vesp.* 24). As it happens, the Via Licinese connects to the Via Salaria near Reate. Vespasian's villa was located at Aquae Cutiliae, over 50 miles from Rome down the Via Salaria. The long trip from Rome had to be broken up, and for this there no suitable site along Via Salaria has yet been found. The villa in the Vigne di San Pietro offered an ideal solution: it was 28.5 miles from Rome and just over 35 miles from Reate. To be sure, stopping there would have lengthened the journey to Aquae Cutiliae, but in compensation since Nero's day it had been fitted out to handle an imperial entourage. Standing in the middle of the triangle whose vertices were Rome, Reate, and Subiaco, "Horace's Villa" could have equally well served as a rest stop for trips between Subiaco and Aquae Cutiliae.

Unlike the Villa Sublacensis, which emperors used well into the third century, Vespasian's Reatine villa fell out of use as early as the reign of Domitian. Vespasian's younger son built an impressive new villa at Castel Gandolfo on the grounds of the later Villa Barberini. This is the time when Domitian might have given his chamberlain Ti. Claudius Parthenius the Vigne di San Pietro property, or sold it to him.

When Parthenius was executed, the property passed to his son Ti. Claudius Burrus and from him to the senator P. Hostilius Firminus. At this point, the connection with the imperial court ended. Later emperors such as Hadrian, Antoninus Pius, and Marcus Aurelius rarely, if ever, passed this way (on the vacation habits of Antoninus Pius and Marcus Aurelius see Mielsch 1997: 158). Judging from the archaeological record, no later than the third century CE a certain stagnation developed on the Vigne di San Pietro site. Without imperial patronage, "Horace's Villa" gradually reverted to what it had formerly been: the kind of place Horace memorably called "*deserta et inhospita tesqua*" (*Epistles* 1.14.19).

In this connection, we can return to Horace and ask whether the new research, discoveries, and interpretations have any impact of the *status quaestionis* of Horatian ownership of "Horace's Villa." As we have seen, no positive proof that this was, or was not, Horace's property emerged between 1996 and 2003. But if the proposed identifications of Claudia Epicharis and Tiberius Claudius Burrus are correct, then the association of both these property owners with the imperial circle is unlikely to be coincidental. It suggests that the property in the Vigne di San Pietro was at some point part of the imperial *fiscus*. Now, according to the Suetonian life, when Horace died in 8 BCE, he left everything to the Emperor Augustus.[12] If some decades after the poet's death we find a property in the small Licenza valley part of the imperial *fiscus*, by Ockham's Razor we can say that this property was very likely the same one that Horace gave to Augustus. If that is correct, then "Horace's Villa" would be Horace's famous Sabinum.

The results of the 1996–2003 investigations were promising but do not constitute a final publication of the site. We learned that, despite 250 years of digging on the site, there is still much good ancient stratigraphy to be uncovered, but the time and resources at our disposal did not permit us to do more than make test soundings and trenches. Below the structures visible on the site—which, as we have seen, mainly date to the first and early second centuries CE (and not to the Augustan age, as previous scholars thought)—earlier remains were found dating to the first century BCE. Doubtless many other features are lurking that probably date to the same period. The garden is a particularly promising area for future research, as Gleason's trial trenches showed. The zone just to the north of the site would also repay investigation. It has been protected for nearly a century by a gravel road (fig. 3, E) which could be easily removed and below which we have reason to suspect additional structures of the villa may be waiting to be discovered.

Looking back over the past 250 years, it seems safe to predict that at some point archaeologists will return to the Vigne di San Pietro and resume the work which came to a halt in 2003. Perhaps when they do, we will receive a definitive answer to the question of whether the poet Horace ever owned the property. However that may be, the newly identified owners—Claudia Epicharis, Burrus, and Hostilius Firminus—are fascinating figures in their own right. Their association with the site will, it is to be hoped, can already give rise to new threads of research by scholars of the Julio-Claudian, Flavian, and Antonine periods. When the excavations resume, we can also expect to find new evidence that will deepen our understanding of how the site was used in the long period from Nero to Trajan. And we will be in a better position to judge whether Rudich was right to rename the site the "Villa of the Imperial Assassins."[13]

GUIDE TO FURTHER READING

For the history and nature of the site and its finds, Frischer, Crawford, and De Simone 2006 gives the most thorough and up-to-date treatment. The classic older treatment was published by Lugli (1926). Mari (1993) gives a compendious account of the archaeology of the surrounding valley. Morley (1996) is a good starting point for reading about the hinterland of Rome, while Mielsch (1997) provides a useful introduction to the villa as a Roman architectural form. For the theme of the villa in Horace's poetry, Schmidt (1997) is a good starting point, supplemented by Bowditch (2001).

NOTES

1   We call the site "Horace's Villa," not Horace's Villa, to indicate that its association with Horace is not certain.
2   The secondary literature on the villa poems of Horace is extensive. Notable recent contributions include Schmidt 1997; Bowditch 2001.

3 Thus, as a result of the new fieldwork, I have had to perform a palinode with reference to my earlier allegation of a disjunction between Horace's description of his
   villa and the actual remains from his period on the site; see Frischer 1995, 1996.
4 I thank Sig. Antonio Muzi, the head guard of the site, for bringing this discovery
   to my attention.
5 Ti. Claudius Parthenius: *RE* III.2.2840 (Stein); *PIR*² C951a; Claudius Burrus: *RE*
   III.1.1070 (Henze); *PIR*² B176.
6 *RE* VIII.2.2506; *PIR*² H225. Cf. Sherwin-White 1966: 171.
7 So Rudich 2006: 324, citing Pliny, *Epistles* 11.23: *hominis compti semper et*
   pumicati.
8 The distances were calculated using GIS software for a route along the corresponding
   modern roads and may, as a result, be slightly inaccurate. But given the range of a
   typical day's travel, 25–35 miles (see Casson 1994: 185), this inaccuracy (which is
   probably less than 5%, perhaps considerably less) will not affect the basic point that
   "Horace's Villa" was a comfortable one day's journey from Rome. On the Via Licinese in antiquity, see Mari 1993: 52, n. 8. Licinese is the modern name for a Roman
   road whose ancient name is not known.
9 Casson's estimates are accepted by White 1984: 138 and are compatible with the
   calculations in Hyland 1990: 254–5, 260–1. On forms of transport generally, see
   Sartorio 1994.
10 Cf. Casson 1994: 180–1: "The emperors and others of high society or of wealth
   took to the road in the grandest imaginable style. They packed a veritable household
   to spare them the ignominy or discomfort of stopping at any inns save those able to
   accommodate a royal party: tents and commodes as well as the usual cooking utensils,
   bedding, and tableware; some of the last could be so precious and fragile it had to
   be carried by hand and not trusted to a jolting wagon. An army of attendants was
   de rigueur. Horace ridicules one Roman worthy who, for the short trip from Rome
   to his villa at Tibur, took along no less than five slaves … The emperor Claudius,
   who liked to play dice, had a traveling carriage fitted as a gaming room …" On the
   escorts and entourage of a traveling emperor, see also Millar 1977: 61–9.
11 Dio 57.72, cited by Millar 1977: 72. Cf. Nero's suicide at the villa of his freedman
   Phaon (Suet., *Nero* 48–9); Domitian's nurse Phyllis buried the emperor's body on
   the grounds of her suburban villa (Suet., *Dom.* 17.3).
12 Near the end of the Suetonian life, we read: "decessit V Kal. Decembris C. Marcio
   Censorino et C. Asinio Gallo consulibus post nonum et quinquagesimum <diem,
   quam Maecenas obierat, aetatis agens septimum et quinquagesimum> annum herede
   Augusto palam nuncupato, cum urgente via valetudinis non sufficeret ad obsignandas
   testamenti tabulas."
13 The Horace's Villa Project, 1996–2003 was a team effort, and there are many people
   and institutions deserving of recognition and thanks for their help. For a complete
   listing, please see Frischer 2006c: xxiii–xxiv.

PART II

Horatian Lyric:
Literary Contexts

CHAPTER FIVE

The Epodes: Genre, Themes, and Arrangement*

David Mankin

The Epode collection

Some time at the end of the thirties BCE Horace published a book of poems which has come to be called the Epodes but which he himself called his *Iambi* (Nisbet 2007: 12; Mankin 1995: 12). The book contains seventeen poems of diverse length, in diverse meters, and with diverse levels of style: the shortest are sixteen lines (*Epodes* [hereafter *Ep.*] 6, 14), the longest is 106 (*Ep.* 5), the first ten are composed in couplets of an iambic trimeter followed by an iambic dimeter, the next six (*Ep.* 11–16) in five (*Ep.* 14 and 15 have the same form) different combinations of iambic and / or dactylic measures, while the last (*Ep.* 17) is in stichic iambic trimeters, and from poem to poem and within single poems the language is at times prosaic, colloquial, and plain, at times poetic, elevated, and adorned with figures, literary allusions, and mythological references (Mankin 1995: 12–14; Watson 2003: 30–5). There is also considerable diversity in the presentation and subject matter. Although most of the poems seem to be in the poet's own voice, in at least one (*Ep.* 2) the speaker is revealed to be someone else, another (*Ep.* 5) is a third-person narrative, and the final poem (*Ep.* 17) is a dialog between Horace and one of the characters from that narrative. The addressees and persons mentioned or referred to include the eminent Maecenas (*Ep.* 1, 3, 9, 14), his even more eminent friend Caesar Octavian (*Ep.* 1, 9), and their enemies Sextus Pompeius (*Ep.* 9), Marcus Antonius, and Cleopatra (*Ep.* 1, 4, 9), but also the Roman people as a group (*Ep.* 4, 7, 16) and a number of more obscure figures: friends (*Ep.* 11, 13), lovers (*Ep.* 8, 11, 12, 14, 15), and especially enemies (*Ep.* 2, 4, 5, 6, 10, 17) whose broad depiction and, when furnished, significant names suggest stock characters rather than actual persons (Mankin 1995: 9). A declaration of friendship for Maecenas in a time of crisis (*Ep.* 1) is followed by mockery of the city slicker Alfius' fantasies of country life

(*Ep.* 2), a (literally) dyspeptic outburst against a joking Maecenas (*Ep.* 3), harsh words from the poet and the "vox populi" for an unnamed ex-slave become a high ranking officer in war time (*Ep.* 4), a narrative about the witch Canidia and her coven murdering a Roman boy to make a love potion (*Ep.* 5), threats against an unnamed, dog-like enemy (*Ep.* 6), an appeal to the Roman people to stand down from civil war (*Ep.* 7), obscene abuse of a randy old hag (*Ep.* 8), joy mixed with anxiety and fear over Caesar's victory in the battle of Actium (*Ep.* 9), ill wishes and imprecations for the smelly sea-traveler Mevius (*Ep.* 10), confessions to Pettius of erotic humiliation (*Ep.* 11), further abuse of the old hag (*Ep.* 12), an exhortation to some downcast drinking companions (*Ep.* 13), an apology to Maecenas for "writer's block" brought on by the ex-slave Phryne (*Ep.* 14), reproaches and threats for the oath-breaker Neaera (*Ep.* 15), another appeal to the Roman people, now to abandon their civil war-torn city (*Ep.* 16), and a futile attempt to placate the vengeful Canidia (*Ep.* 17).

Parian Iambi

For many readers, the diversity of the poems in the Epode collection, which makes it appear something of a crazy-quilt, raises questions as to whether there is a basis for the inclusion of all the diverse pieces or, indeed, any "unity" for the ensemble. As if anticipating such a reaction, Horace has left what look like "clues" to his purpose. Within the Epode book, at *Ep.* 14.7, he refers to his poems as *iambi*, as if to indicate that they all belong to a single literary genre (below), while in *Ep.* 6, which has been called a "programmatic epode" (Schmidt 1977), he identifies as his models the most famous early Greek practitioners of that genre, Archilochus and Hipponax (*Ep.* 6, 11–14):

> caue, caue, namque in malos asperrimus
>   parata tollo cornua,
> qualis Lycambae spretus infido gener
>   aut acer hostis Bupalo.

> Beware, beware, for most savage against evil-doers I raise horns ready for action, just like the son-in-law (= Archilochus) spurned by Lycambes or the relentless enemy (= Hipponax) to Bupalus.

We will return to this passage, but for now it is enough to note that Horace depicts *iambus* as a kind of defensive weapon to be wielded, like the horns of a bull protecting its herd, against "evil" and, as suggested by the names Lycambes ("wolf-rhythm") and Bupalus ("bull-fighter"), naturally hostile aggressors (Mankin 1995: 141–2).

Outside of the collection, Horace uses the term *iambi* in connection with the Epodes three other times. In one passage (*Epistles* 2.2.59–60, probably from early

19 BCE), he distinguishes them from his "lyric" (*carmen* = the *Odes*) and "conversations" (*sermones* = the hexameter poems), while in another (*Odes* 1.16, 22–5, around 29 BCE), he alludes to them in a way (*criminosis … iambis* 2–3) that evokes his bellicose stance in *Ep.* 6, but also suggests he has now, in the *Odes*, "outgrown" that stance (cf. Davis 1991: 75–7):

> me quoque pectoris
> temptauit in dulci iuuenta
> feruor et in celeres iambos
>
> misit furentem.
>
> me also in the sweet time of youth an angry boiling of
> the heart sent raging into swift *iambi*.

But it is the third passage that contains Horace's fullest account of what he had in mind with the Epodes. Looking back at them a decade later, he declares (*Epistles* 1.19.23–5):

> Parios ego primus iambos
> ostendi Latio, numeros animosque secutus
> Archilochi, non res et agentia uerba Lycamben.
>
> I first displayed Parian *iambi* to Latium, having followed
> the meters and spirit of Archilochus, not (his) subject
> matter and words hounding Lycambes.

Horace's main concern here is to vindicate himself and his poetry, both the Epodes and, in the ensuing lines (26–33), the Odes, from charges of "slavish" imitation (Fraenkel 1957: 339–50; Jenny Strauss Clay, Chapter 7 in this volume); hence his claim to "primacy" and his insistence that he did not "follow" his model in his choice of subject matter and the target for his hostile language. But he also amplifies the "clues" furnished by the other passages we have examined. He still, as in *Odes* 1.16 and *Ep.* 2.2, refers to the Epodes with a generic term (*iambos*) which distinguishes them from the Odes, but here he defines their genre in respect to their "meters" (*numeros*) as well as the bellicose "spirit" (*animosque*) alluded to in *Ep.* 6 and *Odes* 1.16 (Fraenkel 1957: 342; cf. Brink 1971: on *A.P.* 79 *Archilochum proprio rabies armauit iambo* [fury armed Archilochus with its fitting (genre of) *iambus*]). They are again, as in *Ep.* 6, associated with Archilochus, but now placed in a broader context with the references to Archilochus' community, the island / city state of Paros (*Parios*), and to Horace's Latin audience (*Latio*).

From what Horace says in these passages it would appear that the key, or at least one of the keys, to the "unity" of the Epodes is their genre: they are meant to recreate in a Latin / Roman setting the ancient Greek tradition of *iambus*, especially as associated with Archilochus. Yet analysis of the Epodes from this perspective is not as straightforward as might be hoped, for although Horace could read complete texts of Archilochus (cf. *Satires* 2.3, 12, a reference to his own copy of the author), if not other iambists, the works of these poets now survive chiefly in short fragments and *testimonia* preserved in references by later writers and in the occasional papyrus scrap or inscription. As such, they have been subject to various interpretations, including an older one in which Archilochus is seen primarily as the inventor of the genre *iambus*, which he employs primarily as a vehicle for plain-spoken, direct, and personally motivated invective against real-life personal enemies. This view has served as the starting point for many discussions of the Epodes, but only a few poems (*Ep.* 4, 6, 8, 10, 12, 15) can be classified as direct attacks and even these, with their occasionally elevated style and allusions and stock characters hardly seem plain-spoken and personal. It has been argued, therefore, that, despite what Horace says, most of his *iambi* are "iambic" in meter only, none of them are truly "Parian," and his claim to "primacy" is not only a sham, but a slight on Latin predecessors such as Catullus. In this view, the Epodes probably owe more to Hellenistic models such as the *Iambi* of Callimachus, in which the poet's aim is to "cross genres" by incorporating types of poetry other than *iambus* (as narrowly defined) into "iambic" form, than to actual archaic *iambi*.[1] More recently, however, some new discoveries (Archilochus' "Cologne Epode" [= fr. 196a West] and the "Telephus Elegy" [= Obbink 2006]), and especially a reassessment of the evidence have led to a quite different interpretation of Archilochus and the iambic genre, one which not only furnishes support to Horace's assertions about the Epodes but also sheds considerable light on their "generic" unity.[2]

In this interpretation, the genre *iambus*, whose main practitioners, Archilochus and Hipponax, but also Semonides of Amorgos, flourished in the mid-seventh to the mid-sixth centuries BCE, may have originated much earlier as a cult song associated with the Greek gods Demeter and Dionysus whose characteristic form would later come to be called "iambic" meter. But *iambi* could also be composed in other measures, including "elegy" and the related "mixed forms" of epodic combinations. The common element, what made it a distinct genre, was that is was, in essence, "blame poetry" that in various ways and with varying degrees of hostility found fault with conduct that was considered inappropriate or dangerous. The sense of what merited blame was determined not so much by the individual iambist's personal experience and sensibilities as by the norms of his society or social group. *Iambus*, then, was composed primarily for an audience drawn from that society gathered as *philoi* ("friends", "fellow citizens") in an assembly or in the predominant social institution of archaic Greece, the symposium (Clay, Chapter 7 in this volume). In either context, the *iambus* was meant to remind the *philoi* of the basis for their *philotēs* ("friendship", "fellowship") by calling attention to and blaming what might be perceived as threats to the customs, institutions, and modes of conduct that united them as an audience. Such iambic blame could take any of a number of different forms. The poet, speaking more or less in his own person but especially as a one of the *philoi* could level a direct attack against somebody, either another of the *philoi* acting "out of line" or an *echthros* ("enemy", "outsider") who has crossed that line. Or he could adopt a persona not his own and reveal "himself" to be guilty of some misconduct by, in effect, "saying the worst things about himself."[3] Or he could tell a story, a kind of "blame narrative" combining such self-indictment with accounts of reprehensible acts. There were also different levels of blame with correspondingly different levels of style (West 1974: 77–11), ranging from admonition and chiding directed at *philoi*, often involving elevated language and literary and mythological allusion, to plainer and more virulent abuse, usually reserved for *echthroi*. It appears, moreover, that the *echthroi* in *iambus* tended to be figures who had originally been *philoi* but had "alienated" themselves through the worst forms of misconduct. It also appears that most such figures were not real people, but stock characters with significant names ("Lycambes", "Bupalus" [above]) embodying or symbolizing what the iambist and his society found most inimical. A scenario, either known to or repeated for the audience, would explain how such an exemplary (in a bad sense) figure had become an *echthros* and serve as a warning against such behavior.

The parallels between all this and Horace's Epodes are not hard to discover.[4] Horace's meters are ones attested, directly or indirectly, for Archilochus, and he has "followed" his model's usage in minute detail (Mankin 1995: 14–22, Watson 2003: 43–6), and it can be argued that the range of his language and style to some degree corresponds to that of Archilochus (Mankin 1995: 12–14). His audience, corresponding to Archilochus' Parians, is likewise either his fellow citizens in some kind of assembly (*Ep.* 7, 16, possibly *Ep.* 4) or his friends in the context of a symposium (*Ep.* 3, 9, 11, 12, 13, 14); while the *amici* (= *philoi*) whom he admonishes and chides (*Ep.* 3, 9, 13, 14) are real people, his enemies, the objects of more severe abuse, are mostly stock characters (above). He, too, speaks in his own person but also can assume a *persona* ("Alfius" in *Ep.* 2), and he frequently "says the worst things about himself" (*Ep.* 1, 3, 4, 6, 8, 11, 12, 14, 15, and 17). Most of the poems pretend to be spoken by the poet or a character, but there is a "blame narrative" (*Ep.* 5) and a "dialog" which suggests that this may also have been a technique of early *iambus* (Mankin 1995: 273, but cf. Barchiesi 2001: 151–2), and within other poems there is considerable use of narration and "talking characters" (*Ep.* 4, 7, 11, 12, 13, 15).

These parallels are significant for clarifying Horace's use of the term "Parian *iambi*," for justifying his claim of "primacy"—no earlier group or collection of Latin poems corresponds so closely to the Archilochean model—and, most importantly, for allowing us to detect at least some level of unity in the Epode collection. But identifying the literary antecedents and genre of that collection takes us only so far, leaving unanswered at least two further questions about the Epodes. Since, as Horace says, he did not simply adopt Archilochus' subject matter and targets of blame, why did he choose the ones that he did? And, an even bigger question, perhaps: why, in late Republican Rome, did he decide to recreate and revive, as it were, the "spirit" of this ancient genre?

Res et agentia uerba

This brings us back to the perception and problem, if it is that, of the diversity of the Epodes. It is possible that this is simply a reflection of the diversity of Horace's model, whether the multifaceted *iambus* of archaic times or, as some will continue to insist, the "genre-crossing" *Iambi* of Callimachus. But a closer look reveals an abundance of verbal echoes, images, mythological allusions, and other "motifs" which connect and shed light on poems seemingly distinct in overall subject matter and address (Watson 2003: 23–30; cf. Carrubba 1969: 21–83). Thus, to cite only a few examples, *Ep.* 1, addressed by Horace in his own voice to his real-life friend Maecenas, seems to many scholars (e.g. Fraenkel 1957: 69–70) one of the "least iambic" poems in the collection, since most of it involves a positive depiction of friendship followed by what appears to be only desultory blame of stock characters (*Ep.* 1, 33–4), while *Ep.* 2, spoken in the *persona* of the stock character "Alfius" (from Greek *alphaino*, "gain"), is more often than not taken as sincerely meant praise of country life hardly miti-gated by the revelation, at the end of the poem (*Ep.* 2, 67–70) that its speaker is a usurer. But the two poems are linked by a verbal reminiscence (*Ep.* 1, 23–4 with *Ep.* 2, 5–6), by agricultural images (*Ep.* 1, 25–30 with *Ep.* 2, 11–12, 61–4), and by a similarity between the usurer that "Alfius" turns out to be and one of the stock characters of *Ep.* 1, the "greedy Chremes," whose name sug-gests "possessions" (Greek *chremata*). These links enhance and add depth to the elements of blame in each poem, providing, for *Ep.* 1, a negative and "unfriendly," if not hostile, alternative to Horace's willingness to face danger and possible death in war for the sake of friendship, and, for *Ep.* 2, giving a clue near its beginning that there is something seriously amiss with the escapist view of country life depicted in it (Mankin 1995: 63–4; Watson 2003: 80–6). Both poems, moreover, have links to other poems as well: the animal imagery (Horace as a mother bird unable to protect her chicks) at *Ep.* 1.19–22 antici-pates similarly disturbing animal images throughout the collection (Watson 2003: 27–8), while verbal echoes of *Ep.* 2 connect it with *Ep.* 16 (Mankin on *Ep.* 16, 41–2, 44, 48–9), in which Horace seeks to persuade his fellow citizens to abandon their civil war-ravaged city to resettle in certain "Fortunate Islands"; here the links, which indicate a similarity between these islands and "Alfius'" countryside, suggest that they, too, are an escapist fantasy, and that Horace, no less than the absurd usurer, is deluding himself and his listeners (Mankin 1995: 244–5).

In addition to connections of this sort, small in scale, if not significance, there are certain themes that run through the collection. Chief among these is a sense of people, events, and even animals and natural objects which are "out of control" either because of because of a vengeful "fury" or because of a kind of "impotence."[5] The first is exemplified by the Roman people, impelled by a seemingly endless cycle of "blind fury" and "culpability" for the ancient murder of Remus (*Ep.* 7, 13–20), rushing headlong into a civil war (*Ep.* 7), but it is also an endemic "contagion" (cf. *Ep.* 16, 61) threatening to turn inward and rupture the *amicitia* of those presumably on the same side (Mankin on *Ep.* 3, 4, 11). The process seems to be depicted symbolically in the "programmatic" *Ep.* 6, where Horace, although verbally attacking an unnamed adversary, suggests that there is an affinity between himself and his target: they are both "sheepdogs," and while Horace is, or proclaims himself, the braver and fiercer of the two, they are at first merely competing in warding off wolves and in pursuit of prey (*Ep.* 6, 1–10). But suddenly there is a shift in the imagery: Horace, in a passage we have already examined, becomes a "bull" protecting his herd and threatening, if provoked, to attack what are now labeled "evil-doers" just as Archilochus and Hipponax attacked their bull-hostile enemies (*Ep.* 6, 11–4), but his adversary, while presumably now numbered among those "evil doers," remains a dog (*Ep.* 16, 15–16). In these "metamorphoses" we are perhaps meant to see the rage-induced changes in perception which can lead a group of people from recognizing their kinship (all "sheepdogs") as "friends" to seeing each other as members of different and hostile "species" ("bulls" vs "dogs"), "instant enemies" (to borrow a phrase from the mystery writer Ross MacDonald) who can or must be attacked, even if it means civil war. Not incidentally, Horace, by identifying himself as an iambist and citing his models, seems in the process to implicate the bellicose "spirit" of the genre itself, as if that, too, has moved out of control.

Yet with all Horace's barking and bull-roaring, *Ep.* 6 ends with an image of passivity (*Ep.* 16.15–16):

> an si quis atro dente me petiuerit,
>   inultus ut flebo puer?

> If someone attacks me with his black tooth, will I
> (merely) weep like an unavenged child?

Although Horace denies the similarity, this is an admission that his adversary, at least, perceives him as an *inultus puer*, much like Canidia's victim in the preceding poem (cf. *Ep.* 5.11–14). It is as if there is something about *iambus* that tends to undermine its angry bellicosity and gives the impression of "helplessness" (cf. Pindar's comment on Archilochus' *amachania* at *Pyth.* 2.54–6 [= Arch. test. 35 Gerber 1999], cited by Watson 2007: 99) or, as modern critics term it, "impotence." The poet and other figures in the iambic scenarios arouse their fury (above) and, in contexts both of conflict and of sexuality, their "manhood," but all too often both prove ineffectual or, even worse, produce unintended consequences ranging from the speaker's own humiliation (so in Horace's "erotic epodes" (*Ep.* 8, 11, 12, 14, and 15), to the near or actual rupture of *philotēs* (as in *Ep.* 6; cf. *Ep.* 3 [below], 4, 11, and 14), to the unloosing of dire forces. This last is depicted most vividly in the "blame narrative" *Ep.* 5, where it is associated with the blackest and most fearful magical arts. Their previous spells having failed, Canidia and her ghastly companions prepare to murder a helpless boy in order to create an especially powerful love potion, but the last words of the dying boy (*Ep.* 5, 87–102) indicate that they will have instead unleashed a terrible ghost which will arouse in the (Roman) crowd a vengeful fury against the witches.

   Epode 5 and the other works featuring Canidia (*Ep.* 17, *Satires* 1.8; cf. *Ep.* 3, 7–6, *Satires* 2.1, 48, 2.8, 95, and, possibly, *Odes* 1.16) are among the strangest and most baffling poems in Latin or, perhaps, any language, but it seems best to take them as largely, if not entirely, symbolic (Mankin 1995: 299–301; Oliensis 1998: 68–90, but cf. Watson 2003: 174–90). It seems to be no accident that Canidia is mentioned in *Ep.* 3, where the silliness of Horace's overreaction to a prank by Maecenas is given a serious, threatening aspect by its comparison with the vengeful acts of another witch, the powerful and murderous Medea, with the manhood-sapping hot winds of Apulia, and the poisonous gift that destroyed the mighty Hercules (*Ep.* 3, 9–18), and if, in *Ep.* 5, Canidia's magic seems to turn back on herself and her companions, in *Ep.* 17 she is given voice to threaten Horace for his blame of her, as if his *iambus*, like her magic, had raised an avenging spirit. There have been many suggestions as to precisely what Canidia and her activities symbolize, but her name seems to point to two associations, with the "dog" (*canis*) and the furiously "dogged" genre of *iambus* (cf. *Ep.* 6), and with "old-age" (*canities*) and the decrepit impotence not only of the poet, but of Rome as it collapses into ruin (*Ep.* 16, 1–2) under the weight of its ancient curse (*Ep.* 7, 17–20).

Annus horribilis

In exploring the possibilities of generic and thematic unity we have generally adhered to the sequence of the Epodes in the collection (e.g. *Ep.* 5 "anticipating" *Ep.* 6 etc., *Ep.* 16 "echoing" *Ep.* 2, not vice versa) and treated or referred to the poems overtly concerned with events in Roman history, the "political epodes" (*Ep.* 1, 4, 7, 9, 16), as if they all belong to the same period of time. The idea that the sequence of the poems, their "internal chronology," as it were, is meaningful, and that this sequence is to be seen as occurring in relation to a particular "external chronology" of historical events, is controversial, but it seems to make more sense of the evidence than other proposals concerning the arrangement and dating of the Epode book and, if correct, offers yet another approach to recognizing not only the unity, but also the purpose of Horace's *iambi*.

To begin with the "external chronology": there is only one poem containing unambiguous references to contemporary historical events, *Ep.* 9, in which Horace is shown addressing Maecenas either just before, or during, or, what seems most likely, just after Octavian's crucial victory over Antony and Cleopatra at Actium (September 2, 31 BCE) and in which he mentions (*Ep.* 9.9–17), as something fairly "recent" (*nuper* 9), the victory over Sextus Pompeius at Naulochus five years earlier (September 3, 36 BCE).[6] A further and less obvious indication of date is furnished by his depiction of his friendship with Maecenas,[7] which began around late 38 or early 37 BCE (Nisbet 2007: 10–12, David Armstrong, Chapter 1 in this volume); the other poems concerned with it (*Ep.* 1, 3, 14) cannot be earlier than that time. But for the remaining twelve poems the apparent absence of indications precise or imprecise has given rise to a number of theories, the most popular of which is that they were composed over a considerable period of time, not just the seven years or so of Horace's friendship with Maecenas, but the twelve years between his ignominious return to Italy (late 42 BCE) after fighting on the losing side at Philippi, when "poverty compelled me to write verses" (*Epistles* 2.2.46–52), and his presence among the victors at Actium (Fraenkel 1957: 24–75; Nisbet 1984 and 2007; cf. Watson 2003: 1–3).

This theory is attractive on several counts, not least because it offers a simple explanation for the diversity of the Epodes: as products of a fairly long period of time, they reflect changes in Horace's attitudes, interests, and level of skill as a poet. But attempts to distinguish the "early" from the "late" epodes tend to rely on rather subjective criteria, such as whether a poem seems "juvenile' (e.g. the crude and obscene *Ep.* 8 and 12) or "mature" (the "*Ode*-like" *Ep.* 13), and, not surprisingly, commentators have arrived at widely different conclusions (Carrubba 1969: 15–17). There is, to be sure, something of a consensus that the "political" poems not addressed to Maecenas must be earlier than those addressed to him, but this is based solely on the assumption that Horace would not or could not have expressed anger (*Ep.* 4), dread (*Ep.* 7), or despair (*Ep.* 16) about Rome's circumstances once he had joined, or rather, been co-opted into Maecenas' (and thus Octavian's) circle.

Even if the criteria for dating the individual poems were more objective, there would still be a basic problem with this approach: it fails to take into account not only the "forward" and "backward" looking connections we have noted between individual poems, but other indications as well which seem to invite a reading of the poems according to the sequence in which they are arranged. These include the procession, as it were, of the meters;[8] ten poems in the same fully iambic combination (*Ep.* 1–10) are followed by a poem in which a dactylic element intrudes (*Ep.* 11), an entirely dactylic poem (*Ep.* 12), a mostly dactylic poem with an iambic element (*Ep.* 13), poems containing a balance of dactyls and iambics (*Ep.* 14, 15, 16), and finally a poem which returns to iambics only (*Ep.* 17). The first word (*Ep.* 1.1) of the collection is *ibis* ("you will go"), the last (*Ep.* 17.81) is *exitus* ("departure"); the sequence of the first ten poems begins

(*Ep.* 1) and ends (*Ep.* 10) with sea voyages, and *Ep.* 14 seems to alert the reader to the fact that the book as a whole is coming to an end.

Guided by such indications, it seems likely that Horace's original audience would have interpreted the poems according to the order in which they encountered them (Schmidt 1977; Porter 1995; Mankin 1995: 10–12). Thus, to consider only the political poems, when they heard or read *Ep.* 1, 4, and 7, they would take these poems as anticipating an imminent war which, when they finally read *Ep.* 9, they might naturally assume to be the Actian War. It would also be natural to take *Ep.* 16, coming "later" in the collection, as referring to a time "later" than that of *Ep.* 9. How much later is not clear, but there is nothing in the book anticipating Octavian's final victory over his civil war enemies in the Alexandrian War (August 30 BCE). This suggests that the Epode book might be supposed to "take place" in something like a single year, an *annus horribilis* with the battle of Actium at its center as it is at the center of the book.

That year, and the book, begin in the spring of 31 BCE, with Octavian preparing for war (Osgood 2006: 371) and Horace pledging to risk the dangers of that war out of friendship for Maecenas (*Ep.* 1); "Alfius", by contrast, imagines a quiet life in an impossible country landscape (*Ep.* 2). During a relaxing symposium, Horace's anger at a jest of Maecenas threatens to disrupt their friendship (*Ep.* 3), but the anger is instead directed at a fellow Roman whom Horace and the Roman crowd regard, perhaps misguidedly, as a dangerous upstart and "fifth columnist" (*Ep.* 4). Meanwhile, Canidia's magic raises a vengeful spirit (*Ep.* 5); as if haunted by that spirit, Horace, asserting himself as an iambist, attacks an adversary whom he perceives as an alien enemy but who turns out to belong to his own "species" (*Ep.* 6), and the Roman people, despite Horace's reproaches, are driven by their "fury" and "blame" for the ancient murder of Remus into civil war (*Ep.* 7). Horace pauses, as it were, to discharge his own fury against a nasty old hag (Canidia?) who has tried to seduce him (*Ep.* 8), and indeed, his reaction to the victory at Actium, although not free of anger against Antony and Cleopatra, runs more to "anxiety and fear" over whether or not that victory will prolong the cycle of civil war (*Ep.* 9; see Mankin 1995: 159–60). As if to avert the danger, he curses the sea voyage of "stinking Mevius," who, like the Greek hero Locrian Ajax, on whom Pallas (Minerva) directed her wrath when she turned it away from Troy (= Rome?) and, it would seem, like the unnamed target of Horace's model, an *iambus* of Archilochus or Hipponax,[9] appears to be kind of "scapegoat" (Greek *pharmakos*) carrying off with him the fratricidal pollution afflicting the Romans (*Ep.* 10; see Mankin 1995: 182–3, but also Oliensis 1998: 91–2). But if, following *Ep.* 10, a change in meter seems to signal a new beginning, it is still only a couple of months (December) after Actium, and, whatever might be happening at Rome, Horace is still caught in his own cycle of blind lust, anger, and self-humiliation (*Ep.* 11), and not only "says the worst things about himself," but gives voice to the hag he had abused in *Ep.* 8 to add her own complaint, a kind of *iambus* within an *iambus* (*Ep.* 12). If his exhortation to companions anxious about the course of events (the as yet unresolved conflict with Antony and Cleopatra?) shows self-possession and a sad wisdom (*Ep.* 13), his uncontrollable passion for a degrading paramour, the freedwoman Phryne, renders him powerless to complete his book of *iambi* (*Ep.* 14). His vengeful anger but also his sorry impotence are once again on display in his denunciation of the faithless Neaera (*Ep.* 15) no less than in his hopeless proposal for the "better part"—as if there were such a thing—of the Romans to escape their collapsing homeland and seek a "Alfian" neverland (*Ep.* 16) and in the futile attempt to placate the destructive fury of Canidia (*Ep.* 17) that brings the book to an ominous and disquieting conclusion.

Criminosis ... modum pones iambis (*Odes* 1.16.2–3)

At the beginning of *Odes* 1, the crisis of civil war and what would prove to be the death-throes of the Roman Republic has not yet passed (*Odes* 1.2); it is only as it becomes evident in the course of the book that Octavian and Rome are in the process of directing their violent energies against non-Roman foes (*Odes* 1.12, 1.21, 1.26, 1.29, 1.35) and that the triumph anxiously anticipated in *Ep.* 9 turns out to be focused on the admirable but safely foreign Cleopatra rather than still divisive figure of Antony (*Odes* 1.37), that it becomes possible to relax (*Odes* 1.38). But Horace presents himself by and large both as a changed man, still subject to powerful emotions, especially love, yet now able to "distance himself" from these, and as a changed poet, no longer an iambist "following" the angry Archilochus, but a lyrist, the heir to Archilochus' old critic Pindar (above; see also William Race, Chapter 8 in this volume) and especially to the Lesbian poets Alcaeus and Sappho, who "moderated" the Parian's fierce Muse (*Epistles* 1.19.28–31; see Clay, Chapter 7 in this volume). If in his previous incarnation, he was, as man and as poet, emblematic of Rome's self-destructive fury and her inability to halt it, he now seems to present himself as an exemplar and his poetry as a source for a "way out" from that terrible cycle.

From this perspective it may be possible to understand why Horace chose to write "Parian *iambi*" when he did. With the Roman world caught up in the crisis of civil war, the ultimate negation of "friendship," he turned to an ancient genre whose function, in its troubled world, had been the reinforcement, through blame, including self-blame, and negative examples, including those set by the irascible poet himself, of the fragile *philotēs* which forms the basis of any community. It is doubtful whether he believed that his or anyone else's poetry could avert disaster, but he may have hoped that his *iambi* might somehow move his friends and fellow citizens at least to ask themselves *quo, quo scelesti ruitis?* (*Ep.* 7.1).

GUIDE TO FURTHER READING

This list is limited to works in English containing surveys and bibliographies of other important studies too numerous to be mentioned here. The standard text of the Epodes, as of all Horace's works, remains Klingner (1959); there are many competent translations, but the inspiration of "Jeffrey" invests that of Christopher Smart (mid-eighteenth century) with special authority. The fragments of the early iambic poets are collected in West (1989–92) and Gerber (1999, with English translation). There are three recent large-scale commentaries on the Epodes, Cavarzere (1992, in Italian), Mankin (1995), and Watson (2003); much of what is said here is "recycled" from the second of these. Outside the commentaries, general introductions to the Epodes include the still valuable Fraenkel (1957: 25–75) and, from a more recent perspective, Watson (2007). For Horace and Archilochus, see, in addition to the commentaries, Barchiesi (2001) and Harrison (2001); for the controversial issue of the relation of the Epodes to the *Iambi* of Callimachus, Heyworth (1993) and Barchiesi (2001); for major themes in the Epodes, (Fitzgerald 1988) and Oliensis (1998: 64–101); for theories about the arrangement of the Epode book, Carrubba (1969) and Porter (1995); and for the historical background, Nisbet (1984 and 2007), Osgood (2006), and Armstrong, Chapter 1 in this volume.

NOTES

* The author is grateful to Jenny Strauss Clay and Gregson Davis for their efforts to improve this piece with careful editing and perceptive comments.
1 For this approach, see Fraenkel 1957: 24–75, Fedeli 1978, and Heyworth 1993; cf. Barchiesi 2001, and Watson 2003: 11–17.
2 See West 1974: 22–39; Nagy 1979: 222–52; Gentili 1988: 107–14, 179–96; Gerber 1991; and Bowie 2001.
3 The quote is from Critias, cited at Ael. *V.H.* 101.3 = Arch. Fr. 295 West.
4 See Mankin 1995: 6–9); cf. Harrison 2001, Watson 2003: 4–11, and Watson 2007.
5 See Fitzgerald 1988 and Oliensis 1998: 64–101, but also Watson 2003: 26–30 and 2007: 99–101.
6 See Mankin 1995: 159–60, but also Setaioli 1981: 1716–28, Nisbet 1984: 9–17, and Watson 2003: 310–13.
7 It would be more obvious if Horace's readers were familiar with his Satires (*Satires* 1.5.27–9, 1.6.47–62, 2.6.40–2).
8 In this respect the Epode book to a degree anticipates the books of the Odes; see Santirocco 1986.
9 Printed by West 1989 as Hipp. Fr. 115; for bibliography on the question of authorship, see Degani 1983: 168.

CHAPTER SIX

Defining a Lyric Ethos: Archilochus *lyricus* and Horatian *melos*[1]

Gregson Davis

The point of departure for this essay is the observation that Horatian lyric is deeply indebted, in its fundamental value-system, to the non-iambic poetry of Archilochus. By "non-iambic" I mean to designate those extant fragments in the Archilochian corpus that do not fall squarely into the category of outright invective. Thus broadly generic, rather than narrowly metrical, criteria will guide my comparative investigation. Since the historical connotations of "lyric" are notoriously slippery, I wish at the outset to clarify my use of the term within the compass of the discussion to follow. My main focus will be on content, rather than form; more precisely, I shall be concerned with the *nexus of ideas* that provide the philosophical underpinning for what I shall be referring to as a lyric *ethos*, or set of values. The premise of my demonstration, succinctly stated, is that the Archaic lyric poet and his Roman imitator share a defining ethos that is rooted in a particular worldview. In what follows I plan to juxtapose key texts of these two poets in order to illustrate a common way of viewing human existence and a common strategy for surmounting those potentially depressing aspects—for example, misery, fear, grief—that appear to be endemic to that existence. In juxtaposing select passages of the two poets in their aspect as *lyrici*,[2] my attention will be directed to the examination of topoi and motifs as bearers of shared ideas and values.

An inherent limitation of my proposed analysis is the fact that I shall be comparing whole poems in the Horatian corpus with fragments of Archilochus, some of which are not only incomplete but also lacunose. Despite the unfortunate lack of a larger context for many of the Archilochian fragments, however, I believe that the case for an intertextual bond of a non-trivial kind between Greek lyric prototypes and Latin imitations is sufficiently strong to warrant a thorough investigation. Horatian *melos* here will be taken to comprise the four books of the *Carmina*, as well as a few poems from the earlier collection of Epodes.

To unpack the concept of a "lyric ethos" forming an underlying "nexus of ideas" I begin with the two poets' frequent reiteration of the principle of vicissitude that governs human experience. The vicissitude motif is not, by itself, sufficient to define a lyric ethos, since it is by no means peculiar to lyric utterance; but the truism functions, for the lyric poets, as a fundamental platform for their system of values. The motif acquires a characteristically lyric inflection in so far as it is intertwined with a larger nexus of ideas. Of the many articulations of this rhetorical principle in Archilochus, I shall select a few passages for their emblematic value and for their affinity with central tenets of Horatian lyric.[3]

(128)

θυμέ, θύμ', ἀμηχάνοισι κήδεσιν κυκώμενε
†ἀναδευ δυσμενῶν† δ' ἀλέξεο προσβαλὼν ἐναντίον
στέρνον ἐνδοκοισιν ἐχθρῶν πλησίον κατασταθεὶς
ἀσφαλέως· καὶ μήτε νικέων ἀμφάδην ἀγάλλεο,
μηδὲ νικηθεὶς ἐν οἴκωι καταπεσὼν ὀδύρεο,
ἀλλὰ χαρτοῖσίν τε χαῖρε καὶ κακοῖσιν ἀσχάλα
μὴ λίην, γίνωσκε δ' οἷος ῥυσμὸς ἀνθρώπους ἔχει.

O heart, my heart, churning with unmanageable sorrows,
rouse yourself and fiercely drive off your foes with a
frontal attack, standing hard by them steadfastly; and
neither exult openly if you win, nor, if your are beaten,
fling yourself down at home in lamentation. Instead,
rejoice in what is joyful, grieve at troubles, but not too
much: be aware what sort of rhythm rules man's life.

The lyric speaker here directs a series of admonitions to himself—or rather to that part of himself that is the seat of emotion, his *thymos*. Vicissitude is represented in this instance as the alternation between victory and defeat in the context of warfare. That war is synecdochic for human experience in general becomes clear with the final gnome that ends the fragment: the alternation (*rhusmos*—"rhythm") is stated as a rule that holds sway over men. The advice given to the *thymos* amounts to a strategy for controlling the emotions. The personified organ is urged not to give way to inordinate joy in times of victory or, on the other hand, to inordinate grief in times of defeat. In short, the speaker advocates a calculated moderation of extreme emotion such that a kind of equilibrium may be achieved. An important corollary is that the attainment of the desired equilibrium rests on a foundation of knowledge—a master-theme of Archilochian verse. Knowledge, in this case, consists in an unblinkered acceptance of the governing principle of vicissitude (*rhusmos*).

Horace's famous ode addressed to Licinius (*Odes* 2.10) in which he articulates the doctrine of the golden mean (*aurea mediocritas*) is manifestly indebted to the Archilochian model—not so much in terms of verbal allusion or echo, but at the level of underlying ideas. As I have argued elsewhere apropos of this ode, the "mean" in Horace's conception is very close to the Aristotelian notion of a relative principle, rather than an absolute or arithmetical midpoint between extremes.[4] Like Archilochus, Horace understands proper conduct in the face of vicissitude to be based on a calculus in which the human actor is careful to temper his emotions according to circumstance. The lyrist is concerned with the adjustment of man's emotional equilibrium. In lines 12–14 of the Horatian ode, hope and fear are the specific emotional poles that correspond to Archilochus' joy and lamentation:

> Sperat infestis, metuit secundis
> alteram sortem bene praeparatum
> pectus.

> A heart well prepared for vicissitude shows hope in
> adverse times and fear in prosperous times.

Horace's *pectus* (heart) here corresponds to the *thymos* in the Archilochian intertext. The final strophe extends the idea of the need to moderate alternating polarities of confident and prudent behavior according to changing circumstances:

> Rebus angustis animosus atque
> fortis appare; sapienter idem
> contrahes uento nimium secundo
>   turgida uela.

> In narrow straits show yourself intrepid and brave: but
> wisely draw in your sails when they are puffed up by a
> wind too favorable.

A very similar exhortation to temper extreme expressions of joy and grief in the interests of equanimity is foregrounded in the opening strophe of *Odes* 2.3:

> Aequam memento rebus in arduis
> seruare mentem, non secus in bonis
>   ab insolenti temperatam
>   laetitia ...

> In hard times remember to keep an even mind; in easy
> times, likewise, a mind curbed from arrogant exultation ...

Though the particular pair of emotions differs in the passages juxtaposed above, the fundamental principle they frame is consistent. As is customary, Horace puts his own peculiar stamp on the recurrent motif of alternation of fortune, since for him it is crucial to reiterate that neither polar state (felicity or infelicity) lasts forever.

In our second Archilochian text, the source of vicissitude in human affairs is attributed to the gods:

(130)

τοῖς θεοῖς †τ' εἰθεῖἀπαντα·† πολλάκις μὲν ἐκ κακῶν
ἄνδρας ὀρθοῦσιν μελαίνηι κειμένους ἐπὶ χθονί,
πολλάκις δ' ἀνατρέπουσι καὶ μάλ' εὖ βεβηκότας
ὑπτίους, κείνοις <δ'> ἔπειτα πολλὰ γίνεται κακά,
καὶ βίου χρήμηι πλανᾶται καὶ νόου παρήορος.

> All things are easy for the gods. Often out of
> misfortunes they set men upright who have been laid
> low on the black earth; often they trip even those who
> are standing firm and roll them onto their backs, and
> then many troubles come to them, `and a man wanders
> in want of livelihood, unhinged in mind.

Although some words in the initial line of the fragment are uncertain, we may assume from what follows that the mutilated gnome ascribes ultimate responsibility for endemic reversal of fortune to the gods (*tois theois*). We may plausibly speculate that the lost sentiment expressed in the garbled line is most probably the equivalent of Horace's "leave the rest to the gods" (*permitte divis cetera*), which occurs in the well-known Soracte Ode (*Odes* 1.9.9)—an injunction that is immediately followed by an assertion of the gods' total control over alternations in nature (epitomized in the abrupt change for storm to calm). Be that as it may, one effect of assigning a divine agency to life's ups and downs is to demarcate those areas of our experience that are within our control from those that are not. When the relentless oscillation of good and bad fortune is graphically represented by the lyrists, the unhappy turn may be represented as extremely daunting in addition to being outside our control, as is the case in the Archilochus text, which focuses on the pole of misfortune and its dire repercussions on the mind of the victim.

With this grim elaboration of the negative pole of experience we may compare such Horatian passages as the portrayal of Fortune's cruelty in the closing strophes of *Odes* 1.34—an ode which we shall discuss later from a different angle:

> Valet ima summis
>
> mutare et insignem attenuat deus,
> obscura promens; hinc apicem rapax
>   Fortuna cum stridore acuto
>   sustulit, hic posuisse gaudet.   (12–16)

> The god [Jupiter] can change the lowest with the
> highest and he weakens the mighty while exalting the
> humble. From one man's head Fortune abruptly snatches
> a crown with strident wings only to place it with glee
> upon another's.

Yet another acerbic description of the role of Fortuna occurs in a passage from the long ode addressed to Maecenas (3.29) in which the goddess' sadistic delight in her gruesome game is the focal point:

> Fortuna saevo laeta negotio et
> ludum insolentem ludere pertinax
>   transmutat incertos honores
>   nunc mihi, nunc alii benigna.

> Fortune rejoicing in her savage work and relentless in
> playing her wanton game transmutes her unstable
> honors, kind in turn now to me, now to another person.

Despite these gloomy formulations, it is important to bear in mind that, in the larger lyric argument, the poets' representation of misfortune, however graphic, is the backdrop against which they draw explicit or implicit attention to the internal means available to mortals to surmount it. In sum, they offer a counsel, not of despair, but of hope. Thus the rhetorical function of the vicissitude motif in the context of lyric discourse is, at bottom, dialectical: it establishes a dark platform (or "foil" to revert to the useful terminology of Bundy in his *Studia Pindarica*) for the disclosure of the antidote or solution—the uninhibited enjoyment of the here and now. Crucial to the lyric strategy, then, is the overt or latent encouragement to dismiss, or at least to impose due limit upon, those emotions of extreme grief that mark our reaction to the irreversible misfortune that is reflected in human mortality. Thus in a famous Archilochian archetype we find the lyric speaker pointing the way to the resources available to us to counter the potentially depressing aspects of random vicissitudes. Fragment 13 assures us that the main antidote (*pharmakon*) to our painful apprehension of misfortune is internal fortitude (*tlēmosynē*):

(13)

> κήδεα μὲν στονόεντα Περίκλεες οὔτέ τις ἀστῶν
>   μεμφόμενος θαλίηις τέρψεται οὐδὲ πόλις·
> τοίους γὰρ κατὰ κῦμα πολυφλοίσβοιο θαλάσσης
>   ἔκλυσεν, οἰδαλέους δ' ἀμφ' ὀδύνηις ἔχομεν
> πνεύμονας. ἀλλὰ θεοὶ γὰρ ἀνηκέστοισι κακοῖσιν
>   ὦ φίλ' ἐπὶ κρατερὴν τλημοσύνην ἔθεσαν
> φάρμακον. ἄλλοτε ἄλλος ἔχει τόδε· νῦν μὲν ἐς ἡμέας
>   ἐτράπεθ', αἱματόεν δ' ἕλκος ἀναστένομεν,
> ἐξαῦτις δ' ἑτέρους ἐπαμείψεται. ἀλλὰ τάχιστα
>   τλῆτε, γυναικεῖον πένθος ἀπωσάμενοι.

> Repining at painful sorrows, Perikles, no one among our
> citizens, no, nor the city itself, will find pleasure in
> festivities: such were the men whom the waves of the

> loud-roaring sea washed over, and we struggle in our
> distress with swollen lungs. But for evils that have no
> cure, my friend, the gods have ordained stern endurance
> as remedy. These things go by turns: now it is to us that
> they have shifted, and we groan at the bloody wound,
> but soon they will pass to others. Come now, with all
> speed endure, and thrust aside this womanish grief.

We cannot be sure that we have the end of the fragment, of course, but we may infer from other passages in Archilochus and his lyric successors that the endurance he prescribes is not of the stiff upper lip variety but rather the sort that liberates us from the grip of numbing grief. Once we have thrust the latter aside we are on our way to a return to the pleasures of the good life. As the first couplet makes clear, excessive mourning, however appropriate and justified, is, at the end of the day, incompatible with the kind of pleasurable experiences summed up in the sympotic milieu (festivities: *thaliai*). Andrew Miller's cogent rendition of the opening lines, in my view, accurately conveys the sense of an underlying tension between prolonged mourning and reaffirmation of life through participation in feasts.

The basic idea of transcending persistent grief through re-engagement in festivity is more clearly expressed in the comparison that Archilochus makes in fragment 11 between lament and the pursuit of pleasure

(11)

οὔτέ τι γὰρ κλαίων ἰήσομαι, οὔτε κάκιον
θήσω τερπωλὰς καὶ θαλίας ἐφέπων.

> Neither by weeping shall I bring about any cure, nor
> shall I make things worse by pursuing enjoyments and
> festivities.

In this elegiac distich of the Parian master we receive an unequivocal articulation of the ethos of lyric, which is so trenchantly summed up in Horace's *carpe diem* imperative. The core pleasures that constitute the *telos* of lyric are attainable only through a considered adjustment of behavior, enabling us to overcome, and in some measure to compensate for, our tendency to fixate on the dark side of our mortal destiny. The happy life, symbolized in the banquet, is grounded in a prior and full acknowledgment of our mortal condition—the philosophically necessary prelude to our recommitment to the present.

In documenting Horace's debt to Archilochus *lyricus* we turn next to a few of the more striking articulations of the sympotic response that we find in the fragments of the Archaic Greek bard. In unpacking briefly these familiar lines I shall be focusing once again on the philosophical underpinnings of some of the poet's more robust claims and exhortations. In Fragment 4, the force of the sympotic prescription is greatly amplified in proportion to the dreary situation that the speaker describes—the more so if the *phylake* or "watch" he deprecates has a military reference.

(4)

ἀλλ' ἄγε σὺν κώθωνι θοῆς διὰ σέλματα νηὸς
  φοίτα καὶ κοίλων πώματ' ἄφελκε κάδων,
ἄγρει δ' οἶνον ἐρυθρὸν ἀπὸ τρυγός· οὐδὲ γὰρ ἡμεῖς
  νηφέμεν ἐν φυλακῆι τῆιδε δυνησόμεθα.

But come now, take the jug and go up and down the benches of the swift ship, pulling the stoppers off the hollow jars; drain off the red wine from the lees. Not even we will be able to stay sober on such a watch as this.

Closely affiliated in its underlying sentiment (drink as antidote to dreary military duty) is the equally robust fragment 2, which has elicited a copious literature of learned exegesis:

(2)

ἐν δορὶ μέν μοι μᾶζα μεμαγμένη, ἐν δορὶ δ' οἶνος
  Ἰσμαρικός· πίνω δ' ἐν δορὶ κεκλιμένος.

In my spear is my kneaded barley bread, in my spear is my wine from Ismaros, and I drink it leaning upon my spear.

This is not the place to review and evaluate the various erudite interpretations of the repeated phrase *en dori* (in my spear). From our perspective it is sufficient to underscore an aspect of the phrase that has received less attention from the critics: its emblematic status as a reflection of an implicit lyric program. If "*en dori*" is meant to encapsulate, in a stark and synecdochic image, the sphere of warfare in general—as I believe it does—then Archilochus' basic point is to show that the sympotic way of life trumps the military. However concretely or literally we understand the phrase *en dori* ("in/on my spear"; "while in field of warfare"), the vigorous assertion of his adherence to the sympotic even in the very midst of campaigning carries a strong ulterior message: the archetypal lyrist is, by his celebrated posture, privileging the lyric over the heroic ethos. The connotation of the participle *keklimenos* ("leaning") is both deliberately paradoxical and iconic, for it vividly suggests the normative reclining position of the banqueter and thus completes the contamination of two spheres of activity normally regarded as separate. The conflation has deeper philosophical ramifications: the lyric poet transgresses the accustomed borders between the two ways of life in a provocative gesture that proclaims the ontological superiority of the *carpe diem* life style.

The devaluation of the heroic in regard to the lyric ethos is also elegantly figured in the so-called Teucer Ode (Horace: *Odes* 1.7), in which a protagonist of the Trojan War experiences an abortive *nostos* that brings him the acute grief of permanent exile from his homeland. By appointing this unlikely hero to be the spokesperson of a quintessentially sympotic response to his lot, Horace dramatizes the exalted place of lyric in his hierarchy of values. The speaker transfigures the epic warrior into an embodiment of the lyric ethos through a speech-act performed by a wreathed symposiast:

> Teucer Salamina patremque
>   cum fugeret, tamen uda Lyaeo
> tempora populea fertur uinxisse corona,
>   sic tristis affatus amicos:
>
> 'Quo nos cumque feret melior fortuna parente,
>   ibimus, o socii comitesque.
> Nil desperandum Teucro duce et auspice Teucro:
>   certus enim promisit Apollo
>
> ambiguam tellure noua Salamina futuram.
>   O fortes peioraque passi
> mecum saepe uiri, nunc uino pellite curas;
>   cras ingens iterabimus aequor.'   (21–32)

> Teucer, though in flight from Salamis and his father,
> nonetheless bound, they say, his wine-soaked temples
> with a poplar wreath, and with these words addressed his
> sad friends: "Wheresoever fortune, better than a father,
> shall take us, we shall go, O comrades and allies. You
> need not despair with Teucer as your leader and
> prophet! For infallible Apollo has promised that there
> shall be a namesake Salamis founded in a new land. O
> men of courage, who have often endured worse
> circumstances with me, now drive away your anxieties
> with wine; tomorrow we shall resume our journey over
> the vast sea."

The embedded speech of the soldier-turned-symposiast recalls the stance of the Archaic lyrist who enunciates the view of the consolatory function of wine in countering the despair that normally attends upon acute misfortune.

The Horatian ode that best exemplifies the worldview in which the symposium trumps the soldier's life is *Odes* 2.7, addressed to the poet's bosom companion, Pompeius. A powerful intertextual link between the two poets occurs in their employment of the motif of the soldier-poet who flagrantly abandons his shield in the midst of battle in order to save his skin. As is well known, the motif originates with Archilochus and becomes conventional in several of his lyric successors (Alcaeus among them). I reproduce the Archilochian prototype:

(5)
ἀσπίδι μὲν Σαΐων τις ἀγάλλεται, ἣν παρὰ θάμνωι,
  ἔντος ἀμώμητον, κάλλιπον οὐκ ἐθέλων·
αὐτὸν δ᾽ ἐξεσάωσα. τί μοι μέλει ἀσπὶς ἐκείνη;
  ἐρρέτω· ἐξαῦτις κτήσομαι οὐ κακίω.

My shield's in the hands of some jubilant Thracian—a
faultless piece of equipment which I left, unwillingly,
beside a bush. Myself, I'm safe. What do I care about
that shield? To hell with it! I'll soon find another one
that's no worse.

Herman Fränkel in his classic and still useful study, *Early Greek Poetry and Philosophy*, has an excellent discussion of the implications of the iconic Archilochian gesture of leaving one's shield behind—a gesture that blatantly devalues the heroic code in favor of what I have been calling the lyric ethos.[5] In Horace's redeployment of the conventional episode, the role of the god Mercury in rescuing the bard from the scene of battle at Philippi is coupled with the allusion to the Archilochus passage:

tecum Philippos et celerem fugam
sensi relicta non bene parmula,
  cum fracta uirtus et minaces
    turpe solum tetigere mento;

sed me per hostis Mercurius celer
denso pauentem sustulit aere,
  te rursus in bellum resorbens
    unda fretis tulit aestuosis.   (9–16)

With you I experienced Philippi and swift flight, my
shield having been left behind unceremoniously, when
our prowess was broken, and menacing warriors touched
the base earth with their chins. But me, overcome with
fear, swift Mercury bore up in a thick cloud through the
enemy lines; while you the wave of warfare sucked back
into the fray and bore over seething waters.

This particular claim of divine intervention finds resonance in a line that occurs in a much mutilated inscription from Archilochus' native Paros, in which there appears to be a reference to Hermes (equivalent to the Roman Mercury) as having saved a warrior from death in battle.[6] Though only a highly plausible restoration by Zielinski, the name Hermes provides further evidence of the dependence of the Augustan poet on Archilochus as a creator of emblematic lyric motifs. In the context of Horace's proclaimed values in the ode to Pompeius, the lyrist represents military campaigns, such as the debacle at Philippi, as an unfortunate hiatus in the pursuit of sympotic pleasures. The safe return of his convivial companion (*sodalis*) from prolonged campaigning enables poet and addressee to resume a way of life that reduces the military pursuit to an aberrant interlude.

Following his Archilochian model, not so much in words as in *weltanschauung*, the Augustan poet posits fear as a grave emotional threat to the lyric system of values. In the extant fragments of Archilochus, rhetorical strategies for exposing the roots of a corrosive and debilitating fear are once again interlinked with the phenomenon of vicissitude, though with a twist. Several fragments attest to the acute fear induced in the human spectator by an abnormal and seemingly contradictory change in the natural order. Fragment 122 incisively illustrates the genesis of this brand of fear, but the presumed identity of the speaker complicates the status of the text as representative, as I would have it, of a basic lyric insight:

(122)

οὐδὲ θαυμάσιον, ἐπειδὴ Ζεὺς πατὴρ Ὀλυμπίων
ἐκ μεσαμβρίης ἔθηκε νύκτ᾽, ἀποκρύψας φάος
ἡλίου †λάμποντος, λυγρὸν† δ᾽ ἦλθ᾽ ἐπ᾽ ἀνθρώπους δέος.
ἐκ δὲ τοῦ καὶ πιστὰ πάντα κἀπίελπτα γίνεται
ἀνδράσιν· μηδεὶς ἔθ᾽ ὑμέων εἰσορέων θαυμαζέτω
μηδ᾽ ἐὰν δελφῖσι θῆρες ἀνταμείψωνται νομὸν
ἐνάλιον, καί σφιν θαλάσσης ἠχέεντα κύματα
φίλτερ᾽ ἠπείρου γένηται, τοῖσι δ᾽ ὑλέειν ὄρος.

> 'Nothing is unexpected, nothing can be shown as
> impossible nor marveled at, since Zeus, the father of the
> Olympians, made night out of noonday, keeping back
> the light of the beaming sun; and upon mankind came
> fear. Henceforth all things are to be believed, all things
> expected by men. None of you should in future be
> amazed, not even to see the beasts change place with
> dolphins and go grazing in the deep, holding the sea's
> resounding billows dearer than land, while dolphins love
> the wooded hills ...'

The quotation marks with which editors conventionally frame this fragment imply acceptance of Aristotle's remark in a famous passage in the *Rhetoric* (1418b.28) to the effect that some matters are better put in the mouth of another person. Specifically, he asserts in regard to this fragment that the persona adopted here is that of a father speaking of his daughter's misconduct. Not surprisingly, most scholars infer that the unnamed father in Aristotle's cryptic account is none other than the notorious victim of Archilochian invective, Lycambes, and that the daughter in question is none other than Neobule (a name elsewhere attested as a target of the poet's invective).[7] The testimony of Aristotle, if indeed it is to taken as "fact" rather than interpretation, would, of course, place the fragment squarely in the realm of invective poetry. My own view accords with that of Campbell: the jury is still out on the identity of the speaking persona. Our uncertainty as to the name of the persona, however, does not invalidate a reading of these lines as a gnomic statement about the genesis of fear in the context of an unexpected natural event. In this particular instance, it is generally accepted in the scholarly literature that a solar eclipse is the phenomenon that injects dread (*deos*) into the hearts of men. Allied to the general fear engendered by the eclipse is the conclusion, on the part of the speaker, that "nothing is unexpected, nothing can be shown as impossible nor marveled at…" The speaker then continues to elaborate on his preamble with a list of conventional *adynata*, or impossible events, that he now reckons are possible and no longer cause for amazement. The rest of the speech is lost except for a few individual words preserved on a papyrus that do not provide substantial information on the further development of the argument. The gist of the preamble, as we have it, is the speaker's reference to the eclipse as validating the global inference that all things are possible and therefore to be expected. In fine, the persona seeks to promote a revised attitude of expectation vis-à-vis our conception of the *adynaton*—a new attitude that he hopes will function as a kind of mental inoculation against the fear humans normally experience when confronted with phenomena in apparent contradiction of nature's laws.[8]

Horace was in all probability influenced by this nexus of Archilochian motifs when he composed the amusing caricature of himself as a challenged Epicurean deviant in *Odes* 1.34:

> Parcus deorum cultor et infrequens,
> insanientis dum sapientiae
>   consultus erro, nunc retrorsum
>   uela dare atque iterare cursus
>
> cogor relictos: namque Diespiter
> igni corusco nubila diuidens
>   plerumque, per purum tonantis
>   egit equos uolucremque currum,
>
> quo bruta tellus et uaga flumina,
> quo Styx et inuisi horrida Taenari
>   sedes Atlanteusque finis
>   concutitur.   (1–12)

> I, a rare and infrequent worshipper of the gods, while
> straying as an adept of a crazed philosophy, am now
> obliged to turn my sails in reverse, and go back over
> courses formerly abandoned: for whereas Jove normally
> splits clouds with his flashing bolts, he has now driven
> his thundering horses and swift chariot through a clear
> sky! This act has shaken up the sluggish earth and the
> meandering streams, Styx no less, and the terrifying
> abode of Taenarus and even the borderlands of Atlas.

Although the Horatian speaker does not actually mention fear as a reaction to the phenomenon of lightning bolts in a cloudless sky, he nonetheless implies, albeit humorously, that a "true" as opposed to an aberrant faith would require one to be alert to the possibility of drastic vicissitude on the natural plane, however bizarre or spectacular a form it might take. Fortified with this insight, it is subtly implied, the ideal lyric speaker should always be fully prepared for the unexpected.[9] The speaker's playful recantation of his philosophically grounded impiety (his adherence to a "crazed philosophy" (*insaniens sapientia*) is meant to underscore his conviction, stated frequently elsewhere in the *Carmina*, that an expectation of change is the cornerstone of wisdom, in so far as it liberates mankind from the stultifying fear of the unknown. Both Horace and his Archaic Greek model take as their point of departure the motif of an abnormal and potentially terrifying natural phenomenon (solar eclipse in the one case, lightning in a clear sky on the other) by way of dramatizing the need to be prepared for any eventuality in the human sphere.

The salient parallels between essential motif patterns that we find in Horace and in extant Archilochian lyric fragments extend to the important realm of the representation of poetic inspiration. In the programmatic ode introducing his first book of *Odes* (1.1) Horace conspicuously singles out the god Dionysus as the main source of his hoped-for success as a lyric poet. The elaborate priamel that structures the ode comes to its pronominal cap in the proclamation:

> me doctarum hederae praemia frontium
> dis miscent superis, me gelidum nemus
> nympharumque leves cum Satyris chori
> secernunt populo ...

> me ivy wreaths, awards for skilled poets, mingle with the
> gods above; me the cool grove and the light songs
> and dances of nymphs joined with satyrs set apart from
> the crowd...

The ivy wreaths and the entourage of nymphs and satyrs unambiguously refer to the god whom Horace here casts as crucial to his poetic program. The Dionysian connection with the central theme of the symposium—the imbibing of wine—is, of course, patent. It is also necessary to emphasize, however, that, for Horace, Bacchus is not only the wine-god, but also the divine source of literary composition.

The place of privilege accorded to Dionysus in Horace's account of his poetic expertise has its counterpart in a famous fragment of Archilochus in which the Greek poet proclaims his credentials:

(120)
ὡς Διωνύσου ἄνακτος καλὸν ἐξάρξαι μέλος
οἶδα διθύραμβον οἴνωι συγκεραυνωθεὶς φρένας.

> ... since I know how to start off the lovely song of lord
> Dionysus, the dithyramb, when my wits are
> thunderstruck with wine.

Especially noteworthy in this two-line fragment is the claim of expert knowledge made by the lyric composer in regard to his poetic craft. The similarities between the two poets' proud display of their poetic credentials are also paralleled at the level of diction, for in a poem describing an uninhibited symposium (*Odes* 3.19) Horace chooses to echo the metaphor of being a bard (*vates*) "thunderstruck" with wine (*attonitus*: line 14), which is a fairly close rendition of Archilochus' συγκεραυνωθεὶς. The particular form of song (*melos*) that Archilochus claims to know in this context is the genre of the dithyramb, which is exclusive to Dionysus. Although the literary form of the dithyramb went through significant evolution from the Greek Archaic period to Horace's day, we can assume, even on the basis of the relatively scattered evidence, that compositions in the genre occupied an elevated stylistic level.[10]

The proud declaration of his "credentials" in dithyrambic composition/performance on Archilochus' part is tantalizingly brief, but we are fortunate to have inscriptional evidence from his native Paros that he may have been responsible for the introduction of the cult of Dionysus on the island. The extra-literary monuments attest, at the very least, to an intimate association between the god and the poet. Above all the fragment, which is the earliest extant reference to the genre of the dithyramb, makes it clear that we are dealing with a type of song (*kalon melos*: "lovely song") that is devoted to the celebration of Dionysus.

A common misconception in the annals of Horatian scholarship on the Odes is that the poet's repeated claim to enjoy a privileged relationship to Bacchus implies unwavering allegiance to light verse. Reinforcing this false assumption is the exegetical cliché that casts Horace's Bacchus-figure as a jolly Roman variation on the formidable Greek divinity. Before demonstrating the close affinity between Horace's Dionysian claims and those of his Archaic Greek predecessor, it will be useful to examine the two *carmina* in which the Roman master portrays an intimate relationship with the Greek god (*Odes* 2.19 and 3.25).

The opening gambit of *Odes* 2.19 unequivocally ascribes to Dionysus/Bacchus the role of teacher and purveyor of esoteric knowledge to his class of nymphs and satyrs.

> Bacchum in remotis carmina rupibus
> vidi docentem—credite posteri—
>   Nymphasque discentes et auris
>   capripedum Satyrorum acutas.

> I have seen Bacchus teaching songs on remote cliffs—
> believe me, posterity—and the nymphs, his pupils, and
> the pointed ears of the goat-footed Satyrs.

On asserting that he has seen Bacchus in person conducting a master-class, the lyrist establishes his credentials as a poet capable of composing a worthy hymn to the god.[11] The subject of the god's instruction, we learn, is none other than *carmina* (songs)—the collective designation that Horace applies to his Odes. The parenthetical apostrophe to future readers (*credite posteri*) is a robust instance of the motif of the poet establishing his "credentials": he has learnt the craft of choral lyric at the very source of divine knowledge.

If the initial strophe enunciates a claim of eyewitness observation of a rehearsal session, the lines that follow make it crystal clear that the speaker is no passive observer, but an active participant in a Dionysian religious community (*thiasos*). As a genuine insider—"participant observer"—rather than merely a chance eaves-dropper, the poet emits the ritual utterance (*euhoe*) that betokens the authentic experience of Dionysian possession (*ekstasis*) (lines 5–8):

> euhoe, recenti mens trepidat metu,
> plenoque Bacchi pectore turbidum
>   laetatur. euhoe, parce, Liber,
>   parce, gravi metuende thyrso.

> euhoe! my mind quivers with a novel fear and a wild
> ecstasy agitates my heart, fully possessed by Bacchus.
> Euhoe! be gentle, Liber, be gentle, O god to be feared
> for your heavy thyrsus!

The rhetorical effect of this claim to ritual possession—the very signature of Dionysian cult—is to *legitimate* the poetic outpouring that occupies the remainder of the *carmen*. It is precisely in order to stress an authorized form of literary production that the speaker reiterates the words *fas* [*est*] (*it is permitted/sanctioned*) in specifying the type of song to be sung (*cantare/iterare*) (9–16) :

> *fas* pervicaces *est* mihi Thyiadas
> vinique fontem lactis et uberes
>   *cantare* rivos atque truncis
>   lapsa cavis *iterare* mella

> *fas* et beatae conuigis additum
> stellis honorem tectaque Penthei
>   disiecta non leni ruina
>   Thracis et exitium Lycurgi.

> *It is sanctioned for me to sing and sing again* of enthused
> Bacchants, of a fountain flowing with wine and copious
> streams of milk, and honey dripping from hollow trunks.
> *It is sanctioned for me also to sing* of the crowning glory
> of a blessed spouse—a glory added to the stars—and of
> Pentheus' palace demolished in a violent overthrow, and
> the destruction of Thracian Lycurgus.

The particular type of *carmen* that has been sanctioned by the "credentials" motif turns out to be on the order of tragic choral lyric. The themes of the speaker's effusions belong to the august domain of Dionysian "resistance" myth (stories of Greek tyrants who reject the new-fangled cult and are duly punished)—a domain that is famously represented in Euripides' *Bacchae*. Commentators have pointed out the actual echoes of Euripidean choral lyric in Horace's account of the miraculous manifestations of Dionysian experience (fountains flowing with wine; copious streams of milk; honey dripping from tree-trunks). So the grandiloquent register characteristic of choral lyric is imitated in the evolving ode with respect to both theme and style. Such discursive heights as the poet now audaciously occupies have been carefully negotiated with the reader in the opening rhetorical moves.[12]

Having annexed choral lyric, the enraptured speaker launches next into a formal hymn to Dionysus that includes, among the glorious exploits of the god, his participation in the Gigantomachia (the battle waged by the Olympian gods against the Giants)—an episode that is traditionally associated with grand style epic discourse (21–5):

> tu, cum parentis regna per arduum
> cohors Gigantum scanderet inpia,
>   Rhoetum retorsisti leonis
>   unguibus horribilique mala;
>
> you also, when the impious band of Giants
> tried to scale the father's kingdom through
> the arduous heights, cast Rhoetus down
> with the claws and dreadful jaw of a lion.

This rhapsodic hymnal passage in praise of the god's accomplishments provides further "proof" of the poet's matriculation as a pupil/devotee of Dionysus: he is capable of producing quasi-liturgical verses of the kind we encounter in the context of choral lyric embedded in Greek tragedy, or in elevated epic discourse on cosmogonic themes, such as we find in Hesiod's *Theogony*. In fine, we are as far removed as can be imagined from any suggestion of a frivolous, downgraded Bacchus.

A very similar turn to an elevated generic plateau characterizes the second ode devoted entirely to Dionysus (3.25), where a set of rhetorical questions addressed directly to the god is posed by an inebriated bard:

> Quo me, Bacche, rapis tui
>   plenum? Quae nemora aut quos agor in specus
> uelox mente noua? Quibus
>   antris egregii Caesaris audiar
>
> aeternum meditans decus
>   stellis inserere et consilio Iouis?

> Where, O Bacchus, are you taking me, fully possessed by
> you? Into what groves, into what caverns, am I being
> driven, at such speed, with a mind that is new? In what
> grottoes shall I be heard rehearsing a song to place the
> eternal glory of illustrious Caesar among the stars and
> the council of Jove?

The speaker's vivid representation of himself as ritually possessed legitimates the abbreviated encomium to Caesar composed in the grand style that is required by the theme.[13] In what amounts to a hymnal prologue, the speaker announces the stylistic heights he is capable of achieving:

> nil parvum aut humili modo,
>   nil mortale loquar.   (17–18)

> nothing trivial or in a pedestrian manner, nothing of
> mortal cast shall I utter.

In sum, Horace pronounces a bold claim to be an authenticated singer of lofty verse—in this case, grand-style praise poetry—a claim analogous to that enunciated in *Odes* 2.19, where the genre in play is choral lyric. In this diptych of Dionysian odes he elevates his tone to a "dithyrambic" level that is consonant with the Archilochian composer of fragment 120 (cited above), who portrays himself as an inspired/inebriated follower of Dionysus. Sporadic excursions into more sublime stylistic terrain on the part of lyric poets serve to establish their poetic versatility. In occasionally donning the mask of Dionysian votary in his *Carmina*, Horace, no less than his great predecessor Archilochus, displays the wide range of his lyric voice.

   The lyric ethos we have been delineating in the Odes is sometimes formulated against the background of opposing attitudes to life. Thus several odes hold up counter-examples to the *carpe diem* philosophy as a way of reinforcing the values of the here and now. *Odes* 1.25, addressed to a hapless female figure, Lydia, presents a salient instance of such a contrapuntal paradigm. The once attractive Lydia is represented as having repudiated the call of Eros in her youth, only to arrive at a pathetic and joyless old age in which a formerly repressed sexual libido returns to haunt her with redoubled force:

> Inuicem moechos anus arrogantis
> flebis in solo leuis angiportu
> Thracio bacchante magis sub inter-
>   lunia uento,

> cum tibi flagrans amor et libido,
> quae solet matres furiare equorum,
> saeuiet circa iecur ulcerosum
>   non sine questu,

laeta quod pubes hedera uirenti
gaudeat pulla magis atque myrto,
aridas frondes hiemis sodali
    dedicet Euro.   (9–20)

In your turn, old and devalued, you will lament in a
deserted alleyway the superciliousness of paramours;
while the Thracian wind steps up its Bacchic orgies with
the advent of moonless skies; meanwhile a blazing
passion and desire, such as normally drives mares to
madness, will run riot in your ulcerous liver, causing you
to complain that joyful youth takes greater pleasure in
green ivy and dark myrtle, and dedicates dry leaves to
the East Wind, winter's drinking companion.

In the speaker's system of metaphors for Lydia's plight, Dionysian rites ("Bacchic orgies") are equated with erotic indulgence, and the sad fate of being excluded from the delights of the symposium is associated with "dry leaves" that betoken advanced age. The castigating tone of these verses certainly has generic affinities with the invective poems of Archilochus, but it is worth noting that Horace's incorporation of "modes of dispraise" into his lyric corpus has the effect of ostensibly blurring the generic line between "iambic" and "lyric."[14]

In this regard Horace is not beyond appropriating the name Neobule, which Archilochus had notoriously conferred upon a female victim of his defamatory verse. He does so, however, in order to further his lyric subtext by transforming the figure of Neobule from an object of verbal abuse to a speaking subject who delivers a brief monologue (*Odes* 3.12), in which she complains about not being free to indulge her passion for a young man named Hebrus:

Miserarum est neque amori dare ludum,
neque dulci mala vino lavere aut ex-
animari metuentes patruae verbera linguae.

Tibi qualum Cythereae puer ales,
tibi tela operosaeque Mineruae
studium aufert, Neobule, Liparaei nitor Hebri,

simul unctos Tiberinis umeros la-
uit in undis...

It is the unhappy plight of maidens neither to give play
to love-making nor to wash down their miseries in sweet
wine, but to waste away dreading an uncle's verbal
lashings. From you, Neobule, Cytherea's winged boy
carries off your wool-basket, your webs, and your pursuit
of industrious Minerva, as soon as Liparean Hebrus has
bathed his gleaming shoulders in the waters of the Tiber ...

Elsewhere in his lyric collection Horace's deploys a contrary rhetorical ploy by emphasizing, rather than blurring, the distinction between iambic and lyric discursive tonalities. This is conspicuously the case of the so-called "palinode" (*Odes* 1.16), which begins with a plea to an unnamed female to put an end to defamatory verses:

> O matre pulchra filia pulchrior,
> quem criminosis cumque uoles modum
>   pones iambis, siue flamma
>   siue mari libet Hadriano.

> O daughter more beautiful than a beautiful mother,
> please put an end to those invective iambic poems in
> whatever way you will, whether with fire or with the
> Adriatic sea.

After inveighing against the dangerous emotion of anger that impels some persons to engage in reckless abuse, he signals his disavowal of iambic and his conversion to a more mellow lyric mode:

> me quoque pectoris
> temptauit in dulci iuuenta
>   feruor et in celeres iambos

> misit furentem. Nunc ego mitibus
> mutare quaero tristia, dum mihi
>   fias recantatis amica
>   opprobriis animumque reddas.   (22–8)

> I, too, in my sweet youthful prime succumbed to
> hot-headed emotions and was driven by anger to
> compose hasty invectives; now I seek to change gloomy
> verses for mild ones, and retract my slurs—provided you
> become my sweetheart and give me back your affection.

By this clever inter-generic stratagem the Horatian persona manages to construct a shifting lyric voice that builds on motifs already present in Archilochian *melos*.[15]

A central tenet of the philosophical outlook germane to lyric song is the devaluation of wealth and its corollary: the extolling of a modest style of living. Modern commentators on Horace's Odes often, and with justification, explain the recurrence of this topos primarily in the context of the Augustan moral program directed against luxury. At the philosophical, as differentiated from the political level, of interpretation, however, Horace's championship of the life of modest means (*paupertas*) is grounded in the perception of the ephemerality of riches and their detrimental effect on mental tranquility. Before examining the Horatian inflexion and elaboration of the disavowal-of-wealth motif, let us briefly unpack the fragmentary Archilochian archetype:

(19)

οὔ μοι τὰ Γύγεω τοῦ πολυχρύσου μέλει,
οὐδ' εἷλέ πώ με ζῆλος, οὐδ' ἀγαίομαι
θεῶν ἔργα, μεγάλης δ' οὐκ ἐρέω τυραννίδος·
ἀπόπροθεν γάρ ἐστιν ὀφθαλμῶν ἐμῶν

I care nothing for the life of Gyges with all his gold, nor
have I ever felt emulous desire; I do not envy the actions
of the gods; I have no craving for a tyrant's greatness,
for all such things are distant from my eyes.[16]

The Lydian ruler Gyges, whose reign was contemporary with Archilochus' *floruit*, is here singled out as the embodiment of excessive wealth. Despite the particularity of the reference, Gyges was by all accounts already a "living legend" before his demise. His precociously proverbial status may be inferred from the generalizing cast of the passage. Thus the scope of the speaker's disavowal includes, but is not limited to, the historical Gyges, and it becomes clear that the ruler is invoked as a representative of a type. What the lyric persona rejects is not simply wealth per se, but a complex of emotions that are commonly associated with contemplation of another's prosperity on the part of the less fortunate. Prominent in this emotional complex are "emulous desire" (*zēlos*), inordinate envy of actions reserved for gods, and a lust for autocratic power ("a tyrant's greatness"). The final line of the fragment portrays the speaker as deliberately distancing himself from such inappropriate desires ("for all such things are distant from my eyes").

The key components in this nexus of disavowed items are reproduced in several signature Horatian odes that unequivocally devalue wealth (*divitiae*) in analogous terms. Amid an abundance of examples I shall concentrate on two odes that feature motifs closely affiliated with those in the basic ensemble highlighted in the Archilochus fragment: *Odes* 1.29 (*Icci beatis*) and *Odes* 2.18 (*Non ebur neque aureum*).

In the short ode addressed to Iccius, the opening line foregrounds the inhabitants of Arabia Felix—a land that in Horace's lyric corpus invariably stands for legendary opulence:

Icci, beatis *nunc* Arabum *inuides*
gazis et acrem militiam paras
    non ante deuictis Sabaeae
        regibus horribilique Medo

nectis catenas?   (1–5)

Iccius, *do you now envy* the Arabians their fortunate store
of treasures and are you preparing to wage war on the
kings of Sabaea, hitherto unconquered, and to join
together chains to shackle the terrifying Medes?

At the very start of the poem the theme of envy (*invidia*) is immediately inter-twined with Iccius' presumed lusting after fabulous loot. The "emulous desire" (*zēlos*) of the Gyges fragment finds its correspondence in the envy that Horace ascribes to a friend who has conspicuously strayed from the path of Socratic wisdom and Stoic enlightenment. The prevailing tone of the ode as a whole makes it clear that the speaker, who has remained faithful to his own philosophi-cal pursuits and lyric ethos, is disappointed at his friend's change of attitude, and is distancing himself from it in no uncertain terms.

In the finale of his implicit critique of Iccius' present desires, the poet professes total surprise that a person who was steeped in the study of philosophy should entertain military ambitions:

> Quis neget arduis
>   pronos relabi posse riuos
>   montibus et Tiberim reuerti,
>
> cum tu coemptos undique nobilis
> libros Panaeti Socraticam et domum
>   mutare loricis Hiberis,
>   pollicitus meliora, tendis?   (10–16)

> Who would deny that rivers in downward course can
> flow backwards up steep mountains, and that the Tiber
> can reverse its course, when you, who showed promise
> of better things, are on the way to exchanging
> Paenaetius' illustrious books, purchased from all over,
> and the writings of the Socratic school for corselets of
> Spanish make?

In what may be fairly described as the signature Horatian ode on the ubiqui-tous theme of devaluation of material possessions (*Odes* 2.18), the anonymity of the addressee serves to focus the reader's attention on the lyric argument, which is elaborated in a particularly graphic style:

> Non ebur neque aureum
>   mea renidet in domo lacunar;
> non trabes Hymettiae
>   premunt columnas ultima recisas
>
> Africa, neque Attali
>   ignotus heres regiam occupaui,
> nec Laconicas mihi
>   trahunt honestae purpuras clientae.   (1–9)

> No ivory or gilded ceiling panels gleam in my house, nor
> are there any beams of Hymettian marble that weigh
> down pillars quarried in far-distant Africa, nor have I

> unexpectedly come into possession of a palace as an heir
> to Attalus, nor do ladies of high birth spin fancy gowns
> of Laconian purple.

The type of the super-rich mogul is represented here by Attalus of Pergamum. As is the case with Archilochus' prototypical evocation of Gyges, the wealth of the Pergamene dynasty had become proverbial in Horace's time, and the epithet "Attalid" was virtually synonymous with legendary riches. Horace had employed the proper epithet in precisely this generic connotation in the inaugural ode of the Tribiblos—a point well grasped by Page who renders the phrase "Attalicis condicionibus" (1.1.12): "in terms such as a Rothschild could offer." [17]

After this very robust disavowal of "conspicuous consumption," the Horatian persona goes on to claim for himself the interior attributes of loyalty and poetic talent (*fides, ingenium*)[18] as inherently superior to external wealth and political power and, in words that distinctly echo the Archilochus fragment, he dissociates himself from any desire to importune the gods:

> At fides et ingeni
>   benigna uena est pauperemque diues
> me petit; *nihil supra*
>   *deos lacesso* nec potentem amicum
>
> largiora flagito,
>   satis beatus unicis Sabinis.   (9–13)

> But devotion and a generous vein of poetic
> talent are mine, and, though my means are modest, the
> wealthy seek out my company; *for nothing more do I
> importune the gods*, nor do I demand more lavish gifts
> from my powerful friend, sufficiently happy as I am with
> my one very special Sabine farm.

In the spirit of Archilochus' vigorous disavowals, the Augustan poet denies any interest in further divine dispensation (cf. "I do not envy the actions of the gods; I have no craving for a tyrant's greatness"). The Sabine Farm—a gift from his super-wealthy patron and close friend Maecenas, is held up as an unpretentious domicile in contrast to the magnificent palatial villas of the Roman aristocracy.[19]

Our comparative overview of ethical stances and motifs shared by Archilochus *lyricus* and Horace in his collection of Odes has sought to document the perception that, as far as Archaic Greek models are concerned, Horatius *lyricus* owes as much to the Parian master as he clearly does to the Lesbian giants Sappho and Alcaeus. This observation is especially cogent in the sphere of articulated world-views, where defining motifs incarnating lyric values that first appear in the extant fragments of Archilochus are prominently adopted in several odes of the Roman lyrist. The list of fundamental interrelated values is substantial: an emotional calculus for dealing with vicissitude (*rhusmos, fortuna*), the sympotic response as antidote to misfortune and hardship, the preservation of life in the here and now as against death in battle (cf. the abandoned shield motif), the appeal to abnormal natural phenomena as furnishing lessons for enlightened human conduct, the proclamation of allegiance to Dionysus as sponsor of inspired *poesis*, the disavowal of excessive wealth. This set of values comprises a system that earns the appellation of a veritable "lyric ethos," one that was first defined for Greco-Roman poetry by Archilochus *lyricus* and that received exquisite reformulation and elaboration in Horatian *melos*.

GUIDE TO FURTHER READING

For philological exegesis of individual fragments of Archilochus, the standard works by West (1974), Campbell (1967) and Gerber (1967) remain indispensable. The extensive commentaries on *Odes* Books 1–3 by Robin Nisbet (with consecutive co-editors M. Hubbard and N. Rudd between 1970 and 2004) are invaluable for their documentation of Greek parallels to passages in the Horatian text, though they do not consistently explore questions of underlying philosophical values and ethos. For the latter, Herman Fränkel's path-breaking study, *Early Greek Poetry and Philosophy* (1975), contains many valuable original insights into the ethos of Archilochus in particular. Several of the major points that inform this synopsis of central Horatian lyric values are more fully developed in my *Polyhymnia: The Rhetoric of Horatian Lyric Discourse* (Davis 1991). The dense volumes of *Enciclopedia Oraziana* dedicated to Horace contain a treasure-trove of studies on various aspects of Horatian lyric by a large array of scholars (see e.g. the entry *melica* by G. Burzacchini).

NOTES

1 I wish to thank Andrew Miller for his constructive feedback on an earlier draft of this essay. Such imperfections that persist in the final version are entirely my responsibility.

2 Though I have provocatively affixed the epithet *lyricus* to Archilochus, it is worth noting that he was not included in the formal Hellenistic canon of the *ennea lyrikoi* (nine lyric poets). The ancient origin of the designation "lyric" and its modern extensions are magisterially discussed by Pfeiffer 1968: 182–3, 205–6. A rationale for a broad definition of *lyrici* as "authors of poetic works whose performance involved song, monodic or choral, accompanied by the lyre or similar stringed instruments," is offered by Burzacchini (1997) under the heading *melica*, p. 68.

3 Greek citations (and numeration) of the Archilochus fragments are from the edition of West 1989–92. English versions of the fragments are from Miller 1996. They are reproduced here with permission of Hackett Publishing Company, Inc.

4   Davis 1991: 167

5   Fränkel 1975: 136–7. See Davis 1991: 89–98 for a discussion of *Odes* 2.7 as a "mode of authentication" of the poet's lyric credentials.

6   See text of the inscription of Sosthenes (A IVa 2-3 = fr. 95 West, lines 2-4).

7   Among commentators Campbell is more cautious than most: "It would be prudent to make no identification at all: it is remarkable that Aristotle himself does not name the father, although he names Charon in connection with fr.22 [19W]" (see Campbell (1967) 154, apropos of fragment 74).

8   Fear as the common or vulgar response to drastic changes in nature is also the subject of another Archilochian fragment (105) which ends in a gnomic utterance: κιχάνει δ' ἐξ ἀελπτίης φόβος ("and out of the unexpected, fear comes on").

9   Cf. "the heart well prepared" (*bene praeparatum/pectus*) of the Licinius ode discussed earlier.

10   For a succinct overview of the evolution of the genre, see the entry by B. Zimmerman in the *OCD* (3rd edn.) under *dithyramb*. For discussion of the epigraphical evidence, see Clay 2001: 110. Cf. also the remarks of T.B.L. Webster in Pickard-Cambridge 1962: 10.

11   Bacchus is depicted in this strophe in the exalted role of *chorodidaskolos*: he is observed in the process of training a chorus composed of nymphs and satyrs. Cf. Fraenkel 1957: 199.

12   See Davis 1984: 107–11.

13   The future cast of the encomium is of the kind that is "voluntative" or self-fulfilling (see Davis 1991: 112).

14   Cf. Davis 1991: 215–24.

15   Horace exploits the posited disjunction between *carmina* and *iambi* in more subtle and humorous terms in *Odes* 1.22 (*Integer vitae*); on which see Davis (1987a) *passim*, with references cited therein.

16   I cite both Greek text and English translation without the customary quotation marks employed by most modern editors in deference to Aristotle's statement that the speaker of these lines is a persona ("Charon the carpenter") other than Archilochus. The attribution of a proxy persona (in the Aristotelian account) does not bear on the authenticity of the lyric sentiments expressed by the "I" in the fragment.

17   See Page 1895 in his commentary on *Odes* 18.5.

18   There may be word-play on *fides*, which can denote the strings of the lyre. In association with poetic talent (*ingenium*) the attributes take on the color of melic skill. Yet another layer of interpretation would arise from the possibility that the phrase constitutes a hendiadys ("devotion in the pursuit of poetic talent").

19   Some scholars have been disposed to challenge Horace's claim that the Sabine estate reflects *paupertas*. For an up-to-date review of the presumed scale of Horace's "Sabine Villa" on the basis of the complex archaeological evidence, see the essay by Bernard Frischer in this volume (Chapter 4).

CHAPTER SEVEN

Horace and Lesbian Lyric*

Jenny Strauss Clay

In dealing with Horace's relation to Early Greek Lyric, we are at a tremendous disadvantage before we even begin, since our knowledge of this body of poetry is, with the exception of Pindar (but even there the manuscript tradition is limited to the epinicians), fragmentary, based in large part on bits of papyrus from the garbage heaps of Egypt, potsherds, grammarians, and anthologists. Doubtless, Horace had in his library the complete works of Sappho and Alcaeus—perhaps purchased during his school days in Athens—as well as the other canonical lyrists. Recent publications of new finds reveal the breadth of the Roman poet's knowledge of this literature that has come down to us in scraps and snippets. But Horace encountered these texts as they were canonized, classified, arranged, edited, and commented upon by the great Alexandrian scholars, many of whom were themselves also poets.

The debate pitting a classicizing—or from our vantage, an archaizing—Horace against a Callimachean one has runs its course; the acknowledgment of the sophistication of Greek lyric has made the old naive/sentimental dichotomy obsolete.[1] It is, to be sure, impossible to ignore the mediation of Hellenistic editorial activity and the influence of Alexandrian poetics, a poetics that embraced the short but highly sophisticated style predicated upon an audience capable of appreciating its subtle games and that both incorporated and nervously looked back at the classical past. Admittedly, all these features are present in Horace's lyric, but we should nevertheless admire the boldness of Horace's attempt to reach back beyond Alexandria to a Greek world remote both in time and in its cultural institutions. What attracted Horace was more than a sense of returning to the roots of his own literary tradition. After all, Ennius had already claimed the title of the Roman Homer. Horace's specific choice of importing first Archilochus and then the Lesbian poets Sappho and Alcaeus was grounded in his conception of the role of the poet and poetry in civil society. For this the bookish

Alexandrians did not offer a model, nor did the neoterics who ostentatiously turned their backs on politics and public life to cultivate their cliquish aesthetics of refinement. To be sure, Horace's friend Vergil, bold in his own way (*audax iuventa*, *Georgics* 4.565), had from the first found a way to integrate Rome (*urbem quam dicunt Romam*, *Ec.* 1.19) and the great world into Greek bucolic landscapes. But Horace's choice of models allowed him to speak as citizen and poet addressing his countrymen as an equal. In addition, it allowed him to level the social hierarchies and the disparities built into the Roman system of patronage and *clientelae*.[2] Already in *Epodes* 7 and 16, Horace had presented himself as addressing the Roman people and both diagnosing the cause of civil strife and proposing a solution—albeit a fantastical one—to escape from a Rome doomed to fratricidal destruction. The podium from which he spoke and the procedures he adopted do not quite mesh with any recognizable Roman institution, which has caused some critical consternation.[3] But Horace's strategy here is paradigmatic also for the Odes: he has in fact adapted to a Roman context a Greek institution, much like the Athenian assembly, where any citizen could speak and propose a motion. The resultant hybrid constitutes a mythical beast whose fluctuating image simultaneously alludes to an ideal while revealing its impossibility.

The setting where most early Greek poetry was performed offered Horace an environment where he could develop his authoritative voice:

> The Greek *symposium* was essentially a meeting of equals, in which social gradations were ignored; even the Hellenistic king at his *symposium* was expected to behave as if he were an equal, and to welcome the *parrhesia* (free speech) of his drinking companions. In contrast the Roman *convivium* was often arranged hierarchically, with couches ranked in order of importance, the *clientes* stacked 'five to a couch' and served inferior food and drink.[4]

The poetry traditionally associated with the Roman convivium, the *carmina convivalia*, apparently involved the praise of famous men, perhaps in an epic manner; Horace himself seems to allude to such songs in his last ode (4.15.29–32).[5] For the Greeks, however, almost all the monodic poetry of the archaic period was performed in a sympotic context. It ranged in subject matter from songs of love and wine, politics, current events, and martial exhortations, to scabrous mimes, consolations, and quiet reflections on the vicissitudes of human life. To be sure, Catullus and his circle had revived the sympotic ambience for their poetry, but they limited themselves to matters of private concern and the more restricted world of the Hellenistic epigrammatic tradition. The Alexandrians composed elegiac verses on sympotic subjects such as wine and love, but these were not sung, but rather were "pseudo-performances composed as book poetry and only fictionalized as song."[6] Horace's symposium is equally fictional; he neither sang nor played the lyre. However, he found in the earlier Greek symposium not only a far more inclusive range of subjects, embracing both the public and the private sphere, but also a setting in which he could speak authoritatively and on an equal footing with a Maecenas or even an Augustus and hold forth on affairs of state. Again Murray:

> Perhaps most important of all was Horace's recognition that the symposium could give to the poet himself a role which would restore to him that social equality and that literary authority which he had lost in the transition of poetry from Greece to Rome.[7]

In addition to allowing Horace to construct an imagined *hetairia* of *philoi*, the symposium with its range of subject matter, both political and private, and social equality based on friendship and common goals, was from its inception a self-conscious institution, a *spectaculo a se stesso*, as Rossi has called it,[8] where the songs sung and the drinking vessels themselves mirrored the activities of the participants. Horace's meta-sympotic poems offer an imaginative reconstruction of an idealized symposium that lent itself to the creation of a setting for a self-reflexive meditation on poetry and its role in a Rome that was rapidly changing and moving into unknown political and social territory.[9]

Finally, the very occasionality of Greek lyric exerted a special attraction for Horace. The specificity of the moment that occasioned the poem, whether an anniversary, the arrival of spring, or the return of the *princeps*—such temporally defined events could be exploited as a stimulus, whether real or fictive, for meditation on that dominant theme of the Odes: time. Temporal indicators like *iam, nunc, dum, nondum,* and adjectives such a *tempestivus* or *decens,* which more often than not indicate temporal appropriateness, are pervasive. To be sure, early Greek lyric, however occasional, also provided for its own re-performance—one thinks of Sappho 1 with its exemplary eternal return of the same. Moreover, the constitution of the sympotic group, whether Alcaeus' *hetairia* or the Sapphic *thiasos,* allowed for a certain degree of continuity that could lead to the re-elaboration of identifiable motifs: for example, the repeated use of nautical imagery to characterize the political fortunes of Alcaeus' group or even the use of stock characters like the Archilochian Lykambes. Horace, however, encountered these poems through the ultimate medium of re-performance: the written text always available, but also removed from the instant of its performance, whether real or imagined. If, moreover, he could not rely on the continuity of his audience, the editorial and poetic practices of his Alexandrian predecessors made possible Horace's exploitation of the poetic sequence and the arrangement of the large-scale poetic book. Yet, however much Horace may mention song and lyre, his readers are obliged—and perhaps even encouraged—to reconstitute the absent music. Moreover, the fictional presence of the addressee points to the absence of the occasion.[10] Only rarely does Horace allude to or dramatize the presence of multiple participants (e.g. 1.27, 1.36, 1.37, 2.7).[11] The lack of music and a genuine sympotic circle brings about a characteristic but anomalous situation: the solitary symposium (e.g. 1.38; cf. 3.14) or at most a symposium *à deux* (e.g. 1.9, 1.11, 1.20, 3. 28) which at once provides a sense of intimacy and an awareness of its loss.

Horace *epistles* 1.19.21–33

In *Epistles* 1.19 addressed to Maecenas and composed after the appearance of his first three books of Odes, Horace offers his most sustained reflections on his relation to his models, Archilochus and the Lesbian poets Sappho and Alcaeus. The passage occurs in a context in which Horace rails against the "servile herd" (*servum pecus*, 1.19.19) of poetasters who can only slavishly and superficially imitate other poets, but even then, only manage to imitate their vices. The well-known lines that follow are worth quoting in full (21–33):

> Libera per uacuum posui uestigia princeps,
> non aliena meo pressi pede. Qui sibi fidet,
> dux reget examen. Parios ego primus iambos
> ostendi Latio, numeros animosque secutus
> Archilochi, non res et agentia uerba Lycamben;   25
> ac ne me foliis ideo breuioribus ornes
> quod timui mutare modos et carminis artem,
> temperat Archilochi Musam pede mascula Sappho,
> temperat Alcaeus, sed rebus et ordine dispar,
> nec socerum quaerit, quem uersibus oblinat atris,   30
> nec sponsae laqueum famoso carmine nectit.
> Hunc ego, non alio dictum prius ore, Latinus
> uolgaui fidicen ...

> I was a leader in setting my footsteps freely in unoccupied territory
> and did not press my foot in others' tracks. The man who has
> self-confidence will rule the hive. I was the first to show forth
> Parian iambus to Latium, following the meter and spirit of
> Archilochus, but not his subject-matter and the words that
> hounded Lycambes; and in case you would adorn me with a lesser
> crown because I was afraid to change his meters and poetic
> technique, manly Sappho tempered Archilochus' Muse with her
> meters; Alcaeus did too, but differing [from Archilochus] in
> subject matter and arrangement of material, he does not seek out
> a father-in-law to tar with black verses nor with his notorious
> poem tie a noose for his betrothed. Him, not proclaimed before
> by another tongue, I a Latin lyrist made known.

In what Fraenkel (1957: 342) calls "one of the most controversial passages in Latin poetry," Horace first claims to have demonstrated his independence, not by following in the footsteps of others, but by confidently breaking new

ground. But he goes on to declare proudly that he was the first to bring Archilochian iambus into Latin. At first glance this statement seems contradictory, for
how can Horace both strike out on his own and *follow* the "the numbers and
spirit" of his model Archilochus? But the contradiction exists only if one misinterprets Horace's understanding of imitation: Horace's claim to innovation is
twofold: he was the first to import Parian iambus into Latin, but he also asserts
that he altered it, by following the meters and spirit of Archilochus, but not his
subject matter. Now the argument becomes more difficult; people may belittle
Horace's accomplishment and blame him for his timidity in retaining Archilochus' meters and style.[12] The self-confidence of Horace's opening claim (*qui sibi
fidet*) seems at odds with such an accusation of timidity and even more with its
acknowledgement. The even thornier lines that follow have given rise to a thicket
of controversy, which cannot be fully addressed here. These difficulties arise
because of the compression of Horace's argument, an argument that I believe
can nevertheless be retrieved. Moreover, the issues raised are critical for understanding how Horace conceived of his evolution as a poet from the Epodes to
the Odes.

In these lines Horace defends himself against the charges of his detractors
by citing precedents, in fact, the unimpeachable precedence of Sappho and
Alcaeus. Their dealings with Archilochus ultimately—though not immediately—
justify Horace's own. Thus Horace claims that he follows the lead of no less
than universally acknowledged masters (*mascula Sappho*!). So what in this
reading did Sappho and Alcaeus do? They toned down Archilochus' poetry, and
they did so by also using different meters, in fact, their own Aeolic meters:
animi and *numeri* go together. In moderating the spirit of Archilochian iambus,
the Lesbian poets also modified his meters. Thus they differed from Archilochus
(I take *dispar* not contrasting Alcaeus with Sappho, but contrasting them with
Archilochus) both in his contents (*rebus*),[13] which did not deal with abusing
father-in-laws and driving girls to suicide, and in his arrangement of material
(*ordine*).

If we take Horace's argument to end here, we are left with an insoluble contradiction; after all, Alcaeus, and presumably Sappho too, changed the subject
matter of Archilochus' iambus, as did Horace. But whereas Horace kept both
the iambist's meter and his spirit, the Lesbians did not. Therefore, they cannot,
at least on the surface, offer a model for what Horace did; like Io in Housman's
"Fragment of a Greek Tragedy," there seems no reason to mention them at all,[14]
and doing so leaves Horace's defense in shambles. But not if we understand why
Horace appeals to his Lesbian models here: they understood an essential principle: that a change in spirit (*Archilochi Musam*) correctly entails a change in form
(*pede*). Furthermore, when, as Horace continues, he later took Alcaeus as his
model and disseminated his poetry in Rome, his policy was exactly the same as
his earlier strategy with Archilochus. Not only did the Roman lyrist retain his
model's meters, he was also vociferously proud of that achievement as he

triumphantly boasts in *Odes* 3.30: *princeps Aeolium carmen ad Italos/ deduxisse modos* ("I was the first to have brought Aeolic song to Italian measures"). Horace implies that he also followed Alcaeus' spirit (though clearly not his material, e.g. attacks on the tyrant Myrsilos). If, Horace suggests to his critics, you blame me for being afraid to change Archilochus' meters, then you would have to fault me equally for adopting Aeolic meters when I took Alcaeus as my model—but no one would do that. You have not understood, you slavish herd, the difference between intelligent and mindless imitation, nor do you recognize that the form or meters of poetry go hand in hand with their spirit.

If this interpretation of the Horatian passage is persuasive (and other readings are either contradictory, or assume that Horace accepts the criticism leveled by his detractors,[15] or involve an excessively technical understanding of the relationship of Aeolic to epodic meters,[16] which I do not believe was on Horace's mind), it constitutes an important statement—and it must be remembered, a retrospective statement, which may not be fully "accurate"—of what Horace saw as his development when he looked back over his poetic career.

For our purposes, what matters is the implication of a certain degree of continuity between the Epodes and the Odes, a continuity not so surprising when one considers the clear links Horace established between the two collections. To enumerate only the most obvious: *Odes* 1.37 answers *Epodes* 9; we may also note the inclusion of several poems in epodic meters among the Odes (e.g. 1.4). More complex, but I believe crucial for an understanding of the interactions between these two works, are the intertextual relations Horace establishes between the Epodes, especially *Epodes* 17 that concludes the collection and *Odes* 1.16, which explicitly mentions the earlier iambic Horace and his present rejection of the *ira* that armed his previous *iambi* (cf. *A.P.* 79), as well as the whole sequence of poems embracing *Odes* 1.14–1.17.

Odes 1–3

Yet in his first lyric collection, Horace's ambitions went well beyond Archilochian iambus and Lesbian lyric. It encompassed the entire canon of the Greek lyric poets (itself to be sure a Hellenistic invention) including, above all—despite occasional demurrals—the prince of poets, Pindar himself. But in a Callimachean gesture the Theban Eagle was tamed and accommodated into Aeolic quatrains. In the dedicatory poem to Maecenas, the opening priamel begins with a nod to Pindar through a description of Olympic chariot races whose victors are raised to the level of the gods (*evehit ad deos*, 1.1.6). This ability to bestow divine status, even if only momentarily, on victorious athletes is a hallmark of Pindaric epinician. At the end of the ode, when Horace speaks of himself, his claim seems at first more modest: his poetry, which he identifies with the Lesbian *barbitos*, while distancing him from the pursuits of others, brings him close to the gods (*dis miscent superis,* 1.1.30; cf. *evehit ad deos,* 1.1.6). In laying claim to such intimacy with the divine, Horace suggests that he may in fact surpass Pindar. However, the grandeur of Horace's closing ambition—to be included within the lyric canon—is abruptly deflated by a grotesque image of apotheosis (cf. *evehit ad deos!*): his banging his head on the starry firmament.[17] Horace continues his unfortunate poetic flight with an even more fantastic representation of his lyric ambition at the close of his second book (2.20): the poet feels goose flesh forming and feathers sprouting between his fingers as he morphs into a swan soaring over the ill-omened Icarian sea (cf. 4.2.2–4). Only in the final poem, 3.30, does he pronounce his ambition fulfilled and his mission accomplished as he orders the Muse with a Pindaric flourish to crown him with the Delphic laurel, simultaneously vatic and triumphal. The basis of this sublime triumph, however, remains the boast of bringing Aeolic poetry to Rome (3.30.13–14):

> princeps Aeolium carmen ad Italos
> deduxisse modos.

> I was the first to have brought Aeolic song to Italian measures.

The tension between expansive Pindaric ambition and the more limited Aeolic form has a Callimachean flavor. But the playful contrast masks an even greater but still Callimachean aspiration: to incorporate the whole canon of lyric poetry into the circumference of Latin Aeolic.[18] The diverse metrical schemes of the Greek lyricists were rendered into a fairly limited number of Aeolic verse forms. But the scope of Horace's ambition has already been hinted at in *Odes* 1.1.52–3 in the chiastic reference to Polyhymnia and the *tibiae* of choral lyric. We are dealing here not with a Hellenistic *Kreuzung der Gattungen,* but with a far bolder generic imperialism in which Roman Aeolic swallows up the entire tradition of Greek lyric. And in what must be a self-fulfilling prophecy, unique in literary history, this would-be prophet of the Muses finally performs a choral celebration *rite greco,* Pindaric in its pomp, but Sapphic in its meter, in a novel ceremony purporting to be an ancient one, before the assembled citizenry in Rome inaugurating the new age: the *Carmen Saeculare.*

To return to the compass of the first book of Odes, sustained reference to Aeolic lyric returns in *Odes* 1.32, a hymn to the *barbitos,* first tuned by the *Lesbius civis,* a poem that has not won much favor from critics.[19] It begins with a self-depreciating (perhaps Catullan) gesture (*lusimus tecum*) and the hope that this Latin song will live "for this year and more."[20] But the focus of the poem is not, as has sometimes been held, amatory verse,[21] but rather involves the tonal shifts so characteristic of Horace's poetry. The mention of Alcaeus as a citizen of Lesbos, actively involved with the political turmoil of his day, sets his music and erotic verse as a comfort and respite from toil[22] and thus anticipates the grandiose final stanza of the lyre's aretalogy. In a Pindaric gesture, as Apollo's glory (*decus*

Phoebi), it soars to Olympus to adorn the feasts of Jupiter, and among mortals it grants sweet alleviation from suffering and cares. In this capacity, it is the poet's prerogative as *vates* to invoke its blessings, which tightly links this ode to the one that precedes (*poscit Apollinem/vates*, 1.31.1; *poscimus*, 1.32.1).

Sappho and Alcaeus

If in 1.32 Horace presented Alcaeus as both the poet of public political and private erotic poetry, in 2.13 he brings on the two Lesbian poets, Sappho and Alcaeus, and splits the two poetic arenas between them, aligning Sappho with the private erotic and restricting Alcaeus to his civic voice.[23] Neither characterization seems especially apt or accurate, but it is important to understand Horace's purpose in creating this *synkrisis*. While the scholarly consensus holds that the poem is meant as a "glorification of Alcaeus,"[24] this misreads the poetic strategy.

2.13 opens with a hyperbolic curse on the man who planted the tree whose fall almost killed Horace. This near-fatal accident leads Horace to a vision of the underworld where we discover Sappho and Alcaeus singing among the shades (21–32):

> Quam paene furvae regna Proserpinae
> et iudicantem uidimus Aeacum
>   sedesque descriptas[25] piorum et
>   Aeoliis fidibus querentem
>
> Sappho puellis de popularibus
> et te sonantem plenius aureo,
>   Alcaee, plectro dura nauis,
>   dura fugae mala, dura belli.
>
> Vtrumque sacro digna silentio
> mirantur umbrae dicere, sed magis
>   pugnas et exactos tyrannos
>   densum umeris bibit aure uolgus.

> How near I was to seeing the realms of dark Proserpina
> and Aeacus passing judgment and the seats allocated to
> the blessed and Sappho bewailing on the Aeolian lyre
> the girls of Lesbos; and you, Alcaeus, proclaiming in
> more full-bodied strain with your golden plectrum, the
> hardships aboard ships, the evil hardships of exile and of
> war. The shades marvel at both as they sing songs
> worthy of sacred silence, but the crowd thronging
> shoulder to shoulder drinks in with its ears preferring
> battles and tyrants driven out.

The intimate feminine contents of Sappho's querulous tunes, whether erotic or not, offer a sharp contrast to Alcaeus' more full-bodied, perhaps in a grander style (*plenius*), masculine hardships. From the songs' contents, we turn to their effect on their audiences: Alcaeus' *stasiotika* are mobbed by a greater throng with his fans pressing tightly to imbibe his rousing accounts of battles and tyrants overthrown.[26] But then (33–40):

> Quid mirum, ubi illis carminibus stupens
> demittit atras belua centiceps
> 　　auris et intorti capillis
> 　　　　Eumenidum recreantur angues?
>
> Quin et Prometheus et Pelopis parens
> dulci laborum decipitur sono
> 　　nec curat Orion leones
> 　　　　aut timidos agitare lyncas.
>
> What wonder, when marveling at the former songs, the
> hundred-headed beast relaxes his black ears, and the
> snakes entwined in the hair of the Furies are refreshed?
> Why even Prometheus and Pelops' father [Tantalus] are
> distracted from their toils by the sweet sound, nor does
> Orion care to hunt his lions or timid lynxes.

These two concluding stanzas are chiastic and pick up on Sappho and the effects of *her* music,[27] which is not as great a crowd-pleaser nor as rousing as the songs of her compatriot, but it lulls—even managing to soothe the hound of hell—and brings respite to the snakes entwined in the Furies' hair. The sweet sound (*dulci ... sono*)—as opposed to Alcaeus' *dura*—beguiles even the great sinners so that they forget their eternal woes. At the ode's conclusion, then, the soothing power of "Sapphic" music succeeds in calming the tormented in hell and the spirits of revenge—as well as the previously irate poet himself: *laborum dulce lenimen.*

If a programmatic statement concerning his poetic models is implied, one could argue that Horace, here at least, awards the palm to Sappho. To strengthen the case, one could also point to the immediately preceding poem where Horace rejects the suitability of three stanzas worth of battles to *mollibus ... citharae modis* (2.12.1–12) *and* manages to smuggle several Sapphic echoes into his praise of Licymnia.[28] While 2.12 alludes to Sappho, the poem that follows 2.13, the Postumus ode, contains clear echoes of Alcaeus,[29] which again suggests that any simple differentiation or hierarchization of Horace's Lesbian models misses the point. We may also note that Book 2 as a whole avoids political topics after the initial ode to Pollio where Horace rather disingenuously retreats to *modos leviore plectro*—since the second book contains poetry far from light verse but rather some of his most famous ethical poetry. Once we dispense with interpreting 2.13 as a pledge of allegiance to either of Horace's models (while incorporating both), we can begin to see how the poem works as a whole: the emphasis on Sappho's calming music at the end counters the blustering anger of the beginning. The wildly exaggerated curse recalls the abuse of the Epodes, especially the parodic *schetliasmos* of *Epodes* 3 against the dire effects of garlic, and suggests that the soothing character of lyric can counter iambic vituperation.[30]

Arte allusiva

Horace's explicit references to his lyric models must be filled out with an examination of his art of allusion. Only a sampling of his modes of echoing, adapting, evoking, inverting, and subverting his poetic forbears can be treated here. One long-recognized characteristic of Horace's style is his use of an opening tag or motto drawn from Greek lyric.[31] Horace was by no means the first to use this trope, which can be documented in earlier Roman as well as Hellenistic poetry. The practice may even go back to archaic poetry itself when an opening tag, perhaps from Homer or Hesiod or another predecessor, may have been thrown out as a challenge for sympotic improvisation; Mimnermus' reflections on Homer (fr. 2 West), Alcaeus' lyrical rendering of Hesiod (347a V.), and Solon's "correction" of Mimnermus (fr. 20 West) may serve as examples. Moreover, papyrus registers reveal that poems were catalogued and identified by their *incipits*.[32] For a Roman poet, the use of such mottos declared generic allegiance to the Greek tradition and at the same time a translation to a new context and frequently the challenge of retaining the original meter. Despite the fragmentary state of our sources that often hinders analysis of these Horatian strategies, it is nevertheless evident that initial mottos are most prominent in the first book of the Odes and diminish thereafter. For example, 1.18 begins with the line:

> Nullam, Vare, sacra vite prius severis arborem
>
> Plant no tree, Varus, before the sacred vine

that translates and retains the meter of Alcaeus fr. 342 V.:

> Μηδὲν ἄλλο φυτεύσῃς πρότερον δένδρεον ἀμπέλω
>
> Plant no other tree before the vine.

Horace's additions here, the name of Varus (we cannot be certain which Varus is meant), and *sacra*, seem minor, but what follows emphasizes a Roman landscape. Unfortunately we do not have the rest of Alcaeus' poem; the theme, praise of wine followed by a warning and exhortation to moderation, appears conventional. But Horace's seemingly insignificant addition of *sacra* becomes central as the poem progresses; *fas atque nefas* (10) point to the barbaric overstepping of religious boundaries while under the influence, as does the reference to the violation of the sacred mysteries of Bacchus. The god himself progresses over the course of the poem from Roman to Greek, from the comfortable *Bacche pater* to the liberating *Liber*, then the punitive *Euhius* of the Maenads' cry, to the Thracian Bassareus of mystery cult and the ecstatic instruments of Cybele in whose procession follow blind Self-love, empty-headed Vainglory, and Fidelity, who, more transparent than glass, babbles away the secrets entrusted to her. Horace has nicely inverted the proverbial—and Alcaic—notion of wine as the mirror and revealer of men's souls (fr. 333 V.) by transferring its transparency to Fidelity, who is usually veiled (cf. *Odes* 1. 35.21–2). The liberator from cares has become the betrayer of secrets; the sacred vine, the desecrator of divine mysteries.

The so-called Cleopatra Ode (1.37) provides another well-known example of the motto technique:

> Nunc est bibendum, nunc pede libero …
>
> Now we must drink, now with foot liberated …

And the Alcaic (332 V.):

> νῦν χρῆ μεθύσθην καί τινα πρὸς βίαν
> πώνην, ἐπεὶ δὴ κάτθανε Μύρσιλος.
>
> Now we must get drunk and drink with all our might
> Since Myrsilos is dead.

The boisterous partisanship of the Lesbian poet is somewhat muted, although Horace's apostrophe to his *sodales* links him to the *hetairia*, whose presence Alcaeus can take for granted and therefore does not need to mention.[33] But Horace recasts the celebration in public Roman and religious terms (*pulvinar deorum, Saliaribus dapibus, nefas*) and transfers the drunkenness (*fortunaque dulci/ ebria, mentemque lymphatam Mareotico*) to the Egyptian queen. After the Alcaic opening, we immediately expect to hear whose death precipitates the festivities, but we wait rather a long time for the other shoe to drop; and when it does, Horace has manipulated us so that we celebrate not so much the death of an enemy as Cleopatra's triumph in her death (*superbo/ non humilis mulier triumpho*). Here as so often with the Augustan poets, the closer the opening echo of a model, the more surprising the subsequent development.

Odes 1.9 may represent the first exploitation of an Alcaic tag in the Odes, although once again, we have only the opening of Alcaeus' poem (338 V.) and cannot know how it progressed.[34] The following poem, 1.10, a hymn to Mercury that concludes Horace's tour de force parade of meters and which ancient sources connect closely with a hymn to the same divinity that stood second in the Alexandrian edition of Alcaeus' poetry book (cf. 308 V.), draws upon materials from a range of sources.[35] Coming on the heels of 1.9, this poem—perhaps not accidentally—characterizes the god, whom Horace has previously identified as the inventor of the lyre as (1.10.7–8):

> callidum quiquid placuit iocoso
>   condere furto ...

> clever to hide whatever he wished in a playful theft ...

The next stanza elaborates on the theme: as we play hide-and-seek through Horace's devious syntax, tracking Apollo's stolen cows, the older god's threats dissolve into harmless laughter. The incident calls to mind the elder Seneca's dictum, perhaps the best ancient definition of *arte allusiva* (*Suas.* 3.7): *non subripiendi causa, sed palam mutuandi, hoc animo ut vellet agnosci.* ("not in order to steal, but in order to borrow openly, with the intention of being recognized").[36] Horace, who elsewhere identifies himself as a *Mercurialis vir*, invites us to discover here—as well as in his immediately previous and earliest unmistakable *incipit* borrowed from Alcaeus in *Odes* 1.9—allusions to Horace's own playful thefts (*iocosa furta*) from his chosen model, Alcaeus.[37] We might say that Horace here puts the *ludus* back into allusion.

Odes 1.14 has been an object of various revisionist interpretations,[38] but here the relation to Alcaeus strikes me as decisive for an understanding of the ode as a political allegory.[39] Unlike the motto technique, on this occasion Horace seems to combine material from several Alcaic poems (*contaminatio*) but, as usual, puts a new twist on his sources. Both 208 V. and 6 V. describe a ship at sea, caught in a storm and badly damaged, seen from the perspective of those on board with whom the speaker identifies himself ("we"). In his discussion of Homeric allegoresis, Heraclitus (first century CE?) cites both poems as exemplary models of allegory (*Prob. Hom.* 5). In the first fragment, "we are borne in the middle [of the storm] along with the ship," which is taking water while the sails are in tatters. In the latter poem, the crew is urged to strengthen the hull and to make for a safe port; the exhortation to remember past hardships and not to dishonor their noble fathers as well as the reference to *monarchia* make clear that we are dealing with political allegory referring to Alcaeus' *hetairia*. A more difficult third fragment, 73 V., involves a battered ship personified as a woman who "struck by a wave no longer wishes to fight against the rain ..." The following lines appear to dismiss the ship and her woes (and the variant νό]στου λελάθων, "let's forget about our return home" guarantees the political metaphor[40]) as the speaker urges his *philoi* "to enjoy yourselves while young, along with Bycchis ..."

Again, the fragmentary state of the Alcaic corpus makes it difficult to trace specific borrowings, but if we admit that Horace drew his inspiration from these poems (and perhaps others), we can observe some telling differences. While Alcaeus pictured himself along with his companions on board a ship that presumably represents his *hetairia* or political faction, the speaker of 1.14 is an observer on dry land; but as Quintilian claims, Horace's ship represents the *res publica* as a whole rather than a specific political party.[41] Horace thus draws attention to the difference between himself and his model's fierce and partisan involvement in the political turmoil of sixth-century Lesbos; here Horace observes, but does not fight. From the shore, Horace watches with alarm as the battered vessel apparently heads out to sea again, although scarcely seaworthy, and urges her to make for port without delay. In 73 V., Alcaeus turned from the damaged vessel (i.e., the battered fortunes of his political partisans) personified as a woman, and encouraged his companions to forget their woes and to enjoy themselves. In Horace, the speaker likewise announces a change of heart, making clear that the ship is not really a ship: formerly she filled him with disgust and weariness, but she has now been transformed into an object of longing and care. Horace thus rewrites Alcaeus by detaching himself from his model's partisan involvement while at the same time reversing the vector of Alcaeus' emotional attachment. If the Greek poet commended to his friends at least a momentary breather from civil strife, Horace here declares a new-found commitment to the welfare of the body politic that, in opposition to the despair of the Epodes, comes to characterize his stance in the Odes.

Horatius sapphicus

Let me now turn to two of Horace's Sapphic poems that both—in very different ways—play complex intertextual games with *phainetai moi* (31 V.) and thus inevitably with Catullus 51 and, in the case of 4.1, also with Horace's own earlier lyric and Sappho 1.

> Cum tu, Lydia, Telephi
>   ceruicem roseam, cerea Telephi
> laudas bracchia, uae, meum
>   feruens difficili bile tumet iecur.
>
> tum nec mens mihi nec color
>   certa sede manet, umor et in genas
> furtim labitur, arguens
>   quam lentis penitus macerer ignibus. (*Odes* 1.13.1–8)

> When you, Lydia, praise the rosy neck of Telephus and waxen arms of Telephus, alas, my liver swells boiling in indigestible bile. Then neither my mind nor color remains in its proper place, and moisture secretly trickles down my cheeks, revealing how I am simmered to the core by slow fires.

Many scholars have detected the Sapphic source for the speaker's symptoms,[42] but several are more visceral, a trait whose significance remains to be interpreted. Moreover, Horace's scenario is completely at odds with his model.[43] In Sappho "that man"—if present at all rather than hypothetical—functions as an imperturbable foil to the speaker's complete loss of all sensory functions: hearing seeing, and speaking.[44] In Horace, the rival, here absent, and the girl are immediately given names, and Lydia's speech, which continually harps on Telephus' name and erotic attractions, is not only heard, but is the cause of the speaker's violent reaction. Moreover, the Horatian persona not only perceives the girl, but voyeuristically interprets the marks on her shoulders and lips as signs of sexual violence. Finally, the jealous anger of the opening stanzas—and their reference to a bilious disposition—undermines the promise of love "till-death-do-us-part" of the close. However we interpret the poem, the ironical self-presentation takes us a long way from Sappho.

Ten years after the publication of the first three books of Odes, Horace returned to lyric. In the programmatic first poem of Book 4, that return is put in Sapphic terms in a variegated intertextual fabric that looks back at his own earlier lyric production and forward to the collection that simultaneously takes up a more overtly Pindaric stance and revisits sympotic and erotic themes.[45]

> Intermissa, Venus, diu
>   rursus bella moues? Parce precor, precor.
> non sum qualis eram bonae
>   sub regno Cinarae. desine, dulcium
>
> mater saeua Cupidinum,
>   circa lustra decem flectere mollibus
> iam durum imperiis: abi,
>   quo blandae iuuenum te reuocant preces.
>
> Are you, Venus, again taking up wars long interrupted? I
> beg you, beseech you, spare me. I am not the man I was
> in the reign of my good Cinara. Desist, savage mother of
> sweet Cupids, bringing me, already stiff at fifty years, to
> my knees with your soft commands. Take yourself off to
> where the tender entreaties of the young call you.

The lyric campaigns of Venus, long in abeyance, have returned "again"—not surprising, since they were only interrupted, *intermissa. rursus* evokes δηὖτε, a hallmark of Greek erotic poetry as well as an emblem of re-performance.[46] Replay constitutes the central theme of the first poem in the Alexandrian edition of Sappho's poetry and thus for Horace becomes programmatic. Sappho invokes Aphrodite to be her ally *again* as she had been in the past in her prior epiphany when the goddess mirrored the repetition *again* and *again* of previous love affairs. Horace accomplishes a similar effect by his self-quotation of *Odes* 1.19.1–4:

> Mater saeua Cupidinum
>   Thebanaeque iubet me Semelae puer
> et lasciua Licentia
>   finitis animum reddere amoribus.

> Savage mother of Cupids and the son of Theban Semele
> and lascivious License force me to surrender my heart to
> love affairs I thought were over and done with.

Already then he was forced to surrender *again* (*reddere*) to love affairs after he had finished with all that. There the simple sacrifice that accompanied his prayer was intended to soften the violence of the goddess's arrival. In 4.1, however, Horace's apotropaic prayer seeks no epiphany, but instead orders Venus to depart and find a more appropriate victim. The young and talented Paulus Maximus will welcome her epiphany and establish a shrine and an elaborate cult adorned with choral dancing of young men and women—described with a sensuous wealth of imagery that recalls the scenery and festivities of Sappho 2. There, to be sure, the goddess was invited to participate in the celebrations in her honor. Here, despite Horace's disavowals and strategies, love again raises his head—unwanted and unexpected—in the form of the young Ligurinus, who precipitates Sapphic symptoms (31 V.), above all a tongue that lapses into unwonted silence. Oxymoron is the dominant figure throughout this poem, playing variations on Sappho's bitter-sweet Eros. The speaker's nocturnal dreams of pursuit and capture return us to Sappho 1 and the infinite loop of love. Her smiling Aphrodite reassured her that "if the beloved now flees, she will soon pursue ... and if she loves not, soon she will love, even against her will." 4.10 re-enacts that moment as Ligurinus, repeatedly looking at himself in the mirror, laments:

> 'Quae mens est hodie, cur eadem non puero fuit,
> uel cur his animis incolumes non redeunt genae?'

> The attitude I have today, why wasn't it the same when
> I was a boy, or why with my present emotions do my
> unblemished cheeks not return?

   Continued attachment to Sappho's poetry becomes apparent in Horace's catalogue of Greek *lyrici* in 4.9.5–12:

> non, si priores Maeonius tenet
> sedes Homerus, Pindaricae latent
>   Ceaeque et Alcaei minaces
>   Stesichoriue graues Camenae;

> nec siquid olim lusit Anacreon,
> deleuit aetas; spirat adhuc amor
>   uiuuntque commissi calores
>   Aeoliae fidibus puellae.

> Not, even if Maeonian Homer holds first place do the
> stately Muses of Pindar and Simonides or Stesichorus or

the threatening songs of Alcaeus, lie hidden nor has time
destroyed what playful Anacreon once composed; even
now the love breathes and the passions live on of the
Aeolian girl who entrusted them to her lyre.

While Horace merely gives passing mention to the *Alcaei minaces … Camenae*
(which considerably narrows Alcaeus' poetics), Pindar and Sappho book-end the
catalogue that culminates in an elaborate tribute to Sappho: *spirat adhuc amor/
viuuntque commissi calores/ Aeoliae fidibus puellae*. The next stanza describing
Helen's seduction by Paris's beauty echoes Sappho 16 V. and contrasts with the
epic values that follow. In Book 4 of Horace's Odes, for all its Pindarizing,
Sapphic poetry no longer stands in opposition to Alcaeus, but rather appears as
the generic complement to Pindar.

GUIDE TO FURTHER READING

The commentaries of Nisbet and Hubbard (1970, 1978), and Nisbet and Rudd (2004)
discuss sources and allusions for each ode. Kiessling, Heinze, Burck (1964) must still be
consulted. The standard edition of the Lesbian poets is Voigt (1971). Campbell's *Greek
Lyric* (1989), offers useful translations, and Page (1955) discusses the major poems.
Greene (1996) collects important essays on Sappho, while Rösler (1980) focuses on
Alcaeus' social and cultural context. Pasquali's exhaustive study of Horace and early Greek
lyric (1964; first published 1920) should be supplemented by Fraenkel (1957), especially
chapter 5, Richmond (1970), and Cavarzere (1996). The best general essay remains
Feeney (1993); equally helpful for an orientation is Barchiesi (2000, 2007); Hutchinson
(2007) is disappointing. Paschalis (2002) includes articles on various aspects of Horace's
Greek lyric predecessors; and McDermott (1985) reviews the older literature. Horace and
the symposium are discussed by Murray (1993) and Davis (2007); for the Greek institution, see the essays in Murray (1990).

NOTES

* I am grateful to my colleague Tony Woodman, and to Bill Race for saving me from
   sundry inanities and infelicities. Only I can be blamed for those that remain.
1 Cf. McDermott 1985 on the history of the debate. One should perhaps speak of
   Sappho and Alcaeus as not so much classicizing, for Horace, as canonical. Morrison
   2007 makes the case that the divide between Hellenistic and Archaic Greek poetry
   has been exaggerated. Sensible remarks by Feeney 1993 and Barchiesi 2007. Macleod
   1983a nicely demonstrates the interweaving of Alexandrian and Archaic elements in
   Odes 2.5.
2 For a measured appraisal, see White 2007 with literature.

3 Cf. Fraenkel 1957: 42–56. For Fraenkel (44), it was "absurd to assume that Horace intended in any way to connect the Roman theme of *Altera iam teritur* with the institutions of a Greek city."

4 Murray 1993: 91, citing Cicero, may exaggerate the contrast between Greek and Roman, but there remains some truth to it.

5 For the evidence and the issues involved, see Zorzetti 1990.

6 Gutzwiller 1998: 150.

7 Murray 1993: 102. For background on the status of poetry in Rome, see Williams 1968: 31–101.

8 Cf. Rossi 1983.

9 See Mindt 2007; also Barchiesi 2000.

10 Heinze 1960; first published 1923.

11 Significantly, in all these odes, there is explicit mention of *sodales* (1.27.7; 1.36.5; 1.37.4; and 2.7.5). In the latter poem, the symposium belongs to the past.

12 If *modos* and *carminis artem* both refer to meter (= *numeri*), then one wonders what meter Horace's critics thought he should use: hexameter? But that makes no sense.

13 The repetition of *res* in line 25 and *rebus* in line 29 has caused some confusion, but it means the same thing in both cases, the actual contents of Archilochus' poetry. The moderating of the *Archilochi musam*, i.e. his *animi*, by the Lesbian poets has already been taken care of. One could say that once the *animi* have been modified, the actual contents are irrelevant, but Horace wants to keep the parallelism between himself and Alcaeus.

14 "Why should I mention Io? I have no notion why."

15 See Macleod 1983b: 270–4, but cf. Woodman 2002. For Horace to admit his lack of courage would also undermine his opening claim: *qui sibi fidet/ dux reget examen* (1.19.22–3).

16 Cf. Fraenkel 1957: 345–47; Mayer 1994; also Cucchiarelli 1999.

17 Nisbet and Hubbard 1970 claim the expression is proverbial, but "to touch the heaven" and to bang into it are quite different matters. Significantly, the latter expression occurs in a comic fragment (*com. adesp.* 531 K.).

18 Cf. Lowrie 1995 who traces a second parade following the Parade Odes with the sequence of *Odes* 12–18 embracing a series of lyric predecessors that includes Pindar (1.12), Sappho (1.13), Alcaeus (1.14), Bacchylides (1.15), Stesichorus (1. 16), and Anacreon (1. 17) with a return to Alcaeus in 1.18.

19 Nisbet and Hubbard 1970: 359: "an agreeable trifle"; cf. Quinn 1980: 182–3, but Putnam 2006: 50 calls it "one of Horace's most engaging odes." Cf. also *Odes* 1.26.10–12.

20 Cf. Putnam 2006: 50–5.

21 Although Alcaeus doubtless treated amatory subjects in his poetry, it is nevertheless striking how little of it has come down to us.

22 See Lyne 1980: 201–3, who notes (202) "Horace therefore paints a picture of Alcaeus and by implication of himself as a man and poet of love and wine, *who had such things in perspective*" (italics in original) in contrast to the elegists as the immediately following 1.33, addressed to Tibullus makes clear. Cf. Feeney 1993.

23 Cf. Davis 1991: 85–6.

24 Cf. Fraenkel 1957: 167. Nisbet and Hubbard 1978: 205 see a "literary judgement in favour of Alcaeus's style"; and Horace "is making a manifesto about his own poetry, which purported to imitate the practical outlook and masculine style of Alcaeus" (219). Woodman 2002, who reviews earlier discussions, is a rare dissenting voice. He claims that Sappho and Alcaeus were "two poetic personalities forming a single exemplar" and that " Horace was decisively influenced by the striking, pervasive and seemingly unprecedented dualism of gender that is found in Catullus' poetry" (60). La Penna 1972, on the contrary, sees Sappho used as a polemic against Catullus.

25 [*Editor's note*: Borzsák's Teubner text opts for the reading *discretas*. For an excellent account of the arguments in support of the reading, *descriptas* (adopted here), see Nisbet and Hubbard 1978: 215–16.]

26 West 1998: 93 is troubled by the *vulgus* and cites 3.1.1–2; cf. *malignum ... vulgus* (2.16.39–40).

27 After describing the impact of Alcaeus' poetry on his auditors, it is perfectly rational to turn to Sappho's; *illis carminibus* (33) should refer to her songs since she has been mentioned more distantly.

28 See Cavallini 1978–79: 378–9, who points out the echoes of Sappho 16 V. in *lucidum/fulgentis oculos* and in lines 21–4 (*Num tu quae tenuit diues Achaemenes/ aut pinguis Phrygiae Mygdonias opes/ permutare uelis crine Licymniae, / plenas aut Arabum domos*). Despite the fence sitting of Nisbet and Hubbard 1978 and West 1998, the identification of Licymnia with Maecenas' wife is untenable; see Davis 1975. Given the Sapphic verbal echoes in the ode, one could recognize the opposition of land/sea in Horace's first stanza as reminiscent of the opening of Sappho 16. Worth exploring would be the relation between the priamel and the recusatio.

29 Nisbet and Hubbard 1978.

30 Cf. Davis 1991: 82–8.

31 Pasquali 1964, first published 1920; Richmond 1970; Cavarzere 1996; Nisbet and Hubbard 1970 and 1978; and Nisbet and Rudd 2004: *passim*.

32 For a nice example, see Campbell 1982: 200–1.

33 Rösler 1980: 255, n. 339.

34 1.4 may also involve a Alcaic tag; cf. 286 V.; cf. Nisbet and Hubbard 1970: 58.

35 Including Stoic notions of Hermes as culture hero, perhaps the *Homeric Hymn to Hermes, Iliad* 24, and *Odyssey* 24. Cf. Cairns 1983, who suggests an Alcaeus sandwich with the central stanza being "entirely Alcaic."

36 Quoted in Conte and Barchiesi 1989: 87.

37 Lyne 2005 sees in the Alcaic sequence (to which he adds 1.11) an elaborate allusion to the arrangement of the Alexandrian edition of Alcaeus' first book. The suggestion is ingenious but, to my mind, ultimately unconvincing.

38 Cf. Anderson 1966; Zumwalt 1977; Woodman 1980; Davis 1989; and Thomas 2007: 58–60. Cf. Seel 1970.

39 Quintilian 8.6. 44 cites 1.14 as an exemplary model of allegory. The political interpretation of the first fragment is confirmed by a papyrus commentary, fr. 305b V.

40 See Porro 1994: 120–1.

41 I am not convinced by Cucchiarelli 2004, 2005 that, like Alcaeus, Horace refers not to the *res publica*, but to his political faction, the Republicans on whose side he fought under Brutus at Philippi and who had not yet decided to give up the cause.

42 Cavallini 1978–9: 377–8 notes that *umor* should be understood as the Sapphic ἴδρως rather than tears.

43 See Konstan 2006: 238–43, who notes: "While preserving the three-person structure of Sappho's and Catullus' poems, Horace has in fact constructed a wholly new scenario" (242); Konstan further argues that Horace may have been the "inventor" of erotic jealousy.

44 On this, I believe correct, interpretation, Wills (1967) and recently Furley 2000. For the view of Sappho 31 as an expression of jealousy, see Page 1955: 26–33.

45 Thome 1995: 146, n. 46, calls 4.1 "eine Hommage an die große Liebesdichterin." Cf. Putnam 1986: 39–42; Nagy 1994; Barchiesi 2000: 172–3; and Thévanaz 2003.

46 Cf. Mace 1993.

CHAPTER EIGHT

Horace's Debt to Pindar

William H. Race

In his survey of Greek and Latin literature, Quintilian unequivocally ranks Pindar and Horace as the greatest lyric poets in their respective traditions:

> Novem vero lyricorum longe Pindarus princeps spiritu, magnificentia, sententiis, figuris, beatissima rerum verborumque copia et velut quodam eloquentiae flumine: propter quae Horatius eum merito nemini credit imitabilem. (Quint. 10.1.61).

> But of the nine lyric poets, by far the first is Pindar for his inspiration, magnificence, ethical maxims, figures of speech, his bountiful store of topics and words, and for his veritable river of eloquence, for which things Horace justly considered him imitable by no one.[1]

> At lyricorum idem Horatius fere solus legi dignus: nam et insurgit aliquando et plenus est iucunditatis et gratiae et varius figuris et verbis felicissime audax. (Quint. 10.1.96).

> But of the lyric poets, Horace is almost the only one worth reading, for at times he rises to grandeur, and is full of sweetness and charm, and versatile in figures of speech, and in his use of words most felicitously bold.

Although Quintilian praises both poets for their use of *figurae* and *verba*, he does so in very different respects: Pindar's inspiration (*spiritu*) and magnificence (*magnificentia*) are paralleled by Horace's occasional rise to grandeur (*insurgit aliquando*), whereas Pindar's bountiful store (*beatissima ... copia*) of topics and words and virtual river (*velut quodam ... flumine*) of eloquence are contrasted with Horace's variety (*varius*) of figures of speech and plenitude (*plenus*) of sweetness (*iucunditatis*) and charm (*gratiae*). It is important to note that Quintilian draws most of his characterization of Pindar's and Horace's poetry from Horace's own comparison of himself with Pindar in *Odes* 4.2.[2] And when it comes to his use of words Quintilian judges Horace to be *felicissime audax*.[3] Indeed, the only significant overlap between the two poets lies in Horace's occasional elevation (*et insurgit aliquando*) and his boldness (*audax*) in the use of words. We shall see that when these two qualities, elevation and boldness, are present in Horace's odes, Pindar's works become relevant.

The Pindaric corpus

In order to assess Horace's debt to Pindar (c. 518–c. 438 BCE), it is necessary to look briefly at Pindar's works to see what Horace was presented with in his great predecessor's poetry. Pindar came at the end of the two centuries (c. 650–450) during which the canonical nine Greek lyric poets composed their vast corpus. In the line of Alcman, Ibycus, Stesichorus, Simonides, and Bacchylides, Pindar composed choral odes, which, unlike the "monodic" poetry of Sappho, Alcaeus, and Anacreon, used complex metrical patterns typically arranged into triads consisting of a strophe, antistrophe, and epode. Whereas monodic poetry repeats metrical verses and stanzas from one poem to another, choral odes exhibit very diverse and often unique metrical structures.

Pindar's poems were organized into seventeen books (papyrus rolls) by Alexandrian editors. They included books of hymns, paeans, dithyrambs, *prosodia*, *partheneia*, *hyporchemata*, *enkomia*, *threnoi*, and epinicians. Of these only the four books of victory odes have come down to us through a continuous manuscript tradition; of the others we have portions or fragments recovered on papyrus or quoted by later authors. The epinicians vary in length from 21 lines (*Pythian 7*) to 299 (*Pythian 4*). The 45 epinicians alone total over 3,400 verses, some of which are very long.[4]

These poems are marked by loftiness of tone, extraordinary inventiveness in vocabulary and expression, extremely complex syntax, elevated style, varied metaphorical expressions, lengthy mythical narratives, maxims, and abrupt transitions. At times Pindar's language is cloyingly lush, at other times succinct to the point of obscurity; often grandiose, it can also be plain, if not homely. Variety (*poikilia*) is its overarching principle.

Pindar' epinicians were designed for public performance by singers and dancers accompanied by lyres and pipes, and some are addressed to the most powerful rulers of their time—Hieron of Syracuse (*Ol.* 1, *Pyth.* 1, 2, 3), Theron of Acragas (*Ol.* 2, 3), and Arcesilas of Cyrene (*Pyth.* 4, 5). The genre flourished in the intense Greek *polis* culture just before and after the Persian Wars (c. 500–450), only to die out with the intellectual and political changes that came in the wake of the Peloponnesian War (431–404 BCE). Like J. S. Bach at the end of the baroque period, Pindar marked the culmination—and completion—of the age of Greek lyric poetry. The grand choral genre continued for a while in the odes of Attic tragedy, but by the fourth century, these too had ceased being composed.

The famous beginning of *Olympian* 1 can serve as a representative sample of Pindar's rich style:

> Best is water, while gold, like fire blazing
> in the night, shines preeminent amid lordly wealth;
> but if you wish to sing
> of athletic games, my heart,
> look no further than the sun
> for another star shining more warmly by day
> > through the empty sky,
> nor let us proclaim a contest greater than Olympia,
> from where comes the famous hymn that encompasses
> the thoughts of wise men, who have come
> in celebration of Kronos' son to the rich
> and blessed hearth of Hieron,
>
> who wields the rightful scepter in flock-rich
> Sicily, culling the summits of all achievements,
> and is also glorified
> in the finest songs,
> such as those we men often perform in play
> about the friendly table. (trans. Race, Loeb, slightly altered)

This opening, essentially one long sentence in a very complex aeolic meter, illustrates many features of Pindar's style. It is in the form of a priamel.[5] It begins with startling brevity, "best is water," but continues for seventeen verses containing dazzling language, similes of fire at night and the sun by day, a direct address to the poet's heart, and the climactic proclamation of the subject, which continues until the poet, Hieron, and celebratory occasion are brought together "about the friendly table." In the course of this poem (of 116 verses), Pindar narrates a complicated story of Tantalus' breach of divine law and of how his son Pelops won his bride by racing against her father Oenomaus at Olympia, and concludes with praise of and advice for his patron Hieron, the king of Syracuse, whom, the poet proclaims, no living person surpasses in noble pursuits and political power.

How could Horace compete with such poetry as this? Pindar praises his victors in the context of competing city-states and from a pan-Hellenic perspective, whereas Horace is working within the structure of a Roman state presided over by a single ruler. In that regard, Horace is much closer to the Hellenistic poets such as Callimachus and Theocritus, who were writing under the auspices of Ptolemaic kings.[6] The intervening Hellenistic period, with its own reappropriation of archaic and classical poetry, exerted a profound influence on the Augustan poets and must always be kept in mind as a filter through which Horace approached archaic and classical Greek lyric.[7]

Horace's professed attitude toward Pindar
and the appropriation of the poetic past

By professing in his opening poem his aspiration to be included among the "lyric bards" (*lyricis vatibus*, 1.1.35), Horace necessarily invited a comparison with Pindar, the greatest lyric poet of all. But within the Odes themselves, he mentions Pindar by name (or directly alludes to him) just four times, all in Book 4 and three of them in one ode: *Pindarum* (4.2.1), *Pindarus* (4.2.8), *Dircaeum ... cycnum* (4.2.25), and *Pindaricae ... Camenae* (4.9.6–8). Yet as we shall see, Pindar's influence can be detected here and there in the first three books, where one can trace a tendency for Horace's programmatic statements to become more "Pindaric" as his poetic persona takes on greater risks and becomes both more civic and more grand.[8] Nonetheless, however boldly he might wish to emulate Pindaric *magnificentia*, two principal factors restrained him: the inflexibility of the Latin language in comparison with Greek[9] and the "monodic" verse-forms (mainly Sapphic and Alcaic stanzas) that he employed.

Outside the Odes, Horace mentions Pindar only in *Epistle* 1.3, probably written in 20 BCE, between the publication of *Odes*, Books 1–3 (23 BCE) and Book 4 (13 BCE). In that poem, while asking Florus about the literary staff that is accompanying Tiberius on his mission to Armenia, he addresses many of the poetic issues that form the background of his own verse; in particular, it treats the issue of poetic appropriation, especially from Greek models, by presenting three types of contemporary poet. The first poet (Titius) represents attempts to incorporate Greek grand-style lyric and tragic models into Latin.

> quid studiosa cohors operum struit? hoc quoque curo.
> quis sibi res gestas Augusti scribere sumit?
> bella quis et paces longum diffundit in aevum?
> quid Titius, Romana brevi venturus in ora?
> Pindarici fontis qui non expalluit haustus,   10
> fastidire lacus et rivos ausus apertos.
> ut valet? ut meminit nostri? fidibusne Latinis
> Thebanos aptare modos studet auspice Musa,
> an tragica desaevit et ampullatur in arte?

> What works is the learned staff composing? this, too, I want to know. Who takes upon him to record the exploits of Augustus? Who adown distant ages makes known his deeds in war and peace? What of Titius, soon to be on the lips of Romans, who quailed not at draughts of the Pindaric spring, but dared to scorn the open pools and streams? How fares he? How mindful is he of me? Does he essay, under favour of the Muse, to fit Theban measures to the Latin lyre? Or does he storm and swell in the tragic art? (trans. Fairclough, Loeb).

His portrayal of Titius (otherwise unknown) is undoubtedly ironic. The phrase "soon to be on the lips of Romans" can mean either "famous" or "notorious." Titius' boldness (*non expalluit*, 10; *ausus*, 11) in quaffing from the Pindaric fountain and disdaining accessible, placid waters, and his apparent interest in theatrical bombast (*desaevit et ampullatur*, 14), are certain indicators of literary failure from the perspective of Horatian aesthetics, as is Titius' striving (*studet*, 13) to adapt Pindar's measures to Latin verse, presumably while writing encomia of Augustus' achievements (*res gestas*, 7).

The second type (Celsus) represents the poet who takes his material directly from ancient authors.

> quid mihi Celsus agit? monitus multumque monendus,   15
> privatas ut quaerat opes et tangere vitet
> scripta Palatinus quaecumque recepit Apollo,
> ne, si forte suas repetitum venerit olim
> grex avium plumas, moveat cornicula risum
> furtivis nudata coloribus.   20

> What, pray, is Celsus doing? He was warned, and must often
> be warned to search for home treasures, and to shrink from
> touching the writings which Apollo on the Palatine has
> admitted: lest, if some day perchance the flock of birds come
> to reclaim their plumage, the poor crow, stripped of his stolen
> colours, awake laughter. (trans. Fairclough, Loeb)

This type of poetic antiquarianism spurns its own resources (*privatas ... opes*, 16) and instead lays hands on (*tangere*, 16) writings stored in the Palatine library. Appropriation of this kind (virtually plagiarism) is compared to the theft (*furtivis*, 20) of plumage that adds superficial color to a plain crow.

In contrast, Horace describes Florus' own poetic efforts in these terms (20–5):

>   ipse quid audes?   20
> quae circumvolitas agilis thyma? non tibi parvum
> ingenium, non incultum est et turpiter hirtum,
> seu linguam causis acuis seu civica iura
> respondere paras seu condis amabile carmen,
>   prima feres hederae victricis praemia.   25

> And yourself—what do you venture on? About what
> beds of thyme are you busily flitting? No small gift is
> yours: not untilled is the field, nor rough-grown and
> unsightly. Whether you sharpen your tongue for
> pleading, or essay to give advice on civil law, or build
> charming verse, you will win the first prize of the victor's
> ivy. (trans. Fairclough, Loeb)

This description mirrors the avowed poetic strategy of Horace. As opposed to Titius' draughts (*haustus*, 9) from the Pindaric spring and Celsus' spurning of his own poetic resources (*privatas ... opes*, 16), Florus, aptly named, flits busily (*agilis*, 21) about thyme-flowers like a bee, possesses a talent (*ingenium*, 22) that is capacious (*non parvum*, 21) and refined (*non incultum ... turpiter hirtum*, 22), and composes charming (*amabile*, 24) poetry that wins the prize of ivy (*hederae*, 25), Dionysius' plant, emblematic of a poetic style ranging from plain to more elevated.[10] Unlike the bombastic Titius and the bookish Celsus, Florus is a lawyer with a sharpened tongue (*linguam ... acuis*, 23), a professional expertise that complements his judicious choice of subject matter and style of poetry.[11]

Many of the elements, some of the vocabulary, and the overall poetic judgment of this epistle can be found in *Odes* 4.2 (published some seven years later), whose first word is "Pindar." It is the most impressive *recusatio* (literary refusal) in Horace's works and probably the most important *recusatio* in Latin poetry.[12] It begins with a warning to anyone foolish enough to strive (*studet*, 1) to imitate (or rival) Pindar:

> Pindarum quisquis studet aemulari,
> Iulle, ceratis ope Daedalea
> nititur pinnis vitreo daturus
>   nomina ponto.

> Whoever strives to rival Pindar, Iullus, relies on
> wings fastened with wax by Daedalus' craft and will
> give his name to a transparent sea.

This implicit preference for nature (the high-soaring Pindar) over mere craft (the artificial wings of Daedalus), is one commonly expressed by Pindar, especially when he depicts his role as poet.[13] Then, without any connective, Horace launches into a five-stanza tour de force, the subject of which is "Pindar":

> monte decurrens velut amnis, imbres   5
> quem super notas aluere ripas,
> fervet immensusque ruit profundo
>   Pindarus ore,

> laurea donandus Apollinari,
> seu per audacis nova dithyrambos   10
> verba devolvit numerisque fertur
>   lege solutis,

> seu deos regesque canit, deorum
> sanguinem, per quos cecidere iusta
> morte Centauri, cecidit tremendae   15
>   flamma Chimaerae,

sive quos Elea domum reducit
palma caelestis pugilemve equomve
dicit et centum potiore signis
    munere donat,   20

flebili sponsae iuvenemve raptum
plorat et viris animumque moresque
aureos educit in astra nigroque
    invidet Orco.   (*Odes* 4.2.5-24)

Like a river rushing down from a mountain, which rains
have swollen above its normal banks, Pindar seethes and
rushes immeasurably on with his deep voice, worthy to
win Apollo's laurel whether he rolls down new words in
his bold dithyrambs and is carried along in rhythms freed
from rules, or sings of gods and kings, the offspring of
the gods, by whom the Centaurs died a deserved death
and the flame of the terrible Chimaera was quenched, or
whether he sings of those whom the palm of Elis brings
home exalted to the skies, whether boxer or horse, and
bestows a gift more valuable than a hundred statues, or
laments a youth snatched from his weeping bride and
extols to the stars his strength, courage, and golden
character, begrudging them to black Orcus.

The first stanza notoriously characterizes Pindar's poetic style as a river rushing
out of control, and is followed by a selective catalogue of Pindar's works in a
cascade of four Sapphic stanzas, including dithyrambs, hymns (and/or paeans),
victory odes, and dirges.[14] These lines show off Horace's ability to emulate Pindaric
style in Sapphic meter while simultaneously disavowing the ambition to do so.
The next two stanzas draw the contrast between Pindar's style and that of Horace:

        multa Dircaeum levat aura cycnum,   25
        tendit, Antoni, quotiens in altos
        nubium tractus: ego apis Matinae
            more modoque,

        grata carpentis thyma per laborem
        plurimum, circa nemus uvidique   30
        Tiburis ripas operosa parvus
            carmina fingo.

A mighty breeze lifts up the swan of Dirce, Antonius,
whenever he heads for the lofty reaches of the clouds.
But I, in the mode and manner of a Matinian bee that
with the greatest effort gathers pleasant thyme around
the grove and banks of well-watered Tibur, compose
painstaking songs in my small way.

Two adjectives referring to Pindar's flight are programmatic, the emphatic first word *multa* and the qualification *altos*, which together emphasize the volume and height associated with Pindaric grand style, while the "swan of Dirce" characterizes Pindar as the sacred bird of Apollo, known for its loud, sonorous song. In contrast, by depicting himself as small (*parvus*, 31) and like a bee (*apis Matinae / more modoque*, 27–8) that gathers pleasant thyme (*grata carpentis thyma*, 29) about the grove (*nemus*, 30) and banks of Tibur, with greatest effort (*per laborem / plurimum*, 29–30) and his songs as painstaking endeavors (*operosa*, 31), Horace provides a compendium of the terms characteristic of the Hellenistic preference for small topics treated with great artistic refinement.[15]

The emphatic verb at the beginning of the next stanza, "you will celebrate" (*concines*), is qualified by "with a grander plectrum" (*maiore … plectro*), which encircles the word "poet" (*poeta*), a pretentious Greek term that Horace uses only one other time in the *Odes* (4.6.30):

> concines maiore poeta plectro
> Caesarem, quandoque trahet feroces
> per sacrum clivum merita decorus   35
>   fronde Sygambros;
>
> quo nihil maius meliusve terris
> fata donavere bonique divi,
> nec dabunt, quamvis redeant in aurum
>   tempora priscum.   40
>
> concines laetosque dies et urbis
> publicum ludum super impetrato
> fortis Augusti reditu forumque
>   litibus orbum.
>
> tum meae, siquid loquar audiendum,   45
> vocis accedet bona pars, et "O sol
> pulcher, o laudande!" canam recepto
>   Caesare felix.
>
> tuque dum procedis, "io Triumphe!"
> non semel dicemus, "io Triumphe!"   50
> civitas omnis dabimusque divis
>   tura benignis.
>
> te decem tauri totidemque vaccae,
> me tener solvet vitulus, relicta
> matre qui largis iuvenescit herbis   55
>   in mea vota,
>
> fronte curvatos imitatus ignis
> tertium lunae referentis ortum,
> qua notam duxit, niveus videri,
>   cetera fulvus.   60

You, a poet with a grander plectrum, will celebrate
Caesar when he leads the fierce Sygambri along the
Sacred Way, crowned with a well-earned garland, than
whom nothing greater or better have fate and the kind
gods given to the world, nor ever will give, even though
the centuries return to the Golden Age. You will
celebrate the festive days and the city's public games at
the prayed-for return of Augustus and the forum free
from litigation. Then, if I can say anything worth
hearing, the best part of my voice will chime in and I
shall sing, "O beautiful day, O praiseworthy one," in my
joy at Caesar's return. And as you step forth, we citizens
will all say more than once, "Hail to the Victor, Hail to
the Victor," and offer incense to the kindly gods. For
you, ten bulls and as many cows will serve as a sacrifice;
for me, a tender calf which has left its mother and is
growing in the deep grass to fulfill my vows, imitating
with its brow the curved flame of the new moon at its
third rising, appearing white where it bears the mark,
but elsewhere brown.

Much has been written about the contrast between the private sacrifice of a tender calf by the poet who includes himself with the citizenry, and the pretensions of the poet who steps forth (*dumque tu procedis*, 49) and sacrifices twenty head of cattle (a grand, public offering). When Horace quotes himself, his words are the generalized words of the crowd; Antonius' words are Pindaric: he utters a "vaunt" in form like those in Pindaric epinicians, where a comparative adjective is negated (e.g., "no city in a century has produced a man more generous than Theron," *Ol.* 2.93–5),[16] but one that is sweepingly extravagant: "than whom (Caesar Augustus) nothing greater or better have fate and the kind gods given to the world, nor ever will give."

Two points are to be made about the poem as a whole.[17] First, Horace contrives to have it both ways. Even as he disavows being able to write in Pindaric style, he composes five Sapphic stanzas of impressive grand-style poetry. Even as he disavows extravagant praise of Augustus, he puts such praise in the mouth of Antonius. These are tactics which he himself has used frequently elsewhere and which are a staple of other Augustan poets.[18] The other point is that the Pindar presented in this poem is a purposeful exaggeration (almost a straw man), meant to set off Horace's more restrained and painstaking—in other words, more Hellenistic—art.

Horace's verbal debt to Pindar

To a great extent because we have a considerable amount of Pindar's poetry, scholars and commentators have proposed dozens and dozens of places where

Pindaric phraseology may lie behind Horace's choice of words. Such parallels are cited in studies like Rummel (1892: 11–14), in standard editions like Keller and Holder (1899), and in the commentaries of Kiessling and Heinze (1984a), Nisbet and Hubbard (1970, 1978), and Nisbet and Rudd (2004). Well over one hundred borrowings, parallels, or similarities have been proposed. But with the exception of one clear citation, the "motto" at the beginning of 1.12, there are no verbatim borrowings, or if there are, they are relatively minor, such as *supremo ... Iovi* "highest Jove" (1.21.3–4) and Διὸς ὑψίστου at *Nem.* 1.60.[19] Even the frequently cited parallel between *Pyth.* 1.39–40 ("Lord of Lykia, O Phoebus, you who rule over Delos and who love Parnassos' Kastalian spring, willingly take those things to heart and make this a land of brave men") and 3.4, 59–64 ("and he who was never about to put his bow on his shoulder, who washes his flowing hair in the pure dew of Castalia, who haunts the thickets of Lycia and the forest of his birthplace, Delian and Patarean Apollo"), which Williams (1969: 52, n. 3) claims is "almost literally translated from Pindar," not only is very different in vocabulary, form, and function in its poem, but also could derive from other sources.[20] Upon close inspection, purported verbal borrowings from Pindar by Horace are surprisingly few, superficial, and rarely exact.[21] In his *Ars Poetica* Horace may have recommended constant reading of Greek examples,[22] but he also heeded his own warning to Celsus (*Epistles* 1.3,15–20) against plundering former poets' works.

Et insurgit aliquando: Horace's grand-style odes

Although Horace is not indebted to Pindar for exact words, the two poets do share generic and formal elements such as hymns and prayers, catalogues, maxims, abrupt transitions, first-person break-off passages, priamels, and mythical narratives. Figures of style include hyperbaton (extreme separation of words that belong together syntactically), negative expressions that serve as litotes and provide variety, and universalizing doublets (e.g., land and sea, human and god). I shall examine in some detail three poems that in spirit most closely approximate Pindaric grandeur: 1.12.3.4, and 4.4.[23]

Of greatest importance is the one poem that announces itself as Pindaric: *Odes* 1.12 opens by quoting the beginning of *Ol.* 2.1–2:

Ἀναξιφόρμιγγες ὕμνοι,
τίνα θεόν, τίν' ἥρωα, τίνα δ' ἄνδρα κελαδήσομεν;

Hymns that rule the lyre, what god, what hero, and what man shall we celebrate?

Although Horace borrows his opening rhetorical gesture and terms from *Olympian* 2, he does not rely further on the poem, but instead adopts many Pindaric maneuvers and even themes to create an original poem, very grand and very startling:[24]

> Quem virum aut heroa lyra vel acri
> tibia sumis celebrare, Clio?
> quem deum? cuius recinet iocosa
>   nomen imago
>
> aut in umbrosis Heliconis oris   5
> aut super Pindo gelidove in Haemo?
> unde vocalem temere insecutae
>   Orphea silvae,
>
> arte materna rapidos morantem
> fluminum lapsus celerisque ventos,   10
> blandum et auritas fidibus canoris
>   ducere quercus.
>
> What man or hero do you undertake to celebrate with
> the lyre or shrill pipe, Clio? What god? Whose name will
> the joyous echo make resound on the shady slopes of
> Helicon, or on the top of Pindus, or on cold Haemus,
> from where the trees hastily followed Orpheus' singing,
> who with his mother's art stayed the rapid course of
> rivers and the swift winds, being so enchanting that he
> even led the listening oaks behind him with his
> melodious strings.

Like Pindar, Horace begins by offering the addressee (in Pindar's case his personified hymns, in Horace's case the Muse Clio) options for themes and manner of treatment. Bundy (1972) has shown how skillfully Pindar adapts hymnal elements derived both from hexameter "rhapsodic" hymns and lyric "cultic" hymns, each with its own conventions. Although the choice is ostensibly given to the divinity, it is the poet who actually determines the selection, as the voice of the divinity blends into (or is subsumed by) the voice of the laudator.

The high-pitched pipe and lyre are the emblems of choral lyric, and the verb *celebrare* puts us firmly in the tradition of praise poetry. But before we get to the actual subjects (deferment is a great part of Pindar's art as well), there is a digression. This is where Horace firmly departs from the procedure of *Olympian* 2, which names its subjects immediately.

A geographical expansion lists three places to which the *iocosa imago* may travel, namely to Helicon in central Greece (associated with Hesiod and his fellow Boeotian Pindar), to northern Greece (the Pindus range) and to Thrace, mention of which leads the poet to the example of Orpheus and a digression on the cosmic power of the lyre and song over nature. We remain entirely within the realm of Greek geography and song:

quid prius dicam solitis parentis
laudibus, qui res hominum ac deorum,   15
qui mare ac terras variisque mundum
    temperat horis?

unde nil maius generatur ipso
nec viget quidquam simile aut secundum.
proximos illi tamen occupavit
    Pallas honores   20

proeliis audax. neque te silebo,
Liber, et saevis inimica virgo
beluis, nec te, metuende certa
    Phoebe sagitta.

What shall I sing before the customary praises of the
father who directs the actions of men and gods and who
governs the sea, land, and sky with the changing
seasons? From him is begotten nothing greater than
himself, nor does anything flourish like him or close to
him. Nevertheless, Pallas has secured the nearest place of
honor, she who is bold in battle; nor shall I be silent
about you, O Liber, or you, O virgin foe of wild
animals, or you Phoebus, feared for your unerring arrow.

This segment begins with a "rhapsodic question" of the sort that Pindar frequently uses to direct his song, for it imparts an aspect of spontaneity, of involving the listener in the very process of composition: "What shall I sing before the customary praises of the father?" Like Pindar, Horace employs the so-called "performative" or "encomiastic" future that fulfills its action at the very moment when it is spoken, even though it pretends to postpone it to the near future (Race 2004: 86–92). This section of the praise (cf. *laudibus*, 14, an extension of *celebrare*) establishes Jupiter beyond all other subjects of song and answers the initial question *quem deum*. But although the poet cannot sing of anything before (*prius*) Jupiter and although none of his children is greater than their father, he nevertheless (*tamen*, 19)[25] proceeds to name those other gods, and thus begins another of what Nisbet and Hubbard (1970: 20) call "the tedious catalogues of 1.12." To many readers they are indeed tedious, as are Pindar's many catalogues of gods, events, victories, and so forth. But looked at closely, they often prove to be masterpieces of composition, like the catalogue of Pindar's works in 4.2. Whenever encountering a catalogue, one must always ask: how is the list organized, what are the attributes of the individual members, and where is it going? After naming Pallas, the poet will not fail to mention (*neque ... silebo*, 21)—a feigned apology for even considering excluding these gods—Bacchus, Diana, and Apollo. Whereas Jupiter rules over all nature and man (sketched in the all-inclusive sea, land, and sky—an amplification of Orpheus' powers), his offspring are depicted as warriors: Pallas is *audax*, Diana is *inimica*, and Phoebus threatens with his sure arrow (*certa sagitta*). This martial aspect signals a theme that will appear later in the poem.

> dicam et Alciden puerosque Ledae,   25
> hunc equis, illum superare pugnis
> nobilem; quorum simul alba nautis
>   stella refulsit,
>
> defluit saxis agitatus umor,
> concidunt venti fugiuntque nubes   30
> et minax, quod sic voluere, ponto
>   unda recumbit.
>
> I shall sing as well of Alcides and Leda's sons, the one
> famous for victories with horses, the other for his
> boxing, and once their clear star shines for sailors, the
> stormy water flows down from the rocks, the winds
> subside, the clouds flee, and, because they have willed it
> so, the threatening swell sinks to rest in the sea.

This segment answers the question *quem heroa*, and is signaled by the prominent future *dicam* (25) and the additive *et*. The obvious candidates for this status are the deified heroes Heracles and Castor and Pollux, the latter of whom are singled out for their sports and their ability to calm the sea and save sailors. This is an example of what Bundy (1986: 73, 83) calls a decrescendo (cf. *unda recumbit*, 32), which typically signals the end of a topic and serves to relax the tension before the introduction of a new subject. Just as the heroes are ontologically intermediate between men and gods, so they function here as transitional figures between "gods" and "men" as topics.

    The next section opens with a *dubitatio* as to how to answer the poem's opening question, *quem virum*.

> Romulum post hos prius an quietum
> Pompili regnum memorem an superbos
> Tarquini fasces dubito an Catonis   35
>   nobile letum.
>
> After them, I am in doubt whether to mention first
> Romulus or Pompilius' peaceful reign, or Tarquin's
> arrogant fasces, or Cato's noble death.

Up to this point, the poem has dealt exclusively with Greek places, gods, and heroes. *Romulum* (33) emphatically announces the turn to Rome. Once again the poet pretends that he is in doubt as to how to proceed. "After them, whom *first?*" This craftily composed stanza neatly sketches Roman history from the

founding of the city (Romulus), through the civilizing reign of Numa Pompilius
and the expulsion of the Tarquins (and hence the establishment of the Republic),
to the Republic's demise with the suicide of Cato the Younger. Shorey and Laing
(1910: 182), who well understood the rhetorical tradition behind this trope,
aptly comment of *dubito*: "the throng of great memories crowds on the soul of
the bard."[26] There is another small touch: by ending this section with a reference
to death (*letum*) he employs a device often used by Pindar to bring a unit of
discourse to a close (Race 1990: 41–57). The death of Cato is also the death of
the Republic.

The three stanzas that follow fill in the intervening historical period with great
commanders who maintained and augmented Rome's power:

> Regulum et Scauros animaeque magnae
> prodigum Paulum superante Poeno
> gratus insigni referam Camena
>   Fabriciumque.   40
>
> hunc et incomptis Curium capillis
> utilem bello tulit et Camillum
> saeva paupertas et avitus apto
>   cum lare fundus.
>
> crescit occulto velut arbor aevo   45
> fama Marcelli: micat inter omnis
> Iulium sidus velut inter ignis
>   luna minores.

> Regulus and the Scauri and Paulus, unstinting of his
> noble life when the Carthaginians were victorious, these
> will I gratefully celebrate with the fame-bestowing
> Muse, and Fabricius too. He, and Curius with unshorn
> hair, and Camillus were made effective in war by stern
> poverty and an ancestral farm with farmhouse to match.
> The fame of Marcellus grows like a tree with the silent
> lapse of time; but among them all the Julian star flashes
> out like the moon among the lesser lights.

It is significant that the final encomiastic future, *referam* (39),[27] is qualified by
the adjective *gratus*, indicating that the poet is especially warming to (and personally invested in) his Roman theme. The use of such words, especially those
related to *charis* or willingness, is frequent in Pindar.[28] And presiding over this
section is the fame-bestowing Latin Muse (*insigni … Camena*, 39). The catalogue culminates in a pair of similes, each introduced by *velut* (45, 47), which
by juxtaposing Marcellus and Augustus serve to single out at last the *virum*
promised in the opening words. There is a rising intensity in the similes similar
to the effect of Pindar, *Ol.* 1.1–7, where the fire at night is surpassed by the sun

in the day. Here the imperceptibly growing tree of Marcellus' fame is outdone by the radiance of the Julian star, which shines like the moon among the lesser heavenly lights.[29]

The last three stanzas bring together the two subjects of *virum* and *deum*, who together will rule the world by beating down enemies and ruling justly:

> gentis humanae pater atque custos,
> orte Saturno, tibi cura magni   50
> Caesaris fatis data: tu secundo
>   Caesare regnes.
>
> ille seu Parthos Latio imminentis
> egerit iusto domitos triumpho
> sive subiectos Orientis orae   55
>   Seras et Indos,
>
> te minor laetum reget aequos orbem:
> tu gravi curru quaties Olympum,
> tu parum castis inimica mittes
>   fulmina lucis.   60

> Father and guardian of the human race, O son of
> Saturn, to you has been entrusted by the fates the care
> of mighty Caesar; may you reign with Caesar next in
> power. Whether he will subdue and lead in a justly-
> earned triumph the Parthians who are threatening
> Latium, or the Chinese and Indians who live on the
> border of the rising sun, second to you he will rule with
> justice over a happy world: but you will shake Olympus
> with your heavy chariot; you will send your angry
> lightning bolts upon polluted groves.

Having initially been called *parentis* (13), Jupiter is now referred to with greater precision as *pater* (49); so too Pindar often returns to a topic with greater specificity (Race 1990: index *s.v.* increasing specification). In a similar fashion the allusive *Iulium sidus* (47) is made more definite in *Caesaris* (51) and *Caesare* (52), specifying the *nomen* (4) whose *iocosa imago* (3–4) will resound on Helicon and beyond. In a larger sense, the entire poem is an extended priamel, selecting its subject from the range of possibilities. The extraordinary blending of god and ruler with which it concludes would not have been understood by Pindar, for the cult of divine rulers appeared only with the Hellenistic age; nor it is likely that Pindar would have thought it appropriate to constrain public poetry within the limits of Sapphic stanzas. He surely would, however, have been able to follow the rhetoric, the movement, and the priamelistic argument of 1.12, whether or not he approved its triumphal message and its wholesale appropriation of Greek culture to Roman ideology.

All these rhetorical and stylistic elements, as I have tried to indicate, make sense when seen as aspects of the encomiastic tradition that Pindar and Horace have in common. Rather than translate Pindaric odes into Latin by a mere change of names, Horace takes the underlying structures and principles of praise and creates poems that are simultaneously "Pindaric" and all his own (Harms 1936: 62). In *Odes* 1.12 he is certainly *audax*; whether or not he displays his boldness *felicissime* has been a matter of dispute.

Book 2 contains few odes that draw on Pindaric forms. The only ode that rises to some grandeur is 2.19, which feigns dithyrambic inspiration. Fittingly, it is immediately followed by the final ode in the book, which portrays the poet's transformation into a Pindaric swan just before the six "Roman Odes" that open Book 3. In a masterful treatment, Eduard Fraenkel demonstrated the extent to which one of those Roman Odes, 3.4, is related to Pindar's epinicians, especially to his *Pythian* 1 and *Pythian* 8.[30] The opening stanza announces its elevated style:

> Descende caelo et dic age tibia
> regina longum Calliope melos,
>   seu voce nunc mavis acuta,
>   seu fidibus citharaque Phoebi.

> Descend from heaven, Queen Calliope, and sing a long
> song with the pipe or, if you now prefer, with a clear
> voice, or with the strings and lyre of Phoebus.

Here are several emblems of the grand, Pindaric style: the Muse Calliope,[31] the long *melos* (in fact this is the longest of the odes with eighty verses), the pipe, lyre, and voice, all features of Pindaric lyric, as are the disjunctive choices offered to the Muse.[32] The poet then suddenly addresses his (supposedly present) audience (*auditis*, 5) and launches into a lengthy passage of self-fashioning:

> auditis? an me ludit amabilis   5
> insania? audire et videor pios
>   errare per lucos, amoenae
>   quos et aquae subeunt et aurae.

> me fabulosae Volture in Apulo
> nutricis extra †limen Apuliae†   10
>   ludo fatigatumque somno
>   fronde nova puerum palumbes

> texere, mirum quod foret omnibus,
> quicumque celsae nidum Aceruntiae
>   saltusque Bantinos et arvum   15
>   pingue tenent humilis Forenti,

ut tuto ab atris corpore viperis
dormirem et ursis, ut premerer sacra
　　lauroque conlataque myrto,
　　　　non sine dis animosus infans.　　　20

Do you all hear her—or does a lovely fantasy delude me?
I seem to hear her and to be wandering about a sacred
grove, through which course pleasant streams and
breezes. As for me, on Apulian Vultur, beyond … ,
when, as a child, I was exhausted from play and
overcome with sleep, fabulous doves covered me with
fresh foliage—which was a marvel to all who inhabit the
nest of lofty Acherontia and the glades of Bantia and the
rich plowland of low-lying Forentum, how I slept with
my body safe from black snakes and bears, how I was
covered over with sacred laurel and gathered myrtle, not
without the gods' help an inspired child.

The passage presents Horace as favored by the gods from birth (cf. 4.3.1–2:
Quem tu, Melpomene, semel / nascentem placido lumine videris …), an inspired
child (*animosus infans*, 20), protected by laurel and myrtle, the emblems of a
poetic range that extends from the grand style associated with Apollo to the
lighter themes, sympotic and amatory, of which Venus is patron. As the poet
continues his self-fashioning, he turns to his adult biography:

vester, Camenae, vester in arduos
tollor Sabinos, seu mihi frigidum
　　Praeneste seu Tibur supinum
　　　　seu liquidae placuere Baiae.

vestris amicum fontibus et choris　25
non me Philippis versa acies retro,
　　devota non extinxit arbor
　　　　nec Sicula Palinurus unda.

I am yours, Muses, yours when I am borne to the steep
Sabine hills, or whether cool Praeneste or sloping Tibur
or limpid Baiae are my pleasure. As a friend to your
springs and choruses, the battle line routed at Philippi
did not destroy me, nor that accursed tree or Palinurus
with its Sicilian wave.

As the Greek Muse Calliope yields to the Latin Muses (*Camenae*, 21), the poet
refers to Roman locales further afield from his boyhood haunts and cites his
protection from death in battle in the losing cause at Philippi in 42 BCE
(cf. 2.7), from a falling tree (cf. 2.13), and from shipwreck. He then projects
future travels:

> utcumque mecum vos eritis, libens
> insanientem navita Bosphorum   30
>   temptabo et urentis harenas
>   litoris Assyrii viator,
>
> visam Britannos hospitibus feros
> et laetum equino sanguine Concanum,
>   visam pharetratos Gelonos
>   et Scythicum inviolatus amnem.

> So long as you will be with me, I shall gladly test
> the raging Bosporus in a ship and the burning
> sands of the Assyrian shore on foot; I shall visit
> the Britons, savages to strangers, and the Concanian
> delighting in horses' blood, and I shall visit the
> quiver-bearing Geloni and the Scythian river—all
> without suffering harm.

The qualification *utcumque mecum vos eritis* (29) indicates that the travel projected here refers to his poetic fame; neatly sketching the boundaries of the civilized Roman world where his poetry will preserve him, it is the geographical equivalent of the temporal "so long as the pontiff climbs the Capitol with the silent Vestal virgin" (*dum Capitolium / scandet cum tacita virgine pontifex*, 3.30.8–9). Having thus established his credentials from infancy to posterity and presented a geographical survey from his birthplace in Apulia to the ends of the Empire, he suddenly turns his thoughts to the man by whom that Empire is controlled:

> vos Caesarem altum, militia simul
> fessas cohortes abdidit oppidis,
>   finire quaerentem labores
>   Pierio recreatis antro;   40
>
> vos lene consilium et datis et dato
> gaudetis, almae.

> You are refreshing lofty Caesar in your Pierian grotto,
> now that he has settled his tired cohorts in towns and is
> seeking to finish his labors; you give him gentle counsel
> and take joy in the gift, nourishing goddesses.

At this point the Muses are brought together with their new subject of song (*vos Caesarem*, 37), and their role has changed from protectors (of the poet) to refreshers and advisors (of Caesar), two functions prominently assigned to poetry in Pindar's epinicians.[33] Then suddenly, mid-line, a mythical exemplum is introduced, which obliquely proffers the type of gentle counsel that has been just mentioned:

       scimus, ut impios
Titanas immanemque turbam
    fulmine sustulerit caduco,

qui terram inertem, qui mare temperat   45
ventosum et urbis regnaque tristia,
    divosque mortalisque turmas
      imperio regit unus aequo.

magnum illa terrorem intulerat Iovi
fidens iuventus horrida bracchiis   50
    fratresque tendentes opaco
      Pelion imposuisse Olympo.

sed quid Typhoeus et validus Mimas,
aut quid minaci Porphyrion statu,
    quid Rhoetus evulsisque truncis   55
      Enceladus iaculator audax

contra sonantem Palladis aegida
possent ruentes? hinc avidus stetit
    Volcanus, hinc matrona Iuno et
      numquam umeris positurus arcum,   60

qui rore puro Castaliae lavit
crinis solutos, qui Lyciae tenet
    dumeta natalemque silvam,
      Delius et Patareus Apollo.

We know how the impious Titans and their unruly horde were brought low by the thunderbolt falling from him who rules the immobile earth and the windswept sea, the cities and the sad realms below, and with just command alone governs the throngs of gods and men. Relying on the strength of its arms, that fearsome upstart band brought great terror upon Jove, as did the brothers who strove to place Pelion on top of cloudy Olympus. But what could Typhoeus and stout Mimas, or what could Porphyrion with his threatening attitude, or what could Rhoetus and Enceladus, the bold hurler of uprooted trees, accomplish as they rushed against Pallas' ringing aegis? On one side stood zealous Vulcan, on another the matron Juno, and he who was never about to put his bow on his shoulder, who washes his flowing locks in the pure dew of Castalia, who haunts the thickets of Lycia and the woods of his birthplace, the god of Delos and Patara, Apollo.

The subject of the forthcoming example is immediately stated: *impios / Titanas* (42–3). The Titanomachy is the quintessential grand-style narrative depicting the last battle that Jupiter had to fight in order to establish his reign in heaven and on earth. The section concludes with a catalogue of the gods who supported Jupiter, especially Apollo (dear to poets), described with an elaboration of detail (the washing of hair, the visiting of cultic sites) that both brings the narrative to a quiet close and projects the ensuing peace. Having concluded his depiction of the Titanomachy, the poet uses *sententiae* to reorient his song:

> vis consili expers mole ruit sua,   65
> vim temperatam di quoque provehunt
>   in maius, idem odere viris
>   omne nefas animo moventis.

> Power devoid of counsel falls under its own weight, but
> power kept under control the gods even promote and
> increase; conversely, they hate strength bent on
> contriving everything impious.

These gnomic statements reprise the theme of *lene consilium* (41). Here is the "advice" of the Muses: that the gods actually increase power that is wielded in controlled measure (*vim temperatam*, 66). The ode then concludes with a catalogue of examples that illustrate the point:

> testis mearum centimanus Gyges
> sententiarum, notus et integrae   70
>   temptator Orion Dianae
>   virginea domitus sagitta.

> iniecta monstris Terra dolet suis
> maeretque partus fulmine luridum
>   missos ad Orcum; nec peredit   75
>   impositam celer ignis Aetnen,

> incontinentis nec Tityi iecur
> reliquit ales, nequitiae additus
>   custos; amatorem trecentae
>   Pirithoum cohibent catenae.   80

> Hundred-handed Gyges bears witness to my maxims, as
> does Orion, the well-known assailant of Diana, brought
> down by her virgin arrow. Heaped upon her own
> monsters, Earth grieves and laments her offspring sent to
> murky Orcus by the thunderbolt; nor has the swift fire
> eaten its way through superimposed Aetna, nor has the
> bird set as a warder over his villainy abandoned the liver
> of lawless Tityus; three hundred chains hold fast
> Pirithous the lover.

Commentators have been puzzled by the inclusion of the mortal lover Pirithous at the end of this list of mythical sinners. Fraenkel (1957: 285) calls it a "concluding diminuendo." If, however, we see that the point is to counsel Caesar to control his *vis*, then the last example, the most human of the overreaching sinners listed, brings it closer to home. Pindar employs a similar motif in his counsel to Hieron at the close of *Pythian* 1 (95–8), when he adduces the negative example of Phalaris, the cruel tyrant of neighboring Acragas.

Although there are occasional rises to grandeur in the remainder of Book Three (e.g., the dithyrambic 3.25) and in the *Carmen Saeculare*, a public paean to Apollo and Diana performed in 17 BCE (Putnam 2000), it is Book 4 that is the most Pindaric, as is commonly recognized (Putnam 1986). We have already analyzed 4.2, which establishes Horace's relationship to Pindar as one not of rivalry but of respect. But two poems later (4.4) comes the most Pindaric of Horace's encomia, the one celebrating Drusus. It has many of the elements found in Pindaric encomia: elaborate similes, apotropaic gestures toward enemies, gnomic statements, praise of ancestors, illustrative *exempla*, dramatic speech, alternation of positive and negative statements, and the vaunt of achievement in superlative terms (*nil … non perficient*, 73), praising the combination of divine assistance tempered by human caution.

The evaluation of this poem depends upon the attitude of individual critics. Those inclined to see poetic praise as inherently sycophantic downplay the success of the poem. Those familiar with Pindaric encomia are inclined to see in the poem a masterful deployment of topics of praise. The poem opens boldly with two elaborate similes, one depicting a young eagle learning to hunt ever more dangerous prey, the other a lion cub stalking its first deer:

> Qualem ministrum fulminis alitem,
> cui rex deorum regnum in avis vagas
>   permisit expertus fidelem
>   Iuppiter in Ganymede flavo,
>
> olim iuventas et patrius vigor   5
> nido laborum propulit inscium
>   vernique iam nimbis remotis
>   insolitos docuere nisus
>
> venti paventem, mox in ovilia
> demisit hostem vividus impetus,   10
>   nunc in reluctantis dracones
>   egit amor dapis atque pugnae,
>
> qualemve laetis caprea pascuis
> intenta fulvae matris ab ubere
>   iam lacte depulsum leonem   15
>   dente novo peritura vidit:

Like the winged bearer of lightning, to whom Juppiter,
the king of the gods, gave dominion over the roving
birds, having found him trustworthy in regard to

fair-haired Ganymede—at first its youth and inherited
strength sends it forth from its nest without knowledge
of toils, and the springtime breezes, once stormclouds
are driven away, teach it unaccustomed maneuvers,
though still cautious, but soon a strenuous impulse sends
it to attack sheepfolds and now its desire for prey and
battle sends it against snakes that fight back; or like a
lion just now weaned from the rich milk of its tawny
mother, which a doe catches sight of, intent on lush
pasturage and about to perish by an untried fang ...

The emphasis on youth and inherited strength (derived in the eagle's case from
its father, in the lion's from its mother) becomes clear when the similes are applied
to the matter at hand:

> videre Raetis bella sub Alpibus
> Drusum gerentem Vindelici; quibus
>   mos unde deductus per omne
>   tempus Amazonia securi   20
>
> dextras obarmet, quaerere distuli,
> nec scire fas est omnia; sed diu
>   lateque victrices catervae
>   consiliis iuvenis revictae
>
> sensere, quid mens rite, quid indoles   25
> nutrita faustis sub penetralibus
>   posset, quid Augusti paternus
>   in pueros animus Nerones.

thus did the Vindelici see Drusus waging war beneath
the Rhaetian Alps. Whence came to them the custom
that through all time has armed their right hands with
an Amazonian axe, I have put off looking into, nor is it
permitted to know all things; but those hordes long and
widely victorious, defeated by the counsels of the young
man, came to realize what mind and talent rightfully
raised in an auspicious house can achieve, as well as the
paternal devotion of Augustus to the young Nerones.

The juxtaposition across verse-end of *vidit* (16) and *videre* (17) completes the
transition from generality to the historical occasion of the ode, Drusus' military
victory over northern tribes (*bella ... Drusum gerentem*, 17–18), focalized from
the perspective of the enemy. Having broached his subject, the *ego* of the laudator intrudes into the poem by means of a relative clause (*quibus*, 18) to digress
on the tribes' strange custom of wielding Amazonian axes. But after introducing
the topic, he then refuses to pursue it any further (*quaerere distuli*, 21). Such a

(feigned) recoil, followed by a gnomic justification, is very much in the Pindaric manner.[34] In the companion encomiastic ode for Drusus and Tiberius (4.14), he simply labels the Vindelici *legis expertes Latinae* (7), "with no experience of Roman law"; here he makes the same point much more vividly by introducing the concrete detail of the Amazonian axes. The *sed* (22), like ἀλλά in Pindar, resumes the main point, that the enemy were overcome by the good counsels of a young man (*iuvenis*, 24) whose intelligence (*mens*, 25) and talent (*indoles*, 25) had been formed by the paternal attention of Augustus. The surprising introduction of *in pueros ... Nerones* (28) at the end suddenly widens the scope of praise to include Drusus' brother Tiberius, another tactic used by Pindar.[35]

A series of gnomic observations on education forms a bridge to the final section of the ode:

> fortes creantur fortibus et bonis;
> est in iuvencis, est in equis patrum   30
>   virtus neque imbellem feroces
>   progenerant aquilae columbam.
>
> doctrina sed vim promovet insitam
> rectique cultus pectora roborant;
>   utcumque defecere mores,   35
>   indecorant bene nata culpae.

> Brave men are born to brave and good fathers: both in steers and in horses appears the excellence of their sires, nor do fierce eagles produce a timid dove. Nonetheless, training increases inborn strength and proper habits fortify the heart, but whenever good habits are lacking, faults mar well-born traits.

Here are played out the long-standing components of success (Shorey 1909): *natura* (φύσις), *doctrina* (τέχνη), and *cultus* (μελέτη): the Nerones have been blessed with the entire gamut of education. The alternation between positive and negative formulations of the same gnomic thought is also common in Pindar.[36] The remainder of the ode elaborates on the *indoles* that the Nerones have inherited from their progenitor, C. Claudius Nero, who defeated Hasdrubal at the Metaurus river in 207 BCE, thus turning the tide of the long war against Hannibal. This section begins with an address to Rome and calls as witness the debt owed to the Nerones: "What you owe, O Rome, to the Nerones, the Metaurus river is a witness and defeated Hasdrubal ..." (*quid debeas, o Roma, Neronibus, / testis Metaurum flumen et Hasdrubal / devictus*, 37–9). Taking the place of a "myth," this historical exemplum is dramatized by a long speech (50–72) of Hannibal, who focalizes the struggle as one between stags (Carthaginians) and wolves (Romans), thereby picking up the animal similes of the opening. It has been disputed since antiquity whether the last stanza should be taken as spoken by Hannibal or by the poet.[37] Either way, it concludes the poem with resounding praise of the Nerones and the Claudians:

> nil Claudiae non perficient manus,
> quas et benigno numine Iuppiter
>   defendit et curae sagaces   75
>   expediunt per acuta belli.

> There is nothing that the hands of the Claudii will not
> accomplish, which Juppiter with kindly protection
> defends and which wise counsels guide securely through
> the perils of war.

The vaunt articulates the double motivation for human success frequently encountered in Pindar: the assistance of a god (*benigno numine*) being supplemented by the human contribution of diligence and wisdom (*curae sagaces*).

This close examination of three major odes has shown how creatively Horace adapted the encomiastic tradition—whose greatest practitioner was Pindar—and made it his own. Space does not permit an examination of the last Pindaric poem in the collection, 4.14, which celebrates the same military victory as 4.4. As is the case with pairs of odes composed for the same occasion by Pindar (*Ol.* 2 and 3 to Theron of Acragas, *Pyth.* 4 and 5 to Arcesilas of Cyrene, and *Nem.* 1 and 9 to Chromios of Aetna), 4.4 and 4.14 emphasize different aspects of their *laudandi*. *Odes* 4.14 gives climactic place to Tiberius and extended praise to Augustus, who is credited with everything but the actual fighting. This poem rounds off the praise of the Claudian branch and prepares for the final ode in the collection (4.15), which turns from deeds of war to celebrate the Pax Augusta.

GUIDE TO FURTHER READING

For an overview of Pindar's works, see Race (1986), *Pindar*. For a detailed examination of Pindaric style, see Race (1990), *Style and Rhetoric in Pindar's Odes*. Still valuable is the sensible discussion of Pindar's influence on selected odes of Horace by Harms (1936), *Horaz in seinen Beziehungen zu Pindar*. There are excellent observations on Horace's indebtedness to Pindar throughout Fraenkel (1957), *Horace*, and especially with regard to *Odes* 3.4 (pp. 273–85) and 4.4, 4.2 and 4.14 (pp. 426–40). Davis (1991), *Polyhymnia: The Rhetoric of Horatian Lyric Discourse*, contains many insightful observations on Horace's appropriation of Pindaric rhetoric. For treatments of Odes Book 4 with many references to Pindaric influence, see Putnam (1986), *Artifices of Eternity: Horace's Fourth Book of Odes*, and Johnson (2004), *A Symposion of Praise: Horace Returns to Lyric in Odes IV*. For Pindaric influence on the *Carmen Saeculare*, see Putnam (2000), *Horace's* Carmen Saeculare*: Ritual Magic and the Poet's Art*, esp. 104–12. For an excellent analysis of

Horace's twin debts to Pindar and to Hellenistic poetry, see Feeney (1993). For a detailed analysis of *Odes* 1.12 and many possible references to Pindar, see Hardie (2003).

NOTES

1 All translations are my own unless otherwise indicated.
2 For Pindar's "river of eloquence," cf. *velut amnis*, 4.2.5; for his "inimitability," cf. *aemulari*, 4.2.1; for Horace's "sweetness," cf. *ego apis Matinae / more modoque*, 4.2.27–8; and "charm," cf. *grata carpentis thyma*, 4.2.29.
3 The two terms point to a tension in Horace's poetry between Hellenistic refinement (implied by the aesthetic judgment in the word *felicissime*) and grand-style boldness (*audax*). Horace associates Pindar's coinage of new words with the boldness of his dithyrambs at 4.2.10–11: *seu per audacis nova dithyrambos / verba devolvit.*
4 The longest verse, in *Pythian* 1, contains 30 syllables. In contrast, an entire Sapphic stanza consists of only 38 syllables, an Alcaic of 41.
5 For a survey of Pindar's and Horace's use of this focusing device, see Race 1982: 73–81 and 122–9, who notes (122), "Next to Pindar's choral lyrics, Horace's *Odes* exhibit the most sophisticated use of priamels."
6 Nisbet and Hubbard 1970: 143–4 and Hunter 2003: 95–6 observe the debt of *Odes* 1.12 to such praise of kings as Theocritus' encomium of Ptolemy II in *Idyll* 17.
7 Feeney 1993 provides an excellent overview of Horace's relationship to Hellenistic poetry. For Hellenistic adaptations of Pindaric and archaic Greek conventions, see Bundy 1972.
8 Cf. 2.20, where the poet becomes a Pindaric swan, lifted on no slender (*nec tenui*, 1) feather, and 3.30, where the poet's work is credited with powers of endurance and the poet himself is crowned with Delphic laurel. See also Kennedy 1975.
9 Latin's limited vocabulary, inability to form nominal compounds, and lack of an article are but three factors that make imitation of Greek extremely difficult.
10 Cf. *me doctarum hederae praemia frontium / dis miscent superis* (1.1.29–30). This poetic register may broadly be called sympotic; see Davis 2007.
11 Refinement (cf. *non incultum*, 22) and precision (cf. *acuis*, 23) are stylistic desiderata of Hellenistic poetics, beginning with Callimachus. In his long epistle (2.2) to the same Florus, Horace states that the good poet "will smooth what is too rough with wholesome refinement (*sano … cultu*, 122–3)."
12 The influence of *Odes* 4.2 on the Western literary tradition is immense. As we have seen, it forms the basis of Quintilian's characterization of Horace and Pindar. The poem was often appended to Renaissance editions of Pindar and helped establish the distinction between the "greater" Pindaric ode and the "lesser" Horatian ode. For the French Renaissance, see Schmitz 1993: 76–98; for the German tradition, see Hamilton (2003).
13 Cf. *Ol.* 2.86–8, 9.100–2, and *Nem.* 3.80–2.
14 For an analysis of this catalogue, see Freis 1983: 30. For a comparison of Horace's catalogue of Pindar's works with other lists, see Race 1987.

15 The fundamental texts are Callimachus' "Prologue to the *Aetia*" and the epilogue
    to his *Hymn to Apollo* (104–13); still basic is the survey by Wimmel 1960.

16 Cf. also *Ol.* 1.103–5 and *Pyth.* 2.58–61.

17 I follow Davis 1991: 133-43. The analysis of Commager 1962: 59–65 is still valu-
    able, as is his survey of Augustan poetics in pp. 1–49.

18 Cf. 1.6 (for Agrippa), 2.1 (for Pollio) and 2.12 (for Maecenas), on which see Davis
    1991: 30–4 and 246–7. Propertius (3.3.7–12), for example, produces a brief cata-
    logue of Roman heroes before pretending to be stopped by Apollo.

19 But the phrase could equally come from Aristonous, *Paean 7*: Ζηνὸς ὑψίστου.

20 The passage from Pindar is a prayer, whereas the description in Horace com-
    pletes a catalogue of warrior gods (hence the reference to Apollo's bow).
    Kiessling and Heinze 1984a: 279 cite Aristonous, *Paean 41–4* (c. 350 BCE),
    which could also be a source (especially for washing in the dew of Kastalia):
    ἀλλ' ὦ Παρνασσοῦ γυάλων | εὐδρόσοισι Κασταλίας | να[σ]μοῖς σὸν δέμας ἐξαβρύ- | νων
    ("O you who soften your limbs with the well-bedewed waters of Kastalia in the
    valleys of Parnassos").

21 Harms 1936: 62: "He selects what suits him at the time, but seldom without chang-
    ing it. For he never simply translates or copies." Kennedy 1975: 18 cites some "verbal
    echoes" in 4.4, but concludes, "The similarity in formal structure and in thought is
    far more important."

22 A.P. 268–9: "handle Greek models by night, handle them by day."

23 *Odes* 1.2 is a paean which shares some features with Pindar's fragmentary *Paean 9*,
    but which, as Cairns 1971: 75–6 shows, owes as much to a tragic chorus in
    Sophocles' *Oedipus Tyrannus* (151–215).

24 Until recently, it has been fashionable for critics to disparage the poem. Nisbet and
    Hubbard 1970: 146 say of its meter: "Sapphic (not altogether appropriate for the
    matter in hand)." In addition, they completely misunderstand the rhetoric of lines
    33–6: "the drift becomes obscure at this point" (155). Perhaps harshest is D. Porter
    1987: 70–7, who calls it "a hollow hulk" (71) and says, "Its emptiness of real human
    issues strikes me as profoundly despairing" (77). In contrast, A. Hardie 2003 prop-
    erly regards the poem as a "grand public ode" (373) and argues in detail for Pindaric
    influence on all levels of subject matter, style, and presentation. While not always
    persuasive in some particular claims, the article successfully explores the range of
    intertextual possibilities.

25 Cf. Pindar's use of ἀλλ' ὅμως (*Pyth.* 1.85; *Nem.* 10.21) and ἔμπα (*Nem.* 4.36) to
    overcome feigned resistance arising from his subject matter or audience.

26 Interpretation of this stanza has been bedeviled by attempts to impose a "Pindaric"
    triadic structure on the poem that would make this stanza a continuation of the
    section on heroes. Brown (1991) clears up much previous confusion (including
    Fraenkel's) and provides an excellent analysis of the rhetoric of the poem from verse
    33 to the end.

27 Striking is the *variatio* of verbal forms for "celebrate" (*sumis celebrare*, 2; *recinet*, 3;
    dicam, 13; *neque silebo*, 21; *dicam*, 25; *memorem*, 34; and *referam*, 39); cf. High-
    barger 1935: 226 and 245 for verbal variety in Pindar's and Horace's poetry.

28 For the so-called the Bereitwilligkeits-Motiv in epinician poetry, see Maehler 1982:
    92.

29 Commentators point out that the simile of the tree resembles one at Pindar, *Nem.* 8.40–2: "Excellence grows like a tree that springs up to fresh dew, when lifted among wise and just men to liquid heaven," but the differences of subject and context are far more striking than are the similarities.

30 Fraenkel 1957: 276–85, whose observations are supplemented by Miller 1998, 2002.

31 Hesiod, *Th.* 79–80 calls Calliope "foremost of the Muses" because "she attends kings." Any ode that aspires to give praise or counsel to kings might well be indebted to Pindar.

32 For a survey of the forms and functions of hymns and prayers in Pindar, see Race 1990: 85–140.

33 For song that provides refreshment after successful toil, cf. *Nem.* 4.1–5; for poetry that provides gentle counsel, cf. *Pyth.* 4.270–6 and 5.65–7.

34 Cf. *Ol.* 1.52–3 ("I cannot call any of the blessed gods a glutton—I stand back: impoverishment is often the lot of slanderers"); *Ol.* 9.35–7 ("But cast that story away from me, my mouth! for reviling the gods is a hateful skill"); *Nem.* 5.14–17 ("I shrink from telling ... I will halt, for not every exact truth is better for showing its face").

35 Cf. *Pyth.* 1.48 ("he and his family") and *Ol.* 8.15 ("your family").

36 D. Young (1987) astutely used Horace's *doctrina sed vim promovet insitam* (33) to elucidate Pindar's *Ol.* 7.53 comment regarding Athene's gift of *techne* to the Rhodians ("when one is expert, even native talent becomes greater").

37 In addition, the manuscripts disagree on *perficient* (future) or *perficiunt* (present).

CHAPTER NINE

Female Figures in Horace's Odes

Ronnie Ancona

Introduction

Female figures in their many guises take on a wide range of images and functions in the Odes.[1] They are muses, and other goddesses; they are real historical figures, sometimes from the past, like Sappho, and sometimes from the present, like Cleopatra, Livia, Octavia, or the unnamed maidens, referred to in *Odes* 4.6.41–4, who are recalled as having sung, along with boys, Horace's *Carmen Saeculare* or Secular Hymn at the Secular Games of 17 BCE. In other instances they are just brief types—the good or bad mother or girl or wife and so on. Even Rome itself is compared to a woman, specifically a mother, as it looks out for Augustus just as a mother would look out for her son: *ut mater iuvenem ... sic ... quaerit patria Caesarem* (*Odes* 4.5.9–16). While the female figures in the love poems are likely the most famous from the Odes, limiting our discussion to those would give too partial a view of this topic and would miss the many ways in which "the female" pervades the lyric collection as a whole.

John Henderson (1999: 178) offers a general statement about approaching ancient Roman society, and, by extension, Roman literature, that is worth presenting here:

> No one who studies the culture of a historical society such as Rome can today avoid the realization that on the one hand it was always founded on the privileging of man over woman, and on the other Classics has been blind to that constitutive fact.

If woman is not privileged, then it is no wonder that she becomes a topic in a way that "man" does not. In addition, examining "woman/women/the female" not surprisingly may elide with looking at sexuality, for woman is *other* and her body/gender/sexuality is implicated in that otherness. "The female" in the Odes themselves and often in secondary scholarship about them is simultaneously foregrounded and marginalized: that "the female" is a "topic" suggests a kind of foregrounding, but that there would be no equivalent for "the male" under-scores its marginalization. When both male and female are open to examination, the gender dynamics in the Odes become far more interesting. In looking, then, at "female figures" we will hopefully also destabilize to some extent the unex-amined male.

Clearly, "women," "woman," and "female" are not interchangeable terms. I have chosen the title "female figures" to be as inclusive as possible. "Figure," of course, suggests "representation" in a way that a term like "women," does not, but as I think will be clear by the end of this chapter, that will not be an inap-propriate move for our discussion, for I do not think the Odes contain much about "women" per se. Further, the term "female" expands our scope beyond the narrowly human, which will be of benefit in the discussion that follows. While "the erotic" will certainly come into play in this chapter, it should not be auto-matically linked to female figures. Desire takes shape without any female figure in those odes that focus on the desiring male alone and/or a desired male, while female figures are at times significant in the Odes apart from the issue of desire.

Are any of Horace's odes ever "about" female figures? Of course poetry just *is*, it is not *about*. Yet, one could argue, I suppose, that *Odes* 1.23, for example, is "about" the figure of Chloe, but so much would be lost by framing a discus-sion of that particular ode solely in those terms. Still further, since Horace's Odes are lyric poetry, one could make a compelling argument that their subject matter (if, with poetry, we can even use that phrase) will never be "female figures," but rather is always on some level the poet, the speaking "I", the first person voice, or the self (whichever term one might want to use). Some scholarship on the issue of poetic address/apostrophe has even argued that in "address," the concern is with the constituting of the poetic self through dialogue as much as it is with what is addressed (Culler 2002: 135–54). Given this, one might wonder why we should focus on female figures in the Odes at all. A compelling argument for doing so might be that unless we do, we will not "see" them and they are there.

Female figures defined

While I will eventually focus primarily on the "human" (for lack of a better word) female figures who inhabit the Odes, I want to start with a larger discussion that makes clear how pervasive "the female" is in Horace's lyric œuvre. (To look at each female figure would be beyond the space limits of this piece.) If one looks through the Odes, one will quickly discover that even in places that have nothing to do with "women" there is a often a female presence. Still further, even in most of the places where one might find a "woman," she is unlikely to resemble any-thing concrete and tangible that one would easily connect with a real-life "beloved" or an historical figure. I have already referred above to the problem of the "aboutness" of poetry. With Horace one needs to push this idea even further, for not only are his poems, like most poems, not "about" something, they just "are," his poems are even more elusive in this respect than most. Often a poem that begins with one thought will conclude with another. For example, *Odes* 1.9 begins with a snow-capped mountain:

> Vides, ut alta stet nive candidum
> Soracte, nec iam sustineant onus
>   silvae laborantes, geluque
>   flumina constiterint acuto?[2] (1–4)

> Do you see how Soracte stands white with deep snow,
> and the laboring trees no longer hold up their burden,
> and the rivers have come to a halt with penetrating frost?

and ends with a girl's badly resisting finger:

> aut digito male pertinaci. (24)

> or her finger unsuccessfully resisting.

Or a poem that professes to do one thing will in fact do (or include) another.[3] For example, *Odes* 1.6 is a disavowal of epic while it incorporates epic language to define love-lyric.[4] After including mention of epic themes about which he will *not* write Horace announces his subject matter:

> nos convivia, nos *proelia* virginum
> sectis in iuvenes unguibus *acrium*
> cantamus ... (17–19)

> I (we) sing about banquets, I (we) sing about the *battles*
> of *fierce* girls with nails sharpened against young men ...
>   (emphases mine)

The language of the disavowed genre (epic) reappears, transformed, in the chosen genre (love poetry). As several scholars have noted, this generic disavowal and inclusion allows Horace to write in a genre (lyric) that appears slight compared with epic, but which he pushes to encompass and therefore become "bigger" than what it disavows.[5] Thus, if we are looking to examine "female figures" we will find them not only in poems that might appear to be "about" them, but also in many poems that appear to be "about" something else.

Categories and presence

The appearance of female figures in the Odes is far more pervasive than one might expect if one had not set out to notice them. Under the rubric of "female figures," which I have chosen to use to encompass "woman," "women," and "the female," one quickly sees that the category "female figures" includes many and disparate types. One could divide them into "divine" and "human," but in doing so would both miss the overlap of these putative categories and would be left with the possibly misleading term "human." For example, is "the muse" or "a muse" human or divine? It depends, in Horace. When Horace addresses the Muse, for example, in *Odes* 2.1.37, as *Musa procax* (impudent Muse), it is the goddess of his literary inspiration to which he refers. Yet, if one looks for example at *Odes* 1.22, the poem addressed to the "human" Lalage, one can see that she operates in that poem as a kind of muse or inspiration. It is the poet's singing about her that provides him with his subject matter (*dum meam canto Lalagen* ... "while I was singing of my Lalage ..." (10) and his magical protection (a wolf runs away from him and his far reaching travels confront him with no dangers from which he is not protected.)[6] The same poem has echoes of both Catullus and Sappho in its final lines:

> dulce ridentem Lalagen amabo,
> dulce loquentem. (23–4)

> I will love my Lalage, sweetly laughing,
> sweetly speaking.

Sappho, Fragment 31, has the beloved "sweetly speaking and charmingly laughing," while Catullus alters that to "sweetly laughing" only. Horace reverts to something closer to Sappho. One can argue that these two historical poets, Sappho writing in Greek at the close of the seventh century BCE and Catullus writing in Latin in the first century BCE, who influenced Horace in countless ways, also serve as muses of a kind for Horace.[7] If we focus on Sappho or Catullus or even Lalage as a muse or an instantiation of the muse, would we then see the muse as "human"? What does "human" mean in odes where most Greek-named figures like Lalage seem to occupy a world that is not simply *either* fictional *or* real? Is Pyrrha in *Odes* 1.5 (discussed below, p. 186) "human"? Or is she a "goddess / whore"? These remarks should make clear why setting up a distinction between human and divine female figures may not be very useful.

Female figures occupy the *Odes* in great variety. At times they may be the "subject" for a whole poem; at other times they make a brief appearance. If one is looking for some sort of unified view of female figures, either "Horace's" view or a view from within the Odes, one will not find it. Their variety is part and parcel of the variety of perspectives one might find surrounding anything else within these poems.

I would suggest that the "female" is a regularly occurring feature of the Odes and not just an occasional one, and that its presence is felt at least as much through repeated, even brief, references as it is through its presence throughout entire poems. If we return to the topic of Horace's relationship to his muse in the Odes, we will see that it is certainly of great importance, in large part because of its repetition. Even if we limit the mention of the muse to the instantiations traditionally connected with poetic inspiration and leave aside figures like Sappho, Catullus, and Lalage, already mentioned, the occurrences are many. The Muse appears singly as *Musa* "Muse" (cf., e.g., *Odes*.1.6.10), or in the plural as *Musae* "Muses" (cf., e.g., *Odes* 1.32.9), the Latin word for Muse being adapted from the Greek. She also appears as *Camena* (Roman goddess identified with the Muse) at *Odes* 2.16.38, there described as a "Greek Camena" (Graiae … Camenae), as *Camenae* in the plural, as at *Odes* 3.4.21, and as *Pierides* (*Odes* 4.8.20) "the ones from Pieria," the name derived from a traditional home of the Muses. In addition, they sometimes appear individually, by name, as in the following examples: Euterpe and Polyhymnia (*Odes* 1.1), Clio (*Odes* 1.12), Calliope (*Odes* 3.4), Melpomene (*Odes* 3.30 and *Odes* 4.3), Thalia (*Odes* 4.6). In *Odes* 3.4 the Muse is portrayed as protector of the poet, where he addresses her as Calliope, in particular, and then switches to the plural Muses, Camenae; while in *Odes* 3.3 he reproaches the Muse as *pervicax* (headstrong) for having him write of things not suitable to his playful lyre:

> non hoc iocosae conveniet lyrae.
> quo, Musa, tendis? desine pervicax
>   referre sermones deorum et
>   magna modis tenuare parvis. (69–72)

> This will not fit a playful lyre. Where, Muse, are you
> heading? Stop, headstrong, reporting the conversations
> of the gods and diminishing great matters with your
> insignificant meters.

Horace begins and ends his initial lyric collection of the *Odes* (Books 1–3) with poems containing significant appearances of the Muses:

Odes *1.1*

> me doctarum hederae praemia frontium
> dis miscent superis, me gelidum nemus
>
> Nympharumque leves cum Satyris chori
> secernunt populo, si neque tibias
>
> Euterpe cohibet, nec Polyhymnia
> Lesboum refugit tendere barbiton.
>
> quodsi me lyricis vatibus inseres,
> sublimi feriam sidera vertice. (29–36)

> Ivy, reward of learned brows, mingles me with the gods
> above, and the cool grove and the nimble bands of
> Nymphs along with Satyrs separate me from the crowd,
> if Euterpe does not withhold the pipes and Polyhymnia
> does not shrink from stretching the Lesbian lyre. But if
> you insert me among the lyric bards, I will strike the
> stars with my lofty head.

In these lines, two of the Muses are mentioned by name, Euterpe and Polyhymnia. Their Greek names and the "Lesbian lyre," a reference to the Greek lyric poetry of Sappho and Alcaeus, both of whom come from the Greek island of Lesbos, along with the use of the word *barbitos*, a Greek word for lyre, indicate Horace's debt to his Hellenic models. The phrase "*lyricis vatibus*," though, with its mix of Greek-based word (*lyricis*) and Latin (*vatibus*) moves us ahead in literary time to Horace as a practitioner of a Romanized Greek lyric. The Muses are here as a kind of necessary presence to maintain Horace's poetic credentials. While the "you" of "if you insert me" recalls the poem's addressee, Maecenas, his close friend and literary supporter, it also points to the listener and reader—the "audience"—who ultimately have the power to determine his literary fame. Still further, it resonates with the Muses whose participation is necessary for the achievement of the poet's goal.

Odes *3.30, 14–16*

> ... sume superbiam
> quaesitam meritis et mihi Delphica
> lauro cinge volens, Melpomene, comam.

> Take on the pride earned by meritorious acts and
> willingly, Melpomene, encircle my hair with Delphic
> laurel.

In the ode that closes Books 1–3, Horace again addresses one of the Muses by name, Melpomene. Here she will crown the poet with laurel, recalling the "ivy, reward of learned brows" from *Odes*.1.1. What Horace leaves open by not supplying a possessive word to modify "meritis" is the question of *whose* "meritorious acts" Melpomene should take pride in—her own as source of poetic inspiration, or rather Horace's for his poetic achievement?

It is clear that the female Muses "surround" Horace's lyric collection of Books 1–3. They are important as he embarks upon his lyric endeavor and as he sees it concluded. However, this is not a simple, stylized, deferential relationship between poet and "source of inspiration". Rather, it is a kind of dance of inspiration, credit, debt and pride.

The Roman Odes (Book 3, 1–6) contain much that is political, moral and serious. Horace assimilates these matters to his lyric genre and "puts the blame" on the "headstrong Muse" (*Musa ... pervicax*) for taking him away from his proper poetic domain (*Odes* 3.3.70) A similar move takes place in the final four lines of *Odes* 2.1. After announcing civil war as the appropriate topic for his addressee Gaius Asinius Pollio's current literary pursuits, Horace bemoans the fact that while Pollio is thus occupied his tragic Muse will have to be absent. Horace then proceeds to evoke the civil war that will be the topic of Pollio's histories. The poem concludes with Horace chastising his own Muse as impudent or licentious "*procax*" for leading him away from themes more suitable to his playful genre. He calls upon her to go with him to Venus' grotto to seek material more suitable to his light verse. Thus the female figure of the Muse is involved in a dynamic way with Horace's generic moves.

The Muses are (in terms of their traditional genealogy) female divinities, daughters of Zeus and Mnemosyne (Memory). The *Odes* are filled with many other goddesses and goddess-like figures besides the Muses. We have seen the Nymphs (divine or semi-divine figures typically associated with nature) already in *Odes* 1.1. In *Odes* 1.4, a poem celebrating the coming of spring, the Nymphs appear again, along with the Graces, who are daughters of Zeus and Eurynome, dancing with the goddess Venus, who oversees the dancers. Venus, the Graces, and the Nymphs appear together again in *Odes* 1.30, a short invocation to Venus to come to the house of Glycera. Many other goddesses appear in the *Odes* as well, for example, Diana, Pallas (as Horace calls Minerva), and Juno.

The goddess Venus, in particular, appears prominently in many of Horace's odes. She is a versatile figure and functions in a variety of ways. She appears "in the background" one might say in several odes, as for example, in *Odes* 1.4 mentioned above. In others she plays a much more dominant role. Venus, of course, is goddess of love and sexuality, but she is also the mother of the Trojan hero Aeneas, whose father is the mortal Anchises. The Julian family, to which Julius Caesar and Augustus belonged, traced their ancestry through Aeneas and his son Iulus, back to this divine figure. Perhaps the best place to see this dual role of Venus is in Book 4 of Horace's *Odes*, the poetic book that appeared a decade after the publication of his original lyric collection. As Horace returns to writing lyric, and love lyric in particular, and moves towards poetry with more direct political reference to Augustus, it is not surprising that Venus becomes a touchstone for Horace's renewed and new poetic aspirations (Putnam 1986).

> Intermissa, Venus, diu
> > rursus bella moves? parce, precor, precor.
> non sum, qualis eram bonae
> > sub regno Cinarae. desine, dulcium

mater saeva Cupidinum,
　　circa lustra decem flectere mollibus
iam durum imperiis: abi,
　　quo blandae iuvenum te revocant preces. (1–8)

Venus, are you stirring up again battles interrupted for a
long time? Spare me, I beg you, I beg you. I am not the
sort of man I was under the reign of good Cinara.
Savage mother of sweet Cupids, stop moving me, fifty
years old, now unresponsive, with your gentle
commands: go away where the alluring prayers of the
youth call you back.

Horace here combines the writing of love poetry and love itself and argues that he is too old for Venus' domain. Another younger figure, Paulus Maximus, is pointed out as a more suitable object for Venus' interest. Yet at the end of the poem, Horace, who has declared himself no longer pleased by boy or woman or parties (29–32), catches himself moved by the young man Ligurinus whom in his dreams he holds captive and then pursues over the Campus Martius. This is a moving poem because of its evocation of the condition of the pathos of growing old and still feeling desire. It challenges notions of suitability and decorum and leads the reader to sympathize with potentially unseemly emotions. This private pathos, though, is tied to the speaker's / Horace's male gender. No such sympathy is provided in the *Odes* for the aging and desiring female (Ancona 1994: 85–93).

Venus frames Book 4 of the *Odes*. The privacy of desire as a response to the commands of Venus in the opening ode of Horace's final lyric collection (*Odes* 4.1) becomes public ritual in the closing ode (4.15). Following his praise of Augustus and the future benefits that will accrue to Rome through his continued power, Horace concludes on a note of ritual prayer and communal song (the word *canemus* "we will sing" is the poem's final word), whose subject will include the offspring or family (*progeniem*) of nourishing Venus (*almae … Veneris*), which includes, of course, Augustus:

　　　　… almae
progeniem Veneris canemus. (31–2)

Venus functions in these framing poems, first, as goddess of love and inspiration for love poetry and finally, as ancestor of the Romans and, in particular, the Julian line. In both she is a mother—at first a cruel mother of sweet Cupids and then the kindly Venus who mothered the Roman race. Just as divine Muses overlap with historical figures like Sappho and Catullus, and with apparently fictional subject matter like Lalage, so Venus, Roman goddess of love, is variously love, inspiration to write love poetry, cruel mother of Cupids and nourishing mother of the Roman state and its leading family. In her political role she blurs the division between divine figure and historical progenitor.

Female figures, in the particular sense of historical types or specific historical individuals, as opposed to the divine, with some exceptions (e.g., Cleopatra in *Odes* 1.37) most often seem to serve a moral, social, or religious function within the Odes, rather than to serve as central figures themselves. For example, in *Odes* 3.30 (discussed above), Horace's fame will increase over time:

> ... dum Capitolium
> scandet cum tacita virgine pontifex. (8–9)

> while the chief priest climbs the Capitoline Hill
> with a silent [vestal] virgin.

In a poem otherwise free of female presence except for Melpomene, the Muse, and Libitina, goddess of burial, whom Horace (at least a great part of him "*multaque pars mei*", 6) will avoid through his poetry, the one "historical" female individual is a generic Vestal Virgin, who silently performs her ritual religious function at the temple to the Capitoline gods. At other times a female figure embodies moral degeneration, as for example in *Odes* 3.6, the last of the Roman Odes. There, the good stern peasant mother (39–40), who raised up virtuous sons, is contrasted with the young girl of the current generation who plans her unchaste loves and, as a wife, not only has illicit love affairs, but does so openly with the knowledge of her husband—and for a price (22–32). Through intermarriage with local women (*coniuge barbara* "with a barbarian wife" *Odes* 3.5.5) Crassus' conquered Roman army forgets about Rome. The hunter who stays out all night is unmindful of his tender wife (*Odes* 1.1.26).

It is interesting to note that the figure of the semi-divine Helen is used, not unlike human female figures, to comment negatively on illicit, foreign love and its ruinous effect on Troy (in the words of Juno in *Odes* 3.3) as well as to comment positively (or at least neutrally) on the enduring quality of passion through the agency of poetry (*Odes* 4.9). In *Odes* 3.3 Helen's interest in Paris is already waning:

> iam nec Lacaenae splendet adulterae
> famosus hospes ... (25–6)

> No longer does the much talked of famous/infamous
> host shine for his Spartan adulteress

She can be seen as a kind of bridge between the morally negative adulterous wife and the noteworthy, poetry-celebrated, subject of desire. Yet *Odes* 3.3 serves as an interesting commentary on *Odes* 4.9, for the desire that seems almost fixed through poetry in 4.9 is shown, in *Odes* 3.3 to be able to undergo change.

In addition to the female figure "types" of young girls, mothers, and wives, there are actual historical female figures in the Odes. Sappho has already been mentioned as a significant influence upon Horace and as an important literary precursor and model. Contemporary figures appear as well. In *Odes* 3.14, a poem in celebration of Augustus' recovery from illness and safe return from Spain in 24 bce, we find mention of Augustus' wife, Livia, and his sister, Octavia, in the context of ritual activities in honor of his return (5–7):

> unico gaudens mulier marito
> prodeat iustis operata sacris
> et soror clari ducis ...

> Rejoicing in her singular husband, let the wife go forth
> having performed ritual sacrifices, and the sister of the
> famous leader ...

In a typically Horatian twist, this public "real" celebration is followed by a turn towards private ("fictive?") rejoicing as Horace requests that the clear-voiced Neaera be brought to join him.

Cleopatra, historical figure

The ode that stands out for its full-scale attention to a historical female figure is *Odes* 1.37, often referred to as the Cleopatra Ode. Much of its success lies in its marvelously ambiguous portrayal of the Ptolemaic queen, Cleopatra VII of Egypt, a central figure for contemporary Roman politics. The ode begins with a call to celebration for the defeat and fall of Cleopatra, opponent, along with Mark Antony, of Octavian, later known as Augustus. The battle of Actium in 31 BCE signaled their defeat and in 30 BCE the two committed suicide. The elimination of this opposition led to Augustus' assumption of the position of leader of the Roman state and the end to years of civil war. Antony is not mentioned in the ode. Cleopatra is its central figure, more important than Octavian. Despite the celebration of her defeat, by the time the reader has reached the end of the poem one is forced to contend with her nobility. This complicates the celebra-tion—for some readers it makes Octavian's triumph all the greater, for others it renders it somewhat tainted. In a time when poets like Horace and Vergil were not completely enthusiastic in their embracing of the new Roman order, the more ironic reading seems to me more appropriate and interesting.

Since our focus is on female figures in the Odes, attention to Cleopatra specifi-cally as "female" will be useful. The positive imagery of celebratory drinking that begins the poem:

> Nunc est bibendum ...

> Now is the time for drinking ...

quickly turns into negative imagery about the queen who is "drunk with sweet
fortune" (*fortunaque dulci / ebria*, 11–12), "wild" (*inpotens*, 10) in her hopes,
and planning mad ruin for the Capitolium and destruction for the state (6–8).
She is described as accompanied by a vile flock of men shameful because of their
disease or vice: (*contaminato cum grege turpium / morbo virorum*, 9–10). This
is a negative reference to Cleopatra's eunuchs, who served as attendants at her
court in Alexandria. They are "men," but shameful ones, because of their
"unmanly" condition. She is a queen, drunk on ambition, surrounded by less
than orthodox men. Mark Antony, "absent" from the poem, may be indirectly
included among her disparaged male companions. What sobers her up is her
defeat at Actium and Octavian's pursuit of her. Octavian is compared to a hawk
chasing gentle doves or a swift hunter chasing a hare. Gone are Cleopatra's hopes.
They are replaced by real fears (*veros timores*, 15). Octavian's purpose is to put
this "deadly marvel/monster" *fatale monstrum* (21) in chains.

> fatale monstrum, quae generosius
> perire quaerens *nec muliebriter*
>   expavit ensem, nec latentis
>   classe cita reparavit oras,
>
> ausa et iacentem visere regiam
> voltu sereno, fortis et asperas
>   tractare serpentes, ut atrum
>   corpore combiberet venenum,
>
> deliberata morte ferocior:
> saevis Liburnis scilicet invidens
>   privata deduci superbo
>   non humilis *mulier* triumpho. (21–32)

the deadly marvel, *who* seeking to perish more nobly,
did *not in womanish manner* fear the sword and did
not reach hidden shores with her swift fleet. She dared
also to look at her palace, lying in ruins, with calm
face; brave, also, at handling fierce snakes in order to
drink up with her body the dark poison; more bold
because of her carefully considered death; refusing,
evidently, to be led back to Rome as a private citizen
by cruel galleys for a proud triumphal procession—a
not humble *woman*.   (emphases mine)

From the perspective of looking at female figures in the Odes it is the attention
to Cleopatra "as woman" in this final section of the poem that is noteworthy.
After the description of her as a *fatale monstrum* (deadly marvel/monster), a
phrase which contains the neuter noun, *monstrum*, there is a switch back to
feminine gender with the relative pronoun *quae* (who), as we leave the simile.

What follows is a description of a noble, proud, and considered response to defeat on the part of Cleopatra. Her suicide prevents her from being brought back to Rome to be displayed in her defeat like a piece of war booty. The lack of fear of the sword and the choice not to hide are called "not womanish" (*nec muliebriter*), while the final reference to her is as a "woman" (*mulier*), who is not humble. This matches the Roman triumph, which is described as *superbo* (proud). Her noble actions are not womanish, but the result is her elevation to "not humble" / proud *woman*. Whether one sees the conclusion of the poem as heightening Octavian's status by his defeat of someone noble, or sees it as a perhaps reluctant admiration of this great enemy queen, it is clear that her gender does affect the way in which she is characterized. Paradoxically, perhaps, her non-womanish actions make her into a proud woman, or at least not a humble one. That this occurs in conjunction with her defeat may allow for a safe admiration. She can be admired when no longer a threat.

If Cleopatra is a major preoccupation of one of Horace's Odes, she is exceptional in that respect. Far more often, as we have seen, female figures in many of the odes will appear in less starring roles. That she is a historical female figure given this much attention is highly unusual.[8] Our survey of female figures has left to the last the ones who are likely most familiar to readers of the Odes, the ones who exist in a literary, likely fictive, but potentially real world— figures like Pyrrha, Chloe, Barine, and Lalage. While a few of these names recur in the Odes (for example, Chloe in *Odes* 1.23, 3.7, 3.9, 3.26), there is little that suggests any major significance to these poetic series (autobiographically based or otherwise).

While some might still refer to some of these figures as Horace's lovers, it is best, I think, to leave them as literary figures who inhabit a world that is not necessarily alien to Horace's own lived world, but who do not necessarily connect with it in any definitive way. These figures generally have Greek names, which sets them apart from the world of the Roman citizen girl and matron. In fact, their removal to a context apart from the upper class Roman activities of marriage and family, to the Greek world of ancient or Hellenistic lyric or to the world of freedwomen in Rome, or other "non-Romans" within contemporary Roman society, allows Horace an imaginative space within which social conventions are, for the most part, irrelevant. *Odes* 2.8 is something of an exception, for there Horace shows with some amusement the danger to marriage posed by Barine, whose name with its Greek ending ("e") is suitable for a freedwoman (Nisbet and Hubbard 1978), who lures away young husbands and still keeps men at her house who have threatened to leave her (Ancona 2005). Of course, figures like the Lesbia / Clodia in Catullus' poetry defy social convention while perhaps also reflecting social reality. However, although Clodia was a member of a famous Roman family, the Chloes and Lalages of Horace, who are conceptually distinct from particular figures in contemporary society, may be more easily invested with whatever one wants to attribute to them. Their very lack of particularity may be part of their poetic appeal.

Female figures in the Love Odes—a brief look

Despite the great variety in images of female figures in the Odes it is Horace's love poems that generally provide us with the most arresting and best-known female figures and it is to an examination of a few of these that I now turn. More than a quarter of Horace's odes involve erotic themes and the majority of these, in turn, involve female figures. Others involve male figures as objects of desire instead (e.g., *Odes* 4.10), or in conjunction with the mention of female figures, as in *Odes* 4.1 (discussed above). Certain themes, postures and perspectives are recurrent throughout these odes and I offer the following discussion of *Odes* 1.5 and 1.11 in order to highlight these recurring features in relation to female figures in the Odes:

Odes *1.5*

Quis multa gracilis te puer in rosa
perfusus liquidis urget odoribus
    grato, Pyrrha, sub antro?
      cui flavam religas comam

simplex munditiis? heu quotiens fidem   5
mutatosque deos flebit et aspera
    nigris aequora ventis
      emirabitur insolens,

qui nunc te fruitur credulus aurea,
qui semper vacuam, semper amabilem   10
    sperat, nescius aurae
      fallacis. miseri, quibus

intemptata nites. me tabula sacer
    votiva paries indicat uvida
      suspendisse potenti   15
        vestimenta maris deo.

What slender youth, filled with liquid perfume, among
many roses, presses on you down in the pleasing cave,
Pyrrha? For whom do you tie back/tie again[9] your
auburn hair, simple in your elegance? Alas, how many
times he will weep for changed trust and gods and
unaccustomed will be astonished at the sea rough with
black winds, who now credulous enjoys you, golden,

who hopes you will be always available, always lovable,
ignorant of the deceptive breeze. Unhappy are they, for
whom you shine untried. A sacred wall shows with a
votive tablet that I have hung up my wet garments to
the potent god of the sea.

This poem has been a Horace favorite for a long time, not only among Latin scholars and readers, but among readers and translators of many other languages. A collection of translations into English and other languages of this single ode has been published by Oxford University Press (Storrs 1959). John Milton's well-known translation is included. While there are many perspectives from which this poem can be discussed, our focus will be the figure of Pyrrha—how she functions within the poem and how that function sheds light on some common features of female figures in Horace's love poems.[10]

As I suggested above, the very nature of lyric suggests that the odes may be seen as *about* the poet or speaker more than they are *about* anything else. This may be especially true of Horace's love lyrics. Thus, when we look at Pyrrha, what we find may be quite elusive. She *exists* on some level to allow for the poet's discourse about her. As the addressee of the poem she is the poetic occasion for the direct address. While this idea of the addressee applies, of course, to male figures as well and to odes that are not love poems, its significance seems to be somewhat different in this context. In much contemporary discussion of Horace's poetry, what has developed is a view of the love odes in which the focus becomes the female figure herself without attention to how and why she is constructed in a particular way. What is then lost is the ability to do something other than mimic the apparent values of the speaker's persona or reject them out of hand. The mimicking might entail a response like the following: *Great Poem. Women are fickle. We (men) understand that. She's alluring and dangerous and we're lucky to get away alive.* The rejecting might entail the following: *Horace was a bachelor. He didn't understand how to, or didn't want to, have long-term relationships. He never had a lasting love, so he's not much of a love poet. No passion here.* While these are caricatures of responses, I present them as a way of showing a particular either/or to be avoided.

Avoiding such caricatures, let us look at various significant aspects of the poem to see how a female figure is implicated in them. The theme of time is an overarching one in Horace's love poems (Ancona 1994). While one might expect from a love poem a moment of present urgency or of mutual engagement, what one finds far more often in Horace is an erotic dynamic that involves multiple temporal perspectives: a lover looking back or looking forward, or a speaker observing the loves of others (but often indirectly involved). This makes for a love poetry of change and distance, of arguments about "timeliness" for love (cf., among others, *Odes* 1.23 and *Odes* 1.25). Even in the poetry of Horace, whose most famous words are probably *carpe diem* (see *Odes* 1.11 below), the day seems very difficult to seize. Injunctions to do so abound, but loving "in the moment" is not often represented in Horace's odes. This somewhat disengaged approach produces some marvelous poetic effects. Love is seen from several angles. Desire is central but hard to grasp or hold on to. Love as potential transgression leads to questions of the possible relations of selves. For example, if the lover in *Odes* 1.22 is *integer* (untouched), how does that affect his ability to engage with another self? How does it affect his sense of personal and geographic boundaries? (cf. Ancona 2002). Horace is not a poet particularly known for his imagery, but the figurative language in the love odes is quite powerful. To name just a few examples, seas, storms, and fire (in *Odes* 1.5) a fawn and spring (in *Odes* 1.23) and leaves and a mare (in *Odes* 1.25) are all images associated with female figures in the love odes. Horace is a master of Latin word order. In the love odes this takes on particular significance as lovers or would-be lovers are joined or separated through the placement of words. For example, a denial of overaggressive erotic pursuit in *Odes* 1.23:

> atqui *non ego te* tigris ut aspera
> Gaetulusve leo frangere *persequor* (9–10) (emphases mine)
>
> but *I do not pursue you* like a fierce tigress or a Gaetulian lion
> to break you

can be seen as belied by the Latin word order. The "*ego*" is chasing the "*te*" and the "*non*" is so far away from the verb it modifies (*persequor*) that one could argue that the literal denial of "I am not pursuing" is in conflict with the emotive force of the final two words of the line *frangere persequor*, "I pursue to break."

In *Odes* 1.5 we can see how many of the issues mentioned above come into play. The distanced quality mentioned above is apparent in the "surprise" ending to *Odes* 1.5. Until *me* (me) in line 13 of this 16-line poem, there is no indication that the speaker is in any way involved. The questions addressed to Pyrrha, the poem's addressee, in lines 1–3 and lines 4–5, the long statement that follows (5–12), and the short one that comes after (12–13 *miseri ... nites*) could easily be made by just an observer. With *me*, though, the perspective shifts and the speaker becomes involved, even if to announce his current uninvolvement. This shifting of perspective is common in the love odes. It is a kind of disengaged engagement. In *Odes* 1.5 we can see how this characteristic is directly connected with a multiple temporal perspective. The speaker watches and questions in the present (note the present verb tenses, *urget*, "presses," 2, *religas*, "you tie back / tie again," 4). He then shifts to comment on the future (*flebit*, "he will weep," 6, and *emirabitur*, "he will be astonished," 8), made more emphatic by the word *quotiens* ("how many times," 5) which introduces the idea of repeated action in the future. However even these comments on the future are framed in light of the present (*fruitur*, "enjoys," 9, and *sperat*, "hopes," 11). Present enjoyment is made more emphatic by *nunc* ("now," 9) while hopes for the future are underscored by the repeated *semper* ("always," 10). The description of the youth as *credulus* ("credulous," 9) and *nescius* ("ignorant," 11) suggests that love in the present is, at the most, fleeting, and involves both ignorance and hopes to be dashed. The allure that Pyrrha has is both exciting and frightening. She has the power to attract and the built-in necessity to disappoint. Her seeming constancy of appeal over time, not unlike that of Barine in *Odes* 2.8 is striking. Generations seem to experience her without her appeal changing over time. This, one might say, is her almost goddess-like quality. She defies the temporal imperative Horace presents elsewhere in poems like *Odes* 1.23 and *Odes* 1.25 where there is a "proper" time or season for love, at least for women, and that proper time is defined by the male speaker. (In *Odes* 1.23 he defines her as ripe and ready, in *Odes* 1.25 as too old.)

Female figures like this are potentially threatening to men, in the *Odes*. They lead to wisdom and disillusionment, but a disillusionment seemingly not tinged with regret. There is no "I wish I had never known Pyrrha" here and in *Odes* 2.8 there is a nervous awe at Barine's powers. Unlike other poems where nature is used by the speaker to define a female figure's appropriate or inappropriate actions (Chloe in *Odes* 1.23 is associated with spring and is therefore defined as "ready" for love, while Lydia in *Odes* 1.25 is associated with winter and therefore defined as too old for love), Pyrrha is defined through figurative language as a natural force that continues over time. She is fire (her name contains the Greek root for fire), she is golden (*aurea*, 9); she shines (*nites*, 13); she is the dark wind (*nigris ... ventis*, 7) and the deceptive breeze (*aurae / fallacis*, 10–11). All participate in the "sea of love," from the youth with his "liquid" perfume, to the fierce sea that he will become amazed at, to the wet clothes of the speaker whose votive offering to the god, Neptune, indicates that he has given up his own voyage of love.

In *Odes* 1.5 we have a triangulated relationship of lovers with an overarching sense of present moment colored by the perspective of past experience and future knowledge. Is the speaker an observer, a commentator, an adviser, a critic, or a voyeur? When one rereads the poem, do the questions the speaker addresses to Pyrrha change? When one has "retired" from involvement with Pyrrha, why does one care who presses on her now?

If Pyrrha is in some sense the female figure of "experience," Leuconoe, in *Odes* 1.11 is her opposite. While in *Odes* 1.5 the speaker questions and comments and, one might argue, shows continued involvement with Pyrrha, although of an altered kind, here the role of speaker is much more direct and involves repeated injunctions to his addressee. Most of the verbs in the poem are imperatives or subjunctives functioning as imperatives. Yet, if the speaker is more direct here in one sense, he is less direct in another, for Horace manages to combine the rhetoric of philosophy with that of the erotic to create a poem that merges philosophical advice (which one typically thinks of as disinterested or objective) with erotic desire (which one typically thinks of as urgent and potentially non-rational).

Odes *1.11*

Tu ne quaesieris (scire nefas), quem mihi, quem tibi
finem di dederint, Leuconoe, nec Babylonios

temptaris numeros. ut melius, quidquid erit, pati!
seu pluris hiemes, seu tribuit Iuppiter ultimam,

quae nunc oppositis debilitat pumicibus mare   5
Tyrrhenum: sapias, vina liques et spatio brevi

spem longam reseces. dum loquimus, fugerit invida
aetas: carpe diem, quam minimum credula postero.

You, do not seek (it is a sacrilege to know) what end for me,
what end for you the gods have given, Leuconoe, nor try
Babylonian numbers. How better it is to endure whatever will
be! Whether more winters, or whether Jupiter has allotted his
last, which now weakens the Tyrrhenian Sea with hostile
pumice-stones: be wise, strain the wine and cut back long
hope because of brief time. While we are speaking, envious
time will have fled: seize the day, trusting to the least extent
possible in the next one.

Leuconoe's name contains the Greek roots for "clear, bright, white" (*leukos*)
and "mind" (*nous*). Her name can equally mean "clear-minded" or "empty-
minded." If she is clear-minded, then she can rationally listen to his rational
advice. If she is empty-minded she can become the empty vessel for his philosophical ideas. If she is clear-minded, she might have a response (positive or
negative) to erotic interest. If she is empty-minded, then a response to erotic
intent might be irrelevant. The poem can be read as a serious philosophical
statement—it is better not to foresee the future, it is better to endure whatever
will be—or as a poem of seduction. Horace has set it up to function as both
simultaneously. Leuconoe is much like the male youth in *Odes* 1.5. The speaker,
though, speaks as if he has wisdom and knowledge and yet argues that knowledge
of the future is not to be sought out and in fact is inappropriate to seek out
(hence the statement that it is *nefas* or "not sanctioned by divine law"). The time
and manner of one's death are not something to be known. The image of the
sea of love, so powerful in *Odes* 1.5, recurs here in a somewhat different form.
Here, the sea itself becomes weakened over time by the pumice stones hostile to
it (*oppositis … pumicibus*, 5). There is an urgency to time's passing. The youth
is ignorant and trusting and has hopes; Leuconoe is told (by the knowledgeable
speaker!) not to seek knowledge of the future and to cut back on hopes. The
upshot is the advice to seize the day, shaped by the context of time passing (and
being jealous (!)—so there is a third party observing here too) and the need to
avoid trust in the next day (or man). *Postero* ("next") does not have a noun to

modify. While most would understand *diem* ("day") one could somewhat humorously see an understood "man," suggesting that trusting in men (including the speaker) is as risky as trusting in time.

Different as Pyrrha and Leuconoe may appear, both are implicated in a version of love defined as a problem of knowledge and time and perspective. Despite the similarity between the male youth of *Odes* 1.5 and the female Leuconoe in *Odes* 1.11, there is something of a gendered perspective here in that one might imagine the male youth of *Odes* 1.5 "escaping" and becoming the Horatian speaker of *Odes* 1.11 who now has "wisdom" and gets to use it for seduction.

Conclusion

There are some who feel a need to "redeem" Horace, when it comes to female figures in the Odes, by pointing to moments of true affection and mutuality in them. I would argue that those moments are hard to find. For example, the *irrupta ... copula* of *Odes* 1.13, line 18, that most see as an "unbroken" bond, can be seen as a "broken into" or "interrupted" bond (Ancona 1994: 125–8). The end of the lovers' dialogue in *Odes* 3.9 occurs in the subjunctive, not the indicative, leaving the door open for change. But does this make these poems any less interesting? I don't think so. Female figures in the Odes are far more pervasive than one might at first have suspected. However, having found them, we see that they are varied and, finally, quite elusive.

GUIDE TO FURTHER READING

Ancona (1994) is the only book-length discussion of the Odes in which gender issues are central. Some of its arguments were anticipated in Ancona (1989); Fredricksmeyer (1994) offers a counter-argument to Ancona (1989). For another view of Horace as a love poet, one may consult Arkins (1993). Lyne (1980) also includes discussion of female figures in the context of Horace as a love poet. Putnam (1986) and Putnam (2006b), as well as several articles by the same author, directly or indirectly address issues of gender when discussing the erotic. For gender implications of the idea of nature as a moral metaphor in *Odes* 1.25, see Ancona (1992). For another discussion of the same ode that takes into consideration issues of gender, see Anderson (1999). Sutherland (1995, 2003, 2005a, 2005b, 2005c) are all very useful for examination of female figures in the Odes. See Davis (1975, 1987a, and 1991) for female figures and issues of genre. On gender and the erotic in Horace, generally, see Oliensis (2007).

Many articles and books that deal with various other aspects of Horace's Odes, of course, may include discussion of female figures. They are too numerous to list here. One may start with the sources mentioned in this chapter and then consult standard bibliographies for Classics or Horace studies. Equally useful may be sources that deal with female figures and/or gender issues, more generally, in Latin Literature. *Diotima: Materials for the Study of Women and Gender in the Ancient World* http://www.stoa.org/diotima/ provides some excellent bibliography.

NOTES

1 I would like to thank Gregson Davis, editor of this volume, for his useful comments and suggestions.
2 Latin text is that of Borzsák 1984. All translations are my own and are fairly literal. They are intended solely as an aid to the reader of this chapter.
3 See Davis 1991, especially chapter 1, "Modes of Assimilation."
4 Davis 1991: 33–4 and 36–9.
5 Davis 1991 *passim* and Lowrie 1997 *passim*.
6 See Davis 1987a for the figure of Lalage functioning as part of the poem's literary-generic affirmation of erotic lyric.
7 See Ancona 2002 and Woodman 2002.
8 For an argument against identification of Licymnia (*Odes* 2.12) with an historical figure, see Davis 1975.
9 The verb *religo* is most often translated here as "tie back," but it can equally mean "tie again" (the "*re*" prefix always has the potential sense of "again" as well as "back").
10 Another approach might focus on the youth as a foil to the speaker, the voice of experience.

CHAPTER TEN

The Roman Odes

Hans Peter Syndikus[1]

The first six Odes of Book 3 differ in significant ways from the rest of Horace's *Carmina*. His lyric collections are usually organized in sequences that vary with respect to meter, theme, and tone—a principle of arrangement that we find already in the major group of small poems of the Catullan corpus (*Carmina* 1–60). In Horace's normal practice, short poems tend to be followed by long, poems graver in tone by lighter; in such juxtapositions the clash of opposites may often appear rather mannered, and it is rare that more than two successive poems employ the same meter.[2] The six opening poems of Book 3, however, are all unusually long, they are all concerned with the political sphere, and they are all written in the Alcaic meter. Another distinguishing feature is the fact that there are no named addressees for this subgroup of Odes. The first stanza of 3.1 serves as a kind of prooemium for the entire sequence: it announces a series of long, celebratory poems, dedicated by the poet as "priest of the Muses" (*Musarum sacerdos*) to "the maidens and boys of Rome" (*virginibus puerisque*). The poet here presents himself in an unexpected role that is reminiscent of the ancient Greek bards, and bears some resemblance to the role he had assumed in the early *Epodes* 16, but seldom thereafter. He seems to envision a large audience for this new group of poems and to ascribe great weight and authority to his bardic pronouncements and to the truths they claim to embody.

Horace evidently intended these poems to constitute a cycle markedly different in character from any of his previously published odes. However, it appears that not all of the six poems were initially conceived as part of a coherent cycle. References to the *princeps* under the honorific title, Augustus, in *Odes* 3.3.11 and 3.5.3 indicate that these two poems were composed after January of the year 27 BCE, when this title was officially conferred. In contrast, *Odes* 3.4 and 3.6 allude to earlier historical events: the former, to the return of the victorious veterans from the civil wars and to plans to help them resettle in the homeland and resume life as peacetime civilians, the latter, to the restoration of ruined temples which, in accordance with Augustus' own words, were all rebuilt in 28.[3] *Odes* 3.4, through its invocation of the Muse and its appeal for the inspiration of a long poem (*longum melos*), features a prooemium markedly different from that of 3.1; *Odes* 3.6 addresses the whole Roman people (*Romane*), rather than merely the young generation. One may conclude, on the basis of these observations, that Horace, in order to achieve a fuller cycle, added other poems to *Odes* 3.4 and 3.6, which he had composed earlier.[4]

Theodor Mommsen's writings have played an influential role in the interpretation of this cycle. In a 1889 speech at a celebration in honor of the Prussian-German monarchy, the eminent historian drew a parallel between the founding of the kingdom and the establishment of a Roman autocratic state under Augustus. Mommsen saw the six Odes as a eulogy to the new ruler no less than to his newly established regime. Numerous passages, he argued, could be read in light of recent events in Roman history:[5] Thus according to Mommsen, *Odes* 3.2 refers to the virtues that the professional soldier in the standing army created by Augustus should possess—an allusion to the newly reorganized citizen cavalry; while the final two stanzas advert to the loyalty and secrecy required by the new imperial bureaucracy. On similar lines, the unshakeable hero of the opening stanzas of *Odes* 3.3 is a reference to the victor of Actium, the baneful Helen is to be understood as Cleopatra, and the exhortation not to rebuild Troy is a warning not to shift the Empire's center of gravity from Rome and Italy to the East, as Antony had envisaged, and might indeed have seemed plausible in the geopolitical circumstances of the time; *Odes* 3.4 celebrates Augustus as the bringer of peace and exponent of clemency, whose regime also included the sponsorship of poetry; the image of the Olympian gods prevailing over the monstrous Titans and Giants of the cosmogony alludes to the victory over the barbarian East; both the fifth and the second poems of Book 3 are interpreted as supporting a definite plan to conduct a campaign against the Parthians—a campaign that was to establish dominion over the East and potentially even over the entire world;[6] the sixth poem is read as indicating support of Augustus' restoration of traditional religious cults and mores, the first steps of which were being undertaken during this period. Mommsen interprets the cycle as a whole as "courtly" poetry, but is careful to distinguish it from servile adulation. In his view, the cycle shows that Horace regarded both the new state that emerged from civil war and its creator as momentous developments that deserved his personal endorsement.

It is undeniable that Horace was writing these poems with the political mood of his own times in mind. As is already clear from *Odes* 1.2 and 1.12, he regards Augustus as Rome's redeemer from the chaos of the civil wars; he expects him to be an agent of reform who would lead Rome to new military victories and expand the bounds of the empire. Yet Horace focuses not so much on what is new—compare his *Epodes* 16 and Livy's preface to his historical works of the same year—but rather on the rebirth of old Roman customs and of everything that had once been great about the Republic. This retrospective focus is in accordance with Augustus' own express ambitions. Paul Zanker has shown[7] that the commander returning from civil war in the glory of victory deliberately decided not to present himself as a quasi-monarch but rather as a restorer of the Republic, at least in principle, while in practice concentrating all crucial state powers in his own hands. Moreover, Horace quite explicitly commends the Emperor's attempts at fostering a moral renewal.[8] This has been recognized by earlier commentators on these poems as Horace's own vision, with Augustus as its guarantor.[9] Hence, the label "Roman Odes"—first attributed to the cycle during the nineteenth century—seems quite apposite.[10]

Odes 3.1

The high register chosen by Horace at the beginning of *Odes* 3.1 signals to the reader that something different from his usual practice is to be expected in the poems to follow:

> Odi profanum vulgus et arceo;
> favete linguis!carmina non prius
>   audita Musarum sacerdos
>   virginibus puerisque canto

> I detest the uninitiated mob and keep them off;
> keep holy silence! As the Muses' priest I sing
> to maidens and to boys songs not previously heard

Much like Pindar's self-fashioning as prophet of the muses, Horace's self- presentation as *Musarum sacerdos*—"the Muses' priest"—announces poems that are without precedent in the previous books of *Carmina* (2–3, "songs not previously heard"). In the manner of a priest preparing a sacred rite, he sends the uninitiated away and commands a respectful silence. The poems that follow are dedicated to the young Romans who, untainted by guilt like the older generation, seem most receptive and responsive to the poet's message.

This prooemium, which inaugurates, not just the first poem, but rather the whole cycle, is followed by a series of ethical insights, presented in the form of impersonal gnomic pronouncements in an equally high stylistic register. On the level of motifs, the first Ode adopts thoughts and even phrases from the prooemium of Book 2 of Lucretius, where he opposes various imperfect lifestyles to the pleasures of a simple farmer's life.[11] In contrast to the universal types of flawed life style in Lucretius, however, Horace's illustrations tend to be more topical in character: the owner of vast landed estates (*latifundia*), the politician surrounded by his crowd of clients, and the super-rich entrepreneur whose new villas jut out into the sea all belong to an upper class whose boundless greed for property and power brings about the ruin of the Roman state in the course of several genera-tions.[12] The prelude foreshadows the decidedly Roman aspect of the themes that characterize the other odes in the cycle. These initial examples do not focus on the disastrous effects of self-serving ambition on the wider community, but rather, as in the Lucretian antecedent, they center on the quandaries of the rich and powerful individual, tormented by sorrows and fears, whose desires eventu-ally succumb to the leveling powers of death. Hence, the positive counter-example is not found in the virtuous families of the old Roman aristocracy but—again following Lucretius—in the life of a humble human being making do with what little he has: in short, the case is made for the simple farmer. The depiction, in the Ode's final strophe, of a felicitous individual life style, along with allusions to the poet's personal situation, has seemed to many critics to be incongruous with the political thematic of the Roman Odes. However, a prec-edent is already provided in the earlier ode, 3.24, in which Horace combines his praise of a simple, carefree individual life style with admonitions regarding the dangers to the state when men of prominence are driven by an inordinate lust for power and money.[13] From Horace's perspective, then, the life style of the individual and its consequences for the community at large are inherently connected.

Odes 3.2

It has been argued that *Odes* 3.2 focuses primarily on military valor; but this interpretation is too reductionist and has the effect of attenuating the poem's thematic unity. What the poet praises is, rather, the old Roman virtues in their interrelated aspects, in which plain living, courage, moral rectitude, and respect for the will of the gods inform a person's entire life. The motif of a simple life style, which was presented in the first Ode as a counter-image to contemporary instances of decadence, is taken up again with a different inflection by the second Ode. Romans, who are addressed directly by the prooemium of the cycle, are to revert to pristine values by adhering to a soldier's life of Spartan austerity. This notion is emphasized through a variation on an old topos: commonly, the tradi-tional rural Italic stock, embodied in Romulus, Cincinnatus, and Fabricius, is depicted as having been reared in a regimen of hard work and privation to become valiant warriors.[14] Horace reverses the direction of history with the ultimate objective of restoring values associated with the plain, traditional way of life.

The first three stanzas envisage in idealized terms an imminent war against the Parthians, in which young Romans will have the opportunity to prove themselves on the battlefield. The portrayal of the Roman horseman pursuing his enemies may actually be consonant with the anticipated circumstances of the campaign; other images, however, correspond more closely to the archaic Homeric world of epic battle-scenes: ladies of the royal court watching the fighting from the city walls; the maiden's anxious anticipation of a single combat between her betrothed and an enemy prince; the comparison of the warrior with a lion; and the depiction of an *aristeia* (display of martial prowess) on the part of a hero who cuts a bloody swath through enemy lines. This series of images makes it clear that the fourth stanza is modeled after ancient Greek gnomic topoi praising paragons of a bygone heroic era. In this respect, the famous glorification of a soldier's death in line 13 (*dulce et decorum est pro patria mori*: "it's fine and honorable to die for one's country") might be considered controversial by today's standards, but it does correspond to the heroic ideal that is vividly represented in these stanzas.[15]

In the following two stanzas (17–24) the poet elaborates on images of ideal virtue in elevated hymnal style. He sees virtue not just as excellence in war, but as encompassing a more comprehensive set of ideals, reminiscent of Stoic conceptions. Horace takes up elements of Stoic ethics by suggesting, in stanza 5, that notions of virtue are independent of shifting attitudes among the population.[16] The portrayal of a personified *Virtus* who is unaffected by external judgments, whether praise or blame, emanating from the masses is none other than the Stoic sage. This profile is further highlighted in the course of the following stanza: the man who embodies virtue is elevated to a level beyond everyday life and is ultimately granted immortality. This outcome is depicted vividly as the reception of a virtuous mortal lifted up by wings into the supernal realm of the gods.[17] Conventional motifs clearly derived from other literary traditions here serve to amplify what were originally quite sober and mundane notions of old Roman virtue.

A wide range of interpretations has been offered for lines 25–6, where Horace speaks of loyal silence (*fideli silentio*) as eventually earning due reward:-

> est et fideli tuta silentio
> merces: vetabo, qui Cereris sacrum
>   volgarit arcanae, sub isdem
>   sit trabibus fragilemque mecum
>
> solvat phaselon.
>
> There is also a sure recompense for faithful silence: I shall ever forbid a person who has disclosed the sacred rites of secret Ceres to dwell under the same roof or to launch a flimsy skiff with me.

Most attempts to explain these lines leave the connection of ideas with the previous stanzas unclear. It is unlikely that Horace here alludes obliquely to behavior in the political sphere, as has often been surmised, since lines 26–32 all point towards a religious violation that is too intimate for disclosure in a public poem. In my opinion, line 25 and, more particularly, lines 26ff seem to deal with the keeping of sacred secrets, such as those enjoined in the mystery cult of Demeter. This notion of keeping secrets is extended in scope to a warning against every kind of immoral, ungodly behavior by the word *incestus* in line 30. Thus, at the core of the final two stanzas stands a warning against *impietas* and an exhortation to *pietas*,[18] with the keeping of the cult secrets of the Eleusinian mysteries serving as an exemplary instance. This final injunction would link up seamlessly with the praise of traditional Roman piety in the earlier stanzas, for we know that Augustus also placed himself firmly within this tradition of religious reform and made robust efforts to instigate a renewed reverence for the gods.[19]

Odes 3.3

The beginning of *Odes* 3.3 is a continuation of the eulogy of the virtuous man (the very personification of *Virtus*) who is, once again, elevated above the merely mortal. Line 1 praises his chief defining attributes: justice and steadfastness (*justum et tenacem propositi virum*). The speaker thereafter elaborates in some detail on his imperturbability in perilous situations in which the unleashed forces of nature threaten his mere humanity.[20] The core ideas expressed in lines 17–24 of the previous Ode are further accentuated: the individual who fearlessly faces an angry crowd, the menacing glare of a tyrant, a raging storm at sea, and Jupiter's lightning, and who is not shaken even by the sight of the end of the world is portrayed in just the same terms as the Sage of the Stoics.[21] Epictetus paints Socrates in the very same colors: revered by the Stoics as the true image of a steadfast wise man, who does not cede to the populace or to the thirty Athenian tyrants, and whose imperturbable mind is not broken by even Zeus himself.[22] Thus these stanzas do not yet deal explicitly with Augustus, but rather draw on a more general thematic profile. After all, fearlessness in the face of a mad tyrant would hardly be appropriate to Augustus.[23]

Lines 21–4 of the preceding Ode, which laud the capacity of Virtus to elevate its practitioner to supernatural status and transport him to Olympus, are also mirrored in the third and fourth stanzas of the present Ode. Through the very power of virtue (*hac arte*) famous demigods like Pollux, Heracles, Dionysus, and even Romulus have been elevated to higher realms. The speaker's list of heroic apotheoses is quite conventional. The same names, including Romulus, are mentioned in several passages by Cicero in illustration of the idea that benefactors of mankind have become gods or demigods.[24] This is the point in the Roman Odes where the name Augustus is first introduced as true to the type: he will one day be enrolled in the ranks of those deified heroes who receive the reward of Olympus in acknowledgment of their deeds in the world of mortals. This inflexion of the deification motif is also conventional in Hellenistic panegyrics of the ruler. Theocritus, for instance, already employs it in his eulogies of Ptolemaic kings.[25]

The mention of Romulus provides an opportunity to move from the praise of a virtuous individual to a broader exhortation, addressed to all Romans, to observe righteous conduct. An epic scene adapted from the *Annales* of Ennius serves as the link. According to Ennius, a council of the gods is convened upon the death of Romulus, in which Romulus' father, Mars, reminds Jupiter of his promise to elevate his sons to divine status in due course.[26] Probably Juno also granted her assent, in this scenario, to his deification. Once this has been granted, Mars escorts his son on a horse-drawn carriage into the heavens. In his adaptation of the motif, Horace describes a council of the gods during which Juno abandons her wrath with which she had persecuted the Trojan descendant, Romulus, and acquiesces in his reception among the gods (lines 30–6).

At the heart of Juno's long speech, however, stands not the figure of Romulus but Juno's wrath towards Troy and her eternal prohibition against the rebuilding the city. Lines 18–30 are an expression of her triumphant joy at seeing her hated Troy buried in the dust. She justifies her hatred by pointing out the moral profligacy of Paris and Helen and the godlessness of the city's founder, Laomedon, who was greedy enough to refuse to pay the agreed wages to Apollo and Poseidon, the gods who had built his city walls. In a nutshell, the same vices are ascribed to the ancient Trojans that a comprehensive cultural critique would also have imputed to contemporary Romans.[27] After her accession to the deification of Romulus, Juno is even ready to endorse Rome's dominion over the whole world, with the boundaries extended as far as the Pillars of Heracles and the Nile—not coincidentally, the very boundaries of Rome's empire as established in the reign of Augustus. Juno also gives her consent to Rome's eventual triumph over the Parthians—on one condition: Troy must never be rebuilt, and must remain for ever deserted. From Juno's perspective, the future of Rome is to be bound up with the irreversible fall of Troy.

Ever since Mommsen, scholars have speculated that Horace in this passage was implicitly opposing plans to relocate the empire's capital from Rome to Troy or Alexandria—plans once ascribed to Julius Caesar.[28] It is hard to imagine, however, that any such scheme would have been seriously considered at this time by Augustus, who allowed himself to be celebrated as the savior of Rome and Italy from the dangers posed by the East, in general, and by Alexandria, in particular,[29] and who held Rome's traditional customs in such high regard.[30] There has to be a more plausible interpretation of Juno's warning. It appears that Troy, in the context of her harangue, comes to symbolize those salient misdeeds that had been related about its citizens, as enumerated by the goddess in lines 18–30, that is, rampant immorality, greed, and godlessness. It is hardly the resettlement in some specific geographical location that the goddess angrily speaks out against, but rather a nefarious way of living that is anathema to the gods. This moral reprimand is made even clearer in the concluding stanzas, 49–52, where the goddess expresses her hope that Rome will not be seduced by the glitter of gold, and that it will not plunder the riches of the world. Hunger for foreign treasures was regarded by cultural critics as lying at the root of Rome's moral decline in the aftermath of the defeat of Carthage (hence subsequent to Rome's attaining sovereignty over the Mediterranean world).[31]

In the sequence of stanzas comprising lines 53–68, Juno reiterates her affirmation of Rome's hegemony over the known world. The future boundaries of empire she now envisions are those of the extreme south and north—deserts of the south and uninhabitable lands in the north—but in even more vehement tones she repeats her verdict against the reconstruction of Troy. In an ominous vein she warns her audience that she herself, with the aid of those Greeks loyal to her, would destroy it again in a new iteration of the Trojan War. This threat is unmistakably aimed at Rome in the event that it failed to return to its old values. One is reminded of the prophecies of doom enunciated in *Epodes* 16. After this peak of excitement and pathos, the ode abruptly comes to a halt with the observation that such epic effusions are not appropriate to the poet's stylistic register:

> non hoc iocosae conveniet lyrae:
> quo, Musa, tendis? desine pervicax
>   referre sermones deorum et
>   magna modis tenuare parvis.

> This type of song will not suit a playful lyre. Where
> on earth are you heading, Muse of mine? Cease your
> impetuous recounting of divine exchanges and
> attenuating grand themes with meager measures.

Odes 3.4

Even if it seemed, at the end of Odes 3.3, as though the poet was going to turn away from his venture into a high stylistic register, he nevertheless returns to it again at the beginning of Ode 3.4. This poem honors the Muses and the values they inspire, not only in lyric poets, but also in ordinary citizens who receive guidance as to what is appropriate conduct in the public sphere. It is not without significance that Horace invokes the Muse Calliope in a poem that associates the Muses collectively with the ruler. In Hesiod's *Theogony* Calliope is called "the most excellent among the Muses who protects kings and inspires them to correct decisions."[32]

In imitation of the Greek lyric poets,[33] Horace calls upon the Muse in the first stanza and asks her to inaugurate, with her charming music, a *longum melos*, that is, a long, meaningful, and sublime poem. That the choice of tone and instrument is left to her is a familiar convention that implies an elevated manner germane to hymns to the gods. In the second stanza the enraptured poet fancies hearing her voice and his being transported to a land where the gods are in attendance, a land full of trees giving shade and of pleasant streams, and where gentle breezes blow. In providing this description, the poet indicates that the Muse has responded to his invocation and inspired his song.[34] In what follows, the poet goes a long way back into his past. He discloses through a childhood anecdote that he was elected by the Muses very early in his life. Just as a number of Greek poets are said to have been singled out by some miraculous act of discrimination in their infancy,[35] Horace here claims to have been saved when he was asleep as a tender child: doves, birds traditionally devoted to the goddess Aphrodite, adorned the infant who had fallen asleep in a remote mountain forest with laurel and myrtle leaves—leaves from trees that were sacred to Apollo and Aphrodite—so as to protect him from all danger. This event is said to have been commonly regarded as a miracle throughout the surrounding countryside (lines 9–20).

In the following stanzas (lines 21–36) the poet apostrophizes the Muses as a group in hymnal style and thanks them for blessing and protecting him, not merely in his childhood, but throughout his life. He says that he feels their presence when he travels to places in Italy that are dear to him to compose his songs. Locations that are far away from cities, tucked away in the mountains or by the sea, appear to him to be haunts of the Muses, along the lines evoked in the second stanza. By his account, he has also been protected by the Muses from mortal perils. He even goes so far as to proclaim that he can endure the wildest storms at sea as well as the extreme heat of the desert, and can visit wild barbarian tribes beyond the limits of the empire without harm to his person, since he is under the protection of the Muses.

Lines 37–41 continue to employ the style of the hymnal invocation, however it is now no longer the poet who is represented as uniquely protected and inspired by the Muses, but also the ruler. The latter is presented as the bringer of peace in the wake of victorious campaigns. In later Augustan literary works, the end of war is usually marked above all by the closing of the gates of Janus' temple; in this case, it is indicated by the resettlement of soldiers returning from civil war to live as peaceful citizens in untroubled circumstances. The Muses are described as rejuvenating the ruler in the Pierian grotto— hence in a musical landscape that is the special abode hospitable to poets (37–40):

> vos Caesarem altum, militia simul
> fessas cohortes addidit oppidis,
>   finire quaerentem labores,
>   Pierio recreatis antro.

> In the Pierian grotto you refresh sublime Caesar,
> aiming to put an end to his labors, as soon as he
> has settled his war-weary cohorts in the townships.

The "gentle counsel" (*lene consilium*) that the goddesses are said to offer Caesar in the following strophe, however, implies far more than participation in the blessings of peace on the part of a man who is exhausted with military campaigning. Following Pindar's sentiments as expressed in his first Pythian Ode, Horace sees lyric song as capable of showing the way to reconciliation and peace in the domain of state affairs and of politics. Just as Pindar had celebrated the ruler of Syracuse, after his victories over the Etruscans and the Carthaginians, as the founder of Etna (Aitnai), a city governed by just laws, so Horace's ruler, having fought and won a grueling war, is depicted as seeking peace.[36] In this respect, Horace mirrors the cultural climate of the first decades after Actium, as can be seen by comparing his poetic themes with parallels in the visual arts. An especially significant reflection of the contemporary mood in the sphere of sculpture consists in the representation of the goddess Pax surrounded by symbols of exuberant fertility on a relief of the Ara Pacis.[37]

Pindar, in his first Pythian Ode, relates how the enemies of the gods (the brood of Giants who rebelled against the rule of Zeus) are imprisoned under the massive boulders of Mount Etna in Sicily; similarly, Horace, in the long mythological narrative of lines 42–64, recounts the futile assault of the Titans and other adversaries against the sovereignty of Zeus and the other Olympians. In Greek art such battles among divine factions were often used as icons of victorious campaigns against barbarian enemies.[38] In the same way, Horace's re-narration of the successful combats of Zeus and the Olympians alludes obliquely to Augustus' victory over the Eastern forces led by Antony and Cleopatra. It was this signal victory, after all, that laid the foundation for the new regimen of peace.

Horace's way of representing these battles is markedly different from its Greek artistic precedents, especially from the famous Pergamon altar with its frieze of the Gigantomachy that displays brute force in confrontation with brute force. In the latter representation, the Giants' flexed muscles indicate extreme exertion, as is also the case of the muscles of Zeus, which, outstretched to the limit, resemble those of Athena who is dragging a giant upward by his hair. The giants fight with primeval instruments—hurling hefty boulders, for instance; but Hecate does not use more sophisticated weapons either: she shoves a torch against the face of her combatant, while Nyx, goddess of night, throws a jar full of poisonous snakes at her enemy. Aphrodite ruthlessly tramples on the face of a villain who is already lying on the ground; the giants' snakes go after their foes with their poisonous teeth, as do the gods' own attack dogs and lions when they bite into their enemies' limbs. On the other hand, Horace's verbal characterization of the Olympians in the heat of combat is fundamentally different: he pits a riot of bulky, clumsy creatures storming heaven against a Zeus who is a calm, composed, and omnipotent sovereign; and the ferocious bands that pile mountains upon mountains and uproot giant trees are met by a corps of majestic, unruffled Olympians who effortlessly crush their rebellion. The figure of Apollo, in particular, which is modeled after Pindar,[39] appears in serene dignity in a static pose, rather than engaged in strenuous combat.

The conceptual ground for this contrast between the two sets of antagonists is summed up in the *sententiae* (gnomic statements) that compose lines 65–8: strength without reason (*vis consili expers*) will collapse under its own weight; strength in appropriate measure (*vim temperatam*) will prevail. This is followed by the observation that the gods despise heinous acts of impiety (*vires/omne nefas animo moventes*). This topic is further elaborated in the final three stanzas: offenders who have lustfully gazed at goddesses are punished in the underworld. Thus in a thinly disguised allusion the earlier theme of Paris' and Helen's immoral conduct—the Troy anathema to Juno–comes to resonate, at the poem's close, with the mention of other impious offenders.

Odes 3.5

The first stanza of *Odes* 3.5 juxtaposes the two figures of Augustus and Jupiter. The belief in a sky-god who exercises his powers through thunder and lightning had been held among the Romans for a long time; but in the future it is Augustus who will be revered as a supreme god manifest on earth (*praesens divus*). The idea that the ruler was the earthly image of a supreme celestial divinity originated in the Hellenistic period,[40] but was subsequently applied to Augustus by many contemporary writers.[41] According to Horace, he will be revered as a manifest deity as soon as he becomes ruler of the entire world, that is, after the incorporation of Britain and Parthia into the empire. It was a widespread assumption during the first decade after Actium that Augustus would fulfill his highest ambitions by expanding his empire to the ends of the earth, particularly through conquering the Parthians—a grand project that Julius Caesar is said to have already contemplated.[42] Augustus might, in his turn, initially have given the impression that he was preparing to pursue these very goals; soon enough, however, he must have realized that such utopian dreams were unattainable by the means actually at his disposal.

The next two stanzas (lines 5–12) make the case for the inevitability of an eventual war against the Parthians. In indignant tones line 5 poses the question whether Crassus' soldiers had not betrayed, and thus brought humiliation on, everything that Rome had come to embody. This was a sentiment shared by many contemporary Romans: the shame brought about by Parthian defeat had to be erased through new victories.[43] Horace goes further by not even mentioning the defeat, but emphasizing instead the disgraceful behavior of the captive Roman soldiers in the aftermath of battle: they are accused of forgetting their Roman identity by marrying into Parthian families, enlisting in the Parthian army, and fighting on behalf of Rome's arch-enemy.

The entire remainder of the poem deploys an historical counter-example to this failure—an anecdote taken from the first Punic War. The action of a consul, Regulus, is hailed as an example of the true Roman character and contrasted with the ignominious behavior of the prisoners of Carrhae. If Crassus' soldiers had followed his noble example, Rome's name would not have been so dishonored. From the many instances in which Cicero cites the paradigm of Regulus it may be inferred that this was a patriotic commonplace in illustrations of the old Roman virtues.[44]

This example from the glorious past is subsequently compared with the present situation. Line 13 commences with the rebuke:

> hoc caverat mens provida Reguli
>
> such base conduct is what the prescient Regulus
> had tried to preclude

Parallels between the famous historical incident and the present situation are next examined in some detail. The captured ensigns on display in Carthaginian temples call to mind the Roman standards still held by the Parthians. The historical record also makes it clear that some free Roman citizens had surrendered to the enemy, and that their shameful, un-Roman conduct had caused great damage to the state. It has frequently been argued that Regulus' policy of not paying ransom for prisoners of war could constitute yet another parallel to contemporary deliberations, that is, that the ransoming of the Parthian captives was under serious consideration by the new regime and that Horace is advocating in this passage against this undertaking. No documentary evidence can be found anywhere for any such plan, however—a plan that seems altogether unlikely on the face of it. It is certainly not mentioned explicitly in Horace's text: *hoc caverat* can only mean that Regulus was attempting to avoid the recurrence of any such behavior on the part of Roman soldiers in the future. Horace's reasoning is that if Crassus' soldiers had remembered Regulus' counsel they would have chosen to die rather than to live a life of dishonor. Regulus' advice was intended to remove for all time any hope for a financial settlement in hostage situations, thus foreclosing any consideration of capitulation.[45] Regulus' fear of setting a bad precedent became a traditional topos. Thus an advocate of old Roman principles argues in Livy during similar deliberations that, according to ancestral customs, military discipline can only be upheld when any notion of paying ransom is firmly repudiated.[46] That Horace subscribes to such an uncharacteristically stringent position has often elicited the reproach of readers. It is by no means incongruent, however, with the speaker's praise in *Odes* 3.2 of the values upheld by the soldier who willingly embraces death in battle (*dulce et decorum est pro patria mori*).

More characteristic of Horace's humane disposition is the ending of this Ode (lines 45–56), which goes some way towards mitigating some of the more austere features in the Regulus portrait. The strain experienced by the consul in the final struggle has now eased. Knowledge of having done the right thing helps him to embrace certain death. When Horace states that Regulus accepts his fate and leaves the scene with equanimity, as though he were seeking respite in the country after tedious days at court, this serene image resolves all earlier tensions.

Odes 3.6

With the apostrophe *Romane*, the first stanza appeals to the entire people of Rome rather than merely its youth. This change of addressee indicates that *Odes* 3.6 was written independently of—and presumably earlier than—the prooemium of the cycle that forms the opening of *Odes* 3.1. The tone is solemn and ceremonial. It reflects a manner of speaking to the community at large that is familiar from the oracle of Delphi and the prophetic visions of the Sibyls.[47] As previously in his *Epodes* 7 and 16, the poet issues a stern wake-up call admonishing an entire people to change its ways and to put an end to centuries of moral decline.

The first four stanzas develop the poet's warning not to neglect the worship of the gods. This accords with the point of view of Augustus, who saw the revitalization of old Roman cults and customs as a key element in the process of stabilizing the disintegrating state. His attitude took material form in a number of grand temples whose construction he commissioned, and in the restoration, during the year 28 BCE, of eighty-two neglected and virtually derelict places of worship in the city.[48] Horace's Ode was most certainly written with these developments in mind; if they were not already underway at the time of writing they were definitely in the planning stages.

The ideas and attitudes presented in this passage not only reflect Augustus' own thinking, but also align with fundamental convictions that were shared by the wider population and can be found in the works of a number of Republican historians. It was by no means unusual for authors to find the reasons for Rome's success in the observance of divine orders and ritual prescriptions, or to find the roots of defeat in the neglect of these practices and the disregard of signs sent by the gods. Cicero, who was evidently following annalist sources, lists three instances from the First and Second Punic Wars in which the disregard, or even flouting, of omens provided by the gods led to crushing Roman defeats. Livy's depiction of the conflict with the Gauls is framed as indubitable proof of this truth.[49] Similarly, the lack of success of Roman expeditions against the Parthians is characterized in our ode as the direct result of negligence in taking the auspices (lines 9–12). The reminiscence in stanza 4 of the hazardous battle against the Egyptian navy serves as a sober reminder of how close Rome came to the brink of outright failure.

The following segment of the poem (stanzas 5–8) introduces the unrelated view that the general deterioration of affairs is the result of moral decline revealed especially in contempt for the institution of marriage. As in *Odes* 3.24, Horace means here to endorse Augustus' policies. As early as the year 28, upon his return from civil war, the sovereign arguably attempted to combat widespread moral lassitude through a new legislative program.[50] In the present ode the consequences of moral failure are seen in a different light than in *Odes* 3.24. Whereas the latter adduces effeminacy and the immoderate pursuit of wealth, *Odes* 3.6—through terms like *inquinare* and *incestus*—emphasizes the violation of a sacred order of existence.[51] The extreme contempt conveyed in the graphic imagery of these lines approximates the conventions of satiric discourse.

The darker the image of moral decline is painted, the brighter its counter-image eventually appears. Stanzas 9–11 describe the previous centuries' proficient and industrious young farmers who, in their adult age, waged victorious wars against such formidable adversaries as Pyrrhus, Hannibal, and Antiochus. The austerity and frugality of their way of life are openly foregrounded, but in the penultimate stanza idyllic images of quiet evenings by the hearth are meant to imply that a life close to nature provides its own intrinsic and ample rewards. One is reminded of a similar state of equanimity attained by Regulus at the moment of his departure in *Odes* 3. 5. The gloomy picture that Horace has painted in the preceding stanzas of this final poem of the cycle lights up, and it is not difficult to recognize which way of life, the past or the present, is to be regarded as superior. The final stanza, however, points to a pessimistic outcome with regard to the present generation. It reiterates the old Greek lament that every new generation is worse than the previous one. Horace seems here to reveal an apprehension that further decline may be all but inevitable. The issue is not resolved in explicit terms, but by recapitulating the opening stanza's vision of rebirth through a return to old forms of religious piety, the icon of a prudent, simple life style seems at least to suggest the possibility of change for the better.

Conclusion

It might appear strange to many readers that Horace, during the first decade of Augustus' unchallenged rule, would use his Roman Odes—precisely that subgroup of his poems most directly addressed to a wider audience—only to look back at the past with a view to sponsoring a restoration of traditional Republican values, rather than to hailing the dawn of a new era in the present (as Mommsen for instance, had assumed from his particular orientation as an historian). Horace's exhortation to return to traditional customs, however, does resonate with Augustus' express goals at that juncture, namely, his promise to bring about a restitution of the Republic.[52] The fourth book of Odes, published fully a decade later, presents a rather different perspective than the one that prevails in the cycle we have discussed. *Odes* 4.5 and 4.15, in particular, no longer advocate that every Roman citizen should be ready to fight in a war; rather they portray a satisfied and peace-loving Roman citizen enjoying the fruits of Augustus' peace—the *pax Augusta*—and seeing him as the sole guarantor of their security and prosperity.

GUIDE TO FURTHER READING

An excellent overview of the most important secondary literature on individual odes, as well as copious annotations on each poem, is to be found in Nisbet and Rudd 2004. In what follows I draw attention to significant scholarly contributions to the understanding of central motifs in the cycle.

3.1.

The ode's Epicurean background is examined by Pöschl 1958: 333ff and Lyne 1955: 162ff. Fenik 1962: 72ff demonstrates motif parallels with Vergil's *Georgics* 2, 461–71. The relationship between the personal dimension of this initial ode and the political thematic of the Roman Odes as a whole is investigated in a study by Solmsen 1947: 337ff.

3.2

André 1969: 31ff shows that the theme of the Ode is not restricted to military valor, but rather is concerned more broadly with traditional Roman *virtus* in its various aspects. Harrison 1993: 91ff and West 2002: 25ff clarify the conventional background of the controversial sentiment expressed in line 13.

3.3

The affinity between Horace's characterization of the resolute and unshakeable individual and the Stoic ideal is the subject of Parker 2002: 101ff. On the conventional list of deified heroes there is a useful study by Bellinger 1957: 91ff. Nisbet and Rudd cast doubt on the view that the admonition regarding a rebuilding of Troy relates to an actual political project.

3.4

Nisbet and Rudd 2004: 53ff assemble parallels for the tradition of the legendary childhood of the poet; the allusion to Pindar *Pythians* 1, in particular, is discussed by Fraenkel 1957: 273–85.

3.5

Pelling 1996 expounds Roman policy regarding the Parthian empire; Wissemann 1982 deals with the topic of the general anticipation of a Parthian campaign in early Augustan poetry. Kornhardt 1954: 85ff treats the tradition of the Regulus story. The underlying connection between the ode's separate motifs is delineated by Haffner 1938: 132ff.

3.6

The theme of dereliction in respect to the maintenance of religious shrines is taken up by North 1986: 251ff. The poem's cultural critique is discussed in relation to its literary precedents by Earl 1966: 45ff. Zanker 1988 shows how the restoration of the temples undertaken by Augustus was aimed at counteracting the widespread complaints against their state of dilapidation.

NOTES

1 The English translation of this essay (from the German original) is by Gregson Davis and Christophe Fricker.
2 Cf. Orelli *et al.* 1886: lv–lvi.
3 *Res Gestae* 2.4; Dio. 53.2.4.
4 Heinze 1960: 190–204 provides a comprehensive justification of this view. Fraenkel 1957: 261 and Nisbet and Rudd 2004: xx concur.
5 Mommsen 1912: 168–84. Mommsen had an unusual knowledge of documentary sources (even arcane ones) from the Augustan Age; hence his remarks form the basis of scholarly discussion to this day. Nisbet and Rudd 2004 affirm that a number of his suggestions are still worth debating. See ibid. 21, 22, 24, 36–8, 54–6, 69–70, 82, 97–9.
6 Mommsen was evidently thinking of a general climate of opinion, rather than of specific war preparations on the part of the Emperor who was known to be rather hesitant to pursue such aims.
7 Zanker 1987: 96–103. Cf. also Kienast 1982: 69–74 and West 2002: 6f. Main sources for this reading are Aug. *Res Gestae.* 8; Suet *Aug.* 31 and 73.
8 Augustus' numerous attempts at framing moral renewal in legal terms as well as his frugal life style indicate how serious a concern this issue was for him. Cf. Suet. *Aug.* 34; Zanker 1987: 161–70; West 2002: 7f.
9 Cf. Orelli *et al.* 1886: 326f. Horace had demanded of a true statesman—i.e., of Augustus—as early as *Odes* 3.24.25–30, that he take measures against moral decline.
10 According to Fraenkel 1957: 260–1, the term "Roman Odes" was already attested as the standard term by T. Plüss in 1882.
11 This form of social critique resembles that of Sallust's. Cf. Syndikus 2001: 7–9; West 2002: 20f.
12 Cf. Sallust *Catiline* 10–13, *Jugurtha* 41.
13 Solmsen 1947: 337–52 illuminates the relevance of 3.24 for any explanation of 3.1. His article is reprinted in Oppermann 1972: 139–65.
14 This view is expressed in *Odes* 3.6.83ff. Syndikus 2001: 26, n. 12 provides a collection of quotations that indicate how widespread this idea was.
15 Cf. Syndikus 2001: 27–8; Nisbet and Rudd 2004: 26–7.
16 Cf. Pasquali 1920: 673–4; Nisbet and Rudd 2004: 28.
17 Inspiration for Horace was arguably provided by Greek examples such as Aristotle's hymn to Arete, PMG 842.
18 Cf. Kiessling and Heinze 1955: 259–60. For a rhetorical reading of the silence topos in relation to encomiastic conventions, see Davis 1983.
19 Cf. Zanker 1987: 108–40; West 2002: 9–10.
20 The stoic Sage exercises all virtues and no outer threats can detract him from his course (see *Stoicorum Veterum Fragmenta* 3. 557–66 and 567–81).
21 Cf. Pasquali 1920: 682; Syndikus 2001: 36, nn. 22–4.
22 Cf. Epict. *Discourses* 1.1.23; 4.1.164—derivative of Plato, *Apology* 32CD.
23 Leiv Amundson 1972 shows that the opening of this Ode was not written with Augustus in mind.
24 Sources are collected in Syndikus 2001: 39, nn. 37–8. This list of exemplars is another indication that justice is not the unifying theme of this Ode, as is often claimed. Other aspects of *aretē* were more important in the life of these heroes.

25 Theocr. *Idylls* 17, 16–33.

26 Enn. *Annals* 1. frs.xxx–xxxiii (Skutsch). This complex seems to be reflected in Ovid, *Met.* 14. 805–22 and *Fasti*, 2.481–96. Skutsch doubts that Juno could have played a role equivalent to Horace's depiction because, according to Ennius, her conversion to an attitude more friendly to the Romans did not take place until the war against Hannibal (see his commentary on I.fr.xxxii and VIII. fr.xvi). These later events, however, do not necessarily preclude an earlier approval of the deification of Romulus.

27 This is supported by the parallels of *Odes* 3.6 and 3.24.

28 Suet. *Caesars* 79.3; Nic.Dam. *Vit.Caes.* 20. 68 (Jacoby).

29 Cf. Horace, *Epodes* 9.11–16; Vergil, *Aeneid* 8.685–88; 705–6.

30 Cf. Fraenkel 1957: 268.

31 *Locus classicus* is Sallust, *Catiline* 10–1.

32 Hesiod, *Theogony* 79–93; Nisbet and Rudd 2004: 54–5.

33 Alcman fr. 27P and Stesichorus fr. 63 P also invoke Kalliope; fr. lyr. adesp. 17P invokes the heavenly Muses.

34 Traditional aspects of this view are examined in Syndikus 2001: 50, nn. 15–20.

35 Evidence is assembled in Syndikus 2001: 52 and Nisbet and Rudd 2004: 53–4.

36 Fraenkel 1957: 276–83 compares central motifs of the first Pythian Ode with the poem discussed here.

37 Cf. Zanker 1987: 90–6, 103–6, 177–88. West 2002: 4 shows that, following Julius Caesar, *clementia* was a component topos of Augustan poetics from its inception. Its political realization had to wait until after Actium.

38 Cf. Hardie 1986: 85–8, 98–101.

39 Pindar *Pythians* 1.39; Cf. Fraenkel 1957: 276.

40 Cf. Call., *Hymn to Zeus* 79–90; Theocr. *Id.* 17. 1–4.

41 Cf. Vergil *Aen.* 1.286–96; 6, 791–800; Horace, *Odes* 1.12.49–60; Ovid *Met.* 15.858–860.

42 Cf. Wissemann 1982: 14–103, 143–4.

43 A well-known example was Appius Claudius's resistance to a peace deal proposed by Pyrrhus: see Plutarch, *Life of Pyrrhus*, 19.

44 The origins and impact of the story of Regulus are examined by Nisbet and Rudd 2004: 80–2.

45 Cf. Syndikus 2001: 75; West 2002: 61.

46 Livy 22.60.7 and 22.61.1. Several details in Livy's version of events of the Second Punic War are mirrored in Horace's account of Regulus' speech. Horace also adopts received ideas from the Annalists.

47 Cf. Syndikus 2001: 83, nn. 9–10; Nisbet and Rudd 2004: 101 on line 2.

48 Augustus, *Res Gestae* 20.4; Suet, *Aug.* 30.2;.31; Dio 53.2. 4–5; Zanker 1987: 107–16.

49 Cicero *De natura deorum* 2.7–8; Livy 5.51.5ff.

50 Cf. Williams 1968: 532–3 and 606–7.

51 Cf. Heinze 1960: 195–6.

52 Although the phrase *respublica restituta* ("the republic restored"), is often ascribed, directly or indirectly, to Augustus in the secondary literature, it is worth quoting the caveat of Gruen 2005: "The phrase ... appears on no official documents and is celebrated by no poet or prose writer of the era."

CHAPTER ELEVEN

Horace: *Odes* 4

Michèle Lowrie

The fourth book of Horace's *Odes* is a supplement to *Odes* 1–3: it reveals retrospectively that the first collection was, after all, incomplete. There are many ways that Horace's last lyric book looks back to and revises his earlier composition in the genre. Signal differences are that Horace now addresses Augustus directly; Maecenas is present, but less conspicuous; the Sabine estate is no longer in evidence as a locus of retreat; Horace is willing to engage in praise poetry; he identifies paper as a medium of poetic transmission; he gradually adopts a communal voice. Since all these issues were fraught in *Odes* 1–3, the changes stand out as conscious choices. But what has really changed? Horace clearly has greater confidence in his own authority. The Augustan regime has had time to settle and memory of civil war—still searingly vivid in *Odes* 1–3—has not faded, but receded. An image of social harmony largely prevails. If that is so, then why write the supplement and not merely bask in success? Success needs representation. One of the questions dogging the interpretation of *Odes* 4 is why Horace opens the collection with an expression of resistance. This question is not merely biographical or historical. The book traces an arc of resistance falling away. In this way Horace dramatizes the socio-political changes since *Odes* 1–3 and comments on lyric's new role in society and, with it, on the role of the lyrist within the new settlement.

Odes 4 looks back not only to Horace's first lyric collection, but also to the intervening *Carmen Saeculare*. The manuscript transmission keeps all books entitled "Odes" together, but the *Carmen Saeculare*, also in a lyric meter (Sapphics), is set apart. The performance conditions of this choral poem in the festival of the *Ludi Saeculares* ("Century games") are unique in extant Latin literature and separate it from Horace's other lyric work (see Michael Putnam, Chapter 12 in this volume). Perhaps because of the extraordinary honor, participation in the games was transformative for Horace. The experience contributed to his adoption of a more confident poetic persona, and talking about the *Carmen Saeculare* adds a choral dimension to Horace's new definition of his lyric task. While *Odes* 4 looks back to *Odes* 1–3 largely through the subtle handling of allusion, Horace mentions the *Carmen Saeculare* (*Odes* 4.6.31–44) explicitly. It is not only the public role, but also the performance dimension now open for lyric that effects a change in Horace's representation of the genre.

I see Horace's need to redefine lyric in an altered sociopolitical and cultural landscape as the underlying reason for returning to the genre, though there is a long tradition of attributing Book 4's creation to external pressure. We know from Suetonius' life of Horace that Augustus himself encouraged Horace to continue working in lyric as well as other genres. He not only commissioned the *Carmen Saeculare* and asked for *Epistles* 2.1, he also made a request for praise of Tiberius and Drusus.

> Scripta quidem eius usque adeo probauit mansuraque perpetua opinatus est, ut non modo Saeculare carmen componendum iniunxerit, sed et Vindelicam uictoriam Tiberii Drusique priuignorum suorum, eumque coegerit propter hoc tribus carminum libris ex longo interuallo quartum addere. (Suetonius, *Vita Horati* 17–18)

> He approved indeed of his writings and thought they would remain for all time to such an extent that he not only enjoined on him to compose the *Carmen Saeculare*, but also the victory over the Vindelici of Tiberius and Drusus, his stepsons, and he impelled him on this account to add a fourth to the three books of odes after a long interval.

This remarkable piece of evidence for the relation of poet to *princeps* has spawned a persistent idea that Horace's resistance to returning to lyric alleged in *Odes* 4.1 derives from lack of commitment: he did not really want to write lyric, but succumbed to Augustus' importunate demand. The remaining book was composed as padding for the praise poems of Drusus and Tiberius (*Odes* 4.4.4.14), which are of inferior quality. The best argument against this reductionist view is the quality of the individual poems and the overall unity of the book (Putnam 1986: 20–4). I would add that artists generally appreciate support from powerful people or institutions as it furthers their careers and note that in Suetonius' quotations, Augustus makes no attempt to control form or content beyond the suggestion of a poem "of that sort" addressed to himself and poetry for Tiberius and Drusus. Peter White has furthermore shown that requests for poetry were part of the give and take of Roman society and not at odds with artistic freedom in the Augustan period (White 1993: ch. 3; Appendix 3; this passage, 113–15). Even if the commission came from the powers above, the artistry of the book is Horace's own.

Overcoming resistance

Odes 4.1 opens with the poet expostulating against the goddess of love, who has returned after a long interval: *intermissa, Venus, diu / rursus bella moues? parce precor, precor* ("Venus, are you again rousing wars long interrupted? Spare me, I pray, I pray," 1–2). This opening is usually taken allegorically of poetry (see section "Allusion and return" below). Venus is emblematic of lyric, particularly erotic lyric, and it is noteworthy, given the book's subsequent trajectory, that Horace restricts his poetry at the beginning to love lyric. His age (6) makes him unsuitable for the genre so defined and he prays that she spare him and turn her attentions to the young (7–8), specifically a nobleman named Paullus Maximus (10–11). The autobiographical information that ten years have passed positions him as socially mature, if still vulnerable to passion. Furthermore, Horace gives an inkling of what is to come by assimilating Venus' purview to warfare (Davis 1991: 66). He will turn out to have greater poetic mastery in this area than initially alleged. Venus' crushing demands indicate he feels a strong compulsion to write. The allegory allows Horace to make these points concretely, in his own person, and his resistance dramatizes both continuity and change. Rather than simply inaugurating a new kind of lyric, Horace redefines his endeavors. Although he does not avow this sort of activity in his own person, the cult of Venus that Horace predicts Maximus will establish allows for an image of choral song and dance by youths and maidens that Horace comes around to embracing in *Odes* 4.6, when he mentions the chorus of the *Carmen Saeculare*. While the Venus of Horatian love lyric looks backward, her return heralds an advance in the sort of representation Horace is willing to accord her.

The rhetoric of inability continues in the second poem, but here Horace abandons allegory and explicitly disavows a specific kind of poetry: the Pindaric mode. As in the first poem, where Venus is diverted rhetorically onto a young nobleman, Paullus Maximus, here Horace sets up Iullus Antonius as the more suitable candidate for composing in the high style. The surrogate for whatever endeavor Horace averts receives indirect praise: he is capable of love or poetic success beyond the poet's reach. The *recusatio* (refusal poem) is often analyzed as courtly discourse: the poet honors someone of higher social status than himself by elegantly refusing to adopt a form alien to his own poetry as a vehicle for praise. The refusal also functions as poetic self-definition, largely through negation. Here, Horace reserves the context for which praise would be appropriate to the end, when it turns out that Augustus is to be celebrated. He starts rather by folding a compliment to the surrogate poet into a discourse more overtly about his own poetic definition. The strategy of negation gives the impression of resistance. Pindaric poetry was choral, and here Horace rather embraces a Callimachean aesthetic of the small, symbolized by the bee over against the swan (25–7). What he does allow for offers an advance over his distance from the choral cult of Venus he attributes to Maximus in *Odes* 4.1. In this poem, he imagines participating as one among many in a public celebration, a hypothetical triumph honoring Caesar Augustus.

The third poem of the book marks another advance in the role Horace is willing to accept. Although he disavows the active life of the athlete and the politician in the opening priamel—form and content both evoke Pindar—he does accept a public role for himself in Roman society. The Muse—that is, his poetry— is responsible for his being pointed out by passersby as *Romanae fidicen lyrae* (23). This phrase uses two different words for lyre, one Greek, one Roman, so the English translation "lyrist of the Roman lyre" appears more redundant than the original. There is furthermore an advance in the embrace of the chorus, although it is restricted to a metaphor for the society of poets: *uatum ... choros* ("choruses of bards," 15). Choral lyric and the figure of the *uates* both represent a more engaged and public kind of poetry than is implied by the lyre, whether *fides* or *lyra*, which has greater associations with monody.

The next several poems further the scope both of what the poetry does and what its poet avows. *Odes* 4.4 celebrates Drusus' victory over the Vindelici. *Odes* 4.5 shows Horace participating in a collective celebration of Augustus' return from a three-year trip to Gaul and Spain in 13 BCE. Although his voice by the poem's end is communal (*dicimus ... dicimus*, "we say, we say," 4.5.38–9), he does address the Emperor directly (*redi*, "come home," 4) in his own at the beginning. By the end of the next poem, where he prays to Apollo on an epic scale in thanks for the Roman foundation, he acknowledges his role as the author of the *Carmen Saeculare*, explicitly described as a choral poem performed by a chorus of youths and maidens (4.6.31–2). Here, he even sets his signature on this poem and the *Carmen Saeculare* alike in the time-honored form of a sphragis: the last line identifies his name and role as *uatis Horati* ("of the bard Horace," 4.6.44). He characteristically displaces his name into another's voice, here one of the maidens imagined as grown-up, married, and reminiscing about her participation in the chorus, but he signs nevertheless. At this point, the arc of staged resistance has come to an end. Horace continues with *Odes* 4.7, a more conventional poem on how the spring leads to thoughts of seasonality and death (Davis 1991: 155–8), and the collection moves on from here, but just over a third of the book's opening sequence is devoted to renegotiating his position as a lyrist in a more public vein.

Allusion and return

One of Horace's techniques for indicating a difference from *Odes* 1–3 is direct allusion, whether verbatim repetition, the significant repetition of a meter, or by staging similar scenes with some reversal. The recurrence of familiar material reinforces the reader's preconceptions of the lyric genre, while the differences

invite comparison and move our expectations forward. Although there are many
instances of this technique in *Odes* 4, let me offer one each of the above types.

   Odes 4.1.5 repeats the opening line of *Odes* 1.19 verbatim (*mater saeva Cupidinum*, "cruel mother of Cupids/desires") and in the same meter (fourth Asclepiadean). The earlier poem has to do with return, since Venus orders the poet "to
give his spirit back to finished loves" (*finitis animum reddere amoribus*, 1.19.4),
so Horace's recollection of this moment at the beginning of *Odes* 4 is layered:
Venus is again returning, but the repetition of a line of previously existing poetry
encourages us to take the return not just of the goddess and erotic lyric, but of
lyric poetry itself. In both poems, the cult of Venus is observed, but the poet's
simple sacrifice on an altar of turf in *Odes* 1.19 is transformed into a multi-media
extravaganza of a cult statue, lyres, reeds, pan-pipes, and a mixed chorus in *Odes*
4.1 (Lowrie 2009a: ch. 4). The human players in the later poem are also more
complex: beyond Venus and his current love, as in the earlier poem, Horace
additionally honors Paullus Maximus and recalls a past love. The later poem is
also one and a half times as long. All in all, the poetic reminiscence highlights
the idea of return and at the same time adds a greater degree of complexity in
various dimensions that will be characteristic of the new collection.

   The repetition of meter also conveys a sense of advance. In *Odes* 1–3, only
two poems use the first Asclepiadean, the first and the last. Both are loci of poetic
self-definition. In *Odes* 1.1, Horace expresses a wish to Maecenas that he may be
included among the "lyric bards" (*lyricis uatibus*, 35). In *Odes* 3.30, he boasts
that he has "created a monument more lasting than bronze" (*exegi monumentum
aere perennius*, 1). The meter returns in *Odes* 4.8, where Horace improves on his
self-won immortality. While he builds up to the claim that he has immortalized
himself in the first collection, in the fourth book, he lays a claim to be able to
immortalize others. A further advance made in this sequence is in acknowledging
more explicitly that poetic transmission depends on writing. Horace's desire to
be included in the "lyric bards" in *Odes* 1.1 nods implicitly to the Alexandrian
canon of nine lyric poets—canon formation implies a book culture (Feeney 1993;
Barchiesi 2000). The monument of *Odes* 3.30 is furthermore an implicit metaphor in this period for a written composition. To trump a monument in bronze
means to surpass statuary or inscription; that paper is more lasting than bronze
goes unspecified, since Horace presents his monument outside material constraints. *Odes* 4.8 builds on these ideas: the Muses have the advantage over
inscription (13–20), but Horace comes clean on poetry's material transmission
with *chartae* ("papers," 21) and, in case we missed it, follows up by repeating
the word in the subsequent poem (*Odes* 4.9, 31). The conceptual progression
would be less salient without the formal marker of a shared, infrequent meter.

   Recurring poem types and standard lyric scenes provide continuity: the sea-
sonal poem (*Odes* 1.4, 4.7, 4.12); the unhappy love triangle (or square or pen-
tagon) (*Odes* 1.13, 1.33, 3.7, 4.11); parties for Maecenas (*Odes* 1.20 and 4.11);
poems about or addressed to Vergilius (*Odes* 1.3, 1.24, 4.12); the abuse of an

aging beauty (*Odes* 1.25 and 4.13); exhortations more or less overt to "pluck the day" before the arrival of old age or death (*carpe diem, Odes* 1.11.8; 4.10). All of these type scenes can be combed for differences—in general, the poet emerges as more mature and less pushy in matters erotic, more maudlin about the passage of time. I will focus briefly on a programmatic scene that offers a reversal, since it defines not Horace's poetics, but the society in which he carves out a role for himself as a lyrist. My discussion owes much to Ahern (1991), Davis (1987b, and 1991: 33–9), and Lowrie (1997: 55–70, 343–9).

Odes 1.6 is the first poem in Book 1 to make an explicit statement both positive and negative about the type of subject matter the poet embraces. He disavows praise of Agrippa and Caesar, specifically regarding Agrippa's military exploits, the rage of Achilles, Ulixes' travels, and the house of Atreus. Style and genre follow along with the subject matter, since the heroes respectively evoke epic and tragedy, both genres associated with a higher style than lyric. Horace juxtaposes two stylistic code words: *tenues grandia* ("I, being slight, [do not try] grand topics," 9). What he does embrace is sympotic and erotic poetry: *nos conuiuia, nos proelia uirginum / ... cantamus* ("we sing of parties, we sing of battles with maidens," 17–19). The exclusion and inclusion of these various topics is attributed to a prohibition of the Muse (*uetat*, "forbids," 10), who externalizes Horace's own poetic choices.

Many of these elements return in the last lyric poem of the last lyric collection, *Odes* 4.15. They are a surprise in this position, because logically we expect programmatic self-definition closer to the beginning of a collection, where the choices will guide reader expectation for what is to come. At the end, such a statement is not so much resumptive of what has preceded, but rather makes a more general statement about the social conditions for poetry. The same elements are turned to a different purpose. A god, here Apollo, makes another prohibition, again directing the poet away from epic subject matter associated with a high style out of lyric's reach. The categories are similarly coded: battles and conquered cities stand for the subject matter, the Tyrrhenian Sea for a generic or stylistic endeavor beyond the capacity of the poet's small sails. What has changed is the reason for the prohibition. In the first collection, Agrippa has recently achieved a needed military success; in *Odes* 4.15, Roman military activity has ceased both at home and abroad because civil war is at an end, foreign foes have been pacified, and peace reigns over the land. Horace has overturned the stock scene. Rather than being merely an issue of poetics, concerning the kind of topic appropriate for the genre at hand, the choice of material has become a question of social order. There is no longer any need for poetry recounting battles because the battles have all been won. Horace has radically altered the familiar topoi.

The changed political conditions result in changed cultural conditions. In *Odes* 1.6, Horace's stated preference for sympotic and erotic topics over military ones comes across as escapist. Lyric provides a refuge from the harsh world of politics— this is an important social function for a society riven by civil war. Many other passages in *Odes* 1–3 support this idea. Conspicuous is Horace's pulling back from giving an account of Pollio's narrative of civil war in *Odes* 2.1; after letting himself be drawn into a gory description of bloodstained waters, he restores his Muse to a "lighter plectrum" (*leuiore plectro*, 40) in the poem's final stanza. But by *Odes* 4, all that is left behind. The Roman world has achieved peace under Augustus with the result that a different kind of song is needed. The last two stanzas offer a picture of a communal celebration of the national founding myth, on days sacred and profane, in a wholesome family context, with both reeds and lyre. Whether the bachelor Horace can fully participate in this song is a question left hanging (see "The communal voice" and "The eclipse of light lyric" below).

Performance, writing, and the power of speech

I refer above to the rites dedicated to Venus in *Odes* 4.1 as a multimedia extravaganza as well as to Horace's new claim to be able to immortalize others in writing in *Odes* 4.8 and 4.9. This collection has a strong interest in the media of poetic production first as poetics, but also as indices of the power of lyric speech. (The argument in this section is developed at greater length in Lowrie 2009a: chs. 3, 4, and 5). Horace is well aware that his own type of speech is less powerful than the lawyers'. He stages his own failure of speech when overwhelmed by love in *Odes* 4.1 with synapheia over lines 35–6. The elision is an icon of what he says, an attestation of his own silence when persuasion is needed: *cur facunda parum decoro / inter uerba cadit lingua silentio* ("why does my tongue fall among eloquent words in too little decorous silence?"). The erotic topos of the tongue-tied lover mobilizes terms (eloquence, decorum) that call rhetoric to mind. By contrast, his honorand Maximus is successful in defending clients—he speaks on their behalf: *pro sollicitis non tacitus reis* ("not silent for his harassed defendants," 14). The negation of his silence (*non tacitus*) stands in contrast to Horace's *silentium*. As the collection progresses and Horace presents himself as more confident in his own power of speech, he sets a limit to the eloquence of lawyers. It cannot bring you back from the dead: *non, Torquate, genus, non te facundia, non te / restituet pietas* ("Your birth will not restore you, Torquatus, nor will eloquence or pious duty," 4.7.24). This statement comes right before the two poems declaring poetry's power of granting immortality—of course verse cannot bring you literally back from the dead, but it can continue to convey representation into the future. In this way, poetry recorded on paper trumps the transient, though powerful, spoken word.

It is perhaps obvious that lawyers' eloquence can affect people's lives by whether they win or lose in court and that writing is the conventional medium, at Rome at any rate, for the preservation of the word. But much of *Odes* 4 is devoted to choral lyric. What power does it have? Horace answers this question elsewhere. In *Epistles* 2.1, a substantial passage treats choral lyric, specifically with regard to its powers. Poets in general are characterized by their utility to the city (*utilis urbi*, 124). Their role is educational: they aid children to form speech correctly, offer moral exempla, and teach prayers. Horace furthermore attributes choral lyric with the power to appease the gods. This brings peace and prosperity.

> poscit opem chorus et praesentia numina sentit,
> caelestis implorat aquas, docta prece blandus,
> auertit morbos, metuenda pericula pellit,
> impetrat et pacem et locupletem frugibus annum.
> carmine di superi placantur, carmine Manes. (*Epistles* 2.1.134–8)

> The chorus asks for help and feels the gods' presence, it begs for the sky's waters, pleasing with a learned prayer, it averts illness, repels fearsome dangers, obtains both peace and a year rich in fruits. The gods above, the shades below are placated by song.

Horace here explicates the ideology of song that underlies his preoccupation with choral lyric in *Odes* 4. I think his resistance in this collection toward adopting the high style associated with this public, powerful, and celebratory genre has to do with the pressures of the ideology of song. He does not want to create excessive expectations, nor to claim a power beyond his capacity. He knows lyric performance is a powerful means of bringing about social cohesion, but we cannot suppose he thinks it really brings peace by appeasing the gods. In *Odes* 4, he never makes such a claim, but rather assigns song the capability, for example, of alleviating cares: *minuentur atrae / carmina curae* ("black cares will be lessened by song," 4.11.35–6). The hesitation he displays about adopting the persona of a choral lyrist demonstrates that he treats the ideology seriously without taking it at face value.

The ideology of song has its pitfalls. Speech is constitutive of the social order (Habinek 2005; Connolly 2007), but there are many other determining factors (wealth and political office to name a few). Roman poets hesitate to claim the mantle of potent song and often present themselves as powerless before alternative discourses, whether other, usually higher poetic genres or 'real-life' discourses like the law. The latter, one might argue, has a greater capacity to form sociopolitical structures than poetry.

Some scholars furthermore take song literally by attributing performance to poetry that talks about it. This move has a long and revered history, attested in "Probus" (Thilo and Hagen 1881–1902; 3.2.328), who argues that Vergil indicates in the *Eclogues* the passages meant to be sung by mentioning song. Over the course of the twentieth century, many have argued that, in addition to the *Carmen Saeculare*, Horace's *Odes* were also sung (Bonavia-Hunt 1969; Lefèvre 1993). The argument often revolves around poems in *Odes* 4 and the best English piece advocating this view is by Ian DuQuesnay (1995), who suggests not only that *Odes* 4.5 was performed on Augustus' return from Gaul and Spain, but also that the book as a whole could have been performed. Let us be clear that no reliable external evidence exists for the performance of any of Horace's odes of the sort that guarantees the exceptional status of the *Carmen Saeculare*, but also that occasional poetry was regularly read aloud whether in formal recitation or privately at parties at Rome in this period. Figuring out how individual odes were performed is beyond our knowledge. For those who want to refer Horace's interest in performance to historical practices, it is important not to collapse the various imagined options. Performance could imply Horace was strumming on the lyre as he sang before a formal or even an informal audience, that he recited either publicly or among friends (the former disavowed, the latter embraced at *Satires* 2.1.35–49), but it could also include the presentation of a book of poems to an important patron (as at Horace, *Epistles* 1.13). These various representations function as generic indices whatever Horace actually did.

Book 4 nods formally to performance in a distinct change in metrical practice from that of the first collection. One of the ways Horace regularizes archaic Greek meters in *Odes* 1–3 is to place a consistent caesura after the fifth foot of both Sapphics and Alcaics. In the *Carmen Saeculare*, which is in Sapphics, there is a substantial loosening of the word break, so that it may come after either the fifth or the sixth foot. It is thought that the performance conditions of this poem impelled the change, so that the more flexible meter could better respond to the music. Horace continues this practice in *Odes* 4. While one might be tempted to think this is an indication these poems were also performed, the persistence in *Odes* 4 of the regularizations Horace established for Alcaics and Asclepiadeans tilts the evidence against this view. Rossi (1998), who traces the scholarship, argues that the restriction of the change to Sapphics indicates that Horace is alluding to the performance context of the *Carmen Saeculare* through this technique rather than using it because of the actual performance of these poems.

Realia aside, the interest *Odes* 4 displays in the media of representation is one element among others unifying the book. Nearly every poem brings up song, ritual utterance, or recording of some sort. Those that do not are either overtly panegyric (*Odes* 4.4) or look back strongly to the lyric modality of the first collection (4.10). Even *Odes* 4.7, *diffugere niues* ("the snows have scattered," 1), with its revision of the classic lyric meditation on the seasons mentions in passing the choral dance of the Graces with the nymphs (5–6). Beyond the more weighty references to choral lyric and the poet's song traced in "Overcoming resistance" (above), song comes up more casually of others' voices in poems 11–14. Phyllis is to learn a song (*modos*) for Maecenas' birthday party (*Odes* 4.11.34–5). A marker of spring is shepherds' songs, sung to the accompaniment of the pan-pipe (*carmina fistula*, *Odes* 4.12.10). Lyce's "tremulous song" (*tremulo cantu*, *Odes* 4.13.5) has been surpassed by Chia, who is "learned at the strings" (*doctae psallere*, 7). The rising of the Pleiades marks the onset of winter in *Odes* 4.14 and Horace tucks in a reference to their forming a chorus (*Pleiadum choro*, 21) although this is not necessary to indicate the season.

Similarly, Horace's interest in recording goes beyond poetic paper, mentioned in "Allusion and return" above, and extends to official recording methods. Time and commemoration are consistent Horatian concerns across his œuvre and here the calendar brings these two together. As often, repetition of a word or motif in close succession indicates more than casual attention. In *Odes* 4.13, a poem lamenting that the poet's wish for Lyce to grow old has actually come true, Horace expresses the inexorability of time's passage with mention of the *fasti*, the official record of time. Costly raiment and jewelry will not bring back time for her (or, by implication, for him): *tempora quae semel / notis condita fastis / inclusit uolucris dies* ("the times once the swift day has put them away, locked up in the public records," 14–16). This poem closes the Venus motif in the collection, at least in her role as a goddess of love, so the *fasti* appear a mere turn of phrase. When they return at the beginning of the next poem, their official character comes more to the fore. Horace asks what public commemoration could effectively eternalize Augustus, whom he calls *maxime principum* ("greatest of princes," *Odes* 4.14.6). The public records mentioned are "inscriptions and the mindful calendar" (*titulos memoresque fastos*, 4). The inference is that these media are potent, but less so than Horace's poetic commemoration, encapsulated in the honorific apostrophe to Augustus. The repetition of the *fasti* from an erotic to a political poem effects once again the transition to a larger-scale lyric Horace makes in this book.

The official record of time enables temporal return for Augustus in a way that is closed off to Lyce. Horace notes that the recent military successes won by Tiberius and Drusus took place on the anniversary (*quo die*, *Odes* 4.14.34) of Alexandria's capitulation to Augustus fifteen years previous (*lustro … tertio*, 37). This method of reckoning time by five-year increments (*lustrum*) again turns the personal toward the public—Horace began the collection with his age calculated as ten five-year periods (*lustra decem*, *Odes* 4.1.6). But, while Augustus may experience circular time through the repetition of like events, it is song, embodied in ritual time, that truly withstands temporal erosion. This medium inhabits the climax of the book: the collection's last word is *canemus* ("we will sing," *Odes* 4.15.32).

This final scene is extraordinary from the perspective of the first collection of Odes. The typical lyric symposium, where friends join on a specific occasion to forget their cares over wine, has been replaced with a scene of communal festivity. The precursor to this scene closes *Odes* 4.5, where Augustus' return from abroad is met with community celebration. In both places, Horace speaks in the first person plural: his voice joins that of the people. In both, there is a generalized sense of ritual time. Horace expresses this in *Odes* 4.5 with two merisms: "night and day" and "sober and drunk" (38–40). Drinking accompanies the festivities ending *Odes* 4.15 through the metonymy of Liber's gifts and the time is again generalized: *et profestis lucibus et sacris* ("on days profane and sacred," 25–6). Even the sober day and profane time are folded into the festivity, which is generalized beyond any specific occasion and rather represents a new modality of civic life.

The scene owes much to several sorts of ritual song. It looks back to the *carmina conuiualia* that Cicero testifies Cato reported as already long gone (on which see Sciarrino 2004 and Goldberg 2005: 4–16). The *Carmen Saeculare* is also an important precedent. Although there are many differences from the *Carmen Saeculare*—here the emphasis is on citizens and their wives rather than their unmarried children, the preeminent gods are Liber and Venus rather than Apollo and Diana, this festivity is generalized beyond a specific occasion— one of the things Horace learns from his involvement in a civic festival is how to create foundational song. Habinek (2005) argues that song at Rome participates in ritual foundation. In the *Carmen Saeculare*, the context of the games as a celebration of civic renewal lent the song a foundational aspect. Here, foundation is thematized. The topic of communal song is not only leaders who have acquitted themselves with virtue (*uirtute functos ... duces*, 29), but also Rome's mythic Trojan ancestry: *Troiamque et Anchisen et almae / progeniem Veneris canemus* ("we will sing of Troy, and Anchises, and the offspring of gentle Venus," 31–2). Venus has been transformed from the goddess of erotic love to the gentle patron of both the Julian clan and the Roman race. Aeneas is not called by name, because Augustus can share the appellation 'offspring of Venus', so that time again repeats as mythic figures find their correlates in the present. Presumably Romulus' foundation is elided since Horace makes a point that civil strife has been laid to rest (*non furor / ciuilis aut uis exiget otium, / non ira*, "civil furor will not drive out peace, nor force or anger," 17–19), and Romulus tends to bring Remus' unhappy end to mind. The foundation celebrated here is entirely peaceful and the role of song is to unite the community.

The communal voice and the eclipse of light poetry

Although *Odes* 4.1 announces the return of Venus and the light sympotic-erotic poetry appropriate to this divinity, both the symposium and love poetry are largely turned in this book to greater purposes. These lyric modalities mark the place of the individual in all his physical limitations and pleasures, so when Horace gradually adopts more of a communal *nos* ("we") at points in the collection, there is both a generic transformation from a slighter to a grander lyric mode and a realignment in the conception of citizenship. Horace in his person mediates two roles, the ordinary citizen, who is one of the crowd at a parade or civic celebration, and the vatic bard, who has the special task of representing the polity to itself in all its guises—from individual, to bard, to leaders of society and of state, to the single leader, who himself symbolizes Rome as a political entity. The first person plural itself mediates between the individual and the group: Horace can refer only to himself with it (e.g, *Odes* 1.6.5, 17), but it can also refer to him as representative of society or genuinely as a member of a group (*Odes* 4.5.38–9; 4.15.25).

Horace's activities as an ordinary citizen—including the same lusts and desires as anyone—are situated in significant city spaces. Ligurinus, the love-interest of *Odes* 4.1, gets into his dreams at night (*nocturnis ... somniis*, 37) with surreal results—visions of pursuit through the air and water. The locus of these visions is the Campus Martius, signally an urban space reserved for sport and civic activity that cannot take place within the city walls. This is where voting takes place when the citizen body is organized into the *comitia centuriata*, that is, according to military rank, since the army must not enter the city. It is an open space that provides an alternative to the Forum, the heart of political activity at Rome (Millar 1998: 16, 197), and other elections took place there as well. When Horace envisions himself in the next poem as shouting refrains among the crowd at a hypothetical triumph of Augustus, we come closer to the civic center: the Forum is mentioned, but because of the holiday is closed for business (*Forum ... / litibus orbum*, "the Forum, bereft of law-suits," *Odes* 4.2.43–4). In the next poem, Horace disavows a number of professions, including the military life: he will not triumph on the Capitoline (*Odes* 4.3.9), the citadel of Rome, but he does advance over his position in *Odes* 4.2, where he was one of the bystanders at the parade. Now bystanders point at him in his role as bard (*Odes* 4.3.22–3).

On the one hand, he remains an individual; sexual desire grounds this aspect, which is embodied in the book's love poems. But Horace time and again presents his love life as coming to an end. Venus had left him alone for some unspecified period before *Odes* 4.1. Phyllis is characterized as the last girlfriend: *meorum finis amorum / (non enim posthac alia calebo / femina* ("end of my loves, for I will not grow hot for another woman after this," *Odes* 4.11.31–4). Lyce has lost her charms in *Odes* 4.13, although she had once "stolen me out from under myself" (*me surpuerat mihi*, 20), and Horace looks back with anguish at her predecessor, Cinara, who died young. Ligurinus returns from *Odes* 4.1 in 4.10; he is still in the flush of youth, but where the first ode of the collection emphasized Horace's subjective desire, here he anticipates the boy's incipient maturity and projects onto him his future regret at his loss of appeal. The point of view is still the poet's, whose implied critique for the boy' refusal is part of a strategy to get him to yield. Drinking and festivity similarly hold the place of individual desire. Maecenas' birthday party—he is aging too—in *Odes* 4.11 will include sacrifice and song. Horace invites Vergilius to drink with him in *Odes* 4.12 at the price of supplying the perfume. They will indulge in a modicum of sweet silliness, while mindful of death (26–8). His addressee may

be the "client of noble youths" (*iuuenum nobilium cliens*, 15), but is not characterized as young himself. Rather, youths laugh at the likes of Lyce (*Odes*,
4.13.26–7) and her contemporaries, including presumably, the poet. Horace has
grown old and sees aging in those around him, but his own individuality is
folded into the greater community, which derives continuity from replenishment
through children.

When Horace imagines himself singing, he speaks in the first person plural as
part of the citizenry: *non semel dicemus 'io Triumphe!' / ciuitas omnis* ("we will
utter 'io Triumph!' not once, the whole polity," *Odes* 4.2.50–1). The refrain will
be repeated and is repeated in the text (49 and 50), but the implication of "not
once" goes further than the particular occasion. This refrain will be sung again
and again at future triumphs. The celebration of Augustus' return at *Odes*
4.5.37–40 is similarly iterated: *dicimus ... dicimus* ("we say ... we say"). This too
intimates that thanksgiving will surpass the moment. Although the authorial
plural at *Odes* 4.8 generalizes of bards, rather than of the citizen body, it still
transcends Horace's individuality: *carmina possumus / donare et pretium dicere
muneri* ("we can give poems and express the value of the gift," 11–12). The
climactic *canemus* ("we will sing," *Odes* 4.15.32) that closes the book is spoken
by normative citizen men, accompanied by their wives and children (*cum prole
matronisque nostris*, 27).

There is a frequent emphasis on children in this book as a means of transmission of cultural values. The Nerones, like the young eagle who opens the poem,
have been shaped by their upbringing under their father's tutelage:

> sensere quid mens rite, quid indoles
> nutrita faustis sub penetralibus
>   posset, quid Augusti paternus
>   in pueros animus Nerones.
>
> fortes creantur fortibus et bonis.
>
> (the enemy) has felt what mind and character, rightly
> nourished in propitious homes, what the paternal spirit
> of Augustus could accomplish over the Nerones as
> children. The brave are born of the brave and good.
> (*Odes* 4.4.25–9)

In the next poem, this idea underlies a compliment to Augustus regarding his
own generation: he is called *dux bone* ("good leader," *Odes* 4.5.5 and 37) and is
himself descended from the "good gods" (*diuis orte bonis*, 1). Hannibal in *Odes*
4.4 expresses admiration for the Romans in terms of generation: they brought
"both their children and aged parents" from Troy to Ausonia (*natosque maturosque
patres*, 55). The Trojans are later mentioned as defending their faithful wives and
children (*pro pudicis / coniugibus puerisque*, *Odes* 4.9.23–4). The Augustan peace
is expressed partially in terms of the legitimacy of offspring: *laudantur simili prole*

puerperae ("child-bearing mothers are praised for their children who resemble their fathers," *Odes* 4.5.23). The several choruses consist of virginal children (*Odes* 4.1.25–6, 4.6.31–2), one of whom will grow up to get married (*nupta*, 41) and presumably bear the next generation of children. The horrors of myth and war are expressed through violence against children: Achilles burns unborn babies even hiding in their mother's wombs (*nescios fari pueros … / etiam latentis / matris in aluo, Odes* 4.6.18–20; Itys' mother mourns him perpetually (*Odes* 4.12.5–8). All these references build up to the book's final image with its emphasis on the continuity from one generation to the next. The citizenry not only looks forward to the future with their children and the tense of *canemus*, but also looks back: they will sing "in the manner of their fathers" (*more patrum, Odes* 4.15.29).

If Horace subsumes his individual lyric "ego" within a more communal voice, a number of questions arise. What becomes of the individual under the empire as constituted by Augustus? Is there still room for sympotic-erotic pleasure, for the whole realm of the aesthetic? Or is there only room among private citizens for private concerns? Is Horace entirely at ease with these new imperial conditions? As a childless and aging bachelor, with eclectic sexual tastes, his image does not fit that of the normative citizen. Can his role as bard entirely compensate for his idiosyncracy as a person? I am not sure these questions can be answered definitively—or rather, I am quite sure they cannot. In this and the next section, I will try to find a way to address them.

Poetry has a special role in *Odes* 1–3 not just as the refuge for the individual from civic violence, but also as the source of counsel against it. Horace builds up to this role through the periodic repetition of the word *antrum* ("grotto") (Lowrie 1997: 323–4). In *Odes* 1.5, Horace speaks at a distance, imaging his former love Pyrrha entangled with her new flame *grato … sub antro* ("in a pleasing grotto," 3). There is no overt political dimension to the poem. In *Odes* 2.1, Horace recalls his Muse, who has been seduced into telling of Pollio's history of civil war and hence into narrating civil war itself; she should join him *Dionaeo sub antro* ("in Dione's grotto," 39). As Venus' mother, Dione evokes the pleasures of love, or rather, of love poetry, since the woman Horace imagines joining him in the grotto is his Muse. The climax of the sequence is *Odes* 3.4, where the grotto belongs to the Muses and it is a refuge for Caesar himself, once he has disbanded his troops. Horace asks the Muses to "restore high Caesar, … seeking to end his labors, in a Pierian cave" (*uos Caesarem altum … / finire quaerentem labores / Pierio recreatis antro*, 37–40). Poetry has a strong political role in this poem, because in addition to providing a refuge for the head of state, it also gives him counsel: *uos lene consilium et datis et dato / gaudetis almae* ("you, gentle [Muses], both give gentle counsel and rejoice in its giving," 41–2). This is a poetic function with a long lineage—Pindar in his poems to tyrants folds counsel into his victory celebrations. Although Horace is generally more confident of his public role in *Odes* 4, there is no equivalent to the progression traced here. It is not at all clear any more that poetry has a counsel-giving role. What is its role then?

In *Odes* 4, Horace explicitly defines poetry's role as praise: *laudes* (*Odes* 4.8.20). But since this passage says only that poetry's praise exceeds that of inscriptions, that it is necessary for continued renown, it is unlikely that Horace conceived of praise as poetry's only role. It is one function among others and these we must infer not from what he says, but from what he does. *Odes* 4 is manifestly celebratory and this aspect accords with Horace's acknowledgment of poetry's importance for praise. The sticking point for moderns is whether this mean Horace engages in panegyric. Don Fowler argues not, that the contradiction between Horace's aesthetic of the small and the big man in politics makes this speech act founder, though this dynamic pertains more to the first than the second lyric collection (1995). I would say that the role Horace adopts for his poetry is to represent Rome to itself in all its complication and that this discursive gesture includes praise without being exhausted by it. The consequence of this argumentative tack is that Horace the individual would not be excluded from the representation. Rather, the citizenry is shown to consist not entirely of normative men as projected by the collective imperial imaginary. These people, in all their individuality, nevertheless participate in the rituals that constitute their society, though when they do so the particularities of their lives and desires are subsumed into the greater, normalizing whole.

The aesthetics of praise

The interpretive crux of *Odes* 4 is whether this book praises Augustus and his adopted stepsons, whether its status as commissioned poetry obviates its aesthetic claims. Here we must confront the historical contexts of this poetry's conception and reception. Often, when facing interpretive problems of this sort, modern scholars will say that the ancients had no objection to praise poetry, they thought commissions were a good thing. It is we post-romantic moderns who are squeamish about praise of the powerful. So far, I agree. Then the argument takes this turn: sincerity is not necessary for poetry of this kind; it was more a question of fulfilling a rhetorical role. Although I am sympathetic to the notion of rhetorical demands beyond the volition of any individual speaker, I have two problems with this argument for poetry of this time. Horace, among other poets writing from the triumvirs through the mid-Augustan period, expends a great deal of energy in the *recusatio*. If praise were entirely unproblematic, it would not be necessary to take indirect routes to guarantee the poet's sincerity. Furthermore, we moderns have claims on the poetry too. Horace could not conceive that his poetry would continue to be read long past the fall of Rome, but he was writing nevertheless for all time. He had an acute awareness of the limits of occasionality. His poetry operates not only within contemporary rhetorical expectations, but also transcends these constraints to produce work that is not disposable. It is meant to last for all time. His poetry needs to succeed in praising in the circumstances of its conception, as well as offer qualities that resist being used up in the occasion.

If we grant that Horace praises, but that his poetry surpasses this rhetorical demand, my task as an interpreter becomes then to defend the aesthetic quality of the poems that do praise, namely *Odes* 4.4, 4.14, and 4.15. These poems celebrate the victories of Tiberius and Drusus, as well as the Augustus peace. They, along with *Odes* 4.9, are the only poems in Alcaics in the book. Since Horace will not attempt Pindaric meters since they seem to him too loose (*numeris* ... / *lege solutis,* "meters untied from the law," *Odes* 4.2.11–12), Alcaeus is the most political poet among the lyrists on whom he habitually models himself. *Odes* 4.9 will offer an inroad to the others, since it is also a praise poem. Praise of the addressee Lollius poses a different problematic from that of the imperial family. On the one hand, what is really hard for modern sensibilities to swallow is the praise of rulers. On the other, the praise of rulers seems to some extent absolute, while the praise of lesser mortals appears contingent or unnecessary.

It is relatively easy in a praise poem to separate out the elements of overt praise from the aspects of that additionally serve other poetic purposes. *Odes* 4.9, for instance, divides into two parts, the first (1–30) a literary history about the role of poetry in the immortalization of famous deeds, the second (30–52) in praise of Lollius. There are nuances: the last two stanzas of the poem are more generalizing and pertain to Lollius only by implication. Horace formally resists a clean-cut division by making the transition from one section to the next in the middle of a stanza. Elroy Bundy (1986) argues for Pindar that all elements of epinician are functional: poetic statements by the speaker ground the utterance; the myth adds glory; gnomic statements situate praise within society's shared values. For *Odes* 4.9, we could argue that the literary history puts this poem in an illustrious line so as to enhance Lollius' praise; the envy motif—common in Pindar—in *liuidas* / *obliuiones* ("spiteful forgettings," 33–4) offers a blocking figure the praise means to overcome; the gnomic definition of the *beatus* ("blessed," 45–52) not only rubs off on Lollius but articulates an ideology shared by speaker, addressee, and reader alike.

Perhaps harder is to turn the argument the other way: even functional elements in a poem contribute to its aesthetic value. My impression is that the following lines will leave most readers cold, particularly since the next two stanzas continue in the same vein: *est animus tibi* / *rerumque prudens et secundis* / *temporibus dubiisque rectus* ("you have a spirit both prudent in affairs and upright in times favorable and doubtful alike," 34–6). Lollius has been consul more than once, resisted the corrupting allure of money, and made his way victoriously through opposing throngs. Since Lollius was defeated by the Sygambri in 16 BCE and left a sizable estate and a reputation for rapacity behind him when he committed suicide, we have a number of interpretive options: Horace is being bitterly ironic;

he is attempting to salvage Lollius' reputation; the historians are vicious and misleading; praise operates strictly rhetorically, independent of countervailing data; Horace is praising an ideal type. These options can be traced from the introductions to this poem in Page (1956) and Syndikus (1973). Clearly it will make an aesthetic difference whether Horace is telling a joke or praising Lollius straight. In each case, however, Horace is representing the ideology, saying, "Here it is, this is what praise poetry looks like; this is how someone who deserves praise should act." Whether true or sincere or not, these are the terms according to which Romans praise other Romans and Horace lays it out in all its bald glory. Mischievous? Sincere, but self-conscious? Handing down counsel to a powerful but flawed man? Any of these options tempers our initial distaste by putting the poet in the position of control.

Odes 4.4 has many aestheticizing trappings that can be paralleled in Pindar or Callimachus: a long (four-stanza) opening double simile, comparing Drusus to an eagle and a lion (1–16); a learned digression on the Amazon axes the Vindelici bear (18–22); gnomic doctrine about education (25–36); a historical digression in mythic vein where Drusus' ancestors are credited with conquering Hasdrubal (37–44) and setting Rome on a peaceful track (45–8), and Hannibal gives a speech about the greatness of the Romans (49–72 or 76). The final stanza, whether in Hannibal's voice or the poet's, glorifies the Claudian clan under Jupiter's aegis. All these elements may lay claim to beauty and can also be analyzed as functional: they contribute to the greater glory of the honorand. The question is whether we can recuperate any aesthetic quality for the bare praise, where Horace says the Vindelici saw Drusus, like the eagle and lion, "waging war under the Alps" (*bella sub Alpibus / Drusum gerentem*, 17–18). When Romans find themselves in Homeric similes or their portraits on heroic nudes, how are we to imagine their reaction? Yes, it was glorifying, but their rhetorical culture gave them an arch appreciation for figuration—they took these gestures as such, with full knowledge of the distance between their contingent selves and Achilles. It is hard to pull off these conventions; all eyes are on how you manage to do so. The drum-roll of resistance, then yielding to Pindarizing in *Odes* 4.1–3 leads up to this: Horace says that Drusus waged war under the Alps. The apparent simplicity of the statement belies the lead-up, which shows that the game is as much about the conditions of utterance as the utterance itself.

Odes 4.14 is the most resistant poem in the collection to modern queasiness about praise. It retails the victories of Drusus and Tiberius for three whole stanzas (9–20) and ends with a hymn to Augustus, including the divine characterization as *praesens* ("present/powerful," 43) and anaphora of the pronoun *tu* an overwhelming nine times (33–52). This is not a mere hint; the last lines have the Sygambri venerating Augustus as a god (*te ... / uenerantur*, 51–2). He is addressed with *o* in both the opening and closing sections of the ode (5, 43). The military successes of his stepsons serve Augustus' greater glory; he is the preeminent power and they fought under his auspices (*auspiciis ...*

secundis, "favorable auspices," 16; *te copias, te consilium et tuos / praebente diuuos,* "with you offering your military resources, your counsel, and your gods," 33–4). The request to celebrate Drusus and Tiberius that Suetonius records Augustus made is met and surpassed by the celebration of the Emperor himself.

I propose a way into an appreciation of this poem along the lines suggested above: even emperor worship is a rhetorical conceit; Horace is exposing Roman ideology and showing what praise poetry looks like. But the strategy that opens up the poem best for me is to return to the question of the conditions of utterance. If Horace sets Augustus' might on display, he is also arrogating power to himself. He appropriates the language of the state. The poem's first line, *quae cura patrum quaeue Quiritium* ("what care of the fathers and the citizens"), refers to the *senatus populusque Romanus* ("the senate and the Roman people"): *SPQR* is the name of the Roman state. As mentioned above, Horace suggests that their inscriptions and records pale before his own immortalizing potential. He has trumped not just other poets, but the state itself. Suetonius tells us that Augustus did not want his brand cheapened by just anyone singing his praises (*Aug.* 89.3). Horace shows he can get away with it and do it better even than official venues. By the end of the next poem, he has celebrated Augustus in both war and peace. If his voice folds into that of the larger *ciuitas,* the state is also absorbed into the polity as a whole. Augustus moreover belongs to a line larger than himself, the progeny of Venus (*Odes* 4.15.32). Horace's song forwards the image of a communal, foundational song that is greater than his own individual poetry can ever be—such is the ideational power of his utterance.

Virtus, decorum, and morals

If Horace creates an idea of song greater than his own poetry can in fact achieve, we return to the question: what can it do? *Odes* 4 provides an opportunity for thinking about what role poetry may play in society; it reveals Roman society's shared values; it praises; it mourns the passage into old age. Many extraordinary events are praised in this book: military victories, the coming of peace. Individual experience reaches to a universal level in the disappointment over a love's fading beauty. A recurrent topic, especially in the last part of the book, is in fact Roman values. These are both elevating and humble. *Virtus* (manly virtue) is an aspiration of male addressees great and small. It is a common word in Horace (over fifty times in the corpus) and has a special role to play here in holding the leaders to the standards of the *mos maiorum* ("custom of the ancestors"). More applicable to women is decorum, which regulates social and sexual mores. Moral virtue is also a topic and is potentially accessible to anyone.

The first occurrence of *uirtus* in the book is at *Odes* 4.4.31, in the context of ancestral valor: *est in equis patrum / uirtus* ("the virtue of their fathers is in horses"). The animal *exempla*—including domestic cows and predator eagles—color the point about the Nerones' good lineage with an epic tinge. The comparison of the contemporary Nerones with their ancestors from the Punic Wars is complimentary, but raises the bar on expectations. They have a high standard to meet. Horace assumes those with *uirtus* have innate abilities, but in *Odes* 4.8 and 4.9 adds the argument that it is not enough for lasting renown, which requires the invention of poetry. Aeacus is the *exemplum* in the former and a whole line of heroes in the latter, but the implication is that what Horace says about the mythic figures also applies to the addressees. It is not just *uirtus*, but also *fauor et lingua potentium / uatum* ("favor and the tongue of powerful bards," *Odes* 4.8.26) that consecrated Aeacus on the Isles of the Blessed. In *Odes* 4.9, a gnome on the need of a bard so that *uirtus* will not be hidden (29–30) provides the link between the mythic figures and the addressee. So far, Horace has only indirectly attributed *uirtus* to any one living man, though Censorinus in *Odes* 4.8 is addressed with a generalizing clause that acknowledges he has done good deeds: *neque / si chartae sileant quod bene feceris, / mercedem tuleris*, "nor will you will win your due if papers keep silent your benefactions," 20–2).

The first direct attribution of *uirtus* is to Augustus: his *uirtutes* are at issue when Horace suggests state recognition is not good enough (*Odes* 4.14.3). Augustus has already clearly won the honor Horace celebrates, but when the word recurs in the next poem, the bar is again high. Current leaders receive celebration because they have lived up to the standards set by the ancestors: *uirtute functos more patrum duces / ... canemus* ("we will sing of our leaders, who have performed virtue in the manner of our fathers," *Odes* 4.15.29–32). These lines frame the final stanza of the collection and cannot be overemphasized. Augustus is both honored for living up to the pattern and warned not to deviate from it. There are no specifics, but the *mos maiorum* pertains to the governance of behavior private and public and extends even to the form of the Roman constitution. Augustus is expected to stay within these guidelines.

Women should observe standards less inherited than cultural givens. As with the men, myth offers exemplary behavior—here to be rejected. Phaethon and Bellerophon, who both flew too high and fell off their mounts from the sky, are adduced as an *exemplum graue* ("heavy model," *Odes* 4.11.26) for Phyllis not to aim too high in love. She has been hankering after Telephus, whose girlfriend is classier (*non tuae sortis*, 22). Rather, she should "follow what she deserves" (*ut te digna sequare*, 29) and stick with Horace. Similarly, Lyce should obey the canon of decorum. Since *decens / ... motus* ("seemly movement," *Odes* 4.13.17–18) has fled her, she should tone down the jewelry and dress. The point is for your social class, age, and appearance all to be in sync. Decorum means finding your like (*Odes* 4.11.31) and doing what is appropriate. This canon of behavior is not restricted to women, but covers the whole private sympotic and erotic sphere. Horace projects onto Ligurinus a future lament about the disparity of his feelings and looks (*Odes* 4.10). Silliness in drink with Vergilius is fine, provided it is restricted to its proper place (*in loco, Odes* 4.12.28).

Beyond *uirtus* and decorum, Horace advocates a kind of virtue in this book that is open to all. Here I will argue for a more democratic Horace than is often depicted. At the end of *Odes* 4.9, he defines the one who deserves "the name of blessed" (*nomen beati*, 47) as he who knows how to use the gifts of the gods, endures modest resources, fears disgrace over death but not dying for friends and country. These virtues may not belong to everyone, but they are accessible to the common people in a way that aristocratic *virtus* is not. If Horace largely celebrates the higher echelons of the Roman aristocracy in this book, his own adoption of a broader voice opens his poetry to community participation. Horace is often pegged as a social climber who sets his own failings, moral and social, on display (Oliensis 1998; Bowditch 2001). In *Odes* 4, it would be easy to emphasize the honor he accords the imperial family at the expense of the people. But let us remember the societal consent needed for Augustus to rule as he did—as he says in his *Res gestae, per consensum uniuersorum* ("by the consent of all," 34.1). All can attain some form of virtue, some honor to greater or lesser degrees. If Augustus continues to deserve the song offered at the end of *Odes* 4.15, he will need to act within the *mos maiorum*. That is Horace's final lyric message.

GUIDE TO FURTHER READING

Odes 4 awaits a magisterial commentary in English on the scale of Nisbet and Hubbard on *Odes* 1 and 2 and Nisbet and Rudd on *Odes* 3. Still essential is Kiessling's German commentary along with its multiple revisions by Heinze. The essayistic commentaries by Syndikus (*Odes* 4 in 1973) and Pöschl (1970) are also illuminating. My favorite school text is Page (1956). West's (2000) translation is accurate, usually elegant, with occasional awkwardness to capture some detail in the Latin. The sole book-length treatments are Putnam (1986), with his characteristically detailed close reading, and Johnson (2004), who folds his individual analyses into a larger discussion of the entire book through the lens of the symposium. Treatments of individual odes can be found in many more general books on Horace. Davis (1991) examines rhetorical strategies for generic self-definition. Lyne (1995) chapters 11 and 12 address Horace's return to public poetry. The reading in the last chapter of Lowrie (1997) leaves it a cliffhanger whether Horace sells out or not and my essay here builds on this interpretation. Oliensis (1998) and Bowditch (2001) focus on Horace's representations of his social relations. Performance and the media of representation have been much discussed for Horace in general, whether historical practices or how Horace talks about them. Poems from *Odes* 4 are prominent in Lefèvre (1993), Nagy (1994) and, in a discussion of *Odes* 4.5, DuQuesnay (1995) suggests the book as a whole was performed, while Rossi (1998) takes the metrical changes in the book as a nod to the *Carmen Saeculare* without indicating actual performance. I treat the debate about the performance of Horace's *Odes* at length in Lowrie (forthcoming), with special emphasis on *Odes* 4 in chapter 4. Habinek (1986) blends a historicizing approach with more poetic concerns.

CHAPTER TWELVE

The *Carmen Saeculare*

Michael Putnam

The *Carmen Saeculare* is singular among poems preserved from classical anti-quity. First, though an ode, it is unique in the Horatian corpus, standing separate from the four collections of lyrics. Secondly, we probably know more about the circumstances of its production, as one of the features in the performance of the *Ludi Saeculares* that the Emperor Augustus celebrated in June, 17 BCE, than we do about any other piece of Greco-Roman literature.[1] Accordingly, it deserves individual treatment. Let us begin by looking at the *Carmen* itself. Then we will turn to its literary background, especially to Latin literature of the preceding half-century.

> Phoebe silvarumque potens Diana
> lucidum caeli decus, o colendi
> semper et culti, date quae precamur
>   tempore sacro,
>
> quo Sibyllini monuere versus   5
> virgines lectas puerosque castos
> dis, quibus septem placuere colles,
>   dicere carmen.
>
> alme Sol, curru nitido diem qui
> promis et celas aliusque et idem   10
> nasceris, possis nihil urbe Roma
>   visere maius.
>
> Rite maturos aperire partus
> lenis, Ilithyia, tuere matres,
> sive tu Lucina probas vocari   15
>   seu Genitalis:

diva, producas subolem patrumque
prosperes decreta super iugandis
feminis prolisque novae feraci
    lege marita,   20

certus undenos deciens per annos
orbis ut cantus referatque ludos
ter die claro totiensque grata
    nocte frequentis.

Vosque, veraces cecinisse Parcae,   25
quod semel dictum est stabilisque rerum
terminus servet, bona iam peractis
    iungite fata.

fertilis frugum pecorisque Tellus
spicea donet Cererem corona;   30
nutriant fetus et aquae salubres
    et Iovis aurae.

condito mitis placidusque telo
supplices audi pueros, Apollo;
siderum regina bicornis, audi,   35
    Luna, puellas.

Roma si vestrum est opus Iliaeque
litus Etruscum tenuere turmae,
iussa pars mutare lares et urbem
    sospite cursu,   40

cui per ardentem sine fraude Troiam
castus Aeneas patriae superstes
liberum munivit iter, daturus
    plura relictis:

di, probos mores docili iuventae,   45
di, senectuti placidae quietem,
Romulae genti date remque prolemque
    et decus omne.

Quaeque vos bobus veneratur albis
clarus Anchisae Venerisque sanguis,   50
impetret, bellante prior, iacentem
    lenis in hostem.

iam mari terraque manus potentis
Medus Albanasque timet securis,
iam Scythae responsa petunt, superbi   55
    nuper et Indi.

iam Fides et Pax et Honos Pudorque
priscus et neglecta redire Virtus
audet adparetque beata pleno
    Copia cornu.   60

Augur et fulgente decorus arcu
Phoebus acceptusque novem Camenis,
qui salutari levat arte fessos
    corporis artus,

si Palatinas videt aequos aras,   65
remque Romanam Latiumque felix
alterum in lustrum meliusque semper
    prorogat aevum,

quaeque Aventinum tenet Algidumque
quindecim Diana preces virorum   70
curat et votis puerorum amicas
    adplicat auris.

Haec Iovem sentire deosque cunctos
spem bonam certamque domum reporto,
doctus et Phoebi chorus et Dianae   75
    dicere laudes.

Phoebus and Diana, mistress of forests, brilliant grace of the heavens, O (you) worshipped and to be worshipped always, grant what we pray for at this time when the Sibyl's verses have advised (5) that chosen maidens and chaste youths sing a hymn for the gods to whom the seven hills have given pleasure.

O nourishing Sun, who on your gleaming chariot bring forth the day and hide it, and are reborn another and the same (10), may you be able to behold nothing greater than the city of Rome. Ilithyia, gracious at fittingly bringing forth offspring in due season, protect our mothers, whether you wish to be called Lucina (15) or Genitalis: goddess, rear our youth and bless the decrees of the fathers concerned with women and their need for wedlock and on the marriage-law, fruitful of new progeny (20), so that the sure cycle of ten times eleven years may bring back singing and games thronged three times in day's brilliance and as often during the welcome of night.

And you, Fates, truthful in your song, (25) as was once ordained and may the steady hand of events confirm it: join happy destinies to those now past. May Earth, teeming with crops and cattle, offer Ceres a wreath of corn; (30) may the healthful rains and breezes of Jupiter nourish the harvest.

Apollo, gentle and calm, with your weapon put away, hear the suppliant boys; Luna, crescent queen of the stars, (35) hear the girls.

If Rome be your monument and if Ilian bands held the
Etruscan shore, a remnant ordered to change their homes and
city in a course that brings no harm, (40) for whom chaste
Aeneas, survivor of his fatherland, without harm through Troy's
conflagration paved a way for freedom, about to bestow more
[good] things than were left behind [at Troy]: gods grant
upright ways to our educable youth, (45) gods, [grant] peace to
[those] in the calm of old age, [grant] to the race of Romulus
both resources and offspring and every distinction. And what
the glorious scion of Anchises and Venus asks of you, with [the
sacrifice of] white steers, (50) may he obtain, superior to his
warring [foe], gentle to the fallen enemy.

Now the Parthian fears our troops, lords of sea and land, and
the axes of Alba, now the Scythians and the Indi, haughty until
recently, seek answers [from us]. (55) Now Fidelity and Peace
and Honor and ancient Modesty and neglected Courage dare to
return, and blessed Plenty, with full horn, makes her
appearance. (60)

Phoebus, prophet both graced with his gleaming bow and
dear to the nine Muses, who through his saving art relieves the
body's tired limbs, if he views with favor the altars on the
Palatine, (65) always prolongs Roman strength and the
prosperity of Latium for a further cycle and to a better age, and
Diana, who holds Aventine and Algidus, gives heed to the
prayers of the Fifteen (70) and lends friendly ears to the appeals
of the youth.

That Jupiter and all the gods pay heed to these [words] I
bear home good and assured hope, I, the chorus taught (75) to
tell the praises of Phoebus and Diana.

Horace begins by immediately apostrophizing the twin patron divinities of the
Ludi Saeculares.[2] Apollo, in his role as sun god, complements his sister, Diana,
since the etymology of both names stresses the notion of brightness. Their clarity
graces the heavens with a universality enclosing day and night while their worship
embraces a temporal sweep that extends from past (*culti*) into future (*colendi*).
But this bow toward the gods' immortality (*semper*) is quickly (and alliteratively)
centered on a specific time to be celebrated (*tempore sacro*). Our prayer is initiated at a moment of poise, of ends and beginnings, of what has happened anticipating, as we will see, a noble era to come.

The focus becomes more particular still (5–8). The writings of the Sibyl had
served as a reminder that the moment had arrived, and a Sibylline poet, apposite
monitor of tradition, had been co-opted to produce an appropriate hymn to be
chanted (*dicere carmen*). He is to imagine a song suitable for such an essential
ritual that also possesses the magic power to serve as a persuasive conduit between
man and god, and to charm into existence what it proposes in words. A select

chorus of virginal youths is a fitting vehicle to accomplish this task: they, too, are time-ridden, adolescent yet chaste, a crucial attribute within the content of their ensuing verses.

Phoebus Apollo now becomes directly *Sol* (9), and the seven hills of the previous stanza are now united to form Rome itself. The emphasis upon luminescence also continues on, in the glimmer of the Sun's chariot and in the word for day, *dies*, which shares a common root with the name Diana. This theme is further extended in two ways. We concentrate on the idea of birth: the sun may come forward and hide itself, be different and the same, but its rebirth and renewal are crucial. Furthermore, through its splendor both it and we behold the majesty of the great city that would literally have surrounded the participants in the ceremony and spiritually served as their ethical center.

In the fourth stanza (13–16) we return to Diana, not as goddess of woods or as a radiant heavenly body but, appropriately for the milieu Horace has been establishing, as a divinity who presides over childbirth. The litany—she is being duly spoken of in a situation that she must likewise duly help sustain—consists of three names, one Greek and two Latin. The first two are standard, with Lucina iterating the sense of *lucidum* and expanding Diana's role from an essentially passive purveyor of light to an active participant in helping protect mothers at their moment of parturition. The third, *Genitalis*, though equally fitting to describe a divinity involved with begetting, is apparently Horace's invention. Especially given the essentially conservative nature of ritual, this is a daring lexical act on the part of the poet. It is as if to say that, even within a religious context which recapitulates past performances, novelty is also an important feature of the rejuvenation as well as of the renewal that the rite as a whole is devising.

Diana's purview opens out still further in the verses that follow, as she is called upon to foster the larger Roman legal and ethical setting that will in its turn promote the continuity of the very ceremonial being performed and witnessed (17–24). Again the poet secures the intent of his utterance by a series of lexical plays. The sequence of *producas, prosperes,* and *prolis,* with its reiteration of the prefix *pro-*, emphasizes the idea of opening out, prominent in the preceding stanza, and also of moving forward in the ethical development of the state. The combination of *producas* and *subolem* linguistically engenders *prolem*, with the latter of which it shares the same root.[3] *Prosperes* in its turn introduces the theme of hope which will reappear on several occasions as the poem progresses.[4] The notions of joining (*iugandis*) and of fertility (*ferax*) likewise initiate topics still to be elaborated. Finally, it is suitable that a law devoted to positive affirmation of marriage should itself be married.[5] The personification helps effect the reason for its existence.

A further piece of etymological wordplay connects stanzas five and six which bring the address to Diana to a conclusion. The goddess is to lend support to the mandates of the fathers. (The implication is that their good offices, as time passes, will further the moral education of those whom the mothers, according to the previous stanza, have brought into existence.) But these *decreta* lexically anticipate the *certus orbis* that will corroborate the present event itself and reinforce its fundamental presuppositions.[6] The poet's mouthpiece serves now as its own producer of decrees to remind us of two aspects of the temporality with which the poem involves us. The first is the span of one hundred and ten years— supposedly the maximum length of a human life—that was apparently the standard period of years separating individual celebrations of the *Ludi*. The second is the present three-day festivity itself, which culminated in the singing of the *Carmen Saeculare* on the Palatine and Capitoline Hills on June 3, 17 BCE.

Years narrow in on days. A larger span of time focuses upon a specific occasion of game and song, certified by the poet's vatic assurance. The day is bright as we would expect when such luminous divinities are being glorified. But the night is also *grata*, welcome as well as attractive. Nothing about the occasion either darkens the day or draws gloom from the night. And the triple iteration of both entertainment and music adds a further magic dimension to the proceedings.

As if further to assert the perpetuation of the event and its positive force, in the seventh stanza the chorus turns to the Parcae, the Fates, and to a commanding pronouncement that both subsumes and confirms their own song (*carmen*, 8) and the *cantus* (22) that supplement it. The Fates, who are as accomplished at truth-telling (*veraces*) as the "married law" of Augustus is efficacious at engendering (*ferax*, 19), also sing. But their words, once uttered, carry the stamp of the unchangeable, ever steady and secure. They are commanded to perform an intellectual marriage that, like the worship of Apollo and Diana, mixes past and future in an eternal act of blessing. Their proclamations (*fata* complements *Parcae* but also further substantiates *cecinisse* and *dictum*) have been presumably positive, already then in the past (*iam*). In the poem's prayer, in this new act of joining, they must now unite these "statements" with further "good" (*bona*) assertions for time to come.

Command now yields back to prayer as we return to the importance of fecundity, now in the natural world as well as among humankind (29–32). Tellus (Mother Earth), Ceres, goddess of grain, and Jupiter, in his role as god of the elements, now become part of the conversation. Their realms are richly intertwined, sonically and lexically. For instance, *fertilis* is linked, both by alliteration and by etymology,[7] to *frugum* and to *fetus*, which can apply to plants as well as animals. *Spicea*, to give another example, refers to a standard offering of a wreath of ears of corn to the goddess of agricultural growth,[8] but a contemporary etymology by Varro finds that "corn [comes from] hope" (*a spe spica*).[9] Horace thus adroitly expands the theme of hope to embrace nature's continued creativity along with man's own necessity to procreate.

Aquae and *aurae* also are clear complementary elements of Jupiter's presence as supportive divinity. Here the adjective *salubres* is salient for adumbrating the dependence of the human upon the celestial sphere. It thus serves as transition to lines 33–6 which are pivotal for the poem as a whole. Now near the poem's center, the poet has his chorus again apostrophize Apollo and Diana, as they had at the start. He also recalls for his readers that these words, and this song, are being chanted by boys and girls. Likewise the repetition of *audi*, poised between the chiasmus formed by *pueros Apollo* and *Luna puellas*, serves as a reminder that the song is also a hymn in which ritual iterations form an essential part in outlining the expectations of prayer.

In these core lines we face one of the poem's few moments of negativity. As far as we can tell from the evidence, public hymns in the Roman past had usually been performed at moments of crisis when divine help was needed to firm up the state's threatened existence.[10] In the year 17 BCE such was not the situation. Nevertheless the phrase *condito telo* and the posture of the boys as suppliants briskly warns us that Apollo, though now presumably mild and calm, is also a god of violence. In fact Servius quotes lines 33–4 to remind us that, for Homer as well as for Horace, this same god is the "source of disease as of health."[11]

At this central point, then, when Phoebus becomes Apollo and Diana Luna for the only occasion in the poem, and the language of ritual regains particular prominence, we have an apotropaic moment, where Apollo, and presumably his sister as well, are beseeched to remain kindly, their ungentle attributes deflected elsewhere.[12] Horace had already posed the possibility in one of his most famous odes (*Odes* 2.10.17–20)

> ... non, si male nunc, et olim
> sic erit: quondam cithara tacentem
> suscitat Musam neque semper arcum
>   tendit Apollo.

> Though the situation be bad now, it will not always be
> so. On occasion Apollo rouses the silent Muse with his
> lyre nor does he always tauten his bow.

The definitive moment has now come for Augustus' patron god to renounce his propensity for physical force and to embrace fully, perhaps even continually, his role as *Musagète*, which is to say as patron of the arts and promoter of man's spirituality.

So far Horace has concentrated on the notions of birth, fertility, generation, and regeneration that complement the grand celebration of the *Ludi*. Equally important has been an assurance of their stability, through the support of the gods, especially of Apollo and Diana, and through confirmation from the Fates. Rome and its seven hills have entered the poem only vicariously. Now the city, its history and its present political and ethical prestige, claims the ode for itself.

We begin with two stanzas (37–44) devoted to the transition from Troy to Rome, from the conflagration of one city to the foundation of the other. The central figure of this metamorphosis is Aeneas, and any reader contemporary with Horace would immediately think of his story as detailed in Virgil's final masterpiece, published probably at his death, two years before the presentation of the *Carmen*. In watching the *opus* of Rome evolve, which is to say here, in generic terms, in condensing and altering epic into lyric, we first turn to the Etruscan shore whose sacred spaces would have been still honored by Rome.[13]

But it is not now Aeneas' heroism that is paramount, not his share in the final battling or the rescue of his father and son. What we watch closely is the scatheless journey on which his squadrons embarked and the personal integrity of their leader. We are dealing specifically with *castus*, not *pius*, Aeneas, and the attribute links him, as an exemplar, with the *castos pueros* who sing this new presentation of his tale, with its revised ethics. The escape from the flames of Troy becomes now not a test of physical prowess but a type of ritual trial by fire that proves Aeneas guiltless of *fraus* because he emerges from the test without hurt. The route traveled is also metaphorical: we are entering on the path of liberty which promises more in the future than was left behind in the past, a theme varied during the course of the poem, as we have already seen.

After this introduction the gods are then called upon to embrace the resultant nation as it enters a new era (45–8). Anaphora and repetition build urgency: the divinities are to make the youth teachable for moral quality and to give the elderly a calm old age. (After all, Apollo, too, is now *placidus*.) Their part is to proffer resources, offspring—a reminder of line 19—and a grace that they already visibly possess (2).[14]

Mention of "the race of Romulus" brings us a step forward in Roman history from Aeneas. The hallowed Trojan hero, transporting Ilium to Etruria, had set a pattern for proper behavior under challenging circumstances. It remained for Romulus actually to establish the race that bears his name. Third in the sequence is Augustus, the unnamed subject of lines 49–52, the refounder of the city and its people, who had brought it internal peace after a century of civil war.

Horace's formulation takes us in two directions. It reinforces the parallelism between Aeneas and Augustus while emphasizing the illustrious quality of that heritage. In particular, the wordplay between *veneratur* and *Veneris* interconnects the Emperor's present posture of prayer to the gods with his own divine legacy. But the poet also calls our attention to a particular moral stance as noteworthy attribute to the Augustan present: he is superior to those against whom he does battle, but gentle to them in defeat.[15]

This formulation is a careful reminder not only of Aeneas–Augustus' other parent, the mortal Anchises, but also of the weighty words which in the Underworld Virgil has father address to son, as ethical prototype for martial Romans to come (*Aeneid* 6. 851–3):

> tu regere imperio populos, Romane, memento
> (hae tibi erunt artes), pacique imponere morem,
> parcere subiectis et debellare superbos.

> Remember, Roman, to rule peoples with might (these
> will be your arts), and to impose a custom for peace, to
> spare the humbled and war down the proud.

What, in Virgil's poem, is an order aimed at future behavior becomes operative in the Roman here and now, in the person of Aeneas' renowned descendant. But the *Aeneid* famously ends with its hero, though he has just been reminded of his father, not sparing his suppliant opponent. In the post-epic world of celebratory lyric the presumption is that Anchises' moral dictum is now respected in the conduct of Rome's leader.[16]

The universe of contemporary Rome occupies the next two stanzas (53–60). First we watch the city's power, the "Alban axes" that stand for the strength of Rome's magistracies,[17] operative on a global scale against foreign enemies. If the future of Rome itself battens on hope, that of its foes rests on fear, as it becomes an oracular source of its intentions toward those who might oppose its sway. By attaching the adjective *superbus* (55) to the Indi Horace turns them into a particular example upon whom Anchises' general maxim could be put into practice. As *nuper* (recently) yields to the use of *iam* (now) in anaphora, the pride of Rome's antagonists gives way before its might.[18] And there is no apparent need to resort to force to achieve this result.

A third use of *iam* links the two stanzas, but we quickly pass from concrete to abstract, from distant, foreign tribes to the world of Roman spiritual well-being, from literal challenges presented the state from outside to figurative personifications whose presence within is essential. The implication is that their imminence could not always have been taken for granted. For *iam* also here implies a differentiation with the past. *Fides, Pax,* and *Honos* are left unqualified, but both the use of "now" and the outright statement that they can dare to return bring to the fore the virtues' previous absence. *Priscus,* which here means not so much old-fashioned as characterizing a time gone by, adds to the poet's point, while *neglecta* admits publicly to a previous period of wrong-doing. The implication is that not so long ago the Romans had misused their manliness which in turn suggests the spate of civil warring that ended only with Augustus. *Pudor* can now come back, incorporated in the person of the new *castus Aeneas,* and *Copia,* magically in view and happy because times have changed, is a fit companion for *Tellus* and *Ceres.*

We have come from the re-creation of the Roman setting, in the ode's initial core, to the re-fabrication and renewal of Roman history and moral values which is the essence of its second segment. We now return to Apollo and Diana, the gods with whom we began and who claimed an intervening central stanza (61–72). The first, who again receives the title Phoebus with which we started, Horace honors with a summary of four of his attributes. He is a god of prophecy (*augur*) and therefore well suited to preside over the present proceedings which look positively to the future. He is also "graced with his gleaming bow" (*fulgente decorus arcu*), a figure of refinement as he was at the poem's outset (2) who will help bestow *decus* (48) on the Roman people. It was his bow that Virgil has Apollo stretch at a crucial moment during the battle at Actium.[19] We presume that such power is still an essential attribute for Rome, if well applied. As colleague of the nine Muses he is an appropriate promoter of singers, poet and poem. Finally as the god of medicine and its health-bringing art (*salutari arte*), he joins with Jupiter's *salubres aurae* (31–2) further to promote the physical well-being of the Romans.

In the third stanza it was the singers' prayer that the god see nothing greater than Rome (12). We now join him in watching the specific altars connected with the celebration on the Palatine itself, altars presumably associated with the magnificent temple that Augustus had dedicated to him there eleven years previously. Horace's language draws together much of what had preceded. *Rem Romanam* is a reminder of the *rem* (47) for which the chorus had previously prayed. *Semper* recalls its use in line 3: the eternal existence of the twin gods spills over into the eternity of Rome's improvement, and *prorogat* picks up the many earlier words beginning with the prefix *pro-* that suggest Rome's positive forward momentum.

But the tense and mood of *prorogat* introduce a surprising but brilliant maneuver on the poet's part. Up to this point in the ode we have had appropriately prayerful uses of the subjunctive or imperative modes when the gods have been apostrophized. Horace has saved the indicative only to tell of Aeneas' accomplishment or of the present impressive state of the Roman world. Now, as if to read Apollo's mind and to suppose his positive acceptance of the hymn's petitions, the poet uses the indicative to announce that the god in fact extends the city's good fortune into a still better time. In presuming Apollo's response, the poet also posits the magic power of his own song, as voiced by his virginal choristers, to effect in fact what it imagines in word and music.

The same holds true for Diana, goddess particularly worshipped on the Aventine. The hymn does not pray that she care for, or give receptive ear to, the fifteen priests in charge of the compendium of Sibylline sayings or to the young singers. It takes for granted that she is doing exactly that by implementing in actuality what all have so powerfully proposed.

We conclude with a look at the chorus whose initial "we" has now become a singular "I," as if to merge with the unique imagination behind their words, with the mind of the master craftsman through whom it has become *doctus*. They reaffirm the hope that has been a theme of the poem, and, by taking home their sense of divine approval, they share the potency of their role as intermediary between men and gods with the whole city for which they stand as synecdoche.

The final stanzas as a group bring to the reader the same satisfactions that would have accrued to the initial participants in the ceremony. We leave poem and celebration with a sense of wholeness. Mention of the city's seven hills (7) is substantiated in our concluding, closer look at the Palatine and the Aventine.[20] The second quatrain's reference to *Sibyllini versus* (5) gains specificity in the mention of the *quindecim virorum* (70), the *Quindecimviri sacris faciundis* who, because they were the interpreters of the Sibyl's words, would have been major figures in implementing the festivity as a whole.[21] Then there is, of course, the chorus which is called to our attention at the poem's outer bounds as well as at its center. The song that it has been bidden to sing at the poem's start (*dicere carmen*, 8) becomes, in the ode's last words, a metonymy for, which is likewise a definition of, what it contains (*dicere laudes*, 76).

Finally we have the patron gods themselves. We end, as we had begun, with mention of Phoebus and Diana. They too, like the chorus, had also appeared in lines 33–6, with change of nomenclature to Apollo and Luna and with the consequent intimation of what havoc the male god at least could wreak, should he chose not to be "gentle and calm" (*mitisque placidusque*, 33). By returning to the initial names at the poem's conclusion Horace's chorus reassures its fellow celebrants, and us, belated participants in the poet's ceremony of words, that the twin gods will indeed fulfill the promise adumbrated by their roles outlined in the poem's course.

The intellectual background of the *Carmen Saeculare* is as rich as its heritage is lengthy, embracing as it does the whole of classical literature, beginning with Homer. The poem amasses much of its force by serving to concentrate the poetic past, of which it is the culmination. In particular the history of Greek lyric, especially the odes of Pindar, is crucial for our understanding of Horace's accomplishment.[22] Nevertheless, the poet's Latin sources are particularly important for an appreciation of his originality. I will limit myself here to a survey of some salient examples.

First and foremost is Catullus' hymn to Diana, the date of whose composition and performance is unknown but is most likely to be placed in the decade before his probable death around 54 BCE, when Horace would have been eleven years old. That Horace drew inspiration from the evolution of his predecessor's delightful lyric is clear. We begin, as does Horace, with an address to Diana in the poem's opening verse, sung, as also the case in Horace, by virginal girls and boys (*puellae et pueri integri*, 2). The third stanza reminds us, as does Horace's opening line, that Diana was *domina ... silvarum* (9–10) while the fourth treats— and Horace's follows suit—of Diana Lucina, goddess of childbirth. Catullus' subsequent lines take us into the goddess's effect on the georgic world where the "good produce" (*bonis frugibus*, 19–20) may be behind Horace's depiction of Tellus as *fertilis frugum* (29). Certainly the earlier poet's final quatrain, with its prayer that Diana help to preserve "the race of Romulus" (*Romuli ... gentem*, 22–4), anticipates the entreaty of Horace's chorus that the gods "grant to the race of Romulus [*Romulae genti*] resources and offspring and every distinction" (47–8).

These parallels point to how the rhythms of Catullus' briefer hymn have served Horace well in stimulating his more expansive celebration. In the earlier poet we move from Diana's role as goddess of wild nature to tutelary divinity of childbearing and her celestial presence as Luna (16). From there we turn to her saving presence, as her monthly progress (*cursu ... menstruo*, 17) helps measure the route of the farmer's yearly progress (*iter annuum*, 18). In the last stanza agricultural nature yields to humankind, the Romans themselves, and to the poet's plea that the goddess continue to keep the people safe (*sospites*, 24).

In Horace we likewise turn from mention of Luna (36) to the outline of an itinerary, but now of a more literal, historically momentous sort: the unscathed course (*sospite cursu*, 40) that leads Aeneas on his journey (*iter*, 43) from Troy to the Italian shore. This development in turn takes us, in both poets, to Romulus' people. But, just as Horace replaces Catullus' georgic vignette, with a precis of Aeneas' route to Rome, so he now extends the earlier poet's reference to the race of Romulus into a full-scale eulogy of Augustan Rome and its potential, but without losing a residue of his model's grace, warmth, and elegance.[23]

Contemporary with Catullus is Lucretius' *De Rerum Natura* whose opening invocation to Venus also was on Horace's mind as he wrote, as much for its general spirit as for particular details. In the second line of each poem our eye focuses on heaven, and Lucretius' address to *alma Venus*, that initiates the same line, anticipates Horace's apostrophe to *alme Sol* that opens his ninth line.[24] Likewise when Horace invents the epithet *Genitalis* (16) for Diana, he may be thinking of Lucretius' use of the rare adjective *genitabilis* (11) to describe the nurturing aspect of the spring wind.[25] But, more panoramically, it is Lucretius' surpassing capture of the brightness, the opening out, and the release of pent-up energy in his brilliant hymn to nature's primaveral re-enlivenment that also suffuses the initial stanzas of Horace's eulogy to the potential of Diana and Apollo further to vivify the Roman world.

We move next to Virgil's famous *eclogue* 4 where the lexical overlap is as much more extensive as the intellectual influence is deeper still. We are, after all, dealing with an event set into motion by an aspect of "Cumaean song" (*Cumaei ... carminis*, 4) just as the ludic setting in the *Carmen* is initiated by "verses of the Sibyl" (*Sibyllini ... versus*, 5). Lucina (10) is at hand to sustain the birth of the miraculous boy who will initiate a new Golden Age, and Apollo (10) now reigns. It is a time of *decus* (11), when the earth (*tellus*, 19) will pour forth its honorific gifts. If traces of *fraus* (31) remain, they will be purged as the boy grows to manhood (we anticipate Aeneas' departure from Troy *sine fraude* [41]). Virgil's constant recourse to the word *iam* to stress the immediacy of the magical events he is describing—the word appears on nine occasions in the poem, most intensely at 4–7 (in anaphora) and at 41–4—is carefully echoed by Horace at lines 53–7. In particular, for Virgil it is the unnamed virgin Iustitia who returns to dwell again among men (*iam redit et virgo*). Her place in Horace is taken by Courage (*iam ... neglecta redire Virtus / audet*, 57–9).

In each case these dreams of hope and expectation are confirmed by the Fates. For already in antiquity Servius calls attention to the parallel between Virgil's line 47:

> concordes stabili fatorum numine Parcae
>
> the Fates in agreement on the unchanging will of destiny

and lines 26–7 of the *Carmen*:

> ... quod semel dictum est stabilisque rerum
> terminus servet, ...

He might have added that in both instances the Fates are called Parcae and that the word *fata* appears in Horace's verse 28 as it does in the line of Virgil already quoted.

But we must also look at the larger intellectual schema which Horace absorbs from Virgil and now comments upon. In the year 40 BCE, the dramatic date for the fourth *eclogue*, such a world as Virgil envisions, a world embodied in a youth at whose coming of age wars cease and nature is spontaneously all-productive, could only be a dream of the imagination. Another decade of civil fighting was still in store for the Romans. But by 17, fourteen years after the decisive victory by Augustus at Actium, dream, at least for Rome's greatest surviving poet, might now be understood as reality. Horace need not resort to allegory. Instead of Virgil's unnamed *puer* grown to manhood, he has in place Augustus, a new Aeneas *sine fraude*, under whom Apollo and Diana will in actual fact bless the Roman people with an existence which in the earlier poet is only a magnificent fancy.

The closest to being contemporary of the major influences on the *Carmen Saeculare* is the fifth poem of Tibullus' second book of elegies. There is reason to date its composition to not long before the poet's own death, probably in 19 BCE, which is to say two or so years before the occasion of the *Carmen*. It is both the longest as well as the most publicly Roman of the elegist's sixteen poems, concerned as it is with the induction of Messalinus, the son of his patron M. Valerius Messalla Corvinus, into membership in the *Quindecimviri sacris faciundis*.

We begin, as does Horace, with an apostrophe to Apollo as Phoebus and we conclude with the same direct address, with the god now joined by his sister (121–2). Meanwhile, we likewise find ourselves, at the start, before the temple of Apollo (1) on the Palatine, with the poet-speaker in the place of Horace's choristers, praying in his own person for the success of the ceremony (*precor*, 4). We behold the god, and then turn to the Sibyl and her connection with the saga of Aeneas (19–22)

> haec dedit Aeneae sortes, postquam ille parentem
> dicitur et raptos sustinuisse Lares:
> (nec fore credebat Romam, cum maestus ab alto
> Ilion ardentes respiceretque deos ...)

> She gave predictions to Aeneas after he is said to have
> lifted up his father and the Lares he had snatched (nor
> did he believe that there would be a Rome when in
> sadness he beheld from the deep Ilium and its burning
> shrines).

As at lines 37–44 of the *Carmen*, we find mention of Aeneas, of Ilium, of displaced household gods (*lares*), and of Troy's burning divinities (*ardentes deos*) which in Horace become the city itself (*ardentem Troiam*).

The Sibyl then takes over the poem to tell of Roman history, from Aeneas battling Turnus, from the founding of Alba Longa and the rape of Ilia, to the present moment when Ceres looks out over the whole world, east and west, as the province of Rome. There have already been allusions to less than noble moments in the city's past. For instance, we hear, at line 24, of "the walls [of Rome], not to be dwelt in by [Romulus'] brother Remus," a reminder of the city's primal fratricide. Now the poet in his own voice turns to an account of the prodigies that preceded the murder of Julius Caesar in 44. When this is concluded, he turns back to his patron god (79–80):

> haec fuerant olim; sed tu iam mitis, Apollo,
> prodigia indomitis merge sub aequoribus.

> These things were once-upon-a-time; but, Apollo, now
> gentle, sink the prodigies beneath untamed waters.

It is striking that Horace uses the same adjective, *mitis*, at his line 33, the only time he addresses the god as Apollo and one of the few occasions in the *Carmen* where, as we have seen, there is a flash of negativity when we realize that the god could on occasion use his weaponry to ill affect. Horace calculates the allusion effectively. By omitting all references to unfortunate moments in Roman history or in the behavior of its patron divinities, the poet replaces Tibullus' prophetic Sibyl as well as the elegist's own gloomy catalogue of prodigies with an assured look at the blessings of the present. Tibullus' descriptiveness yields to the active role of Horace's chorus—and of the genius behind its words—in confirming that of which it tells.

Let us conclude with Horace himself, with a prelude and a postlude. The prelude is *Odes* 1. 21, the only other ode where both Apollo and Diana are central figures and where, again, a chorus of virginal girls and boys is involved. Again we take due note of the qualities of each divinity—Diana's love of the outdoors,

Apollo with his quiver and lyre—though it is the male divinity that receives the final prayer (13–6):

> hic bellum lacrimosum, hic miseram famem
> pestemque a populo et principe Caesare in
>   Persas atque Britannos
>   vestra motus aget prece.

> Moved by your prayer, he will drive tearful war, will
> drive sad hunger and disease from the people and Caesar
> their prince onto the Persians and the Britons.

Nevertheless there are major differences between the poems that the last stanza in particular sets into relief. First is that we are not dealing with a hymn at all but with the training for a hymn. The speaker's posture is that of chorus leader, educating his charges into what each group should sing. In the *Carmen* nothing mediates between singers and the direct expression of their song.[26] It's as if Horace through his mouthpiece wanted nothing to come between himself and the powerful use of his gifts to corroborate the present glory of Rome.

The final verses especially point up differences in content between the two poems. Here there is still a possibility of the presence of war, hunger, and disease (and a reminder of other earlier moments where poets were enlisted to avert their menace). In the Rome of Augustus, now that Apollo is "gentle," there is no need for concern about such negative presences. By the conclusion of the *Carmen* prayer is no longer necessary. The gods are already fulfilling the chorus's requests.

The postlude looks at two Horatian texts written subsequently to the *Carmen*. The first is the sixth poem in Horace's fourth and final collection of lyrics, published probably in 13 BCE. The ode, directed to Apollo, spends its first half viewing the god as the embodiment of the vengeful assailant, especially against the brutal physicality of Achilles. At the central, pivotal stanza, we turn from Troy to Aeneas and Rome, and to an Apollo who is now suddenly the teacher of our poet-speaker whose grace (*decus*, 27) he is asked to defend and upon whom he bestows imagination (*spiritum*, 29), craftsmanship (*artem*, 29), and repute (*nomen*, 30). Then, with equal abruptness, we suddenly find our bard addressing a chorus, as he had in *Odes* 1.21, but this time they are the particular singers of the *Carmen Saeculare* who are asked to adhere to his beat (37–40):

> rite Latonae puerum canentes,
> rite crescentem face Noctilucam,
> prosperam frugum celeremque pronos
>   volvere mensis.

> duly hymning the son of Latona, duly, the Night-
> gleamer, burgeoning with her torch, encourager of crops
> and swift to propel the plunging months.

We end with a glance at one of the female choristers, and with a look into the future (41–4):

> nupta iam dices 'ego dis amicum,
> saeculo festas referente luces,
> reddidi carmen docilis modorum
>   vatis Horati.'

> Now when married you will say: "As the age was
> restoring days of celebration, I myself performed again a
> song friendly to the gods, I, instructed in the modes of
> the bard, Horace."

Horace's ode, therefore, is essentially a vivid contextualization of the *Carmen* itself. Its initial half presents us with the warrior god Apollo carrying out a vendetta against the Greeks and their savage hero. But the inspiration of the *Carmen* allows no entry for either fighting or the cruelty of requital (we are left to imagine whatever Roman dimension to Horace's words that allegory might suggest), and we soon are in the company of Apollo, the teacher (*doctor*, 25) energizing his bard, in turn, to fashion his own charge as *docilis* (43). We find ourselves with the chorus, poised for the moment of performance, but we also anticipate the later reaction of a chorister who at her marriage recalls the day of the festivity and the song itself. In the *Carmen* the ego of Rome's greatest lyricist is suppressed while his appropriately virginal students serve as innocent intermediaries between man and his omnipotent overseers. In telling the intellectual history of the poem's engendering, it is Horace himself who literally has the last word.

My second text is one of our poet's final works, the splendid epistle to Augustus (*Epistles* 2. 1), dated to 12 BCE or shortly later. In its course we learn about the poet's capabilities. He teaches the young, emends uncouth conduct with wise precepts, educates through judicious examples (132–7):

> castis cum pueris ignara puella mariti
> disceret unde preces, vatem ni Musa dedisset?
> poscit opem chorus et praesentia numina sentit,
> caelestis inplorat aquas docta prece blandus,
> avertit morbos, metuenda pericula pellit,
> impetrat et pacem et locupletem frugibus annum: ...

> When would the unwedded girl, together with chaste
> boys, learn prayers, had not the Muse given them a
> bard? Their chorus asks for aid and responds to the
> presence of the divine, ingratiatingly, with learned
> prayer, it beseeches the gods for water, it turns aside
> diseases, repulses fearful dangers, gains both peace and a
> year rich with crops.

In the opening lines Horace refers to the background of the *Carmen*, as the singers absorb from the bard the prayers they will utter. From the subsequent verses we apprehend the approval of the gods: the poet uses the same verb, *sentio*, as he does at the conclusion of the *Carmen* (73), to posit that acknowledgement. *Aquas* looks back to the *aquae salubres* (31) that Jupiter will grant the earth, and *frugibus* to the gifts of Tellus, *fertilis frugum* (29). And Horace now allots to the chorus the same verb, *impetro*, that he gives in the *Carmen* to the Emperor himself (51) in prayer.

Only line 136 claims no reference to the *Carmen Saeculare* because it would jar with the ode's confident tone. There is no need for the apotropaic quality of *carmina* to be in evidence because there are no diseases or dangers to avert. We only need song's affirmative charm to bring about that of which it so persuasively speaks.

The *Carmen Saeculare*, like most great lyrics, lives in and for the moment. But its content is not that of the Horace we usually admire for the brilliance of his poetry on the challenges (and evanescence) of love, on life's losses and the ever-looming presence of death. Here the moment is part of a broader sweep that battens on the Pindaric heritage of public performance rather than on Sappho's exquisite intimacy. The *Carmen Saeculare* is Horace's most outspoken gesture not just to distinctive personalities within the city's center of power—an emperor, a puissant patron, an array of statesmen—but to the community of Rome as a whole. The poet's voice expands beyond that of one individual addressing another, however universal the topics involved, to find utterance through a chorus performing in celebration on an occasion where the nation itself, its past, present and future, is the center of attention. The creative "I" finds outlet in the collective grouping of virginal youth. These, in turn, at the poem's end disperse to dwellings throughout the city. The performers, as representative of the community, are absorbed back into that collective entity as a whole. They bring with them, and share, some of the enchantment their utterance effects and fosters.

GUIDE TO FURTHER READING

Fraenkel's chapter, in his magisterial *Horace* (1957), traces the story of the discovery of the inscription describing the *Ludi Saeculares* and how detailed knowledge of the context in which it was first performed affected the interpretation of the *Carmen Saeculare*. The historicity of the poem, in particular its relationship to Augustus' moral legislation and political achievements, is traced by Williams (1968). Zanker (1987) studies in detail some of the aspects of Augustan artistic propaganda that surface prominently in Horace's words. Among the topics that he examines are the concept of the golden age and the motifs of fertility, abundance and peace.

Augustus' personal presence, both in the poem and as a force for its creation, is White's focus (1993) while Galinsky (1998) attends to the ode's role as a harbinger and exemplification of Rome's spiritual and ethical renewal during the Augustan principate. The intersection of the *Carmen* and Roman religion, what one has to teach us of the other, is Feeney's concern (1998). Putnam's is the first book-length commentary on the poem, examining in detail the hymn itself as poetry as well as its literary background and its role as a magic *Carmen* (Putnam 2000).

NOTES

1   For details on the actual presentation of the *Carmen* see Putnam 2000: 156, n. 67, with bibliography. The *Carmen* is part of literary history by the time Ovid wrote *Tristia* 2 (25–6), probably in CE 9.
2   I discuss the poem at greater length in Putnam 2000: 51–95.
3   For both *subolis* and *prolis* see *OLD s. v.*
4   See Maltby 1991: *s.v. prospere.*
5   The year preceding the performance of the *Ludi Saeculares* saw the promulgation of the *Lex Iulia de maritandis ordinibus* and the *Lex Iulia de adulteriis coercendis.*
6   *Certus* is a form of the participle of *cerno*, of which *decerno* is a compound. *Decretum* is drawn from the latter's perfect participle.
7   See Ovid *F.* 4.631–2 for the connection between *fero* and *fetus.*
8   Horace is probably thinking back to Tibullus 1.1.15–16.
9   Varro *L. L.*5.37 (and cf. the more expansive explanation at *R. R.*1.48.2).
10   See Putnam 2000: 140–3.
11   *tam pestilentiae … quam salutis auctorem* (Servius on *ecl.* 5.66). He quotes the same lines at *Aen* 3.138, with a similar comment. For Apollo's menacing *tela* see Virgil *Aen.* 4. 149 and their prototype at Homer *Il.* 1.46–7.
12   On Apollo and Diana as averters, and on the importance of the etymology of Apollo's name in this regard, see Nisbet and Hubbard 1970 on *Odes.*1.21.13. The deadly power of Artemis-Diana's shafts is already apparent at Homer *Od.* 11.171–3. Lines 33–6 come near to suggesting that their speaker is not the chorus but none other than its teacher, the poet himself, who with a touch of bravado now commands the gods to pay attention to his young charges.
13   We think for instance of the sacred character of Caere (Argylla), northwest of Rome, and of its nearby port (Pyrgi). See especially *Aen.* 8.597–602. Both city and port are mentioned at *Aen.* 10.183–4.
14   It is appropriate that line 47, with its series of requests for prosperity, is the poem's only hypermetric verse.
15   The adjective *lenis* (52) connects him directly to another divinity, Diana (14)
16   Cf. Propertius' paradoxical rephrasing of the Virgilian tension between *pietas* and *ira* at 3.22.21–2.
17   *OLD, s.v. Albanus,* offers *Albanas* (54) as its only example of the adjective's use to mean Roman. But mention of Alba Longa brings with it much Roman history, including the fact that the city was by legend founded by Aeneas' son, Iulus-Ascanius For further detail see Austin 1977 on *Aen* 6.766.
18   Roman *manus potentis* (53) draw some of their power from Diana *silvarum potens* (1), another of several dozen repetitions that add to the poem's ritual force.

19 *Aen.* 8.704.
20 Diana's Mt. Algidus, as the northern demarcation of the Alban range, looks back to line 54.
21 Suetonius (*Aug.* 31. 3) tells us that the surviving writings of the Sibyl were stored in two gilded cases beneath the pedestal of the statue of Palatine Apollo. When Augustus had them placed there is unknown. The statue itself was the work of Scopas (Pliny *NH* 36. 25).
22 For a summary survey of the poem's background in Greek literature, see Putnam 2000: 104–12.
23 The *Carmen Saeculare* was also influenced by Catullus 64. For a discussion see Putnam 2000: 116–18.
24 As if to differentiate his verse from Lucretius' striking apostrophe, Horace here uses the adjective *almus* for the first time in Latin letters in conjunction with a male divinity.
25 *Genitabilis*, which Lucretius adopts instead of the more common *genitalis*, is used in classical Latin only elsewhere in the initial line (fr. 1) of Lucilius, which Lucretius himself may have had in mind.
26 In the earlier ode Horace carefully separates the female and male voices, the first directed to Diana, the second to Apollo. No such division is apparent in the *Carmen* where the apparently amalgamated chorus sings the whole, making for a powerful universality.

PART III

The Satires and Epistles

CHAPTER THIRTEEN

Horace and the Satirist's Mask: Shadowboxing with Lucilius

Catherine Schlegel

Whatever is profound loves masks; ... there is not only guile behind a mask—there is so much graciousness in cunning.[1]

It is not always easy to argue that Romans were profound, but they did love masks (*personae*), famously suspending the masks of their ancestral dead on the atrium walls so as to face, on every entrance and exit from home, the stern gazes of their disapproving forbears. The concept of a permanent, "real" self seems elusive; rather one wears the appropriate mask for each occasion: formal, informal, social, intimate, solitary.

Horace's satiric persona in relation to Lucilius

An important element of Horace's persona in his Satires is built around his remarks about his satiric predecessor, Lucilius. Though Horace could not have known that Lucilius' corpus would finish up as fragments (in contrast to his own pristinely transmitted œuvre), the critique of Lucilius in the Satires leaves us wondering if that might not have pleased Horace. Horace says Lucilius needed an editor and what we have in the extant fragments are very much *disiecti membra poetae* (*Satires* 1.4.62, not said about Lucilius), a random 1300-ish lines or line fragments, out of Lucilius' thirty books of satires, in a collection motivated largely by the whims of ancient wordsmiths.[2] This is not the editing Horace had in mind, certainly, but it is worth a reminder to any reader of Roman satire that Horace's powerful voice has tended to dictate what we think of Lucilius.[3] The problem is exacerbated by the drastic incompleteness of Lucilius' work as it is left to us, and Horace's authoritative complaints tend to compensate for the vast lacunae in our knowledge of Lucilius' poetry, even while other, differing authorities do exist—Cicero, for example, who enjoyed Lucilius and liked to quote him.[4] I am inclined to think that Horace's view was closer to Cicero's than that of his persona in the Satires, that he probably loved Lucilius' poems even more than most Romans; but he had other reasons, rhetorical and strategic, for representing his persona's approach to Lucilius the way he does in his own satires.

Horace works hard in the Satires to style himself as a figure who, among other things, inhibits the darker forces of traditional satire that provide its impulse for attack and invective. Lucilius is enlisted in Horace's satiric project as a figure of contrast, against whom Horace can appear moderate and restrained, poetically and ethically. But he has a sly relationship with Lucilius, whom he designates as his predecessor in satire, calling him the *inventor* in *Satires* 1.10.48. Ennius' *satura* does not register in Horace's genealogy of satire, and Horace appears to take it for granted that Lucilius established the tone and the meter of the genre.[5] The first-person speaker in Horace's Satires initially disparages Lucilius' poetic gifts. This persona generates a complicated satiric agenda throughout the Satires, and his critique of Lucilius is only one piece of that self-defining and genre-defining agenda. The critique allows Horace to establish that his own satire is different from Lucilius', and to differentiate the apparently conventional wisdom about satire (a genre that attacks its audience and is in general uninhibited) from his own poetic criteria so as to persuade the reader that his own brand of satire has no bite and little in common with Lucilius. In *Satires* 1.4 a complex strategy that puts Horace's own father in the place of satire's progenitor, squeezing Lucilius out of the satiric picture, appears to be Horace's oblique method of rehabilitating satire; but it is also a strategy that to an extent undoes itself as the poet practices on Lucilius the kind of satire he eschews—"Lucilian," in short, insofar as it freely notes his predecessor's failings (*vitia*). Yet Horace's poems themselves, whose Lucilian hexameters make frequent tribute to the earlier master, often seem inconsonant with their speaker's overtly expressed criticism of the *inventor*, Lucilius.

Frances Muecke has recently noted that there is more than one Horatian persona in the Satires, and before we investigate some of the ambiguities the Satires present it is worthwhile considering the nature of these personae.[6] The concept in modern literary theory of an author's persona as separate from the historical writer of the work delivered Horace the poet and his poems, the Satires most of all, from a peculiarly vice-like grip of biographical reading. No matter who practices satire, from Ennius to Juvenal to Jonathan Swift (and add here the name of any contemporary satirist who comes to mind), the genre abounds in realistic material. Whether it bites and threatens or cajoles and smiles, it would not work as satire unless devised in reference to actual moments of living. Horace's satires provide rich details of a world we know relatively little about, if we are honest. If we combine the longing to have facts and pictures of the ancient world with the unique admiration that Horace's poetry generated through the ages, the reader's desire that the Satires offer unmediated "reality," without hermeneutic filters, seems to be nearly overwhelming. Thus, at a time when readers of English literature took an author's use of a persona for granted, readers of Horace were explaining the meaning of his satires in terms of the "man himself," that is, the speaker especially of *Satires* Book 1 (where the persona of Horace figures most prominently).[7] That man is the historical individual, the close friend of Maecenas, and he is modest, likable, born to an underclass father who touchingly struggled to do right by his son, and so on. Indeed the details of this "man himself" are as alluring as they can be, and Horace (poet) makes careful use of the figure to engage, persuade, and bamboozle his reader. Horace's speaker in the Satires is simply irresistible,[8] lending believability to the portrait of Horace "himself," or rather enticing readers all the more to think this was a Roman one could, in some real historical life, get to know.[9] The warmth of that Horatian persona artfully advances his case that what he speaks is a kind of satire that will do no harm to the reader, that his satire will not sting and harry and cause shame. The contrast with Lucilius implies, more than it states, that Lucilius wrote satire whose model Horace has no choice but to avoid, that in fact he is constitutionally incapable of writing Lucilian satire because he is temperamentally unsuited to vituperation, and poetically too skilful a craftsman.

Satires *1.4 and Lucilius*

All this nuanced articulation of the speaker's role gets established in *Satires* 1.4, the first of Horace's satires to mention Lucilius. Lucilius will figure again in *Satires* 1.10 and 2.1, but Horace's poetic persona, fashioned in part by the comparison to Lucilius, is clearly drawn in this first of the so-called "programmatic" satires. The poem sets the program rolling at once. The startling first line is a list of fifth-century Athenian writers of comedy, followed in the next lines by Horace's summary of what they did as poets:

> Eupolis atque Cratinus Aristophanesque poetae,
> atque alii quorum comoedia prisca virorum est,
> si quis erat dignus describi quod malus ac fur,
> quod moechus foret aut sicarius aut alioqui
> famosus, multa cum libertate notabant.   5
> hinc omnis pendet Lucilius, hosce secutus
> mutatis tantum pedibus numerisque; facetus,
> emunctae naris, durus componere versus:
> nam fuit hoc vitiosus: in hora saepe ducentos,
> ut magnum, versus dictabat stans pede in uno: 10
> cum flueret lutulentus, erat quod tollere velles:

garrulus atque piger scribendi ferre laborem,
scribendi recte: nam ut multum, nil moror. ecce
Crispinus minimo me provocat: 'accipe, si vis,
accipe iam tabulas; detur nobis locus, hora,   15
custodes; videamus uter plus scribere possit.'
di bene fecerunt inopis me quodque pusilli
finxerunt animi, raro et perpauca loquentis:
at tu conclusas hircinis follibus auras,
usque laborantis dum ferrum molliat ignis,   20
ut mavis imitare. beatus Fannius ultro
delatis capsis et imagine, cum mea nemo
scripta legat vulgo recitare timentis ob hanc rem,
quod sunt quos genus hoc minime iuvat, utpote pluris
culpari dignos. quemvis media elige turba:
aut ob avaritiam aut misera ambitione laborat. (1.4.1–26)

The poets Eupolis, Cratinus, Aristophanes and the other men
who made Old Comedy—if anyone deserved to be denounced
for being a rat and a thief, because he was a rake or a killer, or
notorious somehow—they marked and censured him with total
freedom. Lucilius is their direct descendant, he follows their
path—only the metrics and rhythm are different—he is smooth,
and witty, sharp-eyed, but his poetry was tough; he was flawed
this way: standing on one foot he could make up two hundred
lines in an hour, as if that were some great thing; he ran like a
muddy stream so there was much you'd lift out; he was
garrulous and lazy—lazy in the hard work of writing that is; as
for quantity—I'll say no more. Look, there's Crispinus
challenging me for small stakes: "get your writing pad, please,
I'll get mine and we'll set a place, a time, judges, to see which
one of us can write more." The gods did me well when they
gave me a puny mind with few resources, speaking little and not
often. So you go ahead as you like to do, be the hot air pressed
inside the bellows that puff and puff until the fire softens the
ore. Lucky Fannius! He's brought his bookcases and bust on his
own; while my writings—no one reads them; I'm afraid to recite
in public, and here's why—people don't like this kind of poetry,
since most of them deserve blame, deserve to be found guilty.
Take anyone out of the crowd: he grinds away because of greed
or fearful ambition.

The poem takes a reductive swipe at Lucilius from the start. Lucilius is the offspring of Old Comedy, there is nothing new about him and he has only changed
the meter (*tantum pedibus numerisque*). The Old Comic poets, and consequently Lucilius, went after (*notabant*—advertised and censured) the nogood-
niks of this world.[10] Lucilius is witty and has a sharp nose (*facetus, emunctae*

naris), but he had his faults (*vitiosus*). His verses are harsh (*durus*), as well as careless and abundant (*in hora saepe ducentos / ut magnum, versus dictabat stans pede in uno*), like a muddy stream (*lutulentus*); there's much you'd want to edit out (*quod tollere velles*). He talks too much (*garrulus*) and furthermore he's lazy at the task of writing (*piger scribendi ferre laborem, / scribendi recte*). In lines 12–13 the forceful economy of the line break brings a pause to emphasize both the quantity and the (lack of) quality: Lucilius was lazy about writing—not too lazy to write too much, too lazy to write it well. The satire's opening lines lead up to the first self-flattering contrast: that "Horace" is verbally restrained, and when bad poets (the infamous Crispinus) challenge him to a contest in quantity, he demurs—size doesn't matter. The gods did him a favor, says Horace, and made him a man of puny mind, short on resources, that speaks few words, infrequently (*inopis me quoque pusilli / finxerunt animi, raro et perpauca loquentis*).

The rhetorical meaning of *raro et perpauca* is layered. It affiliates Horace with the poetic movement governed by Alexandrian principles of composition—brevity and elegance—and implies that Horace is a modern poet, unlike old, muddy Lucilius.[11] Poets like Crispinus who can gas on forever clearly have no merit, and this saves Horace from making further direct insults to Lucilius—he has gotten his point across. But Horace also tells of this favor the gods did him (*di bene fecerunt*) in words that betoken incapacity: *inopis, pusilli, raro, perpauca*. His lack of words betray lack of efficacy, and he begins here, while showing he is at an advantage over Lucilius, to articulate the persona that he will repeatedly reinforce in Book I of the *Satires*: a figure too powerless to be a harmful satirist.

He is also unread, he says, not because he writes so little, which would seem to follow, but because in fact he himself is afraid to recite his poems, since the audience doesn't like satire (*genus hoc*, 24). With mock-logic Horace goes on to say (in paraphrase): "look, pick anyone out of a crowd (*turba*); you'll find most people deserve blame because they all have failings (*vitia*), therefore, they all are afraid of poetry and hate poets." (He never says how *all* poetry became satire.) Then he quotes these fearful, hating, blameworthy people, who say (in Horace's paraphrase) "he'll spare no one, not even a friend, if he can knock a laugh out for himself, he's nuts; once he's come up with something in his notebook, he'll make sure the whole world hears it." This writer of verses, as Horace quotes his putative audience, has no shame about shaming others.

Horace wants it both ways in *Satires* 1.4. He is claiming that he does at one level write Lucilian satire—namely, satire that censures people for their flaws and misdemeanors—and he makes the claim by characterizing fearful reactions to what he has written: the satirist portrays himself by portraying people who fear him. It is hilarious, competitive, and fine satire. While Lucilius in his satire did as Old Comedy did, taking notice of, and censuring, social misfits and criminals, Horace takes note and marks down the failings of Lucilius, the Roman satirist par excellence, one much loved by Roman readers. This surely is a confusing move, and as the satire proceeds Horace compounds the confusion. Do either he or Lucilius even write poetry? he asks. Having conflated satire (*genus hoc*, 24) with poetry as a whole, he defends himself by saying he *cannot* be the kind of threat depicted because he is not even a poet. And he takes Lucilius with him, saying that "we" are like writers of the kind of comedy in which a father rages at his son for getting involved with a hooker instead of the nice girl next door; the boy drinks and carries on, to his father's despair—situation comedy, in other words, known as "New Comedy," distinct from the topical political comedy of fifth-century Athens. According to the speaker, that is not really poetry (much less satire, forgotten in the moment), but plain talk (*sermo merus*, 1.4.48) in ordinary prosaic words (*puris verbis*, 54). Then Horace suggests a surprising experiment (56–62): "rip out the regular tempos and rhythm from the verses I write and that Lucilius wrote, change the order of the words around,[12] and it's nothing like what would happen if you did that to Ennius, whose poetry would have greatness even if you tore it (or indeed the poet himself) limb from limb; you would still have the limbs, the *membra*, of the scattered poet" (*disiecti membra poetae*). The experimental *sparagmos* ("dismemberment") is supposed to prove something about satire's fitness to be called poetry. So, does he or does he not write satire at all? "No matter," says our feckless speaker, "we'll work that out another time; our next question is, should one be suspicious of satire?" He then takes up the question of attack, and denies he is constitutionally able to speak or think in such a way. "You delight in doing harm" (*laedere gaudes*, 78) are the words of another imaginary accuser, to which the satirist here responds with inflated indignation (79–103) that he could never be such a one: "oh do beware of *that* black-hearted character, ye Roman" (*hic niger est, hunc tu, Romane, caveto*, 85), the defensive persona intones with epic bombast.

The poem has taken Lucilius down to size at this point, but all of the twists and illogical turns of the argument suddenly come down to an account of Horace's father, who used the same verb that the Old Comic poets Eupolis, Cratinus, and Aristophanes used when marking social misfits: *notare*. It was part of this parent's teaching plan for his son to use the examples of social failures as instruction in what to avoid. Just as *notabant* (5) is redeployed in Horace Sr.'s *notando*, other words too from the beginning of the poem are borrowed to do new work at the end of the poem. Lucilius was poetically *vitiosus*, but it is examples of ethical failings (*vitiorum*, 106) that Horace's father now marks. He advises his son to avoid taking up with married women, *moechas* (112), just as Old Comedy would censure the *moechus* (4). While Lucilius was tough (*durus*, 8) in his writing, Horace's father prepares his son for time to toughen (*duraverit*, 119) his limbs (*membra*, 120) and his spirit for life on his own. The limbs of Ennius flung out of their meter are now the sturdy limbs of the satirist. The operation is hereby complete as the poem ends; the potential influence of Lucilius, flawed poet and Horace's satiric forbear, is erased and this slave-born, impeccable Roman father, *pater optimus*, gets put in Lucilius' place. Lucilius was *piger*, but Horace Sr. is assiduous; while Lucilius' words ran on, muddy, this father's words shape his son for an ethical life, and Horace repeats his lessons for himself now, in silence, his lips pressed tight—*compressis labris*, 138. Lastly, the *turba* (crowd) full of vices in line 25 is now a *turba* of poets which threatens forced recruitment into their ranks, and the poem's comical dithering about whom to call a poet is conspicuously moot. The satirist's persona is now blameless and harmless, and Lucilius astoundingly is made first the persona's foil, then lifted out of Horace's satiric project altogether, like one of Lucilius' own bits of verbal flotsam (which you would want to take out—*tollere velles*, 11) in the muddy stream of his satire.

It is crucial to the comedy in *Satires* 1.4, I think, to acknowledge the reality that Horace does, in fact, compose verse and Lucilius' form of satire, throughout all the poem's loopy argumentation. Some great sense of amusement at the joke of it runs through the poem; it is also tempting to think that if we had more of Lucilius we might see more Lucilian echoes in 1.4. An unusually long Lucilian fragment of ten lines, discussing the difference between *poema* and *poesis*, prompts the hope that when Horace is quibbling in 1.4.39–62 about what poetry actually is and who is a poet, he is playing with Lucilius' definitions in those fragmentary lines: *et maius multo est quam quod dixi ante 'poema'*, "and it (a poesis) is much greater than what I called before a 'poema'."[13]

What is first evident in 1.4, however, is the extreme disingenuousness of the narrator, the Horatian persona, and it may be instructive to look briefly at another great example of the disingenuous persona in the *Satires*. In *Satires* 1.9, probably Horace's best-remembered satire, the persona of Horace plays his broadest role as he claims to be helpless and a victim. Many features of the poem bring the reader into its drama, but the persona who claims incapacity, as he does in 1.4, is the primary player. Without Lucilius at hand as Horace's foil, one may consider the power of this disingenuous persona in 1.9.[14] Here is the drama of the poem, in brief: Horace is interrupted during a peaceful walk on the Sacred Way by a someone who is barely an acquaintance. The man talks constantly, oblivious to Horace's unresponsive silences and desperate wish to escape. His soon-revealed agenda involves his wish that Horace introduce him to Maecenas, and he volunteers to lend his (unwanted) support to Horace in the domain of Maecenas, a domain he not unreasonably assumes to be the usual Roman competitive and hierarchical social environment (Horace primly informs him that Maecenas' household is a wonder of harmony).[15] The interlocutor is eventually taken off to court by the accident of an ongoing lawsuit in which he is involved; this gives the poet the opportunity to end the talking (and the poem) with an allusion to Lucilius: *sic me servavit Apollo*, "thus Apollo saved me."[16] Horace has homogenized a quotation by Lucilius of *Iliad* 20, 443 by putting it into Latin, and thus he makes good on his boast in *Satires* 1.10 that he has the good sense not to mix Latin and Greek the way Lucilius does. As

Horace likes to do in his *Satires*, the action of 1.9 and the poem end simultaneously and abruptly.

Horace's suffering in the course of the walk with the talker (whose only appellation in the poem is the demonstrative pronoun *ille*) is exquisite. He cannot
shake the man, and says "I lay back my ears, like the unhappy donkey who has
too heavy a burden on his back" (*demitto auriculas, ut iniquae mentis asellus, /
cum gravius dorso subiit onus,* 20–1); he envies the man's relatives, who are all
dead. At one point in the poem he recalls that when he was a child an old Sabine
woman had predicted he would be killed by a *garrulus* (1.9, 29–34); later in the
poem he runs into his friend Aristius Fuscus, who mirthfully torments Horace
by refusing to engage in conversation that would exclude the unwanted, ever-
chatting companion. The companion wants a friendship and inclusion in Horace's elite circle, but at every turn advertises how ill-suited he is for it: praising
the wrong poets, gauchely misunderstanding the fine gentility of Maecenas'
household, refusing to let go, showing a gross insensitivity to Horace, the object
of his importunity. Horace elaborates his anguish at every turn.

The power and the humor of the poem rely on a reader who identifies her/
himself with Horace and his suffering in the drama, and who feels the deep
sympathy that we generally reserve for our own troubles. Our recollections of
being bored by a talkative, self-absorbed, needy acquaintance who presumed
upon our good will seem to blot out the memory of ever having been that needy
talkative person; the universally keen appreciation of this satire would suggest
that none of Horace's readers has ever been a tedious importuning talker, but
we all have had to endure one. Modern commentary on *Satires* 1.9 is interestingly rich in invective when it comes to the talkative companion, who is called
all the names that the poem so scrupulously denies him. Routinely he is known
in English as "the Bore," and gives that name to the title of the poem, but "Pest,"
"scheming social climber," "vulgar place-hunter," and "careerist" also come up
in translations and commentaries of this satire. Horace suborns his readers so that
they do the satirist's work for him, happily drawn in by that artless persona who
coincides with a very great poet—a man who is very good with words. That
persona confesses utter verbal impotence in the face of the verbally bloated companion, but the poet coaches his readers to supply the gritty irritation of satire,
while he stays behind his mask, comic and clean and beloved.

In both *Satires* 1.4 and 1.9 more satire (in the sense of obloquy) occurs than
the persona overtly claims. Lucilius' articulated presence as Horace's foil in 1.4
is latent in 1.9. The talkative interloper—alluded to as *garrulus* just as Lucilius
is in 1.4—takes pride in possessing the very capacity for swift and abundant
writing for which Horace criticizes Lucilius in 1.4.[17] Furthermore, Lucilius is the
implied model in 1.4 of the satirist whose critical speech is a danger to his audience; that danger gets its joking tribute in 1.9 from Horace's recollection that
an old Sabine fortune-teller predicted to him once that words he could not escape
would one day kill him (1.9.29–34).

The pains Horace takes to portray his persona as socially and verbally powerless suggest an awareness in the *Satires* of some degree of menace inherent in their genre—whether that menace to the audience is real, or imagined, or simply part of the satirist's pose. Satire's threat to the listener was elaborated in interesting ways by Robert Elliott in a book which theorized that all the forms of literature in the very broad category he defined as satire—broad enough to include traditions from Irish to Eskimo to the sheer invective of archaic Greek iambics—arise from pre-literary speech genres that depend on a belief in the magical power of words to effect action (Elliott 1960). Such speech robs the listener of volition and has the capacity to harm or kill its hearer if the speaker so chooses. Elliott's thesis has much appeal, not least because few of us can fully relinquish the idea that words do have such power. However skeptical one may be of the thesis (Elliott's book was received much more enthusiastically by scholars in English literature than in Classics), it is obvious that Horace associates the speaker of satire with magic and menace, and also that much of the first book of satires seems particularly focused on issues of speech and its failures. In 1.4 Horace speaks few words and infrequently (*raro et perpauca*, 1.4.18), as we have seen, and keeps his mouth shut tight (*labris compressis*, 1.4.138). *Satires* 1.5 makes good on the poet's assertion in 1.4 that he keeps his friends' secrets: the poem has no comment whatever on the obvious political cause for the journey to Brundisium that is its subject, nor about its diplomatic importance, nor about the lethal antagonism of the principals involved, Octavian and Antony. In 1.6 Horace is *infans*—speechless—when he meets Maecenas for the first time; in 1.7 the words of a court-room argument billow and flood and are entirely purposeless until resolved by a bad but potentially terrifying pun. A dubiously competent Priapus narrates *Satires* 1.8 and drives out, by farting in terror, a couple of faux witches—toothless old ladies who have come to Rome's new Esquiline gardens for a bit of conversation with the dead. And in 1.9 Horace is not merely quiet but victimized and verbally helpless. In *Satires* 2.1 Horace explicitly compares his *stilus* (pen) to the "witch" Canidia's poison as a defensive weapon, and he suggests that though we all sometimes need our weapons, he only uses his for self-protection, not to attack; but he also suggests that there is a latent power to menace in the words of satire.[18]

At every turn in Horace's first book of satires the poet expresses a preference for silence and verbal restraint. The anxiety that prompts the *need* for such restraint is the lurking presence of an aggressive satirist who, with his hostile pen, will disable his listeners, will attack, overwhelm, flood, or perhaps kill them.[19] Horace's persona throughout is counterweight to the conventional notion that a satirist is potent and dangerous to those who hear him. He is a man of few words, of low poetic output (and no audience), and, as son of a freedman, he is socially powerless; he is politically disengaged and pointedly uninformed on the trip to Brundisium in *Satires* 1.5; a friend of the great and mighty, yet he lacks the clout even to rid himself of a troublesome companion on the Sacred Way in

1.9. The fact that the persona is a construction that is mostly fraudulent in terms of matching the presumptive historical figure of Horace should not be a distraction from the many artistic tasks this construction performs. Among other things, it allows Horace to hand over to Lucilius (and thereby disavow) the dark materials of satiric invective.

This strategy is at odds with Horace's practice however, in the sense that his satire *is* Lucilian, and in three different satires (1.4, 1.10, and 2.1) Horace says so with different degrees of praise and blame for Lucilian satire. Reading Lucilius even in its fragmentary state gives a vivid sense of the poet's vigor, experimental play and joy in the word; he is, in a sense, congenial to a modern aesthetic and sensibility in the way that Horace was congenial to eighteenth-century Europeans. His failings as Horace sees them might be just what we find pleasing. Spoken out loud Lucilius' verses sound mischievous: they are full of elisions that make lines run on, indeed like a flood or a waterfall, with Walt Whitman-like lists and repetitions, Shakespearean word-play and sound-play, and unrestrained exploitation of bilingualism—the very trait that Horace laments in *Satires* 1.10.20–30 for being language stew, a Latin–Greek pidgin. Horace's competition with Lucilius emerges more overtly and with a new tone in 1.10, when he says that he writes in this genre (*hoc*) because he has no contemporary competition in it, though he will never rival satire's *inventor*, Lucilius. [20] Yet he still calls to mind, immediately after he says this, those old poetic *vitia*, that Lucilius runs muddy and needs an editor:

> hoc erat, experto frustra Varrone Atacino
> atque quibusdam aliis, melius quod scribere possem,
> inventore minor; neque ego illi detrahere ausim
> haerentem capiti cum multa laude coronam.
> at dixi fluere hunc lutulentum, saepe ferentem   50
> plura quidem tollenda relinquendis. (*Satires* 1.10.46–51)

> Here was the kind of poetry which I could write better than
> Varro of Atax did, who'd tried it without success—as had
> certain others too, though I was less than the Inventor; nor
> should I dare to snatch the laurel wreath from his head, to
> which it very rightly clings. But I *did* say that his verse runs
> full of mud, often bearing downstream more words to throw
> out than to leave in.

If you read Lucilius with Horace's criticisms in mind, Horace begins to come off as something of a stiff. What Horace calls muddy and runny (*lutulentus*, et al.) in fact reads as quick, inventive, and effortless; Horace's touted precision and economy begin to seem strained and self-conscious compared with his boisterous, untamed, easy-going model.

Yet upon scrutiny this proves no more just than are Horace's complaints; Horace has indeed transformed Lucilius' genre, though perhaps not precisely in the manner that he implies. True, he has taken out the Greek and clipped the prolixities, but his style of satire, despite sharing the hexametric medium, is very different and the transformation is far from superficial.

To take a concrete example: Porphyrio, a fifth-century commentator on Horace, says that *Satires* 1.5 imitates a poem in Lucilius' third book of satires, known as the *Iter Siculum*, in which Lucilius describes his journey from Rome to Capua and on to the straits of Sicily. Fragments of Lucilius' poem (W94–148/ M96–147) show an enormous difference in tone from Horace's, but discernible similarities make sense of the scholiast's statement that Horace was imitating and competing with (*aemulatur*) Lucilius' satire when he wrote his "Journey to Brundisium." It is evident the two poems contain the same annoyance at the physical discomforts of travel, similar travelogue items, and plausibly similar contests staged as entertainment for the travelers, between two clowns (*scurrae*) in 1.5, and two gladiators in Lucilius (fr. 109–110W/ 117–18M).[21] Lucilius' poem is thought by commentators to be based on a trip he really made, and Horace's poem supposedly is based on an actual trip that is otherwise attested. Frederick Marx suggests that Lucilius' trip was made to inspect land-holdings in Sicily. The trip to Brundisium in *Satires* 1.5 was perhaps a trip ultimately to Tarentum to sign a treaty in 37 BCE, or to Athens in 38 BCE.[22] It seems impossible to establish which treaty is the goal in Horace's journey; but the men making the trip in 1.5 are involved in the murderous politics of the Second Triumvirate. Despite all the company on the journey, who are significant and in some cases congenial (e.g. the poet Vergil), the narrator's telling of his uninterrupted bodily discomforts make him seem a lonely figure, almost exaggeratedly grateful for the moments of friendship along the trip. Eye trouble clouds his vision—he is *lippus*, an ailment that makes for a greater sense of isolation. Furthermore the isolation seems sometimes welcome and intentional. At Anxur some of the important lieutenants of Octavian and Antony arrive, and Horace smears some black medicinal ointment on his eyes.

> huc venturus erat Maecenas optimus atque
> Cocceius, missi magnis de rebus uterque
> legati, aversos soliti componere amicos.
> hic oculis ego nigra meis collyria lippus
> illinere. interea Maecenas advenit atque
> Cocceius Capitoque simul Fonteius, ad unguem
> factus homo, Antoni non ut magis alter amicus. (*Satires* 1.5.27–33)

> Maecenas, excellent man, was coming here, and Cocceius, who were
> both ambassadors sent on an important matter, men accustomed to
> reconciling hostile friends. This is where I smear some black
> ointment on my eyes for my pink-eye. Meantime Maecenas arrives,
> as do Cocceius and at the same time Fonteius Capito—a fellow
> who's groomed to the last detail, no one a better friend to Antony.

This self-blinding gesture is inserted between his statements of the intended arrival and subsequently accomplished arrival of Maecenas, Cocceius, and Fonteius Capito—Antony's man. We know Maecenas belongs to Octavian, but Horace doesn't say so. In 1.5, even though, unlike Lucilius' trip to Sicily, the event is public and has political significance, we only see Horace's emotional view of it, his good cheer or his complaint, so that the road to Brundisium and Horace's *charta* cover the politics of the trip: *Brundisium longae finis chartaeque viaeque est* (1.5.104), "Brundisium is the end of a long page and a long road."[23]

The fact of having the whole of Horace's *Satires* intact gives us extensive material by which to interpret his poetic journey, while the barrenness of Lucilius' fragments leaves us in doubt as to what his poem might have accomplished. Yet nothing we can see suggests a desire in Lucilius to hide things, to play the game of show and not show, tell and not tell that Horace's *Satires* 1.5 displays. It is hard to imagine that Lucilius' poem could have contained anything like the unbearable tensions found in Horace's account. It is difficult to infer or deduce from the fragments something akin to the politics beneath the trip to Brundisium, and all the different sorts of ache about which Horace complains: bad gut, no sleep, hostile "friends," some violence that makes him cover his eyes to avoid looking or seeing, loneliness, sexual frustration and its unseemly results, muddy, runny roads. The lousy roads certainly we can see in the Lucilian fragments, but not ones loaded with the metaphor for both the traveler's diarrhea and the grim journey to the end of the Roman Republic.[24] The journey's only pleasure is in the companionship of friends (laughing, napping, meeting and parting), and otherwise it causes one disagreeable bodily malfunction after another in Horace. As the poem (*charta*) covers up the road (*via*), one can read the muddy, difficult road as the path to power that the participants on the journey are making; the half-blind satirist lets us half see that his own troubled body stands in for the Roman body politic.

The poem following the Brundisium satire in Horace's first book, *Satires* 1.6, is, at first glance, a deferential song of praise for Maecenas, and for the friendship he has offered to Horace; but it also addresses at once, and explores throughout, what we would call in modern terms the "class" difference between them.[25] The poem complicates the friendship between Maecenas and Horace increasingly as Horace speaks of his father, the one-time slave, and of the value and virtue of this man who made him who, and what, he is. Horace ascribes to his father the whole cause of his friendship with Maecenas, but in addition Horace "confesses" to being grateful he does not have to bear the burdens of the life of a man born into the top echelon of Roman society, such as Maecenas presumably bears. With some comic logic Horace says he wouldn't like these burdens because he isn't used to them, and notes that one such burden is the inconvenient mode of travel that a man of high social rank endures. Such a man must be accompanied by a retinue of slaves and carts and loads of luggage, rather the way we guess it must have been in *Satires* 1.5 when Horace met up with Maecenas on the road to Brundisium.

In commenting on this poem to and about Maecenas, Porphyrio notes that line 106 is taken from Lucilius' poem about his journey to Sicily, whose line the scholiast quotes:

> *Mantica* cantheri costas gravitate premebat (fr. 101W/1207M)
>
> "the saddle bag (*mantica*) pressed on the ribs of the nag with its weight."

Horace's line in 1.6 goes like this:

> ... nunc mihi curto
> ire licet mulo vel si libet usque Tarentum
> mantica cui lumbos onere ulceret atque eques armos (1.6.104–6)
>
> "right now if I liked I could go all the way to Tarentum on a simple mule—the saddle bag (*mantica*) will wear his haunches raw with its weight, and the horseman his withers."

The Horatian line reproduces Lucilius' first word, *mantica*, where it is the subject of *premebat*. Packing more in syntactically, Horace's line makes *ulceret* take two subjects, both *mantica* and *eques*, which will wear out the mule in two separate places (*lumbos* and *armos*) not one (Lucilius' *costas*). All Horace's words besides *mantica* are variations on Lucilius': *premebat* becomes harsher in *ulceret*; the saddle bag's force on the animal is an *onus*, not just *gravitas*; the burden moves down the animal's body from *costas* to *lumbos*, and the added subject, the rider, wears down the mule's body nearer the neck at the withers—*armos*.

Horace's version of the line from Lucilius' Sicily poem seems to have traveled into the wrong satire, but what the allusion in fact nicely does is remind us of another reason Horace may be glad not to have Maecenas' status, what he covered his eyes with black ointment not to see. He wants to be napping with Vergil, not plotting the next move in the civil wars and Roman imperial domination.[26] The burden associated with Maecenas' aristocratic status that might really be worth avoiding is doing the bidding of murderous men such as the unnamed Octavian.

Satires 1.6 is in a way a parallel piece to 1.4, in that in both satires Horace's father improbably displaces a major figure in the son's life as a poet.[27] We have seen this operation performed on Lucilius in *Satires* 1.4, so that Horace's satiric-poetic ancestry excludes Lucilius and is inherited instead from his fault-noting father. Maecenas comes from one of the oldest families of Rome (as *Satires* 1.6 announces in its first line), whereas Horace's father was a slave, and *yet*, says Horace, despite the seeming importance of Maecenas in his life, the only significant influence on his character is his father. Grateful to have escaped the burdens of high birth, the narrator of 1.6 illustrates his gratitude when he cites the great inconvenience of travel for the well to do—a fact borne out by his physical discomfort in 1.5.

Physical discomfort for Lucilius' and Horace's personae while traveling south is the unheroic center of both their poems. Horace's persona begins to intermingle features of the poems where he plays his role. Porphyrio saw the allusion to Lucilius in "*mantica cui lumbos ...*" in the context of a journey, but did not ponder Horace's displacement of the line into a poem on a different theme. Horace's allusion to Lucilius' journey satire creates a recollection of *Satires* 1.5 within the context of *Satires* 1.6; Horace made the journey to Brundisium because he had a relationship with Maecenas, which is the subject of 1.6.[28] The burden Horace expatiates on in the latter poem is status—it is terrible to have the responsibilities of noble birth, as illustrated by the example of one who must travel encumbered by companions, slaves, horses, and luggage. But the governing concept slides, for the *onus* in 1.6 is not only the *mantica* on the mule, but also the burden of the relationship with Maecenas, a relationship which Horace rather decisively limits in that poem. But though the *mantica* in Lucilius' poem is the literal weight on the ribs of the *cantherus*, in 1.6.106 the *mantica* becomes a trope for the lightness of solitude, and represents the pleasures of Horace's unencumbered life as he travels with just a pack and a mule. The Lucilian allusion recalls those other travel arrangements in *Satires* 1.5, where, thanks to Maecenas, Horace has an ironically wretched time of it, where his whole body hurt; in 1.6 it is his mule that suffers the discomfort.

Horace's allusive line at 1.6, 106 becomes a mix of references to himself as well as to Lucilius. As he travels on the Sacred Way in *Satires* 1.9.20–1, Horace sees himself as the mule burdened by the words of the talker: *demitto auriculas, ut iniquae mentis asellus, / cum gravius dorso subiit onus*. The talker's words, which Horace cannot stop any more than he can stop the events consequent on the journey to Brundisium with Maecenas and "friends," are the weight on Horace's ears, now that he has taken on the status of a beast of burden. But the Lucilian echo in 1.6 can now in 1.9 call up the psychic burdens expressed in the troubles of sleep and digestion in *Satires* 1.5, where the poet in the course of the journey is burdened by the discomfort of the friendship with Maecenas, and eventually safely released, thanks to his father, in 1.6.

Horace uses Lucilius' so-called failings as a poet to distinguish himself as a satirist from the recognized master of the genre. Against his own claim of verbal incapacity he paints Lucilius as excessive and uncontrolled, a poet (is he a poet?) of speech immoderate in quantity and in *libertas*. Horace also plays with the idea of himself as both verbally poised and controlled, and verbally helpless. This persona can deny to Horace the domineering power that a satirist might wield over an audience, as he carves out some literary territory for himself in contradistinction to Lucilius. Horace will never batter or drown his listener with his satiric words or his malice. Meanwhile, beneath the mask, Horace can make

Lucilius his collaborator, as in his use of the line from the *Iter Siculum*, taking the older satirist's words to braid two journey poems into another poem about Maecenas and their friendship, and to keep the secrets of the road, but not to fully commit himself to that friendship. He can make his quiet point that he does have the *libertas* to stand apart from Maecenas, though he may not say so the way an Old Comic, or Lucilius, could. Still he can rely on the recognizable music of the *inventor* to make his own satire.

GUIDE TO FURTHER READING

Since discussions of Lucilius tend to be driven by a discussion of Horace, and by assumptions about the poets' differences, the reader is urged first to take up Lucilius' fragments and tolerate the frustrations of reading shards of poetry until a sense of Lucilius begins to emerge—which it will. For students investigating Lucilius' text, Warmington's Loeb Library edition (1938) is the most accessible. Marx's magisterial edition and commentary from the beginning of the twentieth century (1904–5) is rewarding for Latinists; Krenkel's edition, *Lucilius, Satiren* (1970a) was roundly chided for attempting to lace Lucilius' fragments together too tightly; White's review of that edition however (1973: 36–44) provides a particularly succinct and clear account of the arrangement in books of Lucilius' fragments. Raschke gives a deeper account of Lucilius' text (1979:78–89); Hooley (2007: 20–6) briefly scans the collection of fragments and the nature of Lucilius' content. Handbooks on Roman satire include outlines of what we know about Lucilius and his poetry; Coffey (1976) is one of the best. Gratwick's 1982 essay is crisp, clear, and pleasantly opinionated. Rudd (1986) lucidly depicts Lucilius in the context of Roman satire; Muecke (2005) gives a fine picture of the literary world from which Roman satire is born. Goldberg (2005: 144–77) is balanced and insightful about how Lucilius belongs to Republican Roman literary history and politics. Petersmann (1999) explores Lucilius' style; illuminating instances of Lucilius' construction of the hexameter line are found in the first half of Morgan's essay (2004).

Fiske's (1920) thorough exploration of Lucilian echoes in Horace is compendious, and though sometimes too adventuresome to be probable, it is a learned and intelligent reader's attempt to grapple with the relationship between the two poets straight from their texts.

All commentaries on Horace's *Satires* necessarily provide information on Lucilius, although the reader should be wary of an over-emphasis on either Horace's decorum or Lucilius' aristocratic *libertas*. Fraenkel (1957) and Rudd (1966) make indispensable introductory reading to Horace's *Satires*. In his 1964a essay Anderson demonstrates the need to read Roman satire in terms of persona theory, which Braund deploys in *The Roman Satirists and Their Masks* (1996). Oliensis (1998) refines and opens the idea, making use of the sociologist Goffman's concept of "face," to replace "persona" as the figure of the poet in the text.

Bloom (1973) still, despite its eccentricities, provides an interesting way to think about how poets experience and use the force of their predecessors; Bloom's idea of influential "flooding" has an echo of Horace's words for Lucilius' muddy flow. The Australian writer

David Foster (1999: 77) says "all satirists are engaged in trying to write themselves out of a particular psychological situation," and credits Horace with having written himself through satire into being a lyric poet.

NOTES

1   Nietzsche 1989: sec. 40.
2   As Henderson 1999: 174 says, "bear in mind that our Lucilius text is actually in shreds (more of a token than a text), and that his descendants each project distinct Luciliuses appropriated to their own profiles."
3   The impulse among critics to ascribe any displeasing element in the *Satires* to Horace's unfortunate need to imitate Lucilius has abated in the last twenty five years.
4   Quotations from Lucilius show up across Cicero's philosophical and rhetorical works, and a few times in letters, with affection, admiration, and sometimes just to say *ut narrat Lucilius*, "as Lucilius tells it."
5   On Ennius' *satura* see Gratwick 1982; also Muecke 2005.
6   Muecke 2007.
7   The singularly important work of Fraenkel 1957, brilliant in so many ways, comes to mind, and similarly Rudd's 1966 study of Horace's *Satires* for instances of a surprisingly naive conflation of writer and satirist. W. S. Anderson (1964: 293) cites the critic of Renaissance satire A. Kernan (1959) "By 'the satirist,' Kernan means not the writer of satire, but the voice speaking in the satires; by careful use of this term he skillfully avoids the error into which we all tend to plunge, namely that of attributing to the writer every idea expressed by the speaker, the writer's creation." In 1900 G. L. Hendrickson noted elements of fiction in Horace's self-portrait in the *Satires*, but as Eleanor Leach 1971: 622 wryly noted of Hendrickson's insight: "his idea of Horatian fiction-making has not been widely accepted."
8   Irresistible until critics caught on to the idea that Horace can be construed basically as a collaborator in the regime of Octavian/Augustus, that is, until Rome, along with imperialism in the twentieth century generally, lost its charm. One may note that as readers of Horace have grown more guarded concerning the persona in the *Satires* there is a concomitant increase in negativity about "the man himself"; see for example (in the vanguard), Henderson 1999: 173–91; Gowers 2005: 55: Horace's "seemingly casual revelations in the manner of Lucilius are in fact the controlled self-presentation of a self-made man." Oliensis 1998 keeps a distance from her skepticism and is cautious to observe that the life lived in the *Satires* is only one of Horace's "faces."
9   The whole vexed question of the persona has led some critics to refer to Horace as "Horace" to be certain no one confuses the speaker of the *Satires* with the historical man Horace (see for example Bowditch 2001: 10). In this essay I will speak of Horace as both the writer and the speaker in the poems, and trust the reader to distinguish the two unless it seems necessary to be alerted to the difference.
10 Much ink has been spilled on the question of Roman satire's antecedents, beginning in antiquity with Quintilian's claim of Roman origins (in his *Institutio Oratio*,

10.1.93) and continuing (seemingly) unflaggingly to today, but the obvious liter-ary/historical inaccuracy of Horace's genealogy for Lucilius nonetheless is not altogether off the mark; Lucilius does have the tone of Old Comedy: the same clarity, invention, scabrous energy, and the same fun—certainly much more than Horace.

11   Though it is clear that Lucilius too must have been influenced by Hellenistic poetry; Gratwick (1982), and Feeney (2005), on the depth to which Latin literature thought in terms of Greek culture. Warmington's introduction and commentary with the fragments of Lucilius make the Greek influences plain throughout.

12   In the midst of the carefully, poetically drawn argument that the medium is not poetry—that it is not precisely what it is—consider Horace's elegantly illustrative line 59, *posterius facias, praeponens ultima primis*, in which the word order perfectly mimics the meaning. See Freudenburg 1993: 147–8.

13   Fr. 407W/344M. Among the extant fragments of Lucilius, these lines discuss what is *poesis* in contrast to *poema* (fr. 401–10W / 338-47M). These and others like them, that talk of rules of spelling and usage, are part of the (to us) unfamiliar ground that early Roman satire covered. Might Horace here be toying with some of those satires?

14   A standard feature of Roman satire is the poet's statement of intent, known to critics as a "program satire," in which the poet defines his genre and lays out his views of satire and its conditions (as for instance Juvenal's well-known remark in his first poem that life in Rome makes it impossible not to write satire). Horace's *Satires* 1.4, 1.10, and 2.1, those that are considered programmatic, all speak of Lucilius.

15   On the normal competitive, not to say spiteful temper of such environments see White 1993: 38.

16   Apropos Horace's line, the scholiast Porphyrio cites a line from Lucilius who is quoting *Iliad* 20.443: "nil ut discrepet ac τὸν δ᾿ ἐξήρπαξεν Ἀπόλλων fiat," 267-8W/ 231-2M.

17   Criticism of this trait is reprised in 1.10.

18   *Satires* 2.1.39–48; Canidia is one of the old women necromancers of *Satires* 1.8, and has a curious role to play in the satires, appearing a third time in the last line of the last poem (2.8.94–5), breathing poisonously over the banquet of satire and of this satire's story, and over the end of Horace's *Satires*. See Oliensis 1991; Gowers 1993b: 161–79.

19   This anxiety about satire seems resolved in Horace's second book by his use of dia-logue, which is a sort of fantasy of *sermo* (conversation) that can approximate an exchange of speech and thus limit satire's potential threat to an audience.

20   Horace never calls his genre *satura* in Book 1, only *sermo* and *genus hoc*, or sometimes just *hoc*. In Book 2 he will call it *satura*.

21   Fiske 1920: 306–16, meticulously discusses the possible echoes between Lucilius' and Horace's journey satires.

22   See Gowers 1993a: 49, 62, summarizing the views of scholarship on the historical possibilities for this trip.

23   Though at 93 lines the poem does not make a very long page.

24   98W/109M: *praeterea omne iter est hoc labosum atque lutosum*, "moreover the whole of this journey is slippery and slimy" (tr. Warmington).

25 See White 1993, 2007 on how *amicus* does the work (of "patron") that we expect
    patronus to do in the etiquette of the literary relationships that the Romans called
    "friendships."
26 At 1.5.48, having stopped at Capua, Maecenas goes to play ball, Horace and Vergil
    to get a rest: *lusum it Maecenas, dormitum ego Vergiliusque.*
27 Schlegel 2005: ch. 3.
28 The trip to Brundisium may well have gone, in fact, *usque Tarentum* (see above,
    1.6.105)—all the way to Tarentum—if the poem is thinking of the embassy in 38
    BCE.

CHAPTER FOURTEEN

Horatius Anceps: Persona and Self-revelation in Satire and Song*

Kirk Freudenburg

The rhetorical and literary mechanisms of the personal poet's persona-work have received much detailed attention in the last half century.[1] Much of this work has concentrated on satire, and on Catullus, not merely because these poets say "I," but for reasons specific to the kind of "I" (or "I"s) they speak.[2] This essay will be less about showing those mechanisms in motion (though I will do a good deal of that) than it will be about how this volume's poet, Horace, frames the issue of "the poet's life in poetry" as a theoretical conundrum, not as a given, and how he stages his own biographical entry into his poems as a game of catch-me-if-you-can by always suspending details of his real life in highly patterned forms that dare us to try to make the whole of it all add up to him, Quintus Horatius Flaccus ("go ahead and try!").[3] Thus, the poet's autobiographical entries into his work I take not as documentary evidence for who he was, but as the first moves of a back-and-forth game played between writer and reader. This is a game (or collaborative project) of self-perusal and display in which both sides agree that all autobiographical details related are to be marked in scare quotes as "autobiographical," even when they are absolutely true to life, and that they therefore should not be pushed too hard.[4] To do so is to fail to understand the game, for to actually "catch" Horace in his game is to lose it.

The downside of persona theory has always been the perceived loss of the poet "himself," whatever that might mean. I will not make a case for our never having had him in the first place, though I think a good case can be made for it. Instead I will offer a different (intertextualist) paradigm for how we have him, and how this should never find us sifting through reported experiences to separate lived truths from the packagings of fiction (i.e., trying to remove the mask). The problem with persona theory is not that it loses the poet, but that it has tended to be used in over-confident and self-congratulatory ways by critics who are apt to tell us "Look! Here you see Horace playing the parasite, and there a running slave!" as if that were to tell us something strange (I have done my unfair share of this myself, and I will do a bit more of it below). Instead, the point of emphasis should rather be that this is the way it always is with written selves, a given fact of any *bio*'s being rendered through, and as, *graphe*. And not just that: it is the necessary way of *bio* itself, and of all selves, whether written or otherwise lived/performed. All selves, in order to become and count as selves, and as a basic condition of their communicability, are embedded in discursive systems. They are defined within these systems as (I'd say "mysteriously individualized"—thus giving the critic something to do) *loci* of referential activity.[5] This is not to say that persona theory, when it uses the resources of rhetorical analysis (grammar, syntax, literary traditions, etc.) to identify the poet as X and not Y and, in fact, never really "himself," does no good. On the contrary, knowing that selves are rhetorically structured and that they can change from poem to poem does much good in that it forces us to think of the self not as a skin-encased biological entity that crashes through time rounded, singular and hard, like the soul of the Stoic *sapiens* (a sentient, imperturbable bowling ball) with a permanent moral core. And yet, to see the self as rhetorically structured is not necessarily to see it for all that it is. For it does no good to replace an old assumption of the poet's "real historical person" contained by the pages of his poetry (*ipsissimus coram*) with that of a "real" poet hiding behind a mask or any number of masks (*ipsissimus latens*) when that mask is not, in fact, a means of his hiding what is real, but the very *means of* his "self"-realization.

In other words, a more dynamic model of cultural interaction needs to be argued for "persona theory" to describe more fully what it needs to describe. Such a model will take into consideration the cultural modeling of the critic's own work, conceding that the self-mythologization of "Horace" is not just something we are witnesses to, but participants in via the myths we know, and the discursive systems we use, to make poets of poets and selves of ourselves. As indicated above, many who have studied the life/literature problem in Roman personal poetry have tended to focus on the connection of *bio* to *graphe* in the poetic expression of the writer's autobiography, often with much fetishization of the "authentic" (*bio*) over the "contrived" (*graphe*), or vice versa. But the focus of much modern autobiographical theory is not centered here at all. Rather, it is on the word's first element: on the *auto* that is both the subject and object of autobiographical writing. In other words, it treats the problem of the self's never really being *auto* in the first place, because it is never really unto itself, or self-defining, or the same (as the Greek αὐτός suggests), but always rendered through cultural forms, and never actually pre-existing those forms as a hard (bowling ball) "self."

In what follows I take for granted that any given written expression of the poet's self is necessarily intersubjective, and only ever meaningful as such. I can perhaps best describe what I mean by this, my "intertextualist" approach to the poet's written self, by slightly altering a quote by Don Fowler (adapted from Fowler [1997] 14 = Fowler [2000] 117, writing on intertextuality) wherein I (**boldly**) insert "**self/selves**" in places where he had "text/s": "We do not read a **self** in isolation, but within a matrix of possibilities constituted by earlier **selves**, which functions as *langue* to the *parole* of individual **self**-production: without this background, the **self** would be literally unreadable, as there would be no way in which it could have meaning." It is as specific moments of play within this system that I offer the descriptions of the poet's literary self-patterning in the pages below. With this analysis I do not intend to suggest that the poet can be nailed down to, or limited by, the specific characterizing references that appear to me to be most prominent at any given moment of his self-description. In this regard the problem that I see dogging discussions of the poet's persona-work (and I must include my own *Walking Muse* in this criticism) is roughly the same problem that Don Fowler saw in the way that some have used the detection of "parallels" (as useful and meaning-rich as such detections certainly are) as a means of establishing authorial intent, and thus of mastering a text and exhausting its meaning. To do so is to make over-confident assumptions about an inter-text's /-self's containability, and it is to ignore the fact that we are the ones who set the terms for framing and containing that inter–self/-text within whatever bounds we happen to think most relevant. Once we start to fashion our poet's "biography" within these (our) terms, we are trading in self-work of a completely different kind: one that finds us out as the authors of Horace.[6]

I begin my study with the famous votive tablet analogy of Horace *Satires* 2.1, 30–4. These lines constitute one of the three or four most resorted-to chestnuts we have for investigating and describing poetry as biographical self-expression (or not) in classical Roman poetry, with the top of that small nut-heap always being occupied by Catullus 16 (*me ex versiculis meis putatis*, 3).[7] But because the votive tablet chestnut comes from this volume's star, I will promote it to number one by structuring much of what follows in this essay around the several ideas that I hope to develop from these lines. And yes, I do propose that these ideas may actually inhere in, or be hinted at by, the Latin, as thoughtful provocations offered up by it—though I won't say that these ideas are "naturally" offered up by it, because I am much too aware of the politics of my own (even philological) intervention, and the rhetorical strategizing and self-congratulation that always goes into making such a statement.

Lucilius: the Overstuffed Life

Horace Satires 2.1.30–4:

ille velut fidis arcana sodalibus olim
credebat libris neque, si male cesserat, usquam
decurrens alio neque, si bene; Quo fit ut *omnis*

votiva pateat veluti descripta tabella
vita senis. Sequor hunc, Lucanus an Apulus anceps. (emphasis mine)

He (Lucilius) shared secrets with his books, as if entrusting them to
his closest pals. Whether things went badly or well, he always went
running there. And so it happens that the old man's *entire life* is on
public display, as if drawn on a votive tablet. I follow him, whether a
Lucanian or Apulian, not sure.

Beware of Horace when he says *omnis*, especially when he uses it in reference to
Lucilius. That adjective, like its bedfellows "no one" and "always," is by definition immoderate. Accordingly, theorist-Horace sometimes uses it to be outra-
geous, and to provoke, as at the beginning of *Satires* 1.4, where he famously
claims that Lucilian satire derives in its entirety from Greek Old Comedy: *hinc
omnis pendet Lucilius.* He goes on to assert that Lucilius did not little more
than—that would be too moderate—no, he did **nothing** more than change the
meters of Old Comedy to make his *Saturae.* As theory, these claims are befud-
dling and laughable, though few have seen fit to laugh at them. For, as is true
of many of the theoretical assertions of *Satires* 1.4 (and the same can be said of
the literary-theoretical *Satires* and *Epistles* more generally) these claims can be
rescued, and Horace dutifully saved, by spending only a little effort, because deep
down they contain ideas that are respectable, and that were very much in play
on the grammatical/theoretical scene of ancient Rome. As I have argued elsewhere, the opening assertions of *Satires* 1.4 don't so much theorize as represent
theorization (a case of "suspended" focalization, Horace using what was already
out there, momentarily playing the hot-headed slayer of the *satura* **tota** *nostra*
thesis), thereby letting us see the absurdity of a decent theory, and a culture war,
taken several steps too far.[8]

He seems to be at it again with the immoderate phrase *omnis ... uita* in the
passage quoted above. There can be no doubt that these lines make true claims
about how Lucilius included lots of details from his own daily life in his poems,
and how this constituted a second major categorizing aspect of the Lucilian
project, an aspect easily overshadowed by the poet's more prominent culture-
warrior image.[9] But here, as before, we have to wonder whether the claim isn't
perhaps being pushed too far. Triggering suspicion in this case is not just the
immoderate *omnis* ("the whole of" Lucilius' life, which is to say not parts, and
not bits and pieces), but also the way the adjective is made to stretch forward to
reach its noun (hyperbaton) all the way from the end of line 32 to the beginning
of line 34. Because this is not a mild case of hyperbaton, but an extreme one,
unlike any other in the *Satires* (actually a highly stylized double-hyperbaton, with
omnis ... vita forming the outer frame, and *votiva ... tabella* the inner[10]), it puts
an inordinate emphasis on the idea that the old man's life **in its entirety** was
contained on a smallish votive painting (a diminutive *tabella* rather than the more
common *tabula*). And thus, every bit as stretched as the bridge from adjective

to noun is the assertion itself. This may simply be a very funny (grand and expansive) way of saying "the man put his whole ... drawn ... life (*omnis ... descripta ... vita*)—and man was it a long one, as this long ... drawn ... hyperbaton proves—on the page!" But I think it must also pose the question: how do you get the whole life of an "old man" (*senis*),[11] that is, everything from baby Lucilius getting his first tooth to old man Lucilius losing his last one, all put down and neatly drawn (*descripta*) inside a smallish pictorial frame? And why, technically speaking, is that old man's "whole life" (*omnis ... vita*) not inside the painting's frame, but entirely outside it, as outer bracket to inner?[12] The problem of containment is further underscored by the assertion that the poet had no discretion whatever in dumping his life into his books: whatever happened, Horace says, whether good or bad, he wrote it down.

But consider the interpretive ramifications: here we have a passage that is sometimes used to show us how easy and automatic it was for Romans to read first-person poetry as the dutifully recorded script of the poet's lived experience. That basic theoretical idea is defensible enough, and it may, as Roland Mayer has admirably demonstrated, have enjoyed near-universal acceptance among Horace's Roman readers, especially those of a more grammatical bent.[13] But, here again, as in *Satires* 1.4, we have a fundamentally defensible theoretical idea put to us in a funny package, and pushed to an absurd extreme, so again we have to wonder whether this is Horace theorizing about Lucilian satire, to again remind us that "he" was an overstuffed mess, or is it Horace staging a way of theorizing about satire (suspended focalization), as if to show us how absurd and uncompromising such theorizing can sometimes be? Thus, what at one level seems to rank as our single best proof that poets, whether slap-dashedly or not, wrote their lives straight into their poetry, and that "they" could be easily accessed from that poetry, at another level seems to express the absurdity of the very idea of a life contained within the narrow confines of a painted page (even one as big as Lucilius' thirty books). For Fowler it was precisely this absurdity ("Romantic Irony") that allowed the poet to speak for himself, giving him a means of dynamic and sublime expression. He writes: "to quote D.C. Muecke's formulation, 'How can a work of art, which of its nature is something that can be finished and therefore something finite and static, express the infiniteness of life?' The answer of the Romantic Ironists was that 'the work of art should itself acknowledge its limitations and by doing so with irony it would take on the dynamic quality that life has and which art should therefore express.'"[14]

With the elaborate *omnis ... vita*, we are reminded not just of how awfully long Lucilius' life was, and how stretched out (like an overstretched hyperbaton) were the thirty books that he slap-dashed that life into. But we are also reminded of how absurd it is to think that a whole life could be put on the written page in any decently full and neatly containable way. What would such a long old life have to look like—natural? overstuffed? cartoonish? neatly balanced?—if it could actually "look" like any single, contained thing at all? Yes, Horace says, poets can cram their lives into their books (score one point against persona theory), but that is not what you will get from me (one point for ... something else, but what? A reduced life, neatly shaved? No real life in poetry at all?).

The point of Horace's scaling back his own self-presentation in satire, and of his patterning his life in new terms of his own, is immediately emphasized at the end of line 34, in the assertion: *sequor hunc, Lucanus an Apulus anceps*. Following Lucilius is not just a thing described by this line, it is something actually done by it, a "speech-act" performed by the words themselves. For with these words (and in the several lines that follow) Horace has begun to tell us about his own life from where it all started, doing so in a satiric poem. And to do that is to do exactly what we have just been told Lucilius did in writing the whole of his life into his poems. He begins where one might expect Horace's life-story to begin, at its south Italian inception, but he immediately gets stuck: being from Venusia, some would say I'm Lucanian, others Apulian. So what am I? I'm on the fence, *anceps*, and could go either way.

As the first line of an autobiography, this makes for an inauspicious start. And as proof of how poets write their lives into their poems, it is pretty thin gruel. But as an illustration of how Horace's Satires both contain and do not contain the life of their poet, in clear contrast to the practices described for Lucilius, it is perfect. Best of all is that word *anceps* "double-sided," here smartly inhabiting the metrically *anceps* position of the hexameter line. The word is commonly used of swords, and this in a poem obsessed with satiric weaponry.[15] But it is a word not just of weapons (*OLD* 1b), but also of words doubly intended, and ironic (*OLD* 2b and 9), and here it describes not a sword or stylus, but the double-edged poet himself. He cannot quite tell us who he is by birth. But he can tell us that he is, by birth, *anceps*. Unless, of course, he's just being ironic.

Life as (always a) metaphor, and the metaphors that write "life"

No one refers to Horace as a Lucanian. Yes, Venusia (modern Venosa) was near the border with Lucania, but Horace is always solidly Apulian elsewhere in his poetry, and he is never again, even remotely, Lucanian.[16] As Frances Muecke has pointed out, Horace here only "plays with the idea of being Lucanian ... to associate himself more closely with Lucilius' fighting spirit."[17] Being from Venus-town (*Venusinus*, 35), though perhaps perfect for a lover, seems somewhat less auspicious for a man born to scrap in satiric fights. Better, then, to lie just a little, in order to have something of the wolf (*Lucanus*) about you, something of the wolf-satirist, **Luc**ilius, and just enough of the "**push**y" Apu**l**ian.[18] This is a much better mix.

Thus we see that as soon as Horace starts writing about himself, he starts edging over boundaries, straying towards other models and writing other lives into himself, making their stories his. Saying that he is part this and part that, that it is hard to decide because the history is contorted, may in fact, be a Lucilian gesture, since biographies of Lucilius typically begin by telling us something uncannily similar: "Gaius Lucilius was a Latin born at Suessa Aurunca, which, situated on the borders of Campania, was in olden times an Oscan city, but had become a part of *Latium novum* or *adiectum*."[19] Or is Horace rather more interested in lending a Catullan tinge to his tale?[20] In either case, he can't help putting us in mind of someone else on his way to, or better, *in order to,* talk about himself. That, my emphatic *in order to*, is the fundamental point I would like to develop in the pages below, in describing the life-writing of Horace: the life-details he gives us are deeply and incessantly structured by other lives and other models, always offered to us in prepackaged, remembered forms, or as a hybrid of various prepackagings. The point I wish to develop from this is not that Horace was a master of disguises— that point has already been made to death, and I have been one of its main proponents. Rather, I want to point out that if Horace presents himself to us in writing through a series of remembered selves, shifting about from this model to that, it is not just because he is "by nature" shifty and, as he says, *anceps*, it is because that is the only self he could ever give us, because that is the way lives become selves in first-person writing.[21] Stop figuring the "self" you write through pre-existing, remembered selves, stop using those selves to model yourself, and you don't just end up looking odd and disconnected. You simply cease to exist.[22]

   To describe how Lucilius put his "life" into his books, Horace deploys a series of comparisons (*velut … veluti*). I say "a series" rather than two because hiding inside these comparisons are other metaphors that further configure, or confuse, or comment upon Lucilius' life-writing work. With the first comparison, Horace tells us that Lucilius went "rushing down" (*decurrens*) to his books with his secrets like a man telling all, whether good or bad, to his most intimate friends.[23] Commenting on line 30, Porphyrion tells us that the idea came from Aristoxenus, who had described the close, tell-all relationship of Sappho and Alcaeus to their books in exactly these same terms, so there is a Greek literary-critical model at work here giving a theorist's "lyrical" justification to Lucilius' unchecked dumping of his life into his books, just as there is a second solid theoretical idea hiding in the votive tablet image that follows it (*ut pictura poesis*).[24] Under the surface, then, are two literary-theoretical analogies that might be used (and probably were used, and that's why Horace uses them) to defend Lucilius' satiric practice: he puts his inner life and his secrets into his poems, treating them like close friends, just as Sappho and Alcaeus did. And his poems are his canvas, vivid and expressive of his life's many colors. Such theories, as attractive as they otherwise normally are, are anything but attractive in the way they are construed here. Instead, the comparisons tell of two kinds of Lucilian indiscretion, two ways in which he failed. With the first, we see Lucilius failing to discriminate between lyric and satire, treating his books as omni-generic grab-bags, suited to anything and everything that he might choose to toss into them, including his deepest desires, and his love songs for his girl. Horace, who is by now dreaming forward to his own lyric œuvre, is perhaps hinting that he, too, will have other sides of his own inner self to share there, but that this will happen not in satire, but where it should happen: in the odes that he will model after Sappho and Alcaeus.[25]

The second comparison carries another damaging jolt in the picture it paints, giving a worst case scenario of the *ut pictura poesis* thesis as it applies to Lucilius. Votive tablets were widespread in the Greco-Roman world, a fact of one's daily life. They captured the deepest of real feelings on the part of the painting's subject (fear, awe, and gratitude), but they did so, as both Anderson and Harrison have shown, often in the most overdone of conventional ways.[26] In fact, the expression of internal emotional states on such paintings was not supposed to be subtle, since the point was to be visually obvious, episodic, and highly symbolic. Although these paintings purported to be of individual, one-of-a-kind experiences (commonly, aretalogical tales charting the subject's imminent doom and rescue by the god), they came in a limited set of by-the-book renderings, with the life you expressed being the one you picked from the book: for the "man rescued by Poseidon" you just needed to pick one from the stack and have your face painted in.[27] The artist could fix you up. Or, if you had been completely wiped out by the shipwreck, you could find a plank of driftwood and paint yourself (*quoniam solent naufragi se pingere et consecrare in aliqua aede*, Pseudo-Acron *ad* Horace, *Satires* 2.1.32)—and how expertly drawn is any random washed-up sailor's picture likely to be?[28] Not only is the votive tablet simile not flattering to Lucilius, a comment on the big, overstuffed life he painted, and on his skills as a painter, it expresses a basic truth about the necessary reductions and elisions and handy distortions that always come with turning one's *bio* into *graphe*, a process that renders the individual as a type, or a hybrid of types, modeled through existing forms.

The idea of the Lucilian life's hyper-emotive, by-the-book figuring is further emphasized by the second link in the hyperbaton's chain, that is, in the adjective *descripta*, which puts us in mind of the rhetorical device of *descriptio* ("vivid description"). Just prior to criticizing the *descripta … vita* of Lucilius, Horace has denied that he himself possesses the "descriptive" skills required to write panegyrical epic:

> neque enim quivis horrentia pilis
> agmina nec fracta pereuntis cuspide Gallos
> aut labentis equo **describit** vulnera Parthi.

> For it is not just anyone you please who can describe
> troops in their ranks bristling with javelins, or Gauls
> dying, their lances shattered, or the wounds of a
> Parthian as he slips from his horse.

Ironically, in making the claim, Horace shows that he knows full well how to draw a by-the-book, epic *descriptio*, and in doing so he indicates just how outlandish these scenes can be.[29]

Look closely at the votive tablet simile and you can actually see by-the-book modeling in play, Lucilian *bio* modeled through existing *graphe*, right under your nose. For, woven into the lines that describe Lucilius' tell-all intimacy with his books is the famous sketch that Ennius drew in the seventh book of his *Annales* of the ultra-discreet friend of Geminus Servilius, the lesser *amicus* in whom Servilius could always confide at the end of a long day.[30] The sketch, purported by Aelius Stilo to describe Ennius himself, draws upon Hellenistic descriptions of "the king's confidant," and constitutes the longest fragment we have from the *Annales*, and Horace will later call it to mind in *Satires* 2.6 in describing his own relationship to Maecenas.[31] But here Lucilius, who has just been described in line 29 as *nostrum melioris utroque* ("nobler than either of us"), is not in the Ennian/ Horatian role of the discreet lesser friend: he is in the role of Geminus Servilius himself, the nobleman (*uiri nobilis … hominis genere et fortuna superioris*, Gell. 12.4) who, after a hard day *de summis rebus regundis* in the forum and the senate, goes to his un-named friend and unloads everything, good or bad, knowing he will keep his secrets safe:

> quoi res audacter magnas paruasque iocumque
> eloqueretur et cuncta malaque et bona dictu
> euomeret si qui uellet tutoque locaret. (Gell. 12.4.4 = Ennius *Annales* fr.
>   273–275 Skutsch)

> (Servilius) would boldly divulge to him his affairs, the big, the small, and
> the funny, and all that's bad and good to say he would blurt out to him,
> should he want to deposit them somewhere safe.

The dear friends Lucilius dumps on after a hard day are his books—an engaging idea that may have come from Lucilius himself.[32] But there's the rub: his books do not keep secrets, they blab and tell all.[33] As mentioned, Horace will redeploy the same iconic figure of Servilius' friend (Ennius?) to describe his relationship with Maecenas, but there, as Labate makes clear, the emphasis is heavily on the satirist's discretion, and how Horace's books keep their secrets, especially when they concern his own nobler friend, Maecenas.[34] Lucilius himself may have mockingly remembered this passage in the Lupus satire of Book 1.[35] We cannot make out what Lucilius might have intended by redeploying the image there, though it is clear that much of the parodic fun of this poem is made at Ennius' expense. But what is clear from Horace's referencing of the image in *Satires* Book 2 is that he uses it to structure our sense of his relationship to Maecenas, to give shape to something unknown, and thereby to make it knowable, by way of something iconic, pre-shaped, and already known, setting that in clear contrast to Lucilius' relationship to his friend-books. By working his own image through the same model, by delivering himself to us in that preconfigured form, we see Horace differently: no longer is he a failed Lucilian satirist, someone too cowardly to cut loose and tell us what we are dying to know. Instead, he is the picture of friendly discretion;[36] that is, if we choose to see him that way. In the end, the act of authorization, and of making the author, lies with us. He becomes the good and discreet satirist only if we choose to authorize the metaphor's validity, and to acknowledge that it has been properly applied (to satire, and to Horace himself). Many (certainly the more devoted of the *fautores Lucili*) would not.

The encultured *auto* of the poet's *bio*

The self Horace gives us in satire (or rather his many selves and self-parts), is shot through with remembered images, remembered patterns of self-presentation, and previous literary selves. Which is to say it is a self shot through with metaphors for itself, and constituted by those metaphors. And it is a self highly attuned to, and delimited by, specific generic demands in a way that, it seems, Lucilius' was not. Horace invites us to peek at the life he lives at the end of *Satires* 1.6: evening strolls through the forum, haggling with vendors, simple meals of chickpeas and leeks, a drop of oil, a dash of salt. Just what you would want from a satirist in control, and of a more philosophical, understated and introspective bent. Within this satire's frame it is a self-expression fitting and perfect, all drawn, as David Armstrong has shown, according to the pattern of "the philosophers day," and thus a life according to kind.[37] Is it Horace's real life? Is this who he really is? The answer is beyond knowing. But what we can say is that this is certainly who he needs to be in this moment, in this poem, in this book. It is an image that does not square terribly well with the Horace we think we know from elsewhere, Horace the skirt-chaser, the wine-connoisseur, the music-mad party-goer or "squeaky clean prick." "He" does not show up in his satires, but in the odes, certainly, sometimes. And in his epodes he can be something else altogether, a powderkeg of confusion and rage mixing Archilochean, Hipponactean, Callimachean, and who knows what other, selves. Not one Horace, generically speaking, but many Horaces are refracted through his various poem types, as through generic prisms.

At *Satires* 1.6.54–62 Horace describes his first encounter with Maecenas. Recommended by "noblest" Virgil (*optimus … Virgilius*), then again by Varius, humble Horace could barely speak when he came into the presence of Maecenas himself. And he had good reason to tremble under the gaze of "king" Maecenas, as peasant to distant and glowering potentate, because he could not hide that he was from the wrong side of the tracks. But did he really tell the king, straight off, that he was the son of a freed slave? To do so would take tremendous fortitude, because that particular bit of biographical information was almost certain to ruin his chances for success and get him tossed back to the scribal salt-mines for good. In its own way, the satirist's telling Maecenas who he was, straight out, is the most stunning example of outspokenness, of his having nothing to hide, and of his saying what had to be said, regardless of the consequences, that one will find in all the satires. It is, in other words, the perfect beginning for a story about a satirist, telling us that his life and his text are in perfect balance, that he was a man "born" to speak in open and honest ways (another biographical beginning).[38] Speaking truth to power is what this man does because that is who he is. Nothing else he will say after that point in his Satires (Gargonius smells like a goat, Crispinus is a nitwit, etc.) will rank with this, the first words out of bashful baby Horace's mouth telling Maecenas "I am a the son of a freed slave."

We have good reason to be suspicious of a picture so perfect, for as Gordon Williams has shown, the *libertino patre natus* mantra of *Satires* 1.6, repeated again at *Epistles* 1.20.20–2, is hard to credit in this, its blunt, uncontextualized form.[39] In the recent American presidential primaries, one of the leading candidates, Hillary Clinton, talked of learning to shoot a gun behind her grandfather's shed in backwater Pennsylvania. The claim may have been completely true, I suspect it was true, but it made even some of her most ardent supporters cringe. Few voters bought it as anything other than a highly selective rhetorical manipulation, a case of the truth being, at some fundamental level, false. My point is that it was a manipulation, certainly, and yet it was the teller's true experience *at the same time*. Gordon Williams makes much the same point regarding Horace's servile family background as the poet describes it in his *Satires* and *Epistles*—and it should be noted that nowhere in the odes is Horace the son of a freed slave.[40] Williams fashions a good social-historical case for Horace's true experience being stretched in the claim *libertino patre natus*, and thus, what from one angle finds the satirist basing his relationship with Maecenas on truth-telling and trust, from another angle finds him playing the blunt satirist, bad birth and all, to very good and profitable effect (Maecenas being had).[41]

But what Williams did not take into account in his study is the clear literary patterning of the claim, and of the entire introductory scenario that it surrounds and is woven into. Several scholars have proposed that the introduction scene of *Satires* 1.6 is modeled after a satire in Lucilius' 30th book, where the poet pictures himself trembling before the throne of Accius, the imperious head of the *collegium poetarum*,[42] and elsewhere, drawing upon an insightful but overstated assertion by G. C. Fiske, I have pointed out that Horace patterns his introduction to Maecenas after that of Bion of Borysthenes to Antigonus Gonatas.[43] As Bion himself tells it in his famous letter to Antigonus, the first words out of his mouth when he came into the king's presence were "I am the son of a freed slave" (ἐμοὶ ὁ πατὴρ μὲν ἦν ἀπελεύθερος, D.L. 4.46), the Greek equivalent of Horace's *libertino patre natus*, and that phrase is repeated as the mantra of his letter to Antigonus, just as it is for Horace in his address to Maecenas in *Satires* 1.6.[44] Thus again, what at one level looks like a simple assertion of fact, at another level is a figurative rendering of that fact (or "fact"), a patterned expression (and falsification[45]) that helps us structure the speaker's relationship to Maecenas in a certain, known way: Horace speaks truth to power the way Bion the cynic spoke to Antigonus. And thus an entire, pre-existing

theoretical apparatus that lionized such relationships between truth-telling philosophers and kings as both helpful and necessary (the "king's confidant")
comes into play to help us imagine the poet's outspokenness in the same terms:
Maecenas needs a man of that *kind* in his house, and that's the *kind* of (royal)
house he runs.[46]

As the philosopher gifted with leisure in *Satires* 1.6, Horace has time to stroll
through the forum at dusk, to read and write and think great thoughts. Life at
the king's court is simple, unharried, and introspective. But the poet's daily
routine undergoes a drastic shift in *Satires* 2.6 to become the exact opposite of
that earlier picture. Replacing it is a picture of overwrought misery: rising before
dawn the poet sets off to meet with Maecenas.[47] He spends the day chasing
about the city, frantically pursuing errands first for Maecenas, then for the
scribes, and so on, but never having any time for himself. Barely able to keep up,
he hates every minute of his daily routine. The reading and thinking and simple
meals told of in *Satires* 1.6 are by now a distant memory. More precisely, they
have become the future longed-for by the harried poet, as he dreams forward to
life on his beloved, but currently unreachable, Sabine estate.[48] But for now he is
stuck in the city, fighting the crowds. "You'd knock down all that stands in your
way if you are running back to Maecenas with something to tell him" (*tu pulses
omne quod obstet / ad Maecenatem memori si mente recurras*, *Satires* 2.6.30–1),
says a stranger elbowed aside by Horace as he hurries back to Maecenas' house.
The interlocutor's passing complaint, whether or not it is a "fact reported" from
the poet's daily life (did Horace really knock people over to get to Maecenas?
Did he knock them with his knee, or did he prefer a quick jab of the elbow?), is
more importantly a way of seeing that life, and of configuring it in iconic, and
searingly satiric, terms: rushing to report back to Maecenas, Horace resembles
the *servus currens* of Plautine comedy, or the parasite Curculio who bowls his
way through a crowd at *Curculio* 280–98, pushing and kicking as he goes, desperate to bring news to the young man who feeds him.[49] The calm philosopher
of *Satires* 1.6 is nowhere in sight. Bion has been reassigned. In his place we have
Horace the kept man, the go-fer, the officious slave. Master Maecenas keeps him
running.

Where, then, is the "true" Horace in all of this, and what can we really know
of his real life, his opinions, and his routines? Granted, not everything he gives
us to behold of himself has a clear precedent in a pre-existing model, cultural,
literary, or otherwise. But it is surprising how often literary fashioning can be
seen to configure even the most mundane and incidental of personal habits and
experiences. This poet, Cucchiarelli has shown, cannot even daub salve on his
eyes without giving them an Aristophanic tinge,[50] and, to stray for a moment
into his odes, he cannot come in from the cold without playing Alcaeus, nor
can he complain of a tree falling on his head without seeming too generically
cute. I want to give a moment's thought to this last incident (*Odes* 2.13)
because it would seem to defy any attempt to take it as anything other than a

reference to something real, a report of something that actually happened back on the farm. And we may well be relieved to think that here, for once, Horace tells us something straight, providing a detail from life without packaging it as someone else's, or as something already known. There is no "tree crashing on head" genre of ancient poetry, though such a poem might well come under the broader heading of "complaints concerning the vicissitudes of fortune,"[51] or the "divine preservation of the protected poet."[52] Even so, say the commentators, "the historicity of the experience should not be doubted."[53] "He makes so much of the episode … that it cannot be fictitious."[54] This tree is special for the unexpected dent it makes on the Horatian corpus (2.13, 2,17, 3.4, 3.8, 3.28), so it is off-limits to doubters. Like an old-growth ash that falls in a sacred grove, it must be left to lie right where it fell, squarely on the poet's unsuspecting head because he says so (*te caducum / in domini caput*, 2.13.11–12; unless it just barely missed him thanks to Faunus [2.17.28] or the *Camena* [3.4.27], or perhaps it was Bacchus [3.8.16–18]), and because you can't make stuff like that up.

So we are told. But even here, in reckoning with a life-detail that is unique in all of Greek and Roman poetry, an event so highly marked as historical fact that Horace tells us in *Odes* 3.8 that it happened on the first of March, we have to reckon with the "accursed" tree's having fallen, for us, in the only place where we could ever hear it fall: in a poem. And there it is no mere tree or fact of the poet's real life. Rather it is a "tree," a symbol wrought from the pliable, tree-like "stuff" (*materies*, *lignum*, *silva*, ὕλη) from which poems and poetic fictions are made.[55] As text, this tree does not lend itself to being un-texted. It must symbolize, even when the point of its symbolization is to say "Look, I'm not a symbol, but a piece of history, a tree-hard fact, authentic and real!" We see this, the inevitability of the tree's communicating as convention, for example, in the way its untimely demise describes a hazard particular to singers, that is, a hazard according to kind, but only if we assume that the lives that singers sing of in their songs were the ones they actually lived. For it is a truism of singing poets who escape into their art that they compose their songs stretched out under a tree. That tree's shade (often symbolizing a patron's favor) is elsewhere protective and pleasant, and it becomes in song a site for wine, lovemaking, wreathplaiting, and for song itself.[56] Back on his farm, the farmer singer says, my tree came crashing down. That is what I mean by the incident's being generically cute. With no scene set, and with no clear sense made for us of how this poet came to be so unluckily situated under a falling tree (or branch), we are left to work out the details for ourselves, using what little we know. Quite justifiably we might wonder: did the poets who sing of composing songs under trees really sit under trees to compose their songs? Is that what Horace was doing under his evil tree? Does the icon of the shade-drenched singer bear any resemblance to the poet's life as it was actually lived, or is that just a funny convention? For most people, having a tree fall on your head is awful. For Horace, it is awful and ironic (like a Greenpeace activist's being devoured by a whale). And that irony can never be escaped in song ("Orpheus sang in the woods, and he drew trees to himself, too, but they didn't crash down on him!" "And wasn't the injurious threat of these songs of a grander sort: that I would hit my head on the stars, *sublimi feriam sidera vertice*?" and so on, irony upon irony). It is a necessary condition of that incident's expression in song, and Horace knows it. "Catch me if you can," he says. "Even when I swear it really happened—and it really did happen—and even when I give you the exact date—March 1—I must always leave you to wonder whether I might not be pulling your leg. You tell me, reader, what is real. In the end, the reality of my life will always be exactly what you make of it."

My point is not that Horace was never hit on the head by a falling tree—I have no reason to doubt that he was. My point, rather, concerns how the legibility of that incident as factual personal history is necessarily ironized by the fact of its being included in, and delivered as, song.[57] This is art that limits life to the terms it has set for life in song and, as such, it will always carry with it the potential for metatheater, even in the most unlikely of places. Rupturing the illusion of a "whole ... drawn out ... life" contained by song, in this case, is not any explicit statement by the speaker, or even a discernable nudge to make us think that we are bumping against the limits of his art. Rather, that acknowledgment of limits met, if it happens, comes from us as something we provide, from our knowing how this game is played, and from our not wanting it to be played on us. We can put scare quotes around the poet's "subumbral disaster" because the generic rules say we can, and because it is now (as a necessary consequence of the poet's asserting something about his "lived experience") our turn to play: "irony is above all a mode of reading, not a mode of writing," so the decision about how to take the poet's account rests with us.[58] Thus, just as we saw before in the analogy of the votive tablet, the very passage that invites us to think of the poet as reliably spilling his life onto the page also poses the problem of our ever having any access to that life in song. But I could reverse the order of this conundrum, as many have done, to make it speak more positively, and to assert that it is actually through patterned speech and remembered words and forms (variously described as artifice, *ludus*, genre, rhetoric, "literariness," culture) that poets say what is personally specific and true (authenticity, true pathos, semantics, factual information, nature), and that it was only there that they ever had a chance to say it.[59] As I have argued elsewhere, and hinted at in passing above, it does no good to insist that Horace, or Catullus, or whoever is "just" a persona if by that one means to imply that he had any chance of being anything else.[60] That is my main problem with the use of the persona (lit. "mask") to analogize the patterning of the poet's words, and of his life: a mask is something that an actor can take off to show who he really is. If the satirist or singer ceases to express himself through artifice, he does not cease to be artificial, he ceases to satirize or sing.[61]

GUIDE TO FURTHER READING

For a basic survey of the rise of persona theory within the field of Roman satire, see Freudenburg (2005: 27–30). Of several recent studies devoted to this topic, Gowers (2003) focuses on Horace *Satires* Book 1, and Mayer (2003) has much to say about Horace within a larger overview of Roman personal poetry. Harrison (2007a) covers all the most significant autobiographical moments in the works of Horace, demonstrating that they consistently combine fantasy not with reality per se, but with contrived effects of realism (Barthes's "reality effect"). For the poetic "I" of the *Odes* specifically, see Horsfall (1998) and Davis (1991: 78–114); on "Lyrische Wirklichkeit" in the *Odes*, with special emphasis on the poet's three accounts of his being saved by gods of music (*Odes* 2.7, 3.4, and 2.17), see Schmidt (2001: 190–212). On the question of persona versus real life in *Epistles* Book 1, see Moles (2002). Selden (1992) is primarily concerned with lyric poetry, especially with Catullus, but in ways that apply to the "theory and practice of impersonation" (p. 498) in Rome more generally.

   Both Gowers and Selden provide ample bibliographical resources for the study of the poet's life in his poems. Gowers (p. 57) insists that "the current emphasis on "persona" is a very necessary corrective to more literal interpretations," but that "there *was* a life-story to be told, an image to be fashioned, a position to be defended, even if these were tailored to generic and rhetorical demands." This is generally the approach of Oliensis (1998), and I largely agree with it, and seek to demonstrate it, in the paper above. Mine is more of an intertexualist/intersubjectivist approach, heavily influenced by the works of Feeney, Barchiesi, Fowler, and Conte (for specific bibliography see above notes 21, 22, 57–9, *et passim*). Approaching the poets' "I" this way, I take very seriously the idea that so-called "real life" itself always necessarily embedded in, and defined by, the very "artifice" (cultural codes, symbols, existing patterns) it is supposed to defy. The bedrock of modern theorizations of autobiography is Lejeune (1975). Among recent works that I have found most helpful are: Olney (1998), Smith-Watson (2001), and especially Eakin (1999).

NOTES

*   Special thanks are due to Denis Feeney, John Henderson, and Dan Hooley for reading this essay in draft and providing incisive comments. Thanks also to Chris Kraus for causing me to think twice (as if once wasn't enough) about double hyperbaton. That is where this essay started from.

1   A basic bibliographical survey of recent works on persona theory, with special attention to works on Horace, is included in the Guide to Further Reading section at the end of this article.

2   In Freudenburg 2005 I explain the dominant place of persona theory within satire studies as conditioned by two factors working in tandem: 1) the satirist's being generically bound to speak the truth plainly, and to elicit our trust; and 2) our need to socialize him. The trouble is, he gets us to trust that he is telling us the truth of

his life, but we do not always like what he tells us. In speaking from the heart, those personal poets who admit to behaving obscenely, or to being possessed of violent and/or prurient desires, have been the ones most frantically theorized, and thereby socialized and contained, by persona theory.

3 Harrison 2007: 35: "we see that in various different types of self-representation, Horace combines strategies of ambiguity and obfuscation, self-deprecation and humour, playfulness and misdirection. The works of one of the most apparently autobiographical poets of antiquity in fact provide a carefully nuanced and often amusingly misleading series of self-presentations."

4 Here I am referencing Lejeune's "autobiographical pact." See Lejeune 1975.

5 For a stellar example of just how hard it is to contain that referential activity, and to keep track of the cultural symbolism that is written into any given moment of the poet's "self-mythologization," see Henderson 1999: 114–44.

6 Smith and Watson 2001: 13: "If we approach self-referential writing as an intersubjective process that occurs within the writer/reader pact, rather than as a true-or-false story, the emphasis of reading shifts from assessing and verifying knowledge to observing processes of communicative exchange and understanding."

7 See the "Latin texts of a contrary tendency" cited by Mayer 2003: 66–71.

8 See Freudenburg 2001: 18, and 2005: 1–2.

9 On the two "poles" of the Lucilian satiric persona, as reflected on by Horace in *Satires* 1.4.1.10, and 2.1, see Labate 1996: 428–9. For a thorough study of the satiric "I" in Lucilius, with a thorough survey of the poet's inclusion of his private life in his poetry, see now Haß 2007.

10 On adjective interlacings or 'double hyperbaton' in Latin poetry, see Hoffer 2007.

11 Biographers of Lucilius habitually put a heavy burden on *senis*, taking it to prove that Lucilius only began writing satire in his old age; see, e.g. Marx 1904: vol.1, p. xxiii, and Warmington *ROL* vol. 3 (1967) ix. But the "entire life" of an old man surely includes his youth. The point is rather just how very long the life he lived, and put into his poems, was.

12 The tablet's description *votiva ... tabella* brackets the whole of line 43, and *omnis ... vita* borders that inner frame at the front and back. For the interlacing of adjective/noun pairs as a means of spatially representing meaning, see Hoffer 2007: 324–6.

13 Mayer (2003) takes for granted that the base-line assumption of grammarians and teachers of rhetoric, especially Servius, Porphyrio, and Quintilian, was also that of Roman readers generally: "what the poet said of himself was rooted in reality" (p. 61). What I am saying is that the poets themselves can have their own ideas about how they write themselves into their poems, knowing exactly what that entails, and that they might regard the commonplace view as sensible and meaningful, or that they might think it a completely unlikely and silly idea, one worth studying or problematizing or sending up in their poems. The Latin works that Mayer attempts to defuse by way of the generally held view, because they seem to posit a strong disconnect between the poet's life from his art, are all works of poetry, by devilish characters such as Catullus, Horace, and Ovid. These are poets who love to poke fun at bean-counting grammarians.

14 Fowler 2000: 9, citing Muecke 1969: 195.

15 E.g. lines 39–43: sed hic stilus haud petet ultro / quemquam animantem et me veluti custodiet ensis/ vagina tectus: quem cur destringere coner / tutus ab infestis latronibus? o pater et rex / Iuppiter, ut pereat positum robigine telum.

16 Sirago (1958) makes clear that Horace only plays with being a Lucanian (*nugans*), and that the playful suggestion happens only in this one instance. Sirago gathered up all references to Horace's south Italian homeland from his complete works to show that: "Horatius igitur usque ad extremos vitae dies Apulum se proclamavit suamque artem ut Apulam praedicavit" (p. 26). On the ethnic identities of, as well as the moral and intellectual assumptions made about, Roman citizens of south Italian origin, see Farney 2007: 179–228.

17 Muecke 1993: 107.

18 Commentators have failed to note that Horace is humorously etymologizing *Apulus* and *Apula* (34 and 38) with **ad hoc pulsis** in 36.

19 Warmington 1967 *ROL* vol. 3, p. ix.

20 Catullus 44 begins: o funde noster seu Sabine seu Tiburs / (nam te esse Tiburtem autumant, quibus non est / cordi Catullum laedere; at quibus cordi est, / quouis Sabinum pignore esse contendunt), / sed seu Sabine siue uerius Tiburs ...

21 Just as cultural presuppositions and pre-existing categories structure continuous sensations into "experience," so do the known habits of self-representation and existing models of identity in first-person accounts of personal experience turn the teller's experience(s) into a "life" readable in letters; see Smith and Watson 2001: 21: "While the experience represented in an autobiographical narrative seems simply personal, it is anything but merely personal. Mediated through memory and language, 'experience' is already an interpretation of the past and of our place in a culturally and historically specific present." Seen this way, constructedness is not a decoration to communication, nor is it an artificializing of something true and authentic, it is a means of communication, a way of becoming a certain kind of subject, and at the heart of communicability itself.

22 Here my debt to Fowler (1997) is obvious. Similarly, on the referential nature of genre itself, i.e. genre as "happening" rather than "thing," see Barchiesi 1997.

23 Harrison 1987: 48 shows that the word *decurrens* carries a sneering aesthetic judgment, implying that Lucilius, like a muddy river (*Satires* 1.4.11), was "always swept irresistibly along his way without pause for a moment of critical reflections."

24 Porphyrio *ad S.* 2.1.30, commenting on **velut fidis arcana sodalibus**: *Aristoxeni[s] sententia est. Ille enim in suis scriptis ostendit Sapphonem et Alcaeum volumina sua loco sodalium habuisse.* For the *ut pictura poesis* theory as the theoretical background of these lines, see Anderson 1982: 32.

25 On the odes as a project dreamed of as the poet's longed-for, but unreachable future in *Satires*, Book 2, see Freudenburg 2006.

26 On the *votiva tabella* as an aesthetic sneer, see Anderson 1982: 30–2, and Harrison 1987: 48–9.

27 Harrison 1987: 48: "Shipwreck is the topic most often associated with painted votives in Latin literature. If the remaining material evidence is trustworthy, the victims—and their savior(s)—seem to have been depicted conventionally on the votives ... without much concern for realism or drama."

28   Anderson 1982: 32: "the votive tablet did *not* correspond to reality. It was a poor version of life, distorted by the incompetence of the artist and by his desire to concentrate all attention upon a lurid, no doubt overemphasized tragedy."

29   On *descriptio* (Gk. διατύπωσις) as a rhetorical device, cf. [Cicero] *ad Her.* 4.51, giving various examples of the device, and noting in conclusion: *hoce genere exornationis vel indignatio vel misericordia potest commoveri*; Juvenal, the epic satirist, is very fond of the device; see Braund (1988: 5–19). On the ironies of Horace's *recusatio* in *Satires* 2.1, see Freudenburg 2001: 82–92.

30   The fragment is preserved by Aulus Gellius at Gell. 12.4 (= Ennius fr. 268-86Sk.). On the informal air of Ennius' "friend" vignette, and its being "more appropriate to Satire than to Epic," see Skutsch 1985: 451, and Mariotti 1951: 129.

31   For Ennius' friend of Servilius sharing the characteristics of the king's confidant, see Skutsch 1985: 450–1. For Horace's reworking of the portrait in picturing his friendship with Maecenas in *Satires* 2.6, see Labate 1996: 438–40.

32   Krenkel 1970: 211–12 suggests that the tell-all relationship of the author to his books described by *Satires* 2.1.30–4 may have come from Lucilius fr. 190–1K *namque so⟨da⟩lis mihi in magno maerore ⟨metuque⟩/ tristitia in summa, crepera ⟨re⟩, inuentus salutis.* Here Lucilius, too, Krenkel asserts, may be referring to his books as his most trusted and loyal friends. Further on this possibility, see also Haß 2007: 180–1.

33   Harrison 1987: 41 describes the way that the literal meaning of *arcana* damages what others (Fraenkel and Williams especially) have taken as an idealized portrait of Lucilius. With it Horace introduces the idea of "the satirist as tattletale or gossip-monger."

34   Labate 1996: 437–41.

35   For verbal connections between the "friend" vignette of Ennius and the famous "battle of the forum" fragment of Lucilius (1228-34Marx = 1252-58Krenkel), with convincing arguments for assigning that fragment to book 1 of Lucilius' satires, see Degl'Innocenti Pierini 1987: esp. 255.

36   Labate 1996: 440: 'Dopo avere negato di esserlo, Orazio resta di fatto un "influente amico dei potenti": l'amico di Servilio infatti si sarebbe comportato esattamente allo stesso modo.'

37   Armstrong 1986: 277 comments on lines 111–29: "A beautiful picture, which leads us, however, into more complex regions of thought as far as Horace's poetic *persona* is concerned. For, as Lejay long ago saw, it is (for all its realistic Roman details) pure convention."

38   For "paternal" figuring of the poet's introduction to Maecenas, and his subsequent inclusion in his circle, see Schlegel 2000.

39   See Williams 1995.

40   The closest he comes to saying so is in the very last poem of *Odes* 1–3 (3.30.12 *ex humili potens*).

41   For the irony of the poet's stated lack of ambition being the key to his getting ahead with Maecenas, see Freudenburg 2001: 69.

42   See Haß 2007: 225–6.

43   See Freudenburg 1993: 205–6; cf. Fiske 1920: 316: "the text of this satire is essentially that of Bion's famous letter to Antigonus Gonatas." A measured view, is that

of Lejay 1911: 174. For a complete analysis of the Bion analogy in Horace, see now Moles 2007: 165–8: 'Horace mobilizes a whole series of items to accentuate the Bion analogy ... readers are challenged to detect Bion's presence' (p. 167).

44   For the letter, see Kindstrand 1976.

45   Even though it may be perfectly true, as in the Hillary Clinton case cited above. There is always the possibility that Horace simply told the truth he was taunted by, not knowing that the taunt had a different cultural precedent and value in the inter- actions between Hellenistic kings and their philosophers, or that Bion's first encoun- ter with Antigonus was a cultural model that resonated deeply with Horace and that he consciously sought to emulate in his own kingly encounter.

46   On the packaging of both Lucilius and Horace as versions of the Hellenistic king's confidant, see above pp. 281–2, and Labate 1996: 439. For the Hellenistic back- ground that shows through the Ennian portrait, see Skutsch 1968: 92–4, and 1985: 450–1.

47   Labate 1996: 439 describes the abrupt contrast between the new portrait and the old in terms of a "crisi della αὐτάρκεια urbana."

48   The lines that dream forward in *Satires* 2.6 (esp. 60–70) focus on the poet having time for his books, and simple meals, and rest, the very things described as character- izing his life in the philosopher's day vignette of *Satires* 1.6. On these lines see Freudenburg 2006: 149–51.

49   For the *servus currens* in Roman Comedy, with full bibliography, see Csapo 1987. For Horace cast momentarily as a comic *servus currens* by these lines, see Labate 1996: 440. In this case, the model behind the lines actually helps fill in what the text itself leaves undecided: the vague phrase *memori mente* "with unforgetting mind" has often been taken as a reference to the poet's devotion to Maecenas, in the sense "with your mind thinking only of him." A better option comes by way of the running slave's many appearances on the Roman comic stage: the slave (or para- site) is routinely intent on delivering an urgent message, as in the *Curculio* instance cited above. He must remember what he has been told and deliver his message as soon as possible.

50   On the satirist's *lippitudo*, see Cucchiarelli 2001: 66–70. On the satiric poets' various literary, generic, and "emblematic" uses of their bodies, see Barchiesi and Cucchi- arelli 2005.

51   For the conventional categorizations possible for the incident, see Nisbet and Hubbard 1978: 202–3.

52   Harrison 2007a: 24 connects the incident to the poet's encounter with the wolf (*Odes* 1.22.9–16) to argue that "the symbolic point of the incident ... is clearly more important than its actual place in Horace's life."

53   Nisbet and Hubbard 1978: 201.

54   Nisbet and Rudd 2004: 65.

55   For Horace's lyric trees as preternaturally expressive features of "a *poetic* landscape, inscribed within a cultural *poetics*," see Henderson 1999: 118 *et passim*.

56   Two significantly placed *loci classici* of the poet singing *sub umbra* are the first lines of Virgil's *Eclogues* 1 (*sub tegmine fagi*), and the last lines of Horace's first book of odes (*Odes* 1.38, *sub arta / vite bibentem*).

57   For incisive comments on a similar ironic tension "between poetry as *ludus* and poetry as the expression of feeling" in Catullus, see Fowler 1989: 112–13; these first

thoughts connecting "Romantic irony" to the "I" of Roman personal poetry were
subsequently developed, with impressive returns, in Fowler 2000.

58 Fowler 2000: 11.

59 Fowler 2000: 9: "by rupturing the illusion—by in a sense destroying his own creation—the poet frees himself from being bound by the text he has created." And
again on p. 10: "I want to concentrate on the most distinctive element in the
concept: the view that the ironic unmasking of reality is not simply a negative act,
but one in which the reader is enabled to accept a sublimity." Cf. Feeney 1998: 1
on the false dichotomization of literature/life in discussions (and routine dismissals)
of Roman religion: "when we tackle what we call 'religion in literature,' we encounter
the same difficulties of referentiality and representation that have become familiar
topics amongst Latinists in recent discussions of love or politics or friendship in 'real
life' and in 'literature.' In all of these areas, as G. B. Conte in particular has clearly
argued, we must recognize that the 'naked facts' beloved of the empirical historicist
are always 'clothed': there is no unproblematic background of reality—religious or
otherwise—against which to plot the different reality of literature, since 'real life' is
itself 'the locus of cultural images and models, symbolic choices, communicative and
perceptual codes.'" The reference is to Conte 1994: 108–10. For further thoughts
on the fetishization of Greek "authenticity" over Roman artifice, see Feeney 1993:
55–60.

60 See Freudenburg 2005: 28–30. I owe the substance of this observation to Henderson
1999.

61 Again, my debt to Fowler 1997 is obvious.

CHAPTER FIFTEEN

Return to Sender: Horace's *sermo* from the Epistles to the Satires*

Andrea Cucchiarelli

The Greek noun *epistolē* would find its way into Latin (*epistula*) at an early date. The word places particular emphasis on the letter's materiality as a thing 'sent' (*epistellein*) to bridge the distance between writer and recipient. Etymologically speaking, then, an "epistle" can only be defined as such, if it is sent. The point is made by Porphyrio in describing the fundamental difference between Horace's *Epistles* and the *Satires* as follows: "*in sermonum nomine vult intellegi quasi apud praesentem se loqui, epistulas vero quasi <u>ad absentes missas</u>*" ("by the title *sermones* he wishes to imply a direct discourse with his audience, whereas the epistles are intended to be "sent" to those not present"; *Satires* 1.1.1).

At the very opening of his collection of "poems for sending,"[1] Horace makes an assertion that ought to command the reader's attention:

> nunc itaque et versus et cetera ludicra pono;
> quid verum atque decens, curo et rogo et omnis in hoc sum;
> condo et compono quae mox depromere possim. (*Epistles* 1.1.10–12)

> So now I lay aside my verses and all other toys. What is right and
> seemly is my study and pursuit, and to that am I wholly given. I
> am putting by and setting in order the stores on which I may
> soon draw.

That a poet writing in hexameters should talk in terms of "setting aside" verse-writing and all other such "playthings" (*cetera ludicra*) carries a powerful irony that many have noticed.[2] But it should also be observed that in these lines Horace is careful to use images that neatly contain and describe his own theory of "epistolary writing": the phrase *condo et compono* puts us in mind of a secret cache, or store, of wines and other victuals that are stashed within the house,[3] and that may soon be called into use (*quae mox depromere possim*). Our collection of "epistles" opens, therefore, with a sense of the poet's being closed off (as if working in his pantry) and completely absorbed in a private moral inquiry. He sends messages because he can communicate in no other way: he is isolated, turned in on himself and distant from his recipients—*et omnis in hoc sum*.

Horace, however, immediately pulls his reader in an unexpected direction by introducing a new theme that will play a fundamental role throughout the entire work:

> ac ne forte roges, quo me duce, quo lare tuter,
> nullius addictus iurare in verba magistri,
> quo me cumque rapit tempestas, deferor hospes.
> nunc agilis fio et mersor civilibus undis,
> virtutis verae custos rigidusque satelles;
> nunc in Aristippi furtim praecepta relabor
> et mihi res, non me rebus subiungere conor. (13–19)

> Do you ask, perchance, who is my chief, in what home I take shelter? I am not bound over to swear as any master dictates; wherever the storm drives me, I turn in for comfort. Now I become all action, and plunge into the tide of civil life, stern champion and follower of true Virtue; now I slip back stealthily into the rules of Aristippus, and would bend the world to myself, not myself to the world.

The image of the pantry, set back deep within the house, is taken up once more only to be suddenly undone, for it turns out that there is no "guide," or even a "Lar" (a *domus*) to protect Horace. Freed from all forms of authority, he becomes an itinerant wanderer in the mold of Ulysses, who finds himself at the mercy of the changing seasons and is forced to rely on the kindness of strangers. But while he may hurl himself into the metaphorical seas of civil life, he also remains a stalwart keeper of true virtue (Stoicism perhaps?); for if he abandons this role then all that remains for him is to "slide back to" the school of Aristippus.[4] Thus the poet, who for an instant we imagined as at home with a hidden treasure-trove of knowledge, now loses himself in a shifting moral tide. The world of the Epistles seems "unstable," tossed by continuous revolutions and reversals. Perhaps such was the turbulent reality of high Augustan Rome (or perhaps this is how things seemed to the poet in his turbulent internal state).[5]

We are able, at this point, to appreciate that a sense of "return" is present already in the perfectly weighted opening verse, expressed through the repetition *dicte ... dicende* ("addressed ... to be addressed"), and the correlation *prima ... summa* ("as before, now and evermore"). Looking back to the first of his *sermones* in hexameters (that is, taking the Satires and Epistles as a paired set that was just now nearing completion)[6] we see that the poet there, too, began by naming his patron, and by examining different ways of life (and of evasion) available to men (*Satires* 1.1.1). Both the Odes and Epodes began by addressing Maecenas. The Epistles thus presents itself as a rethinking, and a closer examination, of ground already covered. In company with the recipients of the book's individual letters (beginning with Maecenas), readers are encouraged to recognise and follow these paths that lead to other poems and other beginnings, putting their own knowledge of Horace to the test.

The frame and beyond: Lollius, Celsus, and Albius

Horace is rightly recognized as possessing a distinct editorial sensibility in arranging his poems in book form. It has been noted that, in effect, one finds in the Epistles a circular arrangement of the letters' addressees. Leaving aside the final send-off that is addressed to the *liber* itself, and thus is not strictly epistolary, as Porphyrio observed ad *Epistles* 1.20.1, we may say that the collection of "epistles proper" opens and closes with letters to Maecenas (who appears one last time in 1.19: one recalls the "return" pattern of the opening lines: *dicte-dicende*). This same correlation is also found in poems 2 and 18, both of which are addressed to the young Lollius Maximus. We might conclude, therefore, that the sequence Maecenas–Lollius, and, in reverse order, Lollius–Maecenas forms the "double frame" of the *liber*.[7]

The fact that a principle of disposition has been recognized in the identity of Horace's recipients seems to offer proof of the editorial complicity between the poet and (at the very least) his select public. If the honorific "frame" structure was indeed apparent to the book's principal honorand, the young Lollius would have been grateful for his own (double) positioning behind the illustrious patron, and others will accordingly have recognized various ways of regrouping the poems, especially their distribution into small groups separating younger addressees from older ones.[8] Nevertheless, notwithstanding observations of this kind, which presuppose a comprehensive "architectural" awareness of the volume in its entirety, it is also important to understand the book's structure as one of a running order of poems read in succession; in other words, taken little by little as the volume "unfolds."[9]

Taken this way, the reader encounters a "second opening" in the first lines of *Epistles* 1.2, the first epistle to Lollius:

> Troiani belli scriptorem, Maxime Lolli,
> dum tu declamas Romae, Praeneste relegi;
> qui, quid sit pulchrum, quid turpe, quid utile, quid non,
> planius ac melius Chrysippo et Crantore dicit. (1–4)

> While you, Lollius Maximus, declaim at Rome, I have been
> reading afresh at Praeneste the writer of the Trojan War; who
> tells us what is fair, what is foul, what is helpful, what not,
> more plainly and better than Chrysippus or Crantor.

Once again a "rereading" is explicitly formulated: *relegi.* In fact, Horace does more than recommend a moral reading of the Homeric poems, which was an approach especially common among the Stoics (one notes the irony of his declaring Homer superior to two of his most important readers and interpreters, the Stoic Chrysippus and the Academic Crantor).[10] The same poet who, in *Satires* 2.3, would worry that his study was overburdened with the weighty tomes of Plato, Menander, Eupolis and Archilochus, whom he considered precious sources of inspiration (lines 11–12), now "rereads" the Homeric poems, looking to them for models of moral behavior.[11] There is a noticeable conflict between the public activity of the young Lollius, intent as he is to be seen "declaiming" Homer in Rome (the shared object of both *declamas* and *relegi* is *Troiani belli scriptorem*), and the undefined but remote writing activity of Horace himself (the epistolary conversation is by definition separate from "recited" literature: Dem. *De eloc.* 225).

We are able to conjure, therefore, an image of the young Lollius, caught up in the dazzling social and literary diversions of Rome, and so busy that Horace almost has to excuse himself for detaining him: *nisi quid te detinet, audi* (5). Horace attempts to capture his attention with a hurried précis of the *Iliad* (the *fable* of line 6), a rich resource for any aspiring writer, full as it is of vice, passion, intrigue and shock. But an individualized purpose can be seen already in *rursus* which marks the transition from the *Iliad* to the *Odyssey*: *quid virtus et quid sapientia possit/utile proposuit nobis exemplar Ulixen* (17–18). With such obvious references to the cups of Circe and to the proverbial song of the Sirens (*nosti,* 23), Horace presses his young recipient to recognize the poem's moral significance, further stressing his opening point by means of an unexpected shift into the first person plural: *nos numerus sumus et fruges consumere nati,/sponsi Penelopae, nebulones, Alcinoique/in cute curanda plus aequo operata iuventus* ("We are but ciphers, born to consume earths fruits, Penelope's good-for-naught suitors, young courtiers of Alcinous, unduly busy in keeping their skins sleek," 27–9). The second part of the epistle, marked by the surprising shift in line 27, is a deliberately strong and sententious proptreptic.[12] Above all, it is the exhortation of a poet who is, by now, himself "great," who addresses himself to a young man of letters so that he might be able to grasp how to link strict moral research to the study of texts—perhaps, one might even assume, with better results than even Horace himself had achieved in his own youth (cf. *posces ante diem librum*, 35–7, eqs. with *Satires* 2.3.1–4).

Materializing before us, then, is an image of Horace the philologist-poet, who rereads and reabsorbs the great texts of Homer, even managing, like a Roman

Aristarchus,[13] to avoid the pitfalls of wild allegorical interpretations, by devoting himself to the moral heart of the *fabula*. It is precisely this image which appears again in the following epistle. This letter, too, is addressed to a young student of letters, and it is even more emphatic about poetry's capacity to "effect." One has the impression, however, that the lone recipient, Julius Florus, has been chosen by Horace almost at random from a select group of eager literary new-comers who make up the *comitatus* of Tiberius, who was himself, at that time, just over twenty years old. Horace could never have foreseen that, with *Claudius Augusti privignus* in line 2, he was naming the successor to Augustus; still it is clear that Tiberius represents the future, engaged as he is in a diplomatic mission (the installation of Tigranes on the throne of Armenia) of considerable signifi-cance. And his fellow travelers, a group of up-and-coming writers, also represent that future. The attentive reader (one prepared to "reread" Horace's text) will remember such figures from an earlier poem, intuiting that history is playing itself out here in *Epistles* 1.4 in terms already known.

In *Satires* 1, 5 a picture was painted of the young Horace, employed in the role of *comes*, or "companion" to Maecenas on his journey to Brundisium. "Fol-lowing the great men," not only in their travels, but also, poetically, in the descriptions of their adventures, was a fundamental problem for the young Horace, as his first epode suffices to demonstrate. During the time of the Satires Horace had maintained a respectful but calculated distance from the *magnae res* ("important affairs of state," as he calls them in *Satires* 1.5.28; cf. esp. 2.1.10–20). But now that his poetic *corpus* was almost complete and his *summa Camena* was coming into view, it was time for Horace to take stock of his achievements, and to consider also his failures. This is the particular urgency behind his flurry of questions to Florus, questions that, in essence, amount to: "who will be the next Horace?" or even, "is there another who will write better poetry than I have?" It is a discussion of literature that follows the epistle's strategic military opening. The switch from one mode to the other is flipped by *operum* in line 6, which we subsequently find out refers to literary works, not military ones. Horace then continues: "who then will choose to write the deeds of Augustus? Who will preserve the memory of our times? What activities is Titius, ambitious Latin translator of Pindar, engaged in? Or is he working on tragedy?" (7–14, noting the barb that protrudes from *desaevit et ampullatur* ("rages and swells") in line 14, which concerns what would continue to be the great *desideratum* of Augus-tan poetry). At this point, it is evident that the choice of Julius Florus is anything but casual, that is, if the information transmitted by Porphyrio is worth crediting. For here we find Florus described in terms that are strikingly reminiscent of those that described the young Horace in *Satires* 1.5: a minor official (a *scriba*) who is also a writer of satires, and a close friend of the powerful envoy, Tiberius.[14] Only time would tell whether the *comitatus* of Tiberius would rank with Virgil, Plotius, Varius, and the other companions that Maecenas took with him on his journey to Brundisium. It seems, however, that Horace wishes to confer upon his young correspondent the role of "satirical witness," that he himself had once fulfilled. Thus again, in his third epistle, Horace is treading old ground, rereading his own works.

It is with the mention of Celsus that Horace turns suddenly towards the topic of imitation, a theme fundamental to the Epistles, already hinted at in *Epistles* 1.2 (especially 18, *utile … exemplar*):

> Quid mihi Celsus agit? monitus multumque monendus,
> privatas ut quaerat opes et tangere vitet
> scripta, Palatinus quaecumque recepit Apollo,
> ne, si forte suas repetitum venerit olim
> grex avium plumas, moveat cornicula risum
> furtivis nudata coloribus. (15–19)

> What, pray, is Celsus doing? He was warned, and must often
> be warned to search for home treasures, and to shrink from
> touching the writings which Apollo on the Palatine has
> admitted: lest, if some day perchance the flock of birds come
> to reclaim their plumage, the poor crow, stripped of his
> stolen colours, awake laughter.

This younger generation of intellectuals and poets had their own spaces for study and research in Rome: as was the case in Ptolemaic Alexandria, attached to the palace of the *princeps* was an impressive library. The god of poetry, as if delving into the practical matters of promoting his cause, has "accepted" (*recepit*) new works and made himself their guarantor: thanks to Augustus, Rome has finally been made over according to the Alexandrian model, establishing herself as a cultural centre as well as a political one.[15]

But even before any god came along to finish the job, Horace himself had stood as a literary guarantor and champion of skilled writers.[16] According to an anecdote passed along by Vitruvius, 7 praef. 4–7 and probably well known to Horace's Roman readers, on the occasion of a poetry contest held in the Museum of Alexandria to honor Apollo and the Muses, Aristophanes of Byzantium exposed several poetasters who had attempted to pass off works of past authors as their own (7 praef. 7). The poet-philologist Horace has no hesitation in telling the careless young Celsus of the ridicule that awaits him: in "rereading" Homer, Horace has made fresh discoveries of content and form, but, analogously, with the help of that marvelous library on the Palatine hill, he may also have noticed certain overly blatant "borrowings" made by Celsus. And, along with Horace, also those directly concerned may object if the detected plagiarism should end up damaging contemporary writers. With this scolding advice from Horace to the young Celsus, one recognizes that the world of literary activities in Rome now adheres to a certain order, and that a ready diffusion of philological consultation can be included among the Emperor's many achievements. And Celsus risks ending up like a comically colorless crow, once he has been stripped of his stolen feathers (*furtivi colores*).

The employment of the animal fable for poets who have been "robbed" and are here transformed into "flocks" of birds (*grex avium*) revives the polemical language that traded on the Alexandrian literary scene, especially within the Ptolemies' "birdcage of the muses." In the first iambus of Callimachus the philologists and men of letters who rush to answer the call of the resurrected Hipponax, appear as *kepph[oi* (fr. 191.6 Pf.), "coots," or "petrels." The intention is to represent them as birds of little brain, who are used to flying in dense flocks.[17] Amid the animal sounds that issue from the mouths of humans in the second iambus we again hear the shrill, imitative song of the *psittakos* (constituting a dig, perhaps, at the "rhetoricians", fr. 192.11 Pf.).[18] Thus, in his passing "avian" comparison of Celsus to a crow, Horace found an efficient means for helping us imagine an Alexandrian polemical setting for his words.

Epistles 1.4 is addressed to a writer, Albius. With good reason interpreters have concentrated on the possible identification of this Albius with the elegiac poet Albius Tibullus. That identification is now commonly accepted.[19] Horace had already addressed himself to a writer of elegies named Albius in *Odes* 1.33. There is nothing new to defend or contradict this claim. Instead I will limit myself to highlighting a structural detail that may pertain to a privileged communication between poets (an observation within the grasp of any reader who is equipped for a proper "rereading"). Despite being separated—at least as far as their publications in book-form are concerned—by a divide of some four (or more) years, both *Ode* 1.33 and our epistle nevertheless display certain similarities which must not be overlooked. Affinities are reflected in tone (consolatory in nature) and theme, and in the fact that both poems open with the vocative *Albi* and close with the figure of Horace himself, named in the first person. In the ode, however, Horace appears on an equal, if not greater footing than his friend, and both he and his addressee are afflicted by matters of the heart: *ipsum me melior cum peteret Venus* ("since I was taken from a better Venus," 13); the epistle, for its part, closes with the comical image of Horace, the "epicurean piglet":[20] *me pinguem et nitidum bene curata cute vises,/ cum ridere voles, Epicuri de grege porcum* ("as for me, when you want a laugh, you will find me in fine fettle, fat and sleek, a hog from Epicurus's herd," 15–16). If Albius, the recipient of the epistle, is truly dedicated to "rereading," he will have taken note of the many similarities shared by the two poems, including their having the same number of verses (16). The qualifications possessed by Albius as a literary "arbitrator," hinted at in the first verse: *nostrorum sermonum candide iudex* ("impartial critic of my 'chats'"), should also include the ability to compare, and to count verses. It is likely, then, that the man addressed— whether or not he is in fact Tibullus—would have been able to figure out from similarities of form and structure that the two poems were directed to the same addressee.[21]

The intellectual challenges exchanged between Horace and his writer friend are part of the very structure and communicative form of the letter itself. This is a letter that ambles, passing through landscapes, feelings and moral sentiments before finally revealing its purpose: it is with *vises* in line 15, put in the future tense as the only precondition for their sharing a good time (*cum ridere voles*, 16), that the letter to Albius enters into the well defined typology of a poem of invitation.[22] From all the many allusions and ironies that render their communication so involved and intense, we sense, as an idea disclosed in the margins of the poem, that these two men have met before (in poetry, of course) and will meet again. Even though Horace undergoes a surprise "porcine" transformation that the Ulysses of *Epistles* 1.2 was able to avoid (*vixisset canis immundus vel amica luto sus* "would have lived as an unclean dog or a sow that loves the mire," 26), and thus he classes himself among the anti-heroic *Proci* (*in cute curanda plus aequo operata iuventus*, 29; cf. 1.4.15: *bene curata cute*), the surprise at the close of 1.4 is less pronounced for the careful, "critical" reader who has been able to think beyond the confines of a single poem. Horace, remember, had already warned him: *nos numerus sumus et fruges consumere nati,/sponsi Penelopae nebulones* ... (1.2.27–8; see also the paradoxical "*nostos* of the Phaeacian" in 1.15.24).

In the middle: the boundary of ten, Maecenas and Aristius Fuscus

Upon leafing through the collection, Albius may have noted that the epistle addressed to him, with its "open invitation," precedes an even more obvious and typical letter of invitation to Torquatus. *Epistles* 1.5, with almost double the number of verses as 1.4, evokes scenarios of pleasant conversation that are Callimachean in nature: *aestivam sermone benigno tendere noctem* ("to prolong the summer night in genial converse," 11).[23] The letter displays the assorted trappings of a sympotic gathering that are symbols of moral values, then it signs off by requesting a reply from Torquatus, adding a final exhortation: *tu quotus esse velis, rescribe et rebus omissis/atria servantem postico falle clientem* ("write back, pray, how many you would like us to be; then drop your business, and by the back-door give the slip to the client waiting in your hall," 30–1). The closing gesture of the poem's last lines is appreciably different from that of 1, 4, but its function is largely the same: to "draw in" the recipient. And this lets us read these two very different invitations as complementary, a diptych.[24] The final "escape" through the back door (*postico falle clientem*, 31) marks a special intimacy between the men, an intimacy from which the nameless readers–*clientes* are locked out.

Earlier, in his first "conversational" effort (the *Satires*), as well as in the one stichic poem of his Epodes, Horace had used the metaphor of escape as a means of "exiting" the book: at the end of *Satires* 2.8 (with *fugimus* of line 93 governing the concluding period), and at the end of *Epodes* 17, with *exitus* of line 81 being the book's last word, set up by the *fuga* of *Epodes* 16.66.[25] The reader should be alert to the possible presence of a first incision in Book 1 of the Epistles between the fifth and sixth poems. For with *Epistles* 1.5 in fact, we are halfway to 1.10, the perfect number of the Eclogues and *Satires* Book 1, a number that will be doubled in *Epistles* 1.20.[26] Philosophical protreptic (made programmatic in *Epistles* 1.1.11) dominates in both poems 2 and 3 (esp. 25–9),[27] and it is still easily identifiable in poem 4 (where it is attributed to Albius). But by poem 5 it is watered down by the convivial atmosphere of the banquet. The idea that Horace is here the *Epicuri de grege porcus* is contradicted only superficially by the subsequent note of "moderation" sounded by *modica … patella* "a modest dish" (1.5.2). The book might have neatly ended its first act here, by promoting the values of a simple and measured symposium, in much the same way that the first book of the *Odes* ends with *Persicos odi, puer, apparatus* "I hate, boy, the Persian pomp."[28]

The motif of Torquatus' escape does not, however, signify a new beginning. In spite of what the numeric structure of the book might have given one to expect, the reader is thrown off guard by the next epistle: addressed to Numicius, it preaches that the key to happiness is found in *nil admirari* ("marvel at nothing")—referring to the man who is courageous enough to observe the mysterious regularity of the stars and the seasons (3–4) without trepidation. Maecenas is not, therefore, addressed anew as he was at this point of the book in *Satires* 1.6. Here his return is delayed to the seventh epistle, where his position as patron (and also as the book's honored dedicatee?) is highly problematic. Horace represents himself as absent or better still, delayed, and that is a delay sensed at the level of the book's arrangement as well—*Sextilem totum mendax desideror* ("I am missed the whole of *Sextilis* [= August]", 1.7.2).

Let's now take another look at what is, for good reason, commonly considered the natural fulcrum of a work based upon twenty compositions: the Virgilian boundary of ten. In the dedicatee of the tenth epistle, Aristius Fuscus, we once again have an elite recipient; like Horace, he is also a man of letters (grammarian and comic poet), included in the select group of friends and acquaintances of *Satires* 1.10.81–3:

> Plotius et Varius, Maecenas Vergiliusque,
> Valgius et probet haec Octavius optimus
> atque Fuscus et haec utinam Viscorum laudet uterque.

> Let but Plotius and Varius approve of these verses; let
> Maecenas, Virgil and Valgius; let Octavius and Fuscus, best
> of men; and let but the Viscus brothers give their praise!

Aristius Fuscus will have appreciated that his poet friend should now have singled him out from among all those old comrades:[29] if in the *Satires* he was featured in the tenth and final composition of the first book in the company of all those others, he now enjoys the exclusive privilege of the tenth spot, although this poem will merely conclude the first half of the collection and not the entire book (one might argue that *Satires* 1.10 also concludes the first half of the *Satires*, if taken as part of two volumes making up the whole).

In the opening lines of *Epistles* 10 Horace confirms the deep affinity that binds him to Fuscus, giving us to think that the two men understand one another completely. But right from the start he defines a crucial difference between them: *Urbis amatorem Fuscum salvere iubemus/ruris amatores* ("To Fuscus, lover of the city, I, a lover of the country, send greetings," 1–2). Here the reader is encouraged to recall that other memorable "urban" appearance of Fuscus in Horace in *Satires* 1.9. There Horace was caught up in the machinations of the so-called "pest," the enterprising man of letters who sought his support in order to gain entry to Maecenas' coterie. The affectionate terms on which the meeting with Aristius had occurred[30] temporarily deceive the poet into thinking that he has found a means of escape. Aristius, however, shows himself to be well versed in the art of *urbanitas*, intentionally playing the fool with a ready wit in order to avoid embarrassment—*male salsus/ridens dissimulare* ("the cruel joker laughed, pretending not to understand," 65–6); *hodie tricensima sabbata: vin tu/curtis Iudaeis oppedere?* ("to-day is the thirtieth Sabbath. Would you insult the circumcised Jews?" 69–70). Thus as Book I of *Satires* draws to its decimal point, we find Aristius Fuscus, the *urbanus*, as a joint-protagonist of *Satires* 1, 9 and then mentioned again in affectionate terms in *Satires* 1.10.

Returning to *Epistles* 1, we see that poem number nine again finds Horace subjected to aggressive social pressure in the person of a young writer who wants acceptance into a select circle (this time, however, Horace is no longer in the prime of life). The result of this solicitation is a masterpiece (and model) of the "calling card." In the course of its thirteen verses, which both open and close with the supplicant, *Septimius*, referred to in glowing terms (*hunc et fortem crede bonumque* ("and believe him brave and good," 13): a frame effect with noticeably "mnemonic" results), the epistle throws light on a complex web of social affairs. On one side we have the young Tiberius, whose name is deliberately split between line 1, where it appears beside that of Septimius, and line 4, where he is praised for his powers of discernment; on the other we have the young Septimius, who is both enterprising and esteemed. Standing between the two men is the poet Horace. It is not entirely clear whether the intentions of the poet are tongue in cheek or mildly malicious, but what is apparent is that the epistle attempts to "repeat" *Satires* 1.9: if Tiberius, albeit somewhat predictably, inherits the discerning patron's role that had previously belonged to Maecenas,[31] Horace behaves rather as he had long ago during that unforeseen encounter on the Via Sacra, proffering a multitude of excuses in order to make a "face-saving escape."[32] Horace thus risks becoming a "dissembler" who intentionally belittles himself to avoid sharing his success with others: *dissimulator opis propriae* ("like a dissembler of my real power," 9).[33] Septimius also resembles that old "pest," from whom he is kept separate only by the light-hearted tone that Horace uses in line 2: *rogat et prece cogit.* The underlying irony in *nimirum*, to which the *novit me valdius ipso* of line 6 responds, is enough to express the satirical potential of the situation. Perhaps, though, the passing of the years, with a change of circumstances and protagonists, the poet's increased fame, or even the simple lack of an Apolline intervention, have blocked Horace's path of escape, forcing him instead to yield to the "ways of the city"—*frontis ... urbanae* (11).[34]

It is as a lover and connoisseur of the city that Aristius Fuscus is called to the fore in the next epistle, a poem that styles itself as an exaltation of the simplicity of a life lived in the country, far from the ambitions and political machinations of the city that are so eloquently portrayed in *Epistles* 1.9. We have no way of knowing whether Aristius Fuscus ever received this letter as a single *charta*; but we can be reasonably sure that, as he thumbed through the *liber*, he would have been amused to find himself right beside a poem where Horace is once again being pressured to give in and cough up a recommendation. As in the Satires, Aristius once again finds himself in the role of a witness to the adventures and misadventures of his poet friend in the "big" city, and once again this happens in the ninth and tenth poems. Again we have the sense of returning, of walking back along that old familiar path that runs along the Via Sacra through the heart of the city, straight back to Book I of the Satires.[35]

In depicting the literary environment of writer friends and illustrious patrons in *Satires* 1.10 at the close of the *libellus*, Horace was reproducing in satire what Virgil had himself previously toyed with in the erotic-elegiac tale of Cornelius Gallus in the tenth eclogue, where he opened a window to an extra-bucolic world of poets and literary genres. In the Epistles the figure of Aristius Fuscus, by evoking the memory of the last two satires of Book I, underlines the passage from the first to the second group of ten poems. This helps to explain the strong closural effect produced by the last words of *Epistles* 1.10, enhanced by the framing repetition of *laetus* in line 44 and line 50 (in one case referring to Aristius, in the other, to Horace himself). In addressing himself to his recipient with *tibi*, the poet at the same time puts a certain distance between himself and his work, and this is a detachment well timed for reaching a significant editorial "boundary": *haec tibi dictabam post fanum putre Vacunae,/excepto quod non simul esses, cetera laetus* ("these lines I am dictating to you behind Vacuna's crumbling shrine, happy on all counts save that you are not with me," 49–50): cf. *Satires* 1.10.92 *i, puer, atque meo citus haec subscribe libello* ("Go, boy, and quickly add these lines to my little book").

"Interval" on the Thirteenth Epistle, Vinnius Asina, and Augustus

Following *Epistles* 1.12, addressed to a certain Iccius who was known to have cultivated an interest in the scientific systems of Lucretius (the cosmic "mysteries" of *Epistles* 1.6 reappear in lines 16–20) the reader finds himself grappling with volumes already polished and ready:

> Ut proficiscentem docui te saepe diuque,
> Augusto reddes signata volumina, Vinni,
> si validus, si laetus erit, si denique poscet;
> ne studio nostri pecces odiumque libellis
> sedulus inportes opera vehemente minister. (1.13.1–5)

> As I instructed you often and at length, when you set out, Vinius, you will deliver these close-sealed rolls to Augustus, *if* he's well, *if* he's in good spirits, *if*—in fine—he asks for them; lest you blunder in your eagerness for me, and by officious service and excessive zeal bring resentment on my poor works.

The plural nouns *volumina* and *libellis* leave no doubt, even in the case of an initial (and naive) reading, that we are not dealing here with one book of the Epistles. If we are to follow the most widely held and probable interpretation,[36] the books in question are Horace's three volumes of Odes. This assumption gains further credence from the lowly and fearful tone adopted by Horace in offering his advice. If approached at an inopportune time, Augustus would hate the poet's work (3–5), and thus he seems, despite the passing of time, the same unpredictable man he was in *Satires* 2.1, where he was compared to a nervous steed—... *cui male si palpere, recalcitrat undique tutus* "stroke clumsily and back he kicks, at every point on his guard" (20). At that time Trebatius beseeched Horace to "at the very least" recognize and praise the virtues of Caesar (as Lucilius had already done with Scipio), and the poet committed himself to fulfilling this request from that point forward (*Satires* 2.1.16–19). Indeed, by the time he was writing Book I of the *Epistles*, the three books of the Odes (even if this applies most obviously to "Roman Odes") must have been considered the realization of that promise.

Nevertheless, even though it treats a work that is separate from the Epistles themselves, *Epistles* 1.13 introduces the idea of the "book" as an entity that the poet sends off, destined for travels, adventures, and receptions that are not always possible to predict, and that one might well expect to be unpleasant. Yet here it is Vinnius Asina, the recipient of the epistle, who assumes the role of "mediator," or better still, "carrier."[37] This anticipates the final poem, where the poet will send off the book itself: in signing off his letter to Vinnius, we sense that Horace is letting his books go, detaching himself from volumes that are so precious to their author.[38]

Inside the frame II: Lollius and Maecenas (in reverse order)

We last encountered Lollius as the book's second "inset" addressee:[39] in poem 2 he was part of the *comitatus* of Tiberius, that group of youths who were no strangers to the Muses and who found themselves following in the footsteps of Horace, "companion" to Maecenas. Then near the center of the book, Horace's *amicitia* has a social purpose in following up on Septimius' ardent wish to be accepted into the circle of Tiberius. In the letters that follow, Horace is once again in intimate dialogue with his friends, including Aristius Fuscus and with Iccius who also cultivates interests *de rerum natura*. In fact, upon the conclusion of the epistle to Iccius, and immediately before the "eccentric" missive to Vinnius, the poet does not fail to turn once again to the task of making a recommendation (the beneficiary this time is Pompeius Grosphus, and it comes with the famous aphorism: *vilis amicorum est annona, bonis ubi quid dest* ("the market-price of friends is low, when good men are in need," 1.12.24); nor does he pass up the opportunity to remember Tiberius' great exploit: ... *Claudi virtute Neronis/Armenius cecidit; ius imperiumque Phraates/Caesaris accepit genibus minor; aurea fruges/Italiae pleno defundit Copia cornu* ("the Armenian has fallen before the valour of Claudius Nero; Phraates, on humbled knees, has accepted Caesar's imperial sway; golden Plenty from full horn has poured her fruits upon Italy," 26–9).[40]

To encounter once again the theme (crudely put) of "literature and power," we have to run up against book's "second frame." In *Epistles* 1.17, a précis of the art of dealing with powerful men (*quo ... pacto deceat maioribus uti*, "on what terms one should handle greater folk"), we once again find ourselves tracking memories of the young Horace in the image of a novice *comes* in lines 52–7: *Brundisium comes aut Surrentum ductus amoenum/qui queritur salebras et acerbum frigus et imbres* ("The man who, when taken as companion to Brundisium or lovely Surrentum, grumbles about bad roads and bitter cold and rain etc."). By now from a distance of many years, *Satires* 1.5 confirms itself as a text relevant to the fragile relationship between patron and client: in that poem the young Horace had proved that he could take a humorous view of his adventures and misadventures (e.g., the rain of lines 94–5), that he could complain, but still avoid (though perhaps just barely) the malice of the plaintive *meretrix*.

It is in moving on to *Epistles* 1.18, however, that the reader re-encounters the problem of client–patron relations in terms that are specific to the scholar–poet: in setting the frame that corresponds to 1.2 the poet revisits that poem's young recipient, Lollius. In the opening lines of 1.18 Horace recalls the journey to

Brundisium, describing it once again in terms of "comfort" (*Brundisium Minuci melius via ducat an Appi* ("which is the better road to Brundisium, that of Minucius or that of Appius," 20: by now it is the parasitic *amicus* who quarrels over the matter). Moving on to lines 39–40, the focus narrows to pursuits of a conspicuously literary kind: *nec, cum venari volet ille, poemata panges* ("nor, when your friend would go a-hunting, will you penning poems," 40; cf. 47–8). The question of his own personal time, or more specifically, how best to protect himself from the immoderate expectations of a socially unbalanced *amicitia*, was clearly a matter of general interest in Horace's day. Staying on the subject of *Satires* 1.5, it is clear that when Horace had described his patron going to play ball while he and Virgil went off to rest (48–9), not only was Horace poking fun at his own physical weakness, but he was also emphasizing the relaxed and unhurried climate of Maecenas' circle. Thus it is interesting to note the pastime that the enterprising Lollius had chosen for himself in order to fill the days of leisure spent with his brother in their native countryside (*rure paterno*):

> ac ne te retrahas et inexcusabilis absis:
> quamvis nil extra numerum fecisse modumque
> curas, interdum nugaris rure paterno:
> partitur lintres exercitus, Actia pugna
> te duce per pueros hostili more refertur;
> adversarius est frater, lacus Hadria, donec
> alterutrum velox Victoria fronde coronet.
> consentire suis studiis qui crediderit te,
> fautor utroque tuum laudabit pollice ludum. (58–66)

> Further, that you may not draw back and stand aloof
> without excuse, bear in mind that, however much you
> take care to do nothing out of time and tune, you do
> sometimes amuse yourself at your father's country-seat:
> your troops divide the skiffs; with you as captain, the
> Actian fight is presented by your slaves in true foemen's
> style; opposing you is your brother, the lake is the
> Adriatic; till winged Victory crowns with leafage one or
> the other chieftain. He who believes that you fall in with
> his pursuits will with both thumbs eagerly commend
> your sport.

The world which this new generation of young writers inhabits is a strange one: the victorious battle of Actium celebrated by Horace in *Odes* 1.37 (and much mythologised by all the previous generation of poets, including Virgil and Propertius) is now, in the time of the *Pax Augusta* (in which this same Lollius had played an active role: lines 54–7), merely a ludic naumachia[41]. What a tremendous struggle it was for Horace to find time for himself on his Sabine estate (the unhoped-for gift of Maecenas) in *Satires* Book 2! But here we have the two brothers, relaxed as were the Scipiones and Lucilius in the golden era of the Republic (cf. *Satires* 2.1.71–4), enjoying the battle of Actium on their pond, dividing between themselves the roles of Antony and Caesar, until the "hasty" Victory should decide who would hold the palm aloft.[42] All the while, in the background, they have the leisurely peace of their ancestral home (Horace had lost his family estate by fighting in another battle, one that was all too real).

After Lollius comes Maecenas (*Epistles* 1.19). And thus we have the powerful patron and the young scholar seeking protection; the past and the present. The book returns to a discussion of literature, the topic with which it began, before finally reaching its conclusion; the third address to Maecenas, coming before the book's send-off, sounds a note of finality.[43]

Clear correspondences with *Satires* 1.10 should call our attention to the retrospective nature of the text; that is, just as the conclusion to Book I of the Satires reconsiders statements made earlier in the book about the poet's predecessor (1.10.1), *Epistles* 1.19 revisits a point taken up in the first poems of the book (particularly in letters 2 and 3), namely, imitation. And as he had done before in *Satires* 1.10, Horace once again turns to ancient comedy—quite opportunely represented this time, as we shall see, by Cratinus—in search of a foundation for his own "literary-critical" reasoning.

The urgency of this theme is underscored, as if set in "negative" relief, by the poet's departure from normal epistolary customs. In place of the conventional opening salutation, we dive straight into a debate that is heavy on mimetic vivacity. According to Demetrius (*De eloc.* 223), it seems that Artemon, the editor of Aristotle's letters, had himself acknowledged the inevitably dialogical nature of the epistolary form. For his part, Demetrius observed that one should be careful to avoid excessive "mimeticism," for example in the over-use of interruptions like the ones employed in the prologue of the *Euthydemus* (which, as one sees in the quotation that Demetrius extracts from Plato's text, include both direct interrogatives and interjections [226]). *Epistles* 1.19 does in fact contain an interrogative pronoun in the *quid?* of line 12, as well as the frequent employment of lively conversational shifts, such as the *scire uelis* of line 35 (not to mention the involvement of the interlocutor in line 26: *ne me foliis brevioribus ornes* "and lest you should crown me with a scantier wreath"). Furthermore, frequent use of "conversational verbs" tangle the page with an overabundance of speech marks (*hoc simul edixi*, 10; from 43 all the way to *"displicet iste locus"*, *clamo* in line 47). *Dicere* is without a doubt an essential verb in any epistle that would seek to address issues of imitation and individual poetic expression, and it is in this light that Horace turns to consider his past experience (add here: *non alio dictum prius ore* of line 32; but previously in 7–8: *ad arma/... dicenda*). In line 10 the idea of "speaking" or "saying" is expressed in the solemn terms of a formal "edict"; the context is as follows:

> "Forum putealque Libonis
> mandabo siccis, adimam cantare severis":
> hoc simul edixi, non cessavere poetae
> nocturno certare mero, putere diurno. (*Epistles* 1.19.8–11)

> "To the sober I shall assign the Forum and Libo's Well; the
> stern I shall debar from song". Ever since I put forth this edict,
> poets have never ceased to vie in wine-drinking by night, to
> reek of it by day.

The form *edixi* appears in the text of current editions: supporting it is the use of the first person singular in lines 17–18 *quodsi/pallerem* (Fraenkel 1957: 340, n. 6) and once again in line 43 *si dixi*, an instance where one encounters an analogous rhetorical-syntactical structuring, with a shift into direct discourse, a saying's attribution at the beginning of the verse, and a consequence among the poet's "public" of learned readers (41–5). On the other hand, nowhere in his works does Horace deliver an edict that resembles this one even remotely. The edict is especially unusual for its authoritarian tone: Horace is generally averse to making such "proclamations" (even within this epistle one should consider the understated demeanor of lines 41–2: it is others who imitate him without being asked!). It's fully conceivable, then, that the alternate reading, *edixit*, might deserve some consideration.[44] But whether or not we wish to attribute the words to Horace or Ennius, the edict of lines 8–9 puts us in mind of an earlier discussion of imitation, understood in much broader social terms. I am referring to a specific section of the first epistle:

> "O cives, cives, quaerenda pecunia primum est:
> virtus post nummos": haec Ianus summus ab imo (1.1.53–5)
> prodocet, haec recinunt iuvenes dictata senesque

> "O citizens, citizens, money you first must seek; virtue after
> lucre." This rule the Janus arcade proclaims from top to
> bottom; this is the lesson the old as well as the young are
> singing.

This request, framing the front end of the book, seems to suggest that there is no great difference between the mania for cash promoted by Janus,[45] and the demands exerted by literary fashions *à la mode*. In any case, there is in both cases a chorus ready to reiterate and acquiesce (*haec recinunt iuvenes dictata senesque* ≈ *non cessavere poetae/nocturno certare mero, putere diurno*). In the book's second epistle Horace had advanced the problem of what could be termed correct poetic and moral "exemplification" (namely the *utile exemplar* of Homer, provided that is correctly interpreted); but now, in his penultimate epistle, addressed to Maecenas, the process of imitation and its potential for debasement are both examined and explained. It is thus, as motifs carved into an outer frame, that Horace has reintroduced themes and forms from the beginning to the end of the book.

"Personal" revelations: Horace's *sermo* from the Satires to the Epistles

According to Demetrius, the letter must reveal something about the character (*ēthos*) of the individual.[46] It might be said, then, that the letter intensifies an existing trait of literary communication; namely, the profound connection already established by Aristotelian theory with the "nature," or better still, the "character" of the individual.[47] From this premise, we can understand just why *Epistles* 1.19 appears so well placed in a collection of epistles written by a poet (and furthermore, with Maecenas as recipient, in a conspicuous position prior to the poet's farewell). Whatever the reasons, polemical or otherwise, that Horace may have had for writing *Epistles* 1.19, he must have seen, in his inevitably "self-revelatory" epistolary collection, the perfect opportunity for expressing his own ideas about the connection between "character" and "poetry"—for that is precisely the issue at stake in his treatment of the topic of imitation. Notwithstanding their specific significance to Horace himself, Archilochus and Alcaeus, the two authors focussed on in *Epistles* 1.19, were considered exemplars of poetry that gave direct access to their own deepest feelings, speaking as strong characters expressed through strong poetic forms.[48] His ability to play on the emotive sensibilities of his reader, especially the young reader, made it seem that Archilochus was endowed with a rather suspicious character;[49] this helps explain the marked distance which Horace places between Alcaeus and one of Archilochus most notorious exploits, the suicide of Lycambes and his daughter—*nec socerum quaerit, quem versibus oblinat atris,/ nec sponsae laqueum famoso carmine nectit* ("looking for no father-in-law to besmear with deadly verses, and weaving no halter for his bride with defaming rhyme," 30–1).

The sum of these factors that push the poet towards self-revelation in the Epistles make it all the more surprising that the first letter should open on a sense of the poet's being closed off: for here, as we have seen, we find Horace adopting a completely introspective stance, interested only in the accumulation of knowledge for his own use. Such a paradox does, however, have a precedent in the first of Horace's *sermones*, in his Satires, for the author of those earlier "conversations" had already depicted himself as a silent, if not taciturn, individual (in *Satires* 1.3, 1.6, and 1.9), a trait which returns again in *Epistles* 2.2.83 (even his patron had shown himself to be a man of few words on the occasion of their first meeting: 1.6.60–1, *respondes, ut tuus est mos,/pauca*). In order to render his hexametric "prose" all the more confidential and to further develop it into a reflection of his own soul, Horace must also resist promoting it. Such a mechanism had been recognised by the poet himself in his satiric predecessor: Lucilius would turn to books as if to "friends" (*sodalibus*), confiding in them his personal secrets, and *for this very reason* (*quo fit ut*) his life "revealed itself" (*pateat*) to everyone through his works, just as if drawn on a *votiva tabella* (*Satires* 2.1.30–4).

Horace has not held back in mimicking some typical epistolary techniques in his letters, and yet one does not have the impression that they engage in genuine exchanges of information or that they are linked to specific situations (here we are touching again on the tired, and by now, exhausted topic of their being fictitious and not "really" sent). Even in the one rare case where we can make a comparison with the poet's satiric predecessor, Lucilius, who also wrote at least one epistolographic poem, we can note a clear difference between them: in fr. 181–3 M. = 186–188 W. Lucilius addresses his recipient in a direct and somewhat resentful tone (to inform him, it would seem, of the actual state of his health); in *Epistles* 1.8, however, Horace sends his recipient a set of playful mediations that render his letter's message distant and abstract.[50]

It would be naive, however, to take the writer's reticence about his practical circumstances and his daily life (and this applies to his addressees as well) as evidence of an incomplete "epistolarity." If Lollius, Celsus, or Iccius, the highly refined Aristius Fuscus, or even the "honest critic" Albius (Tibullus) actually received their letters before reading them in the book, they would have been able to appreciate fully the intimate and confidential nature of those hexametric poems. Herein lies the heart of the matter, for friends and friendship play a crucial role in Book I of the Epistles.[51] Even if the poet addresses himself to one of these friends in order to extract a specific piece of information (e.g., of a touristic nature, to Numonius Vala), or for an invitation to supper (to Torquatus), this is always a starting point for the poet's introspection, for a look within that uncovers (perhaps to set them loose) anxieties and joys that are hidden deep inside. These addressees, therefore, are "friends" in the sense of "confidantes," like the book-*sodales* of Lucilius.

This would also explain why in Book I Horace avoided addressing letters to excessively illustrious figures: if his recipients are of a higher class (such as Tiberius), they are extremely young. Those recipients chosen by Horace as analogues for himself, whether they match him in wealth or in social position, are otherwise generally of his own age. Horace has deliberately chosen to avoid the pattern of the "letter to the king," which instead he will cultivate in the special epistle to Augustus (*Epistles* 1.13 assumes the inapproachability of the prince). In the Epistles and elsewhere, Maecenas himself appears to serve a series of specific purposes, and in this way, he almost ceases to be readable as a real individual;[52] he does not interrupt or disturb the mirror game that takes place between the author and his text: the epistle can thus come back to the one who sent it; it can speak to Horace about Horace.

The fact that Horace regards his poems as a sort of substitute of his own individuality and experience (the *bíos* or *votiva tabella*), means that their very connections to one another, their specific passages and structures, lend themselves to being interpreted in a personalized sense. The poet's emotions, even those of a contradictory or thoughtless nature, are reflected through these "editorial" means. This self-expressive function is much more pronounced in the letter, a poem written to be sent, and that lends itself to be exploring the connections between literature, thought, and personal experience. The first book of the Epistles is even better explained as a message of a poet to other poets and to men of letters (and *sodales*), and it is exactly here that it looks ahead to the great "literary" epistles of Book 2 and the *Ars*.[53] When Horace employs the term *persona* in reference to Aristippus, he takes for granted the term's social significance: in his eyes, the philosopher Aristippus, as opposed to the cynical Diogenes, is capable of switching from one "mask" to the other with masterly self-assurance: crucial is *personamque feret non inconcinnus utramque* ("and in no inelegant fashion will play either part," 1.17.29; but it is worth reading lines 27–32). For Horace, the philosopher stands as a legitimate model of conduct, but only on the condition that he remains in control of his own choices and continues to be open to a range of moral standpoints, never adhering slavishly to any one school. Notwithstanding the poet's initial assertion that he followed no one school, or better still, that he was "self-taught" (1.1.14 and 27), scholars still struggle to pin Horace down to a specific philosophical school.[54] But, beyond the question of his having any specific allegiance, it should be clear that the figure of Socrates is fundamental to Horace's philosophical thinking, especially insofar as Socrates devoted himself to a free and ongoing moral search (no matter how mediated or mythologized that search might end up). It is Horace himself who describes his education and reading, telling us that he attended the Academy in Athens (*Epistles* 2.2.45) and exhorting his reader to use the *Socraticae chartae* as a source of philosophical subjects (*Ars* 309–322). Nevertheless, at the time he wrote the Satires, the young Horace was spied reading Plato in his Sabine villa, evidently intent on using him as a model of "subjects" (*res*) and ideas. Correspondingly, *Satires* 2.4 contains a scenario in the style of a Platonic dialogue that hints specifically at the *Phaedrus*.[55]

The *Phaedrus* could, furthermore, prove the source from which Horace derives his programmatic image of the "pantry" or "storeroom" at the beginning of the first epistle. There, as mentioned above, Horace declares a desire to "store up and arrange," in order later to make use of, his personally acquired wisdom (*condo et compono quae mox depromere possim*, 12). This image finds a precise precedent in Socrates' address to Phaedrus:

No. The gardens of letters he will, it seems, plant for amusement, and will write, when he writes, to treasure up reminders for himself, when he comes to the forgetfullness of old age, and for others who follow the same path, and he will be pleased when he sees them putting forth tender leaves. When others engage in other amusements, refreshing themselves with banquets and kindred entertainments, he will pass the time in such pleasures as I have suggested. (Plat., *Phaedr.* 276d; trans. H. N. Fowler)

The *mox* of Horace alludes precisely to an "old age" (the *gêras* of Plato) during which the individual may finally call upon his "treasure" of knowledge (*hypomnēmata thesaurizomenos*).[56] The opposition Socrates describes between duty and "diversion" (*paidiais*; cf. also 276b, e), finds its analogy in the confrontation of Horace between the "accumulation" of wisdom and the "carefree" fancies of poetry (as well as the pleasures it brings).[57]

With its conspicuous inaugural position, the image of the *Phaedrus* allows Horace to pick up the thread of his satiric "discourse": there was much emphasis (and with good reason) on the importance of the Socratic *persona* in the two volumes of the Satires.[58] And the epistolary Horace seems not to have forgotten his Socratic education: for it was thought that Socrates, even before Plato, had written the first "philosophical" epistles.[59]

Once more, therefore, we find Horace returning to himself, retracing his steps from the Epistles back to the Satires. The introduction of the ant, a patient little hoarder (with its own storage larder: *Satires* 1.1.35, *non incauta futuri*), in the first satire of the first book allowed the poet to communicate the *elementa* of wisdom with a playful smile (ibid., 26), but it would now appear that he must abandon all ditties and tricks of old and dedicate himself to a philosophical didaxis that instructs primarily himself—*restat ut his ego me ipse regam solerque elementis* ("what remains is for me to guide and solace myself with these poor rudiments," *Epistles* 1.1.27).

Farewell

Horace's drive towards freedom (freedom even from the confines of poetry that is sometimes "monumental") may perhaps help to explain his fondness for verbs of movement, which are often connected specifically to the idea of "escape," in poems of closure. In *Epistles* 1.20 this movement of flight is a feature of the book itself:

> Vortumnum Ianumque, liber, spectare videris,
> scilicet ut prostes Sosiorum pumice mundus;
> odisti clavis et grata sigilla pudico,
> paucis ostendi gemis et communia laudas,
> non ita nutritus: fuge quo descendere gestis.
> non erit emisso reditus tibi. (*Epistles* 1.20.1–6)

> You seem, my book, to be looking wistfully toward
> Vertumnus and Janus, in order, forsooth, that you may

> go on sale, neatly polished with the pumice of the Sosii.
> You hate the keys and seals, so dear to the modest; you
> grieve at being shown to few, and praise a life in public,
> though I did not rear you thus. Off with you, down to
> where you itch to go. When you are once let out, there
> will be no coming back.

The idea of "sending," etymologically implied by the word *epistolē*, which the first epistle had redefined, is referred to as something fulfilled in the closing lines: *fuge quo descendere gestis./non erit <u>emisso</u> reditus tibi* (5–6). It is in fact the *liber* that wishes to extricate itself from intimacy with a poet who reminds him of how he had been brought up for a better purpose: the collection of letters had been "nourished" on what common sense discards, on introspection, which is the fruit of a mind entirely obsessed by a desire to "hide" and "set in store" (for itself). Instead, Horace's Epistles now set their sights on Janus, from whose "enticing" call the poet had previously wished to distance himself in the first epistle (*Ianus summus ab imo/prodocet*, 54–5):[60] these letters wish to be on their way, as any epistle would. The *libellus* of the Epistles, we have seen, ambles over paths already trod by the Satires: it rediscovers those poems, observing differences and analogies, and it lets us feel the pleasures of the return. But suddenly, now, there is a risk of following the book along the wrong path, to end up at a dead-end:

> hoc quoque te manet, ut pueros elementa docentem
> occupet extremis in vicis balba senectus. (17–18)

> This fate, too, awaits you, that stammering age will
> come upon you as you teach boys their ABC in the city's
> outskirts.

Here at the end, there is a risk of concluding the journey in a forbidden place, in the very schoolroom that the young Horace thought so beneath his efforts at the end of *Satires* Book 1: *an tua demens/vilibus in ludis dictari carmina malis?* ("what, would you be so foolish as to want your poems dictated in common schools?," 1.10.75–6).[61] Perhaps this was Horace's way of preparing himself for the inevitability of his soon becoming a "classic": and so it is to this "kid" that he is resigned to entrust his self-portrait (his *votiva tabella?*)—... *corporis exigui, praecanum, solibus aptum* ("of small stature, grey before my time, fond of the sun").

GUIDE TO FURTHER READING

While the resources available for the study of the first book of Horace's Epistles are vast, they have become considerably more manageable in recent years thanks to the comprehensive bibliographical synthesis and systemization of the *Enciclopedia Oraziana* (established by F. Della Corte, edited under the direction of S. Mariotti, in three volumes, Rome, 1996–8). I have included references to numerous works in the notes, where my primary concerns were with the philosophical concept of the book, and in particular Horace's poetic-epistolary techniques. Concerning the editorial structures of Horace's poetry books, still seminal is Zetzel (1980: 59–77). The concept of "closure" that I have used in the pages above naturally owes much to Don Fowler 1989.

In working through the argument I laid out above, my reader will recognize that, as far as I am concerned, one of the best "further readings" available for deepening our understanding of Horace's first book of letters is to be found in one's own rereading of Horace himself. For the interpretation of a work that is, so to speak, "posthumous" (in the sense that it pushes past the confines of the poet's mortal frame by inviting us to imagine the poems' subsequent receptions among later readers) new possibilities can always arise from fresh encounters with the Satires, the Epodes, and the Odes. To this end it is also useful to move on from one's own reading of "Horace with Horace" into Persius' reading of Horace, because Persius constantly prompts us to remember our encounters with Horace by recovering and freely mixing into his Satires the themes and imagery of his predecessor (and in particular those of his Epistles) so as to tease out and valorize certain aspects of what they say or might be taken to imply.

For the task of reading "Horace with Horace" commentaries are indispensable. The German commentaries of Kiessling and Heinze (1957; but published in multiple editions since 1930) are still valuable, and the recent commentaries of Mayer (1994) and Fedeli (1997) are both reliable and insightful. The latter is in Italian, and it is especially helplful for providing a rich bibliography and ample bibliographical discussion. Also occasionally useful is the French commentary of Préaux (1968). Fraenkel (1957) remains a fundamental point of departure (and often of arrival) for the study of Horace's Epistles. The pages of his ample book are worth consulting: they are good to think with and, quite often, to disagree with. A complex and stimulating complement to the argument that I have made above, touching as it often does on the concept of freedom (*libertas*) in book one of the Epistles, is Johnson (1993).

NOTES

* I would like to thank Kirk Freudenburg, Luigi Galasso, and Victoria Rimell for their generosity in offering to read and comment upon the pages that follow. Translations of Satires and Epistles are taken, with some slight and rare infidelity, from H. Rushton Fairclough (*Satires, Epistles and Ars Poetica, with an English translation*. Cambridge, MA: Harvard University Press, 1929).

1 The dispute over this matter between Fraenkel 1957: 308–63 and Williams 1968: 1–30, is aptly defined by Harrison 1995b: 48, n. 1, as "a distant Titanomachy." On the audience of the Epistles, both specific addressees and a more general public, see Citroni 1995: 345–59.

2 Harrison 1995: 50; on Horace's *Epistles* 1.1 regarding Maecenas and lyric poetry, see Freudenburg 2002a.

3   See in particular the commentary of Mayer 1994: 90; Fedeli 1997: 989; to the image of the "store" (or "treasure"?) we shall return: pp. 309–10.

4   On the genuine presence of Aristippian thought in Horace, Traina 1991.

5   We will limit ourselves to a brief selection of passages: 1.1.90 and 97–100, 1.2, 41–3, 1.7, 10–13, 1.8, 12, 1.14, 10–13 (at times also a sort of "reversibility" that secures salvation, as we see in the two parables: 1.1 esp. 75 *retrorsum*; 1.7, esp. 33 *repetes*). In the midst of such changing feelings and events is Eutrapelus who appears like a comic hero, in the habit of effecting (for his own amusement) changes in the lives of others: *cuicumque nocere volebat/vestimenta dabat pretiosa* (1.18.31–2)—in his very *cognomen* is contained the notion of "change": *eutrapelos* from *trepo*, and, therefore, "versatile" (so, "astute," "witty": his Latin name was *Volumnius*).

6   This sense of an editorial continuity between the Satires and the Epistles (in the common setting of the satiric genre, i.e., as *sermones*) did not escape the notice of Porphyrio: see again his commentary on *Satires* 1.1.1; cf. also ad *Epistles* 1.1.1. On *Epistles* 1 as belonging to "satire," Braund 1992; an updated bibliographic discussion can be found in de Pretis 2002: 99–101.

7   We refer here to the valuable synthesis offered by Kilpatrick 1996: 305; cf. Radke 1996: 781b; also Fraenkel 1957: 314–15. We might add that it is on the name of Lollius, the consul of 21 BCE (the father of Lollius Maximus?), that the book closes: ... *collegam Lepidum quo duxit* [or *dixit*?] *Lollius anno*.

8   Again, Kilpatrick 1996. The significance of the recipient was not overlooked by the rhetorical tradition of epistolary technique (Demetrius, *De eloc.* 234): it seems all the more natural, therefore, that the recipients could exert an influence over the criteria for collecting and arranging the single epistles into one volume.

9   On the usefulness of reading the Epistles in order, see: Ferri 2007: 125, with bibliography: nn. 16 and 17; also Morrison 2006: esp. 44–5.

10 Mayer 1994: 112 to line 4, elegantly intuits the implication.

11 It also constitutes a return, along with Homer, to the roots of his own schooling, as Horace himself must have been readily aware: *Romae nutriri mihi contigit, atque doceri/iratus Grais quantum nocuisset Achilles* ("At Rome I had the luck to be bred, and taught how much Achilles' wrath had harmed the Greeks," *Epistles* 2.2, 41–2).

12 With many memorable one-liners: *sapere aude*, 40; *nocet empta dolore voluptas*, 55; *ira furor brevis est*, 62 ("dare to be wise"; "pleasure bought with pain is harmful"; "anger is short-lived madness").

13 *Ars* 450: *fiet Aristarchus*.

14 Porph. ad *Epist.* 1.3.1. The sense of a mirroring between Horace and his young correspondent might also be found in the second epistle of the second book, where the poet offers up a good deal of autobiographical information: Freudenburg 2002b. It goes without saying that the differences between the two, not least the "professional" ones, are anything but irrelevant: *seu linguam causis acuis seu civica iura/respondere paras* ("whether you sharpen your tongue for pleading, or essay to give advice on civil law," 1.3.23–4).

15 On the dialectic of centre and periphery in Latin culture and literature see Barchiesi 2005. Alexandria and Rome had already enjoyed two centuries of lively political, diplomatic and cultural relations: Lampela 1998.

16 *Nobilium scriptorum auditor et ultor*, as he will define himself in *Epistles* 1.19.39. On the cure for the *exemplaria Graeca* we naturally call to mind *Ars* 268–9. The accusation of "plagiarism," whether real or assumed, is typical of a lively and competitive cultural environment, previously seen, to cite one example, in the times of Aristophanes: cf. *Nub.* 553–554.

17 Cf. Acosta-Hughes 2002: 41–2. A little further on the image morphs into that of the swarm of flies or wasps: 26–8; *Dieg.* VI, 5 *kat' éilas* (cf. *examen* in *Epistles* 1.19, 23).

18 A zoomorphic transformation into birds appeared previously for the Telchines in the prologue of the *Aitia*, fr. 1.1 Pf. *epitruzousin*. On men of letters and poets as birds see Theocr., *Id.* 7.47 *Moisân orniches* (the "imitators" of Homer); and also Timon., *Sill.* fr. 12 (but previously Pind., *Ol.* 2.86–8); on Horace himself as a bird see *Epist.* 1.20.21 *maiores pinnas nido extendisse loqueris*. On the complex relationship between Horace and Callimachus (as well as relevant bibliography), see Cucchiarelli 2001: 172–9, with bibliography; poets as birds reappear in Persius' *Choliambs* (see Freudenburg 2001: esp. 140–2).

19 See Fedeli's introduction to the epistle (1997: 1056); for cautionary notes, see Mayer 1994: 133, ad v. 1.

20 On this theme see Citti forthcoming.

21 This also has been thrown into doubt.

22 Cf. 1.5.4, *bibes*, with Citti's commentary 1994: 138. On *viso* in the sense of "to go and see, visit" cf. *Satires* 1.9.17; *OLD*, 2077, s.v. 3b. The comparison with Philodemos is relevant, *Epigr.* 27.5–6, Sider, ἀλλ' ἑτάρους ὄψει παναληθέας, ἀλλ' ἐπακούσῃ/Φαιήκων γαίης πουλὺ μελιχρότερα ("but you will see real friends and listen to tales much more delicious than the land of Phaeacians," *AP* 11.44.5–6 = 23, 5–6 G–P), with Sider's commentary 1997: esp. 158–9 (note the Odyssean reference to the Phaeacians).

23 Where one sees at least in part the audacity of the celebrated *Epigr.* 2.3 Pf. = *AP* 7.80.3.

24 It is also worth noting the effect of contrast and humorous variation which characterizes the succession of closures in 1.3 and 1.4: from the *votiva iuvenca* for the return of friends (1.3.36) to the *porcus* which awaits Albius.

25 The lines preceding the end of *Satires* 2.7.117–18 are also strongly "kinetic": *ocius hinc te/ni rapis*; more in Cucchiarelli 2008: 99, n. 2. The idea of escape as liberation, but in the eschatological sense of death, appears at the close of *Epistles* 1.16.78–9.

26 *Epistles* 1.5 also establishes a certain equilibrium in the number of verses it contains (*Epistles* 1–5 number 262 verses, in contrast to the 246 verses of *Epistles* 6–10, which make a total of 508 *verses*). It is only in his debut *libellus*, and in the "prosaic" dimension of the *Satires*, that Horace has perfectly adopted Virgil's decimal structure, placing the "second proem" at the opening of the second half of the collection (*Satires* 1.6.1; cf. obviously *Ecl.* 6.1 *Prima Syracosio* eqs.). But a decimal sequence is clearly identifiable in the first section of the Epodes as well as *Odes* 1 (not without the articulation of the first group of five: a prologic note is recognizable in *Epodes* 6 as well as *Odes* 1.6): Cucchiarelli 2008: 93, n. 1, with bibliography.

27 The grouping in threes, begun in the first three epistles, will be found again in the second part of the book, in 14–16 and 17–19.

28   Here, as if "opposed" to the *Persici apparatus,* are the *Archiacis ... lectis;* add 1.5,
     8 *mitte levis spes* ≈ 1.38.3 *mitte sectari.* On a calmer and more rarefied tone we find
     in *Epistles* 1.5 the dialectic between wisdom and the pleasures of the symposium that
     is typical of Horace: La Penna 1968: lxxxv–lxxxix = 1993: 104–10.

29   On the features that qualify him as a privileged reader of Horace see Biondi
     1996.

30   *Satires* 1.9.61, *mihi carus et illum/qui pulchre nosset* ("a dear friend of mine, who
     knew the fellow right well") (note the acknowledgement of his worldly
     perspicacity).

31   *dignum mente domoque legentis honesta Neronis* ("worthy of the mind and house of
     Nero," 4); cf. *Satires* 1.9.44, *paucorum hominum et mentis bene sanae* ("a man of
     few friends and right good sense"); *domus hac nec purior ulla est/nec magis his aliena
     malis* ("no house is cleaner or more free from such intrigues than that," 49–50).
     Naturally remember also *Satires* 1.6.49–52 and 62–4.

32   See *multa ... dixi cur excusatus abirem* ("I gave him many reasons for excusing me
     and letting me go away," 7); it is the verb which expresses the "escape," previously
     employed by the pest with reference to Horace in *Satires* 1.9.14, *misere cupis ...
     abire* ("you're dreadfully anxious to go away").

33   *Dissimulatio* is an art which, though different, Aristius Fuscus had already practiced
     in *Satires* 1.9.66; furthermore, we would also remind the reader of the reactions of
     the hoi polloi in *Satires* 2.6.50–8 as well as the accusations of "egotism" which will
     be leveled at Horace in *Epistles* 1.19.43–5.

34   Obviously, we would not wish in any way to deny that there were palpable differ-
     ences between the pest and Septimius, at least for the fact that the latter did achieve
     what he desired; Fedeli 1997: 1137–8. It seems that the same Septimius appears
     again in a letter penned by Augustus, but on this occasion it is he who stands as
     witness to the high esteem in which Horace is held by the prince: Suet. *Vita Hor.*
     p. 45, 18–22 Reiff.; Nisbet and Hubbard 1978: 93.

35   A path that also traverses the Odes. Previously, in *Odes* 1.22, dedicated to Aristius
     Fuscus, he found himself in a relevant editorial position: Cucchiarelli 2006: esp. 107,
     n. 70; for the iambic implications of *Odes* 1.22 see Davis 1987a. Like *Satires* 1.9,
     also *Odes* 1.22 contains its own miracle: not the salvation of Apollo but the fleeing
     of the enormous wolf (cf. Gantar 1983: 131–2; Nisbet and Hubbard 1970: 262);
     perhaps it is with a certain sense of playfulness that the poet has also settled on the
     vocative *Fusce,* meaning "of a dark colouring," used between two African references:
     1.22.2 *Mauris iaculis;* 5 *Syrtis ... aestuosas. Odes* 2.6, to Septimius, also touches on
     the theme of retreat in the *rus* (Tibur, or a bucolic Tarentum): this previous lyric
     experience more than qualifies the two recipients of *Epistles* 1.9 and 1.10 for the
     reason that they understand Horace on the theme of ambitious city life. Finally, the
     phonic similarities between *Epistles* 1.9.1 *Septimius, Claudi,* and that of *Odes* 2.6.1
     Septimi, Gadis, must not go unnoticed.

36   Cf. the commentary of Mayer 1994: 204, to line 17 (and also the intro., p. 4);
     it is also true that from the non-technical viewpoint of Vinnius, *carmina* as it stands
     could also mean "poetry" in general, and, therefore, also be connected to the Epistles
     with little difficulty: cf., in a satirical context, *Satires* 1.10.66 and 2.1.63 (Lucilius);
     2.6.22.

37   The scenario has a genuine epistolary precedent: Cic. *Fam.* 11.16.1; Fraenkel 1957:
      350. On the identification of Vinnius the reader should see the comm. of Fedeli
      1997: 1185.

38   *Vade, vale; cave ne titubes mandataque frangas* (19): a previous form of epistolary
      greeting is found at the opening of *Epistles* 1.10.1 *Urbis amatorem Fuscum salvere
      iubemus.* The Callimachean number of 13, perhaps conclusive of the *Iambi* is,
      however, centred on the principle of poetic "multiplicity" (the *polueideia*), and had
      already had a structural relevance for the Epodes, where it was used to mark out
      themes of an obviously lyrical nature (analogously, in *Odes* 1.13 Horace uses tones
      of a strong intensity which may be defined as "iambic"): cf. esp. 88, n. 1. Therefore
      we find once more in *Epistles* 1 a number 13 which is pertinent to the lyric form,
      but now applies to the very collection of the Odes.

39   Note the "motoric" conclusion to *Epistles* 1.2, which neatly fits itself to introduce
      to the heart of the volume: *quodsi cessas aut strenuus anteis,/nec tardum opperior nec
      praecedentibus insto* ("but if you lag behind, or with vigour push on ahead, I neither
      wait for the slow nor press after those who hurry on before," 70–1).

40   The act of submission by the Parthians (and Phraates) appears throughout the official
      iconography, most especially the coinage, and the same is true for the *Cornucopia*:
      together they are seen on the cuirass of Augustus of Prima Porta (e.g., Galinsky
      1996: 155–64). We can say that the book displays a well-planned sequence in which
      Tiberius first appears engaged in a mission, then being courted by both Septimius
      and Horace, and finally he is raised up by his political and diplomatic success (1.3,
      1.9, 1.12).

41   See Mayer 1994: 250, ad lines 61–4. Might we, therefore, end up defining as *cetera
      ludicra* an ode like 1.37? On *amicitia* and *libertas* in *Epistles* 1.18 (as an extension
      of *Satires* 1.4), see Hunter 1985.

42   Going by what Horace himself had said in *Odes* 1.37 (esp. 18–19), such speed would
      have proved decisive even in "Adriatic" waters.

43   This is confirmed by the closing image of the *ludus*, which had already been used in
      the opening of the first epistle: 1.19.46–9 *luctantis acuto ne secer ungui,/… diludia
      posco./ludus enim genuit trepidum certamen et iram* ("and lest, if he wrestle with
      me, I be torn by his sharp nails … I call for a truce in the sports. For such sports
      beget tumultuous strife and wrath") ≈ 1.1.1–6 (from the gladiatorial "game,"
      therefore, to the wrestling): Macleod (1977: 360 = 1983: 263).

44   The *quodsi pallerem* might limit itself to taking up the *quid? si quis* ff. of line 12
      (and, with a certain element of surprise, it would draw the reader's attention
      back to the poet, concluding the historical and etymological excursus of lines 1–11).
      It is possible that Persius, in his text of Horace, had read *edixit*. In the opening quips
      of his sixth satire, in which, addressing the "Horatian" Caesius Bassus, he shows
      himself to be more than familiar with *Epistles* 1.19 (of which he actually intends the
      derivative metrical doctrine: lines 3–4 to be compared with 1.19.23–33), Persius
      writes: *"Lunai portum, est operae, cognoscite cives!" /cor iubet hoc Enni* ("'Citizens,
      you must see Luna's port.' Thus commands the wise Ennius," 6.9–10). In introduc-
      ing a direct citation from Ennius, consisting of a highly prescriptive address
      (*cognoscite cives!*: one would say that this also is an edict), it is possible that
      Persius wished to reproduce in his own work Horace's page: and his line 10 is also

comparable numerically with Horace's own line 10 (*cor iubet hoc* ≈ *hoc simul edixit*).

45   Furthermore, note with regard to the question *edixi/edixit*, the discourse "with the people", as well as the *haec ... prodocet* of lines 54–5: third person singular.

46   *De eloc.* 227: "Just like dialogue, the letter should be full of revelations about the character of an individual (*to ēthikon*). In fact, each person writes letters, so to speak, in the image of their own soul. Of course, it is possible to discern the writer's true character (*to ēthos tou graphontos*) from any form of speech, but none so more than from the epistle." For a comparison between Demetrius and the overall relevance of the autobiographical theme in the Epistles see: Harrison 1995b: 58–9.

47   Aristot. *Poet.* 4.1448b24–27.

48   Of particular relevance is the discussion in Philodemus, *De poem.*: see the TT 126–130 Tarditi; cf. also Sext. Emp. *adv. math.* 1.298 = T 163 Tarditi.

49   An extreme case was the "ban" on Archilochus' works in Sparta, according to the anecdote of Valerius Maximus, 6.3 ext. 1 = T 182 Tarditi (in Plut. *Inst. Lacon.* 34.239b = T 143 Tarditi, the poet himself was banished from Sparta, because he was guilt of *rhipsaspia* "throwing away of the shield"). Cf. Quint., *Inst.* 10.1.60 ... *adeo ut videatur quibusdam, quod quoquam minor est, materiae esse, non ingenii vitium* ("indeed, some critics think that it is due solely to the nature of his subjects, and not to his genius, that any poets are to be ranked above him;" trans. H. E. Butler).

50   Lucilius: *quo me habeam pacto, tam etsi non quaeris, docebo/quando in eo numero mansi quo in maxima non est/pars hominum* ("although you do not ask after me, still I will let you know how I find myself, since I have managed to stay among the number in which the greater part of mankind is not found" [trans. E. H. Warmington]); Horace, lines 3–4, *si quaeret quid agam, dic multa et pulcra minantem/vivere nec recte nec suaviter* ("if he ask you how I fare, tell him that despite many fine promises I live a life neither wise nor pleasant").

51   Of use is Kilpatrick 1986, esp. xiii–xxiv; cf. 1996: esp. 304–6; see also: Harrison 1995b: 60.

52   See: Labate 2005.

53   There certainly would have been no lack of scholarly epistolographers in the Rome of Maecenas and Augustus, even on a technical level: we know, for example, of Valgius Rufus' books *de rebus per epistulam quaesitis*, apparently in the Varronian tradition of *epistolicae quaestiones* (testimonies beginning with the fundamental Gellius, 12.3.1–2, in Cugusi 1979: 501–3; cf. Cugusi 1983: 110–11, 123–4, and also 184.

54   The following all maintain Horace's philosophical independence: Moles 1985 and also 2002; Mayer 1986; Rudd 1993b. Kilpatrick 1986 insists upon Horace's adherence to the Academic School; he was substantially a Stoic (albeit eclectic) according to McGann 1969; on didacticism and philosophy in *Epistles* 1 see now Morrison 2007a.

55   Previously observed by Fraenkel 1957: 136. The *Phaedrus* has some bearing on the theme of friendship, which is fundamental in *Epistles* 1 (see Kilpatrick 1986: xx).

56   The image of the "pantry" is a traditional one in philosophy: see the comm. to line 12 of Kiessling and Heinze 1957: 5; Préaux 1968: 30; Mayer 1994: 90. This passage

of the *Phaedrus* enjoyed a particular fortune in Latin literature, especially in "intro-ductory" contexts: Plin. *Nat.* praef. 17; Gell. praef. 2; Citroni Marchetti 2005: esp. 112–14. Almost at the opposite part of the *Epistles* 1, we might recall the *bona librorum copia* in which Horace hopes may never be lacking, a "supply" as important as that of grain (*Epistles* 1.18.109–10).

57 *et versus et cetera ludicra* (10); cf. 276d … παιδιαῖς ἄλλαις χρῶνται, συμποσίοις τε ἄρδοντες αὐτοὺς ἑτέροις τε ὅσα τούτων ἀδελφά ("…other amusements, refreshing themselves with banquets and kindred entertainments").

58 Anderson's 1963 successful essay on Horace the satirist is in fact entitled "The Roman Socrates".

59 Some of these, obviously spurious, have come down to us. They contain a mixture of popular philosophy, diatribe and cynicism (besides their linguistic character) that suggest that they could actually have been composed before the first century CE: cf. Sykutris 1933: 106–12; and also Costa 2001: xvii and 72–9; Trapp 2003: 29, n. 118. Not too far, therefore, from the time when Horace studied in the Grove of Academus.

60 In the first epistle we also found the Greek equivalent of Vertumnus, the Proteus of line 90.

61 The comparison with the *elementa* of *Epistles* 1.20.17 already appears in Kiessling and Heinze to Hor. *Satires* 1.1.25–6 (a word which "frames," therefore, a good part of Horace's *sermo* from the first satire to the last epistle of Book I, passing through the first epistle).

CHAPTER SIXTEEN

The Epistles

W. R. Johnson

Though Horace was only in his mid-forties when he composed the first book of his Epistles, in that era anyone that age was thought to be entering into the twilight years, and this peculiar collection of verse-letters to friends and acquaintances has a strong flavor of geriatric intimations. It looks back on the life lived only seldom, it looks forward into the dim prospects of the life to come with an anxious hesitation that clouds these epistolary representations of what this poet or his readers might feel and try to think about as they become, gradually yet ever more vividly, aware of the closing of their options and their proximity to the truly irreversible and truly inevitable. Readers of these poems meet with, it is true, constant reminders of the familiar, beloved voice (the sly, wry uncle, the self-deprecating and humorous friend, the ironic phrase-maker and the astonishing craftsman), but they cannot miss the prevalence here of a new, somber tone, they cannot help but feel that their poet has changed, and not entirely for the better. And in fact *Epistles* I is chiefly "about" change, about the kinds of uneasy transformation of identity that arise from meditations on a life that is apparently approaching its conclusion, of minds (hearts, souls) that find their confrontation with the realities of mortality inescapable. *Epistles* I is essentially an old man's book, and though the middle-aged and even the young can read it with varying degrees of pleasure and illumination, it is no wonder if they tend to prefer to it, the Satires or the Odes or even the Epodes or the *Ars Poetica* and *Epistles* 2.

But another set of problems in addition to its slant toward "fast falls the eventide" moods centers on the volume's strange shift in its generic "horizon of expectations." Through the centuries readers of the poem have worried over two questions: 1) Do these poems constitute real letters that were actually sent to real correspondents, or, to put it another way, are these letters representations of actual situations or moments in the poet's life that have called them into existence?; 2) What were the epistolary models that Horace looked to when he decided to employ the form of verse-letter for this set of poems?[1] Precise answers to these questions may not be absolutely necessary for our enjoyment of the poems but, combined with the change in theme and tone that the poems present us with, these questions about their possible actuality and about their generic origin tease us, distract us, as we work to accustom ourselves to their unfamiliar and rather puzzling new territory, as we find ourselves forced to remake ourselves as new readers of this new Horace.

The solution to the first of these readers' troubles, their concern over the actuality of the poet's correspondents has, in recent times, come to seem a less urgent matter than before. Throughout his poetry, Horace frequently mixes the facts of his life and the world around him with fictions that add color and veri-similitude to those facts.[2] Few readers now believe that many (if any) of these verse-letters were literally sent to their poetic recipients. This collection of letters is meant for the eyes and ears of poetry readers at any time and in any place (this intention is emphatically stated in the poem that closes the volume). The occasion for any of these letters (whether mostly real or really fictive) is essentially a gimmick that lets the poet say what he really wants to say: under the surface message to his formal correspondent he unfolds a subtext that has wider meanings (for wider audiences) than the literal meaning of his letter to his designated addressee. The letters of Cicero are often concerned with particular (and ephemeral) matters that have no relevance beyond themselves, but some of the letters, and among them some of the most famous are to be numbered, have an enduring import. Most of these letters were deliberately constructed as messages for posterity and for eventual collection and publication. All Horace's letters, like those of Epicurus, his most likely model, were written to be published and widely distributed, and they were composed in exquisite verse and shaped with his usual eye to exact articulation and precision of syntax. Each of them, then, from the least to the most elaborate, manifests the poet's constant obsession with polish, which means they do not accord with the simplest of epistolary requirements— timely response to what an immediate circumstance or event requires, brevity as against rumination, a clumsy clarity as against limpid elegance. These letters were labored over, and it needed meticulous care to mimic the effortless, breezy conversation with recipients that characterize the best letters (of a certain type, Byron's for instance).

The problem as to the generic formulae of *Epistles* 1 is less likely to be solved in a satisfying manner because it is something of a false problem. We hear of a couple of verse-letters in Latin before Horace wrote his, but these poems seem to have been chatty notes about fleeting experiences, ephemera about ephemera, ordinary letters about ordinary matters, versified.

Horace's letters are mostly about philosophy, that is to say, that are about philosophy as Romans tended to think of it: morality, the way to discern what the good life might consist in, and how, once discovered, to take possession of the *summum bonum*. But Horace, unlike the philosophical epistlers that preceded him (a long tradition here of philosophers inspiring and guiding their protégés) is less interested in instructing his correspondents in what to think and in pre-scribing for them a regimen that will enable them to live the life he wants them to live than he is in describing to them how difficult—now, at this crucial moment in his life—he finds it to come upon the true path he seeks and how inept he feels in following that path whenever he thinks he has got some inkling of it. Probably the closest paradigm he had when he undertook to invent his poetic philosophical letters was Epicurus.[3] But unlike his master (with whom, like Lucre-tius, he sometimes disagreed) he is very far from the luxury of certainty and the pleasures of dogmatism. He is a troubled spirit struggling to find himself as a swarm of conflicts threatens to overwhelm him.[4]

In the penultimate poem of his new collection, *Epistles* 1.19, a letter addressed to Maecenas but meant for the eyes and ears of his contemporaries and of posterity, Horace constructs an elaborate defense of his poetic career, one which focuses on his originality. It was, of course, not unusual for his great contemporaries (in their different ways, Vergil and Propertius) to boast of their pioneer efforts to recreate in Latin verse the spirit and the forms of some of best of non-dramatic Greek poetry (Homer, Hesiod, Callimachus, Theocritus), but Horace's advertisement for himself differs from those of Vergil and Proper-tius in emphasizing both the boldness and the unique technical mastery that were required to make Latin verse capable of accommodating Greek lyric forms and feelings. In claiming to be the first (as it turned out he was also almost the last) to bring some of the sound and much of the spirit of Achilochus, Sappho, and Anacreon into the Latin language (21–35), he ignores his own achieve-ment in his two books of Satires because for them he had, in Lucilius, a bril-liant predecessor. But for the Epodes and especially for the Odes he had no real Latin models, and it seems that it is the Odes in particular, with their astonish-ing variety of themes and meters, that he regards as his crowning achievement. As well he might: those eighty-seven poems distil what is best and brightest in Greek lyric as far as we can judge it from its sad fragments (even some of Pindar's power and majesty find a modest if ironic reflection here and there throughout Horace's lyric volumes), and they represent an amazing triumph over what must at first have seemed both to the poet and his first readers insu-perable technical difficulties. This gift to Latin literature of Greek lyric and the fearless craftsmanship that made possible that gift are what Horace celebrates at the center of this letter to Maecenas: *iuvat immemorata ferentem/ ingenuis oculis legi manibusque teneri* ("it delights me to have given poetry of a kind hitherto unwritten to be read by the eyes and held in the hands of the elite (the happy few," 33–4).

These lines, which close the verse-paragraph in which he flaunts his lyric triumph, are immediately followed by a fierce castigation of the kinds of readers who, unlike the ideal readers he has just identified, disgruntle him.

These are readers who inhabit what may be called the Poetry World. They are critics or poetasters or both who may like what they read of Horace but dare not praise his lyrics publicly. Why? We will never know for certain, but it seems likely that two unintended consequences merge and come into play at this (crucial) moment in Horace's poetic career: 1) the Poetry World is puzzled by and very likely also jealous of the Odes; 2) Horace himself, never one to suffer fools gladly or wisely, has made himself unpopular with many of the Poetry World's denizens by virtue of his contempt for poetry recitations and by virtue of what seems his arrogant refusal to promote or even to damn with faintest praise the work of second-raters. The author of the Satires, who had found fame and enthusiastic acceptance nearly equal to Vergil's, has with his lyric volumes met with unwonted mixed reviews. Not blessed with the thickest of skins, he responds to this unexpected reception with hurt and resentment. He strikes back at his detractors in this poem which is at once something of a swan song (one utterly lacking in Prospero's beneficent farewell to his magic) and, to the Poetry World, a sour adieu.

Despite its placement in the volume, the poem is not, so it seems to me, among the last of the volume's to have been written but among its first. If this were the case, it would reflect some of Horace's mood when he first became aware of how the Odes were being received out beyond the circle of the happy few. And though he may have told himself and the happy few that the opinions of envious idiots didn't matter, those opinions could not be completely ignored because—suppose the idiots right? Because, suppose the gamble he had taken, writing unmusical songs to musical Greek meters, had been a foolish one? Because, suppose what he had on his hands was a colossal flop? The happy few assured him of what he already knew: that it was silly of him to listen to murmurs of the wannabes and the great barely washed. He listened to the happy few and to his own best voice. But that disapproval continued to rankle and fester, because—because that criticism, that set-back ("when sorrows come, they come not single spies"), combined with other feelings that were just now bubbling to the surface, refused to be ignored. He had begun, imperceptibly, to feel his age (*sensim sine sensu senesco*, "slowly, imperceptibly, I grow old," said Cicero's irrefutable Cato the Elder: Cicero, *De Senectute*, 38); he was spending more and more time by himself at the farm that Maecenas had given him, alone, away from the hubbub of Rome, but also away from the cheer and comfort of his friends there. After the immense effort the Odes had cost him (not to mention the deflation that attended their reception, lukewarm and worse), came the usual *post-partum* dismay, a sort of vague misease: after the Epodes and the Satires and after the Odes, where could he turn? And beyond these merely personal anxieties, the world was changing too, the ground beneath his feet was, ever so slightly, shifting. He looked up at Augustus' Palatine, he heard Propertius muttering his asinine slurs, he watched Maecenas falter and flail. What sort of remedies would Lucretius or Philodemus advise? He glanced over some of *De Rerum Natura*. He unrolled some scrolls of Philodemus, looked over some passages of *On Anger* and *On the Good King*. Some images began floating in and out of his mind. He began to hear some tunes in his ear.[5]

Roughly two decades before he began writing the first volume of his verse-letters, in the company of Vergil and other friends, Horace had belonged to a circle of young intellectuals whose center was their elder, Philodemus, an eloquent exponent of Epicurean philosophy and a writer of exquisite light verse. Whatever Horace's attitudes to philosophical pursuits in the years following Philodemus' death (c.35 BCE), it would be natural for him to renew his earlier attachment to this man and his teachings at a point in his life when he felt increasingly at odds with his society, with his vocation, and with himself.[6] That philosophical questions should gradually intrude themselves into his consciousness more insistently than had perhaps been the case in recent years and consequently began suggesting themselves as themes for poetry at this period of his life would not be surprising. What is peculiar about this philosophical turn (and continues to cause some bewilderment in some styles of interpreting these poems) is the unexpected strategy that Horace devised (or stumbled upon) to render them suitable to the kind of poetry that could represent his feelings about himself and his world after the completion of the first collection of lyric poems. (I don't dismiss out of hand the possibility that the speaker of these poems is perhaps fictive, that he is, as he says and is represented as feeling and thinking, a product of the poet's imagination; but, if only in the interest of an economy of effort, I assume that whatever fictions these poems contain grew out of, or at least are somehow linked with, the life that the man Horace was living at the time the poet Horace was producing these poems.)

Their complete self-confidence is what distinguishes the discourse of philosophers who publish explanations of their views on the nature of reality and who offer instructions to their readers which are designed to help possible initiates to choose the path their mentors recommend and then to make steady progress toward the goal those mentors propose as the only one worth reaching. Horace, whose previous voices were everywhere marked by irony and ambivalence, does not depart from this core poetic identity when he sets about turning philosophical rumination into poetry. Instead of offering himself as infallible guru, he mostly presents himself throughout these verse-letters to his correspondents as no more than a fellow-seeker, a companion on the road to wisdom and happiness. He reveals himself as being less a prophet guiding the unenlightened from the wilderness than lost himself, a victim of myopia, who exhorts the nearly blind to stumble along with him toward a clouded and distant refuge, one where they may or may not discover what they are looking for.

This astonishing reversal of roles and the fissure in generic decorum that accompanies it permits Horace to write poems that are satisfying to him in several ways. As a bumbling, hesitant *proficiens* (one who is progressing, one who is "on the way") he can continue yet also elaborate on, and transform, the modest (but shrewd) voice that sustained the Satires and contributes to the Odes not a little of their variety and antithetical structure (commonsense interrupting sublimities and profundities).[7] United with the epistolary form and its refurbished persona, this old voice made new can continue to speak in the colloquial language that he fashioned for the satiric poems (*sermones*, conversations, chats), a style that is shaped from something like "the speech of living men" combined with a maximum of metrical and rhetorical elegance. Finally, it permitted him to explore (and imagine) the complexities and the inadequacies of philosophical thinking when an existing individual (one who is not a philosopher) undertakes to reform himself (change his life); and it, this persona of an unfinished and undogmatic proponent of the need for philosophy in daily life, permitted him, indeed required him, to discover, once again, as he always did, that, for him, irony and ambivalence were the essential tools he needed for shaping, or trying to shape, the messy dissonance of ordinary experience. Even philosophic truth, even the philosophic truth one believes in and tries to trust in, is subject to the operation of *sic-et-non* (yes, but no; no, but yes). [8]

When he turned to his new inspiration, making poetry out of philosophical questions, he was, it seems to me, actually in need of the kind of help that philosophy claims to provide (and that Philodemus had once provided him with). But when he reached for that help, he found it hard to pluck, harder still to hold on to. The truth he wanted seemed at times more a mirage than an oasis. It is not impossible that in writing *Epistles* I Horace worked through his doubts about the efficacy of using philosophy for living.

Maybe he did, in actuality, achieve the equanimity and contentment with life (and mortality) that mark the splendid close of the second poem of his second book of verse-letters, *Epistles* 2:

> vivere si recte nescis, decede peritis.
> lusisti satis, edisti satis atque bibisti:
> tempus abire tibi est, ne potum largius aequo
> rideat et pulset lasciva decentius aetas. (*Epistles*
> 2.2.213–18)

> If you can't live a decent life, make way for those who
> can. You have played enough, eaten enough and drunk
> enough. It's time for you to go away, before young
> people, who can party far better than you can, make fun
> of you when they see you've had a drop too much and
> shove you aside.

This is, of course, a reworking of Lucretian irony (DRN 3.938f), typically a bit gentler than its model (he doesn't call his addressee—or himself—*stulte*, you fool), but these verses, like the entire verse-paragraph it closes (204ff.), show in their low-keyed homage to Lucretius, a clarity, almost a transparency, an untroubled and even cheerful resignation, that the poems of the first volume of verse-letters (with the exception of the superb close of 1.18.106–12) never allow themselves. Though a number of the themes of 2.2 repeat those of the first volume of verse-letters (the onset of the tedium of decrepitude, various unwelcome distractions, his waning poetic powers, and his resolution to have done with poetic composition), this renunciation of the Poetry World and his place in it seems firmer, less uncertain, than similar efforts at renunciation in *Epistles* l, in part because it is addressed to Julius Florus, inmate of the Poetry World, to whom *Epistles* 1.3 was also addressed. But whether the equanimity that sounds at the ends of *Epistles* 2.2 is fact or fiction, whether in real life Horace found peace in philosophy or elsewhere is neither knowable nor, for our present purposes, important. What matters here is the voice and the tone of voice that dominate the first book of verse-letters, the style of speaking which is shaped by struggle, conflict, and a powerful skepticism as to the capacity of philosophy (thinking) to bring aid and comfort to a life (feelings) that stands in pressing need of them.

Much of what Horace says to Julius Florus in *Epistles* 2.2 he had already rehearsed in his petition to Maecenas, the opening (programmatic) poem of *Epistles* 1. His patron, his sponsor, his dearest friend, had apparently been nagging him (again) to continue writing poetry (including, perhaps, some more of the patriotic poetry that he had furnished plentifully in the third of his lyric volumes). Horace had, it would seem, offered Maecenas a variety of excuses for his discontinuation of poetic production—illness, perhaps a disinclination to quit the charms and the leisure offered him by the farm Maecenas had given him, a protracted attack of writer's block. And Maecenas had at last grown weary of these inadequate excuses and begun to make something close to outright demands. Horace is therefore forced to outline a real transformation in his design for living. He has permanently jettisoned poetic production in favor of a serious commitment to living the philosophic life: *nunc itaque et versus et cetera ludicra pono* ("now, accordingly, I put aside my versifying and my other playthings," 10). To call his poetic vocation, his poetic career, his poetic identity, one of his playthings, to equate his poems with wine, women, and boys, is no less a jolt than it was for him a few verses earlier to equate himself with a gladiator (slave) who is ready to retire from the theatre of death. Having consigned such trivia to oblivion, Horace has decided to philosophize, but he cannot make up his mind what philosophical school to attach himself to. Sometimes he feels attracted to something that smacks of a Stoic resolve to devote himself to civic duty and to become a vigorous champion of rectitude (16–17), but at other times, perhaps a bit more frequently, he finds himself pulled in the opposite direction, toward the enlightened, pragmatic hedonism promulgated by Aristippus (18–19). He is anxious here as elsewhere to avoid the dangers proposed by extremes in favor of exploring the spectrum that stretches between antithetical values (he will affirm in the antepenultimate letter of this collection: *virtus est medium vitiorum et utrimque reductum* ("virtue marks the middle ground between two opposing vices, at equal distance from either," 18.9). So, at the outset of his pilgrimage to equipoise (*ataraxia*), he emphasizes here the moral gift, or character flaw, that will all but condemn him to keep choosing eclecticism—with all its concomitant indeterminacies—over the comfort and safety that a single doctrine and its sure dogmas could provide him with. For better or worse, he is his own man: *nullius addictus iurare in verba magistri, / quo me cumque rapit tempestas, deferor hospes* ("I have not sworn allegiance to the prescriptions of any teacher, and when I feel buffeted by the storm I get help wherever I find it," *Epistles* 1.1.24–5). He feels lost, he wants shelter from what shakes him, but (it is the core of this poetry and this life) he cannot yield up his freedom in exchange for what might rescue him from his predicament. Hence, the indecision and the steady current of anxiety that haunt these poems. He distrusts himself, but he distrusts the salvific claims of the major schools of philosophy as much or more. Thus, in liberating himself from his poetic identity and its conflicts (and with them, from Rome and from Maecenas' hold on him), he is heading off into unknown territories.

Epistles 1 contains three letters to Maecenas, one at the beginning, one (19) almost at the end, and one (7) about a third of the way through the collection. Of the 1,006 verses that compose the collection, 256, or roughly one-quarter of them, make up the letters to Maecenas. These letters are all concerned in some way or another with liberation, the final one, as we've seen, about liberation from the Poetry World to which Maecenas had given Horace his first, crucial access and in which Maecenas is still attempting to keep him housed (or imprisoned). In *Epistles* 1.1, when refusing to share in the ideology that defines the Roman people (loving what they love, hating what they hate, 70ff.), Horace makes use of a fable of Aesop's, one in which a wise fox informs a sickly lion that he does not enter into the lion's den because he has noticed that the tracks of other animals that entered there all lead into the den but none lead out of it (see Babrius, 103). At 1.7, 29–33, a less wily fox slips into a a corn-bin through a narrow chink, eats ravenously and finds that its distended stomach will not let it exit the place where it found its luckless feast; a smug weasel provides the poor fox with some obvious advice: "If you want to extricate yourself from the trap you've made for yourself, you'll have to wait until you're once again as lean as you were as when you squeezed yourself in there" (see Babrius 86). A similar fable occurs in Epistles 1.13.34ff.: A powerful stag could drive off a horse from the pasture they both depended on; but once the horse had allied itself with a human rider, though it was now able to drive the stag from the pasture, could never free itself from the rider it had empowered and been enslaved by (see Phaedrus 4.4.).

Maecenas had furnished Horace with real freedom, both in welcoming him into his salon, thereby sponsoring him in the Poetry World, and in giving him his Sabine Farm, which provided him with other kinds of freedom, freedom from Rome with its distractions, obligations and tedium, freedom to relax in solitude, to ponder and to write. In the great penultimate ode of Book 3 (29), Horace had invited Maecenas to come to the farm and leave behind him in Rome all its "smoke and wealth and noise," all the worries that his position at the court of Augustus burdened him with. In that vision of the farm's significance, it is Maecenas who stands in need of being rescued from the city's stresses and strains, and it is Horace who has found a sure antidote to the city's evils, and it is Horace who continues to try to imagine the farm as his own (Roman) version of the garden of Epicurus (the contrast between farm and city also provides the central theme of two other verse-letters, l.10 and l.14).

But *Epistles* 1's steady meditation on the question of what constitutes the good life and its continuing search for an inner freedom that would rid its poet of his false hopes and false fears and give him *ataraxia*, true contentment, equanimity (*aequus animus*: see 1.11.30 and 1,18.11—both the concluding phrases in their respective poems) suggest that the farm seemed sometimes an illusory sanctum. Even when he has fled Rome and its obligations and tedious distractions and found some respite from them on the farm, he still feels beset by the need to move about (*Epistles* 1.8.1–12; 15.1–25), and cannot practice what he preaches to Bullatius: *caelum non animum mutant qui trans mare currunt* ("they change their weather, not their psyches, who speed across the sea," 1.11, 27). The farm, like the salon and the poetic fame, is both a blessing and a curse. Much as he loves it, in so far as it has failed to provide permanent solutions to enduring problems and has masked them rather than resolved them, Horace devotes the core of his volume, the three letters to Maecenas, to attempting to reclaim his freedom from the giver and his gifts. In 1.7, having sketched the story of the greedy fox, he says: "If anyone should compare me to the fox in the fable, I relinquish everything I've been given" (*cuncta resigno*, 34), and he emphasizes the force of this challenge by closing this verse-letter with another anecdote, this one rather lengthy (46–95). A rich Roman gentleman befriends a hardworking auctioneer who, having first resisted the rich man's efforts to make his acquaintance, ends by accepting a generous loan from him, which enables him to purchase a small farm. At first the new farmer is delighted with his move from the city and with his new life, its modest pleasures and the welcome prosperity that accompanies them. But when he suffers a run of bad luck, he angrily returns to the rich man and demands that he be restored to the life he had given up in exchange for the rich man's generosity. It would be too much to maintain that, at this point in his life, Horace's feeling for Maecenas, as reflected in this tale, this poem, and this volume, are nourished by anything like love–hate, but it looks as if, when Horace composed *Epistles* 1, Maecenas has come to symbolize a conflicted mix of feelings and thoughts (affection, gratitude, resentment, regret among them). Like the farm he gave, Maecenas is part of the vortex of confused fragments of a shaken identity that Horace struggles to master or to abolish by writing these poems. (The *cuncta resigno* theme and its hunger for inner freedom are vividly echoed in the closing section of 1.16, with its fierce paraphrase at 63–79 of Dionysus' fierce assertion of his independence to Pentheus in Euripides' *Bacchae*.)

All but hidden in this tangle of discontents and anxieties, just under the surface of the faltering efforts that make up Horace's efforts at reintegration (poetic, psychic, spiritual), is another symbol of what confronts him, another obstacle to his recovery of what Yeats calls "self-delighting." In 1.5 Horace issues a brief, charming invitation to a distinguished friend, Torquatus, to a modest supper party. Torquatus, it seems, might be tempted to refuse this invitation because he is hard at work preparing to plead a case in the law courts, but Horace reminds him that he could sleep in the next day, that he need not trudge off to the courts the morning after a night of gentle inebriation and pleasant conversation since the day after the party was a feast day. The nature of this *dies festus* is briefly and casually alluded to: *nato Caesare*, Caesar's birthday. We don't know much about when, how or how widely the birthday of Augustus, September 23, began to be celebrated (it would probably provide some fun to have Ovid's comments on this question, but he abandoned his *Fasti* well before he got to this date in his version of the Roman, or Augustan, year).[9] Suetonius tells us (*Vita Aug.* 57.1) that "Roman knights celebrated his birthday of their own accord" (as contrasted with honors conferred on him by the senatorial decree) "and always for two successive days."[10] More interesting, but vaguer, is the comment of Dio Cassius (54.1.2): "the birthday of Augustus was honored by the slaughter of wild beasts both in the Circus and in many other parts of the city. This was done almost every year by one of the praetors then in office, even if it was not authorized by a decree ...".[11] What matters more here, the party or the birthday?

We will presently be engaged with Horace's *Epistles* 2.1 which is addressed to the Emperor himself. For the moment it is enough to say that the shadow of the Emperor, however lightly, drifts over *Epistles* 1. First here, where his birthday makes its fleeting appearance, then at the close of *Epistles* 1.12, where Horace offers Iccius a brief glimpse at current events : Agrippa's conquest of the Cantabrians; the surrender of Armenia to Tiberius, which included the return by the Armenian king of the Roman standards that had been infamously lost some three decades before, a glorious recovery that looms large in Augustan propaganda because, as Horace puts in, when King Phraates, on bended knee, submits to Caesar's laws, the goddess Abundance heaps her fruits on Italy from her copious horn (27–9). Then, in the next poem (1.13), Horace gives detailed instructions to the person who will deliver a gift to Augustus, a bundle of poems (perhaps the Odes, perhaps early versions of some of the verse-letters?).[12] The light tone of this poem, with its elaborate, ironic concern for the decorum that the approach to the Emperor demands, suggests some of the finesse that marks the courtly rhetoric of Theocritus and Callimachus when they fabricate poems for their potentates.

Aside from these meager moments, *Epistles* 1 is essentially unbothered by regal intrusions. But that simple phrase, *nato Caesare*, though it seems to slip by us almost unnoticed, sticks at the back of the mind the more one encounters it.

Epicureans celebrated the birthday of their master (as he himself had celebrated it), and they celebrated their own birthdays and those of their friends. One of the loveliest of the poems in the final lyric collection (4.11) is an invitation to a lady named Phyllis to what promises to be a special party on the Ides of April, which happens to be the birthday of Maecenas, a day more sacred (almost) than the poet's own birthday (*sanctiorque/ paene natali proprio*, 17–18; the "almost" is a nice touch that the honoree doubtless delighted in). Birthdays for all Epicureans, not least for Horace, were private affairs. They signified the blessedness of having come into existence, for having become part of Nature's vast and awesome realities, they symbolized one's unique thingness among the other things that made up Nature's joyous plenitude, one's existence and place in the infinite, beautiful dynamic of her (its) processes. The celebration took place in Epicurus' garden, that is to say, in the gardens of his followers which recalled his garden. Though these gardens were often physically located in cities, they were also, in what Auden calls an "otherwhere," a place both inside and outside the City, away from the public, away from the hive, far from, far beyond, the Emperor's reach. So, though there is no harm in an Epicurean's honoring the Emperor, since Epicureans are part of the civic body and, unlike the early Christians a little while later, it costs them nothing, when the occasion demands, to conform to the common, public practice, it is, nevertheless, something of a blasphemy, Epicureanly speaking, to celebrate the Emperor's birthday, for this innovative manner of honoring the Emperor—think of Lucretius in attendance at this party!—involves the act of worshiping his *numen*.

On the surface of *Epistles* 1.5, Horace invites Torquatus to participate in a small gathering which will honor the savior of the Roman empire on the day of his birth, an annual celebration that has become part of what is becoming the new (Augustan version) of the Roman calendar. But suppose the party (real or fictive) is just another Horatian get-together (jovial and sometimes boisterous and carnal), and the poet, in a spirit of subtle mockery, only pretends to Torquatus and his other guests (who will understand his real intent) that what motivates him is his desire to participate in this new ritual, this recent addition to the emergent political and religious ideology, a day that is now another ingredient in the deft fusion of old Roman customs and attitudes with the introduction of new oriental ceremonies and Hellenistic monarchical institutions that characterizes the Augustan renovation, "the Augustan revolution"? In such a reading, the royal birthday becomes, ironically, a good excuse for a bit of private (and unpatriotic and irreligious) merrymaking. (The context of this conflation of tradition and re-invention is neatly sketched by Shaw in his Caesar and Cleopatra: "there was an old Rome and a new, and men standing perplexed between the two...". Horace's ironic call to celebrate the imperial birthday reflects that perplexity with suave wit.)

Horace's complex discontents cluster about the figure of Augustus in the final stage of his poetic career that *Epistles* 1 ushers in, and the growing fascination (and power) of that figure is adumbrated by the spare glimpses of it that we have just examined: the feast day, the extolling of Augustus' triumphs in foreign policy, the gift to him of the roll of poems. These acknowledgements, meager and oblique as they are, of the Augustan presence in Rome and in the poet's own consciousness barely reflect the pressures on him that the Emperor kept applying, sometimes through Maecenas, sometimes directly. The urgency of the Emperor's desire to enlist Horace's talents in the service of his agenda is easily discerned in the sketch of the poet's life written by Suetonius. This version of the poet's life and career, which we seem to have in its entirety, centers firmly on his strained, awkward relationship with Augustus, where, in his letters to the poet, the Emperor's jocular tone barely masks his irritation. Horace had refused the imperial invitation to become his private secretary, and in composing his verse-letters he had failed to include Augustus among his correspondents:

"I hope you realize that I'm vexed with you," wrote the Emperor, "because you conspicuously exclude me from the recipients of your chatty letters. Perhaps you're worried posterity would judge you harshly if you were to number me among your close acquaintances." Augustus, says Suetonius, was eager to have Horace among his admirers because he believed that his poetry would never die (*scripta mansuraque perpetuo*).

And Horace finally gave in. In addition to *Epistles* 2.1, which we're about to glance at, he went on to write a flawless yet unimpassioned hymn that was performed at the Sacred Games of 17 BCE (a crucial moment in the construction of the emerging imperial ideology), and he even produced a fourth book of lyrics, partly in would seem, because, in the words of Suetonius, Augustus vigorously coaxed him into celebrating the military victories of his stepsons, Drusus and Tiberius (*Odes* 4.2 and 4.14). What caused this change of heart, if that is what it was? And what reason had Horace to behave in such a fashion that the Emperor felt called on to beg for his friendship and (more important) for his literary testament to that friendship?

Earlier, there had appeared a splendid victory song (*Odes* 1.12, a miniature Pindaresque poem shorn of music and dance) devoted to Augustus, and scattered throughout the first three lyric volumes there were flattering, if brief, mentions of his triumphs and war and peace.[13] But despite these indications of the poet's approval of Augustus, which he shares with most of the Roman people, the volumes that contain them glow with a powerful, sophisticated hedonism that is coupled with a secure, even arrogant, affirmation of the autonomy of art and the genius of their poet—and with a recognizably Epicurean interest in discovering the meaning of and the way to the good life. The political realm is hardly absent from these poems (this is a Roman book and Horace is very much a creature of his own times), but its place in this poet's hierarchy of values is distinctly relegated to the last of his preferences, well after pleasure, art, spiritual hankerings, and, as the close of the great Maecenas ode emphasizes, 3.29.41–64, intimations of independence (*ille potens sui*). Fully committed to these private, merely personal values, the poet would have no trouble in acquiescing to Maecenas' suggestions that he pay some attention to the evolution of the new regime, and an Epicurean, particularly one who was undertaking to demonstrate his Latin mastery of the forms and feelings of Greek lyric, would not feel degraded by experimenting with the themes and rhetoric of epinician poetry (or by expressing his personal, if rather limited, patriotic fervor). So, Augustus had not been ignored by Horace before *Epistles* 1, but neither had he been represented by him with vivid enthusiasm (*Odes* 1.12 is perhaps the exception that proves the rule; see note 13). At some time the poet's relative neglect of him began to cause the Emperor to fret. He mentioned his displeasure to Maecenas, who passed it on to the poet. Noting the poet's continuing abstention from full-throated praise, the Emperor sent the poet some funny notes, asking for poems, asking for friendship. When the first volume of verse-letters appeared and the Emperor was again missing from the action (save for the droll teasing of 1.13), he perhaps sent the poet a clearer message. So, finally, the poet wrote the Emperor a letter of his very own, and he went on to write the ironic victory songs for the stepsons (and included them in a very short volume of lyric poems, some of them on non-patriotic themes, such as pederasty, death, and the autonomy of art). He could construct these poems, probably, not because he was much bothered by the thought of the petulant Emperor but because he had, by writing *Epistles* 1, pretty well worked through his various anxieties, of which Augustus and his demands were no small part.

Once he had written himself out of his fear of senility and death, of waning poetic power, and of his disenchantment with his discordant identities, once he had taken hold of his inner freedom, the problem of Augustus and all that he symbolized dwindled in importance. He was then free to write Augustus the ironic letter, the ironic hymn, and the ironic victory songs. The final poem in *Epistles* 1 (20) is addressed to this book itself, here represented as a sullen young man, just emerging from adolescence and eager to escape from his master and make his way in the world as a hustler. The poet, after warning the slave of the humiliations he will bring upon himself in his new existence, sets him free to go peddle his wares, but he closes this liberation poem with a gentle self-epitaph which all but ignores his artistry and, skimming over his connection with the corridors of power, emphasizes his contentment with his life and with himself (19–28).

Like *Epistles* 2.2, *Epistles* 2.1, the letter of his own that Augustus had begged for, concerns itself primarily with literary history and literary theory.

At its most trenchant moments, it wittily criticizes the Roman taste for antique poetry and its concomitant aversion to modern poetry (including Horace himself; 63–92). But this preference for the old over the new disappears when "we," the Roman people, come to evaluate the achievements of Augustus: "While you remain with us, we heap you with honors in due season, we erect altars and swear oaths by your divinity [*numen*], affirming that none like you will come to us again, and none like you has ever come to us before" (15–17). Except for Augustus, the truth that informs Horace's complaint about Roman reverence for the antique holds all too true. While elaborating on this fact about Rome's poetic taste with copious illustrations from literary history and with observations about theories of literature, he turns away from the glory of his addressee, but in the closing segment of the poem he resumes his praise of the Emperor. Or rather, he takes up the problem that Augustus creates for himself when he asks Horace for one of his verse-letters, one in which he would figure as one of the poet's cherished correspondents.

Alexander the Great, who was among Augustus's models for his self-representations, had been very good at selecting sculptors and painters to depict him and his *virtus* (231), his courage, his moral beauty, his glory. But he betrayed himself when it came to choosing poets, giving the job of celebrating him in deathless verse to a wretched poetaster, Choerilus. Augustus has proved himself far wiser than Alexander in requesting the service of truly great poets, Vergil and Varius, to hymn his achievements (245–50). Horace therefore frees himself of the duty the Emperor has tried to impose upon him by stating the mere facts: he is a rather pedestrian poet whose signature, in the verse-letters at least, is the plain speech (*sermones*, 250) that he also employed in his satiric poetry, and he cannot lift himself (like Vergil and Varius) to the lofty heights that the Emperor's exploits would require him to climb to. If he attempted to compose what the Emperor asks of him, he might well end with something dreadful. He himself would not be pleased to find himself commemorated in a bad poem by the wrong poet, a poem fit for nothing but wrapping up merchandise one purchases in the markets, frankincense, perfume, pepper. Something vile, something briefly useful and eminently disposable.[14]

If Horace frees his book (*liber* = book and free) in *Epistles* 1.20, in *Epistles*.2.1 he frees himself from the most threatening obstacle to his *ataraxia*, one more insidious and more importunate than those offered by the old age and death or poetic decline or spiritual confusion, the gathering of anxieties that had prompted him to begin the explorations that ended in the composition of *Epistles* 1. Augustus kept pestering him for poems, and that intrusion intensified his distress as the philosophical poems were germinating and beginning to blossom. But it was not so much the man-god himself that imperiled the composition of the new poems and the formation of the renewed integrity that they shaped and were shaped by. Rather, it was the ideology that the Emperor symbolized and has symbolized since then: the capacity of the state to interfere with what a poet (or a man) was striving to think and do and be in his private world. For many if not most of Horace's contemporaries in the Roman Empire such interference might have seemed a natural, inevitable consequence of the end of a long series of civil wars, merely the price one paid for safety and prosperity, for order and for law. For an Epicurean poet that interference was a grave danger to what he valued most: his freedom to free himself from false hopes and false fears, especially those that the state subjected him to. *Epistles* 1 and 2.1 are Horace's challenge to that interference, and they represent his success in countering it.[15]

GUIDE TO FURTHER READING

There are two recent commentaries on the Epistles, both of them very useful: Mayer (1994) for Book 1 and Rudd (1989) for Book 2; but Dilke's commentary for Book 1 (1954) continues to offer rewarding insights as does Brink's (1982). Major interpretations of the Epistles have been offered by McGann (1969), Kilpatrick (1986 and 1990) and Ferri (1993). Helpful discussions of various aspects of the poems are to be found in Oliensis (1998) and Bowditch (2001).

NOTES

1 See descriptions of these models by De Prentis 2002: 33–7; Malherbe 1988: 1–14.
2 See Harrison 1995b: 59.
3 See Ferri 2007: 126–7.
4 For brilliant observations on Horace's dissatisfactions with Epicurus, see Ferri 1993: *passim*.
5 For Philodemus, see the powerful arguments by Armstrong 2004: *passim*.
6 See Freudenburg 2002: 124–5.
7 For the Horatian *proficiens*, see Johnson 1993: 129.
8 Contrast Mayer's version of this 'eclecticism' (1994: 39–43) with the more generous and more satisfactory version offered by Moles 2002: 148–9, 156.
9 See Mayer 1994: 136; Dilke 1954: 90.
10 J. C. Rolfe's Loeb translation.
11 Ernest Cary's Loeb translation.
12 For interesting speculations on this uncertainty, see Oliensis 1998: 190–1.
13 For the suave ambiguities of *Odes* 1.12, see Feeney 1998: 111–13.
14 See Rudd 1989: 10–11.
15 See Moles's eloquent verdict 2002: 157.

PART IV

Reception of Horace's Poetry

CHAPTER SEVENTEEN

The Reception of Horace's Odes

Lowell Edmunds

Discussion of the reception of Horace's Odes has to begin by facing the breadth of the word "reception." Classicists use this word to refer both to present engagement with an ancient text and also to someone else's earlier engagement with an ancient text, even in the lifetime of its author. Reception in this second sense extends almost from the text's creation almost to the present moment. A poet can even participate in his own reception, as Horace participates in that of the Odes with his comments in the Epistles (1.19.21–49). There could be a history of the reception, in the second sense, of a text or of a corpus of texts like the Odes. In fact, it has already been written for the Odes, at least piecemeal, by many hands.[1]

The model of reception in the first sense is a reader's or scholar's interpretation of an ancient text. Classicists are divided, however, on the question of interpretation. Some see it as their goal to pin down the text's original meaning. Others hold that this goal is futile because we cannot step outside our own situation in history and its ineluctable biases, which shape our view of the past. At best, they would say, we can participate in the history of the text's always unfolding, always new meanings. On either view, reception in the second sense, that is, focused on some point between antiquity and now, presents special difficulties. It seems that, if for the first group the original meaning is the true meaning, then the later, different meaning of the intermediate text will always have to be false. For this group, there could be no worthwhile reception, unless it contributed to the ascertainment of original meaning. For the second group, the intermediate text must be subject to the same conditions of interpretation as the ancient one. But are the scholar's biases, accepted by the second group as a working premise, the same with respect to the two texts, the ancient one and its intermediate reception? Can he or she even determine if they are the same? The relation of the two

texts will remain unstable, and it will perhaps be possible, starting from the presuppositions of the second group, to talk about the influence of the later text on
the earlier one.[2]

Reception in the sense of a reader's interpretation of a text is closely associated
with the name of Hans Robert Jauss, who began in his inaugural lecture at the
University of Constance, "Literary History as a Challenge to Literary Theory"
(1967), to argue for what he called an "aesthetics of reception."[3] When Jauss
spoke of aesthetics, he was speaking within a German philosophical tradition in
which the word was still close to its Greek meaning (αἰσθάνειν "to perceive or
apprehend by the senses"). Provided that one keeps Jauss's meaning of the word
in mind, aesthetics is a good rubric for the kind of reception I have been discussing, because it refers to the way one apprehends and interprets a text. But it is
not the only kind. In discussing Horace's Odes, it is useful to distinguish three
other kinds or modes of reception: the material; the social, in particular the educational; and the scholarly. These distinctions are logical and serve as ways of
organizing the following discussion, which will return in the last part of this
chapter to the particular problems of the aesthetic mode. In practice, as will be
seen, these modes are rarely operating independently of one another.

Material mode

The text of the Odes is an ideal object, the original words in their original order,
embodying what Horace meant to say.[4] From the modern editor's point of view,
the material form of the text is at best neutral, though often it is recalcitrant.
The editor's task is to restore what has been corrupted or lost in transmission.
The text's material form looks very different, however, to scholars of the history
and the sociology of the book. In their perspective, its material form is itself
expressive and conveys meaning, and it is "pointless to try to distinguish the
essential substance of the work, which is supposed to remain invariable, from the
accidental variations of the text, which are viewed as unimportant for its meaning."[5]
In the sociological area of their research they have discovered, further, that "what
constitutes a text is not the presence of linguistic elements but the act of construction" by the reader.[6] The material form of the text enters into that construction and thus into reception.[7] In the following discussion of the material reception
of Horace's Odes it will be impossible to specify, for each of the discernible stages,
the exact ways in which material forms have affected constructions of meaning.
My purpose is to set down a hypothesis concerning a mode of reception of the
Odes that tends to be neglected.[8]

At the beginning of their reception, the Odes take the material form of the
papyrus roll, the *libellus* ("book").[9] Publication meant, in the first place, the
copying of the Odes and their distribution to patrons, friends, and important
persons (cf. *Satires* 1.10.81–92).[10] It does not follow that the recipients *read* the

Odes themselves. While in *Epistles* 1.13, on the delivery of the first three books of the Odes to Augustus, Horace seems to imagine both audition and reading ("poems that might catch the ears and eyes"), the former was more likely. It has been said that in Rome at this time "a book of poetry ... was not simply a text in the modern sense but something like a score for private or public performance."[11] The poet himself might put on the first performance of his work. Horace, however, says that he prefers to avoid recitations, except to his friends and if he is compelled (*Satires* 1.4.73).

In the second place, publication meant the private copying of the copies initially released (not "published" in any modern sense) by Horace. It also meant a book trade, as Horace acknowledges in *Epistles* 1.20, referring to the Sosii, booksellers. Though he presents this trade as distasteful (also *Satires* 1.4.71–2), without it he could not have imagined himself, as he did, as known at the limits of the Roman Empire in every direction.

His books would have to earn money for the Sosii and be exported across the sea.[12] A papyrus fragment of the first century CE from Hawara, near Fayum oasis, shows him at the southern boundary of the empire. It is a calligraphic exercise, that of an expert, who has copied out a line of *Ars Poetica* six times.[13] Though it is the only papyrus fragment of Horace, it shows that a global (in Roman terms) market for his work reached even to this outpost. Nothing prevents one from imagining the Odes there, too.

No physical text of Horace appears again, after the time of this fragment, his oldest manuscript, until the second half of the ninth century, the period of the earliest codices of his works.[14] The first of three major changes in the material reception of the Odes, the change from papyrus roll to codex, a book with parchment pages, has long since taken place.[15] The second major change is from codex to printed book. The earliest dated incunabulum of Horace's works came from the press of Antonius Zarotus in March 1474 (Milan). By convention, the incunabulum period of printing is said to end at 1500.[16] It was shortly thereafter that Aldus Manutius published Latin authors in the octavo format. He brought out Horace in 1501–3. The third major change since the *libellus* is from the printed book to the electronic text.

To the ideal object of the textual critic, the text itself, there was attached, at every stage of material transmission some amount of paratext. As soon as it left Horace's hands, his text was liable not only to miscopying but to deliberate rewriting, interpolation, and annotation. When Martial speaks of correcting copies of his poems for friends, his correction (*litura*, lit. "erasure") is a matter of marking (verb *notare*, "to mark," 7.17.7–8) and thus of paratext.[17] Horace might have done the same. As for his readers, when he uses the image of a fugitive slave boy for a published book of poems (*Epistles* 1.20), the indignities the boy is expected to suffer must stand in part for graphic interventions in the book.[18] Modestus and Claranus, the first known scholars of Horace, apparently contemporaries of Martial (10.21), would have entered their glosses in their copies.[19] Marcus Valerius Probus (fl. in reign of Nero, 54–68 CE) is said to have used Aristarchus' critical signs in his text of Horace. He would not have done so if that text had not contained interpolations,[20] and, if there were interpolations, there could have been paratextual matter. The titles of the Odes are an example of the kind of thing that was added as a help. They appear in the codices and then in incunabula and perhaps go back to at least two different post-Proban copies.[21] The grammarian Q. Terentius Scaurus commented on Horace in the time of Hadrian (emperor, 117–38 CE), as did Helenius Acro at the end of the second century and, somewhat later, Pomponius Porphyrio.[22] The manuscripts that came into the hands of the last two would already have carried not only titles (in the case of the Odes) but some amount of commentary.

Acro's commentary is lost. The heterogeneous scholia going under his name, referred to as those of "pseudo-Acro," are preserved in the margins of various manuscripts of the works of Horace.[23] Porphyrio's commentary, on the other hand, is preserved in two manuscripts (Vaticanus, ninth century and Monacensis, tenth century), though not exclusively. Like that of pseudo-Acro, it is also found in the margins of Horace, and that was its original location.[24] A manuscript bearing commentary typically surrounds some lines of verse on three sides, and this format carried over into the incunabulum.[25] From the point of view of the history of the text, this ponderous format is "archaic," and the first edition of Lambinus' Horace (1561) is commendable because his page "appears modern by contrast with its immediate predecessors and contemporaries."[26] A century after Lambinus, John Dryden still used editions of Horace in which the text was surrounded by glosses, and a perceptive reader of Dryden can see how he constructed a Horace of his own out of the various elements on the page, of which the received text was only one. "[I]t becomes inappropriate to insist upon the familiar distinction between text and margin: the marginal glosses become part of the text which the reader makes when interpreting the poetry … "[27]

The tendency toward paratext that had begun already in the days of Horace has gone to astonishing lengths in the most recent of the major changes in the material reception of the Odes. In the Perseus Digital Library, every word of every Ode is glossed or, to put it differently, every word is a link that takes one to a window in which one sees a brief definition; a parsing of the word; a link to its entry in either Lewis and Short or the Elementary Lewis; its frequency in Horace and in other Latin authors; a link to the passages in which the word is attested in other Latin authors in the Perseus database.

Though its aim is pedagogical, Perseus could include, because of copyrights, only older commentaries and reference works. It might, then, seem that the real reception of Horace is taking place elsewhere, in the minds of scholars and intellectuals. On the contrary, now, as in long stretches of European history, by far the largest readership of Horace consists of students. The scholars and intellectuals are the happy few who continue with Horace after their student days. Further, by the hypothesis with which this discussion of material reception began, reading of Horace's Odes in the electronic format will inevitably affect the ways in which they are understood. Experience in the classroom has already shown that students arrive in class with their own commentaries culled from Perseus (no matter if Quinn, say, was required for the course) and sometimes, depending on their assignments, with notes from more recent, scholarly commentaries and also from on-line articles.[28] This kind of preparation encourages a new kind of reading. Again experience confirms often-heard descriptions of the effects of the electronic text: non-linear reading, the loss of the stable page (a screen-full of words is not a page), fragmentation, the "surfing" of multiple, ephemeral units. Such matters as the structure or unity of an Ode, its rhetoric or its imagery, recede in importance. The next generation of scholars and intellectuals will discover new Horaces in the new electronic forms of the text.

Social mode

Education is the main social mode of the reception of the Odes. Apart from the Roman *ludus litterarius*, which is probably not to be conceived of as the "primary" school, preceding the grammarian's, but as the lower-class elementary school, the teaching of Horace was always, until the mid-twentieth century, addressed to an elite.[29] For this reason, one might be expected to refer to this use of Horace in education not as social but as ideological, as an old-time Marxist would surely do.[30] A post-Marxist concept of ideology will, however, be restricted to thinking that is explicitly political: ideologies as "those systems of political thinking, loose or rigid, deliberate or unintended, through which individuals and groups construct an understanding of the political world they, or those who preoccupy their thoughts, inhabit, and then act on that understanding."[31] In the long history of the teaching of Horace to be surveyed briefly here, his value, for those who bother to state their point of view, is almost never political as in the definition of ideology just quoted. His value lies, in certain periods, in his usefulness in rhetorical training; in others, in the cultivation of the mind. For an ideological use of Horace one would look to the celebration in Fascist Italy of the bimillenary of his birth. In a grotesque speech delivered on the Campidoglio in 1935, Ettore Romagnoli, the pre-eminent Italian Classicist of the day, finds the true Horace in the Odes, and, in the Odes, in the civil ones. The *Epistles* begin to show a decline, Romagnoli says, but then Augustus restores the poet's powers by commissioning the *Carmen Saeculare*.[32]

To take up, then, the story of Horace in education, he disliked the idea of his poems becoming school texts. What awaits the book figured as a run-away boy in *Epistles* 1.20 is that "a stammering old age comes upon you as you teach children their ABC's" (17–18). In *Satires* 1.10, Horace backs up the principle that the poet should be content with a few (sc. worthy) readers by asking: "Or are you so crazy that you prefer to have your poems dictated in low schools?"

(72–5). In both passages, he seems to have in mind the Roman *ludus litterarius*. Quintilian, for his part, thinks of the grammarian (*grammaticus*) as the first teacher of the future orator, and approves the teaching of lyric poetry—he mentions Horace—at this stage of a boy's education, though the teacher must choose appropriate parts of the poet's work (*Instit.* 1.8.6). Juvenal, writing a few decades later, mentions, among the grammarian's woes, his having to breathe the smoke from the boys' lanterns, adding that the soot turns the copies of Vergil and Horace black (*Satires* 7, 225–7). Horace ended up, then, as the school text that he did not want to be.

For about the first five centuries CE, the grammarian's school was the primary venue for the reception of Horace's Odes. The grammarian taught the knowledge of speaking correctly and the explication of the poets (Quint. *Instit.* 1.4.2). The commentary of Porphyrio, mentioned above, taken as a document in the history of Roman education, affords a look at how students learned to read Horace in the third century, and it will be necessary to return to this work in discussing the scholarly and the aesthetic modes of reception. In the mode under discussion here, the social function of the grammarian requires notice. His school "was the single most important institution, outside the family, through which the governing classes of the empire perpetuated and extended themselves."[33] To have sweated out a competence in Horace at school was above all a mark of elite status.[34]

Horace's Odes could be taught also at the highest level of Roman education, the school of rhetoric, as Quintilian shows. In discussing the reading matter of the future orator, having awarded Horace the first place among the satirists, he proceeds to say: "Of the lyric poets Horace is also almost the only one worth reading. He sometimes rises to heights, and he is full of pleasantry and charm and versatile in his figures and happily bold in his choice of words" (Quint. *Instit.* 10.1.96).[35] In Tacitus' *Dialogus de oratoribus* (c. 101/2 CE), Marcus Aper, the spokesman for present-day tastes, includes poetry in the orator's training, mentioning Horace in a way that suggests he has the Odes in mind.[36] Quintilian himself, the man and the orator, as distinguished from the author of the *Institutio Oratoria*, is one of the happy few who emerged from the grammarian's school with an appreciation of poetry. He refers in passing to his love of Horace (10.1.94), and his occasional references to individual words show a detailed knowledge of the Odes.[37]

The barbarian invasions of Italy in the fifth century set off changes far-reaching in space and time. For the history of education, the main outline, at least, is clear. The grammarian's and the rhetorician's schools, where the Odes were read, survive in some places into the seventh century, but not beyond. They are succeeded in the Carolingian period by the monastic and by the episcopal or cathedral schools. These new kinds of school differed little from each other at first.[38] They prepared students for life in the monastery or for offices in the church.[39] For some centuries, Horace faded from any regular curriculum, even if there was a learned man here or there who still read him. Talk of "revivals" and "renaissances" in the Middle Ages tends to obscure the fact that such men were few and far between. Alcuin (c. 735–804), summoned by Charlemagne to be the head of his palace school, assumed Horace's cognomen "Flaccus" but had probably never read a line of this poet except in some intermediate source.[40]

Only with the emergence of a new model of education, one including letters and manners, did the study of the pagan poets return.[41] The institutional setting of this model is the cathedral school, which from the mid-tenth century assumes the function of training young men for service at court, whether in secular or in ordained roles. The earliest evidence for the teaching of Horace is a reference from the end of the tenth century to Gerbert of Aurillac's lecturing on Horace in Rheims.[42] Though Gerbert was probably lecturing on the *Satires*, it is in this period that the Odes return to the curriculum.[43] A considerable number of neumed manuscripts, corresponding in date roughly to the rise of the cathedral school, would have had a didactic function, and this school is the likeliest place for their use.[44]

The University of Paris grew out of the cathedral schools of Notre-Dame in the twelfth century; teaching also began at what would become the University of Oxford. In the next century, universities came into existence in Italy, Spain, and Portugal. To follow the fortunes of Horace's Odes in university teaching would be to follow many separate national paths.[45] The same is true for the teaching of Horace in schools in England, Europe, and the other parts of the world to which European culture spread. Readers of this chapter will know something, indeed will have experienced something, of the latest phases of that history in the schools of their own countries. English-speaking readers will be aware of a particular reception of the Odes which began in eighteenth-century England or earlier, soon had reflexes in America, and in some cases continued into their own lifetimes: Horace became the ideal of the gentleman.[46] Though the Satires seem at first to be the foundation of that ideal, the Odes are equally important.[47] The preface to an anonymous edition of the Odes, Epodes, and *Carmen Saeculare* published in London in 1741 begins: "Of all the Gifts of the Muses, Horace's poems are the most useful, and he is the only Poet who can form the Gentleman, as there is none but he who lays before us the Duties of a civil life, and teaches Men to live happily with themselves, with their Equals, and with their Superiors."[48] The gentleman will have read the Odes in school; will in some cases have composed Latin verse in Sapphics and Alcaics; will be able to quote tags and to allude to the Odes when he writes in English. Despite the adverse judgment of the Romantics on the Odes, this ideal, both in England and elsewhere, continued into the nineteenth century and on into the twentieth.[49]

Patrick Leigh Fermor's *A Time of Gifts*, the narrative of a journey on foot across Europe in 1933–4, includes a remarkable document of the gentleman's Horace.[50] In an excursus on the poems he had memorized, Leigh Fermor includes "a number of [Horace's] Odes" and so is led into a further excursus.

"One of them—I. ix. *Ad Thaliarchum*—came to my rescue in strange circumstances a few years later." He proceeds to give a brief, modest account of one of
the great exploits of World War II, his and William (Billy) Stanley Moss's capture
and abduction, on occupied Crete, of the German general Heinrich Kreipe, for
which Leigh Fermor and Moss were awarded the DSO (Distinguished Service
Order).[51]

> It was a time of anxiety and danger; and for our captive, of
> hardship and distress. During a lull in the pursuit [i.e. the pursuit
> by German troops of captors and captive], we woke up among the
> rocks just as a brilliant dawn was breaking over the crest of Mt.
> Ida. ... Looking across the valley at this flashing mountain-crest,
> the general murmured to himself:
>
> Vides ut alta stet nive candidum
> Soracte ...
>
> It was one of the ones I knew! I continued from where he had
> broken off:
>
>   nec iam sustineant onus
> Silvae laborantes, geluque
> Flumina constiterint acuto,
>
> and so on, through the remaining five stanzas to the end. The
> general's blue eyes had swiveled away from the mountain-top to
> mine—and when I'd finished, after a long silence, he said: "Ach
> so, Herr Major!" It was very strange. As though, for a long
> moment, the war had ceased to exist. We had both drunk at the
> same fountains long before; and things were different between us
> for the rest of our time together.[52]

Horace becomes a bond between the twenty-nine-year-old Leigh Fermor and
the forty-nine-year-old general. Able to quote Horace, Leigh Fermor shows that
his background is the same as the general's, and his identity as enemy officer
now shifts in the German's mind to something like social equal from another
country.

Scholarly mode

The treatment of scholarship on the Odes as one mode of their reception amongst
others, which might once have seemed improper, would now be accepted by
many Classicists, at the very least as a working hypothesis. In the course of this
section and the next, support for this hypothesis will emerge.

    The chefs d'œuvre of scholarship are the commentary and the textual edition.
Scholarship on the Odes in the first of these senses began within a century of

Horace's death (cf. on Modestus and Claranus in the first section above). Porphyrio represents a synthesis of grammatical knowledge at the point it had reached in his time. He does not simply report, however, what others before him said but states his own opinion.[53] If he has a particular strength, it lies in his sensitivity to diction or stylistic register. His deficiencies, as they appear to us, are many. He never cites Greek antecedents of the Odes. His knowledge of meter stops at the hexameter. (The metrical study of the Odes by Caesius Bassius [first century CE] somehow failed to get into the grammatical tradition.[54]) Porphyrio is weak on mythology and insensitive to imagery; has difficulties with syntax; has no interest in historical context beyond the identity of persons named in the Odes and no interest in Odes as wholes beyond occasional concern for marking where they begin and end.[55]

Karsten Friis-Jensen's studies of the tradition of medieval commentary on Horace show that the collection of Odes always begins with an *accessus* or introduction.[56] It included a life of Horace;[57] the *materia libri* ("the subject-matter of the book": the different kinds of lyric, as defined by Horace himself in *AP* 83–5); the *intentio auctoris* ("intention of the author": *prodesse* "to be useful" and *delectare* "to delight," from *AP* 333);[58] and the "title of the work" (discussion of the etymologies of *oda*, "ode" and *lyricus*, "lyric"). The commentaries are uneven when it comes to meter, though most medieval manuscripts of the Odes carry either a separate metrical treatise or metrical glosses on individual poems. Each Ode typically has its own *accessus*. Friis-Jensen prints the *accessus* to, and the glosses on, *Odes* 1.20 from six medieval commentaries (from about 1050 to 1200), along with the corresponding parts of Porphyrio and Pseudo-Acro on this Ode.

Taking *levi* ("I sealed [a jar of wine]" 3) as an example, one can get a sense of medieval commentators at work on glosses. Both Porphyrio's correct interpretation of the sense ("sealed," with which he contrasts *relevi*, "I unsealed" at Ter. *Haut.* 460) and Pseudo-Acro's incorrect one (*aperui*, "I opened," *protuli*, "I brought out," for which the same place in Ter. is cited!) reached various places during the Middle Ages. The St. Gall commentary says simply but not incorrectly: *reposui* ("I stored away"). Paris 7641 gives a sophisticated description of the sealing of the container with pitch; then proceeds to consider, with equal seriousness, a misleading textual variant (*aut LENI* ..., "or 'I softened'").

To judge from this sample of glosses, a single citation, Porphyrio's, of an author other than Horace himself, Terence, has determined an incorrect alternate interpretation of *levi* in medieval commentary. Otherwise, it is a matter of *Horatium ex Horatio explanare* ("to explain Horace on the basis of Horace") and of common sense.[59] As for the *accessus* in this selection, they show clearly enough the filters, one moral, the other Christian, through which the sense of an Ode as a whole was made accessible to the medieval reader.[60] Five of the six commentaries present *Odes* 1.20 as spoken by a *villicus* (St. Gall) or *rusticus* (Aleph) attempting, by a display of poverty, to extort gifts from his master, or as Horace using himself as an example of this kind of dishonorable conduct.[61] The Oxford commentary exhibits another strategy. It introduces *Odes* 2.6 (*Septimi Gadis*) with the explanation: "Horace has come to despise this world with its pleasures and in future wishes to subject himself to the monastic rule. For being already weary of these worldly affairs, he meditates in advance on the end of his life and is longing to find a suitable locality to spend his old age."[62] In this way, it was not difficult to answer Jerome's question, "What has Horace to do with the Psalter?"[63] The commentators put these filters in place in order to legitimize the reading of the Odes by medieval students. The rest is glosses. But grammatical interpretation suffices when the temporal distance between the present and the past has been effaced.[64]

Renaissance commentaries cease to be anonymous, and they begin to display scholarly competitiveness. The first humanistic commentary on Horace was that of Landino (Florence, 1482 and often reprinted).[65] Landino takes a new approach to the moral problem of the Odes, assuring Guidobaldo da Montefeltro, to whom he presents his edition, that "the books of Horace are written with skill of such a sort ... that they can help you tremendously, even his lyric poetry, in rousing young men's mental powers and in polishing and enhancing their speech."[66] He goes on to say that the Satires and other works of Horace will then complete the moral part of the youth's education. It is no longer necessary, then, to pretend that the Odes carry useful moral or Christian messages. Though Angelo Poliziano praised Landino in the ode that appears at the beginning of Landino's edition, he criticizes him in his own *Miscellanea* (1489), two collections of about one hundred notes (*centuria*), each on classical texts.[67] The Odes, not much mentioned in the *Miscellanea*, come into their own in the second Quattrocento commentary after Landino's, that of Antonio Mancinelli (Venice, 1492 and often reprinted). He confined himself to the lyric Horace (Odes, Epodes, and *Carmen Saeculare*). He published his work, the purpose of which was didactic, along with Porphyrio, Pseudo-Acro, and Landino, the last of whom he does not mention.[68] The text which he included shows the same incipient critical spirit as in Poliziano's *Miscellanea*.

Editions of Horace proliferated in the sixteenth century. The one most often mentioned is that of Jacobus Cruquius. He published a complete text and commentary (1578), which was preceded by separate editions, including one of *Odes* 4. In 1611, he printed, before his own commentary on each poem, that of the so-called "Commentator Cruquianus," someone he conjured up as the source of notes that he thought were too good to be by Porphyrio or Pseudo-Acro.[69] But it is for another reason that Cruquius is always mentioned, the more interesting work of Landino, Poliziano, and others almost never. The reason is that Cruquius had access to an important manuscript, designated V (Blandinius or Blandinius vetustissimus), which he often cites. This manuscript was destroyed when iconoclasts burned down the monastery (St. Peter, near Ghent) in which it was housed (1566).[70]

For the text of Horace, the edition of Denys Lambin or Lambinus (1561) is a milestone. It is considered the best text before Richard Bentley's (1711 and after) and "still worth consulting."[71] At the same time, despite the advance represented by Lambinus' text, his uncritical adherence to received readings, when his manuscripts offered better alternatives, causes puzzlement. Despite his *Diatribae* against Lambinus on the editing of Horace, Stephanus did little better, nor did Heinsius and other editors. Concerning all of them, the modern editor raises the same question that one also raises concerning the state of Renaissance commentary: why were the same old mistakes (and often the same old commentaries) repeated over and over again?[72]

Textual criticism became modern, that is, "scientific," when it became historical, attempting to establish the ancient text as it originally was, that is, "what the author originally wrote."[73] If the same spirit were brought to the question concerning Renaissance editions raised in the preceding paragraph, one could avoid a teleological history, in which pre-modern editors are only forerunners, sometimes puzzling in their blindness, of their modern counterparts. One could see pre-modern texts as sufficient unto their users. In this perspective, it did not matter much, for the purposes of instruction, what the state of the pre-modern text was (just as, in our contemporary classrooms, the text of the Odes read by students is unlikely to be that of the most recent editions). For higher purposes, the reader constructed his own text (cf. on Dryden above). Petrarch could prize the Odes without needing manuscripts better than the ones he had, or, if he had lived in the time of incunabula or in the sixteenth or seventeenth centuries, better than the editions that he happened to own.[74]

Critical editions currently in use present an interesting spectacle. Almost at the same time, the two Teubner houses both published new editions of Horace, that of Stephan Borzsák in 1984 and that of Shackleton Bailey in 1985. On their own terms, these editions intended progress toward the goal of establishing what Horace originally wrote. The differences between the two are, however, so pronounced that one might conclude that the shared scientific goal has paradoxically led to two different Horace's, each the editor's own construction. One reviewer even found that the older edition of Friedrich Klingner (1959) was preferable.[75] While it would be foolish to claim that these twentieth-century editions are no better than the Renaissance ones, something can be said for the notion of the scholar's constructing his own Horace. In the two most recent Teubner editions, a feature that encourages this notion is the apparatus criticus, on which, as in all critical editions, the text rests both visually and conceptually. Borzsák's is almost baffling. Shackleton Bailey's, to pick out one of its peculiarities, fails twenty-nine times to report when Porphyrio and/or Pseudo-Acro support a reading that he rejects.[76] The difficulty of the apparatus criticus, of which Paul Maas had once complained, might seem to have become a deliberate strategy that the editor employs for his own purposes.[77] The element of judgment, acknowledged in a conservative account of textual criticism as sometimes inevitable, seems to have become predominant.[78]

One might conclude, then, that the critical edition of Horace also belongs to the history of the reception of this poet. The editor's text puts on record not only his scholarly labors but also, in effect, his interpretation of the Odes. In *Odes* 1.23, for example, to be discussed in the next section, to read Shackleton Bailey's text is to read in lines 5–6 not the manuscript's *mobilibus veris inhorruit / adventus foliis* ("spring's approach shivers with flickering leaves") but emendations yielding *mobilibus vepris inhorruit / ad ventum foliis* ("the thorn-bush shivers in the wind with flickering leaves"). The reader, at such a point, takes the apparatus criticus not as the editor's justification for what should be read but as a way of constructing his or her own text consistently with the unfolding of this text within his or her aesthetic perspective.

Aesthetic mode

The commentary and the textual edition, contrary to the view taken in the preceding section of this chapter, are conventionally regarded as in a different category from the rest of the scholarship on an author.[79] It would be more readily conceded that books and articles on Horace, for their part, go under the heading of aesthetics of reception as defined, with reference to Jauss, in the introduction to this chapter. Various Horaces, as everyone can see, have come and gone in the history of classical scholarship, which thus appears to be a history of reception. Even the historicist scholar would assent to this view, though he or she would maintain that scholarship should not abandon the goal of recovering original meaning.

Scholarship can be distinguished from two other kinds of aesthetic reception. One is reading. The other is artistic reception. The latter divides, in turn, into literary (allusion, imitation, and translation) and other than literary (figurative art, emblemata in particular, and musical settings), the latter not to be discussed here.[80] Yet another kind of reception, which profoundly affects aesthetic reception, focuses on the character and life of Horace. The earliest document of this kind is Suetonius' brief *vita*. The detail concerning Horace's immoderate lust and his mirror-lined erotic studio was easily combined with the image of bibulous poet-courtier. In the seventeenth and eighteenth centuries, he became a character in historical fiction. Novels like Marie-Catherine Desjardins's *Les exiles de la cour d'Auguste* (1672), the anonymous *Poète courtesan ou les intrigues d'Horace à la cour d'Auguste* (1705), and Pierre-Joseph de la Pimpie-Solignac's *Les amours d'Horace* (1728) had an eager readership. The figure projected by these novels inevitably affected reading of the Odes, and thus Lessing's "rescue" of Horace became necessary.[81] He defended the poet against the charges arising from Suetonius as well as those of pederasty, atheism, and cowardice.

At the time of its beginnings, modern scholarship certainly did not appear as aesthetic reception, but could be contrasted with reading, as it was by Johann Gottfried Herder (1744–1803) apropos of the Odes. In the last year of his life, Herder completes the fifth and final volume of his *Adrastea*. It includes seven "Briefe über das Lesen des Horaz, an einen jungen Freund" ("Letters on the reading of Horace, to a young friend"). These letters, defining an opposition between research on details of the Horatian ode and grasp of the whole, challenge the views found in Christian Adolf Klotz's *De felici audacia Horatii*, published forty-one years earlier, in 1762.[82] The short-lived Klotz (1738–71) is now remembered, if he is remembered at all, as Gotthold Ephraim Lessing's favorite whipping-boy.[83] But Herder, too, attacked him during his lifetime, already opposing his views on Horace in both the first and the second *Kritische Wäldchen* (1769). In fact, the "Briefe über das Lesen des Horaz" repeat the main points of the *Wäldchen*.[84]

The points that Herder makes are worth reviewing because they come at a turning point in intellectual history, and they define the terms in which the reception of the Odes continues to be understood two centuries later. One must not, says Herder, obscure the ode as a whole by draping it with notes and parallel passages; one must put oneself imaginatively in the situation of the poet, in the occasion that gave rise to the poem. Herder takes the primary characteristic of the Odes to be "Anmuth und Grazie" (his translation of Quintilian's *iucunditas et gratia*, "pleasantry and charm"), which he finds in their prosody (Letter 1). Melodies and prosody are not enough, however. Visual representations (*Bilder*) are also necessary. Each ode chooses for itself and presents a situation, which becomes a picture. Because, however, an ode is musical, it has a beginning, middle, and end (Letter 2). In the second letter, too, comes Herder's main advice to his friend: "So, my friend, in every Horatian ode seek out the mental situation, which the poet wanted to represent and animate; seek in it his standpoint, his course, his goal; then see how he pursued his course; with what difficulty or ease he completes it." The third letter deals with "grace of life" (*Lebensgrazie*); the fourth with friendship; the fifth with a theme that would become perennial, Horace's relations with Augustus; the sixth with translation (Herder here develops a point that he made earlier concerning the unique suitability of the German language for translating Horace). The seventh begins by entering into contemporary debate concerning Horace; then changes direction with the report of the death of the poet Friedrich Gottlieb Klopstock. In the essay following the Letters, he states his main point once again, this time with a valuable description of his own experience of reading an Ode: "I have set myself to it; I come to the end; the whole of the Ode, one over-all impression, in a few, but mighty, touches, lives in my soul; the situation of the Horatian Ode stands before my eyes, and—my book is closed."

Herder's debate with Klotz was soon replayed, in different terms, on an important stage, namely, the new University of Berlin. In twenty-six semesters, in the years 1809 to 1865, August Boeckh (1785–1867) lectured on the "Encyclopedia and Methodology of the Philological Disciplines." In these lectures, published by his student Ernst Bratuscheck in 1886, Boeckh's adversary, Gottfried Hermann (1772–1848) in Leipzig, is for the most part left unnamed.[85] Boeckh held that, like philosophy, philology should investigate itself as a form of knowledge and that the ensuing theory would be the "philological organon."[86] Against Hermann, he held that the ancient languages themselves belonged to the material side of philology. The formal side was concerned only with the activity itself of the scholar, with the "theory of understanding."[87] Boeckh distinguished between an absolute understanding (of the object itself) and a relative one (of the object in relation to other things). Hermeneutics, he said, deals with absolute, criticism with relative understanding. By "criticism," he meant such things as determining the correct reading in a text or deciding a question of authorship.[88] The relation of the two understandings is necessarily circular, "a great circle."[89] The notion of the hermeneutic circle, first formulated by Friedrich Ast (1778–1841) and developed by Boeckh's former teacher, friend and colleague, Friedrich Schleiermacher (1768–1834), thus remained fundamental in Boeckh's concept of philology even as the discipline of Classics was evolving away from it in the direction of historicism, thanks partly to Boeckh himself.[90] Boeckh stands in the line of succession that leads up to today's hermeneutics; he is also one of the grandfathers of historicism in Classics.[91]

But Hermann's sense of philology, that is, the study of language and of literary works, was to prevail and has prevailed, with the stamp given it by Ulrich von Wilamowitz-Moellendorff (1848–1931), up to the present.[92] With Wilamowitz, philology and history became two sides of the same coin. For him and his contemporaries, classical scholarship no longer had the humanistic resonance that it retained even in Boeckh.[93] Though the study of Greco-Roman antiquity might have a formative effect, "there could no longer be a privileged epoch if it was the case that every epoch was equally justified before god (Ranke)."[94] Historicism, meaning in principle the self-sufficiency of separate historical periods and the scholar's task of objective representation, became the rule for both literature and history.[95]

Herder's views were to have a curious brief afterlife. In an article on *Odes* 4.2, Eduard Fraenkel (1888–1970), often called the greatest Horatian scholar of the twentieth century, quoted Herder's strictures on the reading of Horace from the second of the "Briefe." He complained, as did Herder, of scholars who obfuscated the ode with learned commentary.[96] While scholars today might be inclined to place Fraenkel in the camp that he is ostensibly opposing, his evocation of Herder marks a continuing conflict over reception of the Odes in particular and over method in general. It emerged explicitly again in the early 1990s, at the time of the beginning of the current trend of reception studies in Classics, which coincided with, perhaps was prompted by, a loss of faith in historicism.[97] In 1990, Daniel Selden, writing in the inaugural issue of the third series of *Arion*, placed the editorial statement that had opened the first series in 1962, in the context of a history of controversy going back to Boeckh and Hermann.[98] In 1992, Karl Galinsky published a collection of articles entitled *The Interpretation of Roman Poetry: Hermeneutics or Historicism?*[99] In the following year, Charles Martindale's *Redeeming the Text: Latin Poetry and the Hermeneutics of Reception* appeared.[100]

Though the word "hermeneutics" appears in these titles, it would be fair to say that Classics had lost all connection with both the discipline-specific hermeneutics of Boeckh and, if it ever had one, with the philosophical hermeneutics of Wilhelm Dilthey, Martin Heidegger, and Hans-Georg Gadamer. The emergence, out of the philosophical tradition, of a specifically literary hermeneutics in the work of Hans-Robert Jauss was at first either unnoticed or repudiated in Classics.[101] Lately, in the swelling discussion of reception, it has come to be discussed with respect, if not yet applied.[102] The tardiness of Jauss's recognition undoubtedly has something to do with the opacity both of his German and of the English translations of his work. Two metaphors that are central in his presentation of his hermeneutics also cause difficulty, one, dialogue, because it seems facile, the other, horizon, because few are aware of its historical-philosophical depth.[103]

For Jauss, in his rethinking of the tradition of the horizon metaphor, the etymological meaning of the word ὁρίζειν ("to separate, as by a boundary") remains fundamental. A horizon marks the boundary beyond which one cannot see. To read a text is to read it within a certain horizon, within the expectations that the reader brings to it, thus within his or her "horizon of expectations." The text has its own, different horizon, however, that of its author and first readers. In an elaboration of the horizon metaphor, Jauss borrows "fusion [*Verschmelzung*] of horizons" from Gadamer to refer to the encounter of the reader's horizon with the text's. This additional metaphor is misleading if it suggests that understanding as fusion takes place automatically or is somehow predetermined. On the contrary, it has to be attained, and is attainable only through the mediation (an expression Jauss uses more often than fusion), on the reader's part, of the differences between the two horizons.

If I change my position, my horizon will also change.[104] In the re-reading of a text, my horizon of reading will also have changed. I will approach the text with new expectations and new questions. Jauss, taking a suggestion from Edmund Husserl's analysis of horizon, uses the shift of horizons systematically as the basis of an interpretation of Charles Baudelaire's "Spleen II."[105] In this interpretation, Jauss distinguishes three readings. The first is perceptual or aesthetic. It is sequential or "linear," and attempts to make sense of the poem as a whole, without stopping to do research on difficult points; presupposes as much scholarly information as necessary to reach this degree of sense. The first is not necessarily the very first empirically but serves to establish the horizon of the aesthetic perception.[106] One sees immediately another reason for the slow acceptance of Jauss on the part of Classicists. The conventions of classical scholarship do not recognize this kind of reading, even if it is often a visible sub-text or even the surface text in a scholarly publication, but require objectivity, which is usually tied to original historical meaning or to timeless, transhistorical meaning. Jauss's second reading returns, within the horizon of the first, to questions left unanswered by the first and to significance left open. The second stands to the first as "reflective interpretation" to "perceptual understanding."[107] The third reading seeks the first readers' horizon of expectation. It begins "by seeking out the questions (most often inexplicit ones) to which the text was a response in its time." Jauss continues: "An interpretation of a literary text as a response should include two things: its response to expectations of a formal kind, such as the literary tradition prescribed for it before its appearance; and its response to questions of meaning such as they could have posed themselves within the historical life-world of its first readers."[108]

This sequence of readings was the method for the "aesthetics of reception" for which Jauss had called from the time that he assumed his chair at Constance (1967). In the essay on "Spleen II," Jauss was demonstrating reception in the first of the two senses distinguished at the beginning of this chapter. Many Classicists are now interested in reception in the second sense, that is, as focused on some point between antiquity and now. How would Jauss's method apply to this kind of reception?

To answer this question, one has to observe in the first place that this method applies only to a particular kind of reception, that is, to works that can be read as aesthetic wholes, namely, to translations and imitations. To take the example of *Odes* 1.23, of which a reading on Jauss's model is offered below, one could read Austin Dobson's translation (1877) and make comparisons with the results of one's reading of *Odes* 1.23. For the third reading of the translation, however, the Classicist may lack the competence of a scholar of the English literature of Dobson's period. In this respect, Jauss's method presents difficulties to research in the history of the reception of classical texts. This difficulty might be overcome by research conducted jointly by a Classicist and an expert in the relevant field. For the third reading, it would be best if someone in Dobson's time had offered an interpretation of the translation. For that matter, it would be best for the third reading of *Odes* 1.23 if someone in Horace's time had offered an interpretation of this poem. But as Jauss observed wistfully of "Spleen II," "one rarely finds interpretations of individual poems" in the nineteenth century, and the same is of course true of Greek and Latin poems in antiquity.[109]

The history of classical scholarship, however, often offers something like a reading of individual Odes, at least a single reading, beginning with the *accessus* (discussed above) in medieval commentaries. If and when these commentaries are published, it will be possible to reconstruct the medieval phase of reception of the Odes.[110] Commentaries from the Renaissance and thereafter sometimes give summaries of or general reflections on the Odes, and one of these commentaries will be considered apropos of *Odes* 1.23 below. If it were possible to study all of them, at least the outline of a history of the reception of this Ode (or another) could be put together.[111]

The following brief readings of *Odes* 1.23 intend to sketch out Jauss's method and to bring it into relation with ongoing discussion of reception in the field of Classics.

Odes *1.23*

vitas inuleo me similis, Chloe,
quaerenti pavidam montibus aviis
   matrem non sine vano
     aurarum et silvae metu.

nam seu mobilibus veris inhorruit
adventus foliis seu virides rubum
   dimovere lacertae,
     et corde et genibus tremit.

atqui non ego te tigris ut aspera
Gaetulusve leo frangere persequor:
   tandem desine matrem
     tempestiva sequi viro.[112]

You avoid me, Chloe, like a fawn,
seeking in pathless mountains its fearful
mother, not without empty
fear of breezes and forest.

For whether with flickering leaves spring's
approach shivers or green
lizards have parted a bramble
she trembles in heart and knees.

And yet I do not pursue you like a fierce tiger
or Gaetulian lion to crush you.
At last cease to follow your mother,
you who are ripe for a husband.

Two of the first five words are Greek (*inuleus*,[113] *Chloe*), and Horace's simile has a precedent in Greek lyric in Anacreon's comparison of a boy or girl to a fawn abandoned by its mother.[114] The Horace speaking in this Ode is likely to be an "older man" in Chloe's eyes. (As a common noun, her name means "tender shoot.") But as for the allusion to Anacreon, is it something that Horace wants to communicate to the young woman or only to the reader? Are there two relations here, one between Horace and Chloe, the other between Horace and the reader? If -*dam* in *pavidam*, just before the caesura, is heard as the stem of *damma, -ae*, the general name for various members of the deer family, then the paronomasia seems to be something not for Chloe's but for the reader's amusement. The first stanza ends with a curious parallelism "of breezes and forest" (*aurarum et silvae*). Is it a hendiadys, that is, the forest's breezes, the breezes in the forest? Is it a merismus, a whole divided into two parts, like "heaven and earth"? If so, it would mean "everything in the natural environment." Or is it a pair of complementary dissimilars, like "bacon and eggs"?

The second stanza, beginning with *nam*, is going to offer an explanation of *similis* (1). It also answers the question concerning "breezes and forest." The first *seu* clause says "the coming of spring shivers with flickering leaves" (the figure is hypallage, as Porphyrio said). Here are the breezes that were just mentioned. The second clause speaks of green lizards parting a bush. Here is the forest. The breezes and forest at the end of the first stanza were then a totalizing pair. Everything scares the fawn, and in fact everything in the second stanza is about her fear.

In the third stanza, Horace denies the identity that could be imagined for him in the simile he has constructed, that of fierce tiger or Gaetulian lion, that is, the predator that a fawn would have to fear. If he is not this predator, then she does not have to be a fawn. Such is Horace's implicit argument. But now the question of two relations, which the ornateness of the second stanza might also raise, returns. In order to follow Horace's argument, Chloe has to know Greek and Roman poetry well enough to know that as a fawn her natural poetic predators are the "fierce" tiger and the "Gaetulian" lion. Only in this way can Horace bring her into the human reality indicated in the last two lines, in which she is exhorted to give up her attachment to her mother and to accept the human sociobiological agenda in which she is *tempestiva viro* ("ripe for a husband," or "for a man"). It seems as if Chloe might be as sophisticated as the reader. If so, she might have taken Horace's elaborate build-up of the fawn simile as a reflection more of his frustration than of her resistance, and she might feel, with the reader, a certain amusement at Horace's agitated *tandem desine matrem ... sequi* ("at last cease to follow your mother," 11–12). At the end, then, one relation, with Horace on one side and Chloe and the reader on the other.

A second reading returns to the two relations that seemed to be implied by the opening allusion to Anacreon, one between Horace and the reader, the other between Horace and Chloe. If, at the end of the poem, Horace's argument does not work unless Chloe has enough literary sophistication to understand his dismissal of the fawn's potential predators, was Chloe, then, *all along* as sophisticated as the reader, thus in the same relation with Horace as the reader? Faced with this question, one begins to realize that the mind of Chloe is a blank in the reader's mind. (For that matter, the feelings of Horace are never expressed, only inferred from "you avoid me" at the beginning and from the imperative at the end.) The two relations have to be rethought.

Horace's closing argument takes the form of the kind of argument called *modus tollens* (if A, then B; not B; therefore not A), with the premise unstated as such:

> If you are a fawn, I am a tiger or lion.
> I am not a tiger or lion.
> You are not a fawn.

Horace wins. Or does he? At this point, even if Chloe agrees that she is "ripe for a husband," she may not agree that Horace is the man. Horace gives the reader no way of deciding the question.

In the final stanza, another *modus tollens* argument bearing on Chloe's state of mind is implicit:

> If you are not a fawn, you need not follow your mother.
> You are not a fawn.
> You need not follow your mother.

This argument arises directly from the two terms of the Anacreontic simile, mother deer and fawn, with which the poem opened. In those terms, the fawn's independence of its mother is, one assumes, complete once attained. The fawn simply has no further need of its mother and is on its own. But in order to shift from the plane of the simile to the plane of reality, in which the human Chloe is "ripe for a husband," Horace has to argue for the same absolute independence on Chloe's part. Again, Chloe might accept Horace's argument without agreeing that it entailed complete independence of her mother.

Horace's argument as a whole leaves Chloe ways to escape. Though he cancels the fawn simile, she may still be fugitive. If Horace, who allowed Chloe and the reader to see these things, saw them himself, then the poem as a whole looks more like a somewhat self-ironic self-dramatization on the part of a poet who in his right senses would have agreed with Pindar that "We should ... gather the flowers of love / At the moment that fits our years ..." (Pindar fr. 123.1–2 S-M).[115] A second reading of the poem tends, then, to corroborate the conclusion of the first reading, that it was a matter of one relation, with Horace on one side and Chloe and the reader on the other.

As soon as one faces this Ode's "response to expectations of a formal kind, such as the literary tradition prescribed for it before its appearance," as Jauss stipulated for the third reading, one begins to suspect that the concerns of the first two readings were, as could have been expected, the reflex of one's own times. Horace's contemporary readers would have been more aware than we can be, perhaps more than we care to be, of Horace's program of appropriation of, and rivalry with, the archaic Greek poets.[116] A detailed reading of *Odes* 1.23 from this point of view would follow Horace's use of an opening "motto" from

Anacreon, with its affiliations in other archaic poets and also in Euripides, to another allusion (12) to Anacreon at the end of the poem (1 [fr. 1] P = 60 Gent.), and thence to Horace's relation to Anacreon in the rest of his œuvre.[117] When Horace, to make his case to Chloe, repudiates the simile, he also asserts himself as a Roman poet. There is, then, a second (if there was only one) or third (if there were two) relation at work in the Ode, between Horace and the poetic tradition in which he is working.[118]

As for this Ode's "response to questions of meaning such as they could have posed themselves within the historical life-world of its first readers," which was Jauss's other stipulation for the third reading, one again begins by broadening the context in the Odes. Matthew Santirocco has shown how the sequence of *Odes* 1.20–3, opening the second half of the first book, corresponds to the sequence of *Odes* 1.1–4. *Odes* 1.23 thus corresponds to *Odes* 1.4. They share the themes of springtime and love. The striking difference between the two is the figure of *pallida Mors* ("pale Death") in *Odes* 1.4. Whereas death is absent from *Odes* 1.23, it appears in the following ode, to Vergil on the death of Quintilius Varus. In what Santirocco calls a "dynamic" reading, then, the opposition that is explicit in *Odes* 1.4 is implicit in the relation between *Odes* 1.23 and 24. Santi-rocco further discusses *Odes* 1.23–5 as a triad illustrating a familiar Horatian idea: the "centrality of death as. . . the ultimate test of our ability to conform to the decorum of nature."[119] The triad is formed by a consistent theme ("attempts to cling to the past, to deny the passage of time") and by the antithetical relation of *Odes* 1.23 and 25, which frame *Odes* 1.24. In *Odes* 1.23, Chloe is in the springtime of life, the time for love, which she refuses; in *Odes* 1.25, Lydia is in the winter of life, burning with lust that she should give up. Gregson Davis's reading of *Odes* 1.25 shows that behind the plight of the aging Lydia lies "the ethical immaturity Horace criticizes in many [*carpe diem*] odes—the failure to come to terms with one's mortality."[120]

In this broadened context, Horace's advice to Chloe in *Odes* 1.23 has a particular ethical connotation that was invisible to the first two readings, one that takes this advice beyond Horace's immediate self-interest, without canceling it. The image of the fawn thus also appears differently in the third reading. In the first and second readings, its ostensible function seemed to be to serve in an argument that would break down Chloe's resistance to Horace. In the ethical perspective, it has another dimension. One can compare *Odes* 2.5. In this poem, the "heifer" Lalage is now too young for love but the time will come when she is ready. To her unnamed husband Horace advises the patience of which Horace is incapable in *Odes* 1.23 (or perhaps patience is unnecessary if Chloe is old enough). The two poems have in common the imperatives of human time. Even in *Odes* 3.11, where the filly is an image of Lyde's obstinacy (9–12), the adverb in the phrase *adhuc protervo / cruda marito* ("till now unripe for a bold husband") indicates that time has brought her to a new phase of life. The images of young women as animals in Horace differ, then, from the ones in archaic Greek lyric, where the pervasive image of the adolescent girl as a filly or heifer needing to be tamed by education and marriage points to the assumption of a static hierarchic relation of male and female.[121] The youth of the women in the poems of Horace just mentioned does not stand for an inherent female nature.

The sequence of readings, even briefly presented, has shown how the meaning that unfolds within the horizon of aesthetic perception becomes the starting point, in re-reading, for interpretation, and how the third, historicist reading establishes a horizon that can be contrasted with the first two. My first readings were preoccupied with the relations between Chloe and Horace and between Horace and the reader. The third reading suggests that the one between Chloe and Horace had something like an exemplary value, which would be the reason that the feelings on both sides, except for Chloe's fear, are under-characterized. (Her fear, for the sake of the poem's argument, is, one could say, over-determined.) Further, the relation of Horace to the poetic tradition in which he is working has an importance to which, one realizes, no first or second reading in the year 2008 is likely to be sensitive enough.

The sequence of readings also offers an approach to reception in the second sense in which it is being considered in this chapter. *Odes* 1.23 as it has appeared within my horizon of expectation and within its original horizon can be compared with its reading by someone else in the history of reception, provided that sufficient evidence for such a reading can be found. As said earlier, often a translation or an aperçu will indicate a reading. For comparison with *Odes* 1.23 I have chosen the edition of the Odes by André Dacier (1651–1722) because its horizon of expectation is to some extent self-evident and does not need the aid of an expert in seventeenth-century French literature.[122] Dacier, the keeper of Louis XIV's library and a central figure in the intellectual life of Paris, obviously reads Horace from the point of view of the *bel esprit*. He looks for beauty, finesse, grace, and elegance. His comment on *Odes* 1.22 is revealing: "This Ode is of a politeness and a gallantry that one cannot praise too much." For *Odes* 1.23, his comment on *tempestiva sequi viro* (12) is enough to show how he read this Ode: "These kinds of transpositions (i.e. from the metaphorical to the literal) are too rude and I would wish always to avoid them. It is true that some equally violent ones are found in prose and I have often been astonished that even the Septuagint is full of them. I have there noticed some completely like this one in Horace." Dacier is of course exquisitely sensitive to tact, in which he finds Horace lacking at the point in which he turns abruptly from the simile of the fawn to his plea to Chloe. He can forgive Horace only on the basis of a comparison with the Septuagint.

Though Dacier was aware of the allusion to Anacreon in the opening lines of the poem, he was probably unaware of the broader intertextual dimension of the fawn simile, and thus out of touch, in this respect, with the original horizon of expectation as reconstructed above. Likewise, he was unaware of the ethical connotation of the fawn simile discovered in the third reading. In short, Dacier remains, despite his scholarship, ahistorical at heart and thus in the line of Renaissance commentaries discussed above. As for his own horizon, it is comparable with my own in that the affective relationship between Horace and Chloe is what presents itself to him as most important. Though he interprets it differently, from the courtier's point of view, the accessibility of his horizon gives an intimation that, through the separation of present and past horizons, a history of the reception of *Odes* 1.23 could be written showing "how the meaning of the poem has unfolded historically … up to those very questions that guide our interpretation and to which the text in its own time did not yet have to be an answer."[123]

Conclusion

The results of Jauss's method in the case of *Odes* 1.23 provide the basis for concluding reflections on the modes of reception discussed in this chapter. To begin again with the material mode, the comparison of my third with my first and second readings, which brought out the rhetorical character of this Ode, suggests how appropriate it was to reading in the time of the papyrus roll, that is, to performance. My first and second readings were just that, readings, lying on the far side of post-Gutenberg print culture, in the history of which the novel became the most important genre.[124] The reading of novels is the formative literary experience of most of those who read Roman poetry, and in retrospect my readings seem to have tried to "novelize" the poem.[125] (But it was the way in which I could read the poem, and I cannot read it as Horace's first readers did.) My readings were also undoubtedly gender-based, insensitive to the relationship between mother and daughter that, Adrienne Rich said, has been "minimized and trivialized in the annals of patriarchy."[126] The chapter on this relationship in Rich's *Of Woman Born: Motherhood as Experience and Institution* (1976) and Luce Irigaray's *Et l'une ne bouge pas sans l'autre* (1979)[127] touched off an intense discussion that could form the basis of a reading of *Odes* 1.23 quite different from the one I have given.[128]

As for the social mode of reception, I would not have been writing this chapter if I were not one of the happy few who survived four years of high school Latin, including a semester of Horace, and then one day returned to this poet. My preference for Jauss's method and my sympathy with its presuppositions are no doubt a reflex of my having lived through the same (*mutatis mutandis*) crises of the humanities and of the university that inspired Jauss's hermeneutics.[129] The happy few as newly constituted now dwell within the walls of academe. The few are fewer, and they are hardly a social elite.

My discussion of scholarship led to the conclusion that even a critical edition of the Odes could be reckoned in the history of their reception. An editor's reading in the narrower sense, that is, his or her choice of a particular word or words in a particular place, belonged to a reading in the larger, hermeneutic sense, or ought to be construable in this larger sense. As I pointed out above,

Shackleton Bailey reads *vepris* for *veris* in line 6 of *Odes* 1.23, along with other emendations in the next line: "the thorn-bush shivers in the wind with flickering leaves." In this way, he creates a distinction between the movements of thorn-bush and of bramble which would be difficult to integrate into the readings that I have offered.[130] Shackleton Bailey's reading of these lines, like the discussion of it by Nisbet and Hubbard, presupposes that the significance of particulars can be decided in isolation from the poem as a whole, contrary to the hermeneutic principle.[131] The result for interpretation is a stand-off between strongly implanted (and I do not mean unadmirable) conventions of classical scholarship, on the one hand, and hermeneutics (of any kind), on the other. This stand-off is not exactly the same as, but corresponds to, the one described at this beginning of this chapter, the one between the hard-core historicists and the historical relativists.

GUIDE TO FURTHER READING

The *Cambridge Companion to Horace* (Harrison 2007a) contains short surveys, with bibliographies, of the reception of Horace in antiquity, the Middle Ages, the Renaissance, the seventeenth and eighteenth centuries, and the nineteenth and twentieth centuries (Friis-Jensen 2007; Harrison 2007b; McGann 2007; Money 2007; Tarrant 2007). Each covers Horace's whole œuvre. Martindale and Hopkins (1993) is a collection of essays on Horatian influence on British writing from the Renaissance to the twentieth century. Norman Vance (1993) writes about Horace in the nineteenth century, Theodore Ziolkowski (2005) about Horace since 1935. Caroline Goad's (1967) magnificent study of Horace in the eighteenth is the most detailed one we have for any century. Her index points her reader to her discussions of individual Odes.

As for the reception of the Odes in particular, the only book-length study or survey has been that of Eduard Stemplinger (1906). He gives, for each Ode, a bibliography of, and some samples of, translations (German, French, Italian, and English), with brief comments, and, sometimes, also musical settings. His later book (1921) has valuable inventories of judgments on Horace arranged thematically under two main headings: "Moralische Wertung" (3–70) and "Ästhetische Wertung" (71–196). A few Odes have received individual attention in articles or chapters of books. Niklas Holzberg (2007) lists them under the subheading "einzelne Werke" under "Nachleben."

The bimillenary of Horace's death (reckoned as 1992 or 1993) coincided with an upsurge in reception studies. This double impetus produced celebratory collections, one, edited by Charles Martindale and David Hopkins (1993), completely devoted to the reception of Horace. Others, miscellaneous, included articles on reception, those edited by Matthew Santirocco (thematic issue of *CW*, 1994) and by Stephen Harrison (1995), and also a thematic issue of *Arethusa* (1995), to name those in English. Articles on Horace in the Renaissance by Barbara Pavlock (1994) and by Michael Roberts (1995) are of interest. Ludwig's collection (1993) is another that includes reception, including an article by Ludwig himself. The volume of reception studies edited by Helmut Krasser and Ernst Schmidt (1996) includes several articles at least partly on the Odes. Those by Rudolf

Sühnel and Jasper Griffin are on England, the one by Günther Heilsbrunn on the United States. The largest single collection of reception studies is the third volume of *Orazio: enciclopedia oraziana* (1998; all in Italian).

In my category of aesthetic reception, translation is perhaps the most important mode. The two volumes of the *Oxford History of Literary Translation* that have appeared each contain useful overviews of translations of Horace (Gillespie and Hopkins 2005; France and Haynes 2006). The eighteenth, that Horatian century is the one that has been best served. Goad's book has already been mentioned. Arthur Sherbo has edited Christopher Smart's translation of the Odes (1979). Robert M. Ogilvie has written on translation in the seventeenth and eighteenth centuries (1981), Richard Thomas on translation of the Odes, especially *Odes* 4.1 in the nineteenth century (2006). Some of the papers at the conference "Perceptions of Horace: A Roman Poet and his Readers" (University College London on July, 5–6 2007) dealt with translation. Luke Houghton and Maria Wyke are editing these papers for a volume to be published by Cambridge University Press.

Another aesthetic mode, emblemata, will undoubtedly attract further research and perhaps a reprint, namely of Otto Vaenius' *Emblemata Horatiana*. To the bibliography in my note 78, add an article by Leonard Forster (1981) and Stemplinger's discussion (1906: 46–50). In the forthcoming collection just mentioned, Roland Mayer has a paper on Vaenius.

NOTES

1 See Guide to Further Reading.
2 Kallendorf 1994: 156: "Sometimes … meaning flows backwards when we take into account the reader as well as the text."
3 Jauss 1970. Translated into English, along with other pieces, and published under the appropriate title (the translator's): *Toward an Aesthetic of Reception* (Jauss 1982d). The emphasis on the aesthetic in literary history emerges still more decisively in Jauss 1977 = Jauss 1982a. For the historical context of Jauss' reassertion of the hermeneutic tradition see Rosenberg 2003: 247–8.
4 See Edmunds 2001: ch. 1 ("Text").
5 Chartier 2007: ix.
6 McKenzie 1999: 43. Cf. Johnson in the following note.
7 See Johnson 2000: 600–6 on the distinction between reading as neurophysiological-based cognition and as sociocultural construction and on reading as "negotiated construction of meaning within a particular sociocultural context" (603).
8 Cf. Grafton 1997.
9 The diminutive of *liber*, on the semantics of which see Kenney 1982: 15, 30–1.
10 See White 1993: ch. 1 ("Poets and Roman Social Life"), especially the section "Collaborators in a Cultural Marketplace" (47–63), on the social context in which the Odes would first have been communicated and received.
11 Kenney 1982: 12. Cavallo 1999 is fundamental. Cf. Johnson 2000: 616: "vehicles for performative reading in high social contexts" (of the educated elite of the first and second centuries CE).

12 As he imagines, here without distaste, the success of the poet who knows how to combine the pleasant and the useful (*AP* 343–46).

13 Pap. Hawara 24 (*CLA*, Suppl. 1718). There are also multiple copies of two lines from the *Aeneid*. For details see Capasso 1998.

14 For an overview see Tarrant 1983 and for Horace in the ninth century Tarrant 2007: 285–9 ("Carolingian postscript").

15 See Kenney 1982: 25–7 on the change from papyrus and roll to parchment and codex.

16 The date may come from the earliest catalogue of incunabula: Kirchner 1952–6: *s.v.* Inkunabel; same explanation in Glaister 1979: *s.v.* incunabulum.

17 It is always assumed that Martial meant that he was restoring what he wrote the first time and not revising for improvement. Cf. McKenzie [1984–1986] 1999: 36–8.

18 Kenney 1982: 28: "[E]very copy of any text was an edition, being different from every other copy, and ... any reader who cared to take the trouble had always been accustomed to correct, punctuate, and annotate his own books using whatever resources were open to him."

19 Claranus is cited by Porphyrio on *Satires* 2.3.83.

20 Pasquali 1962: 378–9.

21 Pasquali 1962: 379.

22 For Scaurus, Porph. on *Satires* 2.5.92; and see Nisbet and Hubbard 1970: xlvii for the extent of his work, which is likely to have covered the Odes. For the date of Porphyrio: Diederich 1999: 3 (first half of the third century).

23 For these mss. see Tarrant 1983: 186.

24 As his comment on *Satires* 1.9, 52 shows. He refers to mark-up of the text indicating change of speakers. Cf. Diederich 1999: 5–6, 341 (marginal position of comments explains their brevity).

25 Another format: a column of verse in the center of the page flanked by columns of commentary on either side, as in the edition of Horace by Johann Grüninger (Strasburg, 12 March 1498), with also interlinear commentary and rubrication. This is also the first illustrated edition of Horace. See <http://www.slsa.sa.gov.au/exhibitions/treasures/rbrb15797600_184.htm> (accessed November 27, 2007).

26 Kenney 1974: 64.

27 Hammond 1993: 127–8. It is a matter of what the Chaucerian scholar Martin Irvine calls the "textuality of commentary" (in the title of Irvine 1992).

28 I.e. Quinn 1980.

29 Kaster 1983: 339.

30 See the section "The Concept of Ideology" in Edmunds 2002: 65–7.

31 Freeden 1996: 3.

32 Schiesaro 1995: 348–53; Cagnetta 1998: 616. Fleming 2006 argues that fascist appropriation of antiquity should be studied as such, not simply dismissed as abuse; cf. Fleming 2007: 343–6.

33 Kaster 1988: 14. For the literary education offered by the grammarian see 12–13, 16–17.

34 Kaster 1988: ix, 13–14, 26–31. For sweating it out, 16–17.

35 Quint. *Inst.* 10.1.96. At lyricorum idem Horatius fere solus legi dignus. Nam et
    insurgit aliquando et plenus est iucunditatis et gratiae et uarius figuris et uerbis
    felicissime audax. His felicissime corresponds to an element of the famous (it is even
    an entry in the *OED*) characterization of Horace's style by Petronius' Eumolpus:
    curiosa felicitas ("painstaking felicity," *Satires* 1.18.5). On the phrase see Baldwin
    2005.
36 *Dial.* 20.5. Tacitus alludes to *Odes* 1.37.6–10 at *Ann.* 15.37.4.
37 E.g., *acrem tibiam* cited at 8.2.10 from *Odes* 1.12.1–2.
38 Jaeger 1994: 26–7 with works cited in n. 34.
39 Alcuin's propounding of rhetoric as a secular discipline in *De rhetorica et virtutibus*
    is exceptional. See Jaeger 1994: 31–5. "It lacks the distinctive feature of Carolingian
    learning, the submersion of classical models in Christian ones" (34).
40 Stella 1998: 160.
41 Jaeger 1994: 48–52.
42 Tarrant 2007: 288 in "Carolingian postscript" (285–9). On Gerbert at Rheims see
    Jaeger 1994: 56–62.
43 Though to Dante Horace is simply "Orazio satiro" (*Inf.* 4.89). Friis-Jensen 1997:
    66, in conclusion: "The medieval commentaries on the *Odes* which I have seen
    indicate that Horace's Odes were actually read in the arts courses of eleventh- and
    twelfth-century schools, and that some of the texts we have are based on lectures
    in the classroom."
44 A "neume" (probably from πνευμα) is a mark placed above the text (usually added
    interlinearly after the fact) to indicate the contour of a melody. Jaeger 1994
    assumes, I think uncontroversially, 950–1100 for the rise of the cathedral school.
    For lists of mss., arranged in various ways: Piperino 1998: 661–5; Ziolkowski 2000;
    Wälli 2002. For photographs: Piperino 1998: 662–3. For dates: Ziolkowski 2000:
    75; Wälli 2002: 34–6. For use of neuming in schools: Ziolkowski 2004. I was
    unable to obtain Ziolkowski 2007 from a library before the date on which this
    chapter had to be submitted.
45 Separate articles on the reception of Horace in thirty-three countries and in Latin
    America can be found in Mariotti 1998: section 16 ("Orazio nei vari Paesi").
46 For an overview of the connection between social class and the study of Latin from
    the Renaissance to the twentieth century, see Waquet 2001: ch. 8.
47 Ogilvie 1964: 40–1 for Horace and Vergil as the two main school poets; 54–5 for
    imitation of the Odes; 65–6 for the ideal of the gentleman. For imitations of the
    Odes in 1730–40: Stack 1985: 22. For the great importance of Horace in eight-
    eenth-century England, the list of editions in Schweiger 1962: 405–14 is indicative,
    not to mention the reactions to Bentley's edition of 1711 (idem: 406). For English
    translations in this century, idem: 436–9. For Horace in eighteenth-century America,
    Money 2007: 323–4.
48 Anon. 1741: A2. Amongst the attractions listed on the title page one finds: "For
    the Use of SCHOOLS as well as of PRIVATE GENTLEMEN."
49 Vance 1993 on the nineteenth century: Horace "was the common possession of
    well-educated men, benignly presiding over cultivated masculine interchange in life
    and letters" (199; cf. 216). Gaisser 1994 convincingly inserts into this picture an
    "Imperial Horace," based on the Roman Odes, who flourishes from about 1870
    until World War I; cf. already Vance 1993: 210–14.

50 Leigh Fermor 1977.
51 For a good short account see <http://www.explorecrete.com/history/kreipe-follow.htm> (accessed December 15, 2007).
52 Leigh Fermor 1977: 74.
53 Diederich 1999: 5.
54 Mazzarino, *Gram. Rom. Frag.* 129–32, 135–48. See 126 for the problem of authorship. It is now thought that these fragments are by someone else.
55 These generalizations are based on Diederich 1999.
56 Beside pseudo-Acro, medieval commentary on Horace remains mostly unpublished and little studied. See Friis-Jensen 1997: 52–7 for a survey of scholarship; also, more briefly, without striking additions, Friis-Jensen 2007: 295–6.
57 Friis-Jensen 1993: 265–75.
58 Friis-Jensen 1993: 261–4, 278–85.
59 See Diederich 1999: 307–39.
60 So begins an ethical thread in the reception of the Odes. Cf. the discussion of this thread by von Albrecht 1995: 292–9.
61 Friis-Jensen 1997: 62–4 points to the probability of a common source of these five mss.
62 The trans. is that of Friis-Jensen 1993: 287. The Latin is quoted at 287 n. 49. One sees that the literal, i.e. non-allegorical, reading of the Satires studied by Reynolds 1996 in twelfth-century northern European commentaries does not apply to the Odes. But if only one had a book like Reynolds' for the Odes!
63 *Quid facit cum psalterio Horatius?* Letter 22.29.7 = Hilberg 1910–1918.1: 189.
64 Cf. Jauss 1989b: 201 = 1982b: 661–2.
65 Ludwig 1993: 325–6; Bausi 1998. Ludwig explicates Poliziano's ode to Horace, which appears at the beginning of Landino's commentary (327–31).
66 Quoted by Bausi 1998: 307.
67 On Poliziano see Kenney 1974: 4–12.
68 Coppini 1998: 334–35.
69 Nisbet and Hubbard 1970: li.
70 Shackleton Bailey 1991: iv.
71 Brink 1971: 44. For the career of Lambinus: Cecchetti 1998.
72 I am generalizing the question raised by Kenney 1974: 68 thus: "[W]hy did Heinsius and other editors of classical texts persist in following a procedure so well calculated to foster the survival of old and persistent error?" (his emphasis). For Lambinus as editor: 63–7.
73 West 1973: 48. Cf. Maas 1949: 888 (first paragraph). On the historicist turn: Kenney 1974: 19. Cf. Pfeiffer 1976: 154; Timpanaro 2005: 56.
74 Petrarch included Horace, "especially in the Odes," in a list of his favorite poets (BNF lat. 2201). On Petrarch's mss.: Feo 1998: 405–408 (with photographs). On Petrarch as reader: Grafton 1999: 208: "Petrarch's copies of Vergil, Augustine and many other authors mutated as he read and wrote in them into elaborate scripts, discussions between text and margin that sometimes involved several voices." Ludwig 1993: 312–25, on Petrarch's verse "Letter to Horace," with text (359–63).
75 Mankin 1988.
76 Mankin 1988: 271–3.

77 Maas 1949.
78 McDonald 1970. In the bibliography at the end of this article, note the heading: "ON JUDGEMENT IN TEXTUAL CRITICISM." Note that Shackleton Bailey 1990, a defense of his edition, tallies the places in which Nisbet 1986 and Delz 1989 accepted his conjectures (213 n. 1) In Shackleton Bailey 1985, before the edition appeared, he stated: "I do not believe that the resources of conjectural criticism have been exhausted" (153).
79 Note the divisions of Harrison 1995, a useful overview of scholarship on Horace in the twentieth century. The first section is: "Texts and Commentaries." Cf. Fowler 1999: 441: "The commentary is often figured as a more impersonal and objective form of scholarship compared to the monograph or article. …"
80 For figurative art: Cavallero 1998. For bibliography on emblemata: Schweiger 1962: 462–3; Sabbe 1935; Cavallero 1998: 682–5; Iurilli 1998. One can see photographs of Vaenius' emblemata at emblems.let.uu.nl/. Choose "Vaenius, Horatiana emblemata (1612)" under "Emblem Books." Photographs also in Martindale and Hopkins 1993: plates between 142 and 143. For bibliography on musical settings (aside from neumes): Schweiger 1962: 463.
81 "Rettungen des Horaz" (1754).
82 I have not seen this work. Nor have I seen *Vindiciae Q. Horatii Flacci* (1764), with a commentary, or *Lectiones Venusinae* (1770), also published by Klotz. For references see Schweiger 1962: 455.
83 Except that Bursian 1883.1: 444–47 writes more about Klotz than he does about, for example, Scaliger, largely because of Klotz's controversies with Lessing and with the younger Burman. The titles of Klotz's satirical writings, some published anonymously, some under his own name, against contemporary scholars, are quite amusing. Bursian gives the impression that the story has another side.
84 Herder 1877–1913. Vol. 3 for *Wäldchen*. Vol. 24: 199–222 for "Briefe über das Lesen des Horaz, an einen jungen Freund." Vol. 33: Index, for passing reference to Horace.
85 For an excellent synkrisis of Hermann and Boeckh, Bursian 1883. For a narrative of the debate: Hoffmann 1901: 48–62. Sandys 1908: 89 characterizes the two schools as "grammatical and critical" (Hermann) and "historical and antiquarian" (Boeckh). From Sandys's account (95–101) one gets no sense of Boeckh's methodological sophistication.
86 Boeckh 1886: 53. Horstmann 1990: 329–38 argues that it is at best half true to speak of hermeneutics in Boeckh as playing the role of a "philological organon"; that hermeneutics has the same generality as in Schleiermacher. Boeckh clearly distinguishes, however, between a philosophic and a philological hermeneutics.
87 Boeckh 1886: 54–5.
88 Boeckh 1886: 77, 170–1. The term "criticism" came from Schleiermacher. It should be remembered that for Boeckh philology covered everything in the "encyclopedia," all the parts of *Altertumslehre*.
89 Boeckh 1886: 178–9.
90 For Ast and the hermeneutic circle see Flashar 1979: 28–9. But the hermeneutic circle came to Boeckh from Schleiermacher: Boeckh 1886: 75.
91 Hentschke and Muhlack 1972: 91–6.
92 For Hermann's sense: Vogt 1979: 52–4.

93 Momigliano 1955: 177–81 for inheritance in Boeckh of the neo-humanism of Friedrich August Wolf (1759–1824).

94 Hentschke and Muhlack 1972: 105–6, in the conclusion of their not unsympathetic section on Wilamowitz in ch. 3 ("Der historische Positivismus"). They allude to Ranke 1955: 29–30.

95 First use of Historismus (according to Iggers 1995: 130) in Friedrich Schlegel's notes for treatises (*Aufsätze*) on philology, which were never finished: Schlegel 1981: 35 *passim*. One of his central points, with which he credits Winkelmann, is the "immeasurable" difference between antiquity and the present.

96 Fraenkel 1932–3.

97 The first chapter of Kennedy 1993 is a good example. For the recent conflicted return to historicism: Edmunds 2005: 2–5.

98 Selden 1990.

99 Galinsky 1992.

100 Martindale 1993. One can also point to a revival of interest in hermeneutics at that time on the part of ancient philosophers: Laks and Neschke 1991.

101 Edmunds 2005: 6–7.

102 Hexter 2006; Martindale 2007.

103 On problems of the dialogue metaphor see Jauss 1989b: 213–14 = 1982b: 679–80. For a historical survey of the concept of horizon, see Jauss 1989b: 199–207 = 1982b: 660–71. He cites inter alia the article "Horizont" in *Historische Wörterbuch der Philosophie* (Scherner 1974). Gill 1995: 17–18 in valuable comments on the comparability of modern and ancient notions of the person uses the dialogue metaphor, putting dialogue in quotation marks.

104 Gadamer 1965: 232 = Gadamer 1975: 217 in the context of discussion of Husserl.

105 For Husserl: Jauss 1989b: 204 and n. 14 = 1982b: 666–7 and n. 12. I used Jauss's interpretation as a model for my interpretation of Hor. *Odes* 1.9 in Edmunds 1991 (cf. afterthoughts in Edmunds 2001: 43–52).

106 Jauss 1982e: 148 = Jauss 1982c: 824.

107 Jauss 1982e: 143 = Jauss 1982c: 818.

108 Jauss 1982e: 146 = Jauss 1982c: 821–2.

109 Jauss 1982e: 170 = Jauss 1982c: 847.

110 The accessus cited earlier happened to be quoted by Friis-Jensen.

111 To enter into discussion with all of scholarship on *Odes* 1.23 published in, say, the last twenty-five years would lead to the doubling of the length of this chapter. For this scholarship, see Niklas Holzberg's bibliography at <http://www.klassphil.uni-muenchen.de/personen/holzberg.html>.

112 The text is that of Borzsák.

113 In *OLD s.v.* hinnuleus ("apparently adaptation of Greek ἔνελος").

114 Anacreon, frag. 39 D^2 = 63 P = 28 Gent. This fragment is a standard anthology piece and is assumed to lie within the ken of a first reading.

115 C.M. Bowra trans.

116 Overviews of this program: Feeney 1993; Hutchinson 2007.

117 For "motto": Pasquali 1920: 9 n. 1; on Pasquali's use of the term: Cavarzere 1996: 12–13. For allusion to Anacreon: Cavarzere 1996: 178–81, 257–9. For Horace and Anacreon: Davis 1996.

118 Such metrical phenomena as hiatus (3, 7) and diaeresis (*silvae*, 4) should be under-stood in the context of this relation.
119 Santirocco: 1986: 55–60, following a suggestion of Fuqua 1968: 44–6.
120 Davis 1991: 221.
121 Calame 1997: 238–44. (I cite Calame 1997 because it "is the equivalent of a second edition" [vi] of Calame 1977).
122 Dacier 1709, the third edition of this vastly successful work.
123 Jauss 1982e: 170 = Jauss 1982c: 846–7.
124 An often discussed aspect of the change from a script culture to a print culture is the change from hearing to reading or from performance to reading. The monumental study of the printing press as an agent of change, Eisenstein 1979, touches on this particular change at 1979.1: 129–36 (with citation of McLuhan 1962). Large questions concerning the new print culture, particularly the kinds and degrees of fixity that were achieved, are under debate. See the critique of Eisenstein by Johns 1998. This debate will have consequences for the understanding of the reception of Horace in the fifteenth and sixteenth centuries.
125 Fantham 1992: 195: "preoccupation with the novel shapes the questions we ask and the expectations with which we approach an ancient text." Cf. Gill 1996: 122.
126 Rich 1976: 236. Cf. my earlier acknowledgement of an alternate feminist perspective on *Odes* 1.23: Edmunds 2001: 103.
127 Trans. by Wenzel 1981.
128 This discussion has gone on in several fields, including especially psychoanalysis. See Hirsch 1981. For literature, see Hirsch 1989.
129 For the background of literary theory in Germany of the 1960s see Rosenberg 2003.
130 Even leaving aside the question of the "leaves" of a thorn-bush and of objections raised by Nisbet and Hubbard 1970: 277.
131 Jauss 1982e: 141 = Jauss 1982c: 815–16.

CHAPTER EIGHTEEN

The Metempsychosis of Horace: The Reception of the Satires and Epistles*

Susanna Braund

Although for our own era Horace is essentially a lyric poet, there have been long stretches of time when he was known and treasured at least as much for his hexameter poetry. Foremost among the hexameter works was, and is, the *Ars Poetica*, which was viewed as a central didactic work throughout the Middle Ages and which still features regularly in university courses on the history of literary criticism. But for Dante, Horace was "Orazio satiro" (*Inferno* 4.89), an attitude that is typical of the medieval view of Horace as a moralizing poet.

Pagan texts susceptible of ethical interpretation were clearly privileged in late antiquity and throughout the Middle Ages, as borne out by the evidence of the school canon in western Europe, which shows that Virgil, Horace, Juvenal, and Terence were the central pagan poets.[1] All of them were recuperable for a Christian audience through allegorical and/or moralizing interpretations. For example, we know that the man who would later become Pope Sylvester II was giving lectures on Horace, Persius, and Juvenal in the schools of Rheims just before the year 1000, the Horace text in question presumably being his Satires.[2] The different elements of Horace's œuvre, usually grouped as *Odes, Ars Poetica, Satires*, and *Epistles*, are apparently pretty evenly represented in the numerous manuscripts that survive from the ninth century onwards (see Friis-Jensen in Harrison 2007a: 293–4). Significantly, many of these manuscripts are annotated with glosses that indicate the kinds of ethical message derived from Horace; the extreme of this is the representation of Horace as a monk (Friis-Jensen in Harrison 2007a: 294). The Christian environment naturally exerted pressure on those involved in education to justify their pagan texts as ethically edifying. A fine example comes from the introduction (*accessus*) to the standard French commentary on Horace, dating probably from the middle of the twelfth century (Marchionni 2003: 1.6–7; on the dating problems see Marchionni 2003: xiii):

postea librum sermonum addidit, ubi diuersis generibus uiciorum irretitos repre-
hendit. ad ultimum opus suum in epistolis terminauit ibique ad modum boni
agricole uiciis extirpatis uirtutes superseminauit.

Later he added his book of Satires, in which he censured people ensnared in different types of vice. Finally he finished his output with Epistles and in them he
uprooted vices and sowed virtues instead, in the manner of a good farmer.

Two elements in this quotation are important for me: firstly, the close association
of the works we know as Satires and Epistles and secondly, the view of Horace
as cultivator of virtue. In this essay, I shall treat the reception of the hexameter
poems, apart from the *Ars Poetica*, holistically (see Braund 1992: 31, n. 61 for
supporting evidence) and I shall focus on the moral aspect of that reception.

The modern reception of Horace's Satires and Epistles is rich and complex,
as can be seen in recent studies of Horace, including the anthology of translations
in the Penguin volume *Horace in English* (Carne-Ross and Haynes 1996) and
the selections in Gillespie's *The Poets on the Classics* (Gillespie 1988: 116–31),
many of the essays in *Horace Made New* (Martindale and Hopkins 1993) and
the contributions to *The Cambridge Companion to Horace* by Tarrant, Friis-
Jensen, McGann, Money, and Harrison (Harrison 2007a), as well as material in
Bolgar (1954: index *s.v.* Horace) and Highet (1967: 303–21), to mention just
a few pertinent items. If we start with the advent of printing in the fifteenth
century, it should be no surprise that Horace was among the earliest pagan poets
to be printed: the *editio princeps* appeared in 1470, just a year after those of
Virgil, Lucan, and Juvenal. Horace's moralizing hexameter works clearly made a
powerful impact in Italy, France, and England. Translations and imitations of
Horace and poems inspired by him appear in English and the other European
vernaculars from early in the sixteenth century, for example, by Sir Thomas Wyatt
(1503–42) (Highet 1967: 310), via the Italian Luigi Alamanni's epistolary satires
(on this chain of influence see Burrow 1993: 34–7). The complete Satires were
translated into French by François Habert in 1549, into Italian by Lodovico
Dolce in the same year and into English by Thomas Drant in 1566, with his
translations of the Epistles and *Ars Poetica* following in 1567. His translations of
the Satires appear in the tellingly entitled *A Medicinable Morall*, juxtaposed with
translations of Jeremiah (thus McGann in Harrison 2007a: 306–7). As Burrow
astutely observes in his discussion of the sixteenth-century reception of Horace
(Burrow 1993: 27–8), at this point there is no standard of "Horatianism" to
influence the reception of his poems. This makes it particularly fascinating to see
how different poets react to Horace and how they deploy his themes. This topic
is potentially huge—and other scholars have covered some of the ground already
(see the Guide to Further Reading below)—so for the purposes of this essay I
have chosen to examine the reception and refraction of Horace in just a few major
figures: Ariosto in sixteenth-century Italy, Régnier and Boileau in sixteenth-
seventeenth century France, Pope's *Imitations of Horace* in eighteenth-century

England, with the portrayal of Horace by Ben Jonson in his 1601/2 play *The Poetaster*, as my finale. At every point, I shall explore which particular texts and which particular aspects of Horace's persona make the most impact. We will find Horace rewritten and reinvented as a modest and moral courtier who values his independence and protests his loyalty and integrity. The Horace of the Satires seems to offer not exactly a blank slate to later poets but a versatile opportunity to reflect and explore their own concerns.

I start with the Italian reception of Horace's hexameter poetry. Ludovico Ariosto wrote seven *Satire* in *terza rima* during the years 1517 to 1525, poems that blend Horatian themes, concerns, and expressions with the occasional element of Juvenalian declamatory raillery. Small-scale verbal echoes guarantee that Ariosto had Horace's hexameter poems in the forefront of his mind, but much more important are the overarching themes that he takes over from Horace. These include contentment with a modest lifestyle away from the demands of the court and the city, along with the fervent desire for independence from a patron's demands. The mode of exploring these themes is essentially the same in both poets: the autobiographical mode that uses conversation to create the impression of confiding in the addressee, whether through direct address (as used by Horace in *Satires* 1) or dialogue (*Satires* 2) or letter (*Epistles*) (see Burrow 1993: 33–4 on the essential similarities of the hexameter poems).

Ariosto's updated Horatianism can be most readily appreciated by close analysis, such as David Marsh has already performed to show how *Satira* 6 relates to Horace *Satires* 1.6 (Marsh 1975: 319–22). Here I shall examine Ariosto's first *Satira*, written in 1518 and addressed to his brother Alessandro and his friend Ludovico Bagno, in which he substantially reprises Horace *Epistles* 1.7, which is Horace's "apology" to Maecenas for staying away from court. Ariosto's situation is likewise that of not attending on his patron, in his case Cardinal Ippolito d'Este, on his removal to his see at Buda in Hungary, but with the significant difference that Ippolito has just discarded him after fifteen years' service for his failure to accompany him. In other words, Ariosto exploits the Horatian model to produce a justification of his own conduct and a condemnation of Ippolito's, but the result is a blend of Horatian mildness with Juvenalian fierceness.

The combination of satiric voices is evident at the start of the poem. Ariosto begins by asking if he is missed at court (1–9), reprising the idea that Horace is missed (*desideror*, *Epistles* 1.7.2) from Maecenas' entourage, but immediately deplores the flattery endemic there (10–18), in terms more reminiscent of Juvenal's tirade (through his mouthpiece Umbricius) against Greek flatterers in *Satires* 3. He states that his reasons for declining to join his patron were honest and sincere (19–24) and proceeds to catalogue them in the next hundred lines and more: the change in climate would harm him, the food and wines at court are too rich and he cannot expect or afford special culinary treatment, because his patron has been less than generous. He states that he cannot perform the tasks that the patron desires of him (again echoes of Juvenal's third Satire) and

bemoans the patron's lack of appreciation of the praises Ariosto has sung. He
closes this part of the poem by depicting life in court as a form of slavery, in
terms that recall elements in Juvenal *Satires* 5, which is a poem attacking both
patron and client for the humiliating treatment meted out to and accepted by
the humble client. Reverting to a distinctively Horatian voice he then celebrates
the joys of independence (166–92), referring to untrammeled existence in his
father's house and lands, far from court.

If he had finished the poem there, as he explicitly acknowledges he might have
(193–5), the poem would have described a similar trajectory to its model, *Epistles*
1.7, albeit significantly less oblique in its strategies. Horace's poem, which is
addressed directly to his patron, Maecenas, starts by sketching the situation, that
Horace had promised to stay in the country just a few days but has ended up
staying away from Rome for the entire month of August (1–2). His reason is
simple: fear of illness (2–9). In a rather daring assertion of independence, he says
that he intends to extend his absence still longer, once snow has fallen, and
promises to revisit Maecenas in the springtime (10–13). Then, introducing the
dominant strategy of this poem and many others, Horace switches to a more
indirect mode. He contrasts the way that Maecenas has enriched him with
another patron who forces his gifts on an unwilling client (14–23). Reverting to
disarming directness, he promises to deserve Maecenas' generosity (24) provided
Maecenas does not insist on his presence (25–8). Then he again switches to
indirect mode to tell the fable of the fox and the weasel (29–33: to be discussed
below) before returning to the direct mode, asserting that he would not exchange
his prized leisure and freedom (*otia … liberrima*) for all the wealth of Arabia
(34–6). After articulating his ability to decline unwanted gifts from a rich patron
obliquely, in terms drawn from the *Odyssey* (Telemachus declining Menelaus'
gifts; 37–43), he says, quite simply, "small things suit the small" (*paruum parua
decent*, 44) and asserts his pleasure in his country refuge from Rome (44–5). The
remainder of the poem consists of the lengthy elaborated tale of Philippus and
Mena (46–95), telling how a hard-working man of modest means and simple
lifestyle is in effect bought by a patron who changes his lifestyle utterly, ultimately
to the man's misery. Though the miserable client sounds rather like a cipher for
Horace, we can be confident that the patron who "hooks" this "fish" (*piscis ad
hamum*, 74) is not designed as a criticism of Maecenas, but rather as a cautionary
tale. Thus Horace concludes the poem without drawing any explicit moral about
his relationship with Maecenas but instead leaving things vague and abstract
(96–8, my translation):

> qui semel aspexit quantum dimissa petitis
> praestent, mature redeat repetatque relicta.
> metiri se quemque suo modulo ac pede uerum est.

> The person who has once seen how preferable what he's left is to what
> he seeks should hurry right back and seek again what he had abandoned.
> Each is right to measure himself by his own foot-rule.

It is clear that Ariosto's situation bears close, but not exact, resemblance to that of Horace. The important difference is that while Horace addresses his patron directly, Ariosto articulates to his brother and a friend a complaint against his ex-patron. It is this switch of addressee that takes Ariosto further away from his Horatian model in the final seventy lines of his poem. (Burrow 1993: 32–4 comes to a similar conclusion although he reads Horace as more bitter, for example, "Horace's carefully exact *cuncta resigno* ['I give it all back'] becomes a retch.") The thought of his financial difficulties in fulfilling his responsibilities to his family makes him indignant at the meanness of his ex-patron, in much more of a Juvenalian than Horatian voice, and he finally hands over his role to the younger brother he is addressing (196–245). But he concludes the poem by reworking a fable taken directly from Horace *Epistles* 1.7, that of the fox and the weasel. Before arriving at a conclusion about Ariosto's Horatianness, let's take a look at their respective treatments of the fable.

Horace incorporates the fable, one of many moments of indirection in the poem, succinctly in the middle of the poem (*Epistles* 1.7.29–36, my translation):

> forte per angustam tenuis uolpecula rimam
> repserat in cumeram frumenti, pastaque rursus
> ire foras pleno tendebat corpore frustra.
> cui mustela procul: "si uis" ait "effugere istinc,
> macra cauum repetes artum, quem macra subisti."
> hac ego si compellor imagine, cuncta resigno;
> nec somnum plebis laudo satur altilium nec
> otia diuitiis Arabum liberrima muto.

> Once a slim little fox had crept through a narrow opening
> into a bin of corn and after feeding it was trying
> with its full belly to escape again, but could not.
> A weasel close by said to her: "If you want to get out of
>   there,
> you'll try that tiny chink again when you're thin—you
>   were thin when you entered."
> If the fable is directed at me, I give up everything.
> I don't praise "penniless slumbers" when full of chicken
> and I won't change my leisure and freedom for the riches
>   of Arabia.

By contrast, Ariosto alters it, expands it and places it at the conclusion to his much longer poem (*Satira* 1.247–65):

> Uno asino fu già, ch'ogni osso e nervo
> mostrava di magrezza, e entrò, pel rotto
> del muro, ove di grano era uno acervo;

> e tanto ne mangiò, che l'epa sotto
> si fece più d'una gran botte grossa
> fin che fu sazio, e non però di botto.

> Temendo poi che gli sien péste l'ossa,
> si sforza di tornar dove entrato era,
> ma par che 'l buco più capir non possa.
>
> Mentre s'affanna, e uscire indarno spera,
> gli disse un topolino: "Se vuoi quinci
> uscir, tràtti; compar, quella panciera:
> a vomitar bisogna che cominci
> ciò c'hai nel corpo, e che ritorni macro,
> altrimenti quel buco mai non vinci."
> Or, conchiudendo, dico che, se 'l sacro
> Cardinal comperato avermi stima
> con li suoi doni, non mi è acerbo et acro
> renderli, e tòr la libertà mia prima.

I append the English translation by Temple Henry Croker printed in London in 1759 (lines 295–312), itself a curiosity:

> Once on a time, an ass with fasting thin,
> His bones but barely cover'd with the skin,
> Thro' a crack'd wall, a passage far from wide,
> To rob a stack of corn, found means to slide.
> When once got in, he play'd his part so well,
> He neither lost his time nor balk'd his meal:
> Glutted at length, he thinks of a retreat,
> Hence came the proverb, Asses think too late;
> For lo! the wide-stretch'd belly stopp'd his way,
> The reck'ning for the feast the bones must pay.
> At last a mouse, that pity'd his disgrace,
> Taught him the only means to quit the place,
> Quick to disgorge the corn, or wait th'escape,
> Till regularly starv'd to former shape.
>   So, to conclude—if my good Lord has thought
> The service he has had too dearly bought,
> That now both parties satisfy'd may be,
> Let him take back his bribe, and leave me free.

Ariosto well understands that the fable is a signature Horatian device in his hexameter poems, both the Satires and the Epistles, and he has noticed that fables or stories end some of Horace's poems: the fable of the frog puffing herself up (*Satires* 2.3.314–20, followed by a brief six-line sign-off), the story of Philippus and Mena in *Epistles* 1.7 and, surely the most famous case, the town mouse and the country mouse in *Satires* 2.6 (lines 79–117, where the poem simply ends with the fable, with no moral drawn). Ariosto too uses fables to conclude several of his *Satire*, besides *Satira* 1, *Satire* 2, 4, and 5. It seems reasonable to suppose that Ariosto is reproducing the Horatian flavour with some indirection, but in *Satira* 1 he spoils the oblique effect by spelling out in more bitter tones the moral he draws. In sum, the combination of the Horatian themes noted above with the autobiographical stance and confiding tone, the lively incorporation of direct speech and the highly specific details that ground the poem in its context give Ariosto's *Satira* 1 a recognizably Horatian epistolarity alongside the acerbic resentfulness taken over from Juvenal.

The fluctuation between Horatian and Juvenalian tones and strategies that we find in Ariosto is repeated in the emergence of formal verse satire in France in the seventeenth century. Mathurin Régnier (1573–1613) was a key figure in the revival of interest in the Latin verse satirists, particularly in his deployment of alexandrine couplets, in which he was followed by Nicolas Boileau (1636–1711), whose reputation as a satirist eclipsed that of his predecessor. These poets participated in a debate about the relative merits of Horace and Juvenal as models, a debate that constructs Horace as essentially a playful satirist and Juvenal as a more serious satirist thanks to his indignation (Goulbourne 2007: 140; Goulbourne makes the important point that the Roman satirists were usually read in expurgated versions at this time).

In his seventeen satires Régnier often strikes a note of Juvenalian indignation in his sharply observed sketches of immoral individuals. He prefaces the first edition of his poems with the line *difficile est saturam non scribere* (Juvenal 1.30) and explicitly aligns himself with Juvenal rather than Horace at the start of *Satire* 2 (lines 14–17, my translation):

> Il faut suivre un sentier qui soit moins rebatu,
> Et, conduit d'Apollon, recognoistre la trace
> Du libre Juvénal; trop discret est Horace
> Pour un homme picqué ...

> I must follow a path less hackneyed,
> and, guided by Apollo, recognize the tracks
> of Juvenal in his freedom; Horace is too cautious
> for someone nettled ...

Yet in *Satire* 14 he presents himself as a follower of Horace (lines 101–4, trans. Highet 1949: 312):

> Or c'est un grand chemin jadis assez frayé
> Qui des rimeurs françois ne fut oncq' essayé:
> Suivant les pas d'Horace, entrant en la carrière,
> Je trouve des humeurs de diverse manière.

> This highway has felt many poets' tread,
> but by French rhymers is unvisited;
> I enter it, following Horace close behind,
> to trace the various humours of mankind.

And so it proves when we consider Régnier's debt to Horace, which manifests itself in his amiable persona, in the conversational structure of the poems, in echoes of Horace's words and in his adaptation of Horatian material. (On the influence of Horace and Juvenal on Régnier see Highet 1967: 312–13; Colton 2004; Goulbourne 2007: 140–1.) *Satire* 12, for example, is modeled on *Satires* 1.4 (for details see Colton 2004: 39–47), where Horace presents his moral credentials for writing satire, and *Satire* 15 imitates *Satires* 2.3 with its Stoic sermon on madness from an aggressive interlocutor who interrupts the poet's vacation (see Colton 2004: 51–2). *Satire* 8 is closely based upon *Satires* 1.9, in which Horace is assailed by a social climber, and includes verbatim quotations (see Colton 2004: 19–28) and in *Satire* 10 he pillories a bad meal such as depicted in *Satires* 2.8. So, for example, Régnier describes one of the courses like this (*Satire* 10.299–300, trans. Highet 1967: 313):

> Devant moy justement on plante un grand potage
> D'où les mousches à jeun se sauvoient à la nage.

> Next, an enormous plate of soup arrives,
> where famished flies are swimming for their lives.

Writing fifty years after Régnier, Nicolas Boileau also uses Horace and Juvenal as models for his poems. He wrote *Satires*, starting in 1660, and *Épîtres*, starting in 1669, and in 1674 he published his renowned *L'Art poétique*, an imitation of Horace's so-called *Ars Poetica*. Like Régnier, he explicitly presents himself as a successor of the Roman satirists. In *Satire* 9 he names as his models Lucilius, the founder of the genre, and Horace, and uses their names as his justification (*Satire* 9.275–8, my translation):

> C'est ainsi que Lucile, appuyé de Lélie,
> Fit justice en son temps des Cotins d'Italie,
> Et qu'Horace, jetant le sel à pleines mains,
> Se jouait aux dépens des Pelletiers romains.

> So it is that Lucilius, supported by Laelius,
> treated as they deserved in his own times the Cotins of Italy,
> and that Horace, flinging salt by the handful,
> had fun at the expense of Roman Pelletiers.[3]

And just a few lines earlier he echoes Horace in asserting satire's value as a combination of entertainment and instruction (*Satire* 9.267–70, trans. Goulbourne 2007: 139):

> La satire, en leçons, en nouveautés fertile,
> Sait seule assaisonner le plaisant et l'utile,
> Et, d'un vers qu'elle épure aux rayons du bon sens,
> Détromper les esprits des erreurs de leur temps.

> Satire, fertile in lessons and novelties,
> Alone unites the pleasing and the instructive,
> And, with each perfect line of common-sense verse,
> Releases minds from the errors of their times.

This is an adaptation of *Ars Poetica* 343–4 *omne tulit punctum qui miscuit utile dulci, | lectorem delectando pariterque monendo* ("everyone votes for the man who mixes wholesome and sweet, | giving his reader an equal blend of help and delight" (trans. Rudd 1993c) along with the famous lines early in *Satires* 1 where Horace establishes his mode of satire: *quamquam ridentem dicere uerum | quid uetat?* (*Satires* 1.1.24–5: "can't we laugh when we reveal a truth?", trans. Juster 2008).

That said, as in the case of Régnier, we find plenty of Juvenalian moments, tones and themes in Boileau. Notably, his first and sixth *Satires*, sometimes dubbed *Le départ du poète* and *Les embarras de Paris*, an envoi to Paris and a criticism of the ceaseless noise of the city which both date from 1660, are both heavily derivative of Juvenal's third *Satire*. Like Juvenal's Umbricius, who rages at his displacement by corrupt and foreign social climbers, Boileau's Damon is incensed at the fact that moral behavior is not appreciated (e.g. "Le mérite et l'esprit ne sont plus à la mode" [1.22: "Worth and spirit are no longer in vogue"] and "l'honneur a toujours guerre avec la fortune" [1.130: "honor is always at war with fortune"] and that in the city a poet can find neither the support nor the peace to compose; like Juvenal's Umbricius, the speaker is assailed by noise that prevents sleep (6.116 "Ce n'est qu'à prix d'argent qu'on dort en cette ville" translates *magnis opibus dormitur in Vrbe* [Juv. 3.235]).

But, blended with the Juvenalian elements, Horace is more often Boileau's model. *Satire* 7 (1663), on *Le genre satirique*, is an imitation of *Satires* 2.1 while *Satire* 4 (1664), on *Les folies humaines*, is indebted to the lengthy sermon-type condemnation of madness in *Satires* 2.3. *Épître* 11 (1695), *À mon jardinier*, takes as its basic inspiration Horace's address to his farm-manager in *Epistles* 1.14, while *Épître* 10 (also 1695), *Vie et portrait de l'auteur*, is clearly modeled on Horace's reluctant envoi to his eager book in *Epistles* 1.20, though it is a good deal longer and more elaborated. *Satire* 3 (1665), *Le repas ridicule*, is a close imitation, at least in framework and structure, of the comic narrative of an awful feast in *Satires* 2.8, a poem which had already inspired Régnier's tenth *Satire*. Here I shall discuss *Épître* 6 (1677) on *Les plaisirs des champs*, which is in some respects complementary to *Satires* 1 and 6 in its negative view of city life, as an amalgamation of Horace *Epistles* 1.16 and *Satires* 2.6.

The poem is addressed to Chrétien-François de Lamoignon (1644–1709), who was the Advocate-General to the Parlement of Paris and presumably one of Boileau's patrons. In a tactic inspired by Horace's epistolary feints at the beginnings of poems (e.g. *Epistles* 1.10, 1.11, 1.12, 1.13, 1.14, 1.15, 1.16), Boileau's epistle begins "Oui," thus suggesting that it is part of an ongoing conversation (lines 1–2, my translation):

> Oui, Lamoignon, je fuis les chagrins de la ville,
> Et contre eux la campagne est mon unique asile.

> Yes, Lamoignon, I flee the irritations of the city,
> and the country is my sole refuge against them.

He proceeds to provide a description of the "petit village" where he is staying, deploying the tactic with which Horace opens *Epistles* 1.16, anticipating his addressee Quinctius' questions by describing his farm (*fundus meus* line 1) for him (lines 5–16). After describing his setting (lines 4–20) Boileau sketches the idyllic lifestyle he enjoys there (lines 21–42). He then imagines returning to the city and contrasts rural life with the hassles and weariness induced by life in Paris (43–78), here in terms indebted to the picture of city life in *Satires* 2.6 at lines 23–38. He goes on to blame the trials of urban life as obstacles to composing poetry (79–98), e.g. (79–81, my translation):

> Ainsi de cent chagrins dans Paris accablé,
> Juge si, toujours triste, interrompu, troublé,
> Lamoignon, j'ai le temps de courtiser les Muses.

> So overwhelmed by a hundred irritations in Paris,
> Decide if I, always gloomy, interrupted, troubled,
> Lamoignon, have the time to pay court to the Muses.

Then, in strongly Horatian terms Boileau expresses his envy of the escapee from the city (99–100, my translation):

> Qu'heureux est le mortel, qui, du monde ignoré,
> Vit content de soi-même en un coin retiré!

> How happy is the mortal who, forgotten by the world,
> lives content with himself in a remote corner.

and states that it is only possible to compose in the tranquility afforded by the countryside (lines 120–4, my translation):

> J'ai besoin du silence et de l'ombre des bois:
> Ma muse, qui se plaît dans leurs routes perdues,
> Ne saurait plus marcher sur le pavé des rues.
> Ce n'est que dans ces bois, propres à m'exciter,
> Qu'Apollon quelquefois daigne encor m'écouter.

> I need the silence and the shade of the woods:
> my muse, who delights in their lost paths,
> would not any more know how to walk the paved streets.
> It is only in the woods, fit to rouse me,
> that Apollo sometimes deigns to hear me still.

The poem ends with courteous compliments to his patron as someone who truly belongs in the city (125–68) thanks to "le rang, la naissance, | Le mérite éclatant et la haute éloquence" (129–30: "rank, high birth, dazzling merit and lofty eloquence") which summon him "aux sublimes emploies" (131: "to the highest situations") in the maintenance of the laws. Boileau concludes with a request that he not be summoned until autumn arrives and then only to join Lamoignon at his country estate, where he pictures an idyllic existence in which (151–9, my translation):

> Tantôt sur l'herbe assis, au pied de ces coteaux
> Où Polychrene épand ses libérales eaux,
> Lamoignon, nous irons, libres d'inquiétude,
> Discourir des vertus dont tu fais ton étude;
> Chercher quels sont les biens véritables ou faux,
> Si l'honnête homme en soi doit souffrir des défauts;
> Quel chemin le plus droit à la gloire nous guide,
> Ou la vaste science, ou la vertu solide.

> Soon sitting on the grass at the foot of these slopes
> where Polychrene spreads its generous waters,
> Lamoignon, we shall go, free of anxiety,
> to discuss the virtues which you have made your focus;
> to find out which are the real and the false goods,
> if the honorable person in himself must suffer flaws;
> what route guides us to glory most directly—
> boundless knowledge or solid virtue.

In structure and ideas, Boileau's poem resembles *Satires* 2.6 closely. Like the later *Epistles* 1.16, Horace starts by praising his farm (1–4) and disavows any further proprietorial ambitions (4–19). The poem proceeds with a catalogue of the duties Horace faces when in the city (20–39) and then an account of his relationship with Maecenas since he was admitted into the great man's circle nearly eight years ago (40–58). Wistful thoughts of country life follow (59–76), a life of books and sleep and leisure and of simple food and meals at his own hearth surrounded by friends and marked by real conversation (70–6, trans. Juster):

>   ergo
> sermo oritur, non de uillis domibusue alienis
> nec male necne Lepos saltet, sed quod magis ad nos
> pertinet et nescire malum est agitamus: utrumne
> diuitiis homines an sint uirtute beati,
> quidue ad amicitias, usus rectumne, trahat nos,
> et quae sit natura boni summumque quid eius.

>   ... thus would provoke debate—
> though not about some mansion or retreat
> or whether Lepos lacks a dancer's feet—

> but things of more significant concern
> and which are detrimental not to learn:
> Does wealth or virtue give men satisfaction?
> What leads to friendship—calculated action
> or correct acts? And what will reveal
> the nature of the good and its ideal?

Although Boileau has changed the setting of this idealized conversation, the topics discussed are drawn directly from Horace. In other words, in *Épître* 6 Boileau serves up all the key ingredients of Horace *Satires* 2.6, with the added spice of an epistolary opening inspired by Horace *Epistles* 1.16, except, of course, that he omits the fable of the town mouse and country mouse, supposedly recounted by one of his neighbors at such a meal, which concludes *Satires* 2.6.

There are differences, however, firstly in Boileau's consistent representation of himself as a writer and secondly in both poets' treatment of their patrons. Throughout the poem Boileau emphasizes the role of writing in court life at Paris, a theme that never surfaces as such in Horace, and one of his foremost concerns is achieving the conditions in which he can compose poetry. In this he may be responding to a fleeting remark by Horace when he declares that his farm is a fine topic for his poetry once he has escaped the perils of the city (lines 16–19, trans. Juster):

> ergo ubi me in montes et in arcem ex Vrbe remoui,
> quid prius illustrem saturis Musaque pedestri?
> nec mala me ambitio perdit nec plumbeus auster
> autumnusque grauis, Libitinae quaestus acerbae.

> So when I've left my city life to stay
> secure within my mountain hideaway,
> how should I first illuminate my views
> through satire with my heavy-footed Muse?
> My vain ambitions haven't brought me low,
> and neither have the southern winds that blow
> oppressively as autumn's bleakness offers
> vicious Libitina fuller coffers.

Boileau too is concerned for his health, since as he ages he finds the demands of city life harder, but he develops Horace's passing reference to his poetry into a persistent self-presentation as a poet.

Secondly, in *Épître* 6 Boileau chooses to address his patron directly, which leads him into the panegyrical concluding section (125–68), and he chooses to imagine the ideal conversation as taking place at his patron's country seat. By contrast, Maecenas is not addressed in *Satires* 2.6, and the ideal conversation takes place at Horace's modest farm without the great man. That said, Maecenas is of course a presence, implicit or explicit, throughout the poem and his name occurs three times (at lines 31, 38, and 41). It is he who gifted Horace with his farm and it is in his service that Horace faces the vexations of life in Rome. There is no direct panegyric of Maecenas, but the pleasure that Horace takes in being associated with him, for example *hoc iuuat et melli est, non mentiar* (32: "For sure, I'm thrilled, | and it's like honey") is an oblique compliment. So too his account in lines 40–58 of his being admitted to Maecenas' circle. This is highly disingenuous in that it reveals nothing about the great man. In fact, Horace here leaves the exact nature of his relationship with Maecenas obscure, thus parading his discretion and leaving the reader to infer a certain intimacy. In other words, we can form the same conclusion as in the case of Ariosto, above, another poem in which the poet is accounting for his absence from his patron's entourage: that Horace is more subtle and oblique than his later imitators.

Moving to eighteenth-century England, we find that Horace and Boileau were both central figures in Alexander Pope's self-definition (1688–1744) (see Wood 1985). In fact, Pope explicitly associates the two in *An Essay on Criticism* (1711) in lines that criticize French servility while describing the spread of humanist culture (711–14):

> Thence arts o'er all the northern world advance,
> But critic-learning flourished most in France;
> The rules, a nation born to serve, obeys;
> And Boileau still in right of Horace sways.

As Robin Sowerby suggests, Pope's hostility to Boileau is overstated, given his debt to the French poet and critic's *L'Art Poétique* (Sowerby 1993: 160–1): presumably a poet defining himself must distance himself from his influences. Leaving that to one side, and despite his palpable attainment of Juvenalian indignation in the *Dunciad* (1728), it is self-evident that Pope consciously models himself on Horace, and not just in his *Imitations of Horace*. In another excerpt from *An Essay on Criticism* we hear praise of Horace's mode of criticism in terms closely inspired by passages from *Satires* 1.3 (especially lines 49–54 and 68–98) and 1.4, lines 78–105 (653–6):

> Horace still charms with graceful negligence,
> And without method talks us into sense,
> Will, like a friend, familiarly convey
> The truest notions in the easiest way.

This passage also reprises the Neronian satirist Persius' sketch of Horace at *Satires* 1.116–18 (my translation):

> While his friend is laughing, the rascal Horace touches
> every fault in him and, once he's got in, he frolics around his heart,
> clever at dangling the public from his cleaned-out nose.

This characterization of the satirist's role in society is particularly suitable for the shifting political circumstances of the early eighteenth century, as Quintero argues (Quintero 2007: 213): the moralizing satirist of this era prefers the model of friendly critique to caustic tongue-lashing and combines praise of the exemplary with censure of misconduct. Such factors make Horace the ideal model. And Pope is absolutely explicit about the Horatian basis of his project in a letter to Swift dated November 28, 1729 (*The Correspondence of Alexander Pope* ed. George Sherburn, 5 vols. Oxford 1956 III.82) in which he writes about "a system of Ethics in the Horatian way" articulated in ethical epistles. The story of how Pope came to write his imitations of Horace has his friend Lord Bolingbroke suggesting an imitation of *Satires* 2.1 as a response to the savage criticisms directed at Pope's *Moral Essays* (published in 1731 and 1733; see Sowerby 1993: 171). It appears that Pope immediately saw the power of conveying his ethical vision in the form of imitations and it was not long before he shifted his original project of writing the *Moral Essays* and *An Essay on Man* to further imitations of Horace. His imitation of *Satires* 2.1 was published in 1733 and during the next five years there followed his imitations of *Satires* 1.2, 2.2, and 2.6 and *Epistles* 1.1, 1.6, 2.1, and 2.2. As scholars have noted, Pope's imitations cover a considerable range "from close fidelity to the originals to ironic and contemporary comment upon their implications and views" (Sullivan 1992: 231).

It is not difficult to generate a picture of just how intimate was Pope's relationship with Horace, especially if we read the poems alongside the original Latin, which was his intention: in the original publication the Latin text was printed on the facing page. Yet I suggest that key to appreciating Pope's vision are the poems with no specific Horatian models that form part of this project: the *Epistle to Dr Arbuthnot* (1734), which functioned as the prologue to the *Imitations* and the two *Dialogues* (both 1738) that constitute an epilogue, originally entitled *One Thousand Seven Hundred and Thirty Eight: A Dialogue Something Like Horace*. Like Horace's apologetic poems (*Satires* 1.4, 1.10, and 2.1), Pope's three original poems offer self-justification of the satirist's moral integrity. As Niall Rudd has shown, in the *Epistle to Dr Arbuthnot*, Pope combines Horatian detail with a degree of fearlessness in the satiric portraits that he labels Lucilian (Rudd 2005); this is absolutely appropriate in that Horace deploys Lucilius, the founder of Roman satire, as his role model in all three poems. Both the *Dialogues* feature a so-called "Friend" addressing the Poet who Pope himself tells us in a note should be considered "an impertinent Censurer." The thrust of the argument is familiar enough from Horace—that only people who are corrupt need fear the satirist's tongue and that only people who are corrupt will be offended.

Pope's wit is on display in the opening lines of the first of these dialogues when he depicts himself accused of stealing from Horace. The poem begins with the "Friend" intruding upon the Poet and reproving him, in the manner of the opening of *Satires* 2.3 with elements of *Satires* 2.1 added (and an echo of Persius 1.116–17 again in 19–20):

Not twice a twelvemonth you appear in Print,
And when it comes, the Court see nothing in't.
You grow *correct* that once with Rapture writ,
And are, besides, too *Moral* for a Wit.
Decay of Parts, alas! we all must feel—   5
Why now, this moment, don't I see you steal?
'Tis all from *Horace*: *Horace* long before ye
Said, 'Tories call'd him Whig, and Whigs a Tory;'
And taught his Romans, in much better metre,
'To laugh at Fools who put their trust in *Peter*.'   10
But *Horace*, Sir, was delicate, was nice;
Bubo observes, he lash'd no sort of *Vice*:
Horace would say, Sir Billy *serv'd the Crown*,
Blunt *could do Bus'ness*, H–ggins *knew the Town*,
In *Sappho* touch the *Failing of the Sex*,   15
In rev'rend Bishops note some *small Neglects*,
And own, the *Spaniard* did a *waggish thing*,
Who cropt our Ears, and sent them to the King.
His sly, polite, insinuating stile
Could please at Court, and make AUGUSTUS smile: 20
An artful Manager, that crept between
His Friend and Shame, and was a kind of *Screen*.
But 'faith your very Friends will soon be sore;
Patriots there are, who wish you'd jest no more—
And where's the Glory? 'twill be only thought   25
The Great man never offr'd you a Groat.

The Poet's response in both poems is to assert his respect for Virtue, replaying Horace's praise of Lucilius for his celebration of *Virtus* as instantiated in Scipio (*Satires* 2.1.70 and 72): in *Dialogue* 1 he celebrates Virtue before lashing Vice in a colorful passage (141–70) portraying the spread of corruption through the whole of society (137–40):

> *Virtue* may chuse the high or low Degree,
> 'Tis just alike to Virtue, and to me;
> Dwell in a Monk, or light upon a King,
> She's still the same, belov'd, contented thing.

In *Dialogue* 2 he does the same (94–7):

> Yet think not Friendship only prompts my Lays;
> I follow *Virtue*, where she shines, I praise,
> Point she to Priest or Elder, Whig or Tory,
> Or round a Quaker's Beaver cast a Glory.

His justification is his hostility to the flattery that marks life at court, in this recalling Ariosto's Horatian persona (*Dialogue* 2.181–4):

> *Friend.* This filthy Simile, this beastly Line,
> Quite turns my Stomach. *Poet.* So does Flatt'ry mine;
> And all your Courtly Civet-Cats can vent,
> Perfume to you, to me is Excrement.

In his own eyes, the Poet is the champion of truth and virtue. In other words, Pope uses his Horatian persona to take the moral high ground (*Dialogue* 2.197–204):

> Ask you what Provocation I have had?
> The strong Antipathy of Good to Bad.
> When Truth or Virtue an Affront endures,
> Th' Affront is mine, my Friend, and should be yours.
> Mine, as a Foe profess'd to false Pretence,
> Who thinks a Coxcomb's Honour like his Sense;
> Mine, as a Friend to ev'ry worthy mind;
> And mine as Man, who feel for all mankind.

Taken together, Pope's *Imitations* and his original poems offer one of the richest recreations of Horace's satiric persona because they demonstrate how thoroughly Pope identifies with the ethical position he finds in Horace's Satires and Epistles. In Pope above all, the lines between translation and imitation and adaptation are blurred, resulting in what J. P. Sullivan has felicitously called "trans-mutation" (Sullivan 1992: 232) and what we might term metempsychosis.

If there is a rival to Alexander Pope in English literature for the closest iden-tification with Horace, it must be Ben Jonson. Perhaps the most extraordinary and entertaining reception of Horace's Satires consists of Jonson's 1602 play *The Poetaster* (first performed by the Children of the Queen's Chapel in 1601), which was one of the many volleys in the intense poetic rivalries between poets and dramatists at the turn of the century known as the War of the Theatres (see Cain 1995: 23–5 and 30–6). In this play, which was originally entitled *The Arraignment* (this is how Envy, in the first moments of the play, refers to it; see Cain 1995: 19, 277), Jonson devises a plot set in Augustan Rome featuring the leading poets of the day, Ovid, Tibullus, Gallus, Propertius, Horace, and Virgil, as well as Maecenas, along with Augustus and his daughter Julia. During the play there are accusations and counter-accusations of treason against Augustus, which lead to Augustus exiling Ovid during Act IV: the Ovid–Julia sub-plot provides the obligatory romantic aspect of the drama. But the central drive of the play is the conspiracy by the poetaster Crispinus and his sidekick Demetrius, who represent Jonson's contemporaries Marston and Dekker, along with a hilarious braggart captain, Pantilius Tucca, to defame Horace, who represents

Jonson himself (for more details see Joanna Martindale 1993: 54–8 and Cain's edition of the play, Cain 1995). Jonson has incorporated several passages from Horace's Satires into the play, including the whole of *Satires* 1.9, and in the 1616 edition he inserts his translation of the dialogue with Trebatius (*Satires* 2.1) as the final scene of Act III. Dekker and Marston responded to Jonson's attack in their play *Satiromastix, or The Untrussing of the Humorous Poet* (likewise performed in 1601 and published in 1602), in which the same characters appear and which culminates in Horace being crowned with nettles. Jonson's identification with Horace as a model of civility and morality, virtue and wisdom was strong and deep-seated (Cain 1995: 10–14). As Joanna Martindale rightly says (Martindale 1993: 54), "Jonson's use of Horace was not just a question of imitating particular themes and stylistic elements; through allusion to Horace, he defines his poetic role." He uses the character of Horace to settle personal scores but also to raise larger issues about the role of poetry in society (thus Cain 1995: 3–7). In my discussion of the play, I shall try to show how systemic the identification is.

In *The Poetaster* Jonson's Horace is a poet of modest means who has won the support of Maecenas and the approval of Augustus. In the course of the play, he is attacked directly and indirectly by envious poetasters and social climbers; indeed, the theme of envy is established immediately with Envy taking the stage to deliver the prologue before the real prologue itself. We first meet Horace in Act III Scene i, when the poetaster Crispinus waylays him in the street, wanting to curry favor with Maecenas through an introduction from Horace. This scene is a clever adaptation—and in parts a close translation—of *Satires* 1.9, in which Horace is assailed by "the bore" or "the pest," here given life as the character Crispinus. Jonson expands the opening dozen lines of the Latin poem to establish Crispinus as a poetaster, but thereafter follows the original pretty faithfully. The scene starts thus (lines 1–44 using Cain's 1995 edition):

HORACE.	Hmh! Yes, I will begin an ode so; and it shall be to Maecenas.
CRISPINUS. [*Aside.*]	'Slid, yonder's Horace! They say he's an excellent poet. Maecenas loves him. I'll fall into his acquaintance if I can; I think he be composing as he goes i' the street. Ha! Tis a good humour, and he be: I'll compose too.
HORACE.	*Swell me a bowl with lusty wine,* *Till I may see the plump Lyaeus swim* *Above the brim:* *I drink as I would write,* *In flowing measure filled with flame and sprite.*
CRISPINUS.	Sweet Horace, Minerva and the Muses stand auspicious to thy designs. How farest thou, sweet man? Frolic? Rich? Gallant? Ha?

HORACE.	Not greatly gallant, sir; like my fortunes, well. I'm bold to take my leave sir. You'd naught else, sir, would you?
CRISPINUS.	Troth, no, but I could wish thou didst know us, Horace. We are a scholar, I assure thee.
HORACE.	A scholar, Sir! I shall be covetous of your fair knowledge.
CRISPINUS.	Gramercy, good Horace. Nay, we are new turned poet too, which is more; and a satirist too, which is more than that; I write just in thy vein, I. I am for your odes, or your sermons, or anything indeed; we are a gentleman besides: our name is Rufus Laberius Crispinus. We are a pretty Stoic too.
HORACE.	To the proportion of your beard, I think it, sir.
CRISPINUS.	By Phoebus, here's a most neat fine street, is't not? I protest to thee, I am enamoured of this street now, more than of half the streets of Rome again; 'tis so polite and terse! There's the front of a building now. I study architecture too: if ever I should build, I'd have a house just of that prospective.
HORACE. [*Aside*]	Doubtless, this gallant's tongue has a good turn when he sleeps.
CRISPINUS.	I do make verses, when I come in such a street as this. O, your city ladies, you shall ha' 'em sit in every shop like the Muses—[Pauses.] offering you the Castalian dews and the Thespian liquors, to as many as have but the sweet grace and audacity to—[Pauses.] sip of their lips. Did you never hear any of my verses?
HORACE.	No, sir; [*Aside*] But I am in some fear, I must now.

Crispinus proceeds to torment Horace with dreadful verses so that Horace desperately wishes to be rid of him, envying Bolanus (as in the Latin poem) his fierce temper in a desperate aside (III.i.102–15):

> Death! I must crave his leave to piss anon;
> Or that I may go hence with half my teeth,
> I am in some such fear. This tyranny
> Is strange, to take mine ears up by commission,
> Whether I will or no, and make them stalls
> To his lewd solecisms and worded trash.
> Happy thou, bold Bolanus, now I say,
> Whose freedom and impatience of this fellow
> Would long ere this have call'd him fool, and fool,
> And rank and tedious fool, and have flung jests
> As hard as stones, till thou hadst pelted him
> Out of the place; whilst my tame modesty

Suffers my wit be made a solemn ass,
To bear his fopperies—

Crispinus then mentions a lawsuit he must attend and asks Horace to help him
out with the bail, commending himself thus (III.i.161–8, 170–2):

> I protest to thee, Horace, do but taste me once, if I do know myself and mine own
> virtues truly, thou wilt not make that esteem of Varius, or Virgil, or Tibullus, or
> any of 'em indeed, as now in thy ignorance thou dost; which I am content to
> forgive. I would fain see which of these could pen more verses in a day, or with
> more facility than I, or that could court his mistress, kiss her hand, make better
> sport with her fan or her dog … Or that could move his body more gracefully, or
> dance better: you should see me, were it not i' the street.

As in the original, however, Horace declares that he is unable to help. At that
point, Crispinus abandons his lawsuit to press his case for admission to the circle
of Maecenas, in terms virtually identical to those in the Latin poem, to which
Horace replies frostily that Crispinus completely misunderstands Maecenas' criteria. Then Horace's friend Aristius Fuscus comes along but refuses to rescue
him from the pest. Finally, when officials enter to arrest Crispinus, Horace takes
the chance to slip away, leaving Crispinus feeling snubbed and embroiled in his
lawsuit.

In Act IV Scene iii Jonson depicts the plot against Horace that arises from
fierce hostility towards him. He is described by Demetrius as "a mere sponge,
nothing but humours and observation; he goes up and down sucking from every
society, and when he comes home squeezes himself dry again" (IV.iii.104–7) and
by Pantilius Tucca as "a sharp, thorny-toothed satirical rascal" who "carries hay
in his horn" (translating *Satires* 1.4.34) and who "will sooner lose his best friend
than his least jest" (IV.iii.109–11); "'tis all dog and scorpion: he carries poison
in his teeth and a sting in his tail. Fough! Body of Jove! I'll have the slave whipped
one of these days for his satires and his humours, by one cashiered clerk or
another" (IV.iii.115–18). The accusation of treason against Horace is delivered
to Augustus in Act V Scene iii, interrupting a recitation from the *Aeneid* by Virgil.
It calls Horace (298–9, 301–2, 304–5):

> A critic, that all the world bescumbers
> With satirical humours and lyrical numbers …
> And for the most part, himself doth advance
> With much self-love, and more arrogance. …
> And, but that I would not be thought a prater,
> I could tell you he were a translator.

In response to the assertion that anyone he consorts with may need to fear his
tongue Horace utters a denial (316–33):

And why, thou motley gull, why should they fear?
When hast thou known us wrong or tax a friend?
I dare thy malice to betray it. Speak!
Now thou curl'st up, thou poor and nasty snake,
And shrink'st thy pois'nous head into thy bosom.
Out, viper, thou that eat'st thy parents, hence.
Rather, such specklèd creatures as thyself
Should be eschewed, and shunned: such as will bite
And gnaw their absent friends, not cure their fame;
Catch at the loosest laughters and affect
To be thought jesters; such as can devise
Things never seen or head, t' impair men's names
And gratify their credulous adversaries;
Will carry tales, do basest offices,
Cherish divided fires, and still increase
New flames out of old embers; will reveal
Each secret that's committed to their trust;
These be black slaves: Romans, take heed of these.

This reworks Horace's warning from his self-defense in *Satires* 1.4 where he
contrasts himself, with his honest, well-motivated remarks which may stray into
bluntness, with the type of man who criticizes his friends in their absence and
reveals their secrets to all and sundry (lines 78–105, e.g., 81–5, trans. Juster):

> absentem qui rodit amicum,
> qui non defendit alio culpante, solutos
> qui captat risus hominum famamque dicacis,
> fingere qui non uisa potest, commissa tacere
> qui nequit: hic niger est, hunc tu, Romane, caueto.

> The man who knocks a friend behind his back,
> who stands aside when enemies attack,
> who seeks huge laughs and status as a jokester,
> who can invent a tale to be a hoaxster,
> and who can never keep a confidence,
> he's dark! Romans, maintain your vigilance
> with him!

Since Augustus does not for a minute believe the accusations against Horace,
he allows the court poets to convene a mock-court with Virgil as judge to try
Crispinus and Demetrius. Tibullus delivers the indictment, in which Crispinus
and Demetrius are "arraigned, upon the statute of calumny" that "contrary to
the peace of our liege lord Augustus Caesar, his crown and dignity, and against
the form of a statute in that case made and provided, have most ignorantly, fool-
ishly, and (more like yourselves) maliciously, gone about to deprave and calum-
niate the person and writings of Quintus Horatius Flaccus, here present, poet,

and priest to the Muses. And to that end have mutually conspired and plotted at sundry times, as by several means, and in sundry places, for the better accomplishing your base and envious purpose, taxing him falsely of self-love, arrogancy, impudence, railing, filching by translation, etcetera" (209, 214–25). In response, Demetrius eventually explains that they were motivated by their envy of Horace, because "he kept better company for the most part than I, and that better men loved him than loved me, and that his writings thrived better than mine and were better liked and graced. Nothing else" (442–5). Horace responds (447–54):

> If this be all, faith I forgive thee freely.
> Envy me still, so long as Virgil loves me,
> Gallus, Tibullus, and the best-best Caesar;
> My dear Maecenas. While these, with many more,
> Whose names I wisely slip, shall think me worthy
> Their honoured and adored society,
> And read and love, prove and applaud my poems,
> I would not wish but such as you should spite them.

Here Jonson has carefully adapted lines from the conclusion of *Satires* 1.10, the poem in which Horace defends his writing of satire by asserting his desire to please not the masses but a small circle of astute critics (78–90):

> men moueat cimex Pantilius aut cruciet quod
> uellicet absentem Demetrius aut quod ineptus
> Fannius Hermogenis laedat conuiua Tigelli?
> Plotius et Varius, Maecenas Vergiliusque,
> Valgius et probet haec Octauius optimus atque
> Fuscus et haec utinam Viscorum laudet uterque!
> ambitione relegata te dicere possum,
> Pollio, te, Messalla, tuo cum fratre, simulque
> uos, Bibule et Serui, simul his te, candide Furni,
> compluris alios, doctos ego quos et amicos
> prudens praetereo; quibus haec, sint qualiacumque,
> adridere uelim, doliturus, si placeant spe
> deterius nostra.

> Why should I let myself get aggravated
> by that louse Pantilius or bated
> by Demetrius, who snipes at me
> at every chance (though never frontally),
> or smeared by vapid Fannius, that sleaze
> who always mooches off Hermogenes
> Tigellius and acts in nasty ways?
> Let Plotius and Varius heap praise
> upon my verse as well as Valgius,
> Maecenas, Virgil—plus Octavius

> and Fuscus, who are finer men than others—
> and, in addition, both the Viscus brothers!
> ...
> I hope my verse, such as it is, brings joy
> to all of them ...

Then, in a bizarre turn of the plot borrowed from Lucian's *Lexiphanes* (entitled for the "Word-Flaunter" who is purged of bombast by the end of the dialogue: see especially section 21), Horace produces pills to be administered to Crispinus who in due course, accompanied by much moaning and groaning, vomits up his poetaster's words in disgusting gobbets (460–515 *passim*): "*retrograde—reciprocal—incubus—glibbery—lubrical—defunct—magnificate—spurious—snotteries—chilblained—clumsy—barmyfroth—puffy—inflate—turgidous—ventositous—oblatrant—furibund—fatuate—strenuous—conscious—damp—prorumped—clutched—snarling gusts—quaking custard—obstupefact.*" Finally Tibullus administers the oath for good behavior, whereby Crispinus, and Demetrius have to:

> solemnly attest and swear that never, after this instant, either at booksellers' stalls, in taverns, twopenny rooms, 'tiring houses, noblemen's butteries, puisnes' chambers (the best and farthest places where you are admitted to come), you shall once offer or dare (thereby to endear yourself the more to any player, engle, or guilty gull in your company) to malign, traduce or detract the person or writings of Quintus Horatius Flaccus, or any other eminent man transcending you in merit, whom your envy shall find cause to work upon, either for that, or for keeping himself in better acquaintance or enjoying better friends ... Neither shall you at any time, (ambitiously affecting the title of the untrussers or whippers of the age) suffer the itch of writing to over-run your performance in libel, upon pain of being taken up for lepers in wit, and (losing both your time and your papers) be irrecoverably forfeited to the Hospital of Fools. So help you our Roman gods, and the genius of great Caesar. (575–86, 591–7)

Not surprisingly, given the combative motivation of the play, much of the Horatian material incorporated by Jonson comes from or is inspired by the three poems in which Horace articulates his satiric apologia, *Satires* 1.4, 1.10, and 2.1. It is a stroke of genius to combine this with the self-satire of *Satires* 1.9. But Jonson does not end there. Another important element in Horace's self-representation, complementary to his inability to rid himself of the pest, is his assertion in *Satires* 1.6 that he is perfectly content with his humble origins—and this Jonson manages to adapt in what looks like a bit of byplay from earlier in Act V Scene i, when Augustus asks Horace, Gallus, and Tibullus their opinions of Virgil (V.i.75–8):

> What think you three of Virgil, gentlemen,
> That are of his profession, though rank'd higher,
> Or, Horace, what sayest thou, that are the poorest,
> And likeliest to envy, or to detract?

Before delivering his (highly favorable) opinion Horace takes the opportunity to reprove the Emperor for his assumptions about the relationship between status and conduct, uttering a frank speech which seems inspired by the message of *Satires* 1.6, where Horace praises Maecenas for valuing people for their morality and not their blue blood (79–93):

> Caesar speaks after common men in this,
> To make a difference of me for my poorness,
> As if the filth of poverty sunk as deep
> Into a knowing spirit as the bane
> Of riches doth into an ignorant soul.
> No, Caesar, they be pathless, moorish minds
> That being once made rotten with the dung
> Of damnèd riches ever after sink
> Beneath the steps of any villainy.
> But knowledge is the nectar that keeps sweet
> A perfect soul even in this grave of sin;
> And for my soul, it is as free as Caesar's,
> For what I know is due, I'll give to all.
> He that detracts or envies virtuous merit
> Is still the covetous and the ignorant spirit.

Augustus courteously accepts the reproof (94–8):

> Thanks, Horace, for thy free and wholesome sharpness,
> Which pleaseth Caesar more than servile fawns.
> A flatter'd prince soon turns the prince of fools,
> And for thy sake we'll put no difference more
> 'Twixt knights and knightly spirits, for being poor.

In this fleeting exchange Jonson promotes an image of Horace—and by extension of himself—as no malicious satirist but an honest reporter of the truth. In short, in *The Poetaster* Jonson utilizes portions of the Satires to create a witty self-defense against his poetic enemies by deploying Horace the satirist to represent himself in the best possible light.

Jonson's identification with Horace seems exceptionally thorough, yet is a typical phenomenon in the reception of Horace's Satires. The encounter of the later poet with 'Orazio satiro'—whether that be Ariosto, Jonson, Régnier, Boileau, Pope, or others not examined in this essay—results in a kind of metempsychosis. The later poets recreate in their different ways the Horace that they find: whether writing within or without the court, essentially someone who values his freedom and does not compromise his ethical integrity. This is a reflection of and a tribute to the malleable persona that Horace created in the Satires and Epistles.

GUIDE TO FURTHER READING

There are many resources for those wishing to pursue this subject in more depth. Overviews are provided by Charles Martindale (1992: 177–213), J. P. Sullivan (1992: 214–42), and David Hopkins (2005: 218–40). Many of the essays in Martindale and Hopkins (1993) and in Stephen Harrison (2007a) are highly pertinent. These volumes also provide more specialized bibliography.

On Ariosto and Horace see David Marsh (1975: 307–26). On Horace in France see Jean Marmier (1962) and Russell Goulbourn (2007: 139–60). On Ben Jonson's identification with Horace see Joanna Martindale (1993: 50–85). On Pope's recreation of Horace see F. Stack (1985); Robin Sowerby 1993: 159–83); and Ruben Quintero (2007: 212–32). For a meditation on the role of Horace's good humour in his reception see Felicity Rosslyn (1993: 184–98).

The afterlife of the fable of the town mouse and the country mouse (*Satires* 2.6) is particularly fascinating. In English there are translations by Henryson, Wyatt, Drant, Beaumont, Fanshawe, Creech, and Pope and Swift's collaboration. For discussion see David West (1974: 67–80) and David Hopkins (1993: 103–26).

NOTES

* My thanks go to Ian Runacres for help with orthography and bibliography and Daniela Boccassini for help with a query about the French. Above all, I wish to express my profound gratitude to Gregson Davis for his sympathy and his belief that I would, ultimately, deliver: I shall never forget his extreme patience and humanity during the time when I was dealing with the emotional impact of my father's death.

1 As discussed by Friis-Jensen in Harrison 2007a, referring to further work by Munk Olsen, 293–4; on Horace in late antiquity see Tarrant in Harrison 2007a: 281–9.

2 Thus Tarrant in Harrison 2007a: 288, citing G. Glauche, *Schullektüre im Mittelalter* (Munich, 1970).

3 Abbé Cotin (seventeenth century) was renowned for his sermons and poems and the sixteenth century humanist Jacques Pelletier [properly Peletier] wrote translations and sonnets.

CHAPTER NINETEEN

Reception of Horace's
Ars Poetica

Leon Golden

Horace's *Ars Poetica* (designated as *AP* hereafter) is a multifaceted verse-epistle that has had a conscious or unconscious influence on a variety of important literary critics and poets almost continuously from the end of the first century BCE, through the twentieth century. The greatest of the classical literary critics, Aristotle and Horace, have survived many changes of fashion and orientation in literary criticism and theory to stand, sometimes in alien landscapes, as beacons of enlightenment regarding the essential nature and ultimate goals of poetry. Because of the impressive role the *AP* has played for so long a period in the history of literary criticism there is every reason to expect that it will continue to exert its influence in the centuries to come as it tenaciously holds its own amidst competition from the constant ebb and flow of new theories bidding for a place of permanence within the realm of ideas. The passing centuries have borne clear witness that Horace's poem about poetry, skillfully designed but deceptively simple in its outward appearance, has avoided easy transparency in the eyes of its readers and interpreters while achieving far more than a mere transitory claim on their critical sensibilities.

In order to speak of the various ways in which the influence of the *AP* has expressed itself in literary history we will have to draw a structural and thematic map of the poem and, very importantly, attempt to define its essential goal and purpose. First, let us note that the original title of the *AP* was most likely *Epistle to the Pisones*, and adopts the format of a verse-epistle directed by Horace to a friend and his two sons imparting advice about the writing of poetry to the young men who apparently were contemplating literary careers. It was Quintilian in the first century CE who referred to the work as the *Ars Poetica* and that has become the title by which the work has generally been known from that time on. Quintilian's reference to the *Epistle to the Pisones* as the *Ars Poetica* has, however, become the source of significant problems for critics who have sought to understand the overall purpose and essential theme of this poem. The regular use of term *"ars"* would be to designate a technical treatise or textbook that would much more resemble the complexity and style of Aristotle's carefully structured studies of poetry and rhetoric than the much more informal character of Horace's verse-epistle with its comic and satiric interludes scattered amidst serious aphoristic comments about poetry and poets, and all of this set within the context of a relaxed and cordial communication between a great poet and members of his circle of friends. Thus one comment on the poem states "it is a most puzzling work and, despite its skill and humour, little is said about poetry that seems worthy of Horace" (*The Oxford Classical Dictionary*, 2nd edn, 1970: 529). Here is another description:

> The intellectual level of the *AP* is not uniform. Not only are there elements missing which we find in Aristotle's *Poetics* (nothing, e.g., about recognition, reversal, error, or catharsis), but some of the recommendations which *are* made come across as perfunctory. Thus the so-called 'five-act law', the restriction of the *deus ex machina*, and the ban on the fourth speaking part (189–92) sound like mechanical repetitions of received wisdom. Occasionally, too, when he is in danger of stepping into deeper water, Horace draws back.... The *AP*, then, is not a systematic handbook of literary theory; nor, in spite of the respect accorded to it in later centuries, was ever meant to be. It is a lively, entertaining, verse-epistle, written by a well-read man for his friends, who shared his love of poetry and whose company we are invited to join. (Rudd 1989: 34)

Niall Rudd correctly guides us to the understanding that the *AP* belongs to a different genre than the school textbook or Aristotelian style philosophical treatise, despite the fact that for some centuries after the classical period it was often used in this way. The title of *"ars"* with which Quintilian adorned Horace's letter to his friend and his friend's sons has succeeded, as we see from the quotations above, in awakening expectations that clearly have not been met and were not intended to be met by a work framed in the genre of a verse-epistle. It is true that a great deal of what Horace has to say about the theoretical and technical aspects of "poetics" is not original and is derived from earlier thinkers going back to Aristotle and his philosophical successors. These comments, while not original, are often expressed with a memorable eloquence not found in the sources from which they are derived. Where we do see Horace' enormous creativity at work is in the keen respect and appreciation he has for the august and meaningful mission of great poetry in human society and the powerful demands that such a mission makes on those whose privilege it is to carry it out. The view that this poem is an *ars* has remained, however, an important part of the history of the reception of the work. Early editions of the *AP* by Geoffrey of Vinsauf and Badius Ascensius were essentially grammar textbooks to be used by schoolboys to enhance their writing skills. Horace's poem was used in this context as a compendium of rules to be followed by such students. The approach to the *AP* as a school textbook prepared the way for an evolving scholarly tradition in which editors and commentators engaged, and continue to engage, in extended dialogues with each other about such technical issues as variant readings in the manuscripts of the *AP*, the structural divisions within the work, and Horace's sources. Daniel Heinsius's edition of the poem (1610, 1612) is an important step in this direction. O.B. Hardison describes his approach as an editor as follows (Hardison and Golden 1995: 238):

> More significant, he treats the *Art* as a scholar or philologist rather than as a poet. The text has become a succession of questions to be solved by the application of learning and rigorous editorial principles, and it gives the impression of being intended for those who are interested in the Art as a philological problem rather than as a guide to making poetry.

In time, important scholarly editions reflecting the approach of Heinsius have appeared: Richard Bentley (1711), Augusto Rostagni (1930), Otto Immisch (1932), C. O. Brink (1963, 1971), and Rudd (1989). Alongside this scholarly investigation of Horace's text another, very different kind of reception of the *AP* has taken place. This is a reception based on later poets who see the *AP* as a poet's manifesto defining the nature and significance of poetry as a human activity. In this avenue of reception it is poets writing poems about poetry that manifest and extend the influence of the *AP*. Some of these poems make specific and direct references to the *AP* and some are related to Horace's poem only by a kinship to the Roman poet based on the fact that they also reflect his deeply serious commitment to the art of poetry.

Thus the influence of the *AP* will be found in the imaginative way it transmits ideas found in earlier technical treatises on poetry, the tough and insightful way in which it makes us aware of the true nature of poetry, and the forces shaping the temperament and skill of the poet so as to elicit the excellence that alone gives validity to the poetic enterprise.

The vigorous debate about how the *AP* is to be divided into its constituent parts goes on unabated today, but the suggestion most helpful to the theme of this essay was offered by Norden in 1905 when he argued that the poem consisted of two sections, lines 1–294 devoted to *ars*, technical matters relating to the writing of poetry, and lines 295–476 devoted to the *artifex*, the poet, with reference to all factors affecting artistic creativity, achievement, and purpose.

C. O. Brink offers us a useful division of the discussion of *ars* in the *AP* into four parts: I. Poetic unity and *ars* (ll. 1–41); II. The arts of arrangement and diction in Poetry, (ll. 42–118); III. Subject-matter and character in poetry, exemplified by drama and epic, ll. 119–52; IV. Drama, 153–294; and he recognizes the final section of the poem distinct from *ars* as V. The Poet, 295–476

(1971: 75–325). With these categories in mind we will be able to identify a variety of themes in the *AP* and locate their near and distant connections in the works of poets who came after Horace.

We begin tracking the influence of the *AP* in the medieval period. Hardison (Hardison and Golden 1995: 83) describes the reception of the *AP* during this period as follows:

> Beyond manuscripts and quotations, evidence for the medieval influence of *The Art of Poetry* consists of works that comment on the *Art* or imitate it. Again the record is relatively clear. The *Art* was well known in the late classical-early medieval period. Its influence waned between the fifth and eighth centuries but revived during the Carolingian period. Between the Carolingian period and the "twelfth-century Renaissance" the *Art* was widely but irregularly known and used. The situation persisted until the fifteenth century, when the *Art* came to be recognized throughout Europe as the central explanation of classical literary theory.

Hardison points out that the influence of a classical text can be detected from the existence of glosses (explanatory notes regarding individual words) and commentaries (comprehensive interpretations of the entire text) that were devoted to that text. Two glosses, one by Porphyrion and the other by pseudo-Acron, survive from the late classical period and are preserved in manuscripts from the Carolingian period. While we have no manuscripts or commentaries on the *Ars* from the fifth to the eighth century and we find few references or quotations from it during this period, a manuscript tradition must have been maintained to provide a basis for the revival of interest in the *AP* during the Carolingian period. A work entitled the *Scholia Vindobonensia ad Horatii Artem Poeticam* is attributed to an author in the school of Alcuin and dates from the tenth century. The scholia contained in this work are comprehensive enough to approach the format of a commentary and make considerable use of examples from ancient rhetoric. From the Carolingian period on numerous manuscripts survive. In the thirteenth and fourteenth centuries few references to the *Ars* are found by writers in Italy but more numerous references to it are made by northern European authors. Of works appearing at this time that were influenced by the *AP* one of the most interesting is the *Poetria Nova* by the Englishman Geoffrey of Vinsauf, which is dated c.1200 CE. It is written in verse like the *AP* but it undertakes to be a much more comprehensive and detailed survey of the art of poetry than the Horatian original. The *Poetria Nova* does not make specific references to the *AP*, shows a large debt to rhetorical theory, and exceeds the *AP* in length by some 1,500 lines. By calling his work *Poetria Nova,* Geoffrey clearly was calling attention to his goal of innovating on the achievements of Horace's *Ars*.

From the Renaissance to the seventeenth century the influence of the *AP* was recognized by the appearance of numerous commentaries, editions, and translations. In 1503 Iodocus Badius Ascensius published one of the most important of these, which served as popular school texts for students of classical literature.

An important work making reference to the doctrines in the *AP* was published by Julius Caesar Scaliger in 1561 (*Poetices Libri Septem*) and an influential text and commentary on the *AP* was produced by Daniel Heinsius in 1610. Of great importance is the period between 1531 and 1555, when increasing knowledge of the doctrines in Aristotle's *Poetics* were linked by scholars to the literary theory expressed in the *AP*. Herrick (1946) provides a detailed report on how the Horatian and Aristotelian literary doctrines were joined together to form what might be called a "Horatian-Aristotelian" literary theory. Herrick describes the general practice of the time as follows (3):

> Although modern scholarship finds no direct connection between the *Ars Poetica* and the *Poetics*, sixteenth-century scholars agreed that Horace was following Aristotle's theories as formulated in the *Poetics* and *Rhetoric*. Parrhasius (1531), for example, believed that Horace had imitated Neoptolemus and Aristotle. Madius believed that the Horatian epistle is a stream flowing from the Aristotelian spring of the *Poetics*; and the main purpose of his commentary on the *Ars Poetica* was to make clear Horace's "obscure and subtle imitation." Therefore Madius tried to find parallels in the *Poetics* for nearly every statement in the *Ars Poetica*, never doubting, apparently, the direct connection between the Greek and Roman arts of poetry. Madius and his fellow commentators in the sixteenth century were not the only ones who accepted the *Ars Poetica* as a Horatian adaptation of the *Poetics*. For many years after 1555 literary men thought of Horace as the interpreter of Aristotle's criticism.

Modern scholars have shown that it was an error for their sixteenth-century counterparts to attempt a fusion of the *AP* and the *Poetics*, to attempt to create an amalgamation of Aristotle's philosophically rigorous, comprehensive, and systematic treatise on the art of poetry designed for an intellectually elite audience with Horace's informal and sometimes comic/satiric commentary about how and why poetry is to be written and what is required in terms of training and skill of anyone who chooses to become a poet. Scattered through the *AP* are remarks about poetry that may have originated with Aristotle but have most probably come to Horace through intermediaries since, as Herrick notes, "there is no certain evidence in the *Ars Poetica* that Horace was familiar with either Aristotle's *Rhetoric* or *Poetics*" (3). Horace's contribution to literary criticism is very important and highly insightful but it is on a quite different plane than Aristotle's systematic analysis which takes the form of a genuine *ars* or *techne* of poetry.

Sir Philip Sidney's *Defense of Poesy*, published in 1595, provides important examples of the fusion of Horatian and Aristotelian literary criticism. Ideas taken from both great classical critics find their way into Sidney's work. Compare the following passage from the *Defense of Poesy* (220–4) with its combined emphasis on Aristotelian *mimesis* and the Horatian echo in the phrase "a speaking picture with this end, to teach and delight":

Poesy therefore is an art of imitation, for so Aristotle termeth it in the word *mimesis*- that is to say, a representing, counterfeiting, or figuring forth -to speak metaphorically, a speaking picture with this end, to teach and delight

with these passages from the *AP*:

Poets wish to benefit or delight us (*aut prodesse volunt aut delectare poetae*) or, at one and the same time, to speak words that are both pleasing and useful for our lives. (333–4)

Poetry is like a picture (*ut pictura, poesis*). (361)

As Hardison has pointed out, the period from 1650 to 1725 was an era in which Horatian influence flourished. During this time Rochester published his *Allusion to the Tenth Satire of Horace* (1680), Soames his translation of Boileau (1682), Mulgrave his *Essay in Poetry* (1682), Roscommon his translation of Horace's *Art* (1684) and his *Essay on Translated Verse* (1684), Samuel Wesley his *Epistle to a Friend*, Granville his *Essay on Unnatural Flights of Poetry* (1701), and Pope his *Essay on Criticism* (1711). The two works of paramount importance from this period on which we will focus our attention are Boileau's *L'Art poétique* and Pope's extremely important contribution in his *Essay on Criticism*.

Nicholas Cronk (1989) notes that Boileau's *L'Art poétique*, "a poem of 1100 lines, contains over one hundred lines taken directly from Horace's *Ars Poetica* plus another hundred lines borrowed from other poems of Horace."

An illustration of Horace's direct influence on Boileau is the theme he imports into his work at 183 ff, one that is strongly influenced by the powerful, satiric passage at *AP* 419–52, in which the poet is warned to avoid the pitfalls of praise from sycophantic acquaintances and critics seeking to curry favor with him for ulterior purposes. Both poets, in lengthy, related passages, but using somewhat differing images, give passionate voice to bitter mockery toward what both feel is the true poet's worst enemies, friends conniving for favors and the poet's own vanity that seeks to deflect and refute any suggestion of mediocrity or failure on his part.

At the core of Horace's *AP* is a profound respect for the importance and high purpose of poetry, and it is this respect that clearly resonates with Boileau. Both critics react with strong and sincere outrage against the subversion of poetic integrity by false friends and critics seeking to curry favor with the poet and by the flawed artistic temperament that resists penetrating criticism which, given a chance, has the capability to elevate poetic effort to the highest level of artistic achievement.

Boileau evokes a most important Horatian topos: the pressing demand on those who pursue the poetic craft to achieve excellence, alone, or completely fail in their enterprise. Boileau introduces his version of this theme with an amusing anecdote about a physician whose fantastic medical incompetence permitted him to kill off nearly all his patients. His abysmal professional career takes a significant turn for the better, however, when he is afforded the opportunity to advise "one Friend, unkill'd by Drugs, of all his Store" who is incompetently constructing a country house, about the means for successfully correcting his egregious errors. Boileau writes, "in short, to finish this our hum'rous Tale/He *Galen's* dang'rous Science does reject, And from ill Doctor turns good Architect." Boileau then draws this conclusion (881 ff):

> In this Example we may have our part:
> Rather be Mason, ('tis an useful Art!)
> Than a dull Poet; for that Trade accurst,
> Admits no mean betwixt the Best and Worst.
> In other Sciences, without disgrace
> A Candidate may fill a second place;
> But Poetry no Medium can admit,
> No reader suffers an indiff'rent Wit.

These lines echo the thought of *AP* 366–78:

> And you, the older brother, although you have been molded by your father's voice to know what is correct and you are wise in your own right, take and hold in your memory this warning: only in certain activities are we justified in tolerating mediocrity and what is just passable. A run-of-the-mill expert in the law or pleader of cases is a long way from the skill of the eloquent Messala and doesn't know as much as Aulus Cascellius, but nevertheless he has a value. But neither men nor gods nor booksellers have ever put their stamp of approval on mediocre poets. Just as at a gracious meal a discordant musical performance or a thick perfume or Sardinian honey on your poppy seeds give offense because the meal could have been put together without them; in the same way a poem that comes into existence and is created for the gratification of our mind and heart, if it misses true excellence by only a little, verges toward deepest failure.

Boileau concludes his poem with a keen and subtle reference to Horace's view of the service a critic performs for the poet (1082 ff.):

> Yet you shall see me, in that famous Field
> With Eyes and Voice, my best assistance yield;
> Offer you Lessons, that my Infant Muse
> Learnt, when she *Horace* for her Guide did chuse:
> Second your Zeal with Wishes, Heart, and Eyes,
> And afar off hold up the glorious Prize.
> But pardon too, if, Zealous for the Right,
> A strict observer of each Noble flight,
> From the fine Gold I separate th' Allay,
> And show how hasty Writers sometimes stray:

> Apter to blame, than knowing how to mend;
> A sharp, but necessary Friend.

The origin of these remarks go back to the more complex and eloquent lines of Horace's *AP* (30–8):

> O what an unlucky fool I am! I have my bile purged just before spring arrives! No one else could write a better poem. But nothing is worth that effort! Instead, I shall serve in place of a whetstone that has the power to render iron sharp but itself lacks the ability to cut; while not writing anything myself, I will teach what nurtures and forms the poet, from what source his power springs, what his function and duty are, what is proper and what is not and in what direction poetic excellence leads and in what direction failure beckons.

Alexander Pope's *An Essay on Criticism* (1711) enters into a stimulating dialogue with the *AP* on intertwining issues of good literary criticism and poetic excellence during the first third of the *Essay* before that work changes its focus almost completely to the theme of criticism. Pope not only cleverly adapts significant Horatian concepts to his own purposes but from time to time also skillfully enriches their application in a way that enlightens and encourages the reader to consider the issues originally raised by Horace more deeply. While it is poetry and the poet that is the central subject of the *AP*, the role of the critic and criticism is certainly not ignored in Horace's poem. For Horace the principal virtue of the critic is unfailing integrity and loyalty to the highest standards for the creation of poetry, the standard which recognizes, as we have noted earlier, that "a poem that comes into existence and is created for the gratification of our mind and heart, if it misses true excellence by only a little, verges toward deepest failure" (*AP* 377–8). In passages already quoted above in relation to Boileau, Horace describes the way a "an honest and judicious" critic must operate in order to fulfill his duty and obligation to poetry and the poet (*AP* 445–50) "and warns about the dangerous and subversive aspect of the very opposite kind of critic, one disposed to offer deceptive and false criticism" (*AP* 419–37).

In his turn, Pope provides, as we would expect in a poem dedicated to the theme he has chosen, a more comprehensive and extensive treatment of the role and purpose of critics and criticism. Early on in his work he makes a telling point directed at critics that is reminiscent of important advice Horace aimed at would-be poets. Pope writes at 46–51 of the *Essay*:

> But you who seek to give and merit fame,
> And justly bear a critic's noble name,
> Be sure yourself, and your own reach to know,
> How far your genius, taste, and learning go;
> Launch not beyond your depth, but be discreet,
> And mark that point where sense and dulness meet.

Here Pope has borrowed for the benefit of critics the following advice Horace gave to poets: "Pick a subject, writers, equal to your strength, and take some time to consider what your shoulders should refuse and what they can bear" (*AP* 38–9). Pope also follows Horace in finding Greek achievement the model for creativity and excellence in both poetry and criticism. He then connects Greek artistic achievement with the proper partnership that should exist between poetry and criticism. He writes in the *Essay* (92–103):

> Hear how learn'd Greece her useful rules indites,
> When to repress, and when indulge our flights:
> High on Parnassus' top her sons she showed,
> And pointed out those arduous paths they trod;
> Held from afar, aloft, th' immortal prize,
> And urged the rest by equal steps to rise.
> Just precepts thus from great examples giv'n,
> She drew from them what they derived from heav'n.
> The gen'rous critic fanned the poet's fire,
> And taught the world with reason to admire
> Then criticism the muse's handmaid proved,
> To dress her charms, and make her more beloved.

Pope views with approval the admiration that Greek critics expressed for Greek poets and the efforts these critics undertook to serve the muse of poetry by making her "charms ... more beloved." He sees this positive symbiotic relationship in Greek culture undermined and abandoned in his own time by critics who employ their talents not in support and enrichment of poetic achievement but as a negative and destructive process by which they obscure and belittle that achievement. Pope admonishes these contemporary critics as follows (*Essay* 118–27):

> You then whose judgment the right course would steer,
> Know well each ancient's proper character;
> His fable, subject, scope in ev'ry page;
> Religion, country, genius of his age:
> Without all these at once before your eyes,
> Cavil you may, but never criticise.
> Be Homer's works your study and delight,
> Read them by day, and meditate by night;
> Thence form your judgment, thence your maxims bring,
> And trace the muses upward to their spring.

In this passage we note the deft application by Pope to the literary critic of an important piece of Horatian advice to the aspiring poet at *AP* 268–9: "your mandate is to hold Greek models before you by day and to hold them before you by night."

In defending the great poet's right to innovate with skill within the commonly accepted rules of composition, Pope accesses two of the best known maxims of Horace's commentary on poetry. At lines 169–74 of the *Essay* he writes:

> I know there are, to whose presumptuous thoughts
> Those free'er beauties, ev'n in them [Greek poets], seem faults.
> Some figures monstrous and mis-shaped appear,
> Considered singly, or beheld too near,
> Which, but proportioned to their light or place,
> Due distance reconciles to form and grace.
> A prudent chief not always must display
> His pow'rs in equal rank, and fair array,
> But with th' occasion and the place comply,
> Conceal his force, nay seem sometimes to fly.
> These oft are stratagems which errors seem,
> Nor is it Homer nods but we that dream.

Compare to this passage the following two comments, among the most well known and quoted passages in the *AP*:

> Poetry resembles painting. Some works will captivate you when you stand very close to them and others if you are at a greater distance. This one prefers a darker vantage point, that one wants to be seen in the light since it feels no terror before the penetrating judgment of the critic. This pleases only once, That will give pleasure even if we go back to it ten times over. (361–5)

> I am also offended when good Homer nods, but it is permitted for some drowsiness to creep into a long work. (358–60)

In reminding us of these Horatian passages in the *Essay* Pope does much more than pay homage to his great predecessor as a poet/critic. He provides us with a perceptive interpretation of Horace's text that goes beyond the literal meaning to provide an even more penetrating understanding of the passages in the *AP* than their actual author may have contemplated. Both Horace and Pope agree that different perspectives are needed for encountering works of art of varying dimensions and complexities. Horace emphasizes (1) the physical distance from different sized paintings that allows for the clearest and deepest appreciation of them, (2) the degree of perfection of the work of art that allows for more or less intense and rigorous appraisal of it, and (3) the varying richness and complexity of the work that can invite either a mere single encounter with it or multiple revisitings to it. But Pope goes further than this to make explicit what is only left strongly implied by Horace, that the understanding of a work of art requires much more than finding the proper perspective and the right vantage point to view and contemplate the work under consideration. Pope asserts that it is our ability to respond sensitively to poetic genius that is central to our ability to understand and appreciate art. He declares that we must recognize that there "are nameless graces which no methods teach/And which a master hand alone can reach" (144–5). Great artists he admonishes us:

> May boldly deviate from the common track.
> Great wits sometimes may gloriously offend,
> And rise to faults true critics dare not mend;
> From vulgar bounds with brave disorder part,
> And snatch a grace beyond the reach of art,
> Which, without passing through the judgment, gains
> The heart, and all its end at once attains.
> In prospects thus, some objects please our eyes,
> Which out of nature's common order rise,
> The shapeless rock, or hanging precipice.
> But though the ancients thus their rules invade,
> (As kings dispense with laws themselves have made,)
> Moderns beware! or if you must offend
> Against the precept, ne'er transgress its end. (151–64)

Here Pope evokes the inexpressible genius of great art which can avail itself of liberties that can dazzle the mind and spirit, defying the limits of ordinary perception and reason. And it is here that Pope dares to correct his great predecessor by eloquently challenging Horace's precept that "Homer nods" when in fact it is "but we who dream" (*Essay* 174). Pope warns us to beware of finding blame in the work of a great poet's imagination when the fault really lies in the limited or flawed perception of the audience which cannot rise to meet the vision of great poetry on its own level. He compares the great poet to the skilled general whose application of unorthodox strategies startles and confuses those used to observing routine maneuvers. The great poet has the capacity "to snatch a grace beyond the reach of art/ Which, without passing through the judgment, gains the heart/ and all its end at once attains" (*Essay* 155). Such poets, in Pope's view, are like kings who "dispense with laws themselves have made" to reach empyrean heights that justly belong to them. Horace's focus is chiefly on the real and potential errors and faults of poets and not on the discrepancy (which Pope addresses) between creative genius and the limited critical acumen that falls short of understanding and appreciating that genius. Nevertheless, there is no doubt that Horace and Pope share the highest respect for poetic greatness, for we recall that Horace asserted that "a poem that comes into existence and is created for the gratification of our mind and heart, if it misses true excellence by only a little, verges toward deepest failure" (*AP* 377–8). Still the point about the audience's obligation to the great poet is well made by Pope. It is no doubt true that Homer and any poet may nod in a long work or short one, but the audience that is dreamily insensitive to a great poet's creative imagination poses an even greater problem.

We find another fascinating connection between the discipline Pope imposes on the poet and critic and Horace's much more exacting demands. Pope's admonition to the poet and critic is "Trust not yourself; but your defects to know, / make use of ev'ry friend and ev'ry foe" (*Essay* 213–14). In the *AP* Horace makes much more extensive demands on poets striving to overcome defects:

> Nor would Latium be more powerful in courage and in illustrious arms than in literature if the time-consuming effort required for a truly polished revision of the text did not give offense to every single one of our poets. O you, who are descendants of Pompilius, denounce any poem that many a day and many a correction has not carefully pruned and then improved ten times over to meet the test of the well-trimmed nail. (289–94)

Then he offers additional advice that must have had a terrifying effect on young poets like the sons of Piso who are addressed in the *AP* (385–90):

> Never will you say or do anything if Minerva, the goddess of wisdom, forbids it; you have good judgment, you have good sense. But if you shall, one day, write something, let it first penetrate the ears of a critic like Maecius or your father or myself; and then keep a lid on it until the ninth year comes around by storing your pages within your house. You will always be able to destroy anything you haven't published; a word, once released. does not know how to return.

Like Pope, Horace advises the poet to seek out friendly and potentially hostile criticism, but then imposes the unbelievably heavy obligation on the young poet to defer publication of his work for nearly a decade, the time needed for the intense editing and reediting required by Horace so that a poem "worth anointing and protecting with oil of cedar, and preserving in chests of polished cypress" (*AP* 331–2) will see the light of day.

An interesting connection exists between Pope and Horace on the subject of minor errors in poetry. Pope writes in the *Essay* (253–60):

> Whoever thinks a faultless piece to see,
> Thinks what ne'er was, nor is, nor e'er shall be.
> In ev'ry work regard the writer's end,
> Since none can compass more than they intend;
> And if the means be just, the conduct true,
> Applause, in spite of trivial faults, is due.
> As men of breeding, sometimes men of wit,
> T'avoid great errors, must the less commit.

Here Pope appears to follow Horace's thoughts at *AP* 347–53:

> There are, however, mistakes that we are willing to forgive. For the string does not always return the sound that the hand and mind desire, and although you seek a

low note, it very often sends back a high one. Nor will the bow always strike whatever it threatens. But where many qualities sparkle in a poem, I will not find fault with a few blemishes, which either carelessness introduced or human nature, too little vigilant, did not avoid.

Although Pope offered an insightful correction to Horace on the subject of Homer "nodding," he agrees fully with his argument that minor flaws will not sabotage a great poem.

A prominent passage in the *AP* (14–19) argues against the use of the "purple patch" by the poet:

Often, one or two purple patches are stitched onto works that have begun in high seriousness, and that profess important themes, so that they sparkle far and wide; as when the grove and altar of Diana and the circling of swiftly flowing waters through the pleasant fields or the Rhine river or the rainbow are described. *But this was not the place for them.*

Here again Pope picks up on a Horatian insight but then expands and deepens it. He writes (*Essay* 293–304):

> Poets, like painters, thus unskilled to trace
> The naked nature, and the living grace,
> With gold and jewels cover ev'ry part,
> And hide with ornaments their want of art.
> True wit is nature to advantage dressed;
> What oft was thought, but ne'er so well expressed;
> Something, whose truth convinced at sight we find,
> That gives us back the image of our mind.
> As shades more sweetly recommend the light,
> So modest plainness sets off sprightly wit;
> For works may have more wit than does 'em good,
> As bodies perish through excess of blood.

Horace is content to chastise the use of purple patches where they are, in Niall Rudd's words, "incongruous and distracting." The passage from Pope's *Essay* is certainly in agreement with this criticism, but Pope has significantly deepened the Horatian critique for he assigns the addiction of poets to "purple patches" in their use of "ornaments" to their need to "hide their want of art." Pope attributes this type of artistic failure to the inability of some poets to recognize that the brilliant effect for which they aim is best achieved amidst a subdued environment of "modest plainness" and that the effect they aim for is actually destroyed when it is surrounded by a clutter of other "ornamental" images. Pope defines these useless poetic ornaments as "a vile conceit in pompous words expressed [that] is like a clown in regal purple dressed" (*Essay* 320–1), and he chooses a brilliant image to make his point in the final two lines quoted above, "for works may have more wit than does 'em good,/as bodies perish through excess of blood." In this eloquent version of the principle that "less is more," Pope significantly enriches the criticism of the "purple patch" theme in the *AP*.

Lord Byron's *Hints from Horace*, published posthumously, bears a very direct relationship to Horace's *AP*. It reflects a number of the important themes in the original work, sometimes with rather close approximation, and sometimes with innovations not based in full or in part on the actual words of the *AP*. Byron does not hesitate to interject into what is occasionally translation, and more often paraphrase, of Horace's poem, biting satire on poets and critics of his own time in the spirit of *English Bards and Scottish Reviewers*. A noteworthy aspect of Byron's poem is its fascinating use of postclassical examples to illustrate themes common to it and Horace's *AP*. I provide below some striking interrelationships between the two poems. Both Horace and Byron show concern for the selection of topics for exposition by poets. Horace writes (*AP* 38–45):

> Pick a subject, writers, equal to your strength and take some time to consider what your shoulders should refuse and what they can bear. Neither eloquence nor clear organization will forsake one who has chosen a subject within his capabilities. Unless I am mistaken this will be the special excellence and delight of good organization— that the author of the promised poem, enamored of one subject and scornful of another, says now what ought to be said now and both postpones and omits a great deal for the present.

Here now is Byron's version (*Hints* 59–68):

> Dear Authors! suit your topics to your strength,
> And ponder well your subject, and its length;
> Nor lift your load, before you're quite aware
> What weight your shoulders will, or will not, bear.
> But lucid Order, and Wit's siren voice,
> Await the poet, skilful in his choice;
> With native Eloquence he soars along,
> Grace in his thoughts, and Music in his song.
> Let Judgment teach him wisely to combine
> With future parts the now omitted line.

Both Horace and Byron cover much of the same territory, but Byron adds an especially charming descriptive note that defines the genuinely disciplined poet who skillfully chooses his themes as someone who "with native eloquence soars along/Grace in his thoughts, and Music in his song."

A most interesting example of the way in which Byron closely follows Horace's thought in the *AP* while skillfully substituting illustrative examples from English literature for Horace's classical allusions is found in the following parallel passages:

> Either follow tradition or devise harmonious actions. O writer, if you by chance describe once again honored Achilles, let him be weariless, quick to anger, stubborn, violent; let him deny that laws were made for him, let him claim everything by arms. Let Medea be wild and unconquerable, Ino doleful, Ixion treacherous, Io a wanderer in mind and body, Orestes filled with sorrow. If you commit anything untested to the stage and you dare to fashion a novel character, let it be maintained to the end just as it emerged at the beginning and let it be consistent with itself. (*AP* 119–27)

> If some Drawcansir you aspire to draw,
> Present him raving and above all law:
> If female furies in your scheme are plann'd,
> Macbeth's fierce dame is ready to your hand;
> For tears and treachery, for good and evil,
> Constance, King Richard, Hamlet, and the Devil!
> But if a new design you dare essay,
> And freely wander from the beaten way,
> True to your characters, till all be pass'd,
> Preserve consistency from first to last. (*Hints* 173–82)

Byron's examples are apt counterparts to those used by Horace although "Drawcansir" is a striking, and probably a most obscure, parallel to Horace's Achilles. Drawcansir was a farcical character in *The Rehearsal* (1672) by G. Villiers, Duke of Buckingham, who kills everyone "sparing neither friend nor foe." Offering a farcical tyrant as a parallel to Achilles strikes a strange note even though a penchant for violence is present in both characters, but Byron was apparently unable to resist the play on the word "draw" in the line. Otherwise the parallel examples compare well with each other, and both poets stress the need for maintaining consistency in the creation and development of any completely new character invented by the artist's imagination.

Throughout *Hints from Horace* the reader will notice many other important echoes of the *AP*. I call attention to the following: "Ye who seek finished models, never cease to read the works of Greece" (424–5); (cf. *AP* 268–9: "Your mandate is to hold Greek models before you by day and to hold them before you by night"); "two objects always should the poet move, /or one or both,—to please or to improve" (531–2); (cf. *AP* 333–4: "Poets wish either to benefit or delight us, or, at one and the same time, to speak words that are both pleasing and useful for our lives"); "Though all deplore when Milton deigns to doze, /in a long work 't is fair to steal repose" (569–70); (cf. *AP* 359–60): "I am also offended when great Homer nods, but it is permitted for some drowsiness to creep into a long work"); "As pictures, so shall poems be; some stand/

the critic eye, and please when near at hand; but others at a distance strike the sight;/this seeks the shade, but that demands the light,/ nor dreads the connoisseur's fastidious view, / but, ten times scrutinised, is ten times new" (571–6); (cf. *AP* 361–5: "Poetry resembles painting. Some works will captivate you when you stand very close to them and others when you are at a greater distance. This one prefers a darker vantage point, that one wants to be seen in the light since it feels no terror before the penetrating judgment of the critic.This pleases only once, that will give pleasure even if we go back to it ten times over"); "All are not Erskines who mislead the bar./ but poesy between the best and the worst/ no medium knows; you must be last for first;/for middling poets' miserable volumes/ are damned alike by gods and men and columns" (584–8); (cf. *AP* 369–73, 377–8: "A run-of-the-mill expert in the law or pleader of cases is a long way from the eloquent Messala and doesn't know as much as Aulus Cascellius, but nevertheless he has a value. But neither men nor gods nor booksellers have ever put their stamp of approval on mediocre poets … In the same way a poem that comes into existence and is created for the gratification of our mind and heart, if it misses true excellence by only a little, verges toward deepest failure;") "Be this your sober judgment, and a rule,/ and print not piping hot from Southey's school,/ who (ere another Thalaba appears),/ I trust, will spare us for another nine years/and hark ye, Southey! pray—but don't be vex'd—/burn all your last three works—and half the next./ but why this vain advice? once publish'd, books can never be recalled—from pastry-cooks!" (653–60); (cf. *AP* 386–90: "But if you shall, one day, write something let it first penetrate the ears of a critic like Maecius or your father or myself; and then keep a lid on it until the ninth year comes around by storing your pages inside your house. You will always be able to destroy anything you haven't published; a word, once released, does not know how to return.")

And finally (822–44), we find Byron's fascinating paraphrase, tinged with bitter satire, of Horace's famous evocation of the "mad poet" scene that concludes both his and Horace's poem. Below I cite two sets of illustrative passages for comparison. The first pair begins with *AP* 463–6 and is followed by *Hints* 823–6:

> Then I'll tell the story of how the Sicilian poet perished. When Empedocles felt the desire to be considered an immortal god, cool as a cucumber he leaped into the burning fires of Aetna.

> Budgell, a rogue and rhymster, for no good
> (unless his case be much misunderstood),
> When teas'd with creditors' continual claims
> "To die like Cato," leapt into the Thames!

In Horace's poem the role of a poet embracing suicide is filled by a major early Greek philosopher, scientist, poet, and statesman with mystical tendencies, Empedocles. The facts of his actual death are uncertain but a famous legend has him seeking immortality by hurling himself into the active volcano, Mount Etna in Sicily. The sardonic parallel offered by Byron is the "rogue and rhymster" Eustice Budgell (1686–1737), a minor English author who was beset by financial diffi-culties and committed suicide.

The second pair of complementary passages form the conclusion of both Horace's and Byron's poems. The *AP* 470–6 ends this way:

> Nor is it sufficiently clear why he practices the poet's trade. Did he sacrilegiously urinate on the ashes of his ancestors or disturb a gloomy plot of consecrated land that had been struck by lightning? Whatever the cause he is certainly mad and just like a bear—if he has succeeded in smashing the restraining bars of his cage—his morose public recitations frighten off the educated and ignorant alike; once he gets his hands on a person, he doesn't let go until he kills him with his reading—a leech who will not release the skin unless gorged with blood.

Here is the parallel passage in *Hints* 833–44:

> Nor is it certain that some sorts of verse
> Prick not the poet's conscience as a curse;
> Dosed with vile drams on Sunday he was found,
> Or got a child on consecrated ground!
> And hence is haunted with a rhyming rage—
> Feared like a bear just bursting from his cage.
> If free, all fly his versifying fit,
> Fatal at once to simpleton or wit:
> But *him*, unhappy! whom he seizes,—*him*
> He flays with recitation limb by limb;
> Probes to the quick where'er he makes his breach,
> And gorges like a lawyer—or a leech.

Byron follows Horace in using the searing image of sacrilegious causation gov-erning the choice of the poet's vocation and the powerful metaphors of bear and leech to describe the interaction of poet and audience, but there is a signifi-cant difference in tone between the two passages. Byron gives vent to the sarcasm that permeates his poem in the last line of *Hints* when he describes the poet accosting a potential listener to his recitations as one who "gorges like a lawyer—or a leech." There is no doubt that he is engaging in condemnatory satire here of the mediocre poets he has attacked earlier in the poem and of lawyers he does not like much better. The ending of Horace's poem is much more difficult to interpret. Authoritative commentators such as Brink and Rudd have called it a "caricature of poetic inspiration, a picture of error" (Brink 1971) and a "caricature of the mad poet" (Rudd 1989). Yet both of these commentators modify their evaluation in important ways. Brink (1971: 516) writes:

'Error' in what sense? Not surely in the sense that H. was a stranger to imaginative 'madness'. This piece is too arresting for that supposition. The satire on inspiration and the 'death-wish' is one of the great satires in European letters. It fascinates because it is written from inside the experience which it professes to ridicule ... This cautionary story could never have been written without a generous measure of the quality so caricatured.

Rudd (1989: 23), after describing lines 453–76 as the "caricature of the mad poet" notes significantly that "it will help us to keep the *AP* in perspective if we recall that at some of the highest points of Horatian lyric the inspired bard is treated very differently." There is a considerable difference between Byron's *mimesis* and Horace's poem. Byron produces a witty, flippant satire; Horace has written a poem of much greater intensity and profundity. We will need to focus on this point when we consider a great twentieth-century poem that follows in the footsteps of Horace's *AP* as an equally serious poetic meditation on aspects of the nature of poetry but also takes issue with some of the important points of view found in the *AP*.

First we should mention that Horace exerted a significant influence on a group of important nineteenth-century American poets and critics including: William Cullen Bryant (1794–1878); Edgar Allen Poe (1809–49); Ralph Waldo Emerson (1803–82); Henry Wadsworth Longfellow (1807–82); and Oliver Wendell Holmes (1809–94). In the twentieth century two poems of some significance appeared bearing the title of *Ars Poetica*, one by Archibald Macleish in 1925 and another by Czeslaw Milosz in 1961 with a question mark added after the title by the author. These two rather short poems do not approach the magnitude and depth of the long poem, though they grapple with a number of the profound issues raised by Horace, which we are about to discuss.

The *Essay on Rime* (hereafter *Rime*) was written by Karl Shapiro (1913–2000) when he was serving in the United States Army in the Pacific theater of war during World War II. The poem, 2,072 lines of blank verse, was written during a three-month respite from military assignments, and covers an amazing amount of literary and intellectual territory, especially when we realize that the author had virtually no library resources at his disposal and had to depend on recollections from the vast amount of reading he had done prior to his military service. In the poem's "Foreword" he almost immediately addresses, and takes issue with, an important observation in the *AP*. At lines 47–53 Shapiro writes:

> Horace and Pope, this pair may be adduced
> As poets who argued in the voice of rime
> And argued well. But poets prefer to roost
> In arbors rather than the tree of knowledge.
> That bard expelled from Socrates' Republic
> Is held sweet to the world; for understand
> That dialectic is the foe of poetry.

At *AP* 309–11 Horace writes:

> The foundation and source of literary excellence is wisdom. The works written about
> Socrates are able to reveal the true subject matter of poetry and, once the subject
> matter has been provided, words will freely follow.

We see here a great divide between Horace's and Shapiro's view of the relationship between poetry and philosophy and one that puts the two poems in
tension with each other at other points as well.

It is on the topic of the purpose and goal of poetry that both Horace and
Shapiro meditate deeply but come to significantly different conclusions. We have
quoted previously Horace's famous line "Poets wish to either benefit or delight
us, or, at one and the same time, to speak words that are both pleasing and useful
for our lives" (*AP* 333–4). We have also quoted above Horace's lines that: "the
foundation and source of literary excellence is wisdom. The works written about
Socrates are able to reveal the true subject matter of poetry" (*AP* 309–10). For
Horace, the transmission of pleasure and some form of knowledge are the goals
poetry aims at and which justify the high place it occupies in human society.
While Shapiro would certainly agree that poetry should give pleasure to its audience we recall that he asserts his sharp opposition to the idea that poetry is a
vehicle for the dissemination of philosophical wisdom in his emphatic assertion
"that dialectic is the foe of poetry." Moreover, he argues:

> Shakespeare, we think, believed in God and country
> And the nobility of man. What else?
> The greatest poet has left us no account
> of his theology or his metaphysics;
> This in our day is almost tantamount
> To calling him a fool or a barbarian. (*Rime* 1821–6)

In place of providing any formal kind of "wisdom," Shapiro defines a very different goal for poetry to achieve—and here he takes sides with Homer, the "bard
expelled from Socrates' Republic" and not with the dialectic of Socrates, Plato's
teacher, that seeks to unearth some philosophical truth, a process he finds
suffocatingly embedded in the heavily intellectualized poetry of his own mid-
twentieth century culture. He asks:

> Where is the literature
> Of nature, where the love poem and the plain
> Statement of feeling? How and when and why
> Did we conceive our horror of emotion,
> Our fear of beauty? Whence the isolation
> And proud withdrawal of the intellectual
> Into the cool control-room of the brain?

For Shapiro, the goal and purpose of poetry is to evoke the brisk response of the human heart to the emotional richness of life, and especially to love, to Nature and the vast domain of beauty to be found in Nature. These are certainly not subjects to which Horace would be indifferent, but which are not accounted for by his elevation of the "writings about Socrates" to a principal source of poetry's strength.

Our final point of comparison between Horace and Shapiro is perhaps the most important one. It concerns the emotional and intellectual turmoil, the restless driving energy, pressing and oppressing from within, that agonizingly fuels the poet's quest for perfected achievement in the creation of a work of art. How powerful and abiding that force is can be seen from the fact that both Horace and Shapiro make us aware of the intimate connection between the challenges faced by those who follow the artist's vocation and the despair, alienation, and, depressing susceptibility to suicide that so often and so gloomily shadow the lives of poets..

Horace addresses the precarious nature of the poet's life in the vivid final scene of the *AP* (453–76), which has come to be known as "the caricature of the mad poet."

In the twentieth century, C. O. Brink emerged as the most authoritative proponent of the "caricature" interpretation of the culminating passage of the *AP*. Brink's interpretation of this provocative and engrossing vision of an eccentric, alienated, and suicidal poet is based on his view that, for Horace, poetic excellence arises out of an equilibrium existing in the poet of natural talent (*ingenium*) and technical skill (*ars*). Brink argues that the *AP* begins with a paradoxical statement emphasizing that technical skill is required to assure the achievement of unity in a work of art but that natural talent (*ingenium*) is a prerequisite for making the product of technical skill into a successful work of art. He then asserts that the poem ends with another paradox that focuses on celebrating the power of natural talent (*ingenium*) "without which art cannot be" but warns that this natural talent "left to itself would destroy art and its practitioners."

Brink's view that the final scene of the *AP* is a caricature of the mad poet, as I have noted, represents the way the scene has generally been understood. However, Brink also offers us a perceptive intuition about the nature of the poem's engrossing coda that makes it possible to go deeper into the interpretation of the passage. After recognizing that Horace was no stranger to imaginative madness, he writes:

> The satire on inspiration and the 'death-wish'; is one of the great satires in European letters. It fascinates because it is written from inside the experience which it professes to ridicule ... This cautionary story could never have been written without a generous measure of the quality so caricatured. (Brink 1971: 516)

Brink is clearly right that the passage is written "from inside the experience" it is describing and must have been felt by Horace as a reality facing the artist. This theme of the artist's dangerous susceptibility to madness, alienation, despair, and suicide has been recognized, of course, by poets other than Horace including Karl Shapiro in his long poem on the nature of poetry and poets.

In this regard I would like to suggest that Horace, in addition to offering us a caricature, is presenting a seriously grim and authentic vision of the artist's life. Horace has laid down the following fundamental proposition concerning the profession practiced by the poet: while practitioners of all other arts can find a role to play appropriate to very different levels of skill and talent, the unique and terrifying difficulty facing those who pursue the art of poetry is that "a poem that comes into existence and is created for the gratification of our mind and heart, if it misses true excellence by only a little, verges toward deepest failure" (*AP* 377–78). This elevated status of the poet and the extremely high level of excellence demanded for artistic success places an especially heavy psychological and emotional burden on the artist, one that often drives the poet into an eccentric relationship to society and even poses a threat to existence itself. It is this imperiled and alienated life of the poet that is treated with grim humor at *AP* 453–76. It will be to our benefit, as we complete our survey of the reception of Horace's *AP*, to look closely at the passage in question.

As when the evil itch or the disease of kings, or the frenzied madness and wrath of Diana oppress someone, so sensible people are afraid to touch the mad poet, and run away from him. Inconsiderate children pursue and torment him. He, head in the clouds, belches out his poems and loses his way; if, like a fowler his attention is riveted on the blackbirds, he falls into a well or pit, no one will care to raise him up no matter how long he shouts, "Hey, fellow citizens, look over here!" But if anyone takes the trouble to come to his aid and to lower a rope to him, I will say, "How do you know that he didn't throw himself down there on purpose and doesn't want to be saved?" Then, I'll tell the story of how the Sicilian poet perished. When Empedocles felt the desire to be considered an immortal god, cool as a cucumber he leaped into the burning fires of Aetna. Let the right be given, let permission be granted for poets to die. Whoever saves someone against his will does exactly the same thing as the person who murders him. Not just once has he done this, and if he is extricated now he will not become a mere mortal and put aside his infatuation with a death that will make him famous. Nor is it sufficiently clear why he practices the poet's trade. Did he sacrilegiously urinate on the ashes of his ancestors or disturb a plot of consecrated land that had been struck by lightning? Whatever the cause he is certainly mad and just like a bear—if he has succeeded in smashing the restraining bars of his cage—his morose public recitations frighten off the educated and ignorant alike; once he gets his hands on a person, he doesn't let go until he kills him with his reading—a leech who will not release the skin unless gorged with blood. (*AP* 453–76)

Three important themes emerge from this passage relating to the alienation of the poet from the larger community: (1) stigmatization of the poet as an eccentric outsider to the society as a whole, which results in it treating the artist with scorn, fear and contempt; (2) the emotional and intellectual torment that often defines artistic temperament and behavior and leads (3) to the special susceptibility of the poet to self-destruction.

The suicide of Empedocles in Horace's poem, emblematic of numerous suicides by artists, raises a deeper issue than the weird and threatening behavior and appearance of poets. Here we note the psychic pain that stalks the artistic temperament forced into confrontation with troubling issues of life and death in a vocation that permits no evasions or escapes, a vocation which, if in pursuing its goal, "it misses true excellence by only a little, verges toward deepest failure" (*AP* 378). Because of that heavy burden which the artist and few others are doomed to bear, Horace can say of the poet: "Nor is it sufficiently clear why he practices the poet's trade. Did he sacrilegiously urinate on the ashes of his ancestors or disturb a gloomy plot of consecrated land that had been struck by lightning?" Horace clearly suggests that whoever takes on the heavy burden of an artist's life can be considered to be as one who has been condemned by malicious fortune to a disturbing ministry amongst mankind. Karl Shapiro also is deeply affected by the not uncommon suicides of artists. Reflecting on Hart Crane's taking of his life a few years before the writing of his poem Shapiro writes:

> Of all
> The famous suicides of modern art
> From Nietzsche on, this baffles more than any,
> Is the most terrible of all because
> Committed in cold blood, apart from love,
> Apart from hate, apart from sure belief.
> Let us not reckon the statistics of
> Those artists who have left the pencilled note,
> The unpaid debt to life, and with less grief
> Than expectation fell; but only ask
> What deadly distillate of the heart is this
> That kills the man most dearly pledged to live?
> And think is not this dram the same that draws
> The artist into self-imposed exile,
> And some to self-imagined hell, and some
> To infamous hatred of the thing they write? (*Rime* 1424–39)

Shapiro recognizes the same dark forces preying on the poet's mind and spirit as Horace incorporated in his depiction of the "mad poet."

What, then, is the identity of this "mad poet" with whose company we part at the end of the *AP*? For Brink it is a poet consumed by an excess of poetic imagination that is not tempered by the discipline of artistic decorum; and this poet for Brink must be, in some degree, Horace, himself, because Brink has told us that the caricature of the mad poet "could never have been written without a generous measure of the quality so caricatured." Ellen Oliensis (1998: 219) goes even further than Brink in suggesting that the prime candidate "for the role of the murderously exuberant versifier within the *Ars* itself" is "in the most literal and immediate sense" Horace. And it is Horace, she argues, "who clings and clings to his readers for all 476 lines (more lines by far than any other poem in the Horatian corpus) before dropping off into silence—who is the leech of the *Ars Poetica*."

Perhaps the best identification we can make of the "mad poet" of the *AP* would be as a collective designation for all those who have fallen victim to the torments of the artistic temperament from Empedocles to Hart Crane and beyond. The impressive coda of the *AP* ranks as great poetry not because it is great satire (although it is that) but because it is great satire that carries the ring of truth in it across the ages.

GUIDE TO FURTHER READING

An introduction to some important aspects of the reception of the *Ars Poetica* can be found in Hardison and Golden (1995). Detailed discussions of important phases of that reception can be found in Herrick (1946); Spingarn (1976), and Weinberg (1961). For general discussions of the *Ars Poetica* and Horace's concept of poetry and literary criticism see Kilpatrick (1990); Freudenburg (1993); Grube (1965); Showerman (1963). More advanced students may wish to consult Brink (1963, 1971, 1982); Fraenkel (1957); and Rudd (1989).

Bibliography

Acosta-Hughes, B. 2002. *Polyeideia: The Iambi of Callimachus and the Archaic Iambic Tradition*. Berkeley, Los Angeles, and London.

Ahern, C. F., Jr. 1991. "Horace's Rewriting of Homer in *Carmen* 1.6." *CPh* 86: 301–14.

Amundsen, L. 1972. "Die Römeroden des Horaz." In H. Oppermann (ed.), *Wege zu Horaz*, 111–38. Darmstadt.

Ancona, R. 1989. "The Subterfuge of Reason: Horace, *Odes* 1.23 and the Construction of Male Desire." *Helios* 16: 49–57.

Ancona, R. 1992. "Horace *Odes* 1.25: Temporality, Gender, and Desire." *Studies in Latin Literature and Roman History. Collection Latomus* 6: 245–59.

Ancona, R. 1994. *Time and the Erotic in Horace's Odes*. Durham, NC.

Ancona, R. 2002. "The Untouched Self: Sapphic and Catullan Muses in Horace *Odes* 1.22." In E. Spentzou and D. Fowler (eds.), *Cultivating the Muse: Struggles for Power and Inspiration in Classical Literature*, 161–8. Oxford.

Ancona, R. 2005. "(Un) Constrained Male Desire: An Intertextual Reading of Horace *Odes* 2.8 and Catullus Poem 61." In R. Ancona and E. Greene (eds.), *Gendered Dynamics in Latin Love Poetry*, 41–60. Baltimore.

Ancona, R. and E. Greene (eds.). 2005. *Gendered Dynamics in Latin Love Poetry*. Baltimore.

Anderson, W. S. 1963. "The Roman Socrates." In J. P. Sullivan (ed.), *Critical Essays on Roman Literature*, vol. 2 (*satire*), 1–37. London. Reprinted in W. S. Anderson 1982, *Essays on Roman Satire*, 13–49. Berkeley and Los Angeles.

Anderson, W. S. 1964a. "Anger in Juvenal and Seneca." *CPCP* 19: 127–96. Reprinted in W. S. Anderson 1982, *Essays on Roman Satire*, 293–361. Berkeley and Los Angeles.

Anderson, W. S. 1964b. "Roman Satirists and Literary Criticism." *Bucknell Review* 12: 106–13. Reprinted in W. S. Anderson, 1982, *Essays on Roman Satire* (3–10).

Anderson, W. S. 1966. "Horace '*Carm.*' 1.14: What Kind of Ship?" *CPh* 61: 84–98.

Anderson, W. S. 1982. *Essays on Roman Satire.* Berkeley and Los Angeles.

Anderson, W. S. 1999. "The Secret of Lydia's Aging: Horace, Ode 1.25." In W. S. Anderson (ed.), *Why Horace? A Collection of Interpretations*, 85–91. Wauconda, IL.

André, J. M. 1969. "Les Odes romaines. Mission divine, otium et apothéose du chef." In J. Bibauw (ed.), *Hommages à M. Renard*, 31–46. Brussels.

Anon. 1741. *The Odes, Epodes, and Carmen Seculare of Horace.* 2 vols. London.

Appadurai, A. (ed.). 1986. *The Social Life of Things: Commodities in Cultural Perspective.* Cambridge.

Arkins, B. 1993. "*The Cruel Joke of Venus: Horace as Love Poet.*" In N. Rudd (ed.), *Horace 2000: A Celebration. Essays for the Bimillennium*, 106–19. Ann Arbor.

Armstrong, D. 1986. "*Horatius eques et scriba: Satires* 1.6 and 2.7." *TAPhA* 116: 255–88.

Armstrong, D. 1989. *Horace.* New Haven, CT and London.

Armstrong, D. 1997. "Some Recent Perspectives on Horace." *Phoenix* 51: 393–405.

Armstrong, D. 2004. "Horace's Epistles 1 and Philodemus." In D. Armstrong, J. Fish, P. Johnston, and M. Skinner (eds.), *Vergil, Philodemus and the Augustans*, 267–98. Austin.

Astin, A. E. 1967. *Scipio Aemilianus.* Oxford.

Austin, R. G. (ed.). 1977. *P. Vergili Maronis: Aeneidos: Liber Sextus.* Oxford.

Baldwin, B. 2005. "Happy Horace." *The Petronian Society Newsletter* 35. At <http://www.ancientnarrative.com>.

Barbanera, M. 1998. *L'archeologia degli italiani.* Rome.

Barchiesi, A. 1997. "Otto punti su una mappa dei naufragi." *MD* 39: 209–26.

Barchiesi, A. 2000. "Rituals in Ink: Horace on the Greek Lyric Tradition." In M. Depew and D. Obbink (eds.), *Matrices of Genre: Authors, Canons, and Society*, 167–82. Cambridge, MA.

Barchiesi, A. 2001. "Horace and Iambos: The Poet as Literary Historian." In A. Cavarzere *et al.* (eds.), *Iambic Ideas*, 141–64. Lanham, MD.

Barchiesi, A. 2002. "The Uniqueness of the *Carmen Saeculare* and its Tradition." In A. J. Woodman and D. Feeney (eds.), *Traditions and Contexts in the Poetry of Horace*, 107–23. Cambridge.

Barchiesi, A. 2005. "Centre and Periphery." In S. J. Harrison (ed.), *A Companion to Latin Literature*, 394–405. Oxford.

Barchiesi, A. 2007. "*Carmina: Odes* and *Carmen Saeculare.*" In S. J. Harrison (ed.), *The Cambridge Companion to Horace*, 144–61. Cambridge.

Barchiesi, A. and A. Cucchiarelli. 2005. "Satire and the Poet: The Body as Self-referential Symbol." In K. Freudenburg (ed.), *The Cambridge Companion to Roman Satire*, 207–23. Cambridge.

Barker, P. 1977. *Techniques of Archaeological Excavation.* London

Basore, J. W. 1935. *Seneca: Moral Essays.* Cambridge, MA.

Batstone, W. and G. Tissol (eds.). 2005. *Defining Genre and Gender in Roman Literature: Essays Presented to William S. Anderson on His Seventy-Fifth Birthday.* New York.

Bausi, F. 1998. "Landino." In S. Mariotti (ed.), *Orazio: enciclopedia oraziana*, vol. 3, 306–9. Rome.

Beard, M. and M. Crawford. 1985. *Rome in the Late Republic.* Ithaca, NY.

Beard, M. and J. North. 1990. *Pagan Priests.* Ithaca, NY.

Bellinger, A. R. 1957. "The immortality of Alexander and Augustus." *YClS* 15: 91–100.

Berres, T. 1992. "Erlebnis und Kunstgestalt im 7. Brief des Horaz." *Hermes* 120: 216–37.

Biondi, G. G. 1996. "Aristio Fusco." In S. Mariotti (ed.), *Orazio. Enciclopedia oraziana*, vol. 1, 643–644. Rome.

Bloom, H. 1973. *The Anxiety of Influence: A Theory of Poetry.* Oxford.

Boeckh, A. 1886. *Encyklopädie und Methodologie der philologischen Wissenschaften.* E. Bratuscheck (ed.), 2nd edn. R. Klussmann (ed.). Leipzig.

Boileau-Despréaux, N. 1995. In O. B. Hardison Jr. and L. Golden (eds.), *Horace for Students of Literature: the "Ars Poetica" and its Tradition*, 180–209. Gainesville, FL.

Bolgar, R. R. 1954. *The Classical Heritage and its Beneficiaries.* Cambridge.

Bonavia-Hunt, N. 1969. *Horace the Minstrel.* Kineton.

Borzsák, S. 1984. *Q. Horati Flacci Opera.* Leipzig.

Bourdieu, P. 1977. *Outline of a Theory of Practice.* Trans. R. Nice. Cambridge.

Bourdieu, P. 1984. *Distinction: A Social Critique of the Judgment of Taste.* Trans. R. Nice. Cambridge, MA.

Bowditch, P. L. 2001. *Horace and the Gift Economy of Patronage.* Berkeley.

Bowie, E. L. 1987. "One that Got Away: Archilochus 188–92 W and Horace *Odes* 1.4 and 1.5." In M. Whitby, P. Hardie, and M. Whitby (eds.), *Homo Viator: Classical Essays for John Bramble*, 13–19. Bedminster.

Bowie, E. 2001. "Early Greek Iambic Poetry: The Importance of Narrative." In A. Cavarzere *et al.* (eds.), *Iambic Ideas*, 1–27. Lanham, MD.

Bradshaw, A. 2002. "Horace's Birthday and Deathday." In A. J. Woodman and D. Feeney (eds.), *Traditions and Contexts in the Poetry of Horace*, 1–16. Cambridge.

Braund, S. H. 1988. *Beyond Anger: A Study of Juvenal's Third Book of Satires.* Cambridge.

Braund, S. H. 1992. *Roman Verse Satire. Greece & Rome New Surveys in the Classics.* No. 23. Oxford.

Braund, S. H. 1996. *The Roman Satirists and Their Masks.* London.

Brink, C. O. 1963. *Horace on Poetry*, vol. 1: *Prolegomena to the Literary Epistles.* Cambridge.

Brink, C. O. 1971. *Horace on Poetry*, vol. 2: *The 'Ars Poetica'*. Cambridge.

Brink, C. O. 1982. *Horace on Poetry*, vol. 3: *Epistles Book II: The Letters to Augustus and Florus*. Cambridge.

Brown, P. M. 1993. *Horace: Satires I*. Warminster.

Brown, R. D. 1991. "*Catonis nobile letum* and the List of Romans in Horace *Odes* 1.12." *Phoenix* 45: 326–40.

Brunt, P. A. 1988. *The Fall of the Roman Republic*. Oxford.

Bruun, C. 2006. "Inscriptions on Lead Pipes." In B. Frischer, J. Crawford, and M. De Simone (eds.), *The Horace's Villa Project, 1996–2003*, vol. 1, 295–301. Oxford.

Bundy, E. L. 1986 [1962]. *Studia Pindarica*. Berkeley.

Bundy, E. L. 1972. "The 'Quarrel Between Kallimachos and Apollonios' Part I: The Epilogue of Kallimachos's *Hymn to Apollo*." *CSCA* 5: 39–94.

Burrow, C. 1993. "Horace at Home and Abroad: Wyatt and Sixteenth-Century Horatianism." In C. Martindale and D. Hopkins (eds.), *Horace Made New: Horatian Influences on British Writing from the Renaissance to the Twentieth Century*, 27–49. Cambridge.

Bursian, C. 1883. *Geschichte der classischen Philologie in Deutschland von den Anfängen bis zur Gegenwart*. 2 vols. Munich and Leipzig.

Burzacchini, G. 1997. "melica." In S. Mariotti (ed.), *Orazio: enciclopedia oraziana*, vol. 2, 68–76.

Byron, Lord, 1995. "Hints from Horace." In O. B. Hardison Jr. and L. Golden (eds.), *Horace for Students of Literature: the "Ars Poetica" and its Tradition*, 291–312. Gainesville, FL.

Cagnetta, M. 1998. "Bimillenario della nascita." In S. Mariotti (ed.), *Orazio: enciclopedia oraziana*, vol. 3, 615–40. Rome.

Cain, T. 1995. *Ben Jonson: Poestaster*. Manchester.

Calame, C. 1977. *Les choeurs de jeunes filles en Grèce archaïque*. 2 vols. Rome.

Calame, C. 1997. *Choruses of Young Women in Ancient Greece: Their Morphology, Religious Role, and Social Function*. Trans. D. Collins and J. Orion. Lanham, MD.

Cairns, F. 1971. "Horace, *Odes* 1.2." *Eranos* 69: 68–88.

Cairns, F. 1983. "Alcaeus' Hymn to Hermes, *P. Oxy. 2734* Fr. 1 and Horace *Odes* 1.10." *QUCC* 13: 29–35.

Campbell, D. A. 1967. *Greek Lyric Poetry*. London.

Campbell, D. A. 1982. *Greek Lyric*, vol. 1. Cambridge, MA.

Capasso, M. 1998. "Pap. Hawara 24." In S. Mariotti (ed.), *Orazio: enciclopedia oraziana*, vol. 3, 51–2. Rome.

Cappelli, R. 1994. "Le pitture della Villa di Orazio. Prime note." *Atti del Convegno di Licenza, 19–23 aprile 1993*, 117–62. Venosa.

Carandini, A. 1996. *Storia dalla terra*. Turin.

Carne-Ross, D. S. and K. Haynes. 1996. *Horace in English*. London.

Carrubba, R. 1969. *The Epodes of Horace*. The Hague.

Casson, L. 1994 [1974]. *Travel in the Ancient World*. Baltimore and London.

Cavallero, D. G. 1998. "Arti figurative." In S. Mariotti (ed.), *Orazio: enciclopedia oraziana*, vol. 3, 679–90.

Cavallini, E. 1978–79. "Saffo e Alceo in Orazio." *MCr* 13–14: 377–80.

Cavallo, G. 1999. "Between Volumen and Codex: Reading in the Roman World." In G. Cavallo and R. Chartier (ed.), *A History of Reading in the West*, trans. L. G. Cochrane, 64–89. Amherst, MA.

Cavarzere, A. 1992. *Orazio: Il Libro degli Epodi*. Venice.

Cavarzere, A. 1996. *Sul limitare : Il "motto" e la poesia di Orazio*. Testi e Manuali per l'Insegnamento Universitario del Latino, 47. Bologna.

Cecchetti, D. 1998. "Lambin." In S. Mariotti (ed.), *Orazio: enciclopedia oraziana*, vol. 3, 305–6. Rome.

Chartier, R. 2007. *Inscription and Erasure: Literature and Written Culture from the Eleventh to the Eighteenth Century*. Trans. Arthur Goldhammer. Philadelphia.

Citroni, M. 1995. *Poesia e lettori in Roma antica. Forme della comunicazione letteraria*. Rome and Bari.

Citroni Marchetti, S. 2005. "Le scelte di un intellettuale. Sulle motivazioni culturali della *Naturalis Historia*." *MD* 54: 91–121.

Citti, F. 1994. *Orazio. L'invito a Torquato. Epistles 1.5*. Bari.

Citti, F. Forthcoming. *Epicuri de grege porcus. Variazioni su un tema oraziano*. Bologna.

Clay, D. 2001. "The Scandal of Dionysus on Paros (the Mnesiepes Inscription E$_I$ III)." *Prometheus* XXVII. 2: 97–112.

Coffey, M. 1976. *Roman Satire*. London.

Colton, R. E. 2004. *Régnier and Horace*. Brussels.

Commager, S. 1962. *The Odes of Horace: A Critical Study*. New Haven, CT.

Connolly, J. 2007. *The State of Speech: Rhetoric and Political Thought in Ancient Rome*. Princeton.

Conte, G. B. and A. Barchiesi. 1989. "Imitazione e arte allusiva. Modi e funzioni dell' intertestualità." In G. Cavallo *et al.* (eds.), *Lo Spazio letterario di Roma antica* 1, 81–114. Rome.

Conte, G. B. 1994. *Genres and Readers: Lucretius, Love Elegy, Pliny's Encyclopedia*. Trans. G. W. Most. Baltimore and London.

Coppini, D. 1998. "Mancinelli." In S. Mariotti (ed.), *Orazio: enciclopedia oraziana*, vol. 3, 334–45. Rome.

Costa, C. D. N. 2001. *Greek Fictional Letters*. Oxford.

Courbaud, E. 1973 [1914]. *Horace. Sa Vie et sa Pensée à l'Epoque des Epîtres*. New York.

Courtney, E. 1986. "Three Corrections in Horace's Roman Odes." *Phoenix* 40.3: 319–21.

Cronk, N. 1989. "Aristotle, Horace, and Longinus: the conception of reader response." In *The Cambridge History of Literary Criticism*, vol. 3, 199–204. Cambridge.

Csapo, E. 1987. "Is the Threat-Monologue of the *Servus Currens* an Index of Roman Authorship?" *Phoenix* 41: 399–419.

Cucchiarelli, A. 1999. "Hor. *Epistles* 1.19, 28: *pede mascula Sappho.*" *Hermes* 127: 328–44.

Cucchiarelli, A. 2001. *La Satira e il poeta: Orazio tra Epodi e Sermones.* Pisa.

Cucchiarelli, A. 2004–5. "La nave e lo spettatore." *SIFC iv.* 2: 189–206, 3: 30–72.

Cucchiarelli, A. 2006. "La tempesta e il dio (inizi e struttura nei *Carmina* di Orazio)." *Dictynna* 3: 73–106.

Cucchiarelli, A. 2008. "Eros e giambo: forme editoriali negli *Epodi* di Orazio." *MD* 60: 69–104.

Cugusi, P. 1979. *Epistolographi Latini Minores,* 2 vols. Turin.

Cugusi, P. 1983. *Evoluzione e forme dell'epistolografia latina.* Rome.

Culler, J. 1981. *The Pursuit of Signs: Semiotics, Literature, Deconstruction.* Ithaca, NY.

Culler, J. 2002. *The Pursuit of Signs: Semiotics, Literature, Deconstruction,* expanded edition. Ithaca, NY.

Dacier, A. 1709. *Oeuvres d'Horace en latin et françois.* 3rd edn. 10 vols. Paris.

Damon, C. 1997. *The Mask of the Parasite: A Pathology of Roman Patronage.* Ann Arbor.

Davis, G. 1975. "The Persona of Licymnia: A Revaluation of Horace, *Carm.* 2.12." *Philologus* 119: 70–83.

Davis, G. 1983. "Silence and Decorum: Encomiastic Convention and the Epilogue of Horace *Carm.* 3.2." *ClAnt* 2: 9–26.

Davis, G. 1987a. "*Carmina/Iambi*: The Literary-generic Dimension of Horace's *Integer vitae* (C. I, 22)." *QUCC* 27: 67–78.

Davis, G. 1987b. "*Quis ... digne scripserit?*: The *topos* of *alter Homerus* in Horace *C.* 1.6." *Phoenix* 41: 292–5.

Davis, G. 1989. "*Ingeni cumba?* Literary *aporia* and the Rhetoric of Horace's *O navis referent* (C. 1.14)." *RhM* 132: 331–45.

Davis, G. 1991. *Polyhymnia: The Rhetoric of Horatian Lyric Discourse.* Berkeley.

Davis, G. 1996. "The Figure of Anacreon in Horatian Lyric." *Hellas* 7: 63–74.

Davis, G. 2007. "Wine and the Symposium." In S. J. Harrison (ed.), *The Cambridge Companion to Horace,* 207–20. Cambridge.

Degani, E. 1983. *Hipponax: Testimonia et Fragmenta.* Leipzig.

Degl'Innocenti Pierini, R. 1987. "Il concilio degli dèi tra Lucilio e Ovidio." *Atene e Roma* 32: 137–47.

Delz, J. 1989. "Review of Shackleton Bailey 1991." *Gnomon* 60: 495–501.

Deniaux, E. 1993. *Clientèles et pouvoir à l'époque de Cicéron.* Rome.

Depew, M. and D. Obbink (eds.). 2000. *Matrices of Genre: Authors, Canons, and Society.* Cambridge, MA.

de Pretis, A. 2002. '*Epistolarity*' in the First Book of Horace's Epistles. Piscataway, NJ.

De Simone, M. 2006. "The Masonry Structures." In B. Frischer, J. Crawford, and M. De Simone (eds.), *The Horace's Villa Project, 1996–2003*, vol. 1, 121–69. Oxford.

De Simone, M., S. Nerucci, and L. Passalacqua. 2006. "Quadriporticus." In B. Frischer, J. Crawford, and M. De Simone (eds.), *The Horace's Villa Project, 1996–2003*, vol. 1, 97–103. Oxford.

De Simone, M. and L. Cerri. 2006. "The Residence." In B. Frischer, J. Crawford, and M. De Simone (eds.), *The Horace's Villa Project, 1996–2003*, vol. 1, 67–70. Oxford.

Diederich, S. 1999. *Der Horazkommentar des Porphyrio im Rahmen der kaiserzeitlichen Schul- und Bildungstradition*. Berlin.

Dilke, O. A. W. 1954. *Horace: Epistles, Book I*. London.

Dixon, S. 1993. "The Meaning of Gift and Debt in the Roman Elite." *EMC* 37: 451–64.

Doblhofer, E. 1966. *Die Augustuspanegyrik des Horaz in formalhistorischer Sicht*. Heidelberg.

Drummond, A. 1989. "Early Roman clients." In A. Wallace-Hadrill (ed.), *Patronage in Ancient Society*, 89–116. London and New York.

Du Quesnay, I. M. Le M. 1981. "Vergil's First *Eclogue*." In F. Cairns (ed.), *Papers of the Liverpool Latin Seminar*, vol 3. Liverpool.

Du Quesnay, I. M. Le M. 1984 [1958]. "Horace and Maecenas: The Propaganda Value of *Sermones* I." In A. J. Woodman and D. West (eds.), *Poetry and Politics in the Age of Augustus*, 19–58. Cambridge.

DuQuesnay, I. M. Le M. 1995. "Horace, *Odes* 4.5: *Pro Reditu Imperatoris Caesaris Divi Filii Augusti*." In S. J. Harrison (ed.), *Homage to Horace: A Bimillenary Celebration*, 128–87. Oxford.

Eakin, P. J. 1999. *How our Lives Become Stories: Making Selves*. Ithaca, NY and London.

Earl, D. C. 1966. *The Political Thought of Sallust*. Amsterdam.

Eder, W. 1990. "Augustus and the Power of Tradition: The Augustan Principate as Binding Link between Republic and Empire." In K. Raaflaub and M. Toher (eds.), *Between Republic and Empire*, 71–122. Berkeley.

Eder, W. 2005. "Augustus and the Power of Tradition." In K. Galinsky (ed.), *The Cambridge Companion to the Age of Augustus*, 13–32. Cambridge.

Edmunds, L. 1991. *From a Sabine Jar: Reading Horace, Odes 1.9*. Chapel Hill.

Edmunds, L. 2001. *Intertextuality and the Reading of Roman Poetry*, Baltimore, MD.

Edmunds, L. 2002. "Oedipus as Tyrant in Sophocles' *Oedipus Tyrannus or Oedipus and Athens*." *Syllecta Classica* 13: 63–103.

Edmunds, L. 2005. "Critical Divergences: New Directions in the Study and Teaching of Roman Literature," Introduction to seven papers from a conference held 24–25 October 2003 at Rutgers University. *TAPhA* 135: 1–13.

Eisenstein, E. 1979. *The Printing Press as an Agent of Change.* 2 vols. Cambridge.

Elliott, R. C. 1960. *The Power of Satire: Magic, Ritual, Art.* Princeton, NJ.

Fantham, E. 1992. "Strengths and Weaknesses of Current Ovidian Criticism." In K. Galinsky (ed.), *The Interpretation of Roman Poetry: Hermeneutics or Historicism?* 191–9. Frankfurt-on-Main.

Farney, G. 2007. *Ethnic Identity and Aristocratic Competition in Republican Rome.* Cambridge.

Fedeli, P. 1978. "Il V Epodo e I Giambi di Orazio come Espressione d'Arte Alessandrina." *MPhL* 3: 67–138.

Fedeli, P. 1997. *Q. Orazio Flacco, Le Opere, II.4, Le Epistole, L'Arte poetica.* Rome.

Feeney, D. C. 1993. "Horace and the Greek Lyric Poets." In N. Rudd (ed.) *Horace 2000: A Celebration: Essays for the Bimillennium,* 41–63. Ann Arbor.

Feeney, D. C. 1998. *Literature and Religion at Rome: Culture, Contexts, and Beliefs.* Cambridge.

Feeney, D. C. 2005. "The Beginnings of a Literature in Latin." *JRS* 95: 226–40.

Feeney, D. C. 2007. *Caesar's Calendar: Ancient time and the beginnings of History.* Berkeley.

Fenik, B. 1962. "Horace's First and Sixth Roman Odes and the Second Georgic." *Hermes* 90: 72–96.

Feo, M. 1998. "Petrarca." In S. Mariotti (ed.), *Orazio: enciclopedia oraziana,* vol. 3, 405–25. Rome.

Ferri, R. 1993. *I dispiaceri di uno epicuro: uno studio sulla poetica della epistole oraziane.* Pisa.

Ferri, R. 2007. "The *Epistles.*" In S. J. Harrison (ed.), *The Cambridge Companion to Horace,* 121–31. Cambridge.

Filippi, G. 2006. "The 'Horace's Villa' Brickstamps and the Brick Production of the Central Anio River Valley." In B. Frischer, J. Crawford, and M. De Simone (eds.), *The Horace's Villa Project, 1996–2003,* vol. 1, 197–219. Oxford.

Fiske, G. C. 1920. *Lucilius and Horace: A Study in the Classical Theory of Imitation.* Madison, WI.

Fitzgerald, W. 1988. "Power and Impotence in Horace's *Epodes.*" *Ramus* 17: 176–91.

Flashar, H. 1979. "Die methodisch-hermeneutischen Ansätze Friedrich August Wolf und Friedrich Ast—Traditionelle und neue Begründungen." In H. Flashar, K. Gründer and A. Horstmann (eds.), *Philologie und Hermeneutik im 19. Jahrhundert: Zur Geschichte und Methodologie der Geisteswissenschaften,* 21–32. Göttingen.

Fleming, K. 2006. "The Use and Abuse of Antiquity: The Politics and Morality of Appropriation." In C. Martindale and D. Hopkins (eds.), *Horace Made New:*

Horatian Influences on British Writing from the Renaissance to the Twentieth Century, 127–37. Cambridge.

Fleming, K. 2007. "Fascism." In C. W. Kallendorf (ed.), *A Companion to the Classical Tradition*, 342–54. Oxford.

Forster, L. 1981. "Die Emblemata Horatiana des Otho Vaenius." In W. Killy (ed.), *Geschichte des Textverständnisses am Beispiel von Pindar und Horaz: Vorträge gehalten anlässlich des 6*, 117–28. Munich.

Foster, D. 1999. *Studs and Nogs: Essays 1987–98*. Milsons Point, NSW.

Fowler, D. P. 1989. "First Thoughts on Closure: Problems and Prospects." *MD* 22: 75–122. Reprinted in D. P. Fowler 2000: 239–83.

Fowler, D. P. 1994. "Postmodernism, Romantic Irony, and Classical Closure." In I. J. F. de Jong and J. P. Sullivan (eds.), *Modern Critical Theory and Classical Literature*, 231–56. Leiden. Reprinted in D. P. Fowler 2000: 3–39.

Fowler, D. P. 1995. "Horace and the Aesthetics of Politics." in S. J. Harrison (ed.), *Homage to Horace: A Bimillenary Celebration*, 248–66. Oxford.

Fowler, D. P. 1997. "On the Shoulders of Giants: Intertextuality and Classical Studies." *MD* 39: 13–34.

Fowler, D. P. 1999. "Criticism Commentary and Commentary as Criticism in the Age of Electronic Media." In G. W. Most (ed.), *Commentaries-Kommentare*, Aporemata 4, 426–46. Göttingen.

Fowler, D. P. 2000. *Roman Constructions*. Oxford.

Fraenkel, E. 1957. *Horace*. Oxford.

France, P. and K. Haynes. 2006. *The Oxford History of Literary Translation in English*, vol. 4: 1790–1900. Oxford.

Fränkel, H. 1975. *Early Greek Poetry and Philosophy*. Trans. M. Hadas and J. Willis. Oxford.

Fredricksmeyer, E. 1994. "Horace's Chloe ('Odes' 1.23): Inamorata or Victim?" *CJ* 89: 251–9.

Freeden, M. 1996. *Ideologies and Political Theory: A Conceptual Approach*. Oxford.

Freis, R. 1983. "The Catalogue of Pindaric Genres in Horace Ode 4.2." *ClAnt* 2: 27–36.

Freudenburg, K. 1993. *The Walking Muse: Horace on the Theory of Satire*. Princeton.

Freudenburg, K. 2001. *Satires of Rome: Threatening Poses from Lucilius to Juvenal*. Cambridge.

Freudenburg, K. 2002a. "*Solus sapiens liber est.* Recommissioning lyric in *Epistles* I." In A. J. Woodman and D. Feeney (eds.), *Traditions & Contexts in the Poetry of Horace*, 124–40. Cambridge.

Freudenburg, K. 2002b. "Writing to/through Florus: Criticism and the Addressee in Horace *Epistles* 2.2." *Memoirs of the American Academy in Rome* 47: 33–55.

Freudenburg, K. (ed.). 2005. *Cambridge Companion to Roman Satire.* Cambridge.

Freudenburg, K. 2006. "*Playing at Lyric's Boundaries: Dreaming Forward in Book Two of Horace's Sermones.*" *Dictynna* 3: 135–72.

Freudenburg, K. (ed.). 2009. *Oxford Readings in Classical Studies: Horace's Satires and Epistles.* Oxford.

Friis-Jensen, K. 1993. "The Medieval Horace and His Lyrics." In W. Ludwig (ed.), *Horace: L'oeuvre et les imitations, un siècle d'interprétation: Neuf exposés suivis de discussions: 24–29 août 1992*, 257–303. Vandœuvres-Geneva.

Friis-Jensen, K. 1997. "Medieval Commentaries on Horace." In N. Mann and M. Olsen (eds.), *Medieval and Renaissance Scholarship Mittellateinische Studien und Texte*, 51–73. Leiden.

Friis-Jensen, K. 2007. "The Reception of Horace in the Middle Ages." In S. J. Harrison (ed.), *The Cambridge Companion to Horace*, 291–304. Cambridge.

Frischer, B. 1991. *Shifting Paradigms: New Appproaches to Horace's Ars Poetica.* Atlanta.

Frischer, B. 1995. "Fu la Villa ercolanese dei Papiri un modello per la villa sabina di Orazio?" *Cronache Ercolanesi* 25: 211–29.

Frischer, B. 1996. "Horazens Sabinum: Dichtung und Wahrheit." In *Römische Lebenskunst*, 31–46. Heidelberg.

Frischer, B. 1998. "Notes on the First Excavation of Horace's Villa near Licenza (Roma) by the Baron de Saint'Odile and the Abbé Capmartin de Chaupy." In J. Hamesse (ed.), *Roma, Magistra Mundi: Itineraria culturae mediaevalis. Mélanges offerts au Pere L.E. Boyle à l'occasion de son 75e anniversaire, Fédération Internationale des Institutes d'Études du Moyen Âge, Textes et Études du Moyen Âge* 10.1, 265–89.

Frischer, B. 2001. "Ramsay's 'Enquiry: Text and Context'." in B. Frischer and I. G. Brown (eds.), *Allan Ramsay and the Search for Horace's Villa*, 73–104. Aldershot, UK.

Frischer, B. 2006a. "Conclusion." In B. Frischer, J. Crawford, and M. De Simone (eds.), *The Horace's Villa Project, 1996–2003*, vol. 1, 375–385. Oxford.

Frischer, B. 2006b. "Knowledge About Horace's Villa From the Imperial Period to 1911." In B. Frischer, J. Crawford, and M. De Simone, (eds.), *The Horace's Villa Project, 1996–2003*, vol. 1, 20–29. Oxford.

Frischer, B. 2006c. "Preface." In B. Frischer, J. Crawford, and M. De Simone (eds.), *The Horace's Villa Project, 1996–2003*, vol. 1, xxiii–xxiv. Oxford.

Frischer, B. 2007. "Textual Sources." In B. Frischer, J. Crawford, and M. De Simone (eds.), *The Horace's Villa Project, 1996–2003*, vol. 2, 389–592. Oxford.

Frischer, B., J. Crawford, and M. De Simone. 2006. *The Horace's Villa Project, 1997–2003*, Oxford.

Fuqua, C. 1986. "Horace *Carm.* I, 23–25." *CPh* 63: 44–6.

Furley, W. D. 2000. "'Fearless, Bloodless. ... Like the Gods': Sappho 31 and the Rhetoric of 'Godlike.'" *CQ* 50: 7–15.

Gadamer, H. 1965. *Wahrheit und Methode*. 2nd edn. Tübingen.

Gadamer, H. 1975. *Truth and Method*. Trans. Garret Barden and John Cumming. New York.

Galinsky, K. (ed.). 1992. *The Interpretation of Roman Poetry: Empiricism or Hermeneutics?* Frankfurt-on-Main.

Galinsky, K. 1996. *Augustan Culture. An Interpretive Introduction*. Princeton.

Gantar, K. 1983. "Horazens Freund Aristius Fuscus." In P. Händel, W. Meid (eds.), *Festschrift für R. Muth*, 129–34. Innsbruck.

Gentili, B. 1988. *Poetry and its Public in Ancient Greece*. Trans. A. T. Cole. Baltimore.

Gerber, D. (ed.) 1967. *A Companion to the Greek Lyric Poets*. Mnemosyne Supplement 173. Leiden and New York.

Gerber, D. 1991. "Early Greek Elegy and Iambus 1921–1989." *Lustrum* 33: 7–225.

Gerber, D. 1999. *Greek Iambic Poetry*. Cambridge, MA.

Gill, C. 1996. *Personality in Greek Epic, Tragedy, and Philosophy: The Self in Dialogue*. Oxford.

Gill, C., N. Postlethwaite and R. Seaford. (eds.). 1998. *Reciprocity in Ancient Greece*. Oxford.

Gillespie, S. 1988. *The Poets on the Classics: An Anthology of English Poets' Writings on the Classical Poets and Dramatists from Chaucer to the Present*. London and New York.

Gillespie, S. and D. Hopkins. 2005. *The Oxford History of Literary Translation in English*, vol. 3: 1660–1790. Oxford.

Glaister, G. A. 1979. *Glaister's Glossary of the Book: Terms Used in Papermaking, Printing, Bookbinding and Publishing with Notes on Illuminated Manuscripts and Private Presses*. 2nd edn. Berkeley.

Gleason, K., J. G. Schryver, and L. Passalacqua. 2006. "The Garden." In B. Frischer, J. Crawford, and M. De Simone (eds.), *The Horace's Villa Project, 1996–2003*, vol. 1, 71–96.

Goad, C. 1967. *Horace in the English Literature of the Eighteenth Century*. New York.

Gold, B. K. (ed.). 1982. *Literary and Artistic Patronage in Ancient Rome*. Austin.

Gold, B. K. 1987. *Literary Patronage in Greece and Rome*. Chapel Hill and London.

Goldberg, S. M. 2005. *Constructing Literature in the Roman Republic*. Cambridge.

Gordon, R. 1990. "From Republic to Principate: Priesthood, Religion and Ideology." In M. Beard and J. North (eds.), *Pagan Priests*, 177–98. Ithaca, NY.

Goulbourn, R. 2007. "Satire in Seventeeth- and Eighteenth-century France." In R. Quintero (ed.), *A Companion to Satire: Ancient and Modern*, 139–60. Malden, MA.

Gowers, E. 1993a. "Horace, *Satire* 1.5: An Inconsequential Journey." *PCPhS* 39: 48–66.

Gowers, E. 1993b. *The Loaded Table: Representations of Food in Roman Literature.* Oxford.

Gowers, E. 2003. "Fragments of Autobiography in Horace *Satires* 1." *ClAnt* 22: 55–91.

Gowers, E. 2005. "The restless companion: Horace *Satires* 1 and 2." In K. Freudenburg (ed.), *Cambridge Companion to Roman Satire*, 48–61. Cambridge.

Grafton, A. 1997. *Commerce with the Classics: Ancient Books and Renaissance Readers.* Ann Arbor.

Grafton, A. 1999. "The Humanist as Reader." In G. Cavallo and R. Chartier (ed.), *A History of Reading in the West.* Trans. L. G. Cochrane, 179–212. Amherst, MA.

Gratwick, A. S. 1982. "The Satires of Ennius and Lucilius." In E. J. Kenney (ed.), *Cambridge History of Classical Literature*, vol. 2 pt. 1, 156–71. Cambridge.

Greene, E. (ed.). 1996. *Reading Sappho: Contemporary Approaches.* Berkeley.

Gregory, C. A. 1982. *Gifts and Commodities.* London and New York.

Griffin, J. 1984. "Augustus and the Poets: 'Caesar qui cogere posset.'" In F. Millar and E. Segal (eds.), *Caesar Augustus: Seven Aspects*, 189–218. Oxford.

Griffin, J. 1986 [1998]. *Latin Poets and Roman Life.* London and Bristol.

Griffin, M. T. and E. M. Atkins (eds.). 1991. *Cicero, On Duties.* Cambridge and New York.

Grube, G. M. A. 1965. *The Greek and Roman Critics.* Toronto.

Gruen, E. 2005. "Augustus and the Making of the Principate." In K. Galinsky (ed.) *The Cambridge Companion to Augustus*, 33–51. Cambridge.

Gutzwiller, K. 1998. *Poetic Garlands: Hellenistic Epigrams in Context.* Berkeley.

Habinek, T. N. 1986. "The Marriageability of Maximus: Horace *Ode* 4.1.13–20." *AJPh* 107: 407–16.

Habinek, T. N. 2005. *The World of Roman Song: From Ritualized Speech to Social Order.* Baltimore.

Haffner, H. 1938. "Die fünfte Römerode des Horaz." *Philologus* 93: 132–56.

Hamilton, J. T. 2003. *Soliciting Darkness: Pindar, Obscurity, and the Classical Tradition.* Cambridge, MA.

Hammond, P. 1993. "Figures of Horace in Dryden's Literary Criticism." In C. Martindale and D. Hopkins (eds.), *Horace Made New: Horatian Influences on British Writing from the Renaissance to the Twentieth Century*, 127–47. Cambridge.

Hardie, A. 2003. "The Pindaric Sources of Horace *Odes* 1.12." *HSCPh* 101: 371–404.

Hardie, P. R. 1986. *Virgil's Aeneid: Cosmos and Imperium.* Oxford.

Hardison, O. B. Jr. and L. Golden. (eds.). 1995. *Horace for Students of Literature: The "Ars Poetica" and its Tradition.* Gainesville, FL.

Harms, E. 1936. *Horaz in seinen Beziehungen zu Pindar.* Diss. Marburg.

Harris, E. 1989. *Principles of Archaeological Stratigraphy.* 2nd edn. London.

Harrison, G. 1987. "The confessions of Lucilius (Horace, Sat. 2.1.30–34): A Defense of Autobiographical Satire?" *ClAnt* 6: 38–52.

Harrison, S. J. 1993. "Dulce et decorum." *RhM* 136: 91–3.

Harrison, S. J. 1995a. (ed.) *Homage to Horace: A Bimillenary Celebration.* Oxford.

Harrison, S. J. 1995b. 'Poetry, philosophy, and letter-writing in Horace *Epistles* I." In D. Innes, H. Hine, and C. Pelling (eds.), *Ethics and Rhetoric: Classical Essays for Donald Russell on His Seventy-Fifth Birthday*, 47–61. Oxford.

Harrison, S. J. 1995c. "Some Twentieth-Century Views of Horace." In S. J. Harrison (ed.), *Homage to Horace: A Bimillenary Celebration*, 1–16. Oxford.

Harrison, S. J. 2001. "Some Generic Problems in Horace's *Epodes*." In A. Cavarzere *et al.* (eds.), *Iambic Ideas*, 165–86. Lanham, MD.

Harrison, S. J. (ed.). 2007a. *The Cambridge Companion to Horace.* Cambridge.

Harrison, S. J. 2007b. "Horatian Self-representations." In S. J. Harrison (ed.) *The Cambridge Companion to Horace*, 22–35. Cambridge.

Harrison, S. J. 2007c. "The Reception of Horace in the Nineteenth and Twentieth Centuries." In S. J. Harrison (ed.), *The Cambridge Companion to Horace*, 334–46. Cambridge.

Haß, K. 2007. *Lucilius und der Beginn der Persönlichkeitsdichtung in Rom.* Stuttgart.

Heinze, R. 1960. "Die horazische Ode." In E. Burck, *Vom Geist des Römertums: Ausgewählte Aufsätze*, 172–89. Stuttgart.

Henderson, J. 1994. "On Getting Rid of Kings: Horace, *Satire* 1.7." *CQ* 44: 146–70.

Henderson, J. 1999. *Writing down Rome: Satire, Comedy, and other Offences in Latin Poetry.* Oxford.

Hendrickson, G. L. 1900. "Horace *Serm.* 1.4: A Protest and a Programme." *AJPh* 21: 121–42

Hentschke, A. and U. Muhlack. 1972. *Einführung in die Geschichte der klassischen Philologie.* Darmstadt.

Herder, J. G. von. 1877–1913. *Herders Sämmtliche Werke.* Ed. B. Suphan. Berlin.

Herrick, M. T. 1946. *The Fusion of Horatian and Aristotelian Literary Criticism, 1531–1555.* Urbana, IL.

Hexter, R. 2006. "Literary History as a Provocation to Reception Studies." In C. Martindale and D. Hopkins (eds.), *Horace Made New: Horatian Influences on British Writing from the Renaissance to the Twentieth Century*, 23–31. Cambridge.

Heyworth, S. 1993. "Horace's *Ibis*: On the Titles, Unity, and Contents of the *Epodes.*" *Papers of the Leeds Latin Seminar* 7: 85–96.

Highbarger, E. L. 1935. "The Pindaric Style of Horace." *TAPhA* 66: 222–55.

Highet, G. 1949 [1967]. *The Classical Tradition. Greek and Roman Influences on Western Literature.* Oxford.

Hilberg, I. (ed.). 1910–18. *Sancti Eusebii Hieronymi Epistulae.* 3 vols. Vienna and Leipzig.

Hills, P. 2005. *Horace*, Ancients in Action series. London.

Hirsch, M. 1981. "Review Essay: Mothers and Daughters." *Signs: Journal of Women in Culture and Society* 7: 200–22.

Hirsch, M. 1989. *The Mother/Daughter Plot: Narrative, Psychoanalysis, Feminism.* Bloomington.

Hoffer, C. 2007. "The Use of Adjective Interlacing (Double Hyperbaton) in Latin Poetry." In *HSPh* 103: 299–340.

Hoffmann, M. 1901. August Böckh: Lebensbeschreibung und Auswahl aus seinem wissenschaftlichen Briefwechsel. Leipzig.

Holford-Strevens, L. 1988. *Aulus Gellius, an Antonine Scholar and his Achievement.* Oxford.

Holzberg, N. 2007. "Horaz: Eine Bibliographie." <http://www.klassphil.uni-muenchen.de/personen/holzberg.html>.

Hooley, D. 2007. *Roman Satire.* Oxford.

Hopkins, D. 1993. "Cowley's Horatian Mice." In C. Martindale and D. Hopkins (eds.), *Horace Made New: Horatian Influences on British Writing from the Renaissance to the Twentieth Century*, 103–26. Cambridge.

Hopkins, D. 2005. "Roman Satire and Epigram." In S. Gillespie and D. Hopkins (eds.), *The Oxford History of Literary Translation in English*, vol. 3: 1660–1790, 218–40. Oxford.

Horsfall, N. 1981. "Poets and Patron: Maecenas, Horace and the *Georgics*, once more." *Publications of the Macquarie Ancient History Association* 3: 1–24.

Horsfall, N. 1998. "The First Person Singular in Horace's *Carmina.*" In P. Knox and C. Foss (eds.), *Style and Tradition: Studies in Honour of Wendell Clausen*, 40–54. Stuttgart and Leipzig.

Horstman, A. 1990. "L'hermeneutique, théorie générale ou *organon* des sciences philologiques chez August Boeckh?" In A. Laks and A. Neschke (eds.), *La naissance du paradigme herméneutique: Schleiermacher, Humboldt, Boeckh, Droysen*, Cahiers de Philologie 10, 327–58. Lille.

Hunter, R. 2003. *Theocritus: Encomium of Ptolemy Philadelphus.* Berkeley.

Hunter, R. L. 1985. "Horace on Friendship and Free Speech." *Hermes* 113: 480–90.

Hutchinson, G. 2007. "Horace and archaic Greek poetry." In S. J. Harrison (ed.), *The Cambridge Companion to Horace*, 36–49. Cambridge.

Hyland, A. 1990. *Equus. The Horse in the Roman World.* New Haven, CT.

Iggers, G. G. 1995. "Historicism: The History and the Meaning of the Term." *JHI* 56: 129–52.

Innes, D., H. Hine, and C. Pelling. (eds.). 1995. *Ethics and Rhetoric: Classical Essays for Donald Russell on His Seventy-Fifth Birthday*. Oxford.

Irigaray, L. 1979. *Et l'une ne bouge pas sans l'autre*. Paris.

Irvine, M. 1992. "'Bothe Texte and Glose': Manuscript Form, the Textuality of Commentary and Chaucer's Dream Poems." In C. C. Morse, P. R. Doob, and M. C. Woods (eds.), *The Uses of Manuscripts in Literary Studies*, 81–119. Kalamazoo, MI.

Iurilli, A. 1998. "Veen, Otto van." In S. Mariotti (ed.), *Orazio: enciclopedia oraziana*, vol. 3, 503–5. Rome.

Jaeger, C. S. 1994. *The Envy of Angels: Cathedral Schools and Social Ideas in Medieval Europe, 950–1200*. Philadelphia.

Jauss, H. R. 1967 [1970]. "Literaturgeschichte als Provokation der Literatur-wissenschaft." In *Literaturgeschichte als Provokation der Literaturwissenschaft*, 144–207. Frankfurt-on-Main.

Jauss, H. R. 1977. *Ästhetische Erfahrung und literarische Hermeneutik.*, vol. 1 (Versuche im Feld der ästhetischen Erfahrung). Munich.

Jauss, H. R. 1982a. *Aesthetic Experience and Literary Hermeneutics*. Trans. by Michael Shaw. Minneapolis.

Jauss, H. R. 1982b. "Einleitung: Horizontstruktur und Dialogizität." In H. R. Jauss, *Aesthetic Experience and Literary Hermeneutics*, 657–703. Minneapolis.

Jauss, H. R. 1982c. "Der poetische Text im Horizontwandel der Lektüre (Baudelaire's Gedicht: 'Spleen II')." In H. R. Jauss, *Aesthetic Experience and Literary Hermeneutics, 813–65. Minneapolis*. Reprinted from *Romanistische Zeitschrift für Literaturgeschichte* 4: 1980, 228–74.

Jauss, H. R. 1982d. *Toward an Aesthetic of Reception*. Trans. Timothy Bahti. Minneapolis.

Jauss, H. R. 1982e. "The Poetic Text Within the Change of Horizons of Reading: The Example of Baudelaire's *Spleen* II." In H. R. Jauss, *Toward an Aesthetic of Reception*, 111–39. Minneapolis.

Jauss, H. R. 1989a. *Question and Answer: Forms of Dialogic Understanding*. Trans. Michael Hays. Minneapolis.

Jauss, H. R. 1989b. "Horizon Structure and Dialogicity." In H. R. Jauss, *Question and Answer: Forms of Dialogic Understanding*, 197–231. Minneapolis.

Johns, A. 1998. *The Nature of the Book: Print and Knowledge in the Making*. Chicago.

Johnson, T. S. 2004. *A Symposion of Praise: Horace Returns to Lyric in Odes IV*. Madison, WI.

Johnson, W. R. 1993. *Horace and the Dialectic of Freedom: Readings in Epistles 1*. Ithaca, NY.

Johnson, W. R. 2000. "Towards a Sociology of Reading in Classical Antiquity." *AJPh* 121: 593–627.

Juster, A. M. 2008. *The Satires of Horace*. Philadelphia.

Kallendorf, C. W. 1994. "Philology, the Reader, and the 'Nachleben' of Classical Texts." *Modern Philology* 92.2: 137–56.

Kallendorf, C. W. (ed.). 2007. *A Companion to the Classical Tradition*. Oxford.

Kaster, R. A. 1983. "Notes on 'Primary' and 'Secondary' Schools in Late Antiquity." *TAPhA* 113: 323–46.

Kaster, R. A. 1988. *Guardians of Language: The Grammarian and Society in Late Antiquity*. Berkeley.

Keller, O. and A. Holder. 1899. *Q. Horati Flacci Opera*. Leipzig.

Kennedy, D. F. 1999 [1994]. "'Augustan' and 'Anti-Augustan'" Reflections on Terms of Reference." In A. Powell (ed.), *Roman Poetry and Propaganda in the Age of Augustus*, 26–58. Bristol.

Kennedy, D. F. 1993. *The Arts of Love: Five Studies on the Discourse of Roman Love Elegy*. Cambridge.

Kennedy, N. T. 1975. "Pindar and Horace." *Acta Classica* 18: 9–24.

Kenney, E. J. 1974. *The Classical Text: Aspects of Editing in the Age of the Printed Book*. Berkeley.

Kenney, E. J. 1982. "Books and Readers in the Roman World." In E. J. Kenney and W. V. Clausen (eds.), *The Cambridge History of Classical Literature*, vol. 2: *Latin Literature*, 3–31. Cambridge.

Kenney, E. J. and W. V. Clausen, (eds.) 1982. *The Cambridge History of Classical Literature*, vol. 2: *Latin Literature*. Cambridge.

Kernan, A. B. 1959. *The Cankered Muse*. New Haven.

Kienast, D. 1982. *Augustus: Prinzeps und Monarch*. Darmstadt.

Kiessling, A. and R. Heinze. 1955. *Q. Horatius Flaccus, Oden und Epoden*. Berlin.

Kiessling, A. and R. Heinze. 1957. *Q. Horatius Flaccus, Oden und Epoden*. Berlin.

Kiessling, A., R. Heinze and E. Burck. 1964. *Q. Horatius Flaccus, Oden und Epoden*. Berlin.

Kiessling, A. and R. Heinze. 1984a. *Q. Horatius Flaccus, Oden und Epoden*. 14th edn. Hildesheim.

Kiessling, A. and R. Heinze. 1984b [1957]. *Q. Horatius Flaccus, Briefe*, Berlin, 1957. 5th edn.

Killy, W. (ed.). 1981. *Geschichte des Textverständnisses am Beispiel von Pindar und Horaz: Vorträge gehalten anlässlich des 6. Wolfenbütteler Symposions vom 18–22. September 1978 in der Herzog August Bibliothek*. Wolfenbütteler Forschungen, 12. Munich.

Kilpatrick, R. S. 1986. *The Poetry of Friendship. Horace, Epistles 1*. Edmonton.

Kilpatrick, R. S. 1990. *The Poetry of Criticism: Horace, Epistles II and Ars Poetica*. Edmonton.

Kilpatrick, R. S. 1996. "Epistole." In *Enciclopedia Oraziana*, vol. 1, 304–9. Rome.

Kindstrand J. F. (ed.). 1976. *Bion of Borysthenes: A Collection of the Fragments with Introduction and Commentary*. Uppsala.

Kirchner, J. (ed.). 1952–6. *Lexikon des Buchwesens*. 4 vols. Stuttgart.

Klingner, F. 1959. *Horatius Opera*. Leipzig.

Konstan, D. 1997. *Friendship in the Classical World*. Cambridge.

Konstan, D. 2006. *The Emotions of the Ancient Greeks: Studies in Aristotle and Classical Literature*. Toronto.

Kornhardt, H. 1954. "Regulus und die Cannaegefangenen. Studien zum römischen Heimkehrrecht." *Hermes* 82: 85–123.

Krasser, H. and E. A. Schmidt (eds.) 1996. *Zeitgenosse Horaz: Der Dichter und seine Leser seit zwei Jahrtausenden*. Tübingen.

Krenkel, W. 1970a. *Lucilius, Satiren*. Leiden.

Krenkel, W. 1970b. "Zur Literarischen Kritik bei Lucilius." In D. Korzeniewski (ed.), *Die römische Satire*, 161–266. Darmstadt.

Kurke, L. 1991. *The Traffic in Praise: Pindar and the Poetics of Social Economy*. Ithaca, NY.

Kurke, L. 1999. *Coins, Bodies, Games and Gold: The Politics of Meaning in Archaic Greece*. Princeton.

Labate, M. 1996. "Il sermo oraziano e i generi letterari." In H. Krasser and E. A. Schmidt (eds.), *Zeitgenosse Horaz: der Dichter und seine Leser seit zwei Jahrtausenden*, 424–41. Tübingen.

Labate, M. 2005. "Poetica minore e minima: Mecenate e gli amici nelle *Satire* di Orazio." *MD* 54: 47–63.

Laks, A. and A. Neschke (eds.). 1991. *La naissance du paradigme herméneutique: Schleiermacher, Humboldt, Boeckh, Droysen*, Cahiers de Philologie 10. Lille.

Lampela, A. 1998. *Rome and the Ptolemies of Egypt: The Development of their Political Relations 273–80 B.C.* Helsinki.

La Penna, A. 1963. *Orazio e l'ideologia del principato*. Turin.

La Penna, A. 1968. "Orazio e la morale mondana europea." In E. Cetrangolo and A. La Penna (eds.), *Quinto Orazio Flacco, Tutte le Opere*, ix–clxxxiii. Florence. Reprinted in A. La Penna, 1993, 1–217.

La Penna, A. 1972. "Sunt qui Sappho malint." *Maia* 24: 208–15.

La Penna, A. 1993. *Saggi e studi su Orazio*. Firenze.

Leigh Fermor, P. 1977. *A Time of Gifts*. New York.

Leach, E. W. 1971. "Horace's Pater Optimus and Terence's *Demea*: Autobiographical Fiction." *AJPh* 92: 616–32.

Lefèvre, E. 1993. "Waren horazische Gedichte zum 'öffentlichen' Vortrag bestimmt?" In G. Vogt-Spira (ed.), *Beiträge zur mündlichen Kultur der Römer*, Script Oralia 47, 143–57. Tübingen.

Leigh Fermor, P. 1977. *A Time of Gifts*. New York.

Lejay, P. 1911. *Oeuvres d'Horace. Satires*. Paris.

Lejeune, P. 1975. *La pacte autobiographique*. Paris.

Lejeune, P. 1989. *On Autobiography*. Ed. P. Eakin. Trans. K. Leary. Minneapolis.

Lendon, J. L. 1997. *Empire of Honor*. Oxford.

Leppert, M. K. 1974. "Vorarbeiten zur Archäologie und Kulturgeschichte der Villeggiatur der hohen Kaiserzeit." Ph.D. Dissertation. Freiburg.

Lowrie, M. 1995. "A Parade of Lyric Predecessors: Horace C.1.12–1.18." *Phoenix* 49: 33–48.

Lowrie, M. 1997. *Horace's Narrative Odes*. Oxford.

Lowrie, M. 2009a. *Writing, Performance, and Authority in Augustan Rome*. Oxford.

Lowrie, M. (ed.). 2009b. *Oxford Readings in Classical Studies: Horace's Odes and Epodes*. Oxford.

Ludwig, W. 1993. "Horazrezeption in der Renaissance oder die Renaissance des Horaz." In W. Ludwig (ed.), *Horace: L'oeuvre et les imitations, un siècle d'interprétation: Neuf exposés suivis de discussions: 24–29 août 1992*, 305–79. Vandœuvres-Geneva.

Lugli, G. 1926. "La villa sabina di Orazio." *Monumenti Antichi* 31: cols. 457–598.

Lyne, R. O. A. M. 1980. *The Latin Love Poets from Catullus to Horace*. Oxford.

Lyne, R. O. A. M. 1995. *Horace: Behind the Public Poetry*. New Haven, CT.

Lyne, R. O. A. M. 2005. "Horace's *Odes* Book 1 and the Alexandrian Edition of Alcaeus." *CQ* 55: 542–58.

Maas, P. 1949. "Textual Criticism." In *OCD*[1], 888–9.

Macaulay, E. R. 2006. "*Garden Material*." In B. Frischer, J. Crawford, and M. De Simone (eds.), *The Horace's Villa Project, 1996–2003*, vol. 1, 191–5. Oxford.

Mace, S. 1993. "Amour, Encore! The Development of δηὖτε in Archaic Lyric." *GRBS* 34: 335–64.

Macleod, C. 1977. "The Poet, the Critic, and the Moralist: Horace, *Epistles* 1.19." *CQ* n.s. 27: 359–76. Reprinted in O. Taplin (ed.), *The Collected Essays of Colin Macleod*. Oxford, 1983, 262–79.

Macleod, C. W. 1983. "Horatian Imitation and *Odes* 2.5." In O. Taplin (ed.), *The Collected Essays of Colin Macleod*, 245–61. Oxford.

MacMullen, R. 1990. *Corruption in the Roman Empire*. New Haven, CT.

Maehler, H. 1982. *Die Lieder des Bakchylides, 1.2*. Leiden.

Malherbe, A. 1988. *Ancient Epistolary Theory*. Atlanta.

Malinowski, B. 1961 [1922]. *Argonauts of the Western Pacific*. New York.

Maltby, R. 1991. *A Lexicon of Ancient Latin Etymologies. Arca* 25. Leeds.

Mankin, D. 1988. "Review of Shackleton Bailey 1991 and Borzsák 1984." *AJPh* 109: 270–4.

Mankin, D. 1995. *Horace, Epodes*. Cambridge.

Marchionni, R. (ed.). 2003. *Der Sciendum-Kommentar zu den Satiren des Horaz.* Munich.

Mari, Z. 1993. "La valle del Licenza in età romana." *Atti del Convegno di Licenza, 19–23 aprile 1993,* 17–76. Venosa.

Mari, Z. 1995. "La valle dell'Aniene nell'antichità." *Atti e Memorie della Società tiburtina di Storia e d'Arte* 68: 25–52.

Mariotti, S. 1951. *Lezioni su Ennio.* Pesaro.

Mariotti, S. (ed.). 1998. *Orazio: Enciclopedia oraziana,* vol. 3. Rome.

Marmier, J. 1962. *Horace en France au dix-septième siècle.* Paris.

Marsh, D. 1975. "Horatian Influence and Imitation in Ariosto's Satires." *CompLit* 27: 307–26.

Martindale, C. 1992. "Horace, Ovid, and Others." In R. Jenkyns (ed.), *The Legacy of Rome,* 177–213. Oxford.

Martindale, C. 1993. *Redeeming the Text: Latin Poetry and the Hermeneutics of Reception.* Cambridge.

Martindale, C. 2007. "Reception." In C. W. Kallendorf (ed.), *A Companion to the Classical Tradition,* 297–311. Oxford.

Martindale, C. and D. Hopkins (eds.). 1993. *Horace Made New: Horatian Influences on British Writing from the Renaissance to the Twentieth Century.* Cambridge.

Martindale, C. and R. F. Thomas (eds.). 2006. *Classics and the Uses of Reception.* Oxford.

Martindale, J. 1993. "The Best Master of Virtue and Wisdom: The Horace of Ben Jonson and his Heirs." In C. Martindale and D. Hopkins (eds.), *Horace Made New:. Horatian Influences on British Writing from the Renaissance to the Twentieth Century,* 50–85. Cambridge.

Marx, F. 1904–5. *C. Lucilii Carminum reliquiae.* 2 vols. Leipzig.

Mattusch, C. 2008. *Pompei and the Roman Villa: Art and Culture around the Bay of Naples.* New York.

Mauss, M. 1990 [1950]. *The Gift: The Form and Reason for Exchange in Archaic Societies.* Trans. W. D. Halls. New York.

Mayer, R. 1986. "Horace *Epistles* I and Philosophy." *AJPh* 107: 55–73.

Mayer, R. 1994. *Horace. Epistles: Book I.* Cambridge.

Mayer, R. 1995. "Horace's *Moyen de Parvenir.*" In S. J. Harrison (ed.), *Homage to Horace: A Bimillenary Celebration,* 279–95. Oxford.

Mayer, R. 2003. "Personał Problems. The Literary Persona in Antiquity Revisited." *MD* 50: 55–80.

Mazzarino, A. (ed.). 1955. *Grammaticae Romanae Fragmenta Aetatis Caesareae,* vol. 1. Turin.

McDermott, E. A. 1985. "Greek and Roman Elements in Horace's Lyric Program." *ANRW* 2.31.3: 1640–72.

McDonald, A. H. 1970. "Textual Criticism." In *OCD²,* 1048–50

McGann, M. 1969. *Studies in Horace's First Book of Epistles.* Brussels.

McGann, M. J. 2007. "The Reception of Horace in the Renaissance." In S. J. Harrison (ed.), *The Cambridge Companion to Horace*, 305–17. Cambridge.

McKenzie, D. F. 1999 [1984–6]. *Bibliography and the Sociology of Texts.* Cambridge.

McLuhan, M. 1962. *The Gutenberg Galaxy: The Making of Typographical Man.* Toronto.

McNeill, R. L. B. 2001. *Horace: Image, Identity, and Audience.* Baltimore.

Mielsch, H. 1997. *Die römische Villa.* Munich.

Millar, F. 1977. *The Emperor in the Roman World, 31 B.C.-A.D. 337.* Ithaca, NY.

Millar, F. 1998. *The Crowd in Rome in the Late Republic.* Ann Arbor.

Miller, A. 1996. *Greek Lyric: An Anthology in Translation.* Indianapolis and Cambridge.

Miller, J. F. 1998. "Horace's Pindaric Apollo (*ODES* 3.4.60-64)." *CQ* 48: 545–52.

Miller, J. F. 2002. "Experiencing Intertextuality in Horace, *Odes* 3.4." In M. Paschalis (ed.), *Horace and Greek Lyric Poetry*, 119–27. Rethymnon Classical Studies, vol. 1. Rethymnon.

Mindt, N. 2007. *Die Meta-sympotischen Oden und Epoden des Horaz.* Göttingen.

Moles, J. L. 1985. "Cynicism in Horace's *Epistles* I." *Papers of the Liverpool Latin Seminar* 5: 33–60.

Moles, J. L. 2002. "Poetry, Philosophy, Politics and Play: *Epistles* I," in A. J. Woodman and D. C. Feeney (eds.), *Traditions and Contexts in the Poetry of Horace*, 141–57. Cambridge.

Mols, S. 2006. "Fragments of Wall Painting from 'Horace's Villa." In B. Frischer, J. Crawford, and M. De Simone (eds.), *The Horace's Villa Project, 1996–2003*, vol. 1, 267–72. Oxford.

Momigliano, A. 1935 [1955]. "Genesi storica e funzione attuale del concetto di Ellenismo." In A. Momigliano, *Contributo allo storia degli studi classici*, 165–93. Rome.

Mommsen, T. 1912. *Reden und Aufsätze: Mit 2 Bildnern.* Berlin.

Money, D. 2007. "The Reception of Horace in the Seventeenth and Eighteenth Centuries." In S. J. Harrison (ed.), *The Cambridge Companion to Horace*, 318–33. Cambridge.

Morgan, L. 2004. "Getting the Measure of Heroes: The Dactylic Hexameter and its detractors." In M. Gale (ed.), *Latin Epic and Didactic Poetry*, 1–26. Llandysul, Wales.

Morley, N. 1996. *Metropolis and Hinterland: The City of Rome and the Italian Economy 200 B.C.—A.D. 200.* Oxford.

Morrison, A. D. 2006. "Advice and Abuse: Horace, *Epistles* 1 and the Iambic Tradition." *MD* 56: 29–61.

Morrison, A. D. 2007a. "Didacticism and Epistolarity in Horace's *Epistles* 1." In R. Morello and A. D. Morrison (eds.), *Classical and Late Antique Epistolography*, 107–31. Oxford.

Morrison, A. D. 2007b. *The Narrator in Archaic Greek and Hellenistic Poetry.* Cambridge.

Moussy, C. 1966. *Gratia et sa famille.* Paris.

Muecke, D. C. 1969. *the Compass of Irony.* London.

Muecke, F. (ed.) 1993. *Horace Satires II.* Warminster.

Muecke, F. 2005. "Rome's First "Satirists": Themes and Genre in Ennius and Lucilius." In K. Freudenburg (ed.), *The Cambridge Companion to Roman Satire*, 33–47. Cambridge.

Muecke, F. 2007. "The *Satires.*" In S. J. Harrison (ed.), *The Cambridge Companion to Horace*, 105–20. Cambridge.

Murray O. 1990. *Sympotica: A Symposium on the Symposium.* Oxford.

Murray O. 1993. "Symposium and Genre in the Poetry of Horace." In N. Rudd. (ed.), *Horace 2000: A Celebration. Essays for the Bimillennium*, 89–105. Ann Arbor.

Nagy, G. 1979. *The Best of the Achaeans.* Baltimore.

Nagy, G. 1994. "Copies and Models in Horace *Odes* 4.1 and 4.2." *CW* 87: 415–26.

Nauta, R. 2002. *Poetry for Patrons: Literary Communication in the Age of Domitian.* Leiden.

Newman, J. K. 1967. *The Concept of Vates in Augustan Poetry.* Brussels.

Nicolet, C. 1966, 1974. *L'ordre équestre à l' Époque republicaine.* 2 vols. Paris.

Nicolet, C. 1988. *L'Inventaire du Monde: Géographie et politique aux origins de l' empire romain.* Paris.

Nicolet, C. 1991. *Space, Geography and Politics in the Early Roman Empire.* Ann Arbor.

Nietzsche, F. 1989. *Beyond Good and Evil.* Trans. W. Kaufmann. New York.

Nisbet, R. G. M. 1984. "Horace's *Epodes* and History." In A. Woodman and D. West (eds.), *Poetry and Politics in the Age of Augustus*, 161–81. Cambridge.

Nisbet, R. G. M. 2007. "Horace: Life and Chronology." In S. J. Harrison (ed.), *The Cambridge Companion to Horace*, 7–21. Cambridge.

Nisbet, R. G. M. and M. Hubbard. 1970. *A Commentary on Horace: Odes Book I.* Oxford.

Nisbet, R. G. M. and M. Hubbard. 1978. *A Commentary on Horace: Odes Book II.* Oxford.

Nisbet, R. G. M. and N. Rudd. 2004. *A Commentary on Horace: Odes Book III.* Oxford.

North, J. A. 1986. "Review of *Religion and Politics, from Republic to Principate.*" *JRS* 76: 251–8.

Obbink, D. 2006. "A New Archilochus Poem." *ZPE* 156: 10–16.

OCD[1] = Cary, M. *et al.* (eds.). 1949. *The Oxford Classical Dictionary.* Oxford.

OCD^2 = Hammond, N. G. L. and H. H. Scullard. (eds.). 1970. *The Oxford Classical Dictionary*. Oxford.

OCD^3 = Hornblower, S. and A. Spawforth (eds.). 1996. *The Oxford Classical Dictionary*. Oxford.

Ogilvie, R. M. 1964. "Horace and the Eighteenth Century." In R. M. Ogilvie, *Latin and Greek: A History of the Influence of the Classics on English Life from 1600 to 1918*. London.

Ogilvie, R. M. 1981. "Translations of Horace in the 17th and 18th Centuries." In W. Killy (ed.), *Geschichte des Textverständnisses am Beispiel von Pindar und Horaz*, 71–80. Munich.

Oliensis, E. 1991. "Canidia, Canicula, and the Decorum of Horace's *Epodes*." *Arethusa* 24: 107–38.

Oliensis, E. 1998. *Horace and the Rhetoric of Authority*. Cambridge.

Oliensis, E. 2007. "Erotics and gender." In S. J. Harrison (ed.), *The Cambridge Companion to Horace*, 221–34. Cambridge.

Olney, J. 1998. *Memory and Narrative: The Weave of Life-Writing*. Chicago and London.

Orelli, J. K., J. G. Baiter, and W. Hirschfelder. 1886. *Q. Horatius Flaccus*. 4th edn. Berlin.

Osgood, J. 2006. *Caesar's Legacy*. Cambridge.

Page, D. L. 1955. *Sappho and Alcaeus: An Introduction to the Study of Ancient Lesbian Poetry*. Oxford.

Page, T. E. 1895 [1956]. *Q. Horatii Flacci, Carminum Libri IV, Epodon Liber*. London.

Paschalis, M. (ed.). 2002. *Horace and Greek Lyric Poetry*. Rethymnon.

Pappalardo, U. 2000. *Le ville romane*. Naples.

Parker, L. P. E. 2002. "Just tenacious of his purpose ..." *MH* 59.2: 101–6.

Pasquali, G. 1964 [1920]. *Orazio lirico*. Ed. A. La Penna. Florence.

Pasquali, G. 1962. *Storia della tradizione e critica del testo*. 2nd edn. Florence.

Pasqui, A. 1916. "L'opera delle sovrintedenze dei monumenti, delle gallerie, dei musei e degli scavi. Quinquennio 1909–1914. Sovrintendenza dei Musei e Scavi di Roma e del Lazio. Licenza." *Supplemento al Bollettino d'Arte* 3: 11–13.

Pavlock, B. 1982. "Horace's Invitation Poems to Maecenas: Gifts to a Patron." *Ramus* 11: 84–9.

Pavlock, B. 1994. "Horace's Influence on Renaissance Epic." *CW* 87: 427–41.

Pelling, C. 1996. *The Cambridge Ancient History* vol.X. 2nd edn., 21–34.

Perret, J. 1964. *Horace*. Trans. Berthe Humez. New York.

Petersen, L. *The Freedman in Roman Art and Art History*. Cambridge.

Petersmann, H. 1999. "The Language of Early Roman Satire: Its Function and Characteristics." In J. N. Adams and R. G. Mayer (eds.), *Aspects of the Language of Latin Poetry*, 289–310. Oxford.

Pfeiffer, R. 1968. *History of Classical Scholarship from the Beginnings to the End of the Hellenistic Age*. Oxford.

Pfeiffer, R. 1976. *History of Classical Scholarship from 1300 to 1850*. Oxford.

Piperino, F. 1998. "Musica." In S. Mariotti (ed.), *Orazio: enciclopedia oraziana*, vol. 3, 661–77. Rome.

Pope, A. "An Essay on Criticism." In O. Hardison Jr. and L. Golden (eds.), *Horace for Students of Literature: the "Ars Poetica" and its Tradition*, 216–35. Gainesville, FL.

Porro, A. 1994. *Vetera Alcaica: L'esegesi di Alceo dagli Alessandrini all' età imperiale*. Milan.

Porter, D. H. 1987. *Horace's Poetic Journey: A Reading of Odes 1–3*. Princeton.

Porter, D. 1995. "*Quo, quo scelesti ruitis*: The Downward Momentum of Horace's *Epodes*." *ICS* 20: 107–30.

Pöschl, V. 1958. "Die Einheit Der Ersten Römerode." *HSPh* 63: 333–46.

Pöschl, V. 1991. *Horazische Lyrik, Interpretationen*[2]. Heidelberg.

Préaux, J. 1968. *Horace, Épîtres, Livre I*. Paris.

Price, T. D. 1932. "A Restoration of Horace's Sabine Villa." *Memoirs of the American Academy in Rome* 10: 135–42.

Putnam, M. C. J. 1986. *Artifices of Eternity: Horace's Fourth Book of Odes*. Ithaca, NY.

Putnam, M. C. J. 1990. "Horace *Carm.* 2.9: Augustus and the Ambiguities of Encomium." In K. Raaflaub and M. Toher (eds.), *Between Republic and Empire: Interpretations of Augustus and his Principate*, 212–38. Berkeley.

Putnam, M. C. J. 2000. *Horace's Carmen Saeculare: Ritual Magic and the Poet's Art*. New Haven, CT.

Putnam, M. C. J. 2006a. "Horace to Torquatus: *Epistle* 1.5 and *Ode* 4.7." *AJPh* 127: 387–413.

Putnam, M. C. J. 2006b. *Poetic Interplay: Catullus and Horace*. Princeton.

Quinn, K. 1980. *Horace: The Odes*. London.

Quintero, R. 2007. "Pope and Augustan Verse Satire." In R. Quintero (ed.), *A Companion to Satire*, 212–32. Malden, MA.

Raaflaub, K. and M. Toher (eds.). 1990. *Between Republic and Empire: Interpretations of Augustus and His Principate*. Berkeley.

Race, W. H. 1982. *The Classical Priamel from Homer to Boethius*. Leiden.

Race, W. H. 1986. *Pindar*. Boston.

Race, W. H. 1987. "*P. Oxy.* 2438 and the Order of Pindar's Works." *RhM* 130: 407–10.

Race, W. H. 1990. *Style and Rhetoric in Pindar's Odes*. Atlanta.

Race, W. H. 2004. "Pindar's *Olympian* 11 Revisited Post Bundy." *HSPh* 102: 69–96.

Radke, G. 1996. "Lollio Massimo." In *Enciclopedia Oraziana*, vol. I, 781–82. Rome.

Ranke, L. von. 1955 [1854]. *Über die Epochen der neueren Geschichte: Vorträge dem König Maximilian II. von Bayern gehalten von Leopold von Ranke.* H. Herzfeld (ed.). Schloss Laupheim.

Raschke, W. 1979. "The Chronology of the Early Books of Lucilius." *JRS* 69: 78–89.

Reckford, K. 1969. *Horace.* New York.

Reinhold, M. 2002. "Usurpation of Status and Status Symbols in the Roman Empire." In *Studies in Classical History and Society*, 25–53. Oxford.

Reynolds, S. 1996. *Medieval Reading: Grammar, Rhetoric and the Classical Text.* Cambridge.

Rich, A. 1976. *Of Woman Born: Motherhood as Experience and Institution.* New York.

Richmond, J. A. 1970. "Horace's 'Mottos' and Catullus 51." *RhM* 113: 197–204.

Roberts, M. 1995. "Interpreting Hedonism: Renaissance Commentaries on Horace's Epicurean Odes." *Arethusa* 28: 289–307.

Rolfe, J. C., trans. 1914. *Suetonius.* Cambridge, MA.

Rosenberg, R. 2003. "Die sechziger Jahre als Zäsur in der deutschen Literaturwissenschaft: Theoriegeschichtlich." In R. Rosenberg, *Verhandlungen des Literaturbegriffs: Studien zu Geschichte und Theorie der Literaturwissenschaft*, 243–68. Berlin.

Roskams, S. 2001. *Excavation.* Cambridge.

Rösler, W. 1980. *Dichter und Gruppe.* Munich.

Rossi, L. E. 1983. "Il simposio Greco arcaico e classico come spettacolo a se stesso." In *Spettacoli dall' antichità alle corti italiane del' 400: Atti del VII convegno do studio.* Viterbo.

Rossi, L. E. 1998. "Orazio, un lirico greco senza musica." In *Seminari Romani di cultura greca* 1: 163–81.

Rosslyn, F. 1993. "Good Humour and the Agelasts: Horace, Pope and Gray." In C. Martindale and D. Hopkins (eds.), *Horace Made New: Horatian Influences on British Writing from the Renaissance to the Twentieth Century*, 184–98. Cambridge.

Rudd, N. 1966. *The Satires of Horace.* Cambridge.

Rudd, N. 1986. *Themes in Roman Satire.* Norman, OK.

Rudd, N. 1989. *Epistles Book II and the Epistle to the Pisones ("Ars Poetica").* Cambridge.

Rudd, N. (ed.). 1993a. *Horace 2000: A Celebration. Essays for the Bimillennium.* Ann Arbor.

Rudd, N. 1993b. "Horace as a Moralist." In N. Rudd (ed.), *Horace 2000: A Celebration. Essays for the Bimillenium*, 64–88. Ann Arbor.

Rudd, N. 1993c. *Horace: Satires and Epistles; Persius: Satires.* A verse translation. London.

Rudd, N. 2005. "Variation and Inversion in Pope's *Epistle to Dr Arbuthnot*." In *The Common Spring: Essays on Latin and English Poetry*, 161–72. Bristol.

Rudich, V. 2006. "The Ownership of the Licenza Villa." In B. Frischer, J. Crawford, and M. De Simone (eds.), *The Horace's Villa Project, 1996–2003*, vol. 1, 315–26. Oxford.

Rummel, P. 1892. *Horatius quid de Pindaro iudicaverit*. Rawitsch.

Sabbe, M. 1935. "Les Emblemata Horatiana d'Otto Venius." *De Gulden Passer* 12: 1–14.

Sahlins, M. 1965. "On the Sociology of Primitive Exchange." In M. Banton (ed.), *The Relevance of Models for Social Anthropology*, 139–236. New York.

Sahlins, M. 1972. *Stone Age Economics*. New York.

Saller, R. P. 1982. *Personal Patronage under the Early Empire*. Cambridge.

Saller, R. P. 1989. "Patronage and friendship in Early Imperial Rome: Drawing the Distinction." In A. Wallace-Hadrill (ed.), *Patronage in Ancient Society*, 49–62. New York.

Sandys, J. E. 1908. *A History of Classical Scholarship*, vol. 3. Bristol.

Santirocco, M. 1986. *Unity and Design in Horace's Odes*. Chapel Hill and London.

Santirocco, M. (ed.). 1994. *Recovering Horace*. CW 87.5.

Santirocco, M. 1995. "Horace and Augustan Ideology." *Arethusa* 2: 225–43.

Sartorio, G. P. 1994. *Mezzi di trasporto e traffico*. Rome.

Scherner, M. 1974. "Horizont." In J. Ritter (ed.), *Historische Wörterbuch der Philosophie*, vol. 3, 1187–1206. Basel.

Schiesaro, A. 1995. "Horace in the Italian Scholarship of the Twentieth Century." *Arethusa* 28: 339–61.

Schlegel, C. 2000. "Horace and His Fathers: Satires 1.4 and 1.6." *AJPh* 121: 93–119.

Schlegel, C. 2005. *Satire and the Threat of Speech: Horace's Satires Book I*. Madison, WI.

Schmidt, E. A. 1977. "*Amica uis pastoribus*: der Jambiker Horaz in seinem Epodenbuch." *Gymnasium* 84: 401–21.

Schmidt, E. A. 1997. *Sabinum. Horaz und sein Landgut im Licenzatal*. Heidelberg.

Schmidt, E. A. 2001. *Zeit und Form: Dichtungen des Horaz*. Heidelberg.

Schmitz, T. 1993. *Pindar in der französischen Renaissance: Studien zu seiner Rezeption in Philologie, Dichtungstheorie und Dichtung*. Göttingen.

Schweiger, F. L. A. 1962 [1832–4]. *Bibliographisches Lexicon der gesamten Literatur der Römer*, vol. 1. Amsterdam.

Sciarrino, E. 2004. "Putting Cato the Censor's *Origines* in Its Place." *ClAnt* 23: 323–57.

Seaford, R. 1994. *Reciprocity and ritual: Homer and Tragedy in the Developing City-State*. Oxford.

Seel, O. 1970. "Zur Ode 1.14 des Horaz. Zweifel an einer communis opinio." In D. Ableitinger and H. Gugel (eds.), *Festschrift Karl Vretska*, 204–49. Heidelberg.

Selden, D. 1990. "Classics and Contemporary Criticism." *Arion* 3rd ser. 1: 158–66.

Selden, D. 1992. "*Ceveat lector*: Catullus and the Rhetoric of Performance." In R. Hexter and D. Selden (eds.), *Innovations of Antiquity*, 461–512. London.

Setaioli, A. 1981. "Gli 'Epodi' di Orazio nella Critica dal 1937 al 1972." *ANRW* II.31.3: 1674–1788.

Shackleton Bailey, D. 1982. *Profile of Horace*. London.

Shackleton Bailey, D. R. 1985. "Vindiciae Horatianae." *HSPh* 89: 153–70.

Shackleton Bailey, D. R. 1990. "Horatian Aftermath." *Philologus* 134: 213–28.

Shackleton Bailey, D. R. 1991. *Q. Horati Flacci Opera*. 2nd edn. Stuttgart.

Shapiro, K. 1973. *Essay on Rime, with Trial of a Poet*. Ann Arbor.

Sherbo, A. (ed.). 1979. *Christopher Smart's Verse Translation of Horace's Odes: Text and Introduction*. English Literary Studies monograph series 17. Victoria, BC.

Sherwin-White, A. N. 1966. *The Letters of Pliny: a Historical and Social Commentary*. Oxford.

Shorey, P. 1909. "Phusis, Melete, Episteme." *TAPhA* 40: 185–201.

Shorey, P. and G. J. Laing. 1910. *Horace: Odes and Epodes*. Chicago.

Showerman., G. 1963. *Horace and his Influence*. New York.

Sider, D. 1997. *The Epigrams of Philodemos*. Oxford.

Sirago, V. 1958. "Lucanus an Apulus." *Antiquité Classique* 27: 13–30.

Skutsch, O. 1985. *The Annals of Q. Ennius*. Oxford.

Skutsch, O. 1968. *Studia Enniana*. London.

Smith, S. and J. Watson. 2001. *Reading Autobiography: A Guide for Interpreting Life Narratives*. Minneapolis and London.

Solmsen, F. 1947. "Horace's First Roman Ode." *AJPh* 68: 337–52.

Sowerby, R. 1993. "Pope and Horace." In C. Martindale and D. Hopkins (eds.), *Horace Made New. Horatian Influences on British Writing from the Renaissance to the Twentieth Century*, 159–83. Cambridge.

Spentzou, E. and D. Fowler (eds.). 2002. *Cultivating the Muse: Struggles for Power and Inspiration in Classical Literature*. Oxford.

Spingarn, J. E. 1976. *A History of Literary Criticism in the Renaissance*. Westport, CT.

Stack, F. 1985. *Pope and Horace: Studies in Imitation*. Cambridge.

Stella, F. 1998. "Carolingi, scrittori." In S. Mariotti (ed.), *Orazio: enciclopedia oraziana*, vol. 3, 159–67. Rome.

Stemplinger, E. 1906. *Das Fortleben der Horazischen Lyrik seit der Renaissance*. Leipzig.

Stemplinger, E. 1921. *Horaz im Urteil der Jahrhunderte*. Leipzig.

Storrs, R. (ed.). 1959. *"Ad Pyrrham": A Polyglot Collection of Translations of Horace's Ode to Pyrrha*. London.

Strazzulla, M. J. 2006. "The Architectural Terracottas." In B. Frischer, J. Crawford, and M. De Simone (eds.), *The Horace's Villa Project, 1996–2003*, vol. 1, 221–30. Oxford.

Sullivan, J. P. 1992. "Satire." In R. Jenkyns (ed.), *The Legacy of Rome*, 214–42. Oxford.

Sutherland, E. 1995. "Audience Manipulation and Emotional Experience in Horace's 'Pyrrha ode' (*Ode* 1.5)." *AJPh* 116: 441–52.

Sutherland, E. 2003. "How (not) to Look at a Woman: Bodily Encounters and the Failure of the Gaze in Horace's *C.* 1.19." *AJPh*: 57–80.

Sutherland, E. 2005a. "Literary Women in Horace's *Odes* 2.11 and 2.12." In W. Batstone and G. Tissol (eds.), *Defining Genre and Gender in Roman Literature: Essays Presented to William S. Anderson on His Seventy-Fifth Birthday*. New York.

Sutherland, E. 2005b. "Vision and Desire in Horace *Carmina* 2.5." In R. E. Greene (eds.), *Gendered Dynamics in Latin Love Poetry*. Baltimore.

Sutherland, E. 2005c. "Writing (on) Bodies: Lyric Discourse and the Production of Gender in Horace's *Odes* 1.13." *CPh* 100: 52–82.

Sykutris, J. 1933. *Die Briefe des Sokrates und der Sokratiker*. Paderborn.

Syme, R. 1939/1960. *The Roman Revolution*. Oxford.

Syndikus, H. P. 2001 [1972–3]. *Die Lyrik des Horaz. Eine Interpretation der Oden*, vols. 1 and 2. Darmstadt.

Tacitus 1969. *The Annals*, vol. 5, trans. J. Jackson. London and Cambridge, MA.

Talbert, R. J. A. 1984. *The Senate of Imperial Rome*. Princeton.

Tarditi, G. 1968. *Archiloco*. Rome.

Tarrant, R. J. 1983. "Horace." In L. D. Reynolds (ed.), *Texts and Transmission: A Survey of the Latin Classics*, 182–6. Oxford.

Tarrant, R. J. 2007. "Ancient Receptions of Horace." In S. J. Harrison (ed.), *The Cambridge Companion to Horace*, 277–90. Cambridge.

Taylor, L. R. 1925. "Horace's Equestrian Career." *AJPh* 46: 161–70.

Taylor, L. R. 1968. "Republican and Augustan Writers Enrolled in the Equestrian Centuries." *TAPhA* 99: 469–86.

Thévanaz, O. 2003. "Poétiques comparées: De l'Aphrodite de Sappho à la Vénus d'Horace." *EL* 2003: 107–27.

Thilo, G. and H. Hagen (eds.). 1881–1902. *Servii Grammatici qui feruntur in Vergilii Carmina Commentarii*. 3 vols. Leipzig.

Thomas, R. 2006. "Looking for Ligurinus: An Italian Poet in the Nineteenth Century." In C. Martindale and R. F. Thomas (eds.), *Classics and the Uses of Reception*, 153–67. Oxford.

Thomas, R. 2007. "Horace and Hellenistic Poetry." In S. J. Harrison (ed.), *The Cambridge Companion to Horace*, 50–62. Cambridge.

Thome, G. 1995. "Die späte Liebeslyrik des Horaz." In G. Alföldy and T. Hölscher *et al.* (eds.), *Römische Lebenskunst: Interdisziplinäres Kolloquium zum 85. Geburtstag von Viktor Pöschl*, 131–54. Heidelberg.

Timpanaro, S. 1985/2005. *The Genesis of Lachmann's Method.* Trans. G. W. Most. Chicago.

Toher, M. 2005. "Tillius and Horace." *CQ* 55: 183–9.

Traina, A. 1991. "Orazio e Aristippo: le *Epistole* e l'arte di convivere." *RFIC* 119: 285–305. Reprinted in A. Traina, *Poeti latini (e neolatini)*, Bologna 1994: 161–179.

Trapp, M. 2003. *Greek and Latin Letters: An Anthology with Translation.* Cambridge.

Trimpi, W. 1973. "The Meaning of Horace's *Ut Pictura Poesis.*" *Journal of the Warburg and Courtauld Institutes* 36: 1–34.

van Groningen, B. A. 1963. "Ekdosis." <Greek alphabet>*Mnemosyne* 4.16: 1–17.

Vance, N. 1993. "Horace and the Nineteenth Century." In C. Martindale and D. Hopkins (eds.), *Horace Made New: Horatian Influences on British Writing from the Renaissance to the Twentieth Century*, 199–216. Cambridge.

Verboven, K. 2002. *The Economy of Friends: Economic Aspects of Amicitia and Patronage in the Late Republic.* Brussels.

Veyne, P. 1990 [1976]. *Bread and Circuses.* Trans. B. Pearce. London and New York.

Vogt, E. 1979. "Die Methodenstreit zwischen Hermann and Böckh und seine Bedeutung für die Geschichte der Philologie." In H. Flashar, K. Gründer and A. Horstmann (eds.), *Philologie und Hermeneutik im 19. Jahrhundert: Zur Geschichte und Methodologie der Geisteswissenschaften*, 103–21. Göttingen.

Vogt-Spira, G. (ed.). 1993. *Beiträge zur mündlichen Kultur der Römer, Script-Oralia* 47. Tübingen.

Voigt, E.-M. 1971. *Sappho et Alcaeus fragmenta.* Amsterdam.

von Albrecht, M. 1995. "Horaz und die europäische Literatur." *Gymnasium* 102: 289–304.

Wallace-Hadrill, A. 1989. "Patronage in Roman Society: from Republic to Empire." In A. Wallace-Hadrill (ed.), *Patronage in Ancient Society*, 63–88. New York.

Wälli, S. 2002. *Melodien aus mittelalterlichen Horaz-Handschriften: Edition und Interpretation der Quellen.* Monumenta monodica medii aevi: subsidia 3. Kassel.

Waquet, F. 2001. *Latin, or, the Empire of a Sign: From the Sixteenth to the Twentieth Centuries.* Trans. John Howe. London.

Warmington, E. H. 1967 [1938]. *Remains of Old Latin*, vol. 3. Cambridge, MA.

Watson, A. 1975. *Rome of the XII Tables.* Princeton.

Watson, L. C. 2003. *A Commentary on Horace's Epodes.* Oxford.

Watson, L. C. 2007. "The *Epodes*: Horace's Archilochus?" In S. J. Harrison (ed.), *The Cambridge Companion to Horace*, 93–104. Cambridge.

Weinberg, B. 1961. *A History of Literary Criticism in the Italian Renaissance.* 2 vols. Chicago.

Wenzel, H. V. 1981. "And the One Doesn't Stir without the Other." *Signs: Journal of Women in Culture and Societty* 7.1: 60–7.

Werner, K. 2006. "The Mosaics." In B. Frischer, J. Crawford, and M. De Simone (eds.), *The Horace's Villa Project, 1996–2003*, vol. 1, 253–66. Oxford.

West, D. A. 1974. "Of Mice and Men: Horace, Satires 2.6.77–117." In T. Woodman and D. West (eds.), *Quality and Pleasure in Latin Poetry*, 67–80. Cambridge.

West, D. A. 1998. *Horace Odes II: Vatis Amici.* Oxford.

West, D. A. 2000. *The Complete Odes and Epodes by Horace.* Oxford.

West, D. A. 2002. *Odes III: Dulce Periculum.* Oxford.

West, M. L. 1973. *Textual Criticism and Editorial Technique.* Stuttgart.

West, M. L. 1974. *Studies in Greek Elegy and Iambus.* Berlin and New York.

West, M. L. 1989–92. *Iambi et Elegi Graeci* I–II. Oxford.

Wheeler, M. 1954. *Archaeology from the Earth.* Oxford.

White, D. C. 1973. "A New Edition of Lucilius," *CPh* 68: 36–44.

White, K. D. 1984. *Greek and Roman Technology.* Ithaca.

White, P. 1991. "Maecenas' Retirement." *CPh* 86: 130–8.

White, P. 1993. *Promised Verse: Poets in the Society of Augustan Rome.* Cambridge, MA and London.

White, P. 2007. "Friendship, Patronage and Horatian Socio-poetics." In S. J. Harrison (ed.), *The Cambridge Companion to Horace*, 195–206. Cambridge.

Wickham, E. C. and H. W. Garrod. 1901 [1955]. *Q. Horatii Flacci Opera.* Oxford.

Wili, W. 1948. *Horaz und die Augusteische Kultur.* Basel.

Williams, G. W. 1968. *Tradition and Originality in Roman Poetry.* Oxford.

Williams, G. W. 1969. *The Third Book of Horace's Odes.* Cambridge.

Williams, G. W. 1982. "Phases in Political Patronage of Literature in Rome." In B. K. Gold (ed.), *Literary and Artistic Patronage in Ancient Rome*, 3–27. Austin.

Williams, G. W. 1990. "Did Maecenas 'Fall From Favor'?" In K. A. Raaflaub and M. Toher (eds.), *Between Republic and Empire: Interpretations of Augustus and His Principate*, 258–75. Berkeley and Los Angeles.

Williams, G. W. 1995. "*Libertino Patre Natus*: True or False?" In S. J. Harrison (ed.), *Homage to Horace*, 296–313. Oxford.

Wills, G. 1967. "Sappho 31 and Catullus 51." *GRBS* 8: 167–97.

Wimmel, W. 1960. *Kallimachos in Rom: die Nachfolge seines apologetischen Dichtens in der Augusteerzeit.* Wiesbaden.

Wiseman, T. P. 1969. "The Census in the First Century BC." *JRS* 59: 60–5.

Wissemann, M. 1982. *Die Parther in der augusteischen Dichtung.* Frankfurt-on-Main.

Wood, A. G. 1985. *Literary Satire and Theory: A Study of Horace, Boileau and Pope.* New York and London.

Woodman, A. J. 2002. "*Biformis vates*: The *Odes*, Catullus and Greek lyric." In A. J. Woodman and D. Feeney (eds.), *Traditions and Contexts in the Poetry of Horace*, 53–64. Cambridge.

Woodman, A. J. 1983. "Horace, Epistles I, 19, 23–40." *MH* 40: 75–81.

Woodman, A. J. 1980. "The Craft of Horace in *Odes* 1.14." *CPh* 75: 60–7.

Woodman, A. J. and D. Feeney (eds.). 2002. *Traditions and Contexts in the Poetry of Horace*. Cambridge.

Young, D. C. 1987. "Pindar and Horace Against the Telchines (*Ol.* 7.53 & *Carm.* 4.4.33)." *AJPh* 108: 152–7.

Zanker, P. 1975. "Grabreliefs Römischer Freigelassener." *JDAI* 1975: 267–315.

Zanker, P. 1987. *Augustus und die Macht der Bilder*. Munich.

Zanker, P. 1988. *The Power of Images in the Age of Augustus*. Trans. A. Shapiro. Ann Arbor.

Zetzel, J. E. G. 1980. "Horace's *Liber Sermonum*: The Structure of Ambiguity." *Arethusa* 13: 59–78.

Zetzel, J. E. G. 1982. "The Poetics of Patronage in the Late First Century B.C." In B. K. Gold (ed.), *Literary and Artistic Patronage in Ancient Rome*, 87–102. Austin.

Ziolkowski, J. M. 2000. "*Nota Bene*: Why the Classics Were Neumed in the Middle Ages." *Journal of Medieval Latin* 10: 74–114.

Ziolkowski, J. M. 2004. "Women's Lament and the Neuming of the Classics." In A. Haines and R. Rosenfeld (eds.), *Music and Medieval Manuscripts: Paleography and Performance: Essays Dedicated to Andrew Hughes*, 128–50. Aldershot, UK.

Ziolkowski, J. M. 2007. *Nota Bene: Reading Classics and Writing Melodies in the Early Middle Ages*. Publications of the Journal of Medieval Latin 7. Turnhout.

Ziolkowski, T. 2005. "Uses and Abuses of Horace: His Reception since 1935 in Germany and Anglo-America." *IJCT* 12: 183–215.

Zorzetti, N. 1990. "The *Carmina Convivalia*." In O. Murray (ed.), *Sympotica: A Symposium on the Symposium*, 289–307. Oxford.

Zumwalt, N. 1977. "Horace's *navis* of Love Poetry." *CW* 71: 249–54.

Index

Armenia 328
Ars Poetica 1, 28, 309, 367, 368,
    374–5
  reception *see* reception of *Ars
    Poetica*
Athens 263
Attalus of Pergamum 124–5
auctioneers 15, 16
Auden, W.H. 32
Augustus (Octavian) 3, 26–8, 155,
    160, 194, 227, 302, 330,
    331
  and Aeneas 238
  at Philippi 53
  battling for inheritance 36
  birth 36
  birthday 328–9
  cared for by Rome 174
  celebration of *Ludi Saeculares* 231
  chiding Horace for ignoring him
    72
  Circle of 34
  commissioning *Carmen Saeculare*
    211
  confiscation of Horace's property 9
  divine status 61, 62, 63–4, 203
  divinely endorsed power 63–4
  establishing peace 222–3
  Horace's neglect of 331
  in Jonson's *The Poetaster* 385–6,
    389
  name of month of August 23
  offer of post to Horace of private
    secretary 25–6
  pax Romana 9
  praise 194, 227, 330, 331
  praise of 329–32
  promoter of arts and spirituality
    237
  pursuit of Cleopatra 184
  refuge in Muses' grotto 223
  return from Gaul and Spain 183,
    213

  as Rome's redeemer 194
  rule by consent of all 229
Aulus Cascellius 406
Aulus Gellius 19
autobiography in poetry 9, 10, 12,
    15, 53–4, 58–9, 68–70,
    271–2, 273–5

Bacchus 137–8, 158 *see also* Dionysus
Bacchylides 148
Badius Ascensius 392–3, 394–5
Bagno, Ludovico 369
Baiae 21, 22
Bailey, Shackleton 347, 348, 359
Banzi 10, 22
Barine 185, 189
Barker, Philip 80
Baudelaire, Charles 351
Bellerophon 228
Bentley, Richard 347, 393
Bion of Borysthenes 281
birthdays 328–9
blame poetry 96–7
Boeckh, A. 350
Boileau, Nicolas 374–9
  L'Art poétique 396–8
Bolingbroke, Lord 380
books (*libelli*) 338
  copying 338–9
  printing 339, 368
booksellers 339
Borzsák, Stephan 347
Bourdieu, P. 56
Bratuscheck, Ernst 350
Brink, C.O. 393–4, 407–8
Britain 203
Brundisium 38, 59, 261, 263, 264,
    266, 295, 303–4
Brutus 9, 17, 17–18, 22
Bruun, Christer 85
Bryant, William Cullen 408
Budgell, Eustice 407
Bullatius 48